LIBERAL ISLAM

LIBERAL ISLAM

A SOURCEBOOK

Edited by CHARLES KURZMAN

New York • Oxford

Oxford University Press

1998

Oxford University Press

Oxford   New York
Athens   Auckland   Bangkok   Bogotá   Buenos Aires   Calcutta
Cape Town   Chennai   Dar es Salaam   Delhi   Florence   Hong Kong   Istanbul
Karachi   Kuala Lumpur   Madrid   Melbourne   Mexico City   Mumbai
Nairobi   Paris   São Paulo   Singapore   Taipei   Tokyo   Toronto   Warsaw

and associated companies in
Berlin   Ibadan

Published by Oxford University Press, Inc.
198 Madison Avenue, New York, New York 10016

Oxford is a registered trademark of Oxford University Press

Library of Congress Cataloging-in-Publication Data

Liberal Islam : a source book / edited by Charles Kurzman.
p. cm.
Includes bibliographical references and indexes.
ISBN 0-19-511621-6;—ISBN 0-19-511622-4 (pbk.)
1. Islamic renewal.   2. Islam—Essence, genius, nature.
3. Islam—20th century.   I. Kurzman, Charles.
BP60.L53   1998
297.2'7—dc21   97-30284

9

Printed in the United States of America
on acid-free paper

Acknowledgments

Chapter 1. 'Ali 'Abd al-Raziq. *Al-Islam wa usul al-hukm* (Arabic: *Islam and the Basis of Government*). Cairo: publisher unknown, 1925, book 2, part 3. Translated from Arabic by Joseph Massad.

Chapter 2. Muhammad Khalaf-Allah. *Al-Qur' an wa al-dawla* (Arabic: *The Qur' an and the State*). Cairo: Maktabat al-Anjlu al-Misriya, 1973, pp. 55–79. Translated from Arabic by Joseph Massad. Published with permission.

Chapter 3. Mahumd Taleqani. *Majmu'eh-e goftar-e "Pedar Taleqani"* (Persian: *Collection of Speeches of "Father Taleqani"*). Tehran: Mujahedin-e Khalq-e Iran, 1979, pp. 51–53. Translated from Persian by Charles Kurzman.

Chapter 4. Muhammad Sa'id Al-'Ashmawi. *Islam and the Political Order*, edited by George F. McLean. Washington, D.C.: Council for Research in Values and Philosophy, 1993, pp. 95–110. First published as *Al-Islam al-siyasi* (Arabic: *Political Islam*) in Egypt in 1987. Published with permission.

Chapter 5. Muhammad Natsir. "The Indonesian Revolution: Harmony of Life! Freedom of Religion! Unity of the Nation!" translated by Peter Burns in *Revelation and Revolution: Natsir and the Panca Sila* (Townsville, Australia: Committee of South-East Asian Studies, James Cook University of North Queensland, Southeast Asian Monograph Series No. 9, 1981), pp. 112–136. First published in Indonesian in 1955. Published with permission.

Chapter 6. S. M. Zafar. *'Avam, parlimant, Islam* (Urdu: *The People, Parliament, Islam*). Lahore, Pakistan: A'inah-e-Adab, 1980, pp. 304–318. Translated from Urdu by Afroz Taj. Published with permission.

Chapter 7. Mehdi Bazargan. "Din va Azadi" (Persian: Religion and Liberty), in *Bazyabi-ye arzesh' ha* (Persian: *The Recovery of Values*). Tehran: Nehzat-e Azadi-ye Iran, 1983, pp. 59–88. Translated by Mahmoud Sadri. Published with permission.

Chapter 8. Dimasangcay A. Pundato. "Making International Politics More Humane" and "Letter to Secretary Manglapus," in *Christian-Muslim Democracy: Wave of the Future*. Pasig, Metro-Manila, Philippines: Pandan Bookpress, 1991, pp. 312–321 and 419–420. Published with permission.

Chapter 9. Rachid Ghannouchi. "The Participation of Islamists in a Non-Islamic Government," translated by Azzam Tamimi, in Azzam Tamimi, editor, *Power-Sharing Islam?* London: Liberty for Muslim World Publications, 1993, pp. 51–63. Published with permission.

Chapter 10. Sadek J. Sulaiman. "Democracy and *Shura*," unpublished manuscript. Arabic original © 1996 Sadek J. Sulaiman. Translation and introduction © 1996 Dale F. Eickelman. Published with permission.

Chapter 11. Nazira Zein-ed-Din. "Unveiling and Veiling: On the Liberation of the Woman and Social Renewal in the Islamic World," translated by Ali Badran and Margot Badran, in *Opening the Gates: A Century of Arab*

Feminist Writing, edited by Margot Badran and Miriam Cooke (London: Virago Press; Bloomington: Indiana University Press, 1990), pp. 272–276; and "Removing the Veil and Veiling: Towards Women's Liberation and Social Reform," translated by Salah-Dine Hammoud, *Women's Studies International Forum*, volume 5, number 2, 1982, pp. 223–226. The original was published as *Al-Sufur wa' l-hijab* (Arabic: *Unveiling and Veiling*) in 1928. Published with permission.

Chapter 12. Benazir Bhutto. "Politics and the Muslim Woman." Cambridge, Mass.: Unpublished audio recording, Rama Mehta Lecture, Radcliffe College Archive, April 11, 1985. Published with permission.

Chapter 13. Fatima Mernissi. *The Veil and the Male Elite: A Feminist Interpretation of Women's Rights in Islam*, translated by Mary Jo Lakeland. Reading, Mass.: Addison-Wesley, 1991, pp. 1–4, 49–61, 62, 64, 70–81. First published in French in 1987. © 1991 by Fatima Mernissi. Published with permission of Addison-Wesley and Edite Kroll Literary Agency.

Chapter 14. Amina Wadud-Muhsin. *Qur'an and Woman*. Kuala Lumpur, Malaysia: Penerbit Fajar Bakti Sdn. Bhd., 1992, pp. 1–10 and 64–74. Published with permission.

Chapter 15. Muhammad Shahrour. "Islam and the 1995 Beijing World Conference on Women." Unpublished manuscript, an earlier version of which appeared in the Kuwaiti newspaper *Al-Siyasa* (*Politics*), September 30, 1995, p. 15. Arabic original © 1996 by Muhammad Shahrour. Translation and introduction © 1996 by Dale F. Eickelman. Published with permission.

Chapter 16. Humayun Kabir. *Minorities in a Democracy*. Calcutta, India: Firma K. L. Mukhopadhyay, 1968, pp. 9–13, 20–30, 64–70. Published with permission.

Chapter 17. Chandra Muzaffar. "Introduction," in *Universalism of Islam*. Penang, Malaysia: Aliran, 1979, pp. 1–11. Published with permission.

Chapter 18. Mohamed Talbi. "Religious Liberty: A Muslim Perspective," *Liberty and Conscience*. Aldershot, England: Committee for the Defence of Religious Liberty, Spring 1989, volume 1, number 1, pp. 12–20. Published with permission.

Chapter 19. Ali Bulaç. "Medine Vesikası Hakkında Genel Bilgiler" (Turkish: General Information on the Medina Document), *Birikim* (Turkish: *Collection*), no. 38, June–July 1992, pp. 102–111, translated from the Turkish by Duygu Köksal; "Bir Arada Yaşamanın Mümkün Projesi Medine Vesikası" (Turkish: The Medina Document: The Possible Project of Cohabitation), *Bilgi ve Hikmet* (Turkish: *Knowledge and Wisdom*), Winter 1994–1995, pp. 3–15, translated from the Turkish by Betigül Ercan. Published with permission.

Chapter 20. Rusmir Mahmutćehajić. *Living Bosnia*, second edition, translated by Spomenka Beus and Francis R. Jones. Ljubljana, Slovenia: Oslobođenja International, 1995, pp. 153–155, 197–205. First published in Bosnian in 1994. Published with permission.

Chapter 21. 'Ali Shari'ati. "Modern Man and His Prisons," in *Man and Islam*, translated by Fatollah Marjani. Houston: Free Islamic Literature, 1981, pp. 46–62. Edited with the assistance of "The Four Prisons of Man," in *Man and Islam*, translated by Ghulam M. Fayez. Mashhad, Iran: University of Mashhad Press, 1982, pp. 60–99. First published in Persian around 1969. Published with permission.

Chapter 22. Yusuf Al-Qaradawi. *Islamic Awakening between Rejection and Extremism*, revised and edited by A. S. Al Shaikh-Ali and Mohamed B. E. Wasfy. Herndon, Va.: American Trust Publications and the International Institute of Islamic Thought, 1991, pp. 21–46. First published in Arabic in 1981. Published with permission.

Chapter 23. Mohamed Arkoun. "Rethinking Islam Today." Washington, D.C.: Center for Contemporary Arab Studies, Georgetown University, Occasional Papers Series, 1987. Published with permission.

Chapter 24. 'Abdullahi Ahmed An-Na'im. *Toward an Islamic Reformation: Civil Liberties, Human Rights, and International Law*. Syracuse, N.Y.: Syracuse University Press, 1990, pp. 161–187. Published with permission.

Chapter 25. Alhaji Adeleke Dirisu Ajijola. *Islam, Dialogue, Christianity*. Kaduna, Nigeria: Straight Path Publishers, 1992, pp. 85–102. Published with permission.

Chapter 26. Abdul-Karim Soroush. An earlier version of this unpublished paper was delivered as a lecture at the Institute of Islamic Studies, McGill University, April 13, 1995. Published with permission.

Chapter 27. Muhammad Iqbal. *The Reconstruction of Religious Thought in Islam*. Oxford: Oxford University Press, 1930, pp. 139–170.

Chapter 28. Mahmoud Mohamed Taha. *The Second Message of Islam*, translated by Abdullahi Ahmed An-Na'im. Syracuse, N.Y.: Syracuse University Press, 1987, pp. 43–47, 130–137, 146–153, 157–161. First published in Arabic in 1967. Published with permission.

Chapter 29. Murcholish Madijid. "The Necessity of Renewing Islamic Thought and the Problem of the Integration of the Ummat" and "Reinvigorating Religious Understanding in the Indonesian Muslim Community," translated by Muhammad Kamal Hassan in *Muslim Intellectual Responses to "New Order" Modernization in Indonesia*. Kuala Lumpur, Malaysia: Dewan Bahasa dan Pustaka, Kementerian Pelajaran, Malaysia, 1980, pp. 188–198 and 217–233. First published in Indonesian in 1970 and 1972, respectively. Published with permission.

Chapter 30. Mamadiou Dia. *Islam et Humanisme* (French: *Islam and Humanism*). Dakar, Senegal: Nouvelles Éditions Africaines, 1977, pp. 49, 83–87, 114–124, 139–142. Translated from French by Charles Kurzman. Published with permission.

Chapter 31. Fazlur Rahman. *Islam and Modernity*. Chicago: University of Chicago Press, 1982, pp. 130–162. Published with permission.

Chapter 32. Shabbir Akhtar. *A Faith for All Seasons: Islam and the Challenge of the Modern World*. Chicago: Ivan R. Dee, 1991, pp. 202–214. First published in England by Bellew Publishing Co. in 1990. Published with permission.

Contents

LIBERAL ISLAM

Introduction

Liberal Islam and Its Islamic Context

"Liberal Islam" may sound like a contradiction in terms. For centuries, the West has identified Islam with its most exotic elements. Islamic faith is equated with fanaticism, as in Voltaire's *Mahomet, or Fanaticism* (1745).[1] Islamic political authority is equated with despotism, as in Montesquieu's intentionally redundant phrase "Oriental despotism" or Francis Bacon's definition (1612): "A monarchy, where there is no nobility at all, is ever a pure and absolute tyranny; as that of the Turks." Islamic military practices are equated with terror and rape, as in Eugène Delacroix's famous painting "Massacre at Chios" (1824). Islamic tradition is equated with backwardness and primitiveness, as in Ernest Renan's inaugural lecture at the Collège de France (1862), one of the founding documents of modern Orientalism:

> Islam is the complete negation of Europe . . . Islam is the disdain of science, the suppression of civil society; it is the appalling simplicity of the Semitic spirit, restricting the human mind, closing it to all delicate ideas, to all refined sentiment, to all rational research, in order to keep it facing an eternal tautology: God is God.[2]

These themes continue today, as Western perceptions of Islam identify the religion with threatening images of theocracy and terrorism. The Iranian revolution of 1979 and the rise of Islamic radicalism from West Africa to Southeast Asia contribute to the impression that a new Cold War is looming.[3] Within the academic world, too, the study of Islam has devoted considerable attention to radical interpretations of the religion, as witnessed in academic works with alarming titles such as *Radical Islam*, *Militant Islam*, and *Sacred Rage*. Indeed, some Muslims agree with Western Orientalists that Islam is timeless and unchanging, that Muslims must interpret the word of God as literally as possible, and that East and West are mutually exclusive and inexorably opposed. A

---

1. All dates are given in the Christian calendar, also known as the Common Era calendar, unless noted.

2. On despotism, see Lucette Valensi, *The Birth of the Despot: Venice and the Sublime Porte*, translated by Arthur Denner (Ithaca, N.Y.: Cornell University Press, 1993). On violence, see Maxime Rodinson, *Europe and the Mystique of Islam*, translated by Roger Veinus (Seattle: Near Eastern

Studies, University of Washington, 1987), pp. 58–59. On exoticism, see Edward Said, *Orientalism* (New York: Vintage Books, 1978). On Islamic faith, see Norman Daniel, *Islam and the West: The Making of an Image* (Edinburgh: Edinburgh University Press, 1960). The Bacon quotation is taken from *Essays or Counsels* (Boston: Houghton Mifflin, 1908), p. 41; the Renan quotation from Ernest Renan, *Oeuvres complètes* (*Complete Works*) (Paris: Calmann-Livy, 1947), volume 2, p. 333.

3. John L. Esposito, *The Islamic Threat: Myth or Reality?* (New York: Oxford University Press, 1992); Samuel P. Huntington, "The Clash of Civilizations?" *Foreign Affairs*, volume 72, Summer 1993, pp. 22–49; Mark Juergensmeyer, *The Next Cold War?* (Berkeley: University of California Press, 1993); Jochen Hippler and Andrea Lueg, editors, *The Next Threat: Western Perceptions of Islam* (London: Pluto Press, 1995).

Pakistani Muslim, for example, has written: "Those who think of reforming or modernizing Islam are misguided, and their efforts are bound to fail. . . . Why should it be modernized, when it is already perfect and pure, universal, and for all time?"[4]

Yet the Orientalist view of Islam should not be mistaken for the whole of Islam. In historical terms, Islam has consisted of countless varied interpretations, among these a tradition that voices concerns parallel to those of Western liberalism. Exponents of this tradition have expressed resentment that their positions "have been generally ignored by Western scholars and members of the media who appear to prefer to highlight the sensationalism of extremist discourse that captures the attention of Western audiences."[5] Among the concerns of this neglected tradition are opposition to theocracy, support for democracy, guarantees of the rights of women and non-Muslims in Islamic countries, defense of freedom of thought, and belief in the potential for human progress—themes that form the six sections of this volume. Voicing such concerns can be dangerous in some countries, and proponents of this tradition have suffered for their beliefs, as discussed later in this chapter. Others, it should be noted, have benefited from relations with Western counterparts; this book, for instance, may confer a certain legitimacy on the authors who are included.

Just what to call this tradition presents a bit of a problem. I have followed the suggestion of legal scholar Asaf Ali Asghar Fyzee (India, 1899–1981), who wrote: "We need not bother about nomenclature, but if some name has to be given to it, let us call it 'Liberal Islam.'"[6] I use the term *liberal* with several caveats: First, the authors in this collection do not necessarily self-identify as liberals. Second, the authors may not espouse all aspects of liberal ideology, even if they subscribe to some. Third, the term "liberal" has negative connotations in parts of the Islamic world, where it is associated with foreign domination, unfettered capitalism, hypocritical paeans to rights, and hostility to Islam. Fourth, the concept of "liberal Islam" should be viewed as only a heuristic device, not a hard-and-fast category. Fifth, I make no claims as to the "correctness" of liberal interpretations of Islam. I am not qualified to engage in such debates; I wish only to describe them.

A small group of Western scholars has begun to examine liberal Islam, in what amounts to a paradigm shift in the academic study of Islam. Building on earlier studies of regional diversity within Islam, the new focus on liberal Islam heralds an increasing recognition of ideological diversity within Islam. Leonard Binder, for instance, discusses a variety of Islamic thinkers whose tenets overlap partially with Western liberalism and the relations that these tenets have with other elements of Islam. Abdallah Laroui examines the changing concept of liberty in Islam, explicitly noting the debate over the origin and application of the term in the Arabic-speaking world. Kevin Dwyer interviewed human-rights activists in North Africa and detailed their struggles with competing visions of progress and the good society.[7] In

7. Leonard Binder, *Islamic Liberalism: A Critique of Development Ideologies* (Chicago: University of Chicago Press, 1988); Abdallah Laroui, "Islam et Liberté" (Islam and Liberty), in *Islam et Modernité* (*Islam and Modernity*) (Paris: Éditions la Découverte, 1987), pp. 47–63; Kevin Dwyer, *Arab Voices: The Human Rights Debate in the Middle East* (London: Routledge; Berkeley: University of California Press, 1991). Among other studies of liberal Islam, see Ishtiaq Ahmed, *The Concept of an Islamic State: An Analysis of the Ideological Controversy in Pakistan*, Stockholm Studies in Politics, volume 28 (Stockholm: Department of Political Science, University of Stockholm, 1985); Nazih N. Ayubi *Political Islam: Religion and Politics in the Arab World* (London: Routledge, 1991); I. William Zartman, "Democracy and Islam: The Cultural Dialectic," *The Annals of the American Academy of Political and Social Science*, volume 524, 1992, pp. 181–191; John Keane, "Power-Sharing Islam?" in Azzam Tamimi, editor, *Power-Sharing Islam?* (London: Liberty for Muslim World Publications, 1993), pp. 15–31; Glenn D. Paige et alia, editors, *Islam and Nonviolence* (Honolulu, Hi.: Center for Global Nonviolence Planning Project, Matsunaga Institute for Peace, University of Hawai'i, 1993); Amyn B. Sajoo, *Pluralism in "Old Societies and New States": Emerging ASEAN Contexts* (Singapore: Institute of Southeast Asian Studies, 1994); Haddad, *Islamists and the Challenge of Pluralism*; "Islam and Liberal Democracy," symposium in *Journal of Democracy*, volume 7, number 2, April 1996, pp. 52–89; and John L. Esposito and John O. Voll, *Islam and Democracy* (New York: Oxford University Press, 1996).

4. Quoted in Bassam Tibi, *Islam and the Cultural Accommodation of Social Change* (Boulder, Colo.: Westview, 1990), p. 73.

5. Yvonne Yazbeck Haddad, *Islamists and the Challenge of Pluralism* (Washington, D.C.: Center for Contemporary Arab Studies and Center for Muslim-Christian Understanding, Georgetown University, Occasional Papers, 1995), p. 4.

6. Asaf A. A. Fyzee, "The Reinterpretation of Islam," in John J. Donohue and John L. Esposito, editors, *Islam in Transition: Muslim Perspectives* (New York: Oxford University Press, 1982), p. 193.

this book, I intend to contribute to this intellectual project by making the texts of major liberal Islamic thinkers available in English in a single anthology.

In addition, I want here to contribute to the literature on liberal Islam by emphasizing its Islamic context. It is common in analyses of liberal Islam to compare it with Western liberalism, with the implication of judgment according to Western standards; such work runs the risk of criticism such as that leveled against one Western author, who has been accused of being "mostly interested in Muslims who, in effect, speak her mind back to her in terms that she finds familiar, and who reassure her of the supremacy of her own Western values."[8] Insofar as the study of liberal Islam focuses on its Islamic dimension, however, I believe it escapes such criticism. The similarity of liberal Islam and Western liberalism does not imply that liberal Muslims are stale and reassuring imitators of Western philosophy. Many of their writings are firmly rooted in Qur'anic exegesis, in the lives of the Prophet Muhammad and the early Muslims, and in traditional Islamic forms of debate.

The next section traces the development of liberal Islam and its ongoing debate with two other major traditions, customary and revivalist Islam. It then identifies three modes of liberal Islam in terms of their readings of basic Islamic sources. The last section explains the selection criteria for the authors and themes included in this volume and introduces each of them briefly in terms of the three modes of liberal Islam.

The History of a Debate

Virtually every region of the Islamic world has witnessed parallel debates over the past two centuries between three traditions of socioreligious interpretation. These traditions overlap and intertwine and should not be considered mutually exclusive or internally homogeneous, but as heuristic devices the three labels provide significant insight into the recent history of Islamic discourse. The first tradition may be called *customary Islam*, characterized by the combination of regional practices and those that are shared throughout the Islamic world. In Morocco, the

customary tradition includes reverence for saintly figures that some Muslims feel have no basis in Islamic scripture; in Indonesia, the customary tradition includes ritual displays of spirituality and power that express regional cultural traditions.[9] We might also mention drumming in West African Islam and other musical traditions throughout the Islamic world, belief in spirits among Kurdish and other Muslims, celebration of the pre-Islamic New Year and other holy dates in Iran and elsewhere, caste-like social hierarchies in South Asian Islam, belief in persons and objects with magical powers, and so on. With no apparent ill ease, local custom may even contravene injunctions that are commonly acknowledged as pillars of Islamic faith, as in Southeast Asia, where "in some localities pilgrimage to sacred stones is regarded as an acceptable substitute for the *haj*"—the pilgrimage to Mecca—which "is regarded as an Arabian trick to hoodwink the Faithful."[10] The customary tradition represents the great majority of Muslims in most places and times. Yet the customary tradition is not a unitary phenomenon, since each region of the Islamic world has forged its own version of customary practice. Thus the customary tradition tends to be justified in local terms, not global ones: identity (this is the way "we" do things), prudence (it can't hurt to propitiate the powerful, be they spirits or spirit-infused humans), and linkages to the past (loyalty to one's teacher, one's teacher's teacher, and so on).[11]

The second tradition, and the most common alternative to customary Islam, is *revivalist Islam*, also known variously as Islamism, fundamentalism, or Wahhabism. This tradition attacks the customary interpretation as being insufficiently attentive to the letter of Islamic doctrine. Against local deviations, the revivalist tradition urges a renewed emphasis on the Arabic language (the language of revelation), the

8. Mohamed Elhachmi Hamdi, "Islam and Liberal Democracy: The Limits of the Western Model," *Journal of Democracy*, volume 7, number 2, April 1996, p. 83.

9. Clifford Geertz, *Islam Observed: Religious Development in Morocco and Indonesia* (Chicago: University of Chicago Press, 1968).

10. Roy F. Ellen, "Social Theory, Ethnography and the Understanding of Practical Islam in South-East Asia," in M. B. Hooker, editor, *Islam in South-East Asia* (Leiden: E. J. Brill, 1983), p. 65.

11. For other views on customary Islam, see Seyyed Hossein Nasr, *Traditional Islam in the Modern World* (London: KPI, 1987); William A. Graham, "Traditionalism in Islam: An Essay in Interpretation," *Journal of Interdisciplinary History*, volume 23, number 3, Winter 1993, pp. 495–522.

illegitimacy of local political institutions (as usurpers of God's sovereignty), the authority of the revivalists as the sole qualified interpreters of Islam, sometimes drastic expressions of personal piety, and the revival of practices from the early period of Islam. Muhammad ibn 'Abd al-Wahhab's revivalist movement in eighteenth-century Arabia—the prototype for all such movements since—was aimed precisely at ridding the Islamic heartland of the customary tradition, the un-Islamic practices that had returned to the region in the millennium after Islam was revealed. A more recent example is Tayyib 'Uqbi of Algeria (died 1960), who attacked customary Islam as heresy: "I have never performed the circumambulation [of a saint's shrine] . . . nor propitiatory sacrifices. . . . I do not invoke the dead. . . . Invoke whom you will, I shall never surrender to your idolatry."[12]

Many analyses of Islamic debates stop with these two traditions, the customary and the revivalist, and ignore a third major tradition that is the focus of this volume. *Liberal Islam*, like revivalist Islam, defines itself in contrast to the customary tradition and calls upon the precedent of the early period of Islam in order to delegitimate present-day practices. Yet liberal Islam calls upon the past in the name of modernity, while revivalists might be said to call upon modernity (for example, electronic technologies) in the name of the past. There are various versions of Islamic liberalism (several modes are discussed here later), but one common element is the critique of both the customary and revivalist traditions for what liberals sometimes term "backwardness," which in their view has prevented the Islamic world from enjoying the fruits of modernity: economic progress, democracy, legal rights, and so on. Instead, the liberal tradition argues that Islam, properly understood, is compatible with—or even a precursor to—Western liberalism.

These three interpretations of Islam have battled virtually continuously throughout the Islamic world for more than a century, with revivalism making occasionally significant inroads into the customary tradition and liberalism making somewhat less of a mark. Indeed, liberal Islam has more often been victim than victor.

Liberal Islam emerged out of the revivalist movements of the eighteenth century, a fertile period for

Islamic debate.[13] Politically, the great Muslim dynasties of the Mediterranean basin (the Ottoman Empire), Southwest Asia (the Safavid dynasty), and South Asia (the Mughul dynasty) were in various stages of collapse. Evangelically, Islam was continuing to win converts to the west, in West Africa, and the east, in Southeast Asia. Theologically, scholarly migration throughout the Islamic world accelerated, creating an international community of religious scholars who had either studied at the great centers of learning in Arabia or apprenticed under someone who had.

These scholars launched a series of revivalist movements that sought to rid Islam of un-Islamic practices not sanctioned by orthodox sources. The solution, according to the revivalists, was to replace the customary tradition with theologically sound Islamic teaching—namely, the teaching of revivalist religious scholars, who essentially argued that the authority of custom be replaced by the authority of the original sources of Islam, as interpreted by the revivalists.

This international community of revivalist scholars had its intellectual center in the great schools of Arabia, where Muslims from all lands visited as pilgrims or lived as students and then returned to their homes inspired to do battle with un-Islamic customary practices: Muhammad ibn 'Abd al-Wahhab from the Nejd region of Arabia, Shaykh Jibril ibn 'Umar al-Aqdisi from West Africa, Haji Miskin from Sumatra, Hajji Shari'at Allah and Ahmad Brelwi from South Asia, and Ma Mingxin from China.[14]

Liberal Islam has its roots in this revivalist context, in the person of Shah Wali-Allah (India, 1703–1762). Born in the last years of the Mughul dynasty, Wali-Allah inherited his father's position as head of a religious seminary. To complete his education, he traveled to Mecca, the holy site and seminary center in Arabia. On his return, he began to espouse a form of

12. Quoted in Ernest Gellner, *Muslim Society* (Cambridge: Cambridge University Press, 1981), p. 156.

13. The best starting point for cross-regional discussion of this period is Nehemia Levtzion and John O. Voll, editors, *Eighteenth-Century Renewal and Reform in Islam* (Syracuse, N.Y.: Syracuse University Press, 1987). However, research on the period remains fragmentary.

14. William R. Roff, "Islamic Movements: One or Many?" in William R. Roff, editor, *Islam and the Political Economy of Meaning* (Berkeley: University of California Press, 1987), pp. 31–52; John Obert Voll, *Islam: Continuity and Change in the Modern World*, second edition (Syracuse, N.Y.: Syracuse University Press, 1994).

revivalism heralded by later liberals as the intellectual forebear of liberal Islam. Like other revivalists, Wali-Allah perceived Islam to be in danger, sought to revitalize the Islamic community through a combination of theological renovation and sociopolitical organization, and viewed the customary tradition as a major source of Islam's problems.

Wali-Allah, however, developed a considerably more humanistic response to the customary tradition than did the Wahhabis and other revivalists. He was, for example, relatively tolerant of certain practices that other revivalists considered beyond the pale, arguing that Islamic law—while divinely inspired—must be adapted for the needs of different peoples and eras. If local custom is not in accordance with orthodox Islamic prescriptions, "it is not considered desirable to replace it by a different one [Islamic law] which is absolutely unknown to them [the local people]. . . . The basic purpose is that these reforms should be introduced in such a way that [the local people's] faculty of reasoning is satisfied and does not repel them."[15] The importance of human reasoning was a recurrent emphasis in Wali-Allah's work and a major precedent for later liberal Muslim thinkers, as in this Wali-Allah quotation translated by a twentieth-century liberal: "Time has come that the religious law of Islam should be brought into the open fully dressed in reason and argument."[16] Fazlur Rahman (Pakistan–United States, 1919–1988), a liberal whose work is excerpted in chapter 32, summarized Wali-Allah's approach as follows:

> So far as the Law is concerned, Waliy-Ullah did not stop at the medieval Muslim Schools of law but went back to its original sources, the Quran and the Apostolic Tradition and recommended *ijtihad*—exercise of independent judgment as opposed to the imitative following of medieval authorities. . . . The fundamental religious and moral fountains of mankind are the same in all times and climes, he holds,

but have to adjust themselves to and re-express themselves in terms of the genius of a particular age and of a particular people. . . . Islam, being a universal religion, had to find a vehicle of flesh and blood whereby to propagate itself and was bound to be coloured by that vehicle—the Arab tradition and way of life. But in different cultures, this vehicle will obviously undergo a change.[17]

Yet Wali-Allah was in many ways a revivalist. Despite his comments about dealing reasonably with local un-Islamic customs, he was highly intolerant of practices that he felt were equivalent to apostasy, such as visiting the tombs of great men to pray for intercession. Despite his comments about the age of reason—contemporaneous but apparently unconnected with European enlightenment sentiment—Wali-Allah did not place any great stock in "modern" forms of knowledge and deemed traditional Islamic scholarship to be sufficient to meet the demands of the contemporary world: "If I had been convinced that the good of this age depended upon the free circulation of Mathematics, Astronomy, Architecture, Technology and Engineering, I would have devoted my energies to their spread."[18] Instead of these novel forms of education, Wali-Allah emphasized traditional Islamic training and held that only graduates of this training were competent to practice *ijtihad*. On occasion, Wali-Allah appeared to suggest that only he was competent to practice *ijtihad* and that all other Muslims must practice *taqlid* (imitation) and follow his teachings. In statements that come close to messianism, Wali-Allah wrote that God appeared to him in a dream and appointed him leader of the world and reviver of Islam.[19]

An analogous development occurred in Shi'i Islam, with Aqa Muhammad Baqir Bihbihani (Iran, 1705–1790) playing a role similar to that of Wali-Allah. Bihbihani also was born into a leading clerical family and trained in traditional modes. He, too, converted to a position, later known as the Usuli school, that emphasized *ijtihad*. Also like Wali-Allah,

15. Translated in Mi'raj Muhammad, "Shah Wali-Allah's Concept of the *Shari'ah*," in *Islamic Perspectives: Studies in Honour of Mawlana Sayyid Abul A'la Mawdudi*, edited by Khurshid Ahmad and Zafar Ishaq Ansari (Leicester, England: The Islamic Foundation, 1979), p. 346. A somewhat different translation appears in J. M. S. Baljon, *Religion and Thought of Shah Wali Allah Dihlawi, 1703–1762* (Leiden: E. J. Brill, 1986), p. 162.

16. Translated in Aziz Ahmad, "Political and Religious Ideas of Shah Wali-Ullah of Delhi," *Muslim World*, volume 52, number 1, January 1962, p. 26.

17. Fazlur Rahman, "The Thinker of Crisis: Shah Waliy-Ullah," *Pakistan Quarterly*, volume 6, number 2, Summer 1956, p. 45.

18. Translated in A. D. Muztar, *Shah Wali Allah: A Saint-Scholar of Muslim India* (Islamabad: National Commission on Historical and Cultural Research, 1979), p. 204.

19. See the citations in Saiyid Athar Abbas Rizvi, *Shah Wali-Allah and His Times* (Canberra, Australia: Ma'rifat Publishing House, 1980), p. 219.

Bihbihani combined the conservative concept of *taqlid* and the potentially liberal concept of *ijtihad* by restricting the practice of *ijtihad* to competent religious scholars. This view evolved in the nineteenth century into the position that each era must obey a single religious scholar as the *marja'-i taqlid*, or source of imitation, though this concept involves no hint of divine inspiration, as in Wali-Allah's work.[20]

Only in the nineteenth century, however, did liberal Islam begin to distinguish itself more clearly from revivalism, and it did so both intellectually and institutionally. On the intellectual plane, first, liberals began to separate *ijtihad* from *taqlid*, reason from authority. Most of the major figures of nineteenth-century liberal Islam echoed these themes:

Jamal al-Din al-Afghani (born in Iran, 1838–1897): "In their beliefs they [the members of each community] must shun submission to conjectures and not be content with mere *taqlid* of their ancestors. For if man believes in things without proof or reason, makes a practice of following unproven opinions, and is satisfied to imitate and follow his ancestors, his mind inevitably desists from intellectual movement, and little by little stupidity and imbecility overcome him—until his mind becomes completely idle and he becomes unable to perceive his own good and evil; and adversity and misfortune overtake him from all sides.[21]

Sayyid Ahmad Khan (India, 1817–1898) and Sayyid Mahdi Ali Khan (India, 1837–1907): "*Taqlid* is not incumbent [on the believer]. Every person is entitled to *ijtihad* in those matters concerning which there is no explicitly revealed text in Qur'an and *sunna* [the practice of the Prophet]."[22]

Muhammad 'Abduh (Egypt, 1849–1905): "First, to liberate thought from the shackles of *taqlid* . . . to return, in the acquisition of religious knowledge, to its first sources, and to weigh them in the scales of human reason, which God has created in order to prevent excess or adulteration in religion . . . and to prove that, seen in this light, religion must be accounted a friend to science, pushing man to investigate the secrets of existence. . . ."[23]

Taqlid became anathema to liberals of the early twentieth century, as it symbolized the popular influence of the liberals' traditionalist opponents. Jamal al-Din al-Qasimi (Ottoman Syria, 1866–1914), for example, called *taqlid* "a leprosy which has spread widely among the people . . . an infectious disease, a general paralysis, a stupefying lunacy plunging man into apathy and indolence."[24] *Ijtihad*, by contrast, allowed Islam to be interpreted in accordance with the perceived needs of the modern age. Nonetheless, considerable disagreement existed as to what these needs might be: whether to resist European rule or acquiesce, whether to reform traditional schools or establish new ones, whether to relax or restore religious practices. Liberals of this period criticized one another almost as enthusiastically as they criticized customary and revivalist Islam.

The expansion of the right to practice *ijtihad* directly threatened the authority of both revivalist and customary Islamic leaders, in that it urged all Muslims to study Islam for themselves and, in effect, to be their own authority. However, few if any nineteenth-century liberals drew from this the twentieth-century conclusion that the opinions of the people should dictate public affairs. Instead, the liberals sought to impose themselves as tutelary authorities, and their primary means of activism was in the field of educational reform. Though many liberals of this period were themselves the product of traditional religious educations, they deemed these institutions insufficient to meet the needs of the day and sought to reform them or to create new institutions combining traditional and modern approaches. Sayyid Ahmad Khan, for example, founded the Muhammadan Anglo-Oriental College in Aligarh, India; 'Abduh attempted to reform the ancient al-Azhar University in Cairo, Egypt; al-Afghani was involved in the early years of Istanbul University in the Ottoman Empire. In addition, we may cite:

---

20. Juan Cole, "Shi'i Clerics in Iraq and Iran, 1722–1780: The Akhbari-Usuli Conflict Reconsidered," *Iranian Studies*, volume 18, number 1, Winter 1985, pp. 3–34.

21. Nikki R. Keddie, *An Islamic Response to Imperialism: Political and Religious Writings of Sayyid Jamal ad-Din "al-Afghani"* (Berkeley: University of California Press, 1968), p. 171.

22. Christian W. Troll, *Sayyid Ahmad Khan: A Reinterpretation of Muslim Theology* (New Delhi: Vikas Publishing House, 1978), p. 275.

23. Albert Hourani, *Arabic Thought in the Liberal Age, 1798–1939* (London: Oxford University Press, 1962), pp. 140–141.

24. David Dean Commins, *Islamic Reform: Politics and Social Change in Late Ottoman Syria* (New York: Oxford University Press, 1990), p. 71.

- Rifa'a Rafi' al-Tahtawi (Egypt, 1801–1873), trained at al-Azhar in Cairo, who lived for several years in Paris as religious instructor to a group of Egyptian students; on his return to Egypt, he sought to develop a new educational system that incorporated both Islamic and European elements.
- Shihab al-Din Marjani (Russia, 1818–1889) and Ahmad Makhdum Danesh (Bukhara, 1827–1897), both trained in traditional schools at Bukhara, who worked to reform the curriculum in this seminary city by introducing secular subjects.
- Ismail Bey Gasprinskii (Russia, 1851–1914), trained in Islamic primary and Russian secondary schools, who founded a large network of modern (jadid) schools throughout Russia that combined secular and religious education.
- Shaykh Muhammad Tahir Jalaluddin (Sumatra-Malaysia, 1867–1957), Kiyai Haji Ahmad Dahlan (Java-Indonesia, 1869–1923), and Ahmad Surkati (Sudan-Indonesia, 1872–1943), all of whom studied at al-Azhar or in Mecca and later helped to found reformist schools in Southeast Asia.
- Wang Haoran (China, 1848–1918), influenced by al-Azhar and pan-Islamic sentiments centered at Istanbul, who founded reformist schools and Islamic organizations in China.

The distinguishing feature of these new reforms was their introduction of Western subjects into the traditional curriculum, a practice that reflected the liberals' second intellectual contribution: respect for "modernity." While revivalists sought to cure the ills of the Muslim world by refocusing on the seventh-century sources of the Islamic faith, liberals sought to combine this refocus with an additional focus on Western disciplines such as engineering and military science, medicine and natural science, comparative legal studies and social science, and modern languages. For this reason, liberal Islam of the period is generally known by the rubric of "Islamic modernism."

These educational institutions that the liberals reformed or founded, spawning further liberal graduates, formed the first of three institutional bases for liberal Islam. By the early twentieth century, liberals were in charge of al-Azhar in Egypt, the leading schools of the Ottoman Empire, the system of jadid (new) schools in the Muslim regions of Russia, the Aligarh and other leading Islamic universities in South Asia, and the Muhammadiya school system in Indonesia.

The second institutional base, somewhat shakier, was journalism. As literacy increased, Islamic liberals made active use of this new medium to communicate with their followers. Indeed, the names of many leading liberals of the era are associated with periodicals: Namık Kemal's Tasvir-i Efkâr (Herald of Ideas) and Hürriyet (Liberty) in Ottoman Turkish, 1865–1870; Sayyid Ahmad Khan's Tahzib al-Akhlaq (Refinement of Morals) in Urdu, 1870–1896; Gasprinskii's Tercüman/Perevodchik (The Interpreter) in Tatar Turkish and Russian, 1883–1914; al-Afghani and 'Abduh's al-'Urwa al-Wuthqa (The Strongest Link) in Arabic, 1884; Mirza Malkom Khan's Qanun (The Law) in Persian, 1890–1898; Muhammad Rashid Rida's al-Manar (The Lighthouse) in Arabic, 1898–1935; Jalaluddin's al-Imam (The Leader) in Malay, 1906–1908; Rizaeddin Fakhreddin's Shura (Consultation) in Tatar Turkish, 1908–1917; Mahmud Tarzi's Siraj al-Akhbar (The Lamp of the News) in Afghani Persian, 1911–1918; Abdullah Ahmad's Al Munir El Manar (Light of the Victors) in Indonesian, 1911–1916; Abu'l-Kalam Azad's al-Hilal (The Crescent) in Urdu, 1912–1914; Mahmud Khoja Behbudiy's Ayina (The Mirror) in Uzbek Turkish, 1913–1916; and others. Some of these periodicals were short-lived, and some had to be published in Europe because of political pressure in Islamic countries. Still, these journals had a tremendous reach and influence among educated Muslims: for example, Ahmad Faris al-Shidyaq's al-Jawa'ib (Rumors), published in Constantinople, was read "in all countries of the Arabic speech" in the 1870s, according to a British observer, and was even found "in the Nejd [Arabian] merchants' houses at Bombay"; Rashid Rida's al-Manar "was widely read in the Islamic world and was a major factor in shaping Muslim thought from North Africa to Southeast Asia"; Gasprinskii's Tercüman was influential in China.[25]

A third institutional base was an international network of intellectuals centered primarily on Muhammad 'Abduh and his disciples in Cairo. Not only were 'Abduh's books and his followers' newspapers, in particular al-Manar, read throughout the Islamic world—Cairo also became a central site for liberals to visit and study, just as Mecca and Medina had been for revivalists a century earlier. Diverse figures such as Jalaluddin, Dahlan, Syekh Ahmad Khatib

---

25. Hourani, Arabic Thought, p. 99; Voll, Islam, p. 163; H. M. G. d'Ollone, Recherches sur les Musulmans chinois (Research on Chinese Muslims) (Paris: Ernest Leroux, 1911), pp. 380–381.

(Sumatra, 1855–1916) Abdullah Ahmad (Sumatra, died 1933), and Sayid Syekh al-Hadi (Malaya, 1867–1934) from Southeast Asia, Sayyid Ahmad bin Sumayt (Comoros-Zanzibar, 1861–1925), Muhammad Kurd 'Ali (Syria, 1876–1952), Abu Shu'ayb al-Dukkali (Morocco, 1878–1937), 'Abd al-'Aziz al-Tha'alibi (Tunisia, 1879–1944), Ha Decheng (China, 1888–1943), and Abu'l-Kalam Azad (India, 1888–1958) returned from Cairo to spread the liberal message in their own regions. A secondary center for this international network was Istanbul, capital of the Ottoman Empire, whose influential students included Gasprinskii from Crimea, Mehmed Džemaludin Ćaušević (Bosnia, died 1937), 'Abd al-Qadir al-Maghribi (Ottoman Syria, 1867–1956), Numan Chelebi Jihan (Russia, 1885–1918), and Abdal Rauf Fitrat (Bukhara, 1886–1938). A few scholars, such as Musa Yarullah Bigi (Russia, 1874–1949), trained at both Cairo and Istanbul. Numerous others maintained contact with these centers through correspondence, meetings abroad, and the traffic in publications.

Liberals reached the apogee of their power in the first two decades of the twentieth century. During the nineteenth century, liberal reforms had begun at the behest of modernizing monarchs (Mehmet 'Ali in Egypt, Mahmud II in the Ottoman Empire, Ahmad Bey in Tunisia) more interested in military and administrative efficiency than in liberalism or Islam; they had continued under prime ministers (Amir Kabir in Persia, Mithat Paşa in the Ottoman Empire, Khayr al-Din in Tunisia) who introduced liberal educational or political reforms but lasted only several years in office. By contrast, the early twentieth century saw liberal Islam rise to significant political influence in its own right. In colonized regions, Muslim communities came to be represented by liberal organizations such as Ittifaq al-Muslimin (Russia), the Muhammadiya (Dutch Indonesia), and the Aligarh establishment (British India). In still-independent lands, liberals gained state power through constitutional revolutions in Iran (1906) and the Ottoman Empire (1908). Unlike the reforms of the previous century, granted from the top down, these revolutions were foisted upon reluctant monarchs. Among the key supporters of the Persian constitutional movement were Sayyid Muhammad Tabataba'i (Iran, 1843–1921), Sayyid 'Abdullah Behbehani (Iran, 1846–1910), and other religious scholars who participated in the revolutionary mobilization and played large roles in the parliamentary government that fol-

lowed.[26] The Young Turks in the Ottoman Empire made considerable use of liberal clerics such as the Sheyh-ül-Islam, the leader of the clerical establishment in the empire, who told a British interviewer: "Our [Islamic] law, rightly interpreted, is in accordance with the principles of representative government. . . . [The Ottoman Constitution] becomes binding upon those who profess Islam. Especially those who are called to lead, our 'ulama', are bound to help actively in carrying out the Constitution."[27] Liberal religious scholars were not the sole movers in these democratic experiments, and many of the leading figures had to be pressured into maintaining a consistently pro-democratic line by activists among their followers. Nonetheless, state sponsorship gave the liberals a tremendous advantage over their theological opponents.

This advantageous position proved to be temporary. The new democracies in Iran and the Ottoman Empire succumbed to the combined onslaught of revivalist Islam and secular military might. In the Ottoman Empire, a revivalist organization incited a mutiny in the capital, calling for the implementation of the *shari'a*, Islamic law, in place of the constitution. In response, the largely secular armed forces marched on the capital and suppressed both the liberal parliament and its clerical allies. In Iran, revivalists politicked actively against the constitution and parliament and supported the coups d'état of 1908 and 1911.

Elsewhere, revivalists sought to cast liberals as apostates, as in this statement by a Russian Muslim leader: "Whoever believes in God and Muhammad must be an enemy of the modernists. For them the *shari'a* demands the death penalty."[28] Such accusations were inevitable, as the liberals' attempt to learn

---

26. Janet Afary, *The Iranian Constitutional Revolution, 1906–1911* (New York: Columbia University Press, 1996); Mangol Bayat, *Iran's First Revolution: Shi'ism and the Constitutional Revolution of 1905–1909* (New York: Oxford University Press, 1991); Vanessa Martin, *Islam and Modernism: The Iranian Revolution of 1906* (London: I. B. Tauris & Co., 1989).

27. Charles Roden Buxton, *Turkey in Revolution* (London: T. Fisher Unwin, 1909), pp. 170–171.

28. Edward Lazzerini, "Ismail Bey Gasprinskii (Gaspirali): The Discourse of Modernism and the Russians," in Edward Allworth, editor, *Tatars of the Crimea: Their Struggle for Survival* (Durham, N.C.: Duke University Press, 1988), p. 156.

about and from the West exposed them to charges of inauthenticity and betrayal of their own cultural tradition. "The modernist aroused suspicion even about his loyalty to Islam, and he was accused of being a pale reflection of the West and of sacrificing Islam at its altar," according to Rahman.[29] Indeed, this is the image of modernist Islam that appears to have stuck.[30] Many later liberal Muslims have accordingly distanced themselves from liberals of the modernist period. "The tragedy," according to 'Ali Shari'ati (Iran, 1933–1977), "is that, on the one hand, those who have controlled our religion over the past two centuries have transformed it into its present static form and, on the other hand, our enlightened people who understand the present age and the needs of our generation and time, do not understand religion. . . . "[31] Few of the liberal authors in this volume cite 'Abduh and his contemporaries approvingly.

While some liberals of this era were no doubt guilty of these charges, adopting the Orientalist perspective and calling Islam backwards and unsalvageable—"There is no second civilization; civilization means European civilization," according to one Ottoman reformer[32]—most liberals of the modernist period were far more protective of Islamic faith and culture than they are generally given credit for. For most of them, the goal was not to displace Islam but to rejuvenate it.

Indeed, it is ironic that liberal Islam was accused of secularism, since secularism was largely responsible for undermining it. Beginning in the 1920s, educated Muslims who might otherwise have subscribed to liberal Islam now turned in large numbers to secular ideologies such as nationalism and socialism. Widespread secularization undermined liberalism in a second way by creating a sense of crisis within Islam that favored revivalists: "Faith rather than explanation or formulation of Faith, intuitive certainty rather than discursive thought-content becomes the cry of the hour."[33] For example, 'Ali 'Abd al-Raziq (Egypt, 1888–1966; chapter 1) was fired from his position at al-Azhar in 1925 for arguing that Islam leaves the form of government to human invention. This liberal position might not have been considered beyond the pale several years earlier, prior to the abolition of the seventh-century-old Ottoman caliphate by Turkish secularists. Al-Azhar had become more conservative; even 'Abduh's disciple Rashid Rida condemned 'Abd al-Raziq. Western observers contended that liberal Islam had become stagnant.[34]

Still, liberal Islamic thinkers helped to found or shape a number of anticolonial movements in the 1920s and 1930s: 'Abd al-Hamid Ibn Badis's Association of Algerian Religious Scholars, Muhammad Iqbal's All-India Muslim League, Muhammad 'Allal al-Fasi's Istiqlal party in Morocco, and 'Abd al-'Aziz al-Tha'alibi's Destour party in Tunisia. In addition, the decolonization of Islamic countries renewed debates over Islamic governance, for example, in India, Indonesia, Nigeria, and Pakistan, debates in which liberals participated. However, liberal Islam was largely overtaken by other ideological trends during the middle part of the twentieth century.

Since the 1970s, however, liberal Islam has enjoyed a renewed popularity. The timing is perhaps unexpected, since it is precisely the period when Islamic revivalism has also gained adherents. The two traditions have clashed on numerous occasions, usually in intellectual debate but sometimes violently.

29. Fazlur Rahman, "Roots of Islamic Neo-Fundamentalism," in *Change in the Muslim World*, edited by Philip H. Stoddard, David D. Cuthell, and Margaret W. Sullivan (Syracuse, N.Y.: Syracuse University Press, 1981), p. 31.

30. Abdallah Laroui, "Western Orientalism and Liberal Islam: Mutual Distrust?" *MESA Bulletin*, volume 31, number 1, July 1997, p. 7.

31. 'Ali Shari'ati, "Where Shall We Begin?" translated by A. Alidust and F. Rajaee, in *What Is to Be Done?* edited by Farhang Rajaee (Houston: The Institute for Research and Islamic Studies, 1986), p. 21. Mamadiou Dia (Senegal, born 1911) makes an entirely contradictory, but similarly sweeping, critique of earlier liberals: "The paradox of Islamic modernism is that it totally ignores modern problems, which are confounded with ancient themes dressed up as modernity. Thus traditional theology remains at the center of modernist thought. . . ." (Mamadiou Dia, *Essais sur l'Islam* [*Essays on Islam*], volume 1, *Islam et Humanisme* [*Islam and Humanism*] [Dakar, Senegal: Les Nouvelles Éditions Africaines, 1977], p. 115).

32. Quoted in Mohamed Arkoun, *Rethinking Islam*, translated by Robert D. Lee (Boulder, Colo.: Westview, 1994), p. 25.

33. Fazlur Rahman, *Islam*, second edition (Chicago: University of Chicago, 1979), p. 222.

34. H. A. R. Gibb, *Modern Trends in Islam* (Chicago: University of Chicago Press, 1947); Wilfred Cantwell Smith, *Modern Islam in India* (London: Victor Gallancz, 1946; first published in 1943).

Liberals of diverse ideologies are disproportionately the victims of such violence, among them:

- Mahmoud Mohamed Taha (Sudan, circa 1910–1985), who opposed the revivalist Sudanese government's interpretation of *shari'a* law, was executed for alleged apostasy in 1985.
- Subhi al-Salih (Lebanon, died 1986), a former vice-mufti of Lebanon, who argued for "opening of all gates of *ijtihad*" and banning *taqlid*, was assassinated by Shi'i gunmen in 1986.
- Farag Fuda (Egypt, 1945–1992), a liberal politician and columnist who criticized Islamic extremism, was assassinated in 1992.
- Maulvi Farook (India, 1945–1990) and Qazi Nissar Ahmed (India, 1948–1994), both Muslim religious scholars and proponents of rights for Muslims in the Kashmir region of India, were killed in 1990 and 1994, respectively, for opposing the violent tactics of Islamic separatists in the region. Yassin Malik, another critic of violence, was attacked several times in 1994 but survived.
- Mohammad Sa'id (Algeria, circa 1947–1995) and Abderrazak Redjam (Algeria, circa 1957–1995), both prominent activists in the Islamist movement in Algeria, were executed along with several dozen followers by a militant Islamist faction in 1995 after they had publicly objected to the faction's violent methods.

On a less violent scale, a number of the authors included in this volume have been subjected to confrontations that go beyond intellectual debate. Muhammad Khalaf-Allah (Egypt, born 1916; chapter 2) was urged not just to burn all the copies of his work but also to reaffirm his faith in Islam and renew his marriage vows; Mehdi Bazargan (Iran, 1907–1995; chapter 7) was hounded out of the prime ministership and then out of parliament in Iran; Muhammad Shahrour (Syria, born 1938; chapter 15) saw his work banned in several Middle Eastern countries; Abdul-Karim Soroush (Iran, born 1945; chapter 26) has been barred from speaking publicly in Iran and publicly threatened with assassination.

Some liberals are understandably depressed about their unpromising position in contemporary Islamic debates. Indeed, Hassan Hanafi (Egypt, born 1935) has placed this pessimism at the heart of his analysis of Islamic history, arguing that nonliberal interpretations of Arab-Islamic heritage have become so firmly entrenched that Arabs have lost the ability to debate and learn.[35] One scholar concludes that with the rise of Islamic revivalism since the 1970s, "the time for Muslim liberalism has certainly passed."[36] Another scholar suggests that liberal Islam faces an "impossible life": "In one Moslem society after another, to write of liberalism . . . is to write obituaries of men who took on impossible odds, and then failed."[37]

At the same time, however, there are indications that pessimism may be premature. On the intellectual plane, liberal Islamic thinkers are building a more self-confident liberalism that apologizes neither for its liberalism nor for its Islamic essence. The contemporary generation is far more familiar with Western society and education than were previous generations. Many of the authors in this volume received postgraduate degrees in Europe and North America; unlike nineteenth-century liberals who called for the implementation of Western disciplines that they themselves were ill-trained in, their late-twentieth-century descendants approach "modern" themes from a position of strength. 'Abdullahi Ahmed An-Na'im (Sudan-United States, born 1946), Mohamed Arkoun (Algeria-France, born 1928), and Rahman, for example, have been certified by faculty positions at elite Western universities. At the same time, contemporary liberals are more confident than their ancestors in asserting the need for Islamic contributions to modern problems. In part because their familiarity with the West allows them to critique it more confidently, in part because of the renewed self-respect that militant revivalist Islam has generated, contemporary liberals are able to argue that the West is suffering from a spiritual crisis—any number of Western sources can be cited in support—that Islam may help to cure. By contrast, liberal Muslims of a century ago were considerably less critical of the West.

35. Hassan Hanafi, "Al-Juzur al-tarikhiya lazima al-hurriya wa al-dimukratiya fi wujdanuna al-mu'asir" (The Historical Roots of the Impasse with Regard to Freedom and Democracy in our Zeitgeist), *Al-Mustaqbal al-'Arabi* (*The Arab Future*), number 5, January 1979, pp. 130–139. For a discussion of this essay, see Richard K. Khuri, "A Critique of Hassan Hanafi Concerning His Reflections on the Scarcity of Freedom in the Arab-Muslim World," in Şerif Mardin, editor, *Cultural Transitions in the Middle East* (Leiden: E. J. Brill, 1994), pp. 86–115.

36. Aziz Al-Azmeh, *Islams and Modernities* (London: Verso, 1993), p. 33.

37. Fouad Ajami, "The Impossible Life of Moslem Liberalism," *New Republic*, June 2, 1986, p. 27.

A further source of optimism for liberal Islam is the rising level of education in the Muslim world. Literacy allows Muslims to read the Qur'an and other Islamic sources for themselves, rather than rely on religious scholars, and as traditional religious schools have lost their monopoly on education over the past century, an increasing number of Muslims have applied their nonreligious education to develop novel approaches to Islam. Recall the large percentage of nineteenth-century liberals who were trained traditionally; by contrast, many of the authors in this volume are the products of secular educations: Bazargan and Shahrour were trained as engineers, Arkoun and Rachid Ghannouchi (Tunisia, born 1941) as philosophers, Chandra Muzaffar (Malaysia, born 1947) and Shari'ati as social scientists, and so on. In addition to providing the theorists for liberalism, expanding systems of education are providing an audience as well. For example, Shahrour's first book was a best-seller in North Africa, though it had to be copied clandestinely; Shari'ati's work is especially popular among university students; Soroush is frequently discussed by Iranians on the Internet.

A final cause for optimism is the emergence of an organizational infrastructure for liberal Islam. Multidenominational organizations have emerged in Malaysia (Aliran), the Philippines (Christian-Muslim Democracy), Senegal (Yewwu Yewwi), and elsewhere with the aim of fostering peaceful coexistence among religious communities and combating intolerance, Islamic and otherwise. In addition, a number of research institutes have been founded to support research, publications, translations (including several in this volume), and conferences. One of the earliest such organizations was the Islamic Research Institute in Pakistan, which Rahman ran until revivalists forced his resignation in the 1960s. Also in the early 1960s, Bazargan, Mahmud Taleqani (Iran, 1911–1979), and other liberals established the Freedom Movement of Iran, which urged liberal reforms on both Islamic institutions and secular ones. Many similar organizations are located in the West: the International Institute of Islamic Thought in Herndon, Virginia; the Institute for Research and Islamic Studies in Houston, Texas; the World and Islam Studies Enterprise in Tampa, Florida; the Liberty for Muslim World human-rights organization in London, England; and the Ibn Khaldun Society in London and Washing-

ton, D.C., among others.[38] These organizations' activities appear to be aimed both at Westerners, by showing the non-"fanatical" face of Islam, and at Muslims, in the attempt to disseminate liberal perspectives within the Islamic world. As such, they represent the first real effort since the late nineteenth century to generate an international scholarly movement of liberal Islam.

Modes of Liberal Islam

Liberal Islam operates in two intellectual contexts: one Islamic and one Western-oriented. The authors in this volume place different emphases on each, yet all can be analyzed in terms of either context, as Islamic liberals (a subset of liberalism) or as liberal Muslims (a subset of Islam). Much of the academic literature on these authors takes the first approach: Just how liberal are Islamic liberals? Do Islamic variants of liberalism meet Western standards of liberalism? Leonard Binder's erudite analysis of *Islamic Liberalism* largely takes this approach, weighing elements of the thought of leading Egyptian writers against Western traditions. I wish to take the opposite tack: to examine liberal Muslims in light of Islamic tradition.

This context is the one that most liberal Muslims themselves appear to favor, even those such as Mamadiou Dia (Senegal, born 1911; chapter 30), whose work deals more with French Christian theology than with Islamic theologians. Dia and other liberals seem to be highly sensitive to charges of cultural inauthenticity and view their work as a renewal of, not an escape from, long-standing debates within Islam. Dia writes: "Islamic authenticity requires a return to the sources, that is, to the Qur'an and to the [*sunna*], not to take shelter there, to drown current cares there, but to draw from thence elements for the renovation and revitalization of Islamic philosophy."

Taking these Islamic debates as the context, we may identify three principal "modes" of liberal Islam. These involve the relationship of liberalism to the primary sources of Islam: the divinely revealed book

38. See, for example, the listing of web sites presented in Nancy Gallagher, "Middle East and North Africa Human Rights Activism in Cyberspace," *MESA Bulletin*, volume 31, number 1, July 1997, pp. 17–29.

(Qur'an) and the divinely inspired practice of the
Prophet Muhammad (*sunna*), which together constitute the basis for Islamic law (*shari'a*). The first mode
takes liberal positions as being explicitly sanctioned
by the *shari'a*; the second mode argues that Muslims
are free to adopt liberal positions on subjects that the
shari'a leaves open to human ingenuity; the third
mode suggests that the *shari'a*, while divinely inspired, is subject to multiple human interpretations.
I call these modes *liberal*, *silent*, and *interpreted*.
Examples are taken from the authors in this volume
and from other liberal Islamic thinkers whose works
could not be included in this volume for lack of space,
but whose ideas and reputations deserve to be more
widely recognized.

The Liberal Shari'a

The first mode holds that the *shari'a* is itself liberal,
if interpreted properly. For instance, Ali Bulaç (Turkey, born 1951), one of the leading liberal Islamists
in Turkey, argues in previously untranslated articles
(chapter 19) that the Medina Document—by which
the Prophet Muhammad granted rights to non-Muslims living under Muslim rule—presents a model of
how the *shari'a* solves contemporary problems in
a liberal manner. Abdur Rahman I. Doi (India-
Nigeria, born 1933) argues that the Qur'an is the
world's first constitution and that European Christians discovered constitutionalism only centuries
later. Maurice Bucaille (France, born 1920) argues
that the Qur'an prefigures methods of scientific inquiry that secular scientists took centuries longer to
understand. Shafique Ali Khan (Pakistan, born 1936)
and Abdelkébir Alaoui M'Daghri (Morocco, born
1942) argue that the *shari'a* establishes freedom of
thought.[39]

The "liberal *shari'a*" mode of liberal Islam is undoubtedly the most influential form of liberal Islam.
I propose three explanations. First, it avoids the
charge of inauthenticity by grounding liberal posi-

tions solidly in orthodox Islamic sources. Second, it
suggests that liberal positions are not merely human
choices but divine commands (leading to the anoma-
lous position, which Western liberalism suffers from
as well, of justifying liberalism by reference to illib-
eralism, such as "God-given" rights).[40] Third, it appeals to pride of discovery: To argue that liberal
Islam predates Western liberalism is a powerful
rhetorical strategy among peoples who have too
often internalized Western images of inferiority and
backwardness.

Yet this mode of liberal Islamic discourse is most
susceptible to theoretical counterattacks on orthodox theological grounds. The "liberal *shari'a*" must
be argued on the home turf, as it were, of orthodoxy:
the detailed analysis of the meaning of the Qur'an,
the sifting of reliable chains of oral transmission of
the traditions of the Prophet, the very sort of research for which orthodox scholars are extensively
trained. Bulaç and Bazargan, by contrast, are basically autodidacts venturing into textual analysis
for which others are better prepared. I do not mean
to judge this work but rather to point out that it
is a difficult intellectual venture. By contrast, the
other two modes of liberal Islam strategically
shift the field of debate away from these orthodox
strongholds.

The Silent Shari'a

The second mode of liberal Islamic argumentation
holds that the *shari'a* is silent on certain topics. Legal
scholar Muhammad Salim Al-'Awwa (Egypt, contemporary) summarizes this approach as follows:

> If Islam does not "mention" something, this indicates
> one of two things: either that it is not stated anywhere
> in the traditional sources or that Muslims have never
> practiced it throughout their history. In the first case,
> the non-mentioning of something implies that it
> is permitted. The only exception to this rule is the
> subject of worship. . . . In the second case . . . [i]t
> is only natural that Muslims should respond to

39. Abdur Rahman I. Doi, *Constitutionalism in Islamic
Law* (Zaria, Nigeria: Centre for Islamic Legal Studies,
Ahmadu Bello University, 1977); Maurice Bucaille, *The
Bible, the Qur'an, and Science* (Indianapolis, Ind.: American Trust Publications, 1978); Shafique Ali Khan, *Freedom
of Thought and Islam* (Karachi: Royal Book Co., 1989);
Abdelkébir Alaoui M'Daghri, *La Liberté de pensée/Free-
dom of Thought/Hurriyat al-fikr* (al-Muhammadiya, Morocco: Matbaat Fazalat, 1991).

40. On the anomaly of "scripturalist liberalism," see
Binder, *Islamic Liberalism*, p. 244. On the illiberal elements
of Western liberalism, see Michael J. Sandel, *Liberalism and
the Limits of Justice* (Cambridge: Cambridge University
Press, 1982); Michael J. Sandel, editor, *Liberalism and Its
Critics* (New York: New York University Press, 1984).

changes and developments at all times and in all circumstances.[41]

'Abd al-Raziq (chapter 1), the controversial Egyptian scholar, helped to pioneer this trope in the 1920s by arguing that the *shari'a* does not specify the form that the state should take, thus allowing the establishment of liberal democracies. As Islamic scholar Muhammad Sa'id Al-'Ashmawi (Egypt, born 1932) notes in chapter 4: "Of some 6000 Qur'anic verses, only 200 have a legal aspect, that is, approximately one-thirtieth of the Qur'an, including the verses which were abrogated by subsequent ones." He and others have concluded, therefore, that the Qur'an does not dictate the adoption of any particular form of government:

> [T]he *shari'a* of God, as embodied in Qur'an and *sunna*, does not bind mankind in *mu'amalat* (worldly dealings) except by providing a few broad principles of guidance and a limited number of injunctions. The *shari'a* only rarely concerns itself with details. The confinement of the *shari'a* to broad principles and its silence in other spheres are due to divine wisdom and mercy. . . . The fact that the *shari'a* is silent on these points—and we should bear in mind that, as the Qur'an remarks, "God is not forgetful"—means only that the application of the general injunctions of the *shari'a* to the multifarious details of human life, and the confrontation of new problems according to the dictates of *maslaha* (public good) have been left to the discretion of the body of conscious Muslims.[42]

> There is nothing in the Islamic *shari'a* that compels one to bind religion to a state-setting. The *shari'a* does not deal with any specific form of government.[43]

The Qur'an came to ask them [the Muslims] to cease directing queries to the Prophet, peace be upon him, that required revelation. . . . Leaving these matters to the people causes the people to develop and grow, and permits change.[44]

The "silent *shari'a*" relies on Qur'anic exegesis to make its central point. However, its burden of proof is somewhat lower than the "liberal *shari'a*'s" in that it needs only to show positive injunctions for human decision-making abilities in the abstract, rather than for specific liberal practices. It thus removes entire arenas of human action from the field of Qur'anic scholarship, where orthodox training has a distinct advantage, and places them in the field of public debate.

The weakness of the "silent *shari'a*" mode of liberalism is its connotation—which liberals of this mode would no doubt deny—that God's revelation is incomplete. It is vulnerable to the counterargument that God's message encompasses all aspects of human life and that religion and politics are not separate in Islam. 'Abd al-Raziq has been critiqued sharply from this perspective, in the 1920s and since, even by liberals of the "liberal *shari'a*" mode such as Rashid Rida and Muhammad Dia' al-Din al-Rayyis (Egypt, mid-twentieth century).[45]

On occasion "silent *shari'a*" arguments appear to warrant the charge of hostility toward Islamic revelation, as in the case of the socialist organization called the Muslim Committee for a Progressive Nigeria, which opposed the implementation of *shari'a* law in the 1970s on the grounds that it offered "no positive answer for such chronic problems such as starvation, unemployment, rotten cities, high rents, failures of U.P.E. [Universal Primary Education], disease control, etc."[46] Yet other liberal authors of this mode take care to phrase the

41. Muhammad Salim Al-Awa, "Political Pluralism from an Islamic Perspective," in Azzam Tamimi, editor, *Power-Sharing Islam?* (London: Liberty for Muslim World Publications, 1993), pp. 72–73. See also Muhammad S. El-Awa, *On the Political System of the Islamic State* [1975], translated by Ahmed Naji al-Imam (Indianapolis, Ind.: American Trust Publications, 1980), p. 83.

42. Said Ramadan, "Three Major Problems Confronting the World of Islam" [1960], in Ahmad Ibrahim, Sharon Siddique, and Yasmin Hussain, editors, *Readings on Islam in Southeast Asia* (Singapore: Institute of Southeast Asian Studies, 1985), p. 330.

43. Hussayn Fawzi al-Najjar, quoted in Bassam Tibi, "Major Themes in the Arabic Political Literature of Islamic Revivalism, 1970–1985," Part 1, *Islam and Christian-Muslim Relations*, volume 3, number 2, December 1992, p. 202.

44. Muhammad Ahmad Khalaf-Allah, translated in chapter 2. See p. 39.

45. Georges C. Anawati, "Un Plaidayer pour un Islam éclairé (*mustanir*): Le Livre du Juge Mohammad Sa'id al-'Ashmawi, *Al-Islam al-siyasi (L'Islam politique)*" (A Plea for an Enlightened (*Mustanir*) Islam: The Book by Judge Muhammad Sa'id al-'Ashmawi, *Al-Islam al-siyasi* [*Political Islam*]), *Mideo*, volume 19, 1989, pp. 124–125; Binder, *Islamic Liberalism*, p. 153.

46. Peter B. Clarke and Ian Linden, *Islam in Modern Nigeria: A Study of a Muslim Community in a Post-Independence State, 1960–1983* (Mainz, Germany: Grünewald; Munich, Germany: Kaiser, 1984), p. 89.

silence of the *shari'a* in positive terms, speaking of God's "wisdom and mercy," as in the quotation from Sa'id Ramadan (Egypt, mid-twentieth century), in leaving certain matters to human deliberation.

A further weakness of the "silent *shari'a*" mode of liberalism is that it leaves little room to challenge illiberal elements that are *not* silent in the *shari'a*. The Qur'an speaks on a number of occasions, for example, of the propriety of slave owning, the ransoming of prisoners of war, and the maiming of criminals; if these practices are explicitly sanctioned by divine revelation, liberals of the "silent *shari'a*" mode can object only that the Qur'anic message is limited in its application. Shah Wali-Allah, for example, argued that Islam, while universal and timeless, takes on the form of the particular people and age to whom it was first revealed. By implication, certain of the commands and regulations contained in the *shari'a* may be tailored to seventh-century Arabia and not intended to bind all peoples and times. A number of authors in this volume make a similar argument with regard to specific topics, such as the status of women. Taha (chapter 28), by contrast, makes this argument in its boldest form, arguing that large sections of the Qur'an were intended for temporary use only (what Taha calls the First Message of Islam), until the Muslim community was prepared to receive the ultimate truths of Islam (what Taha calls the Second Message), which grant far more human choice and autonomy. According to Taha, the permanent injunctions were revealed first, when the Prophet Muhammad lived in Mecca, before he took temporal power; the temporary injunctions were revealed later, when the Prophet Muhammad ruled the city of Medina, and applied to the needs of the era. Taha argues that the earlier revelation abrogates the later (in contrast to "liberal *shari'a*" authors such as Bulaç who argue that the later experience at Medina abrogates the earlier).

This theoretical position is a difficult one. First, it makes the challenging argument that the *shari'a* is silent even on topics it appears to speak clearly about. Second, it gets drawn back into the home ground of orthodox scholarship, namely, textual analysis of classic sources. Third, it limits portions of revelation in a way that some scholars find heretical. Taha himself was executed by Sudanese authorities, in part on these grounds, in 1985.

The Interpreted Shari'a

The third mode of liberal Islamic argumentation, and the one closest to Western liberal sensibilities, holds that the *shari'a* is mediated by human interpretation. In this view, the *shari'a* is divine, but human interpretations are conflicting and fallible. This trope is the most vulnerable to accusations of relativism, but liberals such as Muhammad Asad (Leopold Weiss, Austria-Pakistan, born 1900) draw on sources within the *shari'a* such as the saying of the Prophet Muhammad: "The differences of opinion among the learned within my community are [a sign of] God's grace."[47] According to another saying of the Prophet: "The Qur'an is malleable, capable of many types of interpretation. Interpret it, therefore, according to the best possible type."[48] Muhammad Bahr al-'Ulum (Iraq, born 1927), a Shi'i religious scholar and prominent supporter of the Iraqi democracy movement, cites two verses from the Qur'an in this regard: "The right to differ in ideas, positions, and methods is acknowledged so that one does not deprive others of their convictions. 'Had your Lord pleased, He would have made mankind a single nation.' (Sura 11, Verse 118) 'There was a time when men were one nation. They disagreed among themselves. . . .' (Sura 10, Verse 19)."[49]

Other liberals argue on empirical grounds that interpretative diversity is one of the hallmarks of the Islamic tradition. Arkoun has stated categorically: "ideological deviation occurs within the framework of Islamic thought each time that an author, echoing more or less faithfully a school, a community, or a tradition, transforms Qur'anic discourse from an *open* into a *closed* cognitive system."[50] Rafik Zakaria (India, born 1920) concludes, "As we have noticed in the course of our survey, on none of the basic issues

47. Muhammad Asad, *The Principles of State and Government in Islam* (Berkeley: University of California Press, 1961), p. 48; see also 'Ali Shari'ati, *Histoire et destinée* (*History and Destiny*), translated by F. Hamèd and N. Yavari-d'Hellencourt (Paris: Sindbad, [1969] 1982), p. 89.

48. Mahmoud Ayoub, *The Qur'an and Its Interpreters*, volume 1 (Albany: State University of New York Press, 1984), p. 23.

49. Ayatollah Syed Mohammad Bahrul Uloom, "Islam, Democracy, and the Future of Iraq," in *Under Siege: Islam and Democracy*, edited by Richard W. Bulliet (New York: The Middle East Institute of Columbia University, 1994), p. 26.

50. Arkoun, *Rethinking Islam*, p. 94.

involving religion and politics, was there at any time consensus among the *'ulama'* [religious scholars]."[51] Ziauddin Sardar (Pakistan-England, born 1951) argues that Islamic epistemology has long emphasized "diversity of ways of knowing" that "are equally valid in Islam."[52] Soroush (chapter 26) argues that religious interpretation, Islamic and otherwise, is always a human phenomenon and subject to multiple perspectives: "Revealed religion, of course, is divine, but not so for the science of religion, which is a thoroughly human production and construction. It is human in the sense that it is imprinted by virtually all characteristics of human beings, both noble and mean."

A third basis for the "interpreted *shari'a*" is normative: that disagreement in interpretation is useful for the community of Muslims. For example, Islamic scholar Yusuf Al-Qaradawi (Egypt-Qatar, born 1926) justifies diversity of opinion in practical terms:

> My worst fear for the Islamic Movement is that it opposes the free thinkers among its children and closes the door to renewal and *ijtihad*, confining itself to only one type of thinking that does not accept any other viewpoints. . . . The end result will be for the Movement to lose the creative minds among its ranks and eventually fall prey to stagnation. . . .[53]

Along parallel lines, Sa'id Binsa'id (Morocco, contemporary) has argued that proper understanding of religious truths requires dialogue; radicals who coerce their opponents into silence can only "worship God in ignorance."[54] 'Abdelfatah Mourou (Tunisia, contemporary), a leading Islamist who protested the movement's growing intolerance, wished to found a more liberal Islamic party in order to garner wider support: "When we enter the political arena, I won't say that those on my side go to heaven and those who oppose me will go to hell. Everything I suggest will be open to debate."[55] 'Abbasi Madani (Algeria, born

1931), considered one of the more liberal leaders of the Algerian Islamic movement, has spoken in favor of democracy in similarly pragmatic terms:

> Pluralism is a guarantee of cultural wealth, and diversity is needed for development. We are Muslims, but we are not Islam itself. . . . We do not monopolize religion. Democracy as we understand it means pluralism, choice, and freedom.[56]

Fahmi Huwaydi (Egypt, born 1937) argues that democracy is so crucial to the development of the Islamic world that if democracy is not already sanctioned in Islam, "We ought to 'invent' it by any means possible."[57]

One of the recurrent themes in this mode of liberal Islam is that human interpretations should not be raised to the same plane as divine revelation, since human interpretations are fallible and open to debate. Yet, ironically, the "interpreted *shari'a*" may be vulnerable to accusations that it reduces revelation to the level of fallible human interpretation. These liberals stand accused of the very confusion that they criticize.

For example, M'Daghri, a Moroccan cabinet minister and proponent of the "liberal *shari'a*," pauses in his defense of freedom of thought in Islam to attack Fatima Mernissi (Morocco, born 1940), whose analysis of debates over women's rights in the early days of Islam is excerpted in this volume (chapter 13). Mernissi's work—he does not mention the author or title by name—"describes the Qur'an as being obscure and contradictory, claiming that there were two movements in strife with each other around the question of women's rights. . . . The whole book is nothing more than sheer, doubtful questioning of the legitimacy of the Qur'an and the *hadith* [traditions of the Prophet], and a series of groundless misgivings levelled to the Prophet's august companions."[58] Mernissi argues on historical grounds that interpretations of revelation may be contested; her critic takes her to be contesting revelation itself, an act that is not covered by the "liberal *shari'a*'s" protections for freedom of thought.

51. Rafik Zakaria, *The Struggle within Islam* (London: Penguin, 1988), p. 288.

52. Ziauddin Sardar, *Islamic Futures: The Shape of Ideas to Come* (London: Mansell, 1985), pp. 102–103.

53. Yousef Al-Qaradawi, *Priorities of the Islamic Movement in the Coming Phase* (Cairo: Dar Al-Nashr for Egyptian Universities, 1992), pp. 143–144.

54. Dale F. Eickelman, "Islamic Liberalism Strikes Back," *MESA Bulletin*, volume 27, number 2, December 1993, p. 167.

55. Reuter's, March 31, 1991.

56. Quoted in Daniel Brumberg, "Islam, Elections, and Reform in Algeria," *Journal of Democracy*, volume 2, number 1, Winter 1991, p. 64.

57. Haddad, "Islamists and the Challenge of Pluralism," p. 18.

58. Alaoui M'Daghri, *La Liberté de pensée*, p. 38.

Mohammad Charfi (Tunisia, born 1946), a human-rights activist, has expressed concerns about such counterattacks:

> You know, here in Tunisia, we are very attached to the notion of interpretation or *ijtihad*. . . . And logically, in order to guarantee the freedom of *ijtihad*, you have to, in effect, suppress punishment for apostasy. Why? Because if you suggest an *ijtihad* that goes against establishment thinking, and if your right to express and argue for your right to express and argue for your *ijtihad* isn't guaranteed, you may be accused of apostasy, of no longer following Islam.[59]

This fear of being accused of apostasy applies to all forms of liberal Islam—indeed, it hangs over all Islamic thought that is not impeccably orthodox—but is especially potent in the case of the "interpreted *shari'a*," given the sensitive nature of its challenge to orthodox scholars. Whereas the "liberal *shari'a*" mode leaps into the fray of orthodox scholarship and the "silent *shari'a*" mode tries to carve out areas where orthodox scholarship does not have the final say, the "interpreted *shari'a*" mode denies that orthodox scholarship ever has the final say. It takes the 1,400–year history of scholarly debate and wields it against the scholars engaging in the debate. Every theoretical advance is taken as evidence of interpretive variation; every great mind is presented as a reframer of divine revelation. Short of renouncing their own history, orthodox scholars can only respond to the "interpreted *shari'a*" by casting it out of the bounds of permissible debate.[60]

Selection of Authors and Themes

The authors in this volume were selected according to the criteria that they be:

- "liberal" in some sense of the word (in particular, those who express opposition to Islamic revivalism)
- "Islamic" in some sense of the word (those who believe that Islam has an important role in the contemporary world, as opposed to secularists)

- widely read in their own countries, if not also beyond national boundaries
- geographically representative of the entire Islamic world
- ideologically representative of the variety of liberal Islam
- temporally representative of the post-caliphate era (1920s to the present) but with special emphasis on the contemporary period

The resulting roster includes 32 authors from 19 countries: 18 from Asia, including 8 from the Middle East, 6 from South Asia, and 4 from Southeast Asia; 12 from Africa, including 8 from North Africa and 4 from sub-Saharan Africa; and 1 each from Europe and North America. Five of the authors are Shi'i, the rest Sunni. Twelve of the selections were first written in the 1990s, 8 in the 1980s, 6 in the 1970s, 3 in the 1960s, 1 in the 1950s, 1 in the 1930s, and 2 in the 1920s (the chapters are arranged in chronological order within each section). Three have never been published; 8 have not been published in English; 9 were published in English but not in Britain or North America; 5 were published in Britain or North America by small research institutes and have not received widespread distribution. The introductions are my work, except where specified.

In order to maintain consistency among the selections, spelling and grammar have been standardized according to U.S. usage, even in selections previously published in English. The name of God has also been translated into English throughout. Transliteration follows the standard Arabic system except that: All diacriticals are omitted save *'ayn* and *hamza*; non-Arabic words are transliterated according to common practice in the country of origin; authors' preferences for transliteration of their names are respected, where these preferences are known; and words common in English are spelled according to English usage. All dates are given in the Christian calendar, also known as the Common Era, except where specified. Quotations from the Qur'an have been translated with the assistance of *Al-Qur'an: A Contemporary Translation*, translated by Ahmed Ali, revised definitive edition (Princeton, N.J.: Princeton University Press, 1988). The editor's annotations are set off with brackets; these annotations have been generated primarily through consultation with John L. Esposito, editor, *The Oxford Encyclopedia of the Modern Islamic World*, 4 volumes (New York: Oxford University Press, 1995); and E. van Donzel, *Islamic Desk Reference, Compiled*

---

59. Dwyer, *Arab Voices*, p. 176.

60. Another possible orthodox response might be to consider past interpretations as having laid the basis for contemporary interpretations. However, the appeal to historical progress is more congenial to liberal Islam than to traditionalists or revivalists. See the discussion of this topic later in this chapter.

from the Encyclopedia of Islam (Leiden: E. J. Brill, 1994). Annotation is omitted where information has not proved to be available.

The pieces have been divided into six sections according to liberal theme:

Against Theocracy

Liberal Muslims object to the implementation of the *shari'a* on several grounds. The traditional argument, pioneered by 'Ali 'Abd al-Raziq (chapter 1) and echoed by Khalaf-Allah (chapter 2), applies the "silent *shari'a*" mode: divine revelation has left the form of government for human construction. The Prophet Muhammad was the leader of the polity, as well as the leader of the faith, but did not establish principles for successor governments. As expressed at the recent founding meeting of the Ibn Khaldun Society: "Since the Qur'an emphasizes a just society rather than an ideological state, the form the state takes is not mandated. . . . [Muslims] should regard the Qur'an as a moral edifice rather than a code of laws. Thus, the new Muslim state will, in effect, be a secular state, with the proviso that the term 'secular state' should not be understood in a negative sense. Such a state can protect religion against political manipulation by state authorities . . ."[61]

A further objection to theocracy focuses on the corrupting influence that political power necessarily has on those who rule in the name of God. Taleqani (chapter 3), a leader of the Iranian revolution, expressed his misgivings about the emerging theocracy in Iran in the last sermon before his death in 1979, criticizing "police restrictions imposed upon the people sometimes in the name of religion, which is the most frightening of all." Similarly, Matori Abdul Djalil (Indonesia, contemporary), former secretary-general of the United Development Party, an Islamic coalition, has stated: "Whenever man acts as the agent of God, then there will be no democracy and theocracy will corrupt. If one group of people say they get legitimacy to govern from God, then they will use God as an instrument against others. And this is fundamentally undemocratic."[62]

Another objection argues that the demand for *shari'a* law distracts Muslims from pressing issues. 'Abd al-Hamid Ibn Badis of Algeria (1889–1940), founder of the Association of Algerian Religious Scholars, argued during the controversy surrounding the abolition of the Ottoman caliphate in the 1920s that certain European powers—in particular, the British—wished to restore the caliphate for their own purposes. He warned against revivalists who offered Islamic cover for these plots: "Islamic nation today, stop being vain and deceived and enslaved by these scare-tactics, even if they do emanate from under cloaks and turbans [clerical garb]!"[63] Fuad Zakariyya (Egypt, born 1927), a philosophy professor, put it this way in the 1980s:

> The important element of [the revivalists'] rosy dream is that the application of the *shari'a* will automatically evaporate all the problems from which we suffer. How? No one knows. Most seem to believe deep in their hearts that divine providence will guard us in the application of the *shari'a*. Afterwards, the forces of heaven will intervene to solve our problems without anyone making any effort.[64]

A final objection suggests that those who call for the implementation of *shari'a* law fundamentally misunderstand the status of *shari'a*. Al-'Ashmawi (chapter 4) notes that the Qur'an refers to *shari'a* as a path, not as a ready-made system of law, waiting to be put in practice. Aziz Al-Azmeh (Syria-England, born 1947) argues that revivalists reduce Islamic law to a handful of symbolic elements, such as bans on alcohol and usury, that are taken to represent the rule of Islam. Yet recasting these elements of faith as law transforms them into modern ideology, a shift that removes the context that provided their original justification.[65]

For Democracy

The second theme, democracy, is largely argued in the "liberal *shari'a*" mode, with special emphasis laid on the concept of *shura*, or consultation, which is taken to allow or require the expression of the

61. "Ibn Khaldun Society—Common Ground," *Trans-State Islam*, volume 3, number 1, Spring 1997, p. 23.

62. Douglas E. Ramage, *Politics in Indonesia: Democracy, Islam, and the Ideology of Tolerance* (London: Routledge, 1995), p. 68.

63. Fahmi Jadane, "Notions of the State in Contemporary Arab-Islamic Writings," in Giacomo Luciani, editor, *The Arab State* (London: Routledge, 1990), pp. 251–252.

64. David Sagiv, *Fundamentalism and Intellectuals in Egypt, 1973–1993* (London: Frank Cass, 1995), p. 117.

65. Al-Azmeh, *Islams and Modernities*, pp. 25–26.

popular will in matters of state. (Let us keep in mind that democracy need not be limited to the specific institutional forms that it has taken in the United States or elsewhere.[66]) Bazargan (chapter 7) and Sadek J. Sulaiman (Oman, born 1933; chapter 10) are this volume's primary proponents of *shura*-as-democracy. Bazargan's son 'Abdul 'Ali Bazargan (Iran, born 1941)—a leading member of his father's opposition group, the Liberation Movement of Iran—has also written extensively on this topic, detailing the precedents for *shura* in the *shari'a* and arguing that "an Islamic government without *shura* is not different from a dictatorship."[67] Similarly, Hassan al-Alkim (United Arab Emirates, born 1958) argues that *shura* does not mean merely consultation but the legislative power of representative bodies: "Islam emphasizes that the people have the right to control their president and to advise him as well as to criticize him."[68] Ebrahim Yazdi (Iran, born 1931), Bazargan's successor as leader of the Freedom Movement of Iran, finds an alternative justification for democracy in the Islamic assertion of faith (*shahada*), "There is no deity but God." According to Yazdi, this belief demands:

> the renunciation of the sovereignty claims and lordship of any one man, or group of men, over other human beings. It is [God's] design and command that man must be his own master and be free to govern himself. Man must not permit anyone to manipulate his will and life. Man must not tolerate despotism and dictatorship.[69]

Muhammad bin al-'Arbi al-'Alawi (Morocco, 1880–1964) argued on analogous lines in 1962, "The right that the rulers have given themselves to formulate a constitution and to appropriate for themselves means to make it pass by forcing the people to vote for it are in flagrant contradiction with the principles of Islam and are contrary to the national interest."[70]

Other authors, such as Al-'Awwa of Egypt (quoted previously), adopt the "silent *shari'a*" mode in support of political pluralism. Indeed, Al-'Awwa dismisses the "liberal *shari'a*" approach explicitly, arguing that *shura* by itself is vague and provides insufficient justification for democratic practices. In the early period of Islam, he writes, "Islam at that time had only prescribed *shura* (consultation) as a method for making the choice. What matters is that the *umma* (community) should be able to exercise its free will in choosing and appointing the ruler. . . . The actual procedure is left for the community to determine, and may therefore differ from time to time and from one place to another."[71] S. M. Zafar (Pakistan, born 1930; chapter 6) adopts a similar stance, arguing that systems of government accountability must be adapted to meet the needs of different communities; parliamentary rule, he writes, is simply the most effective means of ensuring accountability in the contemporary era.

A further approach to democracy is a pragmatic version of the "silent *shari'a*," as exemplified by Muhammad Natsir (Indonesia, 1908–1993; chapter 5), Dimasangcay A. Pundato (Philippines, born 1947; chapter 8), and Ghannouchi (chapter 9). All cite Qur'anic precedent, but their primary argument is the need for democracy in particular national conditions. For Natsir, these conditions are the creation of the Republic of Indonesia out of the highly diverse islands of the Dutch East Indies. Natsir, a nationalist, defends the new democracy as an expression of the characteristics of the Indonesian people. Pundato sees democratic coalitions with Christians as the best way to safeguard the rights of the Muslim minority in the Philippine islands. Ghannouchi speaks to the condition of Muslims living under non-Muslim rule (including secular government by Muslims), arguing that participating in a non-Muslim democracy is better for these Muslims than suffering under a nondemocracy.

A final approach to democracy involves the "interpreted *shari'a*" mode. For example, Zaki Ahmad

66. John L. Esposito and James P. Piscatori, "Democratization and Islam," *Middle East Journal*, volume 45, number 3, Summer 1991, pp. 427–440; Esposito and Voll, *Islam and Democracy*; John O. Voll and John L. Esposito, "Islam's Democratic Essence," *Middle East Quarterly*, volume 1, number 3, September 1994, pp. 3–11.

67. Mehdi Noorbaksh, "Religion, Politics, and Ideological Trends in Contemporary Iran," in Jamal S. al-Suwaidi, editor, *Iran and the Gulf: A Search for Stability* (Abu Dhabi, United Arab Emirates: Emirates Center for Strategic Studies and Research, 1996), pp. 33–34.

68. Hassan Al-Alkim, "Islam and Democracy: Mutually Reinforcing or Incompatible?" in Azzam Tamimi, editor, *Power-Sharing Islam?* (London: Liberty for Muslim World Publications, 1993), pp. 81–83.

69. Ebrahim Yazdi, "Democracy and Human Rights in Islam and Europe," unpublished text of a speech at the International Conference on Europe and the Islamic World, Bonn, Germany, November 15–16, 1995, p. 3.

70. Henry Munson, Jr., *Religion and Power in Morocco* (New Haven, Conn.: Yale University Press, 1993), p. 111.

71. Al-'Awwa, "Political Pluralism," p. 70.

(Egypt, contemporary) identifies four traditions of pluralism within Islam: the practice of the early generations of Islam, centuries of scholarly debates over Islamic jurisprudence, prescriptions in favor of freedom within the *shari'a*, and pragmatic appeals for peaceful coexistence among diverse peoples.[72] On a more theoretical plane, Muhammad Asad, an Austrian convert to Islam, justifies democratic procedures through the fallibility of human interpretation, along with a reference to the "liberal *shari'a*" principle of *shura*:

> Nevertheless, it is difficult to see what alternative there could be, within a legislative body, to the principle of majority decisions? Who is to establish, from case to case, whether the majority or the minority is right? Whose opinion shall prevail? One might, of course, suggest that the final verdict should rest with the *amir* [ruler]; but quite apart from the fact that the granting of such absolute power to any one person militates against the principle of *amruhum shura baynaham* [whose affairs are conducted according to *shura*—Qur'an, Sura 42, Verse 38] so strongly insisted upon by the Law of Islam—is it not equally possible that the *amir* is mistaken, while the view of the majority is right? Is there any Divine guarantee attached to his views?[73]

Rights of Women

Liberal Islamic positions on the rights of women— unlike those on democracy—have to contend with a number of statements in the Qur'an and the *sunna* that appear to run in direct contradiction. For example, verses of the Qur'an discuss male polygamy, men's unilateral right to divorce, men's greater rights of inheritance, and the greater weight of male legal testimony. Traditions of the Prophet discuss veiling, gender segregation, and women's unsuitability for leadership of a Muslim community. Liberal scholars have challenged these statements in several ways. First, they reexamine the statements and find them less hostile to women's rights than previously supposed. Benazir Bhutto (Pakistan, born 1953; chapter 12) and Amina Wadud-Muhsin (United States, born 1952; chapter 14) pursue this strategy with extended discussions of Qur'anic verses that are often interpreted to justify male domination over women. This approach attributes women's exploitation in Islam to prerevelation and postrevelation social customs, not to the message of Islam. Interestingly, some revivalists have adopted similar arguments, most famously Hasan Turabi (Sudan, born 1932), whose widely read 1973 pamphlet on women and Islam states baldly that the seclusion of women and restriction of their rights is a result of customary misreadings of the *shari'a*:

> A revolution against the condition of women in the traditional Muslim societies is inevitable. The Islamists are urged by their own ideals to reform the traditional society and to close the gap between the fallen historical reality and the desired model of ideal Islam. This is even more urgent with respect to the present state of women.[74]

Sometimes combined with this is the separate argument that antiwomen statements refer to the conditions of seventh-century Arabia and are not necessarily applicable to other times and places. These verses are then weighed against more liberal portions of the *shari'a*, which, it is argued, enjoy greater authenticity. Nazira Zein-ed-Din (Lebanon, born circa 1905; chapter 11) takes up this argument, suggesting that God's revelation permitted the continuation of pre-Islamic Arab customs such as polygamy and slavery only in order to ease the Arabs' transition to Islam, and that the Prophet Muhammad died before he could fully eradicate these customs, as Islam intended. Another example comes from Isa Wali (Nigeria, 1929–1967), a government clerk and Islamic scholar whose 1956 articles on women in Islam "provoked a wide-ranging debate throughout northern Nigeria."[75] Wali begins with the standard argument that the *shari'a*'s position on women has been historically misunderstood or ignored, to the detriment of women:

> In order to get a clear picture [of the position of women in Islam] one must start by drawing a clear distinction between custom and religion. People so often confuse the two, that in so many cases custom is even trying to gain an upper hand over the religion.

74. Hasan Turabi, *Women in Islam and Muslim Society* (London: Milestones Publishers, circa 1991), p. 46.

75. John N. Paden, *Religion and Political Culture in Kano* (Berkeley: University of California Press, 1973), p. 290; see also John N. Paden, *Ahmadu Bello: Sardauna of Sokoto* (London: Hodder and Stoughton, 1986), p. 302.

72. Haddad, "Islamists and the Challenge of Pluralism," pp. 7–8.

73. Asad, *The Principles of State and Government*, p. 49.

He goes on to suggest, however, that certain parts of the *shari'a* are in keeping with oppressive customs, such as male polygamy. These injunctions, Wali argues, were only intended to be temporary:

> In a small community, as the Muslim Arabs were then, denuded of its manpower by incessant wars, there was bound to be a surplus of a large number of women who must be protected and supported. Unless these women were legally wedded and got economic support and social esteem, they were bound to become a disgrace and danger to society. Under such circumstances, therefore, a legalized restricted polygamy became a social necessity. . . . It was never meant to be a permanent feature in the society. It was never meant to be an ideal married life. It was allowed in strictly emergency cases as an expediency, rather than as a principle. And, in the absence of such causes now, in the twentieth century, there is no justification for it.[76]

A further approach, a version of the "silent *shari'a*," accepts the seemingly antiwomen statements but argues that they do not prohibit women from organizing to protect their rights. For example, feminists in the Islamic Republic of Iran have succeeded in passing legislation requiring couples to sign a prenuptial agreement granting women divorce rights equal to men. Asghar Ali Engineer (India, born 1940) has criticized Islamic leaders who cling to illiberal elements of the *shari'a* in the name of communal survival:

> Islam allows *ijtihad* (creative interpretation). However in the the Indian subcontinent *taqlid* (unthinking imitation) has reigned supreme and there have been very few instances of *ijtihad*. It is high time that Indian Muslims used the provision of *ijtihad* in secular India. . . . While it may not be possible to scrap Muslim personal law altogether, the Muslims should adopt a resilient and creative attitude towards it. They should accept certain necessary changes in it, such as abolishing triple divorce in one sitting [the male right to divorce his wife by saying "I divorce you" three times].[77]

A final approach to discomfiting statements about women in the *shari'a* involves the multiplicity of in-

terpretations to which these statements are subject. Rather than replace an incorrect interpretation with a more faithful one, this approach suggests that all interpretation is human and fallible. Shahrour (chapter 15), for example, argues that "jurisprudential ruling bears the historical stamp of the era in which it was created and the society in which it was shaped." Mernissi (chapter 13) writes in this "interpreted *shari'a*" mode that the Companions of the Prophet— revered in Islamic scholarship as the source of testimony about the statements and actions of the Prophet—disagreed about basic facets of religious injunctions with regard to women. Indeed, she quotes one Companion as being hesitant to relate testimony out of fear of misspeaking:

> If I wanted to, I could recite traditions about the Prophet for two days without stopping. What keeps me from doing it is that I have seen some of the Companions of the Messenger of God who heard exactly what I myself heard, who saw what I saw, and those men recounted *hadith*. Those traditions are not exactly what we heard. And I am afraid of hallucinating, as they hallucinate.[78]

The Rights of Non-Muslims

The issue of interreligious relations arose in the first years of Islam in the context of Muslim conquest of non-Muslims. The *shari'a* granted non-Muslims, especially the "peoples of the book" (Jews and Christians), the right to continue practicing their own religions, so long as they granted allegiance and paid tribute to their Muslim rulers. Bulaç (chapter 19) takes this system as a model for humane treatment of non-Muslims in the contemporary world.

Yet other authors argue—the "silent *shari'a*"— that Muslims are presented with circumstances somewhat different from those in which the *shari'a* was established. According to Syed Vahiduddin (India, born 1909), the late twentieth century is a period:

> when Muslims are tempted to take an extremely static view of religion. Their preoccupation with issues which are not of capital importance has made them uncompromising not only in inter-religious dialogue but also in inter-Islamic dialogue. . . . In a pluralistic and multi-religious society one cannot

---

76. Isa Wali, "The True Position of Women in Islam," *The Nigerian Citizen* (Zaria, Nigeria), July 14, 1956, p. 3; July 21, 1956, p. 3.

77. Asghar Ali Engineer, *The Rights of Women in Islam* (New York: St. Martin's Press, 1992), pp. 170, 161.

78. See p. 125.

do better than to ponder on the Qur'anic vision of human conflicts:

> To every one of you we have appointed a right way and open path. If Allah had willed, He would have made you one community but that He may try you in what befalls you. So push forward in good works; unto Allah shall you move back all together and He will let you know of that whereon you are at variance. (Sura 5, Verse 48)[79]

The "silent *shari'a*" approach seems particularly conducive in countries where Muslims live under non-Muslim rule. Humayun Kabir (India, 1906–1969; chapter 16) and Pundato (chapter 8) represent liberal responses to such situations in India and the Philippines, both men standing in opposition to Islamic separatist movements. Muzaffar (chapter 17) and Rusmir Mahmutćehajić (chapter 20) speak to a somewhat different situation: in Malaysia and Bosnia-Herzegovina, a slim Muslim majority rules but with far less power over non-Muslim communities than the Prophet and early Muslims enjoyed. Interestingly, these authors do not appeal to early Islamic precedent, preferring to construct arguments around more general Islamic themes of tolerance and diversity. Similarly, in Lebanon, Indonesia, and Egypt, where sizeable minorities are non-Muslim, Sobhi Rajab Mahmassani (Lebanon, born 1911) has argued that discrimination based on religion is impossible in an Islamic system; Abdurrahman Wahid (Indonesia, born 1940), leader of the largest religious organization in Indonesia and founder of that country's Forum for Democracy, has stressed that "an Islamic society in Indonesia is treason against the Constitution because it will make non-Muslims second-class citizens"; and Tariq al-Bishri (Egypt, born 1933) has urged that Christian Copts be included with Muslims as integral partners in Egyptian nationalism.[80]

Mohamed Talbi (Tunisia, born 1921; chapter 18) approaches the topic of interreligious relations in the abstract, arguing in all three modes: He cites positive injunctions towards good treatment of non-Muslims (the "liberal *shari'a*"); he argues that the general injunction of tolerance allows the construction of intercommunal dialogue, regardless of past precedent (the "silent *shari'a*"); and he challenges intolerant elements of the *shari'a*, specifically on the penalty for apostasy, as potentially dubious (the "interpreted *shari'a*"). Like Muzaffar, Pundato, and others, Talbi has translated his liberal positions into political action, joining with liberals from other faiths in ecumenical dialogue and calling for a reduction of religious tensions.

Freedom of Thought

This heading covers the topic of intellectual disagreement, which is at the heart of liberal Islam. Indeed, freedom of thought is logically prior to other liberal tenets, since liberals must defend freedom of thought in order to justify their expression of other positions. Generally discussed under the rubric of *ijtihad* (considered earlier in this introduction), freedom of thought involves the stretching of two boundaries: who may speak and what may be spoken. The question of "who may speak"—that is, who may legitimately practice *ijtihad*—is of crucial importance for liberals without orthodox religious educations. Shahrour (chapter 15), for example, trained in engineering, proposes that his method of analyzing the Qur'an is "scientific," an attempt to undermine the implicitly unscientific methods of traditional scholars. It is fortunate for liberal Islamic scholars that a number of prominent revivalists also lack orthodox educational credentials and often argue themselves that such credentials are not required for the practice of *ijtihad*. Naturally, the holders of such credentials are likely to disagree. As for what may be spoken, this boundary is too fluid to begin to define.

The "liberal *shari'a*" approach to the freedom of thought argues that God has made humans to be thinkers and that the *shari'a* encourages Muslims to investigate and reflect. "This word 'freedom' is the word that God chose for the blessed ones in paradise," wrote Aminu Kano (Nigeria, born 1920).[81] 'Ali Shari'ati (chapter 21) is a particularly influential exponent of this position, combining these views with vehement criticism of religious scholars who would monopolize the interpretation of Islam. Al-Qaradawi (chapter 22) cites specific injunctions on

79. Syed Vahiduddin, *Islamic Experience in Contemporary Thought* (Delhi, India: Chanakya Publications, 1986), pp. 108–109.

80. Ann Elizabeth Mayer, *Islam and Human Rights: Tradition and Politics*, second edition, (Boulder, Colo.: Westview, 1995), p. 128; Ramage, *Politics in Indonesia*, p. 64; Binder, *Islamic Liberalism*, pp. 269–288.

81. Paden, *Religion and Political Culture in Kano*, p. 289.

the toleration of opposing views, especially views on religious obligations, and criticizes extremists who would foist their interpretation of religious obligations upon all Muslims. Along similar lines, Abdelwahab El-Affendi (Sudan, born 1955) opposes revivalist movements that deprive Muslims of the "freedom to sin," thereby depriving them also of "the freedom to be virtuous": "This was certainly not God's purpose when He created man and woman and endowed each with free will."[82] Ghulam Ahmad Parwez (India-Pakistan, born 1903) has argued that the Qur'an's protection of individual freedom is so strong that it overrides all forms of authority: "No person has the right to compel any other person to obey his orders: 'It is not [possible] for any human being unto whom God has given the Scripture and wisdom and prophethood that he should afterward have said unto mankind: Be slaves of me instead of God.' (Sura 3, Verse 79)"[83]

The "silent *shari'a*" approach argues on pragmatic grounds that freedom of thought is useful for the intellectual advancement of the Muslim world and is therefore permissible according to general injunctions in favor of the well-being of the community of believers. Alhaji Adeleke Dirisu Ajijola (Nigeria, born 1932; chapter 25) offers one example of this form of reasoning. Another example comes from Haji Andi Mappetahang Fatwa (Indonesia, born 1939), who defended himself in a 1985 sham trial along these general lines:

> Under the blessing of freedom, people must be given protection in developing the activities of investigation and consequent contemplation. Society must be given the liberty to think and to hold opinions. Such is the society envisioned by a democracy.[84]

Laith Kubba (Iraq-England, born 1954), director of the International Forum for Islamic Dialogue in London, offers a similar argument:

> As Muslims devise strategies for economic growth in a competitive world and redefine their priorities,

their outlook will shift from the abstract concepts and values of Islam to the realities of the Muslim world. They will continue to turn to Islam as a source of personal and communal identity and moral guidance, but they will also critically assess the legacy handed down by previous generations who may have narrowed Islam in ways that had less to do with the essence of the faith than with historical accidents and parochial circumstances.[85]

Kubba's argument also broaches the "interpreted *shari'a*" mode, with the suggestion that religious interpretations may be the product of particular historical conditions. According to Husain Ahmad Amin (Egypt, born 1932), Muslim jurists of the early centuries of Islam went so far as to "invent *hadith*s [traditions of the Prophet] that would incorporate their opinions and could cope with current developments, and then attribute them to the Prophet."[86] The "sociologization" of religious interpretation forms the heart of Arkoun's deconstructionist-linguistic approach (chapter 23) and Soroush's sociology-of-knowledge approach (chapter 26). What distinguishes these authors from nonbelievers' approaches to Islamic interpretation is their firm belief in Islam and in the need for a reinterpretation of tenets more in keeping with contemporary social conditions.

Arkoun has also written on the topic of human rights, which forms a distinct subcategory within the theme of individual freedoms. Arkoun begins by discussing the Universal Islamic Declaration of Human Rights, prepared in 1980 by the Islamic Council for Europe in response to the 1948 Universal Declaration of Human Rights, a document that lies firmly in what we are calling the "liberal *shari'a*" mode. The declaration is entirely grounded in statements from the *shari'a* and argues that "Islam gave humanity an ideal code of human rights 1400 years ago." Arkoun calls this approach "mimetic overbidding; it picks up the enunciations of Western declarations and confers upon them an Islamic origin." Arkoun prefers to ground an Islamic approach to human rights in the social and political conditions of the Islamic world—the actual practices of Muslims, rulers and ruled, that provide precedent for human rights—but is not en-

---

82. Abdelwahab El-Affendi, *Who Needs an Islamic State?* (London, England: Grey Seal, 1991), p. 57.

83. Ghulam Ahmad Parwez, "Two Contrasting Systems," translated in Aziz Ahmad and G. E. Von Grunebaum, editors, *Muslim Self-Statement in India and Pakistan, 1857–1968* (Weisbaden, West Germany: Otto Harrassowitz, 1970), p. 171.

84. Haji Andi Mappetahang Fatwa, "Some Political Views and Attitudes," translated by Peter Burns, *Indonesia Reports*, number 16, June 1986, p. 18.

85. Laith Kubba, "Islam and Liberal Democracy: Recognizing Pluralism," *Journal of Democracy*, volume 7, number 2, April 1996, p. 89.

86. Quoted in Ayubi, *Political Islam*, p. 207.

tirely sanguine about the prospects for this project in the near term.[87]

By contrast, An-Na'im (chapter 24) is somewhat more optimistic. A human-rights activist as well as a scholar, he, too, argues in the "interpreted *shari'a*" mode that the historical context of the early Muslim jurists shaped their interpretation of public law. He appears to feel that present conditions allow an alternative, "enlightened" construction of the principle of reciprocity—the granting of rights to others in return for their granting of rights to you—which he sees as the basis for a nonethnocentric conception of universal human rights.

Progress

The final category in this book refers to authors who view modernity and change as potentially positive developments. This attitude reflects a significant departure from traditional views in Islam, which view contemporary history as decline and continuous departure from the revered early days of revelation. Progress in this view can mean only a recovery of past practices, and, indeed, much revivalist activism has adopted the rubric of "renewal," "renaissance," and "return to first principles." Nonetheless, few revivalists actually desire a full-fledged return to the world of seventh-century Arabia. Imam Ruhollah Khomeini of Iran, for example, was himself an inveterate radio listener and used modern technologies such as telephones, audiocassettes, photocopying, and British shortwave radio broadcasts to promulgate his revivalist message. After the revolution, Khomeini allowed the appearance of women on radio and television, chess playing, and certain forms of music. When other religious leaders objected, he responded: "I feel it necessary to express my despair about your understanding of the divine injunctions and that of the [Shi'i] traditions. . . . The way you interpret the traditions, the new civilization should be destroyed and the people should live in shackles or live forever in the desert."[88]

Liberal Muslims, like the revivalists, seek to ground their interpretation of Islam in a return to original sources. What distinguishes liberal Islam from revivalist Islam, in terms of progress, is the willingness to see change as a good thing in itself. Khomeini and other revivalists are pleased to borrow modern technologies from non-Muslims, but only as a means to the end of reviving the pure practice of Islam, as they interpret it. Liberals, by contrast, consider change itself—though not all forms of change, of course—part of proper Islamic practice.

The most influential liberal Muslim of the twentieth century, Muhammad Iqbal (India, 1877–1938; chapter 27), placed "the principle of movement" at the heart of his theology. Iqbal works in all three modes of liberal Islam: the "interpreted *shari'a*" (Islamic legal systems "are after all individual interpretations, and as such cannot claim any finality"); the "silent *shari'a*" (the Qur'an is "far from leaving no scope for human thought and legislation"); and, his primary mode, the "liberal *shari'a*," whereby he argues that the essence of Islam, properly understood, is evolutionary change. Similarly, Mohammad Akram Khan (Bengal, India, 1868–1968) has suggested, "What is Islam is not stationary, what is stagnant is not Islam. Islam welcomes all creative innovations. Islam never lacked nor ever will lack in providing solutions to any problem in the world, because its gate of *ijtihad* remains open at all times."[89]

Taha (chapter 28) also writes in the "liberal *shari'a*" mode, though he uses the term *shari'a* to refer to one part of the teaching of Islam, the "first message of Islam," as he calls it, which was intended for the people of seventh-century Arabia. Taha argues that, beyond this first message, Islam contains an evolutionary directive that urges Muslims to aspire to a higher plane of religious consciousness, in keeping with the "second message of Islam." Muslims of the late twentieth century, Taha suggests, are ready to move into this higher phase.

87. Arkoun, *Rethinking Islam*, pp. 106–113. An abridged English translation of the declaration is published in *Islam: A Challenge for Christianity*, edited by Hans Küng and Jürgen Moltmann (London: SCM Press; Maryknoll, N.Y.: Orbis Books, 1994), pp. 140–150. See also the "Cairo Declaration of Human Rights in Islam," adopted by the Nineteenth Islamic Conference of Foreign Ministers, August 5, 1990 (United Nations Document A/CONF.157/PC/35); and, more generally, Mayer, *Islam and Human Rights*.

88. Farhang Rajaee, "Islam and Modernity: The Reconstruction of an Alternative Shi'ite Islamic Worldview in Iran," in Martin E. Marty and R. Scott Appleby, editors, *Fundamentalisms and Society* (Chicago: University of Chicago Press, 1993), p. 116.

89. U. A. B. Razia Akter Banu, *Islam in Bangladesh* (Leiden: Brill, 1992), p. 48.

The "silent *shari'a*" approach has tended to be less heterodox. Both Nurcholish Madjid (Indonesia, born 1939; chapter 29) and Shabbir Akhtar (Pakistan-England, born 1960; chapter 32) argue that the blanket rejection of modernity and historical change has ossified Islamic thought, stifled the religion's ability to speak to "modern" Muslims, and sacrificed the positive potentialities of modernity. Similarly, al-Sadiq al-Mahdi (Sudan, born 1935) makes "the case for social change": Because Islam prescribes "no particular system" of government, economics, international relations, or legislation, Muslims are not bound by traditional approaches. Rather than seek shelter in traditionalism or accept Western culture and reject traditionalism entirely, al-Mahdi proposes a third path: "separating Islam from the traditionalist thesis, separating modernization from the acculturation syndrome [that is, the acceptance of Western culture], and establishing a synthesis which is both Islamic and modern."[90]

Within the "interpreted *shari'a*" mode, Hassan Hanafi of Egypt has proposed the compatibility of Islam and progress through the construction of an Islamic liberation theology analogous to Christian ones:

There is no eternal theology which fits every time and every space. Theology is always an expression of the spirit of the time. Every time gave us two spirits: The spirit of the institutional religion, which is always conservative, formal and static. It tries to keep the *status quo* of things. It formulates a theology for the elite and for the upper class. It monopolizes the interpretation, prevents any opposition and even oppresses the masses. The second spirit is progressive, concrete and dynamic. It tries to change the *status quo* of things. It formulates a theology for the masses and for the oppressed classes.

There is no one interpretation of a text, but there are many interpretations given the difference in understanding between different interpreters. An interpretation of a text is essentially pluralistic. The text is only a vehicle for human interests and even passions. . . . The conflict of interpretation is essentially a socio-political conflict, not a theoretical one. Theory indeed is only an epistemological

cover-up. Each interpretation expresses the socio-political commitment of the interpreter.[91]

Similarly, Syed Vahiduddin of India has challenged:

the tacit assumption that Islam, as it unfolded from its birth, was complete and perfect in all its expressions. Hence any supposed deviation from the earliest pattern must carry its own condemnation. But as the Qur'an's vision of God cannot be confined exclusively to any one of its historical expressions, religion itself cannot be a static construct made once and for all without revealing fresh nuances in its historical development. This static concept of religion neglects the truth that at no point of history can all possibilities be exhausted, though a given point in history might be pregnant with implications for the future. History is a process of creative expression; not a perpetual repetition, and hence it is presumptuous to limit Islam to its classical expression.[92]

Rahman (chapter 31) also writes in an "interpreted *shari'a*" mode: "To insist on absolute uniformity of interpretation is neither possible nor desirable." Indeed, he writes, "difference of opinion, provided it is meaningful, has to be assigned a high positive value."[93] Rahman criticizes traditional Islamic thought for clinging to the interpretations of the past rather than meeting the challenge of change. At the same time, he also criticizes revivalists for dismissing earlier interpretations in an attempt to return afresh to original sources. Rahman prefers to develop new interpretations of original sources while studying the interpretations of the past, both to learn from their insights and to understand them as products of their historical environments. Rahman is keenly aware of the difficulties involved in reforming Islamic thought and of the generations of earlier reformers who have largely failed in the attempt. He proposes to effect this reform through a focus on educational institutions, a gigantic task that requires a critical mass of reformist thinkers and reformist ideas. The size of the present book suggests that this movement may, indeed, be reaching its critical mass —that liberal Islam need no longer be considered a contradiction in terms.

---

90. al-Sadiq al-Mahdi, "Islam—Society and Change," in John L. Esposito, editor, *Voices of Resurgent Islam* (New York: Oxford University Press, 1983), pp. 236–239.

91. Hassan Hanafi, *Religious Dialogue and Revolution* (Cairo: Anglo-Egyptian Bookshop, 1977), p. 202; Hassan Hanafi, *Religion, Ideology, and Development* (Cairo: Anglo-Egyptian Bookshop, 1995), volume 1, pp. 417–418.

92. Vahiduddin, *Islamic Experience in Contemporary Thought*, pp. 63–64.

93. See below, pp. 312, 317.

PART I

Against Theocracy

Message Not Government, Religion Not State

'Ali 'Abd al-Raziq (Egypt, 1888–1966) unleashed a storm of debate with this controversial short book. A *shari'a* (Islamic law) judge and an academic at the Al-Azhar University in Cairo, 'Abd al-Raziq argued that Islam does not specify any particular form of government, thus allowing Muslims to create democratic regimes. This reasoning may have been intended to undermine the Egyptian king's claims to the caliphate in the wake of the elimination of the Ottoman caliphate in 1924.[1] However, the argument is worded in general terms, thereby challenging the holistic view of Islam as comprising both spirituality and politics. 'Abd al-Raziq was fired from his judgeship and his academic position and was even criticized by Islamic modernists such as Rashid Rida.[2] Beyond the borders of Egypt, his book "generated violent controversy throughout the Muslim world" and "continues to stimulate debate" today.[3] Other portions of 'Abd al-Raziq's book were translated into English from a French edition in 1982.[4]

I

I saw then that there exist obstacles that are not easily overcome by those who are of the opinion that the Prophet, peace be upon him, in addition to the Message [which he carried], was also a political king and a founder of a political state. I saw that every time these people attempted to avoid a trap, they would fall into the next, and each time they attempted to rid themselves of a problem, the problem would confront them again more intensely than before.

There remains before the reader just one school of thought, and I hope that the reader will find that it offers a convenient starting point. . . . This is that Muhammad, peace be upon him, was a Messenger of a religious call, full of religiosity, untainted by a tendency to kingship or a call for government, and that

1. Albert Hourani, *Arabic Thought in the Liberal Age* (London: Oxford University Press, 1962), pp. 184–192.

2. Georges C. Anawati, "Un Plaidayer pour un Islam éclairé (*mustanir*): Le Livre du Juge Mohammad Sa'id al-'Ashmawi, *Al-Islam al-siyasi* (*L'Islam politique*)" (French: A Plea for an Enlightened [*Mustanir*] Islam: The Book of Judge Muhammad Sa'id al-'Ashmawi, *Al-Islam al-siyasi* [*Political Islam*]), *Mideo*, volume 19, 1989, pp. 124–125.

3. Eric Davis, "'Abd al-Raziq, 'Ali," in John L. Esposito, editor, *The Oxford Encyclopedia of the Modern Islamic World* (New York: Oxford University Press, 1995), volume 1, pp. 5, 7.

4. John J. Donohue and John L. Esposito, editors, *Islam in Transition: Muslim Perspectives* (New York: Oxford University Press, 1982), pp. 29–37.

he did not have a government, nor did he rule, and that he, peace be upon him, did not establish a kingdom, in the political sense of the term or anything synonymous with it. For he was but a messenger like his brethren, the preceding messengers. He was not a king nor the founder of a state, nor did he seek to rule. The above may not be a well-known view, and may in fact be resented by many Muslims, although it has great vision and is based on strong evidence.

2

Before we proceed to prove this, we must warn readers about an error that they may fall into unless they observe [the following] accurately and carefully—namely that the Message in itself obliges the Messenger to have some kind of leadership and authority over his people, but this is nothing like the leadership of kings and the authority they have over their subjects. Therefore, one should not confuse the leadership of the Message with that of kings, since they are so different that they could be opposites. Readers have seen that the leadership of Moses and Jesus with regards to their followers was not a kingly leadership, rather it was similar to the leadership of most messengers.

3

The nature of the honest religious call obliges its carrier to have primarily a perfection of the senses, whereby he will lack nothing in his body, sentiments, or feelings, and have nothing that would repulse. And, he must have—because he is a leader—a strong presence to awe those around him, and an attraction that would make him sympathetic enough that men and women would love him. He must also have spiritual perfection, which is necessary for his communication with the other world.

The Message requires its carrier to enjoy considerable social distinction among his people; and as it has been said: "God does not raise a prophet unless he is loved by his people, and unless he commands authority over his clan."[5] The Message also requires

its carrier to have the kind of strength which will prepare him to influence the minds of people so that they will heed his call. For God, may He be elevated, does not take the Message lightly and does not raise a messenger of righteousness unless He wants his call to be heeded, and that its teachings be engraved on the tables of the world, eternally preserved and intermixed with the realities of this world: "We have sent no apostle but that he should be obeyed by the will of God." (Qur'an, Sura 4, Verse 64)[6] "Surely messengers have been mocked before you; but what they had mocked rebounded on the mockers themselves. Say: 'Travel in the land and see what happened to those who disbelieved.'" (Sura 6, Verse 10) "But God wished to confirm the truth by His words, and wipe the unbelievers out to the last, so that Truth may be affirmed and falsehood negated, even though the sinners be averse." (Sura 8, Verses 7–8) "Our word had already been given before to Our servants, the apostles, that they would be helped. And that certainly, Our armies will be victorious [over them]." (Sura 37, Verses 171–173) "We will certainly help Our messengers and those who believe, in this world and on the day the witnesses take the stand, the day when their excuses will not benefit the evil-doers, and the condemnation and evil abode will be theirs." (Sura 40, Verses 51–52) The status of the Message grants its carrier a wider authority than that which exists between ruler and ruled, and even wider than that of a father over his children.

The Messenger may tackle the politics of his people as a king would, but the Prophet has a unique duty which he shares with no one, namely to communicate with the souls embedded in bodies, and to remove visual obstacles in order to look in upon the hearts embedded in chests. He has the right, nay, he must open up the hearts of his followers in order to reach the sources of love and hate, of good and evil, the passages of thought, the places of obsessions, the origins of intentions, the repository of morality. His is open work in general politics and concealed work

5. As the two Shaykhs [Muslim ibn al-Hajjaj, circa 821–875, and Muhammad ibn Isma'il Bukhari, 810–870] have narrated: "Thus prophets are sent from the best families of their clans . . ." which is part of a long *hadith* [tradi-

tion of the Prophet]. See *Taysir al-wusul ila al-jami' al-usul* [*The Facilitation of Arriving at the Compendium of Fundamentals*, by 'Abd al-Rahman Ibn al-Dayba' (1461–1537)], part 3, p. 320.

6. [Translations of Qur'anic verses are taken, with modifications, from *Al-Qur'an: A Contemporary Translation*, translated by Ahmed Ali, revised definitive edition (Princeton, N.J.: Princeton University Press, 1988).—Editor]

in managing the relationship between partners, allies, master and slave, parents and children, and those relationships that only husband and wife are privy to. He has patronage over that which is manifest and that which is latent in life, as well as the management of the affairs of body and soul, and our worldly and heavenly relationships. He directs the politics of worldly living and that of the next world. The Message gives its carrier—as it is seen and beyond the way it is being seen—the right to communicate with each soul, care for it and manage its affairs, as well as the right to unlimited free conduct for every heart.

4

Readers should note that, in addition to the above, the Message of the Prophet, peace be upon him, specialized in a myriad of things that other messengers did not deal with. For he, peace be upon him, came with a call that God chose for him to rally the people to. And God ordained that he deliver it in its entirety, and that he preside over it in order to complete the call to religion, so that grace be established and conflict not arise, and so that all religion be to God. This Message grants its carrier the kind of extreme perfection that human nature seeks to achieve, the kind of psychological strength that is the end-limit of what God had fated for His chosen messengers, and enough of God's support that would be compatible with this great and general call. In this vein, God has said: "Great have been the blessings of God on you." (Sura 4, Verse 113) "For you are always before Our eyes." (Sura 52, Verse 48). And in the *hadith* [tradition of the Prophet]: "By God, God will never humiliate you."[7] "For—without boasting of it—of all of Adam's children, I am my Lord's favorite."[8]

For this purpose, the authority of the Prophet, peace be upon him, was, because of his Message, a general authority; his orders to Muslims were obeyed; and his government was comprehensive. For nothing that the arm of government can reach is beyond the authority of the Prophet, peace be upon him, and

any imaginable kind of leadership or authority is included in the Prophet's, peace be upon him, reign over the believers.

If it is reasoned that it is possible for a messenger's authority over his people to have gradations, then I would say that Muhammad, peace be upon him, should have the right to exercise the highest possible authority of all messengers, peace be upon them, command the highest possible obedience, have the strength of the prophecy, the authority of the Message, and the influence of the honest call, which God had fated to be raised over the call to wrongdoing and to remain on earth. The authority is sent by Heaven, from God, to him whose divine revelation is delivered by Heaven's angels. This sacred power, special to those worshipers of God whom He had raised as messengers, does not hold within it the meaning of kingship, nor does it resemble the power of kings, nor can the [authority of the] sultan of all sultans approximate it. This is the true leadership of the call to God and of the delivery of His Message, not kingly leadership. It is a message and a religion; it is a prophetic government not a government of sultans.

Once again we warn the reader not to confuse the two kinds of governments, and not to conflate the two kinds of trusteeships—the trusteeship of the Messenger, on account of his being a messenger, and the trusteeship of powerful kings. The Messenger's trusteeship over his people is a spiritual trusteeship whose origin is faith from the heart, and the heart's true submission followed by the submission of the body. On the other hand, the trusteeship of the ruler is a material one. It depends on subduing bodies without any connection to the heart. While the former is a trusteeship leading to God, the latter is one for managing life's concerns and populating the earth. While the former is religion, the latter is the world. The former is divine, the latter is human. The former is a religious leadership, the latter a political one—and there is much distance between politics and religion.

5

7. Reported by 'A'isha [wife of the Prophet, circa 614–678] at the beginning of the Revelation. Recorded by the two Shaykhs.

8. Reported by Anas [ibn Malik, a companion of the Prophet, 710–796], recorded by [Abu 'Isa Muhammad] al-Tirmidhi [collector of *hadith*, died 892].

Having said this, we would like to draw readers' attention to something else. There exist a number of words [dealing with our subject matter] that are used as synonyms, and others as antonyms. A disagreement or a difference in point of view arises as a result of such usage. In addition, this creates a confusion in judgment. Such words are "king," "sultan," "ruler," "commander," "caliph," "state," "kingdom," "government," "caliphate," and so on. If we were to ask if the Prophet, peace be upon him, was a king or not, we would be asking if he, peace be upon him, had attributes other than being a messenger. Would it be correct to state that he indeed founded, or began to found, a political unity or not? Kingship in our use of it here—and there is no embarrassment faced by the reader who may wish to call him caliph, sultan, commander, or whatever pleases him—means a ruler over a people who have political unity and who have civilization. As for "government," "state," "sultanate," or "kingdom," we mean that which political scientists mean by the English words "kingship," "state," or "government" and the like.

We do not doubt that Islam constitutes religious unity or that Muslims form a unified group; or that the Prophet called for that political unity and had in fact achieved it before his death; and that he, peace be upon him, headed this religious unity as its only prayer leader (*imam*), its strong manager, its master whose orders are never questioned. And that in the interest of this Islamic unity, he, peace be upon him, struggled with all his might, and with the victorious support of God, conquered. He, peace be upon him, received the support of God's angels until he delivered his Message and completed his trusteeship. For he, peace be upon him, had the kind of authority over his people that no king before him or after him ever had. "The Prophet is closer to the faithful than they are themselves." (Sura 33, Verse 6) "No believing men and women have any choice in a matter after God and His Messenger have decided it. Whoever disobeys God and His Messenger has clearly lost the way and gone astray." (Sura 33, Verse 36)

And he who wants to term this religious unity a state and this authority of the Prophet, peace be upon him—which was an absolute authority—a kingship or caliphate, and the Prophet himself, peace be upon him, a king, caliph, or sultan, and so on, he is free to do so. For this is a matter of semantics which should not stop us here. What is important in what we have said is the meaning, and that we have specified to the reader with precision.

The crucial thing is to find out whether the leadership of the Prophet, peace be upon him, over his people was the leadership of the Message, or a kingly leadership. And whether the different aspects of his trusteeship that we observe at times in the biography [of the Prophet], peace be upon him, were aspects of a political state, or of a religious leadership. And whether this unity over which the Prophet, peace be upon him, presided was a unity of a state and a government or a religious unity proper, not a political one. And, finally, whether he, peace be upon him, was only a messenger or a king and a messenger.

6

The Glorious Qur'an supports the view that the Prophet, peace be upon him, had nothing to do with political kingship. Qur'anic verses are in agreement that his heavenly work did not go beyond delivering the Message, which is free of all meanings of authority. "He who obeys the Messenger obeys God; and if some turn away (remember) we have not sent you as a warden over them." (Sura 4, Verse 80) "This (Book) has been called by your people a falsehood, though it is the truth. Say: 'I am not a warden over you. A time is fixed in every prophecy; you will come to know in time.'" (Sura 6, Verse[s] 66–[67]) "So follow what is revealed to you by your Lord, for homage is due to no one but God, and turn away from idolators. Had He willed it, they would not have been idolators. We have not appointed you their guardian, nor are your their pleader." (Sura 6, Verses 106–107) "If your Lord had willed it, all the people on the earth would have come to believe, one and all." (Sura 10, Verse 99) "Say: 'O people, the truth has come to you from your Lord, so he who follows the right path does so for himself, and he who goes astray errs against himself, and I am not a guardian over you.'" (Sura 10, Verse 108) "We have not sent you as warden over them." (Sura [17], Verse 54) "Have you considered he take his own lust as his god? Can you act as a trustee for him?" (Sura 25, Verse 43) "We have sent down this Book to you with the truth for all mankind. So, he who comes to guidance does so for himself, and he who goes astray does so for his own loss; on you does not lie their guardianship." (Sura 39, Verse 41) "If they turn away (you are not responsible); we have not appointed you a warden over them. Your duty is to deliver the message." (Sura 42, Verse 48) "We are cognisant of what they say; but it is not for you to compel them. So keep on reminding through the Qur'an whoever fears my warning." (Sura 50, Verse 45) "Remind them: you are surely a reminder. You are not a warden over them, other than him who turns his back and denies, in which case he will be punished by God with the severest punishment." (Sura 88, Verses 21–24)

As the reader can see, the Qur'an clearly prohibits the Prophet, peace be upon him, from serving as a guardian of people, or their trustee, or a subduer . . . or a dominator. Moreover, he did not have the right to force people to become believers. In addition, he who is not a guardian or a dominator is not a king; for the prerequisite to kingship is absolute domination and might, which constitute an authority without limits. And he who was not a trustee over his people is also not a king. For God has said: "Muhammad is not the father of any of man among you, but messenger of God, and the seal of the prophets. God has knowledge of every thing." (Sura 33, Verse 40)

The Qur'an is clear that Muhammad, peace be upon him, had no rights over his people except that of delivering the Message; and, had he, peace be upon him, been a king, he would have had the right to govern his people. For kings have other rights beside the Message, and other sources of legitimation beside the Message, and an influence other than its influence. "Tell them: 'I am not master of my own gain or loss but as God may please. If had the knowledge of the Unknown, I would have enjoyed abundance of the good, and no evil would have touched me. I am only a bearer of warnings and bringer of happy news for those who believe.'" (Sura 7, Verse 188) "You may perhaps omit some of what has been revealed to you, and may be disheartened because they say: 'Why was no treasure sent down to him, or an angel to accompany him?' Yet you have been sent to warn alone, for God takes care of every thing." (Sura 11, Verse 12) "But you are only a bearer of warnings, and a guide for every nation." (Sura 13, Verse 7) "Say: 'I am only a man like you, but it has been communicated to me that your Lord is one and single God, and that whosoever hopes to meet his Lord should do what is right, and not associate any one in the worship of his Lord.'" (Sura 18, Verse 110) "Tell them: 'O people, it is my duty to warn you clearly.'" (Sura 22, Verse 49) "Only this has been revealed to me: that I am a distinct warner." (Sura 38, Verse 70) "Say: 'I am a man like you, (but) it is revealed to me that your God is one God.'" (Sura 41, Verse 6)

As readers have observed, the Qur'an is clear that Muhammad, peace be upon him, was but a Messenger preceded by other Messengers, and it is also clear

that he, peace be upon him, had only to deliver God's Message to people and that he was not commissioned to do anything except deliver it. And it is not incumbent upon him [to ensure] that the people accept what he brought them, nor is it incumbent upon him to force them into believing in it. "If you turn away, remember, that the duty of Our Messenger is to give you a clear warning." (Sura 5, Verse 92) "It is for the Prophet to convey the Message: God knows what you reveal and what you hide." (Sura 5, Verse 99) "Have they not bethought themselves that their companion is mad? He is only a plain admonisher." (Sura 7, Verse 184) "Are the people astonished that a man who is one of them was commanded by Us to warn them and to bring glad tidings to those who believe that they are on sound footing with their Lord?" (Sura 10, Verse 2) "Whether We allow you to see (the punishment) we have promised them, or end your life before (its execution), it is certainly for you to convey the Message; the reckoning is for Us to do." (Sura 13, Verse 40) "Need messengers do anything except to convey the Message in clearest terms?" (Sura 16, Verse 35) "We have sent down this Book to you that you might explain to them what it is that they are differing about, and as guidance and a grace for those who believe." (Sura 16, Verse 64) "If they still turn away, your duty is to warn them in clear terms." (Sura 16, Verse 82) "We have sent you only to give good news and to warn." (Sura [17], Verse 105) "So we have made this (Qur'an) easy in your tongue that you may give good news to those who take heed, and warn the people who are contentious." (Sura 19, Verse 97) "*Ta Ha.*[9] We have not sent down the Qur'an to you that you should be burdened, but as an admonition for him who fears." (Sura 20, Verses 1–3) "The duty of the Messenger is to convey the Message clearly." (Sura 24, Verse 54) "Yet we have sent you only to give good tidings and to warn." (Sura 25, Verse 56) "(Say:) 'I am commanded to worship the Lord of this land He has blessed, to Whom all things belong; and I am commanded to be one of those who submit,[10] and to recite the Qur'an.' Whoever comes to guidance does so for himself; as for him who stays astray, tell him: 'I am only a warner.'" (Sura 27, Verses 91–92) "'But if you deny,

9. [Two letters of the Arabic alphabet. 28 of 114 *suras* of the Qur'an begin with letters.—Editor]

10. ["*Muslim*" means "one who submits" to God.—Editor]

then many a people have denied before you. The duty of the Messenger is to convey the Message clearly.'" (Sura 29, Verse 18) "O Prophet, We have sent you as a witness and a bearer of happy tidings and an admonisher, and to call (people) to (know) God by His leave, and as a lamp resplendent." (Sura 33, Verses 45–46) "We have sent you only as a bearer of good tidings and admonisher for all mankind; yet most people do not understand." (Sura 34, Verse 28) "There is no madness about your companion. He is a warner against the dreadful affliction (that awaits)." (Sura 34, Verse 46) "You are only a bearer of warnings. We have sent you with the truth, to give glad tidings, and to warn. Never has there been a community to which an admonisher was not sent." (Sura 35, Verses 23–24) "(The messengers said:) 'Our duty is to convey the Message clearly.'" (Sura 36, Verse 17) "Say: 'I am only a warner, and there is no other god but God, the One, the Omnipotent.'" (Sura 38, Verse 65) "Say: 'I am not a new Messenger to come, nor do I know what is to be done to me or you. I only follow what is revealed to me. My duty is only to warn you clearly.'" (Sura 46, Verse 9) "We have sent you as witness [of the truth] and harbinger of good news and a warner." (Sura 48, Verse 8) "Obey God and the Prophet, and beware. If you turn away, remember, that the duty of Our Messenger is to give you a clear warning." (Sura 5, Verse 92) "Say: 'God alone has knowledge. My duty is only to warn you clearly.'" (Sura 67, Verse 26) "Say: 'I call on my Lord alone and I do not associate any one with Him.' Say: 'Neither is your loss within my power nor bringing you to guidance.' Say: 'No one can save me from God, nor can I find a place of refuge apart from Him, unless I convey from God and deliver His Message.'" (Sura 72, Verses 20–23)

7

If we were to go beyond God's Book to the *sunna* [practice] of the Prophet, peace be upon him, we would find the matter even clearer, and the argument more insistent:

One of the Prophet's biographers[11] narrates the story of a man who came upon the Prophet, peace be

upon him, to take care of a matter. As he stood before him, an intense shiver and fear overtook him. The Prophet, peace be upon him, said: "Be calm, for I am no king nor a subduer, for I am the son of a woman of Quraysh who used to eat dried meat in Mecca." And it has been said in the *hadith* that when the Prophet was given the choice by the angel Israfil of being a king-prophet or a worshipping prophet, the Prophet, peace be upon him, looked up to [the angel] Gabriel, peace be upon him, as his consultant. Gabriel looked down to the ground, indicating humility. And as the story goes, Gabriel indicated for him to be humble. So the Prophet said: "A worshipping prophet." As is evident, this makes it very clear that the Prophet, peace be upon him, was not a king, and did not seek kingship, nor did he, peace be upon him, desire it.

Look between the two covers of the Qur'an for open or latent evidence supporting those who think that the Islamic religion has a political character, and then look for evidence, as hard as you can, among the *hadith*s of the Prophet, peace be upon him—these pure sources of religion which are within your hands, close to you. If you were to look in them for evidence or anything resembling it, you will find no proof, only guesses, and guessing does not replace Truth.

8

Islam is a religious call to God and is a school of thought, from among many such schools, which seeks to reform a certain type of people, guiding them to what will render them closer to God, may He be elevated, and opening up the path to everlasting happiness, which God had prepared for His righteous worshipers. [Islam] is a religious unity that God sought as a bond linking all people, and with which he wanted to surround all the regions of the earth.

It is a pure sacred call to the people of this world, the red [Arabs] and the black [Africans] among them, that they be beholden to one God, that they be one nation worshipping one God, and that they be brothers in their worship of Him. It is a call to the highest example of worldly peace. That it be adopted with the perfection befitting it [the world]. It is a call to the happiness that God prepared for the world; for this is the mercy of Heaven and Earth and God's bounty for this world. Calling on the world to be a fraternity in religion is a reasonable call. There is in

11. *The Biography of the Prophet*, by Ahmad bin Zayni Dahlan, who died in the year 1304 of the *hijra* [1923 A.D.]. From the book entitled *Iktifa' al-qanu' bima huwa matbu'* [*The Contentment of the Satisfied with What Is Printed*].

the nature of human beings a readiness to achieve it.

Indeed God, may He be elevated, has pledged that this call be heeded. "Think not that God would go back on His promise." (Sura 14, Verse 47) "God has promised to make those of you who believe and do right, leaders in the land, as He made those before them, and will establish their faith which He has chosen for them, and change their fear into security. They will worship Me and not associate any one with Me. But those who disbelieve after this will be reprobates." (Sura 24, Verse 55) "It is He who has sent His Messenger with the guidance and the true faith, so that He may exalt it over every other creed. God is sufficient as a witness." (Sura 48, Verse 28) "Who is more unjust than he who invents a lie against God when he is called to submit? God does not show the evil-doers the way. They want to extinguish the light of God by uttering blasphemies. But God wills to perfect His light, however the disbelievers may dislike it. It is He who has sent His Messenger with the guidance and the true way to raise it above all faiths, however the idolators may dislike it." (Sura 61, Verses 7–9)

It is reasonable to say that the world could adopt one religion and that all human beings could be organized into one religious union. However, for the entire world to adopt one government and to be grouped in a shared political union would be foreign to human nature and have nothing to do with God's will. For this is a worldly aim, and God, may He be elevated, has rendered it a matter to be resolved by our minds, and has left people free to manage it in the manner that their minds, knowledge, interests, desires, and tendencies would guide them. God's wisdom in this aims at maintaining differences among people. "But if your Lord had pleased, He could have made all human beings into one community (*umma*). But they would still have differed from one another, except those on whom your Lord had mercy." (Sura 11, Verses 118–119) In addition, in order that competition continue among people so that [the] population [of the earth] would be achieved. "If God did not make people deter one another, this earth would indeed be depraved. But gracious is God to the people of the world." (Sura 2, Verse 251) And, so that the Book's purpose be achieved and God's will be done.

This is one of the worldly concerns on which the Prophet, peace be upon him, had denied himself the right to pass judgment or arbitration. For he, peace be upon him, stated that "you are more knowledgeable of your worldly concerns." This is a worldly concern; and the world from beginning to end, and all that it encompasses of concerns and goals, is too trivial for God to have it managed by anything beside the minds He endowed us with, and what He had placed within us of sentiments and desires, and what He had taught us of names and of what things are called; all this is too trivial for God to raise a Messenger to deal with, and it is too trivial for God's Messengers to be concerned with and occupy themselves in managing it.

9

The reader should not be alarmed by what he may occasionally observe in the biography of the Prophet, peace be upon him, which may seem to him like government work, as if it had the appearance of kingship and statehood. If the reader were to scrutinize it, he would not find it so. Rather, it was only a means that the Prophet, peace be upon him, would seek for the strengthening of his religion, in support of the call. And it is not strange that *jihad* [religious struggle] is one such means. It is a violent and tough way, but who knows, evil may be necessary at times for good to be achieved. Perhaps, destruction becomes imperative in order that construction take place.

> They have said that it [*jihad*] is not free of problems, and we said that this is God's way in His creation. For the struggle between good and evil and between good thinking and evil thinking will persist in this world until God puts a stop to it. If God were to bring forth the springtime upon an arid land in order to revive what is dead in it, to benefit from its harvest and to grow its plants, would its worth be diminished if it came upon an obstacle in its way and overstepped it, or if it came upon a house with strong foundations and destroyed it?[12]

They said: Have you conquered! and God's messengers were sent not to kill a soul, nor did they come to murder anyone.

12. *Risalat al-tawhid* [*Treatise on Unity*], by Shaykh Muhammad 'Abduh [1849–1905], pp. 122–123.

Ignorance and leading astray, dreams and inanities,
for you have conquered with the sword what you had
first conquered with the pen.

When those of good ilk followed you on their own,
[it was left to] the sword to take care of common and
ignorant people.

If you confront evil with good, you will tire of the
confrontation,

But if you confront it with evil, you shall van-
quish it.

For you have taught them all that they did not know

Including fighting and what it encompasses of
morality.[13]

10

From this, the reader can see that it is not only the
Qur'an which prohibits us from thinking that the
Prophet, peace be upon him, was calling upon us,
along with his religious Message, to found a political state. Nor is it only the *sunna* which also prohibits us from doing so. Rather, along with the Book
and the *sunna* comes the wisdom of reason and what
the meaning of the Message and its nature reveal.
For the trusteeship of Muhammad, peace be upon
him, over the believers is the trusteeship of the
Message, untainted by anything that has to do with
government.

Away with it, for there was no government, no
state, and nothing of the tendencies to politics, nor
of the aims of kings and commanders.

Perhaps, the reader has by now been guided to
what he had questioned about the lack of any aspect of government or the aims of a state during the
prophetic epoch. The reader now knows that there
was no governmental organization, nor were there
trustees or judges, a seat of government, and so on.
Hopefully, the darkness of this dilemma which the
reader faced has by now been transformed into light,
and fire has been transformed into coolness and peace
of mind.

13. Ahmad Bik Shawqi [1868–1932].

Legislative Authority

Muhammad Khalaf-Allah (Egypt, 1916–1997) first gained notoriety in the early 1950s for his literary analysis of the Qur'an. The purpose of the Qur'an, he argued, was not to record historical facts but to exhort listeners to Islam. A number of Qur'anic scholars took offense at the implication that the Qur'an was not factually complete, and Khalaf-Allah was subjected to scathing criticism in the Egyptian press.[1] His work in the 1970s continued to upset traditionalists and revivalists. In *The Qur'an and the State*, excerpted here, Khalaf-Allah goes beyond 'Abd al-Raziq's argument that Islam is compatible with democracy; instead, writes Khalaf-Allah, it lays out the basic tenets of democracy and requires Muslims to work out the implementation. In short, divine revelation does not simply *allow* democracy; it *requires* democracy. "This is a new and novel idea, which cannot be found outside of Khalaf-Allah's thought," according to one commentator.[2] Chapter 3, "Legislative Authority," excerpted here, discusses the revelation of the *shura* (consultation) system of governance and its importance for secular, parliamentary authority. Khalaf-Allah is not an easy author to follow, in Arabic or English, as he tries to build his argument on sound Qur'anic reasoning. His conclusions, however, are straightforward and bold.

|

And seek their counsel in all affairs. And when you have come to a decision, place your trust in God alone.

(Qur'an, Sura 3, Verse 159)[3]

When this verse was revealed by God, Muhammad, son of 'Abdullah, peace be upon him, knew that the *shura* [consultation] system had become obligatory.

From that day on, he would have to perform the duties for which God had chosen him to be a messenger and prophet. He had to explain to the people the signs that were revealed to them. In such a situation, the Messenger's explanation was not simply abstract,

1. Yvonne Yazbeck Haddad, *Contemporary Islam and the Challenge of History* (Albany: State University of New York Press, 1982), pp. 46–53.

2. Fahmi Jadaane, "Notions of the State in Contemporary Arab-Islamic Writings," in Giacomo Luciani, editor, *The Arab State* (London: Routledge, 1990), p. 280.

3. [Translations of Qur'anic verses are taken, with modifications, from *Al-Qur'an: A Contemporary Translation*, translated by Ahmed Ali, revised definitive edition (Princeton, N.J.: Princeton University Press, 1988).—Editor]

in the sense that he cannot limit himself to reciting the verse to the people and writing it on a patch of cloth—rather, he must explain its relevance to them in practice.

In this situation, a practical explanation means transforming the idea from an intellectual value into a social reality that people can use as a resource in their everyday life. . . . What we are referring to— the organic relationship between idea and action— is that to which the bounteous Qur'an had referred in numerous verses when it linked faith and action. Faith according to the bounteous Qur'an is not righteous unless it derives from the spiritual value of acting for the purpose of the general interest, and achieving the good for all. When action does not derive from faith in the principle and doctrine [of religion], it inevitably becomes a harmful act—harmful to he who takes it and harmful to the collectivity.

The Qur'anic verses which juxtapose faith to action are so numerous that we are relieved from citing many of them in this regard. All Muslims have heard them from [Qur'an] reciters, or have recited them from the Qur'an if they are reciters, or during prayers if they are worshippers.

The Qur'anic verse which obliges the Prophet, peace be upon him, to seek *shura* was not the first of its kind; it had been preceded by another revealed verse speaking of *shura*. Whereas our verse is a Medinan verse, the other verse is Meccan.[4] The Meccan verse is the one in which the bounteous Qur'an praises the believers for having Muhammad, peace be upon him, among them, when it states: "And they run their affairs by *shura* among themselves." The difference between the two verses is based on the fact that one of them [the Medinan verse] is obligatory, while the other is not—it limits itself to congratulation.

Explaining this Qur'anic phenomenon is not very difficult. The explanation derives from our perception of the historical situation of the Prophet, peace be upon him, and of Muslims in Mecca and Medina. In Mecca, Muslims were a small minority. They were oppressed, and the call [to Islam] was to a certain extent clandestine. And they were unable—this was their situation—to establish institutions with legis-

lative authorities beside the authority of God, may He be praised and elevated.

Things changed in Medina, where Muslims were the rulers, whom people turned to as the new power, which undertook to rebuild life anew on new foundations—foundations established by the entirety of [God's] revelation. The Prophet and his Companions elaborate the details and make legislation which God delegated to the Prophet and to Muslims. The situation in Medina was such that it allowed the establishment of legislative institutions; and the Qur'an came to demand of the Prophet that he be committed to the establishment of those institutions, now that circumstances allowed them during the Medinan period. The Prophet established the legislative institution in response to this Qur'anic verse.

2

The Prophet, peace be upon him, established the legislative institution relying on the previous verse and another Medinan verse: "And when any tidings of peace or war come to them, they spread the news around. Had they gone to the Messenger or to those in authority among them, then those who check and scrutinize would have resolved it." (Sura 4, Verse 83) Whereas the first verse obliges the Prophet to establish this institution, this verse specifies this institution's fields of action, while simultaneously specifying which form such action is to take. The fields of action are the fields of security, fear, and the like. And the form which such action takes is one whereby Muslims would refer matters that concern them to the Messenger and to those in authority among them, in order that they work through them in their minds and conclude with the opinion that will realize the general interest.

And all this happened at the same time that the Qur'an was still being revealed. What this means is that during the life of the Prophet, peace be upon him, there existed two legislative authorities: God's authority, may He be praised and elevated, and the authority of the Prophet and those in authority among the Muslims. And the field of divine authority is these ideas which provide an image of the divine self and which clarify religious beliefs, and from which derive religious permission and prohibition.

As for human authority, the authority which belongs to the Prophet, peace be upon him, and to those

4. [Meccan verses were revealed to the Prophet in Mecca, prior to the *hijra* [emigration] of 622 A.D.; Medinan verses were revealed to the Prophet in Medina, after the *hijra*. —Editor]

in authority, it is concerned with worldly matters—especially that which deals with security, wars, political, economic, and administrative matters, etc.

Professor Imam Shaykh Muhammad 'Abduh [Egyptian modernist, 1849–1905] settled this matter when he stated: "And he counseled them in the general matter which is the policy of the community in war and peace, in fear and security, and in other concerns of their worldly interests."

What is meant by this is the community's worldly concerns, not a purely religious concern whose realm is that of revelation, which is not of opinion. For if religious matters, like doctrines, worship, what is permitted and what is prohibited, were concerns decided by consultation, then religion itself would have been the work of human beings. Religion is established by God. No one may have an opinion on it, either during the lifetime of the Prophet, peace be upon him, or afterwards. . . .

[We end up with] this statement about God's delegation of worldly concerns to Muslims and their decisions about what they see as benefiting the general interest—this helps us to understand the following Qur'anic verse:

O, believers, do not ask about things which, if made known to you, may vex you. But if you ask about them when the Qur'an is being revealed, they will be unfolded to you. God has overlooked [your failings] in this [respect], for God is forgiving and forbearing. Such things were asked by a people before you, but disbelieved them afterwards. (Sura 5, Verses 101–102)

This verse speaks of events that occurred during the Prophet's lifetime, peace be upon him, when the first Muslims would go to him with questions about unresolved matters, asking him to explain the opinion of religion in these matters. The Prophet would turn to the Lord hoping that He would send down from Heaven a verse that would respond to their queries and answer their requests. The Qur'an came to ask them to cease directing queries to the Prophet, peace be upon him, that required revelation. It requested this from them, explaining the reasons which necessitate it. These reasons are as follows:

1. There is a possibility that an answer to their question may harm them in terms of commissioning them to carry out a strenuous task, or to abandon tasks to which they were accustomed and which their souls enjoyed.

2. When they ask questions at the time when the bounteous Qur'an is being revealed, then it becomes imperative that there be a response and that opinion be given in the matter.

3. For those who came before them, asking many questions and waiting for revelation to answer them—whether to take action or not—was not at all in their interest. Because of this, they became disbelievers.

4. Those matters that change with the change of place and time should be left to the people to decide what they consider to be in their interest in the time during which they live, the place where they reside, and in the community to which they belong.

Leaving these matters to the people causes the people to develop and grow, and permits change. As for turning to Heaven and awaiting revelation that provides a point of view in a certain matter, this would render the decision constant and stagnant, incapable of growing or changing, no matter how much times change and places multiply.

The bounteous Qur'an requests that they cease [posing] these questions so that they would not be like their predecessors and follow their path of disbelief when interests change along with the change in time and place. The stance of the bounteous Qur'an emphasizes that this agrees with historical patterns and social laws.

What we have just arrived at allows us the following conclusion: we must stop directing questions to religious scholars—those questions whose aim is to find out the opinion of these religious scholars in matters of worldly living. Religious scholars can perform the duties of prophets, peace be upon them, in explanation and in analysis of Qur'anic texts—especially that which deals with beliefs, worship, and [social] interactions. But the religious scholars cannot do what the prophets, peace be upon them, could not do.

The bounteous Qur'an obliged the Prophet to seek the counsel of his Companions, to decide with them how to achieve the general interest, and to execute that decision without awaiting revelation. In this vein, God's statement, "And when you have come to a decision, place your trust in God alone," means: execute this decision without waiting for divine opinion.

The establishment of legislative authority is what guarantees the achievement of legislative goals, according to the Qur'anic verse: "And seek their counsel in all affairs." The establishment of such an authority is what makes possible various ways of responding to these numerous questions which people pose as they seek to know the basis or the principle on whose foundations we must conduct our worldly living. Our attitude toward religious scholars should be our attitude toward the Prophet, peace be upon him: that which deals with [Qur'anic] texts, we requested of him that he clarify and explain; for that which did not deal with Qur'anic texts, we turn to the legislative authority, we turn to those who are specialized [in secular governance], those who respond to people's concerns—we turn to those in authority.

3

The Prophet, peace be upon him, established this legislative authority, which oversaw and decided matters with him. There existed no specific place for this institution; rather, its members used to meet with the Prophet, peace be upon him, at any place that they saw fit, or wherever circumstances required them to look into matters. We believe that the mosque or the home of the Prophet, peace be upon him, was the preferred place for such a meeting.

The number of Muslims was so small at that time that it facilitated their meeting at such places for counsel. The Prophet, peace be upon him, used to follow this principle [of *shura*]—which is one of the principles of Islam—during his life as circumstances allowed, and as the particular situation permitted. He used to consult those Muslims who were with him, and he would consult some of his personal friends, if the disclosure or publicity of the matter would have been harmful. He consulted the great majority of his Companions and the Emigrants [those who emigrated with the Prophet from Mecca to Medina] on the day of the battle of Badr, when he found out that the [tribe of] Quraysh had left Mecca for the purpose of war. It did not take long for the Emigrants and the Ansar [residents of Medina who adopted Islam] to give their approval. It has been said that once he received the news of the caravan and of the Quraysh, God's Messenger, may God's prayers and benediction be upon him, consulted with his Companions, with the Ansar being the first among them. God's Messenger said: "Show me the way, O people." Sa'd ibn Mu'adh [al-Nu'man] al-Aws [Companion of the Prophet, died

627] arose, saying, "By God, it would seem that you want us, O Messenger of God." [The Prophet] said, "Yes." Sa'd said:

> I am responding on behalf of the Ansar. For we have had faith in you and we believed you and we witnessed the righteousness that you brought. And as a result of that, we gave you our pledges and our covenants to hear and obey you. So, depart where you wish, for we are with you, for He who sent you has sent you with righteousness, and if you were to show us this sea and then you crossed it, we would cross it with you, with no one of us staying behind. . . .

When the Prophet, may God's peace and benediction be upon him, consulted with his friends, he would accede to their opinion and would not hold fast to his own opinion. Of the narratives that deal with this is an incident which the narrators have told us of: The Companions of the Prophet, God's approval be upon them, would not offer their opinions contradicting what the Prophet had said on worldly matters except after knowing that what he had said was an opinion and not derived from revelation—as they did on the day of [the battle of] Badr. The Prophet came to the source of water closest to Badr and camped by it. Al-Habbab bin Mundhir bin al-Jammuh said, "O, Messenger of God, have you seen this location? If this location was chosen for you by God, it is not our place to object to it, or it an opinion about war and a stratagem?" [The Prophet], peace be upon him, said: "It is rather an opinion about war and a stratagem." Al-Habbab said: "O, Messenger of God, this is not a good location, so rise up with the people until we come upon a source of water that is closer to the people, to camp there and then penetrate [the desert] far beyond it." [The Prophet], may God's peace and benediction be upon him, said to him: "Your opinion has shown the way." And he [the Prophet] followed his opinion.

The Prophet asked his Companions for counsel the day of [the battle of] Uhud. He would consult with them on every matter except that which was revealed to him, which he would execute without counsel, and Muslims would help him execute as well.

All this took place when Muslims were a small minority with the Prophet in Medina. When Muslims increased in number and Islam's rule expanded through conquest to areas far from Medina—when there were men of status and opinion among the

Muslims in every tribe and every village—there had to be a system of counsel that would guarantee, for those who are far from the centers of power and from the seat of the caliphate, participation in legislative decisions that dealt with issues of worldly living.

But the Prophet, peace be upon him, wisely chose not to establish this system. We will mention the [following] reasons:

1. The matter [of *shura*] changes with the changes in the social situation of the people in time and place. The period in which [the Prophet], peace be upon him, lived after the conquest of Mecca—which saw the beginning of the acceptance of God's religion by multitudes of people—was too short to allow for the establishment of such a system. [The Prophet], peace be upon him, died after a few years of the conquest of Mecca. This is in addition to [the Prophet's], peace be upon him, realization that this situation will only increase in magnitude as God opens up realms to his people and subdues people before them.

All of this was an obstacle to the establishment of a basis for counsel that would work for the *umma* [Muslim community] in the year of the conquest and afterwards, during the remaining period of the Prophet's life and the following period when realms were being opened and civilized people were accepting Islam or coming under the sovereignty of Islam.

The rules that applied at that time could not be good for all times, or [else the rules] that applied to the situation of the Arabs in their simplicity would apply thereafter to all peoples. It was wiser, then, for the Prophet, peace be upon him, to leave the establishment of such a system to the *umma*, so that they might establish in every age a system that is suitable for that age and that serves their interests in different circumstances.

2. Had the Prophet, may God's peace and benediction be upon him, established temporary rules for counsel, according to the needs of that time, Muslims would have adopted them as a religious ordinance and would have followed them in every time and places, although this is not a religious matter. . . .

Some would go so far as to say that [the Prophet], peace be upon him, could have established such a system and then stipulated that the *umma* would have the right to change and alter this system so that it would be compatible with the temporal or cultural development of the Muslim people. The answer to such a claim is that people would have continued to consider the words of [the Prophet], peace be upon

him, on a matter of worldly living as a religious injunction. They would have continued thus, although they knew that he, peace be upon him, said, "You are more knowledgeable of your concerns," and, "That which deals with your religion, [refer it] to me, and that which deals with your worldly concerns, you are more knowledgeable of that."

If a just person were to contemplate this matter, and if such a person knew the true feelings, on this matter, of the different classes of believers, the public and private ones, it would be plainly clear to him that it would be difficult for most people to accept changing something that the Prophet, peace be upon him, had established for the *umma*—although they may be permitted to do so. They would go very far in their various interpretations of his position. They would say, for example, that he was committed to the people's right to change and alter [the system] as a sign of his modesty and good manners, and that [in doing so], he was explaining to us this truth in order that we not renege on our opinions, but that, at any rate, his opinion would be the higher one.

3. Had he [the Prophet] established this system on his own account, he would not have been practicing counsel, which God had ordered him to do. It would be impossible for him, peace be upon him, to do this, since he would never disobey any order issued by God, may He be praised and elevated.

And had he established it in counsel with his contemporaries, the Companions and Emigrants, he would have decided the matter according to the opinion of the majority, as on the day of [the battle of] Uhud. The opinion of the majority on the day of Uhud was different from his, and he acceded to the opinion of the majority, which later appeared to be wrong. In addition, he, peace be upon him, did not want legislation to be issued by them, which the *umma* would have been beholden to for all time, and which would have provided the base and foundation for the establishment of Islamic government. It was wiser to leave the establishment of such a system to the *umma* so that they may establish in every age [a system] that their preparation and their scientific and cultural achievement qualifies them to establish.

The conclusion of this section is that the establishment of such a system [of *shura*] was one of those matters that God had delegated to Muslims to establish. He did so purposely, not out of forgetfulness or inattention, for He does not err or forget. Muslims have an interest in establishing such a system. It is up to them to establish it on a basis that is good for the time period in which they live and for the nation to which they belong.

We will state this one more time: God has delegated to Muslims the treatment of such a system on the basis of matters that are connected to worldly interests. Such matters for Him are matters of security and fear. We conclude with this statement from the interpretation of *al-Manar* [*The Lighthouse*, modernist Islamic newspaper, early twentieth century]:

The matter in which there is no doubt is that God has guided us to the best and most perfect of foundations and rules on which to build our government and to establish our state. And he gave us the task of building, thus granting us absolute freedom and full independence in our worldly concerns and social interests. He has done so by making our concerns a matter of counsel among us. Those knowledgeable ones of status, whom we trust, look into these concerns and decide on our behalf in every period that which serves our interests and bestows happiness on our people.

4

Here is a third verse [from the Qur'an] that charts out the path that believers must follow in dealing with matters related to security and fear, that involve issues of their worldly living. In this third verse another issue arises, which is knowledge of the attributes that fit those who are beside the Prophet, peace be upon him, when such matters are discussed—holding a dialogue with him on the matter and participating in decision-making with him.

It is clear that those who are beside him are the people of whom the legislative body consists, during his time and after. This Qur'anic verse is God's statement: "And when any tidings of peace or war come to them, they spread the news around. Had they gone to the Messenger or to those in authority among them, then those who check and scrutinize would have resolved it." (Sura 4, Verse 83)

The people whom the Qur'an calls "those in authority" are those who are beside the Prophet, peace be upon him. The legislative body which they comprise has the right to look into matters and to deduce the legal ruling in the case—deducing it from the

texts or from scholarly works on the basis of the goal of the general good and the general interest.

Thinkers disagree as to who "those in authority" are. One group states that they are the rulers, princes, kings, sultans, allies, and so on. Others deny that this is what is meant by the verse and state that what is meant are specialists who have knowledge, know-how, and experience enough to qualify them to oversee people's concerns. And, that they must be trusted by all people.

Their rejection of the logic of the first group in specifying the meaning of "those in authority" is based on a simple yet strong intellectual foundation. They state those addressed in this verse are the community of believers who were the contemporaries of the Prophet, peace be upon him, and that this address is directing them to refer all matters of security and fear to the Prophet, peace be upon him, and to "those in authority." It is also true that "those in authority" themselves are contemporaries of the Prophet, peace be upon him, and that there was no prince or ruler or king or caliph or the like beside the Prophet. Only the Emigrants, the Ansar, and the Companions stood beside the Prophet. Among them were the people with know-how and status whom the Prophet consulted. It is they whom the Qur'an addressed as "those in authority."

On this basis, it is impossible to interpret "those in authority" to mean ruler, princes, and the like. These [thinkers] go further in explaining to us the reasons for which the first group offered such an opinion—that the people with that opinion are actually those who have authority themselves. Those who have authority wanted the scholars of interpretation and religion to interpret "those in authority" to mean princes, rulers, and the like. In doing so, they were aiming to control the masses. For when the masses are told that obeying rulers, princes, sultans, and caliphs is a religious matter, they submit to them with voluntary, not coerced obedience.

Reaching this interpretation of this phenomenon, and uncovering its motives and goals contains within it the accusation by the [second group of] interpreters, that [the first group] did not explain what is right but what the rulers desire.

We would do better to follow the second group and explain their school of thought in specifying the meaning of "those in authority." Professor Imam Shaykh Muhammad 'Abduh states "that 'those in authority' in our time are these: the great scholars, the commanders of soldiers, judges, big agriculturalists and merchants, the owners of public interests, heads of cooperatives and companies, heads of [political] parties, and the geniuses among the writers, physicians, and lawyers. Those whom the *umma* trusts and to whom they refer their problems, no matter where they are." The people of every country know who among them is trustworthy and whose opinion is the most respected. It is easy for the head of government in every country to recognize them and to call upon them for counsel, if he so wished.

As ['Abduh] states: those countries whose authority derives from the basis of counsel have delegated to the people the right to elect those whom they trust to make the laws and oversee the government's execution of them, and to elect those whom we trust to the courts and to administrative councils, etc.

Such elections will not be considered legitimate by us unless the people have absolute choice in the elections, without governmental or other kinds of pressure, without coaxing or coercion. The purpose of this is that the people [should] know their rights to such elections and their aims. If others were to be elected due to the use of governmental authority or that of some other party, such elections would be illegitimate, and those elected would not have the authority of "those in authority." From this it follows that obeying them would not be a duty legitimated by the [above] verse; rather, the matter would enter the realm of the authority of those who defeat others. This situation is illustrated by the similarity between someone who is forced to elect a man to be a representative of the *umma* for a so-called legislative authority, if he is coerced, and someone who marries or buys [something] through coercion—neither his wife nor his purchase will be permitted to him by God.

The above statements by the Imam ['Abduh] lead us to the conclusion that there are two rules: the rule of selecting "those in authority," and the electoral rule that is applied in those countries that build their authority on the basis of counsel. The Professor Imam's ['Abduh's] mention of the second rule indicates that general elections had not yet been mandated during his lifetime, and that governing was not parliamentary.

Today, we practice our electoral life based on the second rule. We have a parliament, and in it there are a variety of specialized committees overseeing matters from a technical perspective, which they then refer to parliament for a decision. Some people say that this suffices, and that parliament is *shura*, consisting of members who are "those in authority."

It is not exactly so. For "those in authority" are a special type of people. They are experienced in life and have dealt practically with technical and vocational matters, and in doing so, have acquired the know-how which made them trustworthy to the people and capable of handling their concerns. Here we suggest a practical procedure which helps to combine the two rules: the rule of selecting "those in authority" and the rule of general elections, in order that the matter of forming a legislative authority be resolved on a good foundation, in accordance with the first meaning of "those in authority." This suggestion can be summarized as follows:

First, the size of the legislative council should be double the number of electoral districts. There is no objection to reducing the current number of electoral districts, so that the public treasury will not be charged large sums of money.

Second, people will elect one member for each district. This member will serve as the representative of the people. The duty of the people's representative is to convey to the council the desires of the people for reform and the problems of their daily living which inhibit their labor and production.

Third, those who represent the vocational and technical institutions in parliament should be selected on the basis that they will serve as "those in authority." They should look into problems that the people's representatives bring to them, study the solutions, and then make decisions whose execution is obligatory. These decisions must be made with the approval of all members, both those elected by the people and those selected by the vocational and technical institutions.

In this way we combine the old and the new in the counsel system. We take from the old the group of "those in authority," the people with influence, those who participate in the *shura*, and from the new we take the constitutional systems forming parliaments or legislative bodies. This is the only way to establish our modern state on the basis of our traditions and in the spirit of our religion. In doing so, we achieve the general good of all citizens, and we render the rights of the people and those of religion compatible.

Obeying these people is mandated by the Qur'anic text: "Obey God and obey the Messenger and those of you in authority." (Sura 4, verse 58)

The Professor Imam ['Abduh] states on the issue of "those in authority" and their authority, which the bounteous Qur'an has bestowed upon them, that if they were to agree on a matter or on a judgment, they must be obeyed, provided that they be from among us; that they not contradict God's ordinances or the *sunna* [practice] of His Messenger which was handed down to us; that they be selected to look into matters . . . and that they be in agreement over general interests—the only things over which "those in authority" have any authority. As for worship and religious matters, this does not involve those with influence—for that is taken solely from God and His Messenger. No one should have an opinion on these matters, except to understand them.

The people must accept these judgments and submit to them in secret and in public. In this, the people will not be submitting or humbling themselves to any human being, nor lie outside the circle of the unity of God, whose slogan is: "For the lawgiver is God, and judgment belongs to God, who has ordained that you will not worship anyone but Him."

The people will follow God's ordinances, the judgment of His Messenger, may God's peace and benediction be upon him, or their own orders, which were deduced on their behalf by the community of "those in authority" and those with influence, know-how, and experience from amongst them, in whom they have placed their trust, feeling secure in their loyalty and agreement as to what is best for them.

5

The orthodox caliphs [the first four caliphs who followed the Prophet Muhammad] and their just judges knew the heads of the community as well as those with knowledge, sound opinion, and religion. They knew that these were "those in authority" and called upon them when the need arose. The *umma* oversaw their prince, so that if he made a mistake, even the weakest of men or women would reproach him for it.

None of the orthodox caliphs had any sense of chauvinism that would have allowed them to be despotic toward the Muslims if so desired. . . . The orthodox caliphs were loyal to [the principles of] "those in authority" participating in governance and abiding by their opinion on things about which there was no [Qur'anic] text, because of the strength of their religiosity and their justice, and because this was ordained [by God]. Even if [the caliph] desired, he could not adopt—though Islam was at the zenith of its power—a sense of chauvinism that he would use to rule arbitrarily without "those in authority."

The Umayyads [caliphs, 661–750] shook the structure of Islamic authority away from the basis of *shura* by developing a chauvinism in Syria, through which, by trickery and violence, they destroyed the authority of "those in authority" over the rest of the Muslims and kept all authority to themselves. Thus the prince answered to the authority of his group, not to the authority of "those in authority" among the Muslims. Little by little, they strayed from the guidance of religion.

Then came the 'Abbasids [caliphs, 750–1258] with Persian and Turkish chauvinism. Then came power plays among the kings of the different sects with their own chauvinism. Islamic government was no longer based on obedience to God, His Messenger, and "those in authority." Rather, it removed "those in authority" from public authority.

As for obeying God and His Messenger by being just and returning trust deposits to their owners, this varied according to the degree of difference in knowledge and religion among the princes. The judgments of 'Umar ibn 'Abdul 'Aziz [caliph, 682–720] were comparable to the orthodox caliphs in justice—but he was unable to return the greatest trust deposit to its rightful owners, because his chauvinism had monopolized the love of authority and leadership.

Then followed the authority of the Ottoman kings [reigned 1281–1924] with their nationalist chauvinism, and the well-known strength of their Janissary army. These [soldiers] were not selected from "those in authority," nor from those knowledgeable in Islamic jurisprudence, nor those of sound opinion, who would normally have been the people with influence among Muslims. They were mixtures of Muslims and unbelievers whom the sultans took and raised in military style. They then became Muslim soldiers, and then soldiers of different mixtures.

6

What remains is a balancing act between what scholars have concluded and what is taking place in modern states. The [following] text is from the Imam ['Abduh]. He states, may God have mercy on his soul, that there exists only a simple difference between the basic law which the [Qur'anic] verse mandated and the basic laws of the highest forms of government of our time [European governments] —and we are closer to what is correct. They [the Europeans] say that the *umma* is the source of laws. We say the same thing with regard to matters for which there is no Qur'anic reference or mention in the *sunna*, as the Imam [Fakhr al-Din] al-Razi [1149–1209] has stated. And very few things have such references [in the Qur'an].

They [the Europeans] say there must exist those who would represent the people so that what they decide would be as if the people had decided it. We too say the same thing. They say that this is known as elections, and that they have different ways of organizing them. We have not been limited by the bounteous Qur'an to a specific way. We have the right to follow in every age the way we feel will achieve what is intended. [God] called those who represent the people "those in authority," which means those who are distinguished among the people, to whom people's interests are referred, whom the people feel safe in following. They may be confined to the center of government at times, as they were at the beginning of Islam.

They [the Europeans] say that if [the representatives] agree, the government must execute that which they agree upon. And the people must obey. They have the right to bring down the ruler if he does not execute their law. And we say the same thing. This is the real consensus which we consider to be one of the fundaments of our law.

They [the Europeans] say that if they disagree, the opinion of the majority should be followed. We know that the Prophet acceded to the opinion of the majority, even if it was incorrect, as occurred during the battle of Uhud. And this position on his part, peace be upon him, trained us.

The opinion of the majority is not the correct opinion—but it is the one on which people with real interests agree.

Mahmud Taleqani

Taleqani's Last Sermon

Ayatollah Mahmud Taleqani (Iran, 1911–1979) established a reputation as a reformist within the Shi'i Muslim religious establishment in the early 1960s when he helped to lead (along with Mehdi Bazargan, whose work is also included in this volume) a religious movement aimed at revitalizing both Islamic theory and Iranian politics.[1] Arrested and jailed repeatedly by the monarchy for his political opposition, Taleqani was released for the last time in the fall of 1978 and immediately became one of the most respected leaders of the Iranian Revolution. Upon the shah's fall in early 1979, Taleqani began to chart a course somewhat independent of the official policies of Imam Ruhollah Khomeini, particularly in his defense of Islamic leftists and local elections.[2] The final sermon before his death in September 1979, excerpted here, is famous among Iranian oppositionists for its sharp criticism of religious oppression. The sermon's reference to Sanandaj (capital of the Kurdish region of northwest Iran) concerns Taleqani's attempted mediation between Kurds who sought autonomy through local councils—a political structure that Taleqani preferred—and the central government in Tehran, already organizing itself in an authoritarian direction. Taleqani's mediation failed and the councils were crushed militarily.[3] Brief portions of this sermon have been translated in more colorful language by Suroosh Irfani.[4]

Those who follow the Messenger, the Prophet of the common folk, described in the [Jewish] Torah and the [Christian] Gospel, who enjoins righteousness and forbids wickedness, makes lawful what is good and prohibits what is bad, who relieves them of their burdens, and the yoke that lies upon them. Those who believe and honor and help him, and follow the light sent with him, are those who will attain their goal.

(Qur'an, Sura 7, Verse 157)[5]

1. Shahrough Akhavi, *Religion and Politics in Contemporary Iran* (Albany: State University of New York Press, 1980), pp. 117–129; H. E. Chehabi, *Iranian Politics and Religious Modernism* (Ithaca, N.Y.: Cornell University Press, 1990), p. 154 et passim; Hamid Dabashi, *Theology of Discontent: The Ideological Foundations of the Islamic Revolution in Iran* (New York: New York University Press, 1993), pp. 216–272; H. E. Chehabi, "Taleqani, Mahmud," in John L. Esposito, editor, *The Oxford Encyclopedia of the Modern Islamic World* (New York: Oxford University Press, 1995), volume 4, pp. 181–182.

2. Ervand Abrahamian, *The Iranian Mojahedin* (New Haven, Conn.: Yale University Press, 1989); Tahmoores Sarraf, *Cry of a Nation: The Saga of the Iranian Revolution* (New York: Peter Lang, 1990), pp. 149–151.

Those who follow this great Prophet, this exalted leader of humanity, this Prophet of the common folk, who arose from among the masses of the people, from among the illiterates and for them, for their benefit, not from among one specific group, the class specified in the verse "the Messenger, the Prophet of the common folk." This Prophet, whom the other prophets had foretold, fulfilled their prophecy and their mission [as stated in] the verse "described in the Torah and the Gospel." This Prophet came in order to raise the people to righteousness, to free them from wickedness, this Prophet came to make lawful all the good that previous religions had forbade, to remove the yokes and prohibit what is bad. The verse "who relieves them of their burdens": he removes the heavy burdens which lay upon the shoulders of humanity, and opens the bridges that had been closed to the people's mind and thought, to the people's living and life.

This goal was the basis for the moral of "enjoining righteousness and forbidding wickedness," the moral of banning the Kharijites [an early sect of Islam], removing burdens and yokes. What does "burden" mean? It means . . . those impositions of mind and thought and belief which the world of paganism and unbelief had imposed upon the minds and thoughts of the people, the class system which had been imposed and bound upon the mass of the people, those laws and rules and customs which had burdened the people with back-breaking impositions, those deceits which had bound the mind and movement of the people hand and foot. This Prophet came to remove all this and expose these deceits. This was the goal of this Prophet—that is, to free the people, to free them from class oppression, to free them from pagan thoughts which had been imposed upon them, to free them from the ordinances and laws which had imposed for the benefit of one group, one class, over others.

This was the mission of your Prophet, [and] we also must pursue this same mission. These martyrs also were pursuing this same mission, against imposed culture, against imposed economics, against imposed laws, against police restrictions imposed upon the people sometimes in the name of religion, which is the most frightening of all. This is what the bishops and monks and their cooperation with the ruling classes have imposed on the people in the name of religion. This is the most frightening imposition: that which is not of God, which is not on the side of truth, has been bound upon the people hand and foot in the name of God. They have blocked people from evolving, they do not allow the right of protest, they do not allow the right of criticism, they do not allow the right of free activity for people and Muslims and the free people of the world. This too is a "burden." This too is a yoke. These are the yokes for which the Prophet was sent, to save humanity afflicted with all these deceits, so that following this Prophet, we might save ourselves and save others.

The call of Islam is the call to mercy and freedom. The start of each sura begins in the name of two mercies, a general mercy and a specific mercy: "In the name of God the merciful and compassionate" and "We have sent you as a mercy unto all the creatures of the world." [Qur'an, Sura 21, Verse 107] In this mercy is mercy for all people. Even the sinner who is condemned to death—under Islamic law there is mercy for him too, that his sins might be cleansed of his residual evil, and that people may become free [through] mercy to others. His [the Prophet's] *jihad* [religious struggle] was mercy, his *hijra* [migration from Mecca to Medina] was mercy, his laws were mercy, his guidance over principles was mercy—the Islamic order ought to be based on mercy.

If we begin by carrying out this mission of God's mercy for our own people and others, many problems will be solved, many of these convulsions [of post-revolutionary Iranian society] will disappear. Already oppressed people throughout the country do not believe that the mission of Islam and of our revolution [against the shah] is for freedom, because [freedom] has been so little seen in these problems which arose in Kurdistan. If we had tried prevention instead of punishment, if when I went to Sanandaj [the capital of Iranian Kurdistan] I had acted with both hands, if I had contacted these people [the Kurds] under the care of mercy, under the auspices of mercy, and the

---

3. Shahrough Akhavi, "Islam, Politics and Society in the Thought of Ayatullah Khomeini, Ayatullah Taliqani and Ali Shariati," *Middle Eastern Studies*, volume 24, number 4, October 1988, p. 424.

4. Suroosh Irfani, *Iran's Islamic Revolution* (London: Zed, 1983), p. ii.

5. [Translations of Qur'anic verses are taken, with modifications, from *Al-Qur'an: A Contemporary Translation*, translated by Ahmed Ali, revised definitive edition (Princeton, N.J.: Princeton University Press, 1988).—Editor]

armed bands had been removed from them, those armed bands imposed on them, imposed on them by the evil traitorous regime [of the shah], then perhaps these problems would not have occurred, or would have occurred less. . . .

But we have not yet recognized the goal of Islam. We all talk about the Islamic revolution—ask yourself, what is the goal of Islam? This group, that group, "they curse one another." [Qur'an, Sura 29, Verse 25] This one contradicts that one, this one calls that one reactionary, this one calls that one deviationist. But we have not yet recognized what Islam demands, what the purpose of Islam is. If the goals are recognized, if we start on the path toward the goal, many of these confrontations will be reduced. . . .

Shariʻa: The Codification
of Islamic Law

Muhammad Saʻid Al-ʻAshmawi (Egypt, born 1932), chief judge of the High Court of
Appeals and the High Court of State Security, may well have passed sentence on the
Islamic radicals who have waged a campaign against the authoritarian Egyptian state. In
the book excerpted here, he condemns the radicals in a different manner, criticizing the
theological basis for their calls for an "Islamic state." His "vigorous" attack[1] on what he
calls "political Islam"[2] provoked "intense reactions" when it was published in Egypt in
1987, angering conservatives—including the head of the state-run Islamic university, the
Shaykh al-Azhar—and pleasing liberals, even oppositionists who infrequently sympathize
with top state officials.[3]

Since the adoption of the Egyptian Constitution in
1971, which states that "the principles of Islamic
Law (*shariʻa*) are a principal source of legislation,"
the question of the codification of the *shariʻa* has
taken on a political dimension. This concerns the
ruling as well as the opposition parties, the moderate religious scholars (*'ulama'*), as well as preachers who know how to play upon tensions. Because
of such politicization, discussion of the law does not
rise above the level of political agitation and superficial reflection and feelings. This politicization is
to the detriment of serious approaches which seek
to be impartial.

Thus, the first Egyptian Congress of Justice organized in Cairo in April, 1986, proposed in one of
its recommendations "the elaboration of projects of
law drawing from the *shariʻa* and a revision of all
laws in effect in order to bring them into conformity
with the *shariʻa*."

1. Nazih N. Ayubi, *Political Islam: Religion and Politics in the Arab World* (London,: Routledge, 1991), p. 203.
2. This was the original title of ʻAshmawi's book. Other
writings of ʻAshmawi are now available in English in Carolyn
Fluehr-Lobban, editor, *Against Islamic Extremism* (Gainesville, Fl.: University Press of Florida, 1998).
3. David Sagiv, "Judge Ashmawi and Militant Islam in
Egypt," *Middle Eastern Studies*, volume 28, number 3, July
1992, pp. 531–546; Georges C. Anawati, "Un Plaidayer pour
un Islam éclairé (*mustanir*): Le Livre du Juge Mohammad

Saʻid al-ʻAshmawi, *Al-Islam al-siyasi (L'Islam politique)*"
(French: A Plea for an Enlightened [*Mustanir*] Islam: The
Book of Judge Muhammad Saʻid al-ʻAshmawi, *Al-Islam al-
siyasi [Political Islam]*), *Mideo*, volume 19, 1989, pp. 91–128;
William E. Shepard, "Muhammad Saʻid al-ʻAshmawi and the
Application of the Shariʻa in Egypt," *International Journal
of Middle East Studies*, volume 28, number 1, February 1996,
pp. 39–58.

That recommendation raises many questions. Is it true, as has been said here and there, that the recommendations of the Congress reflect more the opinion of the religious scholars than of the judges, and if so is one speaking of the opinion of all the judges or of only a part of them? Is it a matter of applying the *shari'a* in a sense that implies the abrogation of all Egyptian laws and their recodification in a specific manner—or is it a matter of maintaining present laws once they have been amended so as to suppress any dispositions contrary to the *shari'a*? Was the recommendation adopted on the basis of serious and impartial studies or did it reflect merely the conflicts which trouble Egyptian political life? Finally, should one conclude that our judiciary has renounced the prestigious patrimony it built up during a whole century and which is rightly its pride and that of all Egypt?

Our people—or better still, the entire Arab people—hold a very high opinion of the Egyptian judiciary. They have the right to expect, when it faces a matter as delicate as this, that it does so with the seriousness and serenity which ordinarily characterize its work. They expect to find in its recommendations the rigor and logic it devotes to editing and researching its judgments.

It is with such serenity and rigor that we intend to reflect here on the problems posed by the codification of the *shari'a*. First, we shall give the term a precise definition. To do so we shall refer to the dispositions of the Qur'an and the prophetic tradition regarding the Prophet (*sunna*), and then to the Egyptian legislative and constitutional texts in which it is mentioned. By comparing its senses in these two types of norms we shall be able to determine to what degree the two understandings are concordant or contradictory. Only then will we know how to modify or complete our legislation.

The Term *Shari'a* in the Qur'an

The term *shari'a* appears as such only once in the Qur'an: "Men we set thee upon an open way (*shari'a*) of the Command; therefore follow it" (Sura 45, Verse 18), but one finds there three other terms from the same root (Sura 42, Verse 13; Sura 5, Verse 48; Sura 42, Verse 21). In all these places *shari'a* signifies not judicial norms but the route or the way. The Qur'anic sense is the one given in all the dictionaries of the

Arab language: the verb *shari'a* signifies to go to water, and the names *shar'a* and *shari'a* mean either to give to drink or the road or the slope leading down to the water.[4]

At first *shari'a* was used in the sense of a path or way of God. To this were integrated the legal rules revealed in the Qur'an; then those which appear in the prophetic verbal traditions (*hadith*), and later the exegesis, glosses, opinions, personal opinions (*ijtihad*s), religious opinions (*fatwa*s), and judgments—in brief, all that completes and clarifies these fundamental rules in order to constitute Islamic jurisprudence (*fiqh*) as this has taken shape in history. In the profane sciences, one can use a word in the sense it has acquired in the course of a long history; nothing authorizes us to do so when it is a matter of a Qur'anic term. There any changes of meaning lead inevitably to deforming the sense of the text and thus to corrupting Revelation. Authentic Islamic fundamentalism should always begin by rediscovering the sense had by the Qur'anic term at the time of their revelation, based upon the Qur'an itself and on the ancient sources. To restrain oneself to only their present sense leads to grave danger for Islam and for the whole society.

The Term *Shari'a* in Egyptian Law

In Article 7 of the Penal Code of 1937 one finds, "In no case are the dispositions of the present Code to limit the personal rights defined by the *shari'a*"; moreover, Article 1(a)(2) of the 1948 Civil Code states that in the absence of any applicable legislative decision, the judge will rule according to precedent, or lacking that, according to the principles of the *shari'a*, or where this is silent the judge will have recourse to natural law and the rules of equity." That text introduced for the first time in Egyptian legislation the expression "principles of the Islamic *shari'a*." The legislation did not clarify what is to be understood by that expression. Nevertheless the preparatory work of the Civil Code shows that it means the combination of principles common to the different schools of Islamic jurisprudence.[5] In other words,

4. *Lisan al-'Arab* [*Dictionary of Arabic*], article on "*Shara'a*."
5. Collection of Preparatory Work for the Civil Code, volume 1, pp. 184, 189, 191.

in 1948 the legislature chose the usual meaning of the term.

Since then Article 2 of the 1971 Egyptian Constitution ("the principles of the Islamic *shari'a* are a principal source of legislation") was modified by the constitutional amendment of May 22, 1980: "The principles of the *shari'a* are *the* principle source of legislation." Although the 1971 Constitution is not accompanied by an explanatory memorandum or a collection of preparatory works permitting one to know what the legislature understood by "principles of the Islamic *shari'a*," there is every reason to think that in the constitution this expression has the same meaning as in the Civil Code: in this sense the report of the *ad hoc* commission charged with preparing the 1980 amendment indicates explicitly that "by this expression the commission has in mind the set of principles common to the school of Islamic jurisprudence."

It is not necessary to state that there is nothing in the preparatory works, or in similar references, which aid in knowing the intention of the legislator in using the phrase "principles of Islamic *shari'a*," which could be considered as contradicting the text. In effect, if the text does not allow us to decide between the two senses of the term *shari'a*, it is only such documents that allow us to know what was willed by the legislator. It would be purely arbitrary to say that this text makes implicit allusion to the first sense of *shari'a*. There is no reason why the legislator would make allusion in such legislative texts as the Constitution or the Civil Code to "the way of God." Such terms come naturally from morality and piety, but have nothing to do with legal language. Furthermore, the word "principles" signifies properly the essential bases on which something is founded and nothing else, whereas the way of God constitutes an indivisible whole which includes at the same time both the foundations and the edifice constructed thereupon. At most one could say that the principles or foundations are moral or cultural rules; that they are not, in any case, legal norms.

Consequently, the expression "principles of the Islamic *shari'a*" designates without the shadow of a doubt "the set of principles common to different schools of Islamic jurisprudence."

If, despite that objective demonstration, one continues to think that it designates the only Qur'anic legal norms, we would say that these norms cannot constitute the principles or foundations of the *shari'a*

because they are fashioned in different places and are not general norms. Moreover, they cannot serve as a basis for other norms if they are considered as the totality of the norms. That would be possible only if one understands by this that they constitute the bases from which Islamic jurisprudence deduces and derives its other norms, in which case one returns to our point of departure, namely, that the "principles of the *shari'a*" designate the totality of the norms common to the different schools of Islamic jurisprudence (*fiqh*).

This does not dispense us from examining the legal norms mentioned in the Qur'an and comparing them with Egyptian legislation to see to what point they are or are not in conformity and whether or not it is necessary to codify and rework Egyptian legislation in order to remove any lack of conformity.

Legal Norms in the Qur'an

Of some 6,000 Qur'anic verses, only 200 have a legal aspect, that is, approximately one thirtieth of the Qur'an, including the verses which were abrogated by subsequent ones. This shows that the principal object of the Qur'an is moral in nature: it is concerned to inscribe the fault in the soul of the believer, to elevate his conscience and morality in order that it might be its own proper *shari'a* in the sense of the way leading to God. Also, even when a Qur'anic law is applicable, this should be in the context of faith and justice, beyond any judicial partiality or deviation. On the other hand, judicial norms being by nature local and temporary, God more often left expressly to humans the work of regulating the details and the freedom to review them with a view to possibly substituting others in function of the needs of each country and epoch. Let us examine these norms.

In civil matters, the Qur'an contains only one normative verse: "God has permitted selling, and forbidden usury" (Sura 2, Verse 275), but it does not specify what should be understood by selling and by usury. Despite this general authorization of selling, the exegetes from the strictest to the moderate, basing themselves on certain *hadith*s, had prohibited certain forms of selling such as the sale of the entire fruits of a tree (*muzabana*), a sale before the harvest (*muzaqala*), the sale of a fixed portion prior to the harvest (*muzara'a*), etc.

We have shown elsewhere[6] what distinguishes usury which is forbidden by the Qur'an from the regulations concerning interest in Egyptian law: in substance, illicit usury is in reality only a loan at excessive cost. By exploiting the need of the borrower this results in his having to reimburse many times over the cost of the principal and could result in his being enslaved if he proved incapable of paying off the debt. It is reported that the Prophet himself had ordered the enslavement of a man named Sorak because he had not paid off the loan he had contracted.

As that verse was the only one containing an objective norm in civil matters, all provisions regarding relations between people (mu'amalat) had to be worked out by Islamic jurisprudence. That is why the Egyptian legislature was able to indicate in its preparatory work for the Civil Code that most of the dispositions of the Code "could easily be from the different dispositions of schools of Islamic shari'a." And when in 1981, in the context of projects of Islamization of law, the project of the code of behavior (mu'amalat) intended to replace the actual Civil Code was presented to the general assembly of the Supreme Court of Cassation its report stated: "If our Constitution stipulated that the shari'a is the principal source of legislation, that does not imply that we should reject our Civil Code of 1948 whose elaboration lasted over twenty years and whose solutions, resulting from deep study, are derived in large part from norms of the shari'a. This is pointed out in the explanatory memorandum which, moreover, makes explicit the foundation in Islamic jurisprudence of a number of these dispositions." Thus that assembly, as true representative of the Egyptian judiciary, decided definitively the question of the codification of the shari'a in civil matters.

There remain nonetheless two problems which merit closer examination: that of interest on debts, which for some constitutes a form of usury prohibited by religious law, and that of insurance contracts which some consider—wrongly in our view—as speculative contracts and hence as illicit. These two questions should be the object of a debate, as open as possible, to which the judges and all religious scholars should contribute, a debate that is really free

6. See M. S. al-'Ashmawi, *Al-Riba wa'l-fa'ida fi'l-Islam* (*Usury and Interest in Islam*) (Cairo: Dar Sina, 1988).

and limited solely by a frame of authentic free opinion (ijtihad) as described above.

In matters of procedure, the Qur'an has only one verse relative to the proof of debts: "O believers, when you contract a debt one upon another for a stated term, write it down . . . with the certification of two male witnesses" (Sura 2, Verse 282). The sense of this verse, limited to the certification of a debt, has been extended by Islamic jurisprudence to all evidence, including that in penal matters. One can legitimately hold then that extension is valid in one specific country and epoch and not in other circumstances. The objective of religious scholars when they have imposed a specific form of evidence in relation to Qur'anic punishments was to restrict as much as possible their application so that the civil punishments could be applied to all crimes, including those subject to a Qur'anic punishment.

In the manner of personal law, all Egyptian legal prescriptions relative to marriage, divorce, and inheritance are taken explicitly from the Qur'an, the prophetic tradition regarding the Prophet (sunna), and some prescriptions of Islamic Law which the legislature has considered to be the most adequate to the needs of society.

In penal manners, the Qur'anic penalties (hudud) strictly speaking are four: theft (amputation of the hand), calumnious accusation of fornication (80 lashes), adultery (100 lashes) and brigandage (execution, crucifixion, banishment or jail). The penalties for apostasy and drinking alcohol are not strictly speaking Qur'anic penalties, as the first is based on the two hadiths and the second was set by 'Ali ibn Abi Talib [the Prophet's son-in-law and fourth caliph, reigned 656–661] by analogy with the penalty for the calumnious accusation of fornication.

At any rate, many conditions must be fulfilled in order that these Qur'anic penalties be applied. The most important is that one be in a community of pious and honorable believers who have installed political, economic and social justice. This is necessary so that the judgment rendered in the name of religious law not be utilized for other purposes, and that the chastisements imposed in the name of Islam not be applied to Muslims by unjust governments or by harsh tribunals on the basis of arbitrary arrests or false witness, as has been too often the case throughout Islamic history and even more so in our day.

Contrary to a broadly accepted idea, Islam does not require that society apply systematically the

Qur'anic punishments. On the contrary, it enjoins it to show tolerance and clemency. Thus, Muhammad said: "Strive to be merciful one to another in the application of Qur'anic punishments." Each time society, by tolerance, avoids the application of Qur'anic punishments, it acts according to the spirit of Islam and the request of its Prophet. That same rule specifies that when a judge is presented with a crime subject to a legal punishment he should withhold application of that punishment if any doubt subsists as regards the facts, the witnesses, the victims or the author of the crime, according to the prophetic verbal traditions (*hadith*): "avoid the application of the legal penalty (*hudud*) in case of doubt." Thus it is reported that under the caliphate of 'Umar ibn al-Khattab [reigned 634–644], a woman came and admitted in the presence of 'Ali ibn Abi Talib to having committed adultery subject to the legal punishment. 'Ali said to 'Umar: "Commander of the believers, this woman does not take account of the gravity of her words." And they agreed that there was therefore doubt which would withhold the Qur'anic punishment despite her admission.

These Qur'anic punishments are so surrounded by conditions that in practice they are practically inapplicable; moreover, to these general conditions are added particular conditions for each penalty. Take for example theft: the object of theft must be marked by the seal of the owner and be in a well-guarded place, which excludes pilfering, open plundering and pick pocketing; it must have a money value; the robber must not be in great need; finally, for the majority of jurists the Qur'anic punishment for theft cannot be applied if the robber has some "quasi-ownership" on the goods stolen, as is notably the case with public goods. For the punishment of fornication, there are required four reliable witnesses who have seen the crime with their own eyes from beginning to end and can swear "that a thread could not have passed between the man and the woman"—conditions which have not been satisfied once in the whole history of Islam. As for the punishment for robbery, all schools of Islamic jurisprudence (*fiqh*) agree that it should not apply if the bandit repents before having been apprehended, in conformity with the end of the verse regarding that punishment: "except for such as repent, before you have power over them" (Sura 5, Verse 34).

More broadly, the majority of jurists think that the Qur'anic punishments cannot be applied against one who repents after the crime and before the execution of the punishment: an adage says for example "no amputation for the repentant." This is because for the Prophet these chastisements are purificatory punishments which should be applied only with the consent of the sinner and should be withheld if he repents, that is, if he wishes to escape it. Thus, the Companions came one day to find the Prophet in order to report that a woman guilty of fornication had begun to be stoned but had fled; being caught again the punishments had been inflicted till death. The Prophet then became angry and said: "Why did you not abandon her to her fate?" It is better then not to apply a penalty to a guilty person who does not willingly accept it.

As regards the law of the talon [retribution], the Qur'an refers to it only in the case of injuries, wounds, blows and homicide: "O believers, prescribed for you is retaliation, in the case of murder" (Sura 2, Verse 178). As regards the talon for blows and wounds, it is evoked only in a verse alluding to a Jewish law and not as a rule to be applied to Muslims ("We have prescribed for them [i.e., for the Jews] a life for a life, an eye for an eye, a nose for a nose, an ear for an ear, a tooth for a tooth. Wounds fall under the law of the talon"—Sura 5, Verse 45). The law "an eye for an eye, a tooth for a tooth" was introduced in Islamic Law by jurists on the basis of the adage "the Law of our predecessors binds us as well except for what was abrogated" and a prophetic verbal tradition (*hadith*) which alludes to it without mentioning it explicitly. Thus, Islamic thought confuses *shari'a*—that is to say, the Qur'anic norm—with Islamic jurisprudence (*fiqh*)—that is to say, what results from the free opinion (*ijtihad*) of jurists. As a result it has thought the law "an eye for an eye, a tooth for a tooth" to be a religious prescription and an integral part of the *shari'a*. In fact, if that law was a fundamental law which God wished to impose on Muslims it would not have been left to the evaluation of jurists, but clearly stated in the Qur'an. Further, jurists who cite the adage "the law of our predecessors binds us as well except for what was abrogated" use it in a selective manner. They ignore it in the case of numerous earlier prescriptions which were not abrogated—for example, that which condemns to death one who strikes his parents.

The law of the talon poses another problem: it is not applicable when the victim or those responsible for him pardon the guilty person, whether or not that person has made financial recompense (*diya*). But to admit that a pardon may annul the penalty is, in our modern societies, extremely dangerous, for one risks thereby encouraging the guilty to put all sorts of pressure on the victim to obtain their pardon and to escape chastisement. It is enough to know a little of penal justice to know the extent to which pressure can be put upon victims in order that they modify or falsify their testimony so that the evidence can be subject to controversy in the judicial process. What will happen if these pressures would make it possible to stop the process itself? Our judicial system authorizes the retraction of an action as a civil matter, but not in a criminal matter for that would threaten the whole society, which is the reason why such a retraction is reserved solely to the public prosecutor. That system is better adapted to actual social conditions and does not contravene *shari'a*.

Since the Revelation, its four or six penalties (*hudud*) have never sufficed to stop criminality, which has always taken many forms. Islamic doctrine had to invent another institution, that of civil penalties (*ta'zir*). Through these, public authority—executive or legislative as the case may be—could designate as criminal any act it judged prejudicial to public security, to the rights of persons, to their goods or to their honor. It could punish such acts by the penalty it considered necessary, including even capital punishment. In our opinion, these civil penalties constitute the heart of the Islamic penal system. This very flexible system allows for the repression of all forms of criminality according as they appear. It can apply itself also to crimes punished by Qur'anic punishment wherever their conditions are not fulfilled. It permits the application of punishment for infractions under the law of the talon even when those culpable have been pardoned by the victim or those responsible for him, as is foreseen in the Egyptian penal code now in force. In other words, our entire penal law depends upon civil penalties and thus does not infringe at all upon *shari'a*. The penal code differs only in the results to which its free opinion (*ijtihad*) concludes in conformity with the social conditions of the epoch.

It is thus, in substance, that the issue of the codification of the *shari'a* must be posed: taking into account the profane as well as the religious points of view. The whole issue of conflict between the penal code and the *shari'a* is false, for Egyptian civil law, its penal law and its personal statutes are in confor-mity with the dispositions of *shari'a* and Islamic jurisprudence (*fiqh*). But when it comes to a political slogan, a pretext for self-seeking or a springboard to power, what was revealed by God is mixed with what was created by humans. Such a mixture risks destroying not only Islamic jurisprudence but the Egyptian legal system, which has resulted from a century of jurisprudential and doctrinal development.

Before concluding, we would suggest here some issues directly involved in our subject.

1. Those who accuse the Egyptian legislature of having turned things upside down in 1883 by replacing the provisions of the *shari'a* by the current legal system should begin by studying more closely the legal system in force in Ottoman Egypt (1517–1883), which they abusively liken to *shari'a*. During that period, the law, which derived from the sultan, ceased upon his death. If certain provisions remained in vigor, that was by the sole force of custom. The magistrates named by Istanbul were not remunerated, but could place a tax upon trials. Of this they kept a part for themselves and sent the rest to the Minister of Foreign Affairs with a view to assuring the renewal of their appointment—a system designed by nature to seriously corrupt the judiciary. The competence of judges was limited to civil affairs. During the entire Ottoman period there were only two known cases of an application of the Qur'anic punishments and in these the principle, "Avoid the application of the legal punishment (*hadd*) in case of doubt," was not well understood. As regards civil punishment, the judge could enter in only when there was a conflict between two people. His competence was limited to establishing the facts; the police authority pronounced judgment and carried out its execution. Further, if a criminal endangered the security of the State the judge lost all competence in favor of the police authorities. Judges had no independence, the instructions and charges were not organized, the judgments—whether from the judge or from an entirely different authority—were not provided with reasons and there were neither procedures of appeal nor a system of defense for the accused.

Could one say that the Egyptian Legislature of 1883 wanted to reject the *shari'a* when it sought to reform a corrupt state in which absolute power was the rule? This it did by elaborating a legal system which was clear, healthy and modern, and founded upon legislative codes over which the Egyptian judiciary has watched for a century. Should one accuse it of having substituted order for disorder, the power of the judiciary for that of the prince, modernity for backwardness?

2. Islamic jurisprudence is certainly general and exhaustive, but it dates from the first centuries of Islam. Since the 4th century A.H. (10th century A.D.), the door of independent opinion (*ijtihad*) was closed and Islamic thought ceased to enrich itself, to develop and innovate. By contrast, since 1883 in Egypt jurisprudence and legal theory have developed an original and modern outlook which, drawing on the best in Islamic Law, have given it a new completeness, variety, precision and force. That theory and jurisprudence have spread through numerous Arab countries, thus constituting an imposing patrimony which everyone today—people, judges and governments—should protect and not allow to be endangered.

3. Regarding the verse "When news comes to them, be it a matter of security or fear, they broadcast it; if they had referred it to the Messenger and to those in authority among them to ask their advice they would have known if they should trust it, for one refers habitually to their opinion" (Sura 5, Verse 83), exegesis cites this dialogue between the Prophet and Mu'adh ibn Jabal [died 627], his governor in Yemen: "How do you decide litigation between persons?" Muhammad asked him. "By means of the Qur'an," he responded. . . . "And if not?" . . . "By means of the tradition regarding the Prophet (*sunna*)," . . . "And if not?" . . . "By the opinion that I form through my efforts at independent opinion (*ijtihad*)."

On the basis of this verse and tradition it is said that independent opinion (*ijtihad*) constitutes an obligation for Islam. This has been surrounded with such restrictions that it has come down to repeating the judgments of the predecessors and sustaining the privileges proper to an elite. Because of the confusion between *shari'a* and Islamic jurisprudence (*fiqh*) and between rules relating to cultural practices ('*ibadat*) and rules concerning relations between people (*mu'amalat*), this group has come to constitute itself into a kind of clergy.

Because of such confusion, Islamic jurisprudence (*fiqh*) lost sight of the fact that independent opinion (*ijtihad*) could not be practiced in the same way in matters regarding cult and those between people (*mu'amalat*). As regards the first, being regulated by the foundations of the law (*usul*)—that is to say, essentially the Qur'an and the tradition regarding the Prophet (*sunna*)—the only free opinion possible is

that of reasoning by analogy on the basis of these laws (*usul*). As the second was practically absent in these foundations and must govern deeds and situations unknown at the time of the Prophet and the first development of Islamic jurisprudence (*fiqh*), it is logical, even necessary, that it be the object of a free interpretation (*ijtihad*). In such cases this must go beyond simple analogy or deduction on the basis of earlier opinions; with a view to the general welfare and in response to social conditions it must be truly creative. If jurists had been capable of theorizing the experience of 'Umar ibn al-Khattab, they would have left us a theory of the temporality of norms. Unfortunately, with but a few exceptions, they did not go beyond a casuist logic.

One finds nonetheless, among some, the beginnings of this type of reflection in this sense. Thus the great Hanifite jurist, [Muhammad Amin] Ibn 'Abidin [circa 1783–1836], wrote: "Numerous legal rules change in function according to the times, by reason of the modification of customs, of necessity or of the change in times. If they do not change they would cause difficulties and harm people, thereby restricting the rule of *shari'a* which directs us to smooth out difficulties and to avoid all prejudice." A similar observation can be found from [Muhammad] Ibn Qayyim [al-Jawziyya, 1292–1350]: "God the All-Powerful did not limit the pointers and directives of justice to but one path, rejecting the others as useless; on the contrary, from this Law it appears clearly that His intention is to establish law and justice; also, when one finds this path one should prescribe to what it decides and declares to be necessary." On his part, the Hanbalite [Najm al Din] al-Towfi [died 1316] specifies:

> If a text implies any damage to the general interest (*maslaha*), it is the latter which should prevail.—But some say, that is against the text.—On the contrary, it reinforces the text, which was revealed in order to safeguard human welfare.—But, some would say, the text is better situated to know where their welfare lies, because it comes from God or His Prophet.— The text is unchanging, whereas human concerns are changing. To take into consideration that interest is to take into consideration that text in its integrity, and to respect the prophetic verbal traditions (*hadith*): "You are more in touch with worldly affairs."

Does Egyptian common law, aside from some exceptions, propose anything other than the installation of justice in society? Does not the action of the

Egyptian judiciary, developed by serious and persevering work, seek to establish justice, law and security? If there is still someone who, after all that, could pretend that Egyptian courts and laws impede *shari'a* and the government of Divine Revelation, we would refer to what we have said above [in an earlier chapter of 'Ashmawi's book] regarding the terms *shari'a* and *hukm* [government], and recall the adage of Islamic jurisprudence according to which: "where one finds the common interest there is situated the Law of God." Politics is the art of being in conformity with the spirit of that Law, and not with its letter; general welfare comes before the letter of the law. Supposing—and this is only a supposition—that there did exist in Egyptian legislation a text contrary to such and such a text or opinion of Islamic jurisprudence (*fiqh*), would not the opinion cited above justify recourse to a decision in the interest of society—for example, in order to avoid discord or to avoid an ordeal which might not help anyone?

4. In a recent article, a judge wrote: "We should note that when the codes still in force were promulgated it was not specified that they were founded upon the dispositions of *shari'a*, which shows that there was no such intention on the part of the legislator. But the application of the *shari'a* requires the existence of an intention for anything related to religion. Hence, we should revise these dispositions which do not seem to contradict the *shari'a* and then repromulgate the whole Code."[7]

That position is untenable: if in Islam in matters of cult the proclamation of intention is obligatory for individuals—though not for states and governments—in matters of daily behavior (*mu'amalat*) only external acts are considered ("God alone knows inner thoughts"); contracts and transfers of property have force without their authors having to make known their intentions. No one has ever pretended that a public official had to declare his intention in order that the laws he promulgates be valid. And how could that be done? Must that intention be proclaimed by the Chief of State or the government, by the Speaker of the People's Assembly or the presidents of the legislative commissions, or must it be subject to an examination of conscience by members of the legislative assembly? Must one be content with the majority opinion or require unanimity? Must one say that the lack of intention or a doubt in that regard suffices to render the law illicit?

Such proposals would constitute a prohibited innovation (*bid'a*). We have established, with great effort to overcome all doubt, that there is no contradiction between Egyptian legislation and Islamic Law (*shari'a*); or if not that it is so small that it can be transcended either on the basis of independent opinion (*ijtihad*) or because of the general welfare and the need to avoid discord and trouble command one to recognize reality as it is. Would one now present that *bid'a* pretending that Egyptian legislation, though in conformity with *shari'a*, does not specify the intention of the legislator and hence that the intention needs to be proclaimed before promulgating that legislation anew? That would mean suppressing the Egyptian laws in order to repromulgate them in a given sense in order that certain persons would have a special right of surveillance or guardianship. Would that not mean dismantling our entire legal and judicial system in order to rebuild them upon new bases and intentions made up from all sorts of pieces which are neither those of the ancients nor those of anyone else? . . .

Such political conceptions of religion are extremely dangerous for Islam and for its *shari'a*. They imply the worst threats to Egypt; they would break in two its legal and judiciary systems, as well as the country itself, and declare an end to contemporary Egyptian Islamic Law, all without this being required by anything in religion or in *shari'a*.

---

7. *Majallat al-qudat* [*Judges' Journal*], numbers 3–4, March–April, 1986, p. 44.

PART II

Democracy

The Indonesian Revolution

Born in Sumatra, Muhammad Natsir (Indonesia, 1908–1993) was among the first Indonesians to receive a European education. He combined this Western training with his Islamic beliefs to create a modernist interpretation of Islam, which he promoted as leader of the modernist wing of the Consultative Congress of Indonesian Muslims (the Masjumi party) during the 1940s and 1950s.[1] After Indonesia regained its independence, Natsir rose to the prime ministership, serving for a year in 1950–1951. Thereafter, through his speeches and interviews, he "became identified as the champion of liberal parliamentary democracy."[2] In the following essay from 1955, Natsir urges Muslims to accept the secular Indonesian state (analogous to the Kabir and Zafar essays in this volume). In 1958, Natsir appears to have abandoned these views, siding with an Islamic revolutionary movement in Sumatra, serving several years in prison, and emerging with far more rigid theological positions. The younger generation of Indonesian Islamic reformers, represented by Nurcholish Madjid in this volume, viewed Natsir as a recalcitrant member of the old guard.[3]

We fought for an [independent] state and initiated the Revolution on 17 August 1945. But it was not on 17 August 1945 that the struggle for freedom was begun.

The struggle, pitting political force against political force, between the people of Indonesia and the Dutch colonial government is more than nine years old. In a political sense, the struggle began in 1905 [actually 1911—Translator] with the establishment, by Haji Samanhudi [died 1956] and his friends, of the *Sarekat Dagang Islam* [Islamic Business Association]. The *Sarekat Dagang Islam* was followed in 1908 by *Budi Utomo* [High Endeavor Association].

1. Howard M. Federspiel, *Persatuan Islam: Islamic Reform in Twentieth Century Indonesia* (Ithaca, N.Y.: Modern Indonesia Project, Southeast Asia Program, Cornell University, 1970); Deliar Noer, *The Modernist Muslim Movement in Indonesia, 1900–1942* (Singapore: Oxford University Press, 1973).

2. Peter Burns, *Revelation and Revolution: Natsir and the Panca Sila* (Townsville, Australia: Committee of South-East Asian Studies, James Cook University of North Queensland, Southeast Asian Monograph Series No. 9, 1981), p. 31.

3. Mark R. Woodward, "Natsir, Mohammad," in John L. Esposito, editor, *The Oxford Encyclopedia of the Modern Islamic World* (New York: Oxford University Press, 1995), volume 3, pp. 239–240.

In 1912 the *Partai Sarekat Islam* [Islamic Association Party] came into existence—the first-ever mass organization. That was the moment when we began to pit political strength against the imperialists by drawing on the political strength of the common people.

But really, with regard to the fight for Indonesian independence—or, at the very least, for self-defense against subjugation—it had all begun much earlier than that. One may note down the name of heroes such as Sultan Hasanuddin [sultan of Gowa, 1653–1669], Teungku Cik de Tiro [religious scholar of Aceh, died 1890], Imam Bonjol [Sumatran revivalist, died circa 1837], Diponegoro [Javanese prince, died 1855], Sultan Hidayat [presumably Hidayatullah, sultan of Banjar, reigned 1860–1862], and others of the great inexhaustible spirit of self-sacrifice.

We know that, in some regions, it was only at the end of the 19th century, or the beginning of the 20th, that the arms of the imperialists were able to subdue popular resistance. In some parts of our homeland—such as Sulawesi, Sumatra and elsewhere—it seems that our people did not quickly lay down their weapons. They were conscious of their weakness with regard to weapons and material resources but they had weapons which were not material, weapons immaterial—as people would now say—that is to say: the weapons of conviction and firmness of purpose in defending themselves against colonialism.

The Colonial Domination of Man over Man

With such weapons as were available, the people opposed the great and varied armament of the colonialists. Their non-material strength lay in their conviction of God's instruction: that they should hold themselves accursed if they were to let themselves be subjugated. Such beliefs as these are rooted in their very flesh and blood. Truly, there is no possible reconciliation between religious faith and colonial domination. The spirit of faith is a spirit opposed to tyranny, "to the exploitation of man by man," as people say these days. They would feel as though they had not fulfilled the divine command, as though their religion was not yet perfected were they to allow themselves, or their folk, to be exploited

by other groups or races. And that was as it ought to have been, for the religion they confessed numbered among its most important teachings, this, that one should oppose every case of the exploitation of man by man in any form whatever.

In its essence the teaching of Islam constitutes a revolution in opposing and wiping out every form of exploitation. Whether the exploitation bears the name of capitalism, imperialism, colonialism, Communism or Fascism—that's a question left to whoever wishes to be concerned with nomenclature. Such then is the spirit of freedom alive and burning in the minds of the Muslims of Indonesia. For centuries this spirit has been the source of strength for our people and it was this spirit too which built up and up and impelled us to proclaim, in the year of 1945, the independence of the Republic of Indonesia.

The Meekest Nation

The world, on hearing the Proclamation [of Indonesian independence], was astounded and amazed because all of a sudden, our nation took a form other than what had been portrayed from the beginning. [The Dutch] had given the Indonesian people the title *"het zachtste volk der aarde"* (the softest people in the world)—gentle of spirit in the sense of willing compliance and being content under the rule of the acknowledged masters. But this most gentle folk now, suddenly, has undergone a metamorphosis, a radical change.

If formerly they might have been likened to sheep or goats which only follow, now, suddenly they became like tigers showing such courage and extraordinary valor that they have astounded men in foreign lands. Then there occurred events such as those in Surabaya, Semarang, Bandung and elsewhere through the length and breadth of the Indonesian archipelago. It seemed as though our people had buried deep in their souls a treasury of velour which, at its appointed time, was to burst out. In a condition of utter lack and without arms to oppose the allied armies which were bringing back the Dutch, it was that non-material weapon which rose among the Indonesian people. Raised by the leaders and men at the forefront of the Revolution, it touched a chord in the hearts of the multitude by means of a spiritual call which has often reverberated in the ears of that multitude.

The Call "*Allah-u-akbar*" (God Is Great)

We heard the call and the cry on the radio to marshal the hidden energy. Millions of our people, men and women, old and young still recall the appeal of Bung Tomo [Sutomo, revolutionary leader, 1920–1983] through Radio Surabaya [in 1946]. He summoned the theologians, the religious teachers, through the whole of Indonesia with the call "*Allah-u-akbar.*" We greatly value it, that there should have been a young hero such as Bung Tomo. It was not just that he appeared bravely at the front leading the struggle, but also that he knew what many people don't often know: that is, he knew where lay the key of strength in this nation of ours. He opened the lock on the hearts of the multitude with the words "*Allah-u-akbar.*" He knew where to find friends. He also knew who were the friends who could rouse up energy and stir it to a high pitch. He sought those friends among the spiritual guides, whose names are never seen in newspapers and never inserted in the lists of leaders of political parties. He sought out spiritual guides— the ones called '*ulama*' and *kiayi*—in the villages. He called and cried aloud, saying: Let us together open the lock to the hearts and minds of the people with the words "*Allah-u-akbar.*" And in that way all the energy desired seethed up and flooded over in abundance. So it was too with material requirements.

The young *pemuda* [freedom fighters], there being that summons which held the key to their hearts, without hesitation constituted themselves as defensive forces, as barriers to protect their homes and villages, to fortify their homes and villages from the bullets of the enemy. Many of them fell as heroes, knights and martyrs. The women folk too did not want to be left behind; not even the very old were content to sit at home. For that, they received neither wage nor salary; nor were they ordered to go. The only orders they received came from their own hearts, which had responded to the cry "*Allah-u-akbar.*"

Holy Sign

That holy call became a sign for those who gave the call. It was clear to them that there was a motivating force among the Indonesian people which could marshal energy to confront disasters coming from the outside. And this was no mere motivation which could stir and unite people to crush an enemy who wanted to oppress; it was also capable of drawing out energy and power on a large scale such that, if one were skilled enough to direct it, it could build and give content to this nation of ours. Every leader is fortunate who is aware of this, and who knows also how to use this great force. And, on the other hand, sad is the fate of the state if its leaders have not the skill to use this potential, so that it explodes and becomes incendiary, or remains completely unexploited. At present we are searching for the way, and we have these questions to answer:

- What meaning do we wish to give our nation state?
- How do we give meaning to Independence?

Such questions we must answer, in the interests of future generations, the young men and women who will replace us.

The Great Task

We face a great task and duty in the story of our people. Our nation is writing its history in the setting of world history.

We must answer the questions above together. Giving meaning to Independence: for us this is an action within the framework of expressing thanks and gratitude. We return thanks to God who, in such a short time (namely, just five years) favored us with such a mighty achievement in the form of our own, independent, Indonesia. This Republic of Indonesia of which we have taken possession is, we feel convinced, the gift of God for which we must thank Him.

There is much lacking in this republic of ours. Many are its shortcomings. There is much which we find unsatisfactory. However, with all its blemishes clinging to it, we must accept the Republic with feelings of gratitude and of benediction. For the faithful of Islam the expression of gratitude for a blessing is an obligation.

But it must be borne in mind that expressing thanks for divine favor is not merely being glad and joyful while releasing every instinct for pleasure and luxury. Expressing thanks for divine favor entails acceptance with consciousness of the way things are with all their potential weaknesses and strengths latent within them. Receiving with the intention of making improvements. Improving that which is still not good, strengthening that which is not strong, while making whole that which is still imperfect. That's what it means to express thanks for divine favor. And it's definitely not a matter of rejection, or of using scorched-earth policies, after having seen the many blemishes in what you hold in your hands.

Disgruntled people—those who, having received, feel a sense of deprivation—they are not the ones who know how to express thanks. There is but one teaching, one guide—to which we adhere—namely the word of God, the gist of which is:

> If you know how to show gratitude, I shall multiply many times what you have received. But, if you are thankless, unappreciative and unable to value it, spending your time in complaint and rejecting all of it because it is not enough, know then that my punishment is bitter punishment indeed. (Qur'an, Sura 14, Verse 7)

We do not wish to become ungrateful reprobates. Such is the Republic of Indonesia we received, come let us nurture it, strengthen it and cultivate it from within with every good basis for healthy growth hereafter.

Because of that, answering the question, "What is the best way we can improve and perfect the blessing we have received?" is not so difficult for the faithful of Islam. We have been blessed with a homeland of such fertile earth and such good climate. Neither very hot nor very cold. It does not rain in flooding torrents as it does it in other tropical regions. Its heat is not a blazing, burning heat, which dries up and makes the fields of grass into fields of stone and sand. Our nation is a very prosperous land and abounds in natural wealth. Meanwhile, if we contemplate its human resources—again the praise is to the Lord—we would not be shamed, were we to be compared with the peoples of other nations. Our nation has a high culture. The culture referred to does not mean only the fruits of intellectual cleverness; it also refers to fine character and disposition which is pervaded by its internal basis of *tasamuh* (indulgence, forbearance), a basis of tolerance, people say nowadays. Discord and violent controversy are not one of our qualities.

Tolerance

In other nations—as in India for example—religious problems between the Hindus and Islam often cause discord and difficult troublesome problems leading to fights and large-scale bloodshed never knowing peace. In our country, things are not like that. This is a positive benefit; something most glorious in the ranks of our people.

The wealth of natural resources remained comparatively undeveloped by the imperialists during those hundreds of years. It's just some few percent which they took at the end. There is not yet here any large-scale industrialization as there is in the West. Industrialization of a revolutionary kind, which shakes the structure of society, has not yet built up to anything very disturbing in our society.

Feudalism, which distinguished the status of one group from that of another, was not something which reigned unchecked in our homeland. Our people possessed a quality which lived deeply rooted in their very bones, to wit: the quality to which we often refer as *gotong-royong* [mutual aid]. The conflict between what they call capitalism and the proletariat in our country has not—all praise to God—become basic, as has happened in Western nations since mid-way through last century.

In brief, it can be said we have a homeland still clear of the seeds of that which is capable of causing upset. This is something fresh and new which we want to develop. This is the base of our development. One might even say that a nation possessing the qualities and the geographical and sociological situation which Indonesia has, with a populace of between 75 to 80 million, is a state possessing special gifts, capable of making its own road into the future, consonant with the environment and the climate and the humanity of Indonesia itself.

Our Own Method

There would be no point were we to go looking for methods which may or may not work well in other countries. There would be no point in our adopting wholesale all those other systems and methods. We can look for our own methods and systems, in accord with our material and our talents, in accord with the mentality of the great part of our people.

For us of the Muslim community, we are permitted to experience it just as it was instilled into his disciples by our Master, the Prophet Muhammad—may the Lord bless him and give him peace—thirteen and a half centuries ago. They also staged a great revolution to raise a very weak community into one of high degree, one which had great capacities. It was, to wit, a saying of the Prophet that, when we recall it today, gets right to the point. The occasion of his utterance was the joyful return of the people from the battles that had culminated in victory; they were glad and rejoicing because they had finally accomplished a difficult task with brilliant results. Said he: "We have just come back from a minor battle, from the lesser struggle" (*raja' na mina jihadi' l-asgar*)—even though that struggle had resulted in the shedding of blood and the loss of life, even though it had been murderous and utterly destructive. Yet in spite of this, he spoke of it as a small-scale battle, a minor battle—*jihad asgar*. And he went on to say, the community would confront another phase in the development of the revolution, called the *jihad akbar*, the greater struggle, greater than anything before, in which there would no sound of swords—nor of rifles—in which there would be no killing and being killed, no incendiarism, but which nevertheless would be more difficult than the holy struggles of the past. The struggle—the *jihadu' n-nafs*—would be a struggle to develop one's own personality, to build up the identity of the Community, building up national strength and capabilities. This holy struggle would be more difficult than the struggle or battle with just the one slogan: "Kill the enemy—as many as possible." This battle of the self (*jihadu' n-nafs*) is a struggle needing an organized plan, perseverance and a farseeing view, constant and enduring patience. Such a holy battle, the struggle to build up personal identity, and the Community, is a long-term struggle, a difficult struggle for those who seriously and earnestly want to carry it through!

It does not seem wrong to compare our struggle at this time to what our Master, the Prophet Muhammad—may the Lord bless him and give him peace —meant by the phrase of *jihad akbar* (the greater struggle).

In this regard we give thanks that we have guides in how to build up personality and how to build up society.

The Prophet Muhammad as a Revolutionary Leader

Muhammad—may the Lord bless him and give him peace—was a revolutionary leader. One of the elements of his revolution was the abolition of every form of *the exploitation of man by man* and *the elimination of poverty and misery*, as people put it these days.

Every teaching of Islam is, both in content and direction, concerned with the abolition of the exploitation of man by man and the elimination of poverty.

He said: "Poverty and misery are next to godlessness." So poverty and misery are not to be let loose to rage unchecked around us, as they lead mankind into a state of rebellion against God. Good men may fall from grace, if poverty and misery reign unchecked. If character is not to deteriorate, if demoralization is to be checked, one method of curing it is *wipe out poverty and misery*. In the practical instruction given by Islam, every single one of us must use his own strengths and powers to increase and multiply production, to increase output so that we can elevate the quality of life of mankind and can mete out, in an orderly and fair way, the riches and the necessary goods. Why, *zakat* [obligatory Islamic tax] is only a small part of the system, and so too is *sadaqa* [voluntary charity]. Nonetheless, rampant misery and poverty can be abolished just by *zakat* and *sadaqa*, provided that they are administered in an orderly way.

Freedom from Poverty, Suffering, and Oppression

The whole system put forward as a way of life by Muhammad—the Lord bless him and give him peace —is clear and explicit in its broad outline. That is, it is to create a society which lives in harmony. We, as the community of Islam, are not permitted to allow ourselves to accept poverty and misery. We have been commanded not to forget our fate here on earth. We have been told to use anything and everything about us, by deploying the forces of nature, things of metal, the products of the oceans, and so on to facilitate the harmony of life. God provided all of that for mankind. And all of that can elevate the life of man, so that it becomes a life of harmony and brilliance and man can feel the blessings of divine favor.

The System of Production

According to the teaching of Islam, capital, or wealth, should not be accumulated without bringing about an increase in production. Gold and silver are not to be stored up just to be looked at and counted over repeatedly; they should be put into the wheels of production, invested in the productive process to increase happiness and the common welfare. God has pronounced His threat to men who accumulate unproductive property, namely on those called *yak-nizuna' dh-dhahab*, that is: people who store up unproductive gold and silver to no useful purpose (Sura 9, Verse 34).

Wealth must not be static; it must be put into circulation so that the unemployed get work and the level of production can meet the needs of society. Or, in other words: while capital must be made productive, it is desirable that the employers or those who command capital should not be motivated exclusively by the profit motive but should give great weight to development and the needs of the community.

Basic Human Rights

In the search for the good life and the well-ordered community, philosophers and sociologists as well as freedom fighters from all over the world have come to an agreement framed in a charter named "[The Universal Declaration of] Basic Human Rights." The United Nations has a separate section for drawing up what they call *basic rights* for mankind. Nearly all the free nations of the world have recognized those basic rights as a conceptual basis to be made into a foundation for the development both of nations and of essential human nature.

Those basic human rights include, among other things, the rights to free speech and the free expression of opinion, the freedom to profess a religion, the right to a decent standard of living, the right to strike when this is necessary—yes, all sorts of rights. The charter of basic human rights is so arranged as to remind men that there should be no person under the exploitation of other men. It reminds each person, himself, that he should refuse to be used as a tool by other men. This is definitely a step in the right direction.

But it is not clear what these basic human rights have achieved. It has not yet been absorbed into the consciousness of each individual exactly what is his right, what is not his right, so that among the communities of the human race, those basic rights have yet to be fully realized.

Man is instructed to fight for his rights. He must strive to attain his rights. Those *who hold those rights* will not just acquiesce to be taken over by him *to whom the rights properly belong*: he will defend that which he believes belongs to him. As a consequence of this *being-aware-of-rights* and that *not-yielding-of-rights* there is a clash between the *holders* and the *entitled.*

Organized labor says: "We have the right, you refuse to concede it; we shall use the strike weapon." The employers say: "No, we want to see how strong you are. We are not going to concede even the slightest part of those rights without a struggle!"

And so a fight ensues with rights won and lost, and from the seizing of rights there arises a kind of system usually dubbed, these days, as "the struggle for life"—a snatching of life based on claim and counter claim, the consequence of which is that the strongest emerge on top while the weakest goes to the wall.

In western nations, it is this "struggle for life" outlook which holds sway at the moment, the search for life—even though other people might be crushed in the process.

But, we may ask, is that indeed the only road by which to achieve life and social welfare? The teaching of Islam, in confronting this vexed problem, holds a different outlook. Without in any way diminishing the necessity for each individual to know what his rights are, Islam first and foremost teaches that it is not a matter of "What are my rights?" but, for a Muslim, "What are the obligations which I have to fulfill?" . . .

The basis of the Islamic approach to this problem has already been laid down by the great Prophet Muhammad himself—may the Lord bless him and give him peace—when he said, "No man has perfect faith who does not love his brother (man) as he loves himself." It is on this basis that Islam holds the opinion that the employers' group and the workers' group do not constitute two classes each representing particular exclusive interests that conflict with each other and cannot be brought together. Islam considers both employer and worker as factors of industry each having his function, responsibility and share, each of the same importance in the process of producing the commodities which society needs. . . .

The Islamic way of settling problems on the basis of mutual affection and mutual understanding and respect for the interests of the other party is the best way. That is without increasing hatred and enmity as is entailed by the concept of class conflict, which does nothing to reduce the possibility of the new danger in the tyranny of the trade unions. With the achievement of harmonious relations between employers and workers, organizations will change in nature and they will function as executive bodies which care for and elevate the degree of mutual understanding between management and the workers themselves. Thus, they will no longer represent two class heroes which in mutual confrontation are already under the power of mutual suspicion and mutual distrust! . . .

Such is the essential teaching of Islam in bringing groups closer together, one stratum with other strata in society. It makes obligation the point of emphasis, that is *what each one, individually, has to carry out.*

Hence Islam teaches two kinds of obligation, namely *fardu 'ain* and *fardu kifaya*. *Fardu 'ain* is individual duty, the duty of the individual towards his God. This cannot be passed on to someone else, just as worship, the fast and the pilgrimage cannot be contracted out wholesale to other people. Next to *fardu 'ain* there is *fardu kifaya* which must be carried out for one's fellow men, for society. Each individual must perform his *fardu kifaya* for the community. These two *fardu* or duties may not be ignored. Should one be withdrawn, all that remains is 50 percent: it is not whole. In this second type there are included what people now speak of as the *social*, the *economic*, and the *political*. Call it economic, call it political, call it social: it's all actually [embraced] within Islam.

Values of Religion

Religion and the profession of religion in Islam have such a close connection to *humane values* that the estimation of a man's religious profession is based on what he does and how he does it to fulfill his responsibilities towards humanity. There are warnings in the Qur'an for the man who makes an insincere pretense of religion—called "one who makes a lie of his religion"—even though he bobs up and down [in fake prayer] five times in each 24 hours and fasts through the whole month of Ramadan. He will yet be known as the man who made a lie of his religion if he will not cast the slightest glance to the side to alleviate the plight of the orphans, the poor and destitute. "Do you know who it is who made his religion into a lie?"—so runs the rhetorical question in the Qur'an, which it then goes on to explain and answer itself, namely: "people who do not care for orphans, who do not protect the poor, those who let misery flourish, who feel quite content living to themselves, who give not the slightest regard to beggars." Those are the people who make a lie of their religion. Such is the teaching of the Qur'an (Sura 107, Verses 1–4).

The values of the individual and the worth of his religious profession are measured by the attitude he adopts with regard to the community. If we wish to be constructive, we must strive to bring about a society which, structurally, has the qualities of *tasamuh* [tolerance] and *gotong-royong* [mutual aid]. The spirit of *gotong-royong* internally is a fertilizer for the fulfillment of *fardu kifaya*. There is no longer any doubt that such a system fits exactly with the mentality of the Indonesian people. In this Indonesia of ours there is no chance that any system based on the conflict of group with group or class with class will emerge. The system which meshes with the Indonesian national mentality is harmony of life as a fixture, but there is *gotong-royong* as well. Such is the teaching brought by the Great Leader of the Revolution, the Prophet Muhammad—may the Lord bless him and give him peace.

Fanaticism

[The Prophet] brought a teaching for the abolition of what is called *ta'assub* or what people often refer to by the term "fanaticism" (although the expression fanaticism is not an exact translation of *ta'assub*). But let's use the word fanaticism meaning fanaticism in the broadest sense. Fanaticism in ideas, fanaticism in defending one's race and kin group. In this connection I had better put something forward, because often people assume that Islam is opposed to the very existence of races or nations—in short, they say, Islam repudiates the existence of race, as though those who have embraced Islam have lost their nationhood altogether. Such is not the truth. We can be dutiful Muslims while, at the same time, we sing with joy *"Indonesia, my native land"* [the Indonesian national anthem]. How are we going to lose our "Indonesianness" seeing that it was God Himself who made us into distinct races and nations such as can be seen at present, all over the surface of the earth. We must be able to be happy and to rejoice in showing to the outside world that this is how we, the people of Indonesia, are: this is our language, this is our culture, this is our hand-drawn *batik* fabric, these are our vital statistics, such are our carvings, such is our music, and so on.

There's nothing wrong in all that. We are even ordered to make our cultural contribution to the culture of the world at large. As a nation we are a member of the larger family of nations.

There is no need for the Muslim to have to strip himself of his nationality and culture. In the teaching of Islam, it is said that humanity has been made in different groups: different nations and different races. Even their languages vary. This is *fitra*, or "natural," as people say nowadays. The end of the verse says *li't-ta'arafu*: so that you might become mutually acquainted the one with the other. How boring it would be were we to see all the people of this world of no more than one skin color. If white, then all white; if black, then all black! In that case, in pursuit of variety—wanting to taste it—we might fly to the moon or to the stars in search of other people.

Equality of Rights

Therefore, the natural condition or the effective law of God in effect among humankind will stay that way. But let us not feel, just because we have white skins, that we are, at once, superior to the nation whose skin has the color of the *sawo* fruit so that we feel we have acquired the basic right to take them under our imperial protection. Or, should we by chance have *sawo*-colored skins, let us not feel ourselves to be superior to people with black skins. That kind of thing is not healthy nationalism. That has evolved into racial conceit, racial arrogance, xenophobia. Such a concept of nationalism is indeed forbidden by Islam. Islam is a system which does away with racial fanaticism, narrow chauvinism—that which Westerners nowadays call *racism*. That way of thought, which Islam prohibits, is, according to our religious scholars (*faqih*), '*asabiya jahiliya*.

I want to say, once again, that, far from wanting to wipe out nations and nationhood, Islam has set down the bases for prosperous life on both the na-

tional and ethnic levels—on the basis of mutual respect, mutual acquaintance, give and take. If we are the Indonesian nation, take pride, if it pleases, in being Indonesian! But, beware, let us not slide into narrow chauvinism, headed in the direction of fascism or totalitarianism.

Do *not* rest assured that fascism or totalitarianism (or the rest) will not be able to grow in this our nation. It could quite easily grow. Fascism and the like constitute a mode of thought independent of whether skin color be white or black or ripe *sawo*, etc. We must be careful that fascism and the like do not grow in this democratic nation of ours which holds to the sovereignty of Almighty God. This is the responsibility of every Muslim.

Racism Is a Monstrous Disease

Racism is acknowledged to be one of the sources of the sicknesses of the world, giving rise to war after war. Chauvinism gives rise to forms of racism which are more dangerous for society, as for example the rise of fascist and totalitarian thought and other examples of the same sort of thing. [Adolf] Hitler [German Nazi leader, 1889–1945] said that the "*Herrenvolk*" was the master race; the rest were mixed races which could not be left to live their own lives; they needed the domination of the master race.

All of that evolves from '*asabiya jahiliya*.

For those groups who would be happier listening to, or would be quicker to accept, what we are propounding here if it were written in a foreign-language publication—say English—I would like to introduce them to a professor named [Arnold Joseph] Toynbee [1889–1975], one of the most excellent English historians of the present time. He writes in his book, *Civilization on Trial*, as follows: "The world at present has two diseases for which men have yet to discover the cure. They are *racism* and *alcohol*." In a full and frank analysis, Toynbee declares that racism and alcohol are sources of the world's commotion. Toynbee goes on to say: "If there is one system which can smash racism and the problem of alcohol, it is Islam alone."

Toynbee is not a Muslim; he is a Christian. As a scientist he looks at facts as facts. He simply analyzes one state of affairs after another. Such were the words of Toynbee, speaking frankly and honestly.

Accountability, Parliament, and *Ijtihad*

Pakistan was created in 1947 as a Muslim homeland for South Asians, but its founders disagreed whether the new nation should be organized democratically or theocratically, with secular government or Islamic government, Western civil laws or Islamic *shari'a* law.[1] The debate over these issues was initially settled in favor of the secularists, but the succeeding decades did not dampen the controversy. By 1980, when the following selection was published, the secularist position was largely out of favor, and the military regime was set to impose *shari'a* law—hence the importance of this work by S. M. Zafar (Pakistan, born 1930). As secretary-general of the defunct Muslim League (Pagara Group), Zafar enjoyed Islamic credentials; as a lawyer and head of the Pakistan Human Rights Organization, Zafar was keenly interested in ensuring the rule of civil law. Zafar argues in this excerpt that an elected parliament is both grounded in Islamic precedent and necessary for holding the government accountable in the modern world.[2]

In the title of this chapter I have combined three topics because there is a very close and deep relation between the three. In Islamic teachings, distinction is commonly made between matters of religion (*'ibadat*) and worldly matters (*mu'amalat*).

"Religious matters" connote the relation between humankind and God, and "worldly matters" connote the relation between humans and [other humans]. Religious matters are generally bilateral; as an analogy, the shortest distance between two points is a straight line. Thus religion brings humankind closer to God. Through religion, humans realize the existence of the authority of God.

In Islam, the details and shape of religious matters are determined. If they are presented properly with complete morals, then it is to be hoped that in society, there will be a majority of people who will be familiar with God's divinity and authority, and it is hoped that this sort of people, to please God, will try to fulfill His every command.

With respect to religion, the responsibility of the government is to manage and arrange its institutions

1. Leonard Binder, *Religion and Politics in Pakistan* (Berkeley: University of California Press, 1963); Mumtaz Ahmad, "Pakistan," in John L. Esposito, editor, *The Oxford Encyclopedia of the Modern Islamic World* (New York: Oxford University Press, 1995), volume 3, pp. 289–293.

2. Ishtiaq Ahmed, *The Concept of an Islamic State: An Analysis of the Ideological Controversy in Pakistan* (London: Frances Pinter, 1987), pp. 36, 150–162.

related to religious matters, that is, the mosques, *Halal* Consideration Committee [to evaluate permissible Islamic practices], *hajj* [pilgrimage] policy, the respect of Ramadan [the month of dawn-to-dusk fasting], and so on. But if the government doesn't do even this much, then all persons must still perform their religious duties. And we all know that several respected scholars, even while living in non-Muslim communities, still fulfilled their religious duties. And they reached a high level of spiritual attainment.

But worldly matters are different from religious matters. This is not a bilateral relationship. Rather, on one side, it is a relation among people, and on the other side, it includes the authority of the rules determined by God. In worldly matters, a person's responsibility is not as it is in religion. Rather, on the contrary, in worldly matters, responsibility often falls on more than one person, or on a group. In other words, this relation isn't represented as one line, but rather as a triangle, rectangle, or other various geometric figures. With respect to the laws pertaining to worldly matters, Islam in some places gives full details, and in other places describes them only in brief. And for the application of these laws according to a specific situation, the necessity [of knowing] the specific details always arises. And when the situation itself changes, then of course the specifics of the situation also change. That is, just as when dots are put in various places, new triangles, rectangles, polygons are continually formed, so worldly matters can be construed in multiple forms.

However, one single thing must definitely be remembered: that with respect to worldly matters, one dot is fixed: the commands of God, described in the form of a law.

By way of example, take one small business regulation. There is a command that one must give the correct measurement of goods being sold. This rule has taken on the form of a triangle. Now if goods-sellers don't give the correct measurement then they act against God's command, and they earn God's displeasure. They are responsible on the Day of Judgment. But the issue doesn't end here. The rule is not enforced in action. Goods-buyers are also involved in this matter, and it is their right to receive the correct amount of goods. Even though sellers are answerable to God, [the buyers] don't receive any benefits, and therefore, they have the right to ask in return that the existing God-given govern-

ment authority should assist them in this matter, and this government should save them from the person who sells them short. And when the government, having acknowledged their rights, makes a law which can save buyers from dishonest sellers, or can punish them, then the triangle becomes complete. Otherwise, a gap is left.

Let's extend this example and see that if the government announces that the weights for measuring goods will be issued with the government's official stamp, then instead of three, four dots appear on the field. The goods buyer, the seller, the government official who issues the correctly calibrated, government stamped weights, and then this command [of God] that goods must be weighed properly. If these dots are connected to one another, then instead of a triangle, then a square or rectangle is formed. At this time, with respect to the government official who is appointed to work on the weights, the law must be made that at the time of the issuance of the weights, [the official] shouldn't do anyone a favor or short-change anybody. For example, the Electricity Act is a law under which the people who connect electrical meters must follow the special instructions issued, and those who don't follow this are criminal.

We will now extend this example even further. If the government announces that [the business of] manufacturing the weights and stamping them shall be given to a particular company, and the weights issued by this company will be provided by government workers and officials to the shop owners, then a new point appears. Now if we connect all of these dots together, then this time a pentagon is formed. And there will be a separate law made regarding this company. Thus we see that just as new details come before us, it is necessary to make new laws.

These laws are not given in the Qur'an or in *hadith* [traditions of the Prophet], nor could they be given. Then who will make them? One lone ministry of law itself cannot make so many regulations relating to society's hundreds and thousands of divisions. And no matter how wise and devout an emperor or sultan is, he can't keep an eye on all aspects of society. For this work, such an institution is necessary whose members have some connection with worldly matters and in which, after thorough debate, the process of making laws is established—not only so that in this institution every point of view and every school of thought and ideas has the opportunity to be completely and freely expressed, but also so that if the majority within this institution cannot make just laws, then the public can hold this institution accountable, and having removed its members, can install new members in their place. Parliament is the only such institution which can fulfill the above conditions, necessities and demands.

In all of Pakistan's constitutions, legislative work has been handed over to the Assembly or Parliament. In the present 1973 Constitution too, this capacity has been given to Parliament alone. Moreover, this Constitution was made by a Constitutional Assembly, which was a truly representative institution. When Governor-General Malik Ghulam Muhammad dissolved the Constitutional Assembly in 1954, then a decision of the Supreme Court compelled him to establish a new Constitutional Assembly. Therefore the new Constitutional Assembly was elected and in 1955 it made a Constitution. Likewise, the 1973 Constitution was also made by an officially elected Assembly and was ratified.

Now [we shall] study the various clauses of this constitution. Among them most are such that in order to categorize them, one cannot refer to Qur'an or *hadith*. For example, in the 1956 Constitution, the federal structure that was created and the way balance was brought about between East and West Pakistan was the result of the particular conditions of Pakistan. To seek precedent for this from the time of the [first] four caliphs or to seek justification in the Qur'an and *hadith* is useless and impossible. Moreover, we cannot find any precedent in the history of Islam for making rules related to the way the budget should be presented in Parliament, which issues can be debated but not voted upon, if the budget cannot be ratified what effect would this have on the government, and all of the other items and articles [in the Constitution] designed to control the government's right to impose taxes and bring into debate its wrong policies.

The rule that the government can impose a tax on the people only after having had the [tax] law ratified in the representative assembly of the people was accepted 200 years ago and now it has been proven that without representation whatever revenue the government collects would not be a tax, but rather a penalty or fine.

In Pakistan, where there are several reasons for the bad tradition of avoiding taxes, there is also another reason: that Pakistan most of the time has not had a representative government. With respect to *zakat* [religiously mandated contributions], the question arises whether the government itself can collect *zakat* from the public or not. On this point, Islamic scholars have different opinions.

In our opinion, however, money like *zakat* also cannot be collected from the people and its correct expenditure cannot be made until the people's representative assembly approves the corresponding law. And for every revenue that a government must collect from any person because the government wants to spend it for a particular collective purpose, that person has the right to hold the government accountable. Once *Hazrat* [his excellency] 'Umar Farooq ['Umar ibn al-Khattab, second caliph, 634–644] was asked how his garment was made so long when the fabric he had obtained in the spoils of war were insufficient. *Hazrat* 'Umar Farooq answered that he had his garment made by adding his son's share. And because of this answer, the questioner had his objection satisfied.

But today, in a country which has a population of more than 70 million, how many questions can every citizen who enters the mosque ask of the responsible person [at the mosque], when that citizen won't know the answer to 99 percent of the questions and will have in turn to ask the secretary of the relevant department, who will not be praying at the mosque. To solve this problem, the present Assembly is arranged so as to reserve a one-week period to answer such questions, during which time the people can call the government and its employees to account. In that period, a detailed system of asking questions is determined, [taking into account] which question is connected with which day and with which department. And permission is also given during this period to ask further questions about previous questions.

In the laws of Islam, the most prominent is the law of accountability. No [school of] Islamic jurisprudence denies that Muslim government is liable to accountability and impeachment. All government agents, judges, and civil servants are accountable for their own actions. [There is the] concept of the Day of Judgment, according to which all people will have to give a complete account of all of their good and bad actions. Its application is not only to religious matters, but to worldly matters as well, and due to the immediacy of worldly matters, this rule also applies to the government.

The Prophet, peace be upon him, says, "Watch out, among you every person is a leader and every person is responsible for their own people, and the greatest leader of the Muslims, who governs all, is also answerable to the people." And *Hazrat* 'Umar says, "If even one goat's kid is lost on the banks of the Euphrates River, then I am afraid that God will question me about it." Not only God will question us, but as has been said before, worldly matters are not only between God and people, and [the questioning] must be thorough between people and people also. Consequently, the people should also question the government; parliament is the best means for this, and the thorough interrogation of the government can only be done by a representative assembly.

In addition to the necessity of making general rules and being accountable, there is a very clear necessity of an Assembly in matters of *ijtihad* [Islamic interpretation]. First of all, we don't accept that the gate of *ijtihad* is closed forever. Who closed it? Why was it closed? And how long will it remain closed? These are the kind of questions for which history doesn't have any clear answer. If the purpose of *ijtihad* is the application of wisdom and learning, then to say that *ijtihad* is no more, is a negation of Islam. Admittedly, we understand that in the name of *ijtihad* permission cannot be given for changing Islam's teachings and its rules. This is the reason that at the end of the 8th century *hijri* [late fourteenth century A.D.] and especially at the beginning of the 9th century *hijri* [early fifteenth century A.D.], Islamic theoreticians became worried that an attempt was being made to change the basic worldly matters of Islam through *ijtihad* and that this should be stopped somehow. To preserve the community from this kind of *ijtihad*, these Islamic theoreticians curtailed even their own rights, and prevented themselves and others from practicing *ijtihad*. Moreover, that time was a period of decline in Islamic history. Therefore, for the benefit of the community, the consensus was reached that *ijtihad* should be left alone for the time being. But it is true that this attempt is in no way synonymous with permanently closing the gate of *ijtihad*. Now this is a period of Islamic revival, and it is very necessary that attention should be given to *ijtihad*. In this connection, we all know about the contribution from 'Allama [Muhammad] Iqbal [Indian philosopher, 1877–1938; see chapter 27]. He called the decision of the Turkish Assembly *ijtihad* and he himself participated in *ijtihad* [to decide] that the burden of the caliphate could be shouldered by a single assembly.

We admit that the conditions of *ijtihad* are very severe and that Islamic jurisprudence makes it very difficult. The conditions that religious scholars have established for *ijtihad* are as follows:

1. In addition to the knowledge of Qur'an, a person should be familiar with literature also. He should have complete knowledge of the text of the Qur'an; he should know when every verse was revealed and what the circumstances of its revelation were; he should be well acquainted with the literal meaning of every word in the Qur'an; and besides this, he should know what connotations are hidden within these words.
2. He should have memorized the entire Qur'an.
3. He should have complete mastery of the science of *hadith* and command of at least 3000 major *hadith*s.
4. He must be very devout and pious.
5. He must be completely familiar with the science of Islamic jurisprudence (that is, with all five branches of *fiqh*).

In addition to these conditions, Imam [Abu Hamid Muhammad] Ghazzali [1058–1111] and Imam [Fakhr al-Din] Razi [1149–1209] placed strongest emphasis on the intellectual ability of those who practice *ijtihad*. Of course, in fulfilling the aforementioned conditions, their knowledge increases. Thus it is clear that the conditions of *ijtihad* are very difficult.

Today, for any citizen to fulfill these conditions is especially difficult, because now, in addition to the aforementioned knowledge, it is also important that the person who practices *ijtihad* should be familiar with the needs of the current period, and he should know the rules of economics and be familiar with the rules of atomic energy. In addition, he should have complete mastery over problems of sociology and psychology.

These days, one cannot find people who can retain an encyclopedic range of knowledge in their memories. In fact, in every field of knowledge, so much advancement has occurred that it is completely impossible for one person, spending his entire life acquiring knowledge of Qur'an and *hadith*, to be able to obtain familiarity with and knowledge of other fields. Likewise, the scientist, doctor, or economist is busy in his own field, obtaining mastery and knowledge. Will that person be able to achieve sufficient status in the knowledge of Qur'an and *hadith* which would give him the right to perform *ijtihad*? Under these conditions, if there is no institution in which all fields can be combined, then Muslim society will have to survive on guesswork for new laws. But the answers to all of the questions raised by the needs of the present period cannot be answered through guesswork. Therefore, only an Assembly where the religious scholars sit down with the other representatives of the public and hold thorough debate on every issue can make the laws.

Ziauddin Sardar, a research scholar at Shah 'Abdul 'Aziz University in Jiddah [Saudi Arabia], wrote a book entitled *The Future of Muslim Civilization*[3]; in this book, he has made a very important point on the subject of *ijtihad*. "I reached the conclusion that *ijtihad* on an individual basis is impossible. However, if the work of *ijtihad* is handed over to an institution in which there is the opportunity to bring together all fields of knowledge, then *ijtihad* will be possible and easy."

This is the only reason that the Islamic scholars of Pakistan have supported a parliamentary system. In 1950 and 1951 the religious scholars [*'ulama'*] of Pakistan collectively supported the [proposal] that the elected assembly be allowed to pass legislation. When Pakistan's draft constitution was being prepared in 1955, the whole *'ulama'* of Pakistan analyzed [the constitution] on only one point: whether anything in it was against Islam. They presented some recommendations, including one that national elections should be held very soon. However, nobody from that institution rejected the Assembly as a lawmaking body. Likewise, in the popular revolution of 1977, the political parties in favor of a religious approach took part vigorously and strongly pushed for elections. Thus it is correct to say that the people of Pakistan and the *'ulama'* think alike that through election, permanent institutions should be established; that the national government should also be established through elections; that if somehow the government becomes less acceptable, then it can be removed and a new government should be elected.

Quaid-i-Azam [Great Leader] Muhammad Ali Jinnah [1876–1948, the founder of Pakistan] thought differently. Instead, he wanted to make Pakistan a modern democratic state [as distinct from an Islamic state]. Now in Pakistan, in the name of Islam, this experiment is under way, and for this reason it is im-

portant that we should decide about the government system with complete faith and security, so there won't be any lack of practical support.

In Pakistan, democracy has not failed. Rather, since the desire for democracy is now in [the people's] hearts and minds, we can conclude that the powers who oppose democracy and want to stop its progress have failed. But in this situation, we again are standing at the crossroads of democracy and monarchy.

The sort of temperaments that have an inclination toward dictatorship consider parliament their rival and generally view a parliament that has a certain degree of autonomy troublesome for them. [Adolf] Hitler [German Nazi leader, 1889–1945] called parliament a club of idle dreamers. [Benito] Mussolini [Italian fascist leader, 1883–1945] thought of parliament as nothing more than a forum for his own speeches. In Pakistan too, political tensions, quarrels, and disputes have continued to arise regarding the authority of the president and prime minister vis-à-vis the Assembly. It was due to these quarrels that [Pakistani Governor-General] Malik Ghulam Muhammad [1895–1956] dissolved the Constitutional Assembly [in 1954] when a legal document was introduced into this Assembly weakening the powers of the president.

In the 1973 Constitution, there was a specific clause added to the law which weakened the authority of the Assembly and increased the authority of the prime minister, making the latter very powerful. Thus it is clear that parliament plays an important role in limiting the increase in the powers of the current ruler and making him adhere to one [system of] law and keeping the president and prime minister within decided limits. How can this institution be rejected on the grounds that it is un-Islamic? In short, to call un-Islamic the institution which provides a means of accountability and a means of collective *ijtihad* and which can stand in the way of dictatorship is very unjust to Islam and presents Islam incorrectly. The result of this line of reasoning is that Muslims are frightened of accountability and avoid *ijtihad*, and Muslims think that a kingdom, monarchy, and even dictatorship are valid styles of Islamic government, even though they are not.

On the contrary, accountability, *ijtihad*, and democracy are Islam's true foundation, by means of which Islam establishes a just and equitable society. And as long as the human intellect cannot create any institution better than parliament, there should

---

3. [English-language edition published in 1987 in London by Mansell.—Editor]

be no problem in adopting this institution. Moreover, as the great Andalusian Muslim scholar Abu Ishaq Shatibi [died 1388] said, once we distinguish between religious matters (*'ibadat*) and local custom (*'adat*), every society should adopt only those religious practices which are determined solely by Islam. As for worldly matters, which fall under the category of *'adat*, there is a concession that traditional ways and customs can be adopted on the condition that they should not conflict with the rules of Islam.

We think that parliament is a logical necessity and mandatory for accountability and *ijtihad*. There is no substitute for this institution in the contemporary era. If we don't adopt it, there are only two prospects before us. One is this, that as under the communist system, ultimate permanent power will be given to a political party like the Communist Party, and this would be the only party or group in the nation which is responsible for writing the Constitution and laws and applying them. In this situation, no matter what decision the leaders make, obedience becomes compulsory, and freedom of thought and of ideas disappears.

The second prospect is that a single *'ulama'* council is set up which can perform the work of legislation, relying for the most part on conjecture and occasionally resorting to *ijtihad*. But this is an extremely dangerous prospect, because in such a situation lie the origins of popishness. Furthermore, [grounds for] confrontation between the people and the *'ulama'* are generated. 'Allama Iqbal was strongly opposed to this proposal and he wrote that to give special authority to one group of the *'ulama'* is a grave error. Instead, *Hazrat* 'Allama [Iqbal] presented the counter-proposal that the *'ulama'* should be in Parliament as representatives of the people, so long as laws are made in an Assembly where the debate allows total freedom of opinion.

Thus the best and most perfect way is this: the *'ulama'* should retain its connection with the people, and [its members] should be sufficiently popular on the strength of their knowledge and wisdom and the power of their character and nature, that they will be voted into the elected Assembly.

7

Religion and Liberty

Born into a devout family of merchants, Mehdi Bazargan (Iran, 1907–1995) was a French-trained engineer, a lay Islamic scholar, and a long-time pro-democracy activist. A deputy prime minister when the nationalists came briefly to power in the early 1950s, Bazargan also participated with Ayatollah Mahmud Taleqani (chapter 3) and others in a reform movement in the early 1960s aimed at democratizing the Shi'i clerical establishment.[1] Bazargan was imprisoned several times during the 1960s and 1970s for his nonviolent opposition to the shah of Iran through groups such as the Liberation Movement of Iran, which he cofounded in 1961, and the Iranian Human Rights Association, which he co-founded in 1977. When the shah was forced out of Iran by revolution in 1979, Imam Ruhollah Khomeini appointed Bazargan as provisional prime minister, but he resigned within a year, complaining that radical clerics were undermining his government. He continued to serve in the Iranian parliament for several years, harassed by his radical opponents, then lived in a sort of political limbo until his death in early 1995, a barely tolerated symbol of opposition to the radical-Islamic government.[2]

O Prophet, We have sent you as a witness and a bearer of happy tidings and an admonisher, and to call [men] to God by His leave, and as a lamp resplendent.

(Qur'an, Sura 33, Verse [45])[3]

The European Renaissance and the Church

In one of the nights of the month of Ramadan of 1981, we gathered in a friend's house to break fast and hold vigil. On that occasion, an old friend and colleague of mine, Mr. 'Ezzatallah Sahabi [Iran, born 1932], delivered a speech on the European origins

1. Ann K.S. Lambton, "A Reconsideration of the Position of the *Marj'a al-Taqlid* and the Religious Institution," *Studia Islamica*, volume 20, 1964, pp. 115–135.

2. H. E. Chehabi, *Iranian Politics and Religious Modernism* (Ithaca, N.Y.: Cornell University Press, 1990); Manochehr Dorraj, "Bazargan, Mehdi," in John L. Esposito, editor, *The Oxford Encyclopedia of the Modern Islamic World* (New York: Oxford University Press, 1995), volume 1, pp. 211–213.

3. [Translations of Qur'anic verses are taken, with modifications, from *Al-Qur'an: A Contemporary Translation*, translated by Ahmed Ali, revised definitive edition (Princeton, N.J.: Princeton University Press, 1988). Bazargan's slightly different numbering of verses has been edited to conform to the other selections in this collection.—Editor]

of the notion of freedom.[4] He argued that the roots of modern liberalism lie in the 17th century, when the feudal governments of Europe were struggling to free themselves from the hegemony of the pope and the [Catholic Christian] church. In those days independent and sovereign nation-states did not exist. Every town or principality was under the tutelage of a lord or noble. These nobles and feudal rulers were, in turn, under the influence of the local priests and the Holy See of Rome. The most chaotic of these countries happened to be Italy. Here a philosopher emerged by the name of [Niccolò] Machiavelli [1469–1527], whose book *The Prince* outlined the philosophy that came to be known as Machiavellianism.[5]

Pursuant to the liberation of the states from the hegemony of the Catholic church and the pope, free and scientific thought sought to liberate itself from the terrible hegemony of the Inquisition. As a result, the hold of the religious tradition and authority over people's thoughts and lives was loosened; but it took a toll on the lives of such great scientists as Galileo [Galilei, 1564–1642]. Investigating minds and blossoming intellects could no longer suffer the rigidity, stagnation, and tyranny of the Catholic clergy.

The next step in the European Renaissance was the religious reformation and Protestantism that was ushered in under the leadership of Martin Luther (1483– 1546), John Calvin (1509–1564), and others. Protestants rejected the superstitions and religious restrictions of Catholicism. They aimed to return Christianity to its pristine simplicity, spirituality, and liberty. The same was true of the quest for the freedom of art and culture.[6] The movement culminated in the quest for social and political liberties demanded by the great French Revolution (1789–1799) and other democratic regimes. The forerunners of this movement were [Jean-Jacques] Rousseau [1712–1778], [François-Marie] Voltaire [1694–1778], [Charles de Secondat, baron de] Montesquieu [1689–1755], and other Encyclopedists [French philosophers of the eighteenth century], who were generally anti-clerical, atheistic, or agnostic.

The speaker went on to propose that Western democracy and individual liberties, their service to human civilization and progress notwithstanding, have been incapable of responding to human needs, economic problems, and social inequities. Hence the advent of socialism, communism, and existentialism in the wake of nationalism and liberalism, and the indefatigable search for freedom and justice.

Religious Scholars[7] and Freedom

Let us return now to the original question: whether or not the liberal political and intellectual movement that triggered Europe's great leap forward was an essentially anti-religious, anti-church, and anti-clerical movement.

We need to first explore the origins of the church's opposition to freedom. The question is whether this antagonism was due to particular doctrinal and historical circumstances or a result of universal properties of all religions at all times. The answer seems simple enough. Setting aside the question of the truth and authenticity of religion, it seems reasonable to expect that God who, by definition, is omniscient, omnipotent, sovereign, and aware of the good and evil is better qualified to judge what is proper for human beings than human beings themselves. Does this belief leave any other option for believers than unconditional surrender to God's will? Furthermore, the priests and church, considering themselves successors of Jesus and representatives of God—and any religious scholars who consider themselves custodians and guardians of the people of God—would necessarily expect the people to follow and revere them, and to subordinate reason and science to the revealed commandments.

You realize that this doctrine leaves no room for the freedom and will of the people to administer their

---

4. [Sahabi, the son of Bazargan's long-time colleague Yadallah Sahabi, had emerged as leader of the left wing of Bazargan's Freedom Movement of Iran. While remaining liberal, Sahabi is more critical of Western-style liberal democracy than Bazargan. A subtext of Bazargan's speech is a defense of liberalism against the left wing of the Freedom Movement, as well as against anti-democratic forces in the Islamic Republic.—Translator]

5. For further information on this thesis and its comparison with other social philosophies, see my book *Be'sat va ide'olozhi* [*Prophetic Mission and Ideology*], part I.

6. The Renaissance of the 15th and 16th centuries commenced with a renewed interest in the Greek art in Italy, particularly after the advent of the print technology.

7. [The author uses the terms *'ulama'* and *ruhaniyat* interchangeably. Both are translated here as "religious scholars."—Editor]

own affairs and to question—much less reject—the representatives of God who claim immunity from error as successors to the Prophet. Thus it seems that human reason and religious rule are mutually exclusive. Contrary to the Prophet's words—"The government can survive unbelief but not injustice"—it seems that the absolute rule of religious scholars would be necessary for the salvation of society, unless society renounces religion altogether. Consequently, democracy, science, investigation, expertise, and erudition seem to be the necessary results of denouncing religion and the religious scholars, while the acceptance of the sovereignty of God and the stewardship on earth of the church or religious scholars would lead to tyranny, enslavement, inquisition,[8] and violence. Ironically, then, the "heavenly" rule of God on earth would require surveillance, censorship, arrest, and torture. Violence against insiders and outsiders alike would be deemed the very essence of justice and charity. In such a society, the minutest criticism, discord, and transgression in matters ritual, administrative, political, and even personal would be considered as a transgression against God and His representatives.

According to the foregoing account, religious governments, not unlike Marxist states, cannot tolerate the freedom of ideas and criticism. Free expression and assembly, as well as strikes or demonstrations would be unthinkable; and the ruling party's judgment and execution would be swift and categorical. Both religious and Marxist governments recognize freedom and rationality only for their docile followers. For everyone else, freedom signifies nothing but corruption, confusion, promiscuity, and denunciation of the ruling ideology and regime.

Freedom and Love

Not long ago in our country [Iran], parents used to tightly swaddle their infants (this practice may still persist in the countryside). The idea was to keep the baby from causing trouble and courting danger. In my father's household there was an old compassionate woman from the Kerman region by the name of Mirza Baji, may she rest in peace. She would teach us the recitation of the Qur'an and the prayers. She had many children, none of whom survived. After her children grew too old to be swaddled, she told us, she would tie them down with a piece of rope so they would not wander by the side of the pool and drown, or engage in dangerous games while she was away doing chores.

Restrictions, as this anecdote demonstrates, are not necessarily hostile measures. One should not attribute the oppressive rule of the medieval church entirely to ill-intent and enmity. Indeed, many of the fathers of the church seem to have been devout, kind, and innocent of abuse or arrogance.[9] It follows, then, that any religion and religious leadership that considers itself responsible for the realization of divine rule over the people, will of necessity become oblivious to human life, rights, and dignity, and will resort to coercion. This will eventually breed ignorance, slavery, and violence. People, in their turn, will sooner or later free themselves from the yoke of religious tyranny. Sometimes they do so without losing their basic belief in God, but often they end up hating religion along with the religious rulers.

That is why—throughout Western civilization, whether under democracy, fascism, or socialism—the idea of the separation of religion and state and the notion of the secular (that is, non-religious, and in a sense, anti-religious) form of government prevails. The more progressive the ideology, the more anti-religious the government.

What Divine Religion Is Really Like

Now, the question is whether all of God's emissaries, particularly the founders of Islam, approved of the medieval Christian practices. Are religion and freedom essentially mutually exclusive? Were God's prophets instructed to instigate bloody revolutions on earth, beheading skeptics, destroying anti-revolutionaries, sowing the seeds of hatred and discord, and swaddling or tying down the youths in the schoolyard of religion, like our late Mirza Baji?

The Qur'an explains the mission of the prophets both directly, through commandments, and indirectly, through the explication of the general divine plan of creation. What we learn from the story of the

8. [Inquisition is] contrary to the Qur'an, which states: "O you who believe, avoid most suspicions: some suspicions are indeed sins. So do not pry into others' secrets and not backbite." (Sura 49, Verse 12)

9. The Holy Qur'an, too, states that "there are priests and monks and scholars among them, and they are not arrogant." [Sura 5, Verse 82]

prophets and our own slogan, "There is no god but God," is that the mission of the prophets has been to liberate human beings, not to enslave them. But liberation from what and from whom?

First, from the idols or imagined gods, that is, from the illusion of idolatry. Second, from the deception of the devil, or the temptations of the flesh, and in a wider sense, from compulsive worship of worldly goods. Third, from religious imposters, false guardians of temples and religions who propagated idolatry and opposed the prophets. Fourth, from the kings, louts, and possessors of the power and the riches, and the oppressors of the time.

In Suras 7, 10, 11, 14, 21, 23, 26, 27, 29, 37, and others that recount the prophets' struggles, we frequently find the supreme command, "O people of God, worship none other than God." Noah stated: "Do not worship anyone but God." [Sura 11, Verse 26] In suras such as 20 and 28 that speak specifically of *Hazrat* [his excellency] Moses, God commands Moses and Aaron to say to the pharaoh, "Send the Children of Israel with us (that we may take them to their own territory and nation), and do not oppress them." . . . They were not told to curse or humiliate him but to "speak to him gently, so he may take heed or come to have fear (of God and the consequences of His action)." [Sura 20, Verses 47, 44]

We are told, with regard to Satan: "Did I not commit you, O children of Adam, not to worship Satan who is your acknowledged foe?" (Sura 36, Verse 60) We are commanded to resist the tyrannical temptation of the flesh, and to reject the rule of tyrants: "And do not follow the squanderers." And: "The patrons of unbelievers are idols [and devils] who lead them from light into darkness. They are the residents of Hell, and will there for ever abide." (Sura 2, Verse 257)

God would not liberate us from the darkness and the tyrants to enslave us at the hand of His prophets and messengers. The Qur'an unequivocally announces: "There is no compulsion in religion." [Sura 2, Verse 256] It even urges the exalted Prophet [that is, Muhammad] not to worry about the derision and rejection of the idolaters and those who oppose him and indulge in sin: "And if your Lord had willed, all the people on the earth would have come to believe, one and all. Are you going to compel the people to believe except by God's dispensation?" (Sura 10, Verses [99–100]) In Sura 33, Verses 45–48, the Prophet's office is defined and limited to serving as

witness and example, bearing glad tidings and admonishment, calling to God, and providing a guiding light. It recommends tolerance in the face of harassment of the infidels and the hypocrites and reliance upon God. You see, God Himself abhors the imposition and propagation of religion by force and coercive measures. Nor does he wish the instantaneous destruction of the unbelievers and the hypocrites.

Truly, there is a great difference between God's religion and the religion born of human illusion and ill-intent!

God not only leaves people free to be "either thankful or ungrateful" [Sura 76, Verse 3] and gives a grace period when they sin; He also assists believers and unbelievers alike on their chosen paths.[10]

God's relationship with people is not based on coercion, enslavement, enmity, or violence, but on freedom and love. With regard to virtues we have [the Qur'anic phrase] "God loves"; with regard to vices we have "God does not love." If we have troubles, they are the result of our own desires and deeds: "God did not surely wrong them, they wronged themselves." (Sura 9, Verse 70) Certainly there is accountability, but there is no pressure or coercion.

Satan and Freedom

You must wonder why God has given us permission to sin, and whether an Islamic government would give us such a permission! You would be even more astounded when you consider that God Himself created Satan. When Lucifer refused to follow God's will and was expelled from the heaven, God gave him until Judgment Day to try to entice human beings to indulge in rebellion, destruction, and injustice.

The presence and influence of Satan on the human mind constitutes an opposing force or a counter-pole to the power of creation, reason, and prudence. It exposes us to temptation and confusion, that is, it forces us to question and to choose. Free will is a gift that God has endowed upon humanity. The question why humanity is blessed with such a gift cannot be addressed here in the detail it deserves. Suffice it

---

10. Sura 17, Verse [20]: "We bestow the gifts of your Lord on these and those, for the gifts of your Lord are not restricted." The answer to the first question, whether Islam has left people to do whatever they wish in this world without any obligations or limits, will be addressed at the end of this article.

to say that the ultimate reason and effect of this free-dom is the realization of humankind's status as "God's steward" on earth. Freedom is essential for our creativity and spiritual evolution. Had free will been denied to us we would follow an inevitable path guided by animal instincts. Protected against doubt, we would remain as stationary in our position as ants, horses, and pigeons. Free will and liberty, fraught with weakness, confusion, and concerns as they are, provoke us to concentrate, think, decide, and move. As such, they are the tools of extraordinary evolu-tion and progress among human beings as compared to animals. Reason, perception, will, and morality are all results of free will and liberty.

Freedom is God's gift to His steward on earth, humankind. Whoever takes away this freedom is guilty of the greatest treason against humankind.[11]

Religion and Politics

We have stated that the confrontation of the medi-eval church and the liberation movements led to the separation of religion and politics in the West. This conflict also accounts for the widespread disenchant-ment of intellectuals and scientists from religion, which has continued well into the 20th century. The situation has been totally different in the Islamic world.

Among Sunni Muslims [the majority sect in Islam] and under the [Sunni] caliphs, government dominated religion and the religious scholars. The caliphs were the religious as well as the temporal leaders of the society. They were the ones who desig-nated leaders of the Friday prayers, governors, and ministers. Judges too were either appointed by the caliphs, or incapable of challenging their rule. The caliphs were commanders in chief, supreme judges, and treasurers. They considered themselves the em-bodiment of the Qur'anic verse: "O believers, obey God, and obey the Messenger and those in authority among you." (Sura 4, Verse 62) They thus claimed to be absolute sovereigns and autocrats. The farther we get from the early days of Islam, the more we encounter this kind of tyranny. After the "rightful caliphs" [the first four caliphs of Islam], the right of citizens to criticize and disagree with their leader was abrogated.

Among the Shi'i scholars it was different differ-ent. As long as they were an oppressed minority, they did not address questions of government and politi-

cal rule. In the wake of the rebellions against the Umayyad and 'Abbasid caliphs [reigned 661–750 and 750–1258, respectively], and in the course of the gradual independence from the regime of Baghdad, the Sunni and the Shi'i governments in Iran reverted to the ancient regime of absolute monarchy. Al-though a number of monarchs, such as Mahmud Ghaznavi [971–1030] or the Deylamis [also known as Buyids], Safavis, and Qajars [Persian dynasties, reigned 945–1055, 1502–1736, and 1794–1925, re-spectively] were religious-minded and ostentatiously righteous, and although they generally held reli-gious scholars in high esteem, religion and politics remained, for all intents and purposes, separate. The leaders of the Shi'i religion were independent of the state and inattentive to social, administrative, and political affairs. They received their tithes and other religious contributions directly from the people and the merchants. Up until the Iranian Constitutional Revolution [1906], religious scholars seldom en-gaged in juridical functions. A handful of them exe-cuted religious penalties within their jurisdiction. However, they largely concerned themselves with education, scholarship, and the issuing of edicts. Since the supreme religious leaders were the recipi-ents of many complaints from the people, they would occasionally protest and lecture the government, or else, they would briefly interfere in the executive functions of the state. Other than these episodic events though, the separation of the religion and politics remained a practical reality. Even in our days, the religious handbooks known as "Explanation of Questions"[12] devote entire chapters to the ritual de-tails of prayers, fasts, and pilgrimages to Mecca, but ignore discussion of morality and education, much

---

11. The charter of the Freedom Movement of Iran, May 15, 1961, declares: "The servitude of God requires refusal of servitude of any other master. Gratefulness to God is contin-gent upon gaining freedom and utilizing it to attain rights, justice, and service." The question arising from this proposi-tion, whether Islamic government should refrain from check-ing corruption and decadence in society, will be addressed at the end of the article.

12. [Such compilations of religious opinions are a rela-tively modern phenomenon in Shi'i ritual observance. Akin to the Jewish tradition of "Responsa," these essays are authored by independent religious scholars who aspire to be a "source of imitation" for other Shi'i Muslims. Those who choose to follow the religious edicts of a particular "source of imita-tion" seek his views on specific subjects in these essays.— Translator]

less social and political issues.[13] Kings had no right to interfere in the affairs of religion, and religious scholars did not concern themselves with the affairs of government.

Religious scholars had a prominent, if temporary and partial, role in the Constitutional Revolution. They helped draft the constitution and participated in the first terms of parliament, and in the ministries of education and justice. But they soon withdrew. In the struggles after September 11, 1941 [the installation of Muhammad Reza Shah Pahlavi by the British], in the nationalist movement and the nationalization of the oil industry [in 1951], only a handful of religious scholars were enthusiastically engaged. In the wake of the coup d'état of August 19, 1953, and in the activities of the movement of national resistance, these gentlemen had a limited role and little aspiration for leadership.[14]

After [the religious protests of] June 5, 1963, the "Movement of the Religious Scholars," with the decisive and unequivocal arrival of Imam [Ruhollah] Khomeini [1902–1989] on the scene of struggle and politics, seized the initiative and leadership of the [1979 Iranian] revolution and the Islamic Republic [instituted in 1979]. Young religious scholars, politically active intellectuals, and revolutionary seminary students were particularly attuned to his message. The separation of religion and state, explicitly rejected in the struggles of nationalists as well as Islamic intellectuals since the 1940s, was condemned and nullified during the [1979] revolution. The doctrine of "Mandate of the Jurisprudent" was explicitly introduced into the constitution of the Islamic Republic of Iran as a paramount principle. The religious scholars cast their shadow upon the government.

13. The late martyr Muhammad Baqir Sadr [Iraqi religious scholar, 1935–1980] states in one of his essays, translated [from Arabic into Persian] under the title *Hamrah ba tahavol-e ijtihad* [Accompanying the Evolution of *Ijtihad* (Islamic Interpretation)]: "the move toward *ijtihad* among the Shi'is was almost coeval with their withdrawal from politics . . . and this departure from politics . . . gave rise to the idea that the proper arena for religious thought is . . . bringing the individual—not the society—into compliance with religion. Thus it was that in the opinion of religious jurisprudence, *ijtihad* came to be applied to the Muslim individual rather than Muslim society."

14. [The author played a crucial and well-documented role in these events.—Translator]

The "Mandate of the Jurisprudent" or the sovereignty of religious scholars that is now being propagated with the help of the state propaganda, is an important and subtle issue that needs to be scrutinized from religious, legal, historical, social, and political viewpoints. It should be implemented in such a way as not to violate the authenticity of Islam and human freedom, as outlined in the Qur'an and the tradition.

Religion and the Nation

Let me now turn to the question of the relationship of religion to government and, by implication, the question of Islamic government.

The relationship of God and people has been outlined. We have established that the monotheistic religions and Islam, in particular, have lavished great respect and care on individual rights. They all consider mankind as free, responsible, and autonomous. The question is whether an Islamic government would set certain limits on individual and group freedom; or whether it would sanction unconstrained liberty? If there is to be a measure of constraint and discipline, then how and by whom would it be implemented?

The Qur'an and *sunna* [the practice of the Prophet] clearly answer this question. With regard to the essence and precepts of religion and the laws of creation, God is the only lawgiver: "There is no rule but that which belongs to God." From this point of view, the prophets and holy books explicate the evolutionary path and fundamental imperatives that God has laid out for humanity. They inform us of our final destiny and responsibilities. The exalted Prophet did not consult anyone concerning divine commandments. Muslims, the people of the book, the hypocrites, and the idolaters were equally excluded from the sacred realm of revelation: "a Book whose verses are set clear and distinct, which comes from God most wise and all-knowing" (Sura 11, Verse 1); and elsewhere: "So judge between them in the light of what has been revealed by God, and do not follow their whims[. . .]." (Sura 5, Verse [49]) In a country with an Islamic government, God is the undisputed and absolute sovereign: "Have they taken others beside Him as protectors? It is God who protects; it is He who gives life to the dead, for He has power over every thing. In whatever matter you disagree the ultimate judgment rests with God." (Sura 42, Verses [9–10]) The world-view and the ideology, the philosophical anthropology, and the constitutional laws—

that is, the foundations of the government—should be based on, and inspired by the Book and *sunna*. Ordinary laws, too, should not contradict those ordinances. It is entirely proper, even necessary, that the parliament of an Islamic country is comprised of people's representatives who are acquainted with the tenets of Islam, and who are God-fearing, reasonable, prudent, and trustworthy; so they legislate in accordance with Islam's fundamental tenets and ultimate goals. (Iran's previous constitution [of 1906] stipulated that five first-tier religious scholars, selected by the religious leadership, should be present to ascertain that the laws were in accordance with religious principles. However, this provision was never implemented.)

But as regards the administration of the country, the text of the Qur'an undeniably proposes that the affairs and governance of the nation be based on *shura* [consultation]. In Sura *Shura* (Sura 42), Verses [36–38] and 41–43 describe the commonwealth of the faithful as solidary and cooperative, in keeping with the motto "their affairs (the management of affairs) are settled (by) consultation among them." (Sura 42, Verse 38)[15] Even the Prophet himself, who was the fulcrum of revelation and the beloved of the faithful was ordered to "take counsel with them in the affair" (Sura 3, Verse [159]) even with the rude individuals at the bottom of society who sought pardon upon the exposure of their transgression.

The practice of the Prophet and 'Ali [ibn Abi Talib, the Prophet's son-in-law, reigned 656–661], who consulted their disciples and followers and implemented the majority's opinion, even where it was against their own convictions,[16] is a clear illustration of the Islamic system of government. It signifies the principle of people's participation in their own affairs, their self-determination, and, to use the contemporary parlance, the national sovereignty. The *hadith* [tradition of the Prophet] that states: "Every one of you is a shepherd (of the community),

and all are responsible for their dependents and herd," also expressed a reciprocal social responsibility and public involvement, and in a different manner announced the principle of democracy, "sovereignty of the people over the people" (11 centuries before Europe). Islamic government cannot help but be at once consultative, democratic, and divinely inspired.

Thus, in Islamic government the relations among individuals and the administration of society are predicated upon relative shared freedom and mutual responsibility. The religious duty to "call others to virtue and to warn them against vice," to stand for justice and truth, presuppose freedom of opinion and criticism. It is the same for [the duty of] guiding the perplexed, educating the ignorant, defending the oppressed, and finally advocating truth, patience, and mercy, which appears throughout the Qur'an, the *sunna*, and the prayers.[17] In emphasizing the freedom of expression and belief, it is enough to listen to the opinions of others and select the best of them. . . .[18] Islam permits difference of opinions even within the realm of the tenets of religion, let alone in administrative and governmental issues. Shi'i theology, under the rubric of *ijtihad* [Islamic interpretation], has left the gate of such debates open until the end of the time and the resurrection of the messiah (may God hasten his rise). This has been the Shi'i position throughout history.

There are two issues that need to be clarified at this juncture: Whether following a religious authority or a "source of imitation" in the Shi'i faith means blind and unquestioning emulation, and more importantly, whether the opponents of Islam and the opponents of Islamic government have the right to express their opinions. Concerning the first issue, it should be stated that, based on the Qur'anic verses and Islamic commandments, the relationship between God and the people is direct and unmediated. The role of the prophets, *Imams* [in Shi'i theology, the infallible heirs of the Prophet], and infallible saints is merely

---

15. The word "among" means among those who are members of society and responsible and the owners of the property in question, not those without work and responsibility, for instance employees and laborers. . . .

16. The same verse that states "and consult them concerning the affair" [Sura 3, Verse 159] advises the following: (after consultation and the soliciting of opinions), once you have reached a decision, then place your trust in God. That is, have confidence in the virtue of its [the decision's] outcome.

17. In the dawn and dusk prayer called "The Manuscript of Imam Sajjad" [Zayn al-'Abidin 'Ali ibn al-Husayn, circa 656–714], we read: "O our nurturing teacher, grant us success in this day and this night and in all our days so we can practice goodness, avoid evil . . . defy falsehood, serve the truth, guide the confused, and help the weak. . . ."

18. Sura 39, Verses 17–18: "So give glad tidings to My creatures. Those who listen to the Word and follow the best it contains, are the ones who have been guided by God, and are men of wisdom."

to call people toward God and to make them responsible before Him.[19] There is no doubt that one should learn from those who are better informed and more virtuous. But this does not mean relinquishing individual responsibility and free will. The Qur'an states: "Do not follow that of which you hast no knowledge. Verily the ear, the eye, the heart, each will be questioned." (Sura 17, Verse 36) In a similar vein, the Ruler of the Faithful ['Ali] advises his governor in Egypt: "Never use the excuse that you are just obeying orders with closed eyes. You are personally responsible before God." Also, the Prophet is quoted as having said: "There is no obedience of a mortal in disobedience of God." 'Ali even held his subjects (that is, citizens) responsible for advice and sympathetic criticism of their leaders.

The second issue is more delicate. Unfortunately our Shi'i jurisprudence and religious scholars, having been excluded from governmental affairs in the past, have not elaborated on the principles and rules of Islamic government, or the limits of freedoms such as are discussed these days. Thus it is hard to provide a definitive answer to this question. While religious manuals and books have sometimes discussed these issues . . . Shi'i scholars have generally ignored these issues. We have one book, *Tanbih al-umma va tanzih al-milla* (*A Reminder and a Cleansing for the Faithful*), by Mr. [Muhammad Husayn] Na'ini [1860–1936], and other lectures and books after September 1941.[20] Furthermore, there is no practical model for a flawless Islamic government, except for the 10 years of the exalted Prophet's rule in Medina, peace be upon him [622–632]; five years of the tumultuous rule of 'Ali [656–661]; and the five months' rule of Imam Hasan [son of 'Ali, 661], culminating in a peace treaty with Mu'awiya [reigned 661–680]. It is indisputable, though, that the struggles and the mission of all prophets, including those of the last Prophet, involved debating the idolaters and enemies.

19. Sura 12, Verse 108: "Say: 'My way, and that of my followers, is to call you to God with full perception. All glory to God, I am not an idolater.'" See also Sura 41, Verse 5.

20. For instance, *Hokumat dar Islam* [*Government in Islam*], by [Haydar 'Ali] Qalamdaran; *Be'sat va ide'olozhi* [*Prophetic Mission and Ideology*], by [Mehdi] Bazargan; *Hokumat-e Islami* [*Islamic Government*], by Yahya Nuri; and *Medina-ye fazeleh, ya sistem-e hokumat dar Islam* [*Learned Medina (Utopia), or the System of Government in Islam*], by 'Ali Tehrani. Also, Imam Khomeini has presented his own opinion of Islamic government in his *Velayat-e faqih* [*Mandate of the Jurisprudent*].

They heard their opponents' arguments calmly and never heaped invectives and threats on them. They tolerated and welcomed debate. This was the practice of the Prophet of Islam, when he was weak in Mecca as well as when he was strong in Medina. The Qur'an commanded him to be kind and tolerant. Verses revealed in Medina bid the Prophet to give refuge to the idolaters who were in a state of war with him, so they would have an opportunity to hear God's message. If they were not persuaded, then they were to be returned, unharmed, to their homes.[21] The infallible *Imams* debated a host of critical, even derisive opponents. Nevertheless, they never mistreated or abused them in any way. The leader of the faithful ['Ali] during his rule waived the oath of allegiance and those who refused it continued to enjoy full civil rights and privileges. He did not banish the "hypocritical" groups, even though he was aware of their conspiracies and enmity. All his battles were defensive. He never initiated a battle. Nor did he ever tire of admonishing his enemies. The extent of freedom of opinion and criticism in the early days of Islam was such that when the second caliph, 'Umar [ibn al-Khattab, reigned 634–644], asked during a public address, that the faithful correct him if he ever wanders from the straight path, an ordinary citizen rose and told the short-tempered commander: "If you wander from the straight path I will straighten you with my sword!"

Certainly apostasy—that is, the denial of God and departure from the nation of Islam—has a severe penalty, up to and including death. Professor Marcel Boisard, professor of the college of law at Geneva and author of the book *L'Humanisme de l'Islam* (*The Humanism of Islam*), suggests that the cause of this severity may have had to do with the political aspect of the act, not the religious nature of it.

The most regrettable consequence of wrapping personal opinions and political and administrative decisions in the garb of religiosity and then presenting them as pure Islam is that to oppose these decisions would be to fight with God! In this manner, the inevitable blending of politics and spirituality exposes Islamic society to the tyranny of the medieval church, with the concomitant eclipse of freedom,

21. Sura 9, Verse 6: "And if an idolater seeks protection, then give him asylum that he may hear the word of God. Then escort him to a place of safety, for they are people who do not know."

truth, virtue, progress, health, and prosperity. In the words of the exalted Prophet: "A community in which the rights of the weak cannot be enjoyed without a stuttering tongue (a certain difficulty and fear) will never be cleansed of corruption." . . .

Islam—based on the Qur'anic principle, "Some of us should not take others as our guardians"—recognizes no person, whether actual or legal, as an absolute sovereign qualified to usurp the divine rights of human beings to freedom and honor.

The Qur'an declares: "You have indeed a noble example in the Prophet of God." (Sura 33, Verse 21) It is edifying to note his protective attitude and behavior toward individuals, even the Hypocrites. In a dark and inclement night, the Prophet, peace be upon him, while returning from the battle of Tabuk, reached a dangerous precipice. Accidentally (or miraculously!) a flash of lightning revealed a group of the Hypocrites, who were lurking to scare the Prophet's camel and send him hurtling to the bottom of the valley. Although this conspiracy was foiled, the Prophet did not publicize the conspirators' plans and did not seek revenge. He even made the camel driver Huzayfa ibn Yaman, who had witnessed the event, take an oath not to recount the event for as long as he lived. Another tradition has it that the son of 'Abdallah ibn Ubai [died 631], the leader of the Hypocrites, who had caused numerous problems for the Prophet and his companions, came to the Prophet and asked for permission to kill his own father. The Prophet reminded him that he was duty-bound to respect and protect his father at all times. 'Abdallah, however, continued to conspire against the Prophet until the end of his life. After 'Abdallah's death, the Prophet said, "Had God not commanded it, I would not pray on his body."[22] "You have indeed a noble example in the Prophet of God"!

Freedom as a Vital Necessity for Government and Religion

Let me reiterate: freedom means freedom to oppose, criticize, and object—even if the criticism is untrue and unjust. Where there is freedom there are oppo-

22. These two narratives are taken from *Mosir-e enqelab-e Islami* [*The Course of the Islamic Revolution*], notes dated September 12, 1980, by Ayatollah Hajji Sayyid Abolfazl Zanjani.

nents and currents that disturb routine stability and normalcy. Otherwise, freedom would be meaningless and useless.

This notion of freedom is hard for many zealous—if sincere—people to digest, as they consider such a freedom unwise and deleterious to the survival of the nascent Islamic Republic [of Iran]. They may even consider it a blunder on their part to have allowed this notion of freedom to prevail in the constitution of the Islamic Republic of Iran.

However, omniscient, compassionate God has not only sanctioned freedom in many affairs, he has made it the very foundation of survival and revival in the world. Let me elaborate on this point.

Opposition, the Cause of Movement and Life

In general, an object in a given force field will, of necessity, behave in a calculable and predictable way. For any object, whether a stone, a plant, or a human society, force means movement. For example, a piece of metal that is released within earth's gravitational field will fall in a straight line. Its position and velocity are calculable at every moment. Similarly, the behavior of a human being who is motivated only by the demands of his or her appetite is predictable. However, if in the place of one force, two or more forces are introduced—for example if a powerful magnet is placed in the path of the falling piece of metal—its trajectory and velocity will change. It will, to use a poetic expression, be freed from the slavery of a single cause of motion. The scenario is most intriguing when the affected object has the power to choose its level of susceptibility to the external influences. That is, when it has "free will." In this case, the person whose choice is not readily predicable and calculable for others—or even for oneself—could be said to possess "free will."

Therefore, freedom requires, as the case of Satan's temptations teach us, the existence of an oppositional force, along with a power of choice on behalf of the individual or the society. Opposition promulgates movement and change, which may, in turn, lead to decline or progress, depending on the choice of the agent involved.

Motion and change in the case of inanimate objects, even constructed objects such as machines, lead to erosion and deterioration (in the jargon of thermodynamic theory, the increase of entropy). In other words, inanimate objects aim at final rest and quiet.

However, objects endowed with life, particularly human beings, thrive on movement and opposition. They acquire new capabilities and aptitudes and accumulate experience and virtue because of opposition and change. Movement, a result of need, agitation, and love, is a blessing and a source of survival and evolution, while rigidity is a cause of stasis, decline, and death. Animals and human beings, once they feel need, danger, or attraction, tend to move, willy-nilly, either toward the object of their desire or away from the source of danger. Therefore, without opposition, as a source of motivation or agitation there would be no progress.[23] The oppositional motivator can lead to reform and revival.[24]

Our Islamic Revolution, our nationalist struggles, revivalist Islamic associations and movements, the earlier Constitutional Revolution of Iran—the awakening and activism of the Eastern countries in general after several hundred years of slumber and humiliation—were all the result of the encounter with Western civilization. The wondrous European Renaissance too was a result of conflicts, dissatisfactions, and objections to medieval Christian hegemony.

Similarly, the missions of the prophets were in the past the source of conflicts that revolutionized towns and tribes that were wallowing in the darkness of idolatry and the cesspool of corruption and inequity.

Conflict, one of whose quintessential representations for human beings is Satan, is the cause of a plethora of blessed events, from the natural cycle of life here on earth to the higher cycle of resurrection in the hereafter. The Qur'an frequently compares the colossal events of Judgment Day with seasonal rain and the revival of life on earth. Rain itself is the result of atmospheric disturbances and opposing forces of cold and warm weather systems. The science of meteorology has established, through hourly reports from weather stations, that rain-bearing continental weather fronts are comprised of successive fronts of dense clouds. These clouds are the result of expanding, rising, and condensing warm tropical weather

and its collision with the cold and heavy weather systems that flow from the northern regions. The heavy winds occupy the lower areas and push the warm humid weather up.[25]

The Opponents of Freedom

The opponents of freedom resort to the adage: "A head that does not ache does not need to be wrapped." Their argument goes like this: We know we are on the true path. We believe in Islam and possess good will and proper judgment. What need is there for further inquiry and learning? We can simply devote ourselves, body and soul, to the realization of the true doctrine. The entire nation and its leadership support this endeavor. Why should we let the enemies of God and the republic, the supporters of America, or those who do not follow our line—in short, people of suspicious intent or judgment—to muddy the waters, confuse minds, disturb society, and weaken the government? Such freedom and criticism will provide fodder for foreign radio propaganda which will, in turn, cause our youth to hesitate or deviate from the straight path. It is thus better to remove all the impediments from the path of the revolution and to conduct our affairs quickly and effectively—that is, without the nagging distractions of free expression and opposition.

These gentlemen, even if they are sincere, are deluded and naive about their own monopoly of the truth and about the notion of freedom. Freedom is not a luxury; it is a necessity. When freedom is banished, tyranny will take its place.

In the first place, those whose belief system is based on reason and truth are not afraid of opponents' criticism and propaganda. In the words of Sa'di [Persian poet, 1184–1292], "He who has clear accounts, has no fear of accountants."

Secondly, freedom of expression, opposition, and criticism awakens the negligent and holds back treason, monopoly, and tyranny. If the objections are unjustified, let the accused respond and thus dispel the clouds of suspicion and slander. This will strengthen the national resolve. The Qur'an considers such examinations as the means of separating

23. See my 'Eshq va parastesh, ya termodinamik-e ensan [Love and Worship, or the Thermodynamics of Humanity].

24. It is obvious that opposition in this context is an external force, different from materialist-dialectical opposition, involving an internal antithesis that is said to be inevitable, global, and social.

25. See [my] book Bad va baran dar Qur'an [Wind and Rain in the Qur'an] where many verses (more than 115 passages) are quoted that bear witness to this argument. [A series of citations follows.—Editor]

the good from the bad.[26] Conversely, suppression of freedom is an indication of a fundamental weakness or flaw in the government's intentions or actions. Consider the following Qur'anic debate: a believer in the pharaoh's family reasons with his affluent and powerful kin to listen to the message of Moses: "If he is a liar, his lie will be his own loss; but in case he speaks the truth, some of what he predicts will befall you." (Sura 40, Verse 28) In response, the pharaoh reiterates the argument of all dictators, tyrants, and zealots: "I show you only what I see (is right); and guide you but to the right path." [Sura 40, Verse 29] How can people exercise their religious obligation to call others to virtue and to warn them against vice in an Islamic society, without the freedom of conscience and expression, and in the absence of political and legal security? These are duties that Muslims are recommended to fulfill lest evil-doers dominate them and their prayers remain unanswered.

Thus the survival of a just system and its progress on the path of virtue and excellence is guaranteed by the freedom of expression and legal opposition. The protection of religion against abuse, ignorance, superstition, and deviance, too, requires that the mace of excommunication and compulsion be removed from society and the media. It is necessary to avoid painting a varnish of religiosity and godliness on human affairs, save that which necessarily and authentically belongs to religion. It is also necessary that some room is left for reflection and maneuver in all debates.

We have established, under the rubric of "Religion and Nation," that God addresses people themselves immediately and directly, without intermediaries. Everyone is directly responsible, and people's reason, knowledge, thought, perception, reflection, and will are the ultimate arbiter. We have the Qur'anic injunction, "If you do not know, then ask the keepers of (knowledge and) remembrance," (Sura 21, Verse 7) which indicates that it is proper to inquire, and to augment one's knowledge. In the meantime, the Qur'an has envisioned, without censure, the existence and expression of disagreements and differences of opinion among the faithful. It recommends the disagreements with the rulers to be referred to the Prophet and to God; which in our days, would mean the body of religious knowledge.[27]

Disagreement becomes unacceptable and disruptive only when it takes place at the executive level and when the responsible managers, instead of harmony and disciplined cooperation, engage in discord and in-fighting, each playing their own tune and doing their own thing. The principle of division of powers and their mutual non-interference and orderly checks and balances pervades Iran's old and new constitutions, and those of other parliamentary democratic systems. People and their representatives have a right to discuss, investigate, supervise, and decide public affairs within certain limits and without interfering in the progress, rigor, and effective management of the executive affairs as determined by the legislature. And now let me address the questions that were posed earlier:

The First Question

Has Islam abandoned people to do whatever they please? Is there no responsibility and restraint in this world?

Being free and autonomous is one thing, and being responsible for one's beliefs and actions quite another. God has given us freedom of opinion and action within certain parameters, but He has given us plenty of warning through His messengers and holy books, that rebellion, disbelief, and injustice will have dire results that will follow from our actions both in this life and in the hereafter. The consequences may be heeded and avoided beforehand, or they may be understood only after they have materialized, as stated in Sura 30, Verse [41]: "Corruption has spread over land and sea from what men have

---

26. Sura 3, Verse [141]: "This is so that God may try the faithful and destroy the unbelievers." Sura 3, Verse [154]: "God had to try them to bring out what they concealed in their breasts, and to bring out the secrets of their hearts, for God knows your innermost thoughts."

27. The text of Sura 4, Verse [59], is as follows: "O you who believe, obey God, and obey the Prophet and those in authority among you; and if (mutual opposition occurs and) you are at variance over something, refer this (matter and disagreement) to God and the Messenger.[. . .]" It is noteworthy that on five or six other occasions the faithful are told to obey God and the Prophet; only in this occasion is the phrase "those in authority" added, and that is qualified by the phrase "among you" (which could mean elected rulers). It is further stipulated that in case there appears a disagreement between the people and the rulers it should be referred to the other two authorities [God and the Prophet].

done (and do) themselves that (God may let) them taste a little bit of what they have done: They may come back [to the right path]."

God bestows both freedom and guidance concerning the consequences of actions. His mercy is infinite and His vengeance great. Thus freedom exists; so do responsibility and restraint. The choice is ours.

The Second Question

Should the Islamic government and the religious scholars in the leadership not check crime and treason? Should chaos and license rule?

First, the issue of individual liberty in violation of others' rights has been addressed in the first question. Absolute freedom of choice, as we understand it in the Qur'an, prevails in the relationship of God and man—not in that of society and the individual, where mutual rights and responsibilities are at stake. God may forgive transgression against His laws but, as we know, God cannot forgive people for transgressing against the rights of people. We do not enjoy the same level of freedom in our dealings with other people as we do in our personal relationship with God.

Second, religious scholars, as religious scholars, have no rights or responsibilities save those delegated to them within the democratic system of the Islamic government.

Third, self-defense and the prevention of injustice and corruption in an Islamic society are not only warranted but required. The principle of "neither inflicting nor suffering harm" is paramount in Islam, both on the individual and the societal level. Since everyone is entitled to enjoy a measure of freedom and honor, the freedom of all is necessarily limited. Furthermore, being a beneficiary of social privileges creates mutual responsibilities that the Islamic government, derived from people's will, is duty-bound to supervise.

The details of this issue and the form of intervention of the state and participation of the people, which should be exercised with utmost justice and mercy, are a separate discussion that should be analyzed under the rubric of Islamic government.

Christian-Muslim Democracy

Muslims are a minority of under 10 percent in the Philippines, concentrated largely on the island of Mindanao. The Moro National Liberation Front, the largest organization representing the Muslims, has waged a war of independence since the 1970s. In 1982, the Reformist Group headed by Dimasangcay A. Pundato (Philippines, born 1947) broke from the front, objecting to the undemocratic internal structure of the movement and the socialist leanings of the movement's leaders, and accepting autonomy rather than independence as the goal of the movement.[1] In the mid-1980s, the Reformist Group joined other pro-democracy forces in peaceful protest against the dictatorship. When the dictatorship fell in 1986, the Reformist Group, along with other Muslim groups such as the United Muslim Democrats of the Philippines, worked with the government to improve the position of Muslims in the Philippines, while the MNLF resumed its war of independence. In the speech and letter published here, Pundato explains his commitment to the democratic process and urges even closer cooperation among Christians and Muslims.

Making International Politics More Humane

Peace be upon all of you!

Let me recall the peroration of a speech delivered before the 94th American Newspaper Publishers As-

sociation Convention in Honolulu, Hawaii, on August 24, 1980:

> I ask you, publishers of America, to please help us open the eyes of your policymakers. Democracy is still the wave of the future. Help us make it less bloody to ride with the wave.

The speech demolished the pretensions of the erstwhile dictator of the Philippines, who had gone to Hawaii with a grand entourage to address that convention.

It was the dictator who was originally the only one invited to explain the situation in the Philippines.

1. W. K. Che Man, *Muslim Separatism: The Moros of Southern Philippines and the Malays of Southern Thailand* (Singapore: Oxford University Press, 1990), pp. 197–199; Che Man, "Moro National Liberation Front," and Cesar Adib Majul, "Philippines," in John L. Esposito, editor, *The Oxford Encyclopedia of the Modern Islamic World* (New York: Oxford University Press, 1995), volume 3, pp. 132–133 and 326–328; Majul, *The Contemporary Muslim Movement in the Philippines* (Berkeley, Calif.: Mizan Press, 1985).

When the organizers of the convention discovered an unfilled time slot in the program, they asked the speaker to address them.

The speaker was then in self-imposed exile in the United States, waging a campaign for freedom and democracy for the Philippines. He was carrying on the tradition of the Filipino intellectuals and propagandists in Spain and Europe towards the end of the 19th century who were fighting for reforms in the Philippines, then a colony of Spain.

The speaker was Raul S. Manglapus [Philippines, born 1918]. That his efforts, together with thousands of Filipino exiles and immigrants to the United States, were efficacious is borne by the fact that the Philippines, after the glorious non-violent People Power Revolution in 1986, is once again a free and democratic republic. Today, as chairman of the Center for Christian-Muslim Democracy, he is the host of this conference.

Similarly, there were Muslim Filipinos waging a campaign for freedom and democracy for the Muslims in the Philippines. I was among the Muslim idealists shuttling between the Philippines and other parts of Asia, the Middle East, and the United States, seeking support for our armed resistance and economic sanctions against the Philippines to hasten the crumbling down of the dictatorship.

As Secretary Manglapus pointed out in one of his speeches in the United States, the Muslims battling the dictatorship were inspired by the Qur'anic precepts on freedom and democracy.

Though the Christian opposition and the Muslim rebels were not formally coordinated along organizational lines, theirs were parallel moves. Their Holy Books, the Bible and the Qur'an, provided the foundation for such commitments.

In 1985, the Reformist Group of the Moro National Liberation Front (MNLF), of which I am Chairman, giving substance to this thesis, entered into a Memorandum of Agreement with the Ninoy Aquino Movement to work jointly for freedom and democracy in the Philippines.

This turned out later to be the first-ever formal agreement forged between a Moro front and a Filipino movement based in the United States.

Earlier in time, however, in 1982, at a meeting in Singapore with the Filipino martyr Ninoy Aquino [1932–1993], we renewed our commitment to support his struggle for the restoration of democracy in the Philippines. That he did not live long enough to see the full flowering of his vision gives us pain, yet we feel consoled that he did not die in vain.

I must modestly admit that our efforts evinced some fruition. A number of structural reforms affecting Muslims were introduced in the 1987 Philippine Constitution. Treatment of, and attitude towards, Muslims have generally improved.

The creation of the Office of Muslim Affairs (OMA) which vastly improved the strengthening of Muslim cultural practices and traditional institutions in the Philippines had somehow provided a sustaining force to further buttress this recognition.

It is under the regime of President Corazon Aquino [1986–1992] that the Muslim Filipinos were able to fully appreciate the realization of one of their aspirations as a people: that of the total implementation of the Code of Muslim Personal Laws of the Philippines, when President Aquino appointed more *shari'a* [Islamic law] judges and directed the conduct of *shari'a* training seminars and the administration of the *Shari'a* Bar Examinations this year.

Even the participation of our country in international Qur'an reading competitions has been expanded. While before, our participation in such assemblies was limited to the one being regularly held in Malaysia, under our present dispensation we are also participating in the Qur'an reading competition in Bangkok, Thailand, and in Jakarta, Indonesia.

More than ever, the conduct of the annual Muslim pilgrimage to Saudi Arabia has been so well coordinated. The Department of Foreign Affairs and other agencies of government have been actively involved in this yearly affair.

More, however, has to be done for the Muslims. Thus, under the mandates of the 1987 Constitution, an Autonomous Region in Muslim Mindanao was organized. Today, the Autonomous Region has gradually but steadily been addressing the administrative needs and development requirements of the region.

In many colleges and universities offering political science courses throughout the world, in scholarly journals, in the popular press, there is a perceptible timidity in articulating how deeply anchored democracy is in Islamic Law.

Even in countries like Pakistan that have adopted the Western manifestation of democracy, that is, relying on suffrage for legitimizing or changing leaders, there is only a minimal resort to the ideological claim that Islam not only allows democracy but in fact prescribes and enjoins it. The silence suggests there is general acceptance that the practice of democracy was an inheritance from its association with Great Britain rather than the carrying out, though in Western form, of an Islamic precept.

The debate in Pakistan that singularly stood out with a touch of Islamic ideology was on the status of women: whether in an Islamic society a woman can be elected Head of State. Those in favor had recourse to Sura 2, Verse 228, of the Glorious Qur'an, that serves as foundation for democracy:

> And women shall have rights similar to the rights against them, according to what is equitable. Never will I suffer to be lost the work of any of you, be he male or female. To men is allotted what they earn, and to women what they earn.

In a brief but masterly discourse in Marawi City, Philippines, on his conferment of an honorary Doctor of Laws at the Mindanao State University on May 6, 1976, Dr. Hassan 'Abdallah A. Sheikh [born 1934], Saudi Arabian Minister of Education, disproved those disparaging "Islamic law as not fit for ruling and guiding societies."

He said that "to understand the extent of dignity and freedom granted by Islam to its followers, it would be wise to briefly mention some of the modern articles that comprise the Human Rights Declaration adopted by the United Nations on December 10, 1948."

Then he cited and explicated verses of the Qur'an and passages from the *sunna* [practice] of the Prophet to illustrate that the modern call for freedom and dignity was vouchsafed by Islamic law centuries earlier.

Observers must not be taken too much by forms in the assessment of democracy in Islamic countries because democracy is covered by Sura 42, Verse 38, of the Holy Book: "Those . . . who (conduct) their affairs by mutual consultation. . . ." Leaders are urged to seek counsel from the wise. This is the essence of Sura *Al-Shura* [Sura 42], Verse 36, of the Qur'an, and I quote:

> Pass over (their faults) and ask for (God's) forgiveness for them, and consult them in affairs (of moment). Then, when those (have) taken a decision, put thy trust in God.

Today, when Eastern Europe, the USSR, and China are in the grip of democratic fervor, in many instances toppling communist regimes outright, it seems it is easier to hold that democracy is more germane to them than in Islamic countries or countries with predominantly Muslim populations. The democratic wave is irresistible.

Earlier, some countries in Western Europe and Latin America restored democracy in their system. In celebration and to bear witness to the significance of such a tide, a conference on newly-restored democracy was held in Manila, Philippines, in June 1988.

It is safe to say that over three-fifths, perhaps even four-fifths, of the world's populations are Christians and Muslims. To grasp an idea of how numerous Muslims are, consider that China and the USSR each have at least over 100 million Muslims in their midst.

I think that this conference is the first, or at least one of the first, held to begin seeing in the proper international perspective how powerful, creative and human Christian-Muslim Democracy is.

If political movements and governments are formed by religious values that affirm dignity and freedom, values enshrined in the Holy Books, the Bible and the Qur'an, our world would be a kinder, more generous, progressive, dynamic and peaceful world.

Islam is "Heaven's message to all mankind, Arabs, non-Arabs, wealthy or poor, black or white." And it precisely admits a bond with Christianity, which shares similar principles and roots with it. Thus, the Qur'an in Sura *Al-'Imran* [Sura 3], Verse 84, states:

> Say ye: We believe in God, and the revelation given to us, and to Abraham, Ismail, Isaac, Jacob, and the tribes, and that given to Moses and Jesus, and that given to (all) Prophets from their Lord; we make no difference between one another of them; and we bow to God (in Islam).

Certainly more research and exchange of views between Christian and Muslim Democrats are in order. Experiments on the juxtaposition of the democratic underpinnings of the two religions are essential. And such experiments are best effected not only in the quiet of the library but in actual maneuvering in the political arena.

Thus, the formation of the United Muslim Democrats of the Philippines was keenly followed by some Christian and Muslim groups in Indonesia.

It is true, Christians in the predominantly Muslim population of Indonesia are not discriminated against in appointments to high civilian and military positions. But the possibility of actually organizing a similar party in Indonesia compelled them to serious thought, and how they plied with questions the Filipinos who attended the religious leaders' conference on national development.

The members of the European community, essentially Christians, are familiar with the Muslim world.

Some have deeply imbibed the Islamic culture—for example, Spain—because of long historical association. Some have fought against it, as in the Crusades. Some have colonized portions of it, and even as de-colonization has become a reality, their links are as firm as ever because millions from former colonies have settled in Europe. I understand there are at least three million in France. There is a vast reservoir of knowledge of the Muslim world and Islam in the European community.

I think, however, that the impetus for the study of Christian-Muslim Democracy as an aid to making international politics more humane and attuned to the raising of the dignity and freedom of the individual is undeniably ardent in this part of the world. But to paraphrase a Christian acceptance of a sad predicament, the intellect and the morale are willing, but the resources are weak.

In the manner of Raul S. Manglapus speaking before the American Newspaper Publishers Association, but admittedly with less eloquence,

I ask you, members of the European community: please help us in our endeavor to plumb the depth of Christian-Muslim Democracy. Christian-Muslim Democracy is the Wave of the Future. Help us spread it wide and fast so more may happily ride with the wave.

And finally, allow me to close this note with Sura 49, Verse 13, of the Glorious Qur'an, and I quote:

Mankind! We created you from a single (pair) of a male and female, and made you into nations and tribes, that ye may know each other, not that ye may despise (each other).

Peace be upon you. Thank you.

Letter to Secretary Manglapus

Dear Secretary Manglapus: Last June 9 [1990], at the conference on "Christian-Muslim Democracy: Wave of the Future," I was very elated to affirm with Her Excellency, President Corazon C. Aquino, together with Honorable Siegbert Alber, Honorable Gunter Rinsche, Honorable Carlos Robles-Piquer, Honorable Gabriele Sboarina (all of the European Parliament), and Honorable Exequiel B. Javier, Mr. Amado Luis Lagdameo, and yourself, our shared commitment to freedom, justice and democracy.

I decided then to seek membership in the Center for Christian-Muslim Democracy, though not in the manner of Saul who underwent a conversion and became St. Paul, because I needed no conversion as far as dedication to freedom and democracy is concerned.

I, in fact, joined the Muslim armed rebellion when the dictatorship that was toppled in 1986 trampled freedom and democracy underfoot in southern Philippines. And later, when I was based abroad, I signed agreements for a joint struggle against the dictatorship with Christian groups who had similar commitments to democracy and freedom.

The Center, I believe, is the best entity to study and spread the creative force of the ideology of Christian-Muslim democracy.

The MNLF (Moro National Liberation Front) Reformist Group counts at least 16,000 members and a far larger number of sympathizers. I will not be so presumptuous as to aver that by a unilateral decree, all of them would be instant adherents of Christian-Muslim Democracy. While I could claim their loyalty, I must admit I would have to explain to a sizeable portion of them this twin-ideology which I believe would be the most puissant guiding force to lift this country from its general malaise and the quagmire of indirection.

But I know enough of leadership to know of their longing for hope and stability, know enough of their rational capacity to expect that, afforded sufficient enlightenment, they would be as staunch believers of Christian-Muslim Democracy as I am.

And from their eventual advocacy and day-to-day affirmation and living out of the ideology of Christian-Muslim Democracy, I trust the larger Muslim community would be one with them in this inspiring ideology rooted in the Holy Qur'an and the Holy Bible.

Signed, Dimasangcay A. Pundato, June 12, 1991

Participation in Non-Islamic Government

Rachid Ghannouchi (Tunisia, born 1941) received a philosophy degree at the University of Damascus and, after a year of study in France, returned to Tunisia in 1969 as a high school teacher. The following year, Ghannouchi helped to establish a reformist movement that opposed the secular socialism of the ruling party in Tunisia and proffered a modernist interpretation of Islam. This movement, formalized as the Islamic Tendency Movement—now called the Renaissance party—grew to become the leading political opposition in Tunisia, and Ghannouchi its leading figure. After a decade in and out of prison for his political activities, Ghannouchi left Tunisia for Europe in the early 1990s. While similar movements elsewhere in North Africa have turned to armed revolt and antidemocratic rhetoric, Ghannouchi continues to resist radicalization.[1] In this paper, Ghannouchi argues for democratic power-sharing as a nonviolent means to effect a transition to Islamic rule.

Introduction

This paper attempts to answer the question related to the position of Islam regarding the participation of its followers in establishing or administering a non-Islamic regime.

1. Marion Boulby, "The Islamic Challenge: Tunisia since Independence," *Third World Quarterly*, volume 10, Number 2, April 1988, pp. 590–614; Khalid Elginty, "The Rhetoric of Rashid Ghanushi," *Arab Studies Journal*, volume 3, number 1, Spring 1995, pp. 101–119; Emad Eldin Shahin, "Ghannushi, Rashid al-," in John L. Esposito, editor, *The Oxford Encyclopedia of the Modern Islamic World* (New York: Oxford University Press, 1995), volume 2, pp. 60–61.

Prior to attempting to provide an answer to this question certain facts need to be underlined:

First: the fact that a concept for an Islamic government does exist, and that it is the religious duty of Muslims, both individuals and groups, to work for the establishment of such a government.

Second: the fact that such an Islamic government, in the circumstances under discussion, is non-existent, and that had it been in existence, a Muslim would have no option but to support it and work for the reformation of such elements of corruption as might exist within it.

Third: the fact that the present circumstances do not seem to favor the establishment of an Islamic government. So much effort has been exerted in order to establish such a government, and despite their failure so far, it is the duty of all Muslims to continue the effort and cooperate in order to fulfill God's commandment and establish justice on earth.

The Holy Qur'an says: "O you who believe! stand out firmly for God, as witnesses to fair dealing, and let not the hatred of others towards you make you swerve to wrong and depart from justice. Be just, that is next to piety, and fear God. For God is well-acquainted with all that you do." (Sura 5, Verse 8)

In the same sura, Verse 49 reads: "Judge between them by what God has revealed, and follow not their vain desires," while Verse 44 reads: "Those who do not judge by what God has revealed, they are unbelievers."

Exceptional Circumstances

The scope of this discussion does not apply to the normal situation when the Muslim community can establish the system of its intellectual, political, economic, international and other relations on the basis of Islam and in conformity with its faith and cultural heritage—the heritage which continues to be deep-rooted in the hearts and souls of Muslims despite the attempts of Western colonial occupation to undermine its fundamental principles.

The discussion here focuses on the exceptional situation when the community of believers is unable to accomplish its goal of establishing the Islamic government directly. In this case the community is faced with tough options.

Realism and flexibility are among the most important features of Islamic methodology. These features explain the fact that this religion is an eternal way of life that is suitable for all times and all places. Furthermore, the lives of human communities, including the community of Muslims, are in continuous dynamism just like the life of an individual human being. Fluctuations between health and sickness, victory and defeat, success and failure, progress and slipping back, strength and weakness are only natural. Therefore, it is imperative that a religion which came for the purpose of improving the life of all humans wherever and whenever they exist should have the capacity to respond to all emerging situations and forms of development through which the Muslim communities may pass. And in doing so, such a religion would have to draw the main straight

lines as well as the bending ones; that is, it would not just be content with drawing the lines for the absolute fundamentals during normal circumstances, but would also define the rules and mechanisms which ought to be followed and observed during exceptional extra-ordinary circumstances. In this way the believers remain in close contact with the fundamentals of the *shari'a* [religious law] in the situations of both strength and weakness.

The *Fiqh* (Jurisprudence) of Requirements and Necessities

The Muslims' heritage of jurisprudence is the greatest and richest legal or canonical heritage ever possessed by any single community, so much so that the Muslims can justifiably be called the community of jurisprudence. The greatness of this jurisprudence stems from the fact that it is founded upon major legislative foundations known as *'ilm al-usul* (the science of fundamentals), which is a great Islamic science.

This science was studied thoroughly and developed over the years by highly talented and authoritative scholars. The apex of this development was reached by Al-Andalusi [Abu Ishaq] Al-Shatibi [died 1388] whose studies and thoughts were complementary to those of his predecessor Imam [Abu 'Abdallah Muhammad] al-Shafi'i [767–820]. The learned scholars who dedicated their lives to this important realm of knowledge believed in the greatness of Islam; they thoroughly studied the revelation (Qur'an), the *sunna* [practice of the Prophet], and the heritage of jurisprudence. They also took into consideration the various practical experiences and applications of jurisprudence throughout the centuries together with the sum of knowledge acquired by man during their own time.

Through this collection of the sources of knowledge, and in the light of their understanding of the purposes and objectives of Islam, they formulated a set of fundamentals for legislation whose ultimate goal is to serve the interests of man—the very essence of the message of Islam.

Al-Shatibi says: "From our exploration of the *shari'a*, we have concluded that it was only set up to serve the interests of man. This is a conclusion no one can dispute, even [Fakhr al-Din] Al-Razi [1149–1209]. Canon laws were made for only one purpose:

to serve the interests of humans in this life and the hereafter. God says in the Qur'an: 'We sent you not but as a mercy for all creatures.' (Sura 21, Verse 107) 'God does not wish to place you in difficulty, but to purify you, and to complete His favor to you.' (Sura 5, Verse 6) 'In the Law of Equality there is (saving of) life to you.' (Sura 2, Verse 179)"[2]

In his book *Al-Muwafaqat*, Al-Shatibi details the types of requirements which Messengers were sent to fulfill in the lives of humans. He categorized them into "essential requirements" without which life would be ruined; these requirements include the protection of faith, of life, of progeny, of wealth and of the mind. Then he spoke of the "special requirements" without which man would be in distress and hardship. They include the requirement to enjoy lawful and good things in life. Finally, he spoke of "ameliorative requirements" whose absence would not seriously undermine life. These include the various manners related for instance to eating and drinking etc. The fulfillment of such requirements is ahead at improving the quality of life.[3]

The general inclination in contemporary Islamic political thought is to adopt Al-Shatibi's concept of the purposes of religion, namely that religion was revealed only to fulfill and protect the needs and interests of mankind in this life and the hereafter, as a general framework for tackling new problems with the Muslim society. Within the framework of this general perspective or purpose of the *shari'a*, the details of religion find their appropriate place as branches of the fundamentals. Within the same perspective, all new problems in the lives not only of Muslims but of all humanity, can find proper solutions that guarantee the fulfillment of their requirements.

In this way evils can be averted without any need for violating the provisions of God's divine law, since this law already includes general principles from which new deductions can be made whenever life progresses or changes. Some of these principles apply to standard situations and normal circumstances, while others deal with exceptional situations and extraordinary circumstances. An example to the latter is the principle of "necessities eliminate pro-

hibitions" (necessity knows no law). This principle is a Qur'anic principle. God says:

> But if one is forced by necessity, without willful disobedience nor transgressing due limits, then is he guiltless. (Sura 2, Verse 173)

Similar to this are the principle of balancing between the better and the worse and opting for that which seems to best serve the general interest of the people, and the principle of outcomes or consequences according to which acts are judged on the basis of what they lead to. The decisive criterion in all cases is the fulfillment of the needs of humans and serving their best interests.[4]

Power-Sharing in a Non-Islamic Government

The general rule in judging the acts of humans is that all actions are permissible unless a prohibition is specified. The prohibition in this case is derived from the commandment to implement the law of God and not to resort to adopting laws other than His. It is therefore a must for all Muslims to do what they can in order to obey God's commandment and establish His governance. But what if the Muslims are unable to do so? The rule is that we are obliged to do only that which we can: "No soul shall have a burden laid on it greater than it can bear." (Sura 2, Verse 233)

The Islamic government is one in which:

1. Supreme legislative authority is for the *shari'a*, that is the revealed law of Islam, which transcends all laws. Within this context, it is the responsibility of scholars to deduce detailed laws and regulations to be used as guidelines by judges. The head of the Islamic state is the leader of the executive body entrusted with the responsibility of implementing such laws and regulations.
2. Political power belongs to the community (*umma*), which should adopt a form of *shura*, which is a system of mandatory consultation.

If this kind of government is possible, it is then the duty of the believers to spare no effort in establishing it. However, if this is not possible, what must the community do?

---

2. Abu Ishaq al-Shatibi, *Al-Muwafaqat* [*fi usul al-shari'a*] [*The Correspondences on the Methodology of Islamic Law*], volume 2, pp. 6–8.

3. Ibid.

4. Ibid.

On the basis of the general fundamentals of Islam and its purposes of accomplishing the needs and serving the rest of the public (and these include the protection of faith, souls, wealth and the prevention of evils), it is incumbent upon the community of the faithful to avoid passivism and isolationism. Every Muslim has a responsibility toward the task of establishing the Islamic government. If such a task is not possible, then Muslims must endeavor to accomplish whatever can be accomplished.

Power-sharing in a Muslim or a non-Muslim environment becomes a necessity in order to lay the foundations of the social order. This power-sharing may not necessarily be based on Islamic *shari'a* law. However, it must be based on an important foundation of the Islamic government, namely *shura*, or the authority of the *umma*, so as to prevent the evils of dictatorship, foreign domination, or local anarchy. Such a process of power-sharing may also aim to achieve a national or a humanistic interest such as independence, development, social solidarity, civil liberties, human rights, political pluralism, independence of the judiciary, freedom of the press, or liberty for mosques and Islamic activities.

Can any Muslim community afford to hesitate in participating in the establishment of a secular democratic system if it is unable to establish an Islamic democratic one? The answer is no. It is the religious duty of the Muslims, as individuals and as communities, to contribute to the efforts to establish such a system. In this way, the Muslims would seek the establishment of the government of rationale due to their inability to establish the government of *shari'a* —as Ibn Khaldun [historian 1332–1406] put it.[5]

Documented Cases

Several events can be quoted from the Qur'an, the *sunna*, and Islamic history to prove that Muslims, as individuals or as communities, are permitted to participate in establishing or administering non-Islamic governments in order to achieve good and avoid evil.

In one chapter of the Qur'an we are told the story of Yusuf (Joseph), who was thrown into the well by his brothers and was then rescued, to end up in the Pharaoh's palace in Egypt where he was subjected to trial and seduction. It is worth noting that this young man, who was imprisoned and mistreated, seized the moment when it was right and expressed readiness to take charge of the most important office in the Pharaoh's government, believing it was his duty to rescue many nations that were threatened by famine and drought. He did not wait for the Egyptian people to renounce paganism and embrace his monotheist religion so as to form the foundation for an Islamic government.

What that young man had in mind was the fact that religion has come to serve the people and fulfill their essential needs. Yusuf had the conviction that rescuing the people from starvation, and consequently from annihilation, could not wait. He saw that he was able to help, and he did help. Through his effective participation in administering the affairs of the people he performed his other responsibility of calling for Islam and admonishing the people to reform their lives and renounce evils.

The detailed narration of the story of Yusuf in the Qur'an is a clear testimony that his approach is commendable. What happened with Yusuf can happen to Muslims anywhere and at any time. In similar circumstances, Muslims have no option but to participate politically in establishing and administering non-Islamic governments in order to serve the interests of the *umma* and prevent evils. Failing to do so will lead to undermining these interests and to allowing evils to spread and dominate society.

The second example is that of the Negus (the Emperor of Ethiopia) who lived during the early years of Islam. The Prophet advised some of his companions who were being severely persecuted to migrate to Abyssinia, describing the Negus as "the king in whose country none is wronged." The presence of the small Muslim community in Abyssinia resulted in the Negus embracing Islam, although he did not effect any amendments to his government in the direction of implementing the *shari'a*, as such an attempt could have threatened his kingship and endangered the lives of his guests. The story of that noble king has been documented in Islamic history and continues to be narrated to this day. The Prophet instructed his followers to perform a prayer for the king's soul when the news of his death reached them.

Commenting on this, Ibn Taymiyya [1263–1328] said, "We know definitely that he could not implement the law of the Qur'an in his community because

---

5. Ibn Khaldun, *Al-Muqaddima* [*The Introduction*].

his people would not have permitted him to. Despite that, the Negus and all those who are similar to him found their way to the pleasure of God in eternity although they could not abide by the laws of Islam, and could only rule using that which could be implemented in the given circumstances."[6]

The third example is that of *hilf al-fudul*, that is the pact or alliance of *al-fudul*.[7] This was an agreement among several pre-Islamic Arab tribes to support the wronged, maintain close relations with relatives and take good care of them. The Prophet did witness the signing of the alliance prior to his prophethood, and said afterwards that if he were to be invited to a similar alliance in Islam he would have accepted without reservation. He further stressed that any good and noble contract made in *jahiliya* [the pre-Islamic era] is automatically endorsed by Islam.[8] It is thus concluded that the community of believers may participate in an alliance aimed at preventing injustice and oppression, at serving the interests of mankind, at protecting human rights, at recognizing the authority of the people and at rotating power-holding through a system of elections. The faithful can pursue all these noble objectives even with those who do not share the same faith or ideology.

The fourth example is that of 'Umar ibn 'Abd al-'Aziz [682–720]. This Umayyad caliph, whose rulership did not exceed two years, is considered by historians and scholars to be the fifth guided caliph because of his piety and justice, although more than half a century separated him from the last of the four guided caliphs [the first successors to the Prophet]. Although he was a king who inherited kingship, he was unhappy with the monarchy, and in principle did not approve of it. However, he could not alter the system and was unable to restore the right of the *umma* in a consultative-style government due to the accumulation of corruption over the years. Nonetheless, he managed to significantly reform many bad practices, and restored justice and fairness. By accepting the monarchy, which he did not approve of,

he was able to do many good things, and no one said he was wrong or misguided in his actions.

Contemporary Considerations

An Islamic government is based on a number of values which if accomplished in their totality, would result in a perfect or near-perfect system. But it may not be possible for all such values to be implemented, and therefore some must suffice in certain circumstances in order for a just government to exist. A just government, even if not Islamic, is considered very close to the Islamic one, because justice is the most important feature of an Islamic government, and it has been said that justice is the law of God.

['Abdallah] Ibn 'Aqil [circa 1294–1367] defined *al-siyasa al-shari'a* (Islamic administrative policy) as the actions which bring the people closer to good and distance them from evil, even if such actions were not advocated by the Prophet or revealed from the Heavens.

He further explained that describing these actions using the phrase "those that conform with the Islamic law (*shar'*)" in order to imply that such actions should not contradict the *shar'*, is justified. However, if one means by such a phrase that such actions must specifically be mentioned in the Qur'an or the *sunna*, then this is wrong and can be taken to imply that the companions of the Prophet themselves went wrong. After all, they initiated many new policies and took numerous measures in order to fulfill the needs of the society in response to new developments or changing circumstances.[9]

In contemporary times, numerous examples can be cited to show that Islamic individuals and groups have entered into alliances in order to prevent evil or in order to serve the community within a non-Islamic framework. This is happening despite the fact that many scholars still insist that such measures should not be pursued.[10] With due respect, these scholars make life difficult for the Muslims unnecessarily. Their opinions impose restrictions on a policy which is definitely permissible and lawful,

---

6. Ibn Taymiyya, *Al-Fatawa [Religious Judgments]*, volume 19, pp. 218–219.

7. [The term's meaning is debated; see C. Pellat, "*Hilf al-fudul*," *Encyclopedia of Islam*, second edition, volume 2, edited by B. Lewis, et al. (Leiden: E. J. Brill; London: Luzac and Company, 1971), p. 389.—Editor]

8. Muslim [ibn al-Hajjaj, 821–875] and Abu Da'ud [al-Sijistani, 817–889]. [Both men are authors of *hadith* collections.—Editor]

9. Ibn Qayyim al-Jawziyya [1292–1350], *Al-Turuq al-hukmiyya [The Ways of Governance]*, p. 13.

10. [Abul A'la] Mawdudi [1903–1979], *The Islamic Government*; Dr. M[uhammad] Abu Faris, *Tahrim al-musharaka fil-hukuma [The Illegality of Participation in the Government]*.

and which is intended to equip the Muslims with the ability to react positively in situations that can be very difficult indeed.

To cite only a few examples of such situations:

First: About one third of the Muslims in the world are minorities in the countries they live in, that is to say they have no hope in the foreseeable future of governing their countries in an Islamic way. Many of these Muslim minorities face threats of exile or annihilation due to ethnic cleansing and other pressures. What options does Islamic jurisprudence have for them? Some people have been suggesting that such minorities should emigrate to countries that have Muslim majorities. If this were possible, and it is normally impossible, what good would it do them? Or is such a suggestion another plot against the Muslims in order to drive them out of their homes? There are those who advise Muslim minorities to isolate themselves and wait, but this too contradicts the very essence of the Islamic message, which encourages the faithful to be positive, active and involved.

The best option for such minorities is to enter into alliances with secular democratic groups. They can then work towards the establishment of a secular democratic government which will respect human rights, ensuring security and freedom of expression and belief—essential requirements of mankind that Islam has come to fulfill.

The accomplishment of such important values in any society will immediately transform it, in the Islamic conception, from *dar al-harb*, a land of hostility and war against Islam, to a land of peace and tranquillity. Al-Imam Al-Nawawi [1233–1277] defines *dar al-harb* as the country in which the faithful cannot practice their religious duties freely, and consequently emigrating from it becomes an imperative duty.[11] True democracies are not like this; they guarantee the freedom of worship and belief.

Second: There are many Islamic communities or movements that exist in countries that have Muslim majorities but which happen to be ruled by dictatorships claiming to be Islamic or by dictatorships hostile to Islam. Such Islamic movements may not be able to reform the regime or change it alone. Does the *shari'a* object to cooperation and alliance

11. Imam Al-Nawawi, *Al-Arba'un hadithan* [*Forty Hadiths*].

between these movements and secular parties that also work and struggle to topple the dictatorships and establish secular democracies that would respect humans and guarantee their liberties? No, not at all.

Third: Similarly, the Islamic groups which exist in Muslim majority countries governed by dictatorships may be able to attract majority support from the public and establish an Islamic government. However, such a transition may incite hostility towards them from within their own country or from other countries, rendering the newly-formed Islamic government susceptible to oppression or other forms of pressures that may end with its collapse.

Is there any reason why such groups cannot agree or coordinate either secular groups in ordeal to isolate the existing oppressive power and establish a secular democracy, postponing the long-term objective of establishing an Islamic government until circumstances permit? Certainly, there is nothing against that.

It should be emphasized that the choice in this case is not between Islamic government and a non-Islamic one, but between dictatorship and democracy.

Fourth: The Islamic groups which exist in countries colonized by foreign powers. Is there any reason why they should not form a united front with the secular groups in order to confront the common enemy of a national alternative, in which the Muslims would have a better life than under the colonial authority? Certainly, there is nothing to prevent them from doing so.

Conclusion

If the establishment of the Islamic government is the short or long-term goal of every Islamic group in order to implement God's commandments, the *shari'a* does take into consideration the possibility that such a goal may not be easily accomplished, and therefore an alternative is provided. Under exceptional circumstances, Islamic groups may forge alliances with non-Islamic groups in order to establish a pluralistic government system in which power is held by the majority party.

Such an alliance may also exist for the purpose of deterring aggression or getting rid of a dictatorship. In all cases, the alliance must not include provisions that would in any way undermine Islam, or impose restrictions on those who work for Islam and who seek to establish its system in the land.[12]

These arguments are based on:

- the principle of supporting that which brings good and suppressing that which produces evil.
- the rule that what an imperative duty is essentially dependent on is imperative in itself.
- the rule of consequences or outcomes.
- the principle of necessity.

What is most important is that a Muslim must remain positive and actively engaged in the effort to implement the revealed laws of God, whether partially or in their totality, depending on circumstances and resources. The essence of God's laws, for which all divine messages were sent, is the establishment of justice for mankind.

"We sent aforetime our Messengers with clear signs and sent down with them the Book and the Balance (of right and wrong), that men may stand forth in justice." (Sura 57, Verse 25)

It should however be emphasized that the problem facing the concept of power-sharing does not lie in the difficulty of convincing the Islamists to accept democracy, pluralism and power-sharing. The current general trend in Islamic circles is to adopt power-sharing—even in a secular style government—as a means for achieving mutual goals such as national solidarity, respect for human rights, civil liberties, cultural, social and economic development, and the deterrence of external threats.

The real problem lies in convincing the "other," that is the ruling regimes, of the principle of "the people's sovereignty" and of the right of Islamists—just like other political groups—to form political parties, engage in political activities and compete for power or share in power through democratic means.

The punishment of the Islamic victors in the Tunisian and Algerian elections—which have regrettably been taking place with the consent of Western democracies and the support of local "secular theological elites"[13] that are allied with the oppressive regimes in both countries—provides a decisive evidence that the root of the problem in the Muslim world lies in the hegemony of despotism. Our main task now is to combat despotism in favor of a genuine and true transition to democracy.

---

12. Dr. Salah Al-Sawi, *Al-Ta'addudiya al-siyasiyya fi al-dawla al-Islamiyya* [*Political Pluralism in Islamic Government*, 1992], p. 142.

13. Dr. Bashir Nafi' article in *Al-Hayat* [*Life*], number 10984, March 9, 1993.

Democracy and *Shura*

Sadek Jawad Sulaiman (Oman, born 1933), like many Omanis who came of age before the oil era, left his country in the 1950s. He worked as a journalist in Kuwait prior to his return to Oman in 1973. From 1976 until 1983, he worked for Oman's Ministry of Foreign Affairs, where he was director of political affairs (1977–1979) and ambassador to the United States (1979–1983). Since 1983, he has divided his time between Washington and Oman. This chapter was first presented as a talk in August 1996 at the al-Hiwar (Dialogue) Center in Washington, D.C., a discussion group of Arab intellectuals, diplomats, and businessmen. Sulaiman's comparison between the Qur'anic principle of *shura* and democracy as it has developed in the United States may at first appear unexpected. Sulaiman explains: "Many Arabs understand democracy as a slogan. Only by understanding it in history and practice does its compatibility with *shura* emerge."[1] In the context of the Gulf states, Sulaiman's argument—that the "logic of *shura*, like the logic of democracy, does not accept hereditary rule, for wisdom and competence are never the monopoly of any one individual or family"—is bold and innovative.

The subject of this discussion is vital for initiating a change in Arab public life, for the relationship between democracy and *shura* touches the essence of our national existence (*qawmiyya*). It determines the quality of our civic experience and the world we would like to leave for future generations. For this reason the subject merits our full attention.

Democracy

Democracy literally means rule by the people, and this distinguishes it from any pattern of governance

not deriving its legitimacy from the people's choice. Americans define democracy in the words of their 16th president, Abraham Lincoln [1809–1865]: "Rule of the people, by the people, for the people." The definition I usually offer is "public participation in decisions affecting public life."

This participation can be either direct or indirect. In direct participation, the people decide the results by a majority vote. They discuss the issue at hand, then reach a decision representing the collective wisdom. Something akin to this happens in "town meetings." A clear example is when people vote on a "proposition"—a term Americans use when an issue that has generated considerable controversy is referred to the public for resolution. Proposition 187

1. Interview with Dale F. Eickelman, November 9, 1996.

in 1995 in California, denying public services to illegal immigrants, is a notable example of direct participation. Another is the referendum in 1995 by which Canadians in Québec rejected the separation of their province. With indirect participation, the people do not specifically decide issues but elect people to represent their views and make decisions. The elected representatives perform this task within the written parameters of a constitution.

The American constitutional system is based on indirect participation, and the republican system in American constitutional law is centered on the principle of representation. It is appropriate to note, however, that the dynamism of the media in recent years has generated more direct participation in policy-making and legislating. The influence that media talk shows and opinion polls have on elected officials is unmistakably clear.

Democracy's core principle is equality, the affirmation that all people are equal. Any discrimination among people on the basis of race, gender, religion, or lineage is inherently invalid. All people are endowed with inalienable human rights. To secure these rights, governments derive their legitimacy from the consent of the governed.

The chief characteristics of the democratic system are:

1. Freedom of speech, whereby citizens are able openly to state their views on public issues without impediment or fear, regardless of whether such views are critical or supportive of the government. In the democratic system, it is important for officials to know how the people feel about policies they adopt and decisions they make.
2. Free elections in which citizens regularly, in accordance with precise and constitutionally protected procedures, elect people they entrust with the affairs of governance. Elections legitimize all levels of representation, from the city council to the presidency of the state.
3. Majority rule and minority rights: In the democratic system, decisions are made by the majority, based on the general conviction that the judgment of the majority is more likely to be right than that of the minority. But majority rule does not give a free hand to the majority to do as it wants. Embedded in the democratic principle is the commitment that certain fundamental citizens' rights shall not be violated—for example, freedom of speech, freedom of the press, freedom of assembly, and the free exercise of religion.

4. Political parties in the democratic system play an important role. By means of political parties, people freely associate on the basis of their convictions about how to achieve a fulfilling life for themselves, their family, and their posterity.
5. Separation between the legislative, the executive, and the judiciary, whereby constitutional checks and balances among these three branches of government prevent potential exploitative practices.
6. Constitutional authority is the supreme authority on the validity of any statutory law or executive directive. Constitutional authority means supremacy of the rule of law, not the rule of individuals, in the resolution of any public matter.
7. Freedom of action for individuals and groups, provided they do not infringe on the common good. From this derives the freedom to own property, the freedom to work, the freedom to pursue personal goals, and the freedom to form various associations and corporations.

These elements are common to any bona fide democratic system. They are particularly well articulated in the American constitutional system under which we live and whose characteristics, as a great and unique experience in the formation and evolution of nations, we try to understand.

The essentials of the American democratic experience were present at its origin but expanded in scope and evolved in application over time. For example, even though the principle of equality as a foundational idea was firmly established in the Declaration of Independence in 1776, the right for free men to vote on an equal basis was not granted until 1850. Black males were not allowed to vote until the 15th constitutional amendment in 1870. Females, both free and slave, were not given the right to vote until the 19th constitutional amendment in 1920. Finally, the poll tax was not abolished until the 24th constitutional amendment in 1964.

Thus we see that the American state, one considered an exemplar of democratic systems, although based on a constitution, did not have its constitutionality complete at birth, nor is it complete today. This is because the democratic principle, although recognized as a universal human principle since ancient times, continues to demand better fulfillment in the experiences of all nations. We also see that the democratic principle is one thing and our endeavors to realize its requirements, something else. In this latter sense, there is no such thing as an ideal democratic society. We must distinguish, on the one hand, between societies that uphold the democratic principle and endeavor to attain its fulfillment, and societies whose rulers reject the democratic principle, exercise autocratic rule and privilege, and deny equality as a moral imperative.

Shura

As a concept and as a principle, *shura* in Islam does not differ from democracy. Both *shura* and democracy arise from the central consideration that collective deliberation is more likely to lead to a fair and sound result for the social good than individual preference. Both concepts also assume that majority judgment tends to be more comprehensive and accurate than minority judgment. As principles, *shura* and democracy proceed from the core idea that all people are equal in rights and responsibilities. Both thereby commit to the rule of the people through application of the law rather than the rule of individuals or a family through autocratic decree. Both affirm that a more comprehensive fulfillment of the principles and values by which humanity prospers cannot be achieved in a non-democratic, non-*shura* environment.

I do not see *shura* as rejecting or incompatible with the basic elements of a democratic system. The Qur'an mentions *shura* as a principle governing the public life of the society of the faithful rather than a specifically ordained system of governance. As such, the more any system constitutionally, institutionally, and practically fulfills the principle of *shura*—or, for that matter, the democratic principle—the more Islamic that system becomes.

There are cultural specifics rooted in the history of every nation that might justify differences in how the democratic principle is applied, but no Arab or Islamic cultural specifics explain the level of civic degeneration with which we Arabs are afflicted today. It is neither an Arab particularity nor an article of the Islamic faith that freedom of speech be suffocated in our national experience, that our people be denied free elections, that our affairs be conducted without the benefit of consensus, and that peaceful political activity be forbidden to our masses. It is neither Arabic nor Islamic that our nation's fate should rest in the hands of a few persons unbound by constitutional restraints.

Some people claim that Arabs are not yet ready for democratic or *shura* governance and that they do not appreciate the democratic principle and values needed to embrace the rule of law, as opposed to the rule of individuals. Such a claim is perverse, unfair, or bad judgment. Any nation that emerged from the civilization of Islam was enjoined to exercise *shura*. Such nations were nurtured with the principles of justice, equality, and human dignity, values which sustain and enhance the human experience. Such nations simply cannot be less qualified to exercise democracy than other nations.

I regard democracy and *shura* as synonymous in conception and principle, although they may differ in details of application to conform to local custom. They reject any government lacking the legitimacy of free elections, accountability, and the people's power, through the constitutional process, to impeach the ruler for violation of trust. The logic of *shura*, like the logic of democracy, does not accept hereditary rule, for wisdom and competence are never the monopoly of any one individual or family. Likewise, *shura* and democracy both reject government by force, for any rule sustained by coercion is illegitimate. Moreover, both forbid privileges—political, social, economic—claimed on the basis of tribal lineage or social prestige.

Shura and democracy are thus one and the same concept. They prod us to find better and better realizations of the principles of justice, equality, and human dignity in our collective socio-political experience. These principles merit implementation in national life across the entire Arab homeland. Let us hope that *shura* or democracy—the choice of terms makes no difference—will find supporters who aspire to a new Arab renaissance.

PART III

Rights of Women

Unveiling and Veiling

Nazira Zein-ed-Din (Ottoman Lebanon, born circa 1905), the daughter of a high-ranking Lebanese judge, was a theological prodigy. In the summer of 1927, as a young woman, she began to research Islamic teachings on the subject of *hijab*, the modest clothing required of Muslim women. She was motivated by the contrast between recent incidents in Syria, where women were prevented from leaving their homes without the veil, and Turkey, where secular reformers encouraged women to remove the veil.[1] Zein-ed-Din published her findings—excerpted here—in 1928, arguing that veiling was anachronistic and that Islam, properly understood, treats women as the equals of men, perhaps even their betters. The book was immediately controversial. Within a year, she had published a follow-up volume containing letters of support and vehement criticism, including the accusation that a young woman could not have written such a work.[2] Zein-ed-Din's subsequent career has been difficult to trace.

Two Views: One View on the Unveiled World and the Other on the Veiled World

Ladies and gentlemen, in the beginning I compared opposites, the numbers of the veiled and the unveiled. I found that the veiled are not more than a few million Muslims living in towns. Those in the villages of the Islamic world and more than 1700 million in other nations are not veiled. They have rejected the veil that they had previously worn. I have noticed that the nations that have given up the veil are the nations that have advanced in intellectual and material life. Such advancement is not equaled in the veiled nations. The unveiled nations are the ones that have discovered through research and study the secrets of nature and have brought the physical elements under their control, as you see and know. But the veiled nations have not unearthed any secret and have not put any of the physical elements under their control but only sing the songs of a glorious past and ancient tradition. With such singing they sleep in stagnation.

I have seen many intellectuals of the nations where women are still veiled advocating unveiling, but I haven't seen anyone in the unveiled nations advocating or preferring the veil. That is, I haven't seen

1. Bouthaina Shaaban, "The Muted Voices of Women Interpreters," in Mahnaz Afkhami, editor, *Faith and Freedom: Women's Human Rights in the Muslim World* (Syracuse, N.Y.: Syracuse University Press, 1995), p. 65.
2. "Biographical Note," *Women's Studies International Forum*, volume 5, number 2, 1982, p. 223.

anyone who has tried unveiling and then has preferred the veil. Even if some Westerner in his hypocritical words makes the veil appear in a favorable light, he is only pleased with the beauty of the Oriental veil while at the same time he would reject the veiling of his mother, wife, sisters, and daughters because of the harm in the veil he favors for others.

I cannot imagine that in the advanced nations which have discovered the secrets of nature and harnessed its powers, which have not let anything pass without examining it to the fullest, where the struggle between right and wrong is continuous until right becomes victorious, nations which have produced works on social subjects we view as masterpieces of literature and sociology, have neglected to study veiling and unveiling to understand the benefits and disadvantages. I cannot think that our own ignorance brings us any greater understanding of what honor is than the unveiled nations possess in learning nor that our conduct is superior to theirs, nor that their women going outside unveiled enjoying their freedom is evidence of their lower conduct and corrupt morals.

Yes, I looked into all that and I could not but consider it evidence of their superior education and elevated conduct. When our esteemed ladies who wear the veil go to a Western country, they take off the veil and the men accompanying them do not prevent them from doing this the way they do when they are at home or after they return. This is because we have more faith in the conduct of Westerners than in our own conduct. The conduct of Westerners has been influenced by mingling with women and thus Western men have based their habits and morals on logic and reason looking to benefits and positive results while our conduct and morals are based on our customs whatever they may be.

I shall never forget a conversation between an Eastern man advocating the veil and an unveiled Western woman who enjoyed her freedom and independence. The Easterner said to the Westerner, "Our nature cannot accept your customs. Our customs are more noble than yours and our men support our women. The man according to his right walks in front of his wife but in your country the woman walks in front of the man as if she were the provider."

The Western woman said, "If you really want to protect your wife please let her go in front of you so that you can watch out for her for the way our men do, rather than letting her walk behind you so that she would misuse her freedom and get hurt."

The Eastern man paused and said, "Truly, Westerners ground their customs in reason. Reason alone should dictate custom."

It is not fitting for us to say that we who are only a few million, most of whom are not advanced, are more honorable than the one and a half billion people (in the world), most of whom are more advanced than we are.

It is not honorable for us to deny our shortcomings and believe we are perfect and claim that our customs are the best customs for every time and place. This conceit and false presumption is a barrier to the reform we seek. When the nation feels its shortcomings, that is the first step in its advancement.

It is inconceivable that we claim to be defenders of honor while the veil is our strongest shield. We must understand as everyone else does that honor is rooted in the heart and chastity comes from within and not from a piece of transparent material lowered over the face.

We have to realize, as the advanced unveiled world does, that good behavior and honor come from sound upbringing grounded in noble principles and virtues. We are shortsighted if we think that the veil keeps evil away from women and that those in the rest of the world exceeding one and a half billion are all in the wrong while we are in the right.

He Who Bears Falsehood to the People Has to Provide Evidence to Them

I have mentioned the above, ladies and gentlemen, fearful that I might be confronted by someone who does not use logic and reasoning to make his points, but relies on untruths concerning the advanced unveiled nations. He may look where vice is but he does not wish to rise up to see where virtue resides. He might have seen their baser women and generalizes from them, subsuming the noble and honorable in his generalization, and hurls accusing arrows of untruths at them even though human beings should not be like flies pouncing on tails (of animals) and ignoring their heads.

He does not dare to lord scientific and industrial knowledge over the unveiled nations because these are tangible matters. Therefore he accuses them of lack of morals and good conduct because these are not tangible. Thus he is overwhelming in this even though his accusation is false.

You know gentlemen, nations are like trees whose rotten fruits fall to the ground and vermin, humans and animals go after them. Those who are wise and advanced look only to the good and ripe fruits, by which the tree is identified.

My antagonist seems to be ignorant of that or is playing the role of the ignorant. He wants to know the tree by the fallen fruits he sees beneath it. Moreover, he does not want to recognize that in every nation, however advanced, there is a lower class overcome by corruption whose morals and conduct have deteriorated because they did not have the chance to be educated and to develop so that they could reach the higher level in the nation.

Gentlemen, we should do our best to see to it that the majority in our nation are able to have an education and the means to develop. Then it would be possible for us to be proud before our nations. . . .

We should not believe everything we hear and take our evidence from falsehood, especially evidence that brings great evil to the nation by obstructing reform and maintaining continual backwardness.

We should abstain from hurling lies and falsehoods at others, which is alien to morality and decent debate and only brings down those who lie. Instead we should subscribe to truth, sound reasoning, unbiased knowledge, and correct behavior. In accordance with the will of God Almighty and the will of His Prophet, may God bless him. . . .

How Men Should Support Women

Gentlemen, you have heard the response of the Western woman to the Eastern man who was proud to support his woman and to walk in front of her. Yes, let men support women in principle. Every man supports his own wife spending money on her, but he has no authority over any other woman. A verse from the Qur'an was sent by God about this in relation to Sa'd ibn al-Rabi from al-Naqba and his wife Habiba; the words are related specifically to husband and wife. Men should know that authority is limited by the benefit deriving from it. Therefore, men should attain high moral development as God wants and society requires. This would make women strong and self-dependent, for when people have virtue, dignity, and honor they turn away from evil, not out of fear of punishment, nor because of reward, nor because of an immovable obstacle, but because evil is ugly

and such a person would not allow herself to engage in lowly acts.

The Prophet, God bless him, said, "I was sent to help you attain the highest morality." Does not the highest morality come from the soul? Pieces of cloth over faces shall never be a measure of morality.

The Veil (Niqab) Is an Insult to Men and Women

It is not beneficial to men and women that men should just support women physically and financially, nor is it beneficial that man rule over those whom the shari'a [Islamic law] did not give him the right. It greatly harms the two sexes that every man continues to insult his mother, daughter, wife, and sister, suspiciously accusing them of bad morals and keeping them confined to a cage, as the venerable Qasim Amin [Egypt, 1865–1908] said, "With their wings cut off, heads bent down, and eyes closed. For him (man) is freedom and for them (women) enslavement. For him is education and for them ignorance. For him is sound reasoning and for them inferior reasoning. For him is light and open space and for them darkness and imprisonment. For him are orders and for them obedience and patience. For him is everything in the universe and for them part of the whole he has captured."

May God be merciful to Qasim and bless his pen, about which "The Poet of the Two Countries" has said, "He tears down the ugly and builds the beautiful, returning to the sunna [the practices of the Prophet] of the Drawer. He sheds light even when he writes with the dark water of the night."

Unfortunately, if the veil (hijab) implies the inability of the woman to protect herself without it, it also reveals that man, however well brought up and in spite of supporting the woman, is a traitor and a thief of honor; his evil should be feared and it is better that the woman escapes from him.

You, Man, the Supporter

If some women, because of the ignorance into which you have cast them, have not recognized the insult to them and to men by the veil, is it easy for you, the man who has kept himself free seeking perfection and good conduct, to bear this insult that comes to you and to your mother, daughter, wife, and sister?

Does the woman who escapes from you, or approaches you lowering the veil over her face, or turns her back on you, confirm your high status, as she might think and say and you might think and say, or is it a great insult? Does this constitute the woman's decorum, chastity and modesty? If so, then men should not be without these precious attributes; let them wear veils and let them meet each other and meet women lowering veils over their faces the way women do. . . .

On Man's Superiority in His Rights to Inheritance, Legal Testimony, Polygamy, and Arbitrariness in Divorce as Evidence Not to His Advantage but against Him

I noticed in some of the articles written against women and their liberation, as well as against their removal of the veil, that the authors boast of the fact that in his Holy Qur'an, God favored men over women—mind and soul—in three different matters:

First, God made a woman entitled to inherit only half of what a man inherits.

Second, God considers her testimony (legally) worth only half of his.

Third, He, the Almighty, allowed a man to marry up to four wives and divorce them at will, without their consent.

The authors of these articles conclude from this that the woman is mentally and spiritually inferior. Hence they think that God, the Almighty, decided to favor a man over a woman in these three areas. But as far as I am concerned, I conclude otherwise. I understand the argument to be against men rather than in their favor.

Indeed, I examine Islam through the greatest words of God and the sayings of His Prophet. I then see God enthroned in greatness, freedom, equality, justice, goodness, and perfection. I become so overwhelmed and so elated that I feel my soul about to leave my body. I only wish that those who pretend to protect Islam and raise its banners would look in the same way as I do and see what I see. I wish they did not look at Islam through the narrow vision of commentaries and interpretations which interpret Islam in ways they want to see it. Islam is far beyond that. It is much greater.

God's permissibility only showed man's cruel heart, his inability to submit to truth and justice, and his immoral character, acquired from the worst pre-Islamic customs. Such a character, as is well known, is in contradiction with the nature of noble human mentality.

Man subjected to slavery those he deemed weak among women as among men, treating them according to his whims like merchandise or cattle. Had it not been for the viciousness in his mind, his misguided soul and cruel heart, God would not have granted him then such allowances that He disliked and which were meant to vanish with time.

We have thus far seen [in earlier sections of the author's book] what the woman's condition was, under the yoke of man throughout the world in general and in pre-Islamic Arabia in particular, just before the Qur'an was revealed to our Prophet, God bless him and grant him salvation.

God dislikes slavery. He dislikes polygamy and any violation of women's rights. God loathes divorce. His divine throne shakes every time the word is uttered on earth, as I will explain in detail below in a discussion of divorce [not included in this excerpt].

God revealed His holy message all filled with the spirit of freedom, justice and equality among people. He does not differentiate between them for His esteem, except on the basis of their faith in Him. How would then the Almighty condone the enslavement of His human creation in whom He instilled life, and for whom He ordered angels to bow in honor and respect? Did God, we might ask, instill life in the strong who take others into slavery but not in the weak who are enslaved by others? Of course not! God gave life to all. Yet, since the days of Adam, peace be upon him, man has disobeyed God and gone astray.

If Adam himself, who was a prophet, "disobeyed God's order and went astray," what of his male offspring who have realized their strength and became misguided by it? In their arrogant ways, they took into slavery whoever they saw as weak.

God sent His Prophet, peace and salvation be upon him, to mankind in that corrupt land of ignorance. He warned him in these holy words: "If you were rude and arrogant, people would desert you." And as goes one of the Prophet's own sayings: "Teach others, be lenient not harsh, preach but do not alienate anyone."

In his book *Al-Islam ruh al-madaniyya* [*Islam, The Spirit of Civilization*], Shaykh [Mustafa] Al-Ghalayini [Ottoman Empire-Lebanon, 1886–1945] wrote: "It was considered wise in Islam not to totally abolish some of the reprehensible traditions such as polygamy, as there were so many difficulties involved." He also went on to say: "Slavery and harsh treatment of captives are odious acts by Islamic standards. Slavery was considered inherited from the era of savageness. Politically, however, it was not ruled absolutely forbidden in those days." In fact if all those customs had been entirely abolished by God, several problems would have ensued. The least of these is that men would have broken away from God's religion and deserted His Prophet. Moreover, not many of His commandments would have been obeyed.

In pre-Islamic Arabia, women as well as male slaves were under the domination of financially powerful men who owned them and enjoyed them at will. These materialistic men used to get as infatuated with their wealth as they were with themselves. A man in those days would own as many as one hundred women and a large number of male slaves. Like property or cattle they were inherited as a part of an estate. How can we then take it for granted that they could be set free from man's ownership and made equal to him in every way, at the same time, and not in a gradual fashion? God said in the Holy Qur'an, "And if We willed it for them to either kill themselves or leave their land, only a few of them would." [Sura 4, Verse 66] Thus it was out of God's wisdom to eliminate some of these reprehensible customs, while leaving traces of them to turn men's attention to Him so they would not give up His religion and abandon His Prophet.

As for a woman's legal testimony, should the fact that it is considered worth only half of that of a man's be grounds for women's mental inferiority? If so, a non-Muslim's legal testimony for or against a Muslim is not accepted; can that also be considered evidence for non-Muslims' mental inferiority? Or was it rather a decision resulting from some unusual circumstances in those days?

In the final analysis, it was no other than God's kindness to the woman to consider her testimony worth half that of a man's. The latter interpreted it as a privilege and became satisfied with it. In reality, legal testimony is no other than a bothersome obligation. It is as if God wanted to reassure men and relieve women from such an obligation at the same time. It seems as if testimony were expressly ruled outside a woman's competence, so that only men would be called upon to testify in courts. There is no reason to believe that God decided that because of a deficiency in the woman's faith or intelligence. Women possess a great deal of goodness and spiritual righteousness, and as the Prophet's saying goes, "One good woman is better than a thousand improper men."

Through God's wisdom, the persistence of a few traces of those bad customs is a way of soothing the minds of those who practice them. His wisdom is revealed in several ways and verses. In the tradition of His Prophet, God bless him and grant him salvation, there is proof that the dangers in the persistence of such traces of vile traditions are removed. Thus their impact is reduced and they become acceptable rather than offensive.

God knew that people with insight would erase all traces of reprehensible customs, following this way the wisdom implied by those Qur'anic verses and Prophet's teachings. God was indeed aware that such wisdom was not unknown to His people. Hence he allowed the taking of slaves but was eager for their freedom, in the same way that He was yearning to abolish polygamy and end discrimination between men and women in their rights. This is one of the interpretations suggested by the famous scholar Muhammad 'Abduh [Egypt, 1849–1905].

Below however is another quotation from [Muhammad] Jamil Bayhum [Lebanon, 1887–1978], the author of *Al-Mar'a fi al-tarikh wa al-shara'i'* [*Woman in History and Religious Legal Systems*]:

> Some commentators have interpreted these opinions as implying a ban on polygamy, because allowing it must depend on fairness in treatment while such indiscriminate justice is highly improbable. But this is in no way an uncommon interpretation as long as laws are subject to considerations of culture and civilization. Just as Christians were somehow able to discover that their religion prohibits polygamy, when it actually did not object to it, it would be easy for Muslims to enact legislation forbidding polygamy, in appreciation of the general world condition, progress and the advancement of women.

Indeed that would be easier for Muslims than making laws condoning all the vile sins such as drinking alcohol, prostitution, usury and idolatry, or disapproving of some of God's ordinances like stoning, requital or other legal punishments. Such laws are constantly being enacted.

Don't you see that slavery was discontinued in Islamic countries like everywhere else and that punishment is administered to whoever engages in it? Don't you see that polygamy has become considered evil by enlightened communities around us, and that the great independent Islamic nation of Turkey has banned it and reserves for it the harshest of punishments?

Don't you see that, through government laws, Islamic countries have made a woman's legal testimony equal to a man's both in witnessing legal punishment as well as in other cases? They gave her equal right for inheriting land, and in Turkey, a woman's right is equal to that of a man for testimony in all cases and transactions, and in inheritance for any kind of property.

By enacting laws to eliminate those vile traditions, the Islamic governments were not in contradiction with God's message and the teachings of His Prophet. Those governments understood the reasoning behind those teachings. They abolished slavery and ended any discrimination between man and woman. Not only did they interpret the surface meanings of those Qur'anic verses and Prophet's teaching; but also they interpreted their essence in depth in the manner of people with insight and reason.

This is indeed an important and broad subject. To cover it with a presentation of convincing evidence would require lengthy explications that are beyond the scope of my present lecture series. God willing, I shall deal with it in a special lecture.

Nevertheless, I think that we should realize right now the reason which led to the persistence of those reprehensible customs and why they had such an impact on the absolute equality of man and woman and amongst men (as slaves and free men). Perhaps that reason is man's cruelty, his error, arbitrariness, and the evil side in his character prevailing over the good side. That is what led God's wisdom, to permit something reprehensible that He never condoned as fair and just.

Right now, we must realize that this reason for that has nothing to do with a woman's faith or her intelligence. In no way was the inequality between a helpless slave and a powerful free man a result of mental or spiritual deficiency so that inequality between man and woman in the matters mentioned should result from her mental and spiritual deficiency.

If God had truly condoned slavery, polygamy and inequality between man and woman, He would not have made the man accountable for expenditures for the woman's dowry, her support and that of her children's which are equal or greater than what she misses in inheritance. If so, indeed, God would not have established laws leading to the disappearance of slavery and the avoidance of polygamy; and His Prophet would not have preferred females over males in several matters. In fact, here are some of his sayings:

> When you give to your children, be fair in your giving and give equally. If I personally had a preference to make (in giving to my own), I would prefer giving to my daughters.

> Whoever goes to market and buys something to bring back home, especially for the females in his family, will enjoy God's care, and whoever is in God's care will be protected from all suffering.

> Purchasing a choice gift for members of your family is like giving charity. Priority should go to the females, because bringing joy to a female is like crying humbly in fear and respect of God and whoever cries in fear of God will be spared from the fires of Hell.

Therefore if females were deficient in mind and in faith, they would not be worthy of such preferential thoughts by the Prophet of God. He is much beyond preferring stupidity over intelligence, and a lack of faith over an abundance of it. He once also said, "Fear God in your treatment of the weak, slaves and women."

As for this last piece of advice given by the Prophet of God, we must stand facing Mecca, humbly and in reverence, in order to hear it. He uttered it from his death bed, at a time he was in distress, because he had not completely removed all of the differences between the slaves and the free, and between men and women. He uttered the following final words, his voice stammering, until his very last word:

> Prayer . . . Prayer . . . If any slaves are in your possession, do not burden them with what they are unable to do. God. God . . . of Women. They are in your hands. . . . You took them with God's trust.

He uttered these words and passed away. Peace be upon you, o Prophet of God, peace be upon you, o beloved of God. Peace be upon you, Lord of the first and last prophets. Peace be upon you the day you were born, the day you died, and the day you will be resurrected.

Politics and the Muslim Woman

Benazir Bhutto (Pakistan, born 1953), twice prime minister of Pakistan (1988–1990 and 1993–1996), is known more for her political activities than for her religious scholarship. Following the overthrow and execution of her father, Prime Minister Zulfikar Ali Bhutto, Benazir Bhutto adopted the leadership of his Pakistani People's Party and opposed the Islamic regime of General Zia-ul-Haq. She spent years in jail, under house arrest, and in exile. As a political leader in an Islamic country, Bhutto has naturally been sensitive to charges that Islam prohibits women from holding such positions.[1] In the speech excerpted here, from her period of exile, she argues that Islamic law does not treat women as inferior to men or incapable of leadership.[2]

I think one of the first things that we must appreciate about the religion of Islam is that there is no one interpretation to it. Islam has certain religious aspects and has some aspects which relate to relations between man and man in society. Just as we have different religious sects in Islam, upholding different religious views—whether it is the Shi'is, the Sunnis, the Malakis, the Hanafis, the Barelwis[3]—so, too, we have different interpretations with regard to the more secular aspects of the duties incumbent upon the Muslim.

I would describe Islam in two main categories: reactionary Islam and progressive Islam. We can have a reactionary interpretation of Islam which tries to uphold the status quo, or we can have a progressive interpretation of Islam which tries to move with a changing world, which believes in human dignity, which believes in consensus, and which believes in giving women their due right.

I know that some authors have speculated that women in Islamic countries can never achieve self-actualization or a degree of assertiveness unless they look at this from a non-Islamic point of view. I don't agree with that at all. I believe that Islam within it provides justice and equality for women, and I think that those aspects of Islam which have been highlighted by the *mullas* [religious scholars] do not do a service to our religion. When I use the term *mullas*,

1. Benazir Bhutto, *Daughter of Destiny* (New York: Simon and Schuster, 1989), pp. 368, 392.

2. See also Benazir Bhutto, "The Fight for the Liberation of Women" (Remarks at the Fourth United Nations Conference on Women, Beijing, China, September 4, 1995), *Women's Studies Quarterly*, volume 24, numbers 1–2, Spring-Summer 1996, pp. 91–97.

3. [This list includes the two largest sects of Islam, Sunnism and Shi'ism; two schools of thought within Sunnism, the Hanafis and the Malakis; and a revivalist sect founded in northern India in the late nineteenth century, the Barelwis.—Editor]

please don't try to think of them in the same terms as the clergy. Christianity has a clergy. Islam does not have a clergy. The relationship between a Muslim and God is direct. There is no need for somebody to intervene. The *mulla*s try to intervene. The *mulla*s give their own interpretation. But I think there are growing movements, as more and more people in Muslim countries, both men and women, achieve education and begin to examine the Qur'an in the light of their education, they are beginning not to agree with the *mulla*s on their orthodox or reactionary version of Islam.

Let us start with the story of the Fall. Unlike Christianity, it is not Eve who tempts Adam into tasting the apple and being responsible for original sin. According to Islam—and I mention this because I believe that Islam is an egalitarian religion—both Adam and Eve are tempted, both are warned, both do not heed the warning, and therefore the Fall occurs.

As far as opportunity is concerned, in Islam there is equal opportunity for both men and women. I refer to the Sura *Ya Sin* [Sura 36, Verses 34–35], which says: "We produce orchids and date gardens and vines, and we cause springs to gush forth, that they may enjoy the fruits of it." God does not give fruits, orchids, or the fruit of the soil just for men to enjoy or men to plow; he gives it for both men and women. What, in terms of income and opportunity, is available, is available to both man and woman. Sura *an-Nisa* [Sura 4, Verse 32]: "To men is allotted what they earn, and to women what they earn."

As regards the law of inheritance, some scholars make a great degree of the fact that inheritance law gives twice the amount to a son, and half the amount to a daughter [Sura 4, Verse 11]. Well, maybe if you look at it in isolation, but not if you look at it in the whole aspect, because it is made abundantly clear that the woman's share is for the use of the woman alone. A man gets two-thirds. One-third—the equivalent of the woman's—is for his own use. The addition one-third that a man gets is to provide provision for his wife and children. This is the obligation on the man. He gets that extra share so that he can provide for the family, the wife and the children. The wife is not responsible for the welfare of the husband, nor is she responsible for the welfare of the children. The wife is not even responsible for suckling her own child. If she chooses not to suckle her child, she does not have to. If she chooses to suckle her child, it is for the husband to provide her with the provisions. . . .

But when it is the case, for instance, of parents, then the Qur'an says, "For parents, a sixth share of the inheritance to each if the deceased left children." [Sura 4, Verse 11] It does not say that the father must get double and the woman must get half. . . . It goes on again to make an equal application when it says, "If the man or woman, who has left neither ascendants nor descendants, but has left a brother and a sister, each one of the two gets a sixth. If more than two brothers and sisters, they shall share [one third of the estate after payment of legacies and debts]." [Sura 4, Verse 12] . . . On the whole, the Qur'an proves that it has a balanced outlook whether it refers to men or to women.

As far as forgiveness and reward are concerned, similar conditions are set down for both men and for women. I refer to Sura "The Clan" [Sura 33, Verse 35]: "Men who surrender unto God, and women who surrender, and men who believe, and women who believe, and men who speak the truth, and women who speak the truth, and men who persevere in righteousness, and women who persevere, and men who are humble, and women who are humble, and men who give alms, and women who give alms, and men who fast, and women who fast, and men who guard their modesty, and women who guard their modesty, and men who remember God much, and women who remember, God has prepared for them forgiveness and a vast reward." There are no special considerations set out for the male sex to show that in the eyes of God they are deserving of special considerations.

In Sura "Repentance" [Sura 9, Verse 71], again emphasis is laid on equal advice to men and women: "The believing man and the believing woman, all loyalty to one another, they enjoin noble deeds and forbid dishonor. They perform prayer and say the alms, and obey God and His Messenger. On them will God have mercy." If it is a matter of entering paradise, again Sura Luqman [Sura 31, Verse 8] says: "If any do righteousness"—be they male or female—"and have faith, they will enter paradise." As regards theft, if you look at the Sura "Tablespread" [Sura 5, Verse 38]: "As for the thief, both male and female, cut off their hand."

Now this doesn't have to do with Muslim women, but I would like to add at this juncture that within Islam there are two kinds of interpretations: One is the rigid interpretation, and one is a conceptual interpretation. Thus, in the rigid or *mulla*-istic sense, "Cut off their hand" would mean "Cut off their hand" even today. But in the conceptual analysis of Islam, "Cut off their hand" would mean "Adopt those means which will prevent thievery occurring again." And again, these means may change with the advance of society. It may involve psychiatric help, it may involve having them kept in a separate home, but the main idea is whether you look at it rigidly, "Cut off their hand," or whether you look at it conceptually, "Do not provide the means for them to do that theft again."

When it is adultery, again: "The adulterer and adulteress, give them a hundred stripes." [Sura 24, Verse 2] That is Sura "Light." Again I would say that there is the rigid interpretation and the conceptual interpretation, and I think that most progressive Muslims believe in the conceptual interpretation because they believe Islam is a dynamic religion for all times and ages.

In behavior toward parents, in the Sura "Israelites" [Sura 17, Verses 23–24] it again says, "Be kind to parents [. . .] and out of kindness lower to them the wing of humility and say, 'My Lord, bestow on them your mercy, even as they cherished me in childhood.'" The reference is both to men and women. And that is the predominant theme of the Qur'an. The references are to men and women. The references are not to men as being characteristic of certain qualities and separate qualities for women. It is not a reference to the male sex as being endowed with some superior attributes and to the woman as being endowed with inferior attributes. The attributes are the same. Both are the creatures of God. Both have certain rights. Both have certain duties. Both have certain obligations. If they want to go to Heaven, they have to behave in a special manner. If they want to do good in this earth, they have to give alms to the needy, they have to help orphans—the behavior is applicable to both men and women. It is not religion which makes the difference. The difference comes from man-made law. It comes from the fact that soon after the Prophet died, it was not the Islam of the Prophet that remained. What took place was the emergence or the reassertiveness of the patriarchal society, and religion was taken over to justify the norms of the tribal society, rather than the point that the Prophet had made in replacing the tribal society with a religion that aimed to cut across narrow loyalties and sought to create a new community, or *umma*, on the basis of Islam and the message of God.

Now there are certain interpretations within the Qur'an Sharif [the Holy Qur'an] which are extremely ambiguous. Some people interpret them in favor of the conservatives; some people interpret them in favor of the reactionaries. One of these occurs in Sura "The Romans" [Sura 30, Verse 21]: "He created from you help-mates from your self that you might find rest in them." This is an interpretation that progressives will give: Because it says, "He created from you," it does not say, "He created from men." "He created from you" means He created from mankind, or the human race, help-mates. But then other interpretations are given which claim what it said is, God created out of you, out of man, mates that you might find rest in them. And the conservatives use this to say that women were created for men to find rest. Or rather, that they were created to be in the service of man rather than being equal to man.

Arabic is a very complex language. It is a language that many Muslims don't even understand, because Islam is not only in the Arab countries, but has spread far and beyond. These scholars and these *mulla*s usually argue on these points. One *mulla* will say that God created women for rest and therefore women are to be used by men. Another one will say no, He created them from amongst yourself. So it depends very much on the matter of interpretation. But which way should interpretation go? Should it go against the basic grain of the entire message of the religion, or should it be in consonance with the basic message of that religion? When the basic message of Islam was for justice and for equality, when it came as a religion to liberate mankind from superstition and ignorance, to provide education and improvements, then I think it is quite clear for modern Islamic thinkers that it is a religion which did not provide for discrimination and ought to be interpreted in the light of its main thematic message, rather than to make ambiguous statements go against the basic theme of the message.

There are many other aspects of Islam which are taken up, again, to provide controversy on whether men and women are equal or not. One of these is the law of evidence. Now the law of evidence: in one specific part of the Qur'an, it is said that if you are going to take a loan or a debt, two men are needed or four women. Now this "two men are needed or four women" has been changed by certain societies, including Pakistan under the present military ruler [Mohammad Zia-ul-Haq, 1924–1988], to mean that the worth of a woman is half that of a man, and that if a woman is killed, compensation will be paid that is half that of a man; and if in a court of law there is evidence, then the woman's evidence will be worth half that of the man. There is no justification for this whatsoever because if the evidence of a woman is worth half that of a man, it would have been clearly stated in the Qur'an. It would not have been related to debts or loans, it would have said that in matters pertaining to legal affairs the evidence of a woman will be half that of a man, or it would have said that in the matter of murder the compensation will be half that of a man. Instead, in terms of compensation, the Qur'an Sharif goes on to say that if you can have retributions, a slave for a slave, a free man for a free man, a woman for a woman, or if the parties agree, they can come to an agreement on blood money or they can set a slave free [Sura 4, Verse 92]. Now the Qur'an says, "set a slave free." It doesn't say that if a woman is murdered set half a slave free. The Qur'an itself makes no distinction at all. It is man and it is the *mulla*s who claim to be the clergy of Islam—and no clergy exist in Islam—who make these discriminations and who give the wrong impression of our religion not only to the outside world but to Muslims ourselves.

The law of evidence, which some Muslim countries following reactionary paths have adopted, conveniently forgets that the first witness to Islam was a woman, and that was the Prophet's wife, Khadija [died 619]. The only witness to the martyrdom of the third caliph 'Uthman [reigned 644–656] was his wife, Nila. So when women themselves have been accepted in early Islam as sole witnesses, then what right do those people have, who come much later, to declare that women are worth only half a man's evidence and that if they are killed, their compensation should be half.

The other aspect that is pointed out that women are discriminated against is the question of inheritance, which I have already dealt with. I don't think I'll say more on that.

The third is the right of divorce and polygamy. It is often said that Islam provides for four wives for a man. But in my interpretation of this, and in the interpretation of many other Muslims, that is simply not true.

What the Qur'an does say, and I quote: "Marry as many women as you wish, wives two or three or four. If you fear not to treat them equally, marry only

one. [. . .] I doubt you will be able to be just between your wives, even if you try." [Sura 4, Verses 3 and 129] So if God Himself and His message says that He doubts that you can be equal, I don't know how any man can turn around and say that "God has given me this right to get married more than once."

. . . The Prophet Muhammad, throughout the life of his first wife, Khadija, never married again. The Prophet's son-in-law, and who was more or less like an adopted son, *Hazrat* 'Ali [circa 596–661], during the lifetime of his first wife, *Bibi* [Madame] Fatima [circa 605–633], never married more than once. The marriages that took place later were more out of necessity of warfare, widows, or even of tribal connections. Thus to say that a man could be allowed to marry four times, at will, is not something that you can find a strong argument for in the Qur'an.

And if you look at Muslim society, it is not often that the vast Muslim population goes on marrying two, three, four [wives]. It is something that is related just to the privileged class. They can afford to do that. And they didn't, as the caliphate ruled and the Muslim empire ruled, they didn't just marry two, three, or four women, they went on to keep harems with hundreds of concubines. None of that had anything to do with Islam, either.

A woman in Islam, when she marries, does not take her husband's name. That is again something that has come about more as a matter of exposure to other customs or traditions. A woman in Islam is an identity in her own right. She is not an extension first of her father and then an extension of her husband. She asserts herself from the moment she is born; she is a person with the characteristics she develops, and she keeps her own name. The ideal of identity is just being appreciated in the West, where many people are beginning to keep their own name.

Aside from these provisions from the Qur'an Sharif, which I have been drawing your attention to, I would like to say that within Islamic history there are very strong roles for women. For instance, the Prophet's wife, Bibi Khadija, was a woman of independent means. She had her own business, she traded, she dealt with society at large, she employed the Prophet Muhammad, peace be upon him, when he was a young boy, and subsequently, Bibi Khadija herself sent a proposal [of marriage] to the Prophet. So she is the very image of somebody who is independent, assertive, and does not conform to the passive description of women in Muslim societies that we have grown accustomed to hearing about. Bibi Khadija was fifteen years older than the Prophet, and she was also known, not only as the wife of the Prophet, but as the Mother of all believers.

Bibi Khadija is a symbol, one can say, for all the sects of Islam. Within the two major sects of Shi'ism and Sunnism, both sects provide for [other] powerful role models for women. The Shi'ite sect provides for Bibi Fatima, the daughter of the Prophet, who from a very small age saw the humiliation that her father faced in spreading his message. When he was taunted, when things were thrown at him, it was Bibi Fatima who was by his side. When they had to face confinement and exile, she, along with her mother, was with him. Hers is a figure of endurance. It is not only a figure of endurance, but after the death of the Prophet, hers is also a figure fighting politically for what she considers is her usurped right—usurpation in terms of the caliphate going to Abu Bakr [reigned 632–634] instead of going to Hazrat 'Ali, and also usurpation in what she considers to be her property seized unlawfully by the caliphate. So she is a woman who does not accept what has happened to her after the death of the Prophet. She goes to the Helpers, she speaks to them of her plight, and she adopts a political role until her death.

Within the Sunni version there is Bibi 'A'isha [wife of the Prophet, circa 614–678], who is also put forward as a politically astute woman, who, after the death of the Prophet, was responsible for many of the Traditions that have been handed down to us, who was the one who proposed the caliphate of Hazrat 'Uthman, and held out the shirt of the Prophet Muhammad, and said that, "Even before this shirt has decayed, you have to ordain someone like Hazrat 'Uthman." She made her views known. She was an extremely bold person. Not only did she make her views known; when she opposed

something, she went to the battlefield and fought against it.

So when we have such powerful role models of women—of the mother, Bibi Khadija; of the daughter, Bibi Fatima; of the wife, Bibi 'A'isha—then one must ask, why is it that today in Muslim countries, one does not see that much of women? One does not hear that much of women. Why is it that women are secluded? Why is it that women are subject to social control? Why is that women are not given their due share of property? . . . It has got nothing to do with the religion, but it has got very much to do with material or man-made considerations. . . .

I have tried to show you Islam as being a very liberal religion toward women, as giving women their own identity, giving women the right to choose their husbands: If they are not happy with their spouse they don't have to keep him. When the divorce law [the nuptial agreement between a man and woman] is written, it is a contract of how you live together; you can write in that contract that "I want the right to divorce you"; you can write in that contract that "in the event of divorce I want to be maintained according to the style that I am accustomed to."

All these considerations are there, and yet women are backward, and they are backward not because Islam has made them backward, but because the societies that they live in are societies which have upheld the privileged class and which have subsisted on a policy of discrimination against a wide segment of the population. . . .

Before I conclude on this aspect of the powerful role within Islam of women, I would like to quote from the Qur'an, the Sura "The Ant" [Sura 27, Verse 23]: "I found a woman ruling over them, and she has been given abundance of all things, and hers is a mighty throne." It is not Islam which is averse to women rulers, I think—it is men.

13

A Feminist Interpretation of Women's Rights in Islam

Fatima Mernissi (Morocco, born 1940), "one of the best known Arab-Muslim feminists," was part of the first generation of Moroccan women to be granted access to higher education. She studied at the Mohammed V University in Rabat and went on to receive her doctorate in sociology in the United States in 1973. She returned to Morocco to teach at her alma mater and currently works at a research institute in Rabat. "She is a recognized public figure in her own country," and her work has been translated into several European languages.[1] According to a fellow academic, Mernissi is the first Muslim woman in the Middle East to succeed "in extricating herself from the issue of cultural loyalty and betrayal" that plagues so many Muslim feminists torn between their double identities.[2] According to a fellow African Muslim, Mernissi represents "the aspirations of women who, while remaining Muslims, wish to live in modernity."[3] One of the recurring themes of Mernissi's work is the mistreatment of women in Islamic societies. In this excerpt, Mernissi argues that the Qur'an and other Islamic sources have been systematically mis-interpreted on the subject of the position of women.

"Can a woman be a leader of Muslims?" I asked my grocer, who, like most grocers in Morocco, is a true "barometer" of public opinion.

"I take refuge in God!" he exclaimed, shocked, despite the friendly relations between us. Aghast at the idea, he almost dropped the half-dozen eggs I had come to buy.

"May God protect us from the catastrophes of the times!" mumbled a customer who was buying olives, as he made as if to spit. My grocer is a fanatic about cleanliness, and not even denouncing a heresy justi-fies dirtying the floor in his view.

A second customer, a schoolteacher whom I vaguely knew from the newsstand, stood slowly ca-ressing his wet mint leaves, and then hit me with a

1. Amal Rassam, "Mernissi, Fatima," in John L. Esposito, editor, *The Oxford Encyclopedia of the Modern Islamic World* (New York: Oxford University Press, 1995), volume 3, pp. 93–94.

2. Leila Ahmad, "Feminism and Feminist Movements in the Middle East," *Women's Studies International Forum*, volume 5, number 2, 1982, pp. 153–168.

3. Fatoumata Sow, "*Le Harem Politique*" (The Political Harem), in *Fippu, Journal de Yewwu Yewwi pour la libération des femmes* (*Fight Back, Journal of "Liberation through Con-sciousness" for the Liberation of Women*) (Dakar, Senegal), number 2, April 1989, p. 33.

hadith [tradition of the Prophet] that he knew would be fatal: "Those who entrust their affairs to a woman will never know prosperity!" Silence fell on the scene. There was nothing I could say. In a Muslim theocracy, a *hadith* is no small matter. The *hadith* collections are works that record in minute detail what the Prophet said and did. They constitute, along with the Qur'an (the book revealed by God), both the source of law and the standard for distinguishing the true from the false, the permitted from the forbidden—they have shaped Muslim ethics and values.

I discreetly left the grocery store without another word. What could I have said to counterbalance the force of that political aphorism, which is as implacable as it is popular?

Silenced, defeated, and furious, I suddenly felt the urgent need to inform myself about this *hadith* and to search out the texts where it is mentioned, to understand better its extraordinary power over the ordinary citizens of a modern state.

A glance at the latest Moroccan election statistics supports the "prediction" uttered in the grocery store. Although the constitution gives women the right to vote and be elected, political reality grants them only the former. In the legislative elections of 1977, the eight women who stood for election found no favor with the six and a half million voters, of whom three million were women. At the opening of Parliament, there was not one woman present, and the men were settled among their male peers as usual, just as in the cafes. Six years later, in the municipal elections of 1983, 307 women were bold enough to stand as candidates, and almost three and a half million women voters went to the polls. Only 36 women won election, as against 65,502 men![4]

To interpret the relationship between the massive participation of women voters and the small number of women elected as a sign of stagnation and backwardness would be in accordance with the usual stereotypes applied to the Arab world. However, it would be more insightful to see it as a reflection of changing times and the intensity of the conflicts between the aspirations of women, who take the constitution of their country seriously, and the resistance of men, who imagine, despite the laws in force, that

power is necessarily male. This makes me want to shed light on those obscure zones of resistance, those entrenched attitudes, in order to understand the symbolic—even explosive—significance of that act which elsewhere in the world is an ordinary event: a woman's vote. For this reason, my misadventure in a neighborhood grocery store had more than symbolic importance for me. Revealing the misogynistic attitude of my neighbors, it indicated to me the path I should follow to better understand it—a study of the religious texts that everybody knows but no one really probes, with the exception of the authorities on the subject: the *mulla*s [religious scholars] and *imam*s [prayer leaders].

Going through the religious literature is no small task. First of all, one is overwhelmed by the number of volumes, and one immediately understands why the average Muslim can never know as much as an *imam*. [Muhammad ibn Isma'il] Al-Bukhari's [810–870] prestigious collection of traditions, *Al-Sahih* (*The Authentic*), is in four volumes with an abstruse commentary by one [Muhammad ibn 'Abd al-Hadi] al-Sindi [died 1726], who is extremely sparing with his comments.[5] Now, without a very good commentary a non-expert will have difficulty reading a religious text of the ninth century. . . . This is because, for each *hadith*, it is necessary to check the identity of the Companion of the Prophet who uttered it, and in what circumstances and with what objective in mind, as well as the chain of people who passed it along—and there are more fraudulent traditions than authentic ones. For each *hadith*, al-Bukhari gives the results of his investigation. If he speaks of X or Y, you have to check which Companion is being referred to, what battle is being discussed, in order to make sense of the dialogue or scene that is being transcribed. In addition, al-Bukhari doesn't use just one informant; there are dozens of them in the dozens of volumes. You must be careful not to go astray. The smallest mistake about the informant can cost you months of work.

What is the best way of making this check? First of all, you should make contact with the experts in religious science (*faqih*s) in your city. According to moral teaching and the traditional conventions, if

4. Morocco, Ministère de l'Artisanat et des Affaires Sociales, *Les Femmes marocaines dans le développement économique et social, décennie 1975–1985* [*Moroccan Women in Social and Economic Development, the Decade 1975–1985*].

5. Al-Bukhari, *Al-Sahih* (*Collection of Authentic Hadiths*), with commentary by al-Sindi (Beirut, Lebanon: Dar al-Ma'rifa, 1978). The *hadith* quoted by the schoolteacher is in volume 4, p. 226.

you contact a *faqih* for information about the sources of a *hadith* or a Qur'anic verse, he must assist you. Knowledge is to be shared, according to the promise of the Prophet himself. *Fath al-bari* by [Ibn Hajar] al-'Asqalani (he died in year 852 of the *hejira* [1372–1449 A.D.]) was recommended to me by several people I consulted. It consists of 17 volumes that one can consult in libraries during their opening hours. But the vastness of the task and the rather limited reading time is enough to discourage most researchers.

The schoolteacher in the grocery store was right: the *hadith* "those who entrust their affairs to a woman will never know prosperity" was there in al-'Asqalani's 13th volume, where he quotes al-Bukhari's *Sahih*, that is, those traditions that al-Bukhari classified as authentic after a rigorous process of selection, verifications, and counter-verifications.[6] Al-Bukhari's work has been one of the most highly respected references for 12 centuries. This *hadith* is the sledgehammer argument used by those who want to exclude women from politics. One also finds it in the work of other authorities known for their scholarly rigor, such as Ahmad ibn Hanbal [780–855], the author of the *Musnad* and founder of the Hanbali school, one of the four great schools of jurisprudence of the Sunni Muslim world.[7]

This *hadith* is so important that it is practically impossible to discuss the question of women's political rights without referring to it, debating it, and taking a position on it. . . .

According to al-Bukhari, it is supposed to have been Abu Bakra [died circa 671] who heard the Prophet say: "Those who entrust their affairs to a woman will never know prosperity." Since this *hadith* is included in the *Sahih*—those thousands of authentic *hadith* accepted by the meticulous al-Bukhari—it is a priori considered true and therefore unassailable without proof to the contrary, since we are here in scientific terrain. So nothing bars me, as a Muslim woman, from making a double investigation—historical and methodological—of this *hadith* and its author, and especially of the conditions in which it was first put to use. Who uttered this *hadith*, where, when, why, and to whom?

Abu Bakra was a Companion who had known the Prophet during his lifetime and who spent enough time in his company to be able to report the *hadith* that he is supposed to have spoken. According to him, the Prophet pronounced this *hadith* when he learned that the Persians had named a woman to rule them. "When Kisra died, the Prophet, intrigued by the news, asked: 'And who has replaced him in command?' The answer was: 'They have entrusted power to his daughter.'"[8] It was at that moment, according to Abu Bakra, that the Prophet is supposed to have made the observation about women.

In 628 A.D., at the time of those interminable wars between the Romans and the Persians, Heraclius, the Roman emperor, had invaded the Persian realm, occupied Ctesiphon, which was situated very near the Sassanid capital, and Khusraw Pavis, the Persian king, had been assassinated. Perhaps it was this event that Abu Bakra alluded to. Actually, after the death of the son of Khusraw, there was a period of instability between 629 and 632 A.D., and various claimants to the throne of the Sassanid empire emerged, including two women.[9] Could this be the incident that led the Prophet to pronounce the *hadith* against women? Al-Bukhari does not go that far; he just reports the words of Abu Bakra—that is, the content of the *hadith* itself—and the reference to a woman having taken power among the Persians. To find out more about Abu Bakra, we must turn to the huge work of Ibn Hajar al-'Asqalani.

In the 17 volumes of the *Fath al-bari*, al-'Asqalani does a line-by-line commentary on al-Bukhari. For each *hadith* of the *Sahih*, al-'Asqalani gives us the historical clarification: the political events that served as background, a description of the battles, the identity of the conflicting parties, the identity of the trans-

6. Ibn Hajar al-'Asqalani, *Huda al-sari, muqaddimat Fath al-bari* [*The Traveller's Guide, Introduction to "The Creator's Conquest"*], commonly known as *Fath al-bari* [*The Creator's Conquest*]. It comprises al-Bukhari's text with a commentary by al-'Asqalani. The *hadith* that concerns us here, on the necessity of excluding women from power, is found on p. 46 of volume 13 of the edition of Al-Matba'a al-Bahiya al-Misriya (1928) and on p. 166 of volume 16 of the edition of Maktaba Mustafa al-Babi al-Halabi fi Misr (1963). (Future page references are to the 1928 edition.)

7. The Muslim world is divided into two parts: the Sunnis (orthodox) and the Shi'ites (literally, schismatics). Each group has its own specific texts of *fiqh* (religious knowledge), especially as regards sources of the *shari'a* (legislation and laws). The Sunnis are split between four *madhahib* (schools). . . . The differences between them most frequently relate to details of juridical procedures.

8. 'Asqalani, *Fath al-bari*, volume 13, p. 46.

9. See Hodgson, *Venture of Islam*, volume 1, p. 199.

mitters and their opinions, and finally the debates concerning their reliability—everything needed to satisfy the curiosity of the researcher.

On what occasion did Abu Bakra recall these words of the Prophet, and why did he feel the need to recount them? Abu Bakra must have had a fabulous memory, because he recalled them a quarter of a century after the death of the Prophet, at the time that the caliph 'Ali [reigned 656–661] retook Basra after having defeated 'A'isha [wife of the Prophet, circa 614–678] at the Battle of the Camel.[10]

Before occupying Basra, 'A'isha went on pilgrimage to Mecca, where she learned the news of the assassination of 'Uthman [caliph, 644–656] at Medina and the naming of 'Ali as the fourth caliph. It was while she was in Mecca that she decided to take command of the army that was challenging the choice of 'Ali. Days and days of indecision then followed. Should she go to Kufa or Basra? She needed to have an important city with enough malcontents to aid her cause and let her set up her headquarters. After numerous contacts, negotiations, and discussions, she chose Basra. Abu Bakra was one of the notables of that city and, like all of them, in a difficult position. Should he take up arms against 'Ali, the cousin of the Prophet and the caliph, challenged maybe but legitimate, or should he take up arms against 'A'isha, the "lover of the Beloved of God" and the "wife of the Prophet on earth and in paradise"?[11] If one realizes, moreover, that he had become a notable in that Iraqi city, which was not his native city, one can better understand the extent of his unease.

It can be said that Islam brought him good fortune. Before being converted, Abu Bakra had the hard, humiliating life of a slave in the city of Ta'if, where only the aristocracy had the right to high office. In year 8 A.H. (630 A.D.) the Prophet decided that it was time for him to undertake the conquest of Ta'if. He had just conquered Mecca, making a triumphal entry into that city, and now felt himself strong enough to

subdue the inhabitants of Ta'if, who were still resisting Islam. But they put up a strong defense. The Prophet camped outside the city and besieged the citadel for 18 days. In vain. The chief tribe that controlled the city, the Banu Tamim, and their allies were entrenched in the fort and used bows and arrows against the attackers, causing casualties among Muhammad's army. Twelve of his men were killed, causing him distress, as he had hoped to win without losses. Each soldier was a Companion; he knew their families; this was not an anonymous army. He decided to lift the siege and depart. But before doing so, he sent messengers to proclaim around the fort and the besieged city that all slaves who left the citadel and joined his ranks would be freed.[12] A dozen slaves answered his call, and Abu Bakra was one of them. The Prophet declared them free men, despite the protests of their masters, and after their conversion to Islam they became the brothers and equals of all.[13] In this way, Abu Bakra found both Islam and freedom.

And then we see him a few years later, a notable in an Iraqi city, the incarnation of Muhammad's dream—that all the poor, the humiliated of the world, could accede to power and wealth. The rapid rise of this one Companion summarizes very well what Islam meant for a man like Abu Bakra, who would never have been able to imagine leaving his native city as a free man and especially changing his social status so quickly: "You, the Arabs, were in an unspeakable state of degradation, powerlessness, and profligacy. The Islam of God and Muhammad saved you and led you to where you are now."[14] In fact, since his conversion Abu Bakra had scaled the social ladder at a dizzying pace: "Abu Bakra was very pious and remained so throughout his life. His children were among the notables of Basra as a result of their fortune and their erudition."[15] . . .

So why was he led to dig into his memory and make the prodigious effort of recalling the words that

---

10. 'Asqalani, *Fath al-bari*, volume 13, p. 46.

11. On this dilemma and the division that it occasioned, see 'Asqalani, *Fath al-bari*, volume 13, p. 49. On the political implications and the philosophical debates that the Battle of the Camel aroused, see the extraordinary description by [Abu Ja'far Muhammad] Tabari [died 922] in his *Tarikh al-umam wa al-muluk* [*History of Imams and Kings*] (Beirut, Lebanon: Dar Al-Fikr, 1979), volume 5, pp. 156–225.

12. [Muhammad] Ibn Sa'd [784–845], [*Kitab*] *al-tabaqat al-kubra* [*The Great Book of Classes*] (Beirut, Lebanon: Dar Sadir, no date), volume 3, p. 159.

13. Ibn Sa'd, *Al-Tabaqat*, p. 159.

14. 'Asqalani, *Fath al-bari*, volume 13, p. 622.

15. ['Izz al-Din] Ibn al-Athir [1160–1233], *Usd al-ghaba fi [ma'rifat] al-sahaba* [*The Lions of the Forest, on Knowing the Companions of the Prophet*] (Beirut, Lebanon: Dar al-Fikr li al-Tiba'a wa al-Tawzi', no date), volume 5, p. 38.

the Prophet was supposed to have uttered 25 years before? The first detail to be noted—and it is far from being negligible—is that Abu Bakra recalled his *hadith* after the Battle of the Camel. At that time, 'A'isha's situation was scarcely enviable. She was politically wiped out: 13,000 of her supporters had fallen on the field of battle.[16] 'Ali had retaken the city of Basra, and all those who had not chosen to join 'Ali's clan had to justify their action. This can explain why a man like Abu Bakra needed to recall opportune traditions, his record being far from satisfactory, as he had refused to take part in the civil war. Not only did he refrain from taking part, but, like many of the Companions who had opted for nonparticipation, he had made his position known officially. 'A'isha, who often used to accompany the Prophet on military expeditions, knew the procedure for the negotiations that took place before the military occupation of a city and had conducted matters correctly. Before besieging the city, she had sent messengers with letters to all the notables of the city, explaining to them the reasons that had impelled her to rebel against 'Ali, her intentions, and the objectives that she wanted to attain, and finally inviting them to support her.[17] It was a true campaign of information and persuasion, a preliminary military tactic in which the Prophet excelled. And 'A'isha was going to use the mosque as the meeting place for a public discussion to inform the population before occupying the city. Abu Bakra was thus contacted from the beginning in his capacity as a notable of the city.[18]

'A'isha did not take this course of action only because of faithfulness to Muhammad's methods. There was a more important reason. This was the first time since the death of the Prophet that the Muslims found themselves on opposite sides in a conflict. This was the situation that Muhammad had described as the worst possible for Islam: *fitna*, civil war, which turned the weapons of the Muslims inward instead of directing them, as God wished, outward, in order to conquer and dominate the world. So 'A'isha had to explain her uprising against 'Ali. She reproached him for not having brought the murderers of 'Uthman, the assassinated third caliph, to justice. Some

of those who had besieged 'Uthman and whose identity was known were in 'Ali's army as military leaders. Many Muslims must have thought as 'A'isha did, because a large part of the city of Basra welcomed her, giving her men and weapons. After driving out the governor who represented 'Ali, 'A'isha set up her headquarters in Basra, and with her two allies, Talha [ibn 'Ubayd Allah al-Taymi, died 656] and al-Zubair [ibn al-'Awwam, seventh century], members of the Quraysh tribe like herself, she continued her campaign of information, negotiation, and persuasion through individual interviews and speeches in the mosques, pressing the crowds to support her against the "unjust" caliph. It was year 36 A.H. (656 A.D.), and public opinion was divided: should one obey an "unjust" caliph (who did not punish the killers of 'Uthman), or should one rebel against him and support 'A'isha, even if that rebellion led to civil disorder?

For those who held the first opinion, the gravest danger that the Muslim nation could face was not that of being ruled by an unjust leader, but rather of falling into civil war. Let us not forget that the word "*islam*" means "submission." If the leader was challenged, the fundamental principle of Islam as order was in danger. The others thought that the lack of justice in the Muslim chief of state was more serious than civil war. A Muslim must not turn his back when he sees his leader commit injustices and reprehensible acts (*munkar*): "The Prophet said: 'If people see *munkar* and they do not try to remedy it, they incur divine punishment.'" Another version of this *hadith* is: "Let him who sees a situation in which *munkar* is being perpetrated endeavor to change it."[19] This was the argument of the group that assassinated Anwar Sadat [1918–1981] of Egypt, and is representative of the very prolific literature of the Muslim extremists of today.[20]

At Basra in year 36 the dilemma that confronted a Muslim—whether to obey an unjust caliph or to take up arms against him—was not just being posed in the circles of the ruling elite. The mosques were veritable plenary assemblies where the leaders came to discuss with the people they governed the decisions to be taken in the conflict between 'A'isha and

---

16. Mas'udi [died 956], *Muruj* [*al-zahab*] [*Meadows of Gold*], volume 2, p. 380; and the French translation of this work, *Les Prairies d'or* [*Prairies of Gold*], volume 3, p. 646.

17. Tabari, *Tarikh*, volume 5, p. 182.

18. 'Asqalani, *Fath al-bari*, volume 13, p. 46.

19. 'Asqalani, *Fath al-bari*, volume 13, pp. 50 and 51 for the first version, and p. 44 for the second.

20. See the analysis of Hamied N. Ansari, "The Islamic Militants in Egyptian Politics," *International Journal of Middle East Studies*, volume 16, number 1, 1984, pp. 123–144.

'Ali, and it must be pointed out (after reading the minutes of those meetings) that the people spoke up and demanded to be informed about what was going on. The ordinary people did not even know what the quarrel was about; for those citizens the important problem was the absence of democracy. It seemed mad to them to get involved without knowing the motives that were driving the leaders and the conflicts that divided them. They gave as the reason for their refusal to get involved on either side the lack of democracy in the selection of the caliph. In one of the debates that took place at the Basra mosque when 'A'isha's partners were invited by the people to explain their motives, a young man who did not belong to the elite made a speech that illuminated a whole area that was not very clear in the dynamics of Islam at the beginning and is often "forgotten" today—the nondemocratic dimension of Islam, which was noted and felt as such by the ordinary people. This young man took the floor in the Basra mosque, an act that would cost him his life, and addressing the allies and representatives of 'A'isha who were pushing him toward subversion, said to them:

It is true that you *Muhajirun* [the original migrants from Mecca][21] were the first to respond to the Prophet's call. You had the privilege of becoming Muslims before all the others. But everyone had that privilege later and everyone converted to Islam. Then, after the death of the Prophet, you selected a man from among you without consulting us [the common people, who were not part of the elite]. After his death, you got together and you named another [caliph], still without asking our advice. . . . You chose 'Uthman, you swore your allegiance to him, still without consulting us. You became displeased with his behavior, and you decided to declare war without consulting us. You decided, still without consulting us, to select 'Ali and swear allegiance to him. So what are you blaming him for now? Why have you decided to fight him? Has he committed an illegal act? Has he done something reprehensible? Explain to us what is going on. We must be convinced if we are to decide to take part in this war. So what is going on? Why are you fighting?[22]

Thus the decision not to participate in this civil war was not an exceptional one, limited to a few members of the elite. The mosques were full of people who found it absurd to follow leaders who wanted to lead the community into tearing each other to pieces. Abu Bakra was not in any way an exception.

When he was contacted by 'A'isha, Abu Bakra made known his response to her: he was against *fitna*. He is supposed to have said to her (according to the way he told it after the battle):

It is true that you are our *umm* [mother, alluding to her title of "Mother of Believers," which the Prophet bestowed on his wives during his last years]; it is true that as such you have rights over us. But I heard the Prophet say: "Those who entrust power [*mulk*] to a woman will never know prosperity."[23]

Although, as we have just seen, many of the Companions and inhabitants of Basra chose neutrality in the conflict, only Abu Bakra justified it by the fact that one of the parties was a woman.

According to al-Tabari's account, Basra, after 'A'isha's defeat, lived through many days of understandable anxiety. Was 'Ali going to take revenge on those who had not supported him, one of whom was Abu Bakra? "In the end 'Ali proclaimed a general amnesty. . . . All those who threw down their arms, he announced on the day of the battle, and those who returned to their homes would be spared."[24] "'Ali spent some days on the battlefield; he buried the dead of both sides and said a common funeral prayer for them before returning to the city."[25]

Nevertheless, everything was not quite so simple, if we take the example of Abu Musa al-Ash'ari [614–662], another Muslim pacifist who had refused to get involved in a civil war that he regarded as senseless. Abu Musa al-Ash'ari lost both position and fortune. However, it is true that the situations of Abu Musa and Abu Bakra are not comparable, except for their refusal to get involved. Abu Bakra's support was solicited by 'A'isha, the losing party, while that of Abu Musa was sought by 'Ali, the victor. Abu Musa was none other than a governor in 'Ali's service, his representative, and the symbol of the Muslim state as the head of the Iraqi town of Kufa. 'Ali, before

21. [Bracketed comments in indented quotations in this chapter are the author's, not the editor's.—Editor]

22. Tabari, *Tarikh*, volume 5, p. 179.

23. 'Asqalani, *Fath al-bari*, volume 13, p. 46.

24. Mas'udi, *Muruj*, volume 2, p. 378; and the French translation, volume 2, p. 644.

25. Tabari, *Tarikh*, volume 5, p. 221.

proceeding to Basra, then occupied by 'A'isha, sent emissaries to Abu Musa demanding that he mobilize the people and urgently send him troops and weapons. Not only did Abu Musa personally choose not to obey his caliph, but he also thought himself obligated to "consult with" the population he governed. He decided to involve the people, whom he called together in the mosque for information and discussion, and to enlighten them about the position of the Prophet on the subject of civil war. Abu Musa recited to them the *hadith* condemning *fitna*, and ordered them to disobey the caliph and not answer his call to enlist. For him, the duty of a Muslim in the case of *fitna* was absolute opposition to any participation. He recited many *hadith* at the Kufa mosque, all of them against *fitna*—against civil war plain and simple. It was not a question of the sex of the leader![26] Al-Bukhari assembled all *hadith* on the subject of civil war in a chapter entitled "*Al-Fitna*"; among them was Abu Bakra's *hadith*—the only one to give as a reason for neutrality the gender of one of the opponents.[27]

What is surprising to the modern reader who leafs through the chronicles of that famous Battle of the Camel is the respect that the people, whatever their position toward the war, showed to 'A'isha. Very rare were the occasions on which she was insulted—and even then it was never by one of the political leaders, but by some of the ordinary people.[28] The historians recall that only the Shi'i chroniclers (the pro-'Ali ones) find fault with 'A'isha. Why, then, did Abu Bakra distinguish himself by a completely unprecedented misogynistic attitude?

Abu Musa al-Ash'ari was dismissed from his post and banished from Kufa by 'Ali. He was replaced by a governor who was less of a pacifist, and above all more tractable.[29] If this happened to Abu Musa, the situation of other "pacifists" who were less highly placed was very delicate indeed. It would seem providential to also remember having heard a *hadith* that intimated an order not to participate in a war if a woman was at the head of the army.

Abu Bakra also remembered other *hadith* just as providential at critical moments. After the assassination of 'Ali, Mu'awiya [ibn Abi Sufyan] the Umayyad [circa 605–680] could only legitimately claim the caliphate if Hasan [624–669], the son of 'Ali and thus his successor, declared in writing that he renounced his rights. And this he did under pressure and bargaining that were more or less acknowledged.[30] It was at this moment that Abu Bakra recalled a *hadith* that could not have been more pertinent, under political circumstances that had unforeseen repercussions. He is supposed to have heard the Prophet say that "Hasan [the son of 'Ali] will be the man of reconciliation."[31] Hasan would have been a very small baby when the Prophet, his grandfather (through his daughter Fatima), would have said that! Abu Bakra had a truly astonishing memory for politically opportune *hadith* which curiously—and most effectively—fitted into the stream of history.

Once the historical context of a *hadith* was clarified, it was time to go on to its critical evaluation by applying to it one of the methodological rules that the religious scholars had defined as principles of the process of verification.[32] The first of these rules was to consider "this religion as a science," in the tradition of Imam Malik ibn Anas (born in year 93 A.H. [710–796 A.D.]), who was considered, with [Abu 'Abdallah Muhammad] Shafi'i [767–820] and Abu Hanifa [circa 699–767], one of "the three most famous *imams* in Islam because of their contribution to the elaboration of the knowledge that enables the believer to distinguish the permitted from the forbidden."[33] Malik ibn Anas never ceased saying:

> This religion is a science, so pay attention to those from whom you learn it. I had the good fortune to be born [in Medina] at a time when 70 persons [Companions] who could recite *hadith* were still alive. They used to go to the mosque and start speaking: The Prophet said so and so. I did not collect any of the *hadith* that they recounted, not because these people were not trustworthy, but

---

26. Tabari, *Tarikh*, volume 5, p. 188.
27. Bukhari, *Sahih*, volume 4, pp. 221ff.
28. Mas'udi, *Les Prairies d'or*, volume 2, p. 645.
29. Tabari, *Tarikh*, volume 5, p. 190.

30. 'Asqalani, *Fath al-bari*, volume 13, pp. 51ff; Mas'udi, *Muruj*, volume 3, pp. 4ff; and al-Tabari, *Mohammed, Sceau des prophètes* [*Muhammad, Seal of the Prophets*] (Paris: Sindbad, 1980), volume 6, p. 95.
31. 'Asqalani, *Fath al-bari*, volume 13, p. 56.
32. For assistance with the research for this chapter, I am indebted to Professor Ahmed al-Khamlichi, Chairman of the Department of Private Law, Faculté de Droit, Université Mohammed V, Rabat, Morocco.
33. Ibn 'Abd al-Barr [978–1070], *Al-Intiqa' fi fadl al-thalath al-a'imma al-fuqaha'* [*The Selection, on the Merits of the Three Founding Jurists*] (Beirut, Lebanon: Dar al-Kutub al-'Ilmiya, no date), pp. 10, 16.

because I saw that they were dealing in matters for which they were not qualified.[34]

According to him, it was not enough just to have lived at the time of the Prophet in order to become a source of *hadith*. It was also necessary to have a certain background that qualified you to speak: "Ignorant persons must be disregarded." How could they be considered sources of knowledge when they did not have the necessary intellectual capacity? But ignorance and intellectual capacity were not the only criteria for evaluating the narrators of *hadith*. The most important criteria were moral.

According to Malik, some persons could not under any circumstances transmit a *hadith*:

> Knowledge [*al-'ilm*] cannot be received from a mentally deficient person, nor from someone who is in the grip of passion and who might incite *bid'a* [innovation], nor from a liar who recounts anything at all to people. . . . And finally one should not receive knowledge from a shaykh, even a respected and very pious one, if he has not mastered the learning that he is supposed to transmit.[35]

Malik directs suspicion at the transmitters, emphasizes the necessity for Muslims to be on their guard, and even advises us to take the daily behavior of sources into consideration as a criterion for their reliability:

> There are some people whom I rejected as narrators of *hadith*, not because they lied in their role as men of science by recounting false *hadith* that the Prophet did not say, but just simply because I saw them lying in their relations with people, in their daily relationships that had nothing to do with religion.[36]

If we apply this rule to Abu Bakra, he would have to be immediately eliminated, since one of the biographies of him tells us that he was convicted of and flogged for false testimony by the caliph 'Umar ibn al-Khattab [reigned 634–644].[37] This happened during a very serious case that 'Umar punished by execution—a case involving *zina* [fornication], an illicit sex act. In order to end the sexual licentiousness and promiscuity that existed in pre-Islamic Arabia and in an effort to control paternity, Islam condemned

all sexual relations outside marriage or ownership as *zina*, encouraging women and men to marry and labeling celibacy as the open door to temptations of all kinds. It gave men the right to have several wives and to divorce them easily and replace them by others, provided that it was all within the framework of Muslim marriage.

'Umar, the second caliph of a new community still under the influence of pre-Islamic customs, had to act rapidly and severely to see that a key idea of Islam, the patriarchal family, became rooted in the minds of believers. Capital punishment for *zina* would only be applied if four witnesses testified to having seen the adultery with their own eyes and at the same time. These were conditions so difficult to prove that it made this punishment more a deterrent than a realistic threat. It was necessary, moreover, to avoid having enmities and slanders lead to the condemnation of innocent persons. If there were only three witnesses who saw the accused *in flagrante delicto*, their testimony was not valid. In addition, any witness who slandered someone by accusing him of the crime of *zina* would incur the punishment for slander—he would be flogged for false testimony.[38]

Now this was what happened in the case of Abu Bakra. He was one of the four witnesses who came before 'Umar to officially make the accusation of *zina* against a well-known person, a Companion and a prominent political man, al-Mughira ibn Shu'ba [died 670]. The four witnesses testified before 'Umar that they had seen al-Mughira ibn Shu'ba in the act of fornication. 'Umar began his investigation, and one of the four witnesses then admitted that he was not really sure of having seen everything. The doubt on the part of one of the witnesses made the others subject to punishment by flogging for slander, and Abu Bakra was flogged.

If one follows the principles of Malik for *fiqh* [Islamic jurisprudence], Abu Bakra must be rejected as a source of *hadith* by every good, well-informed Malikite Muslim.

To close this investigation, let us take a brief look at the attitude of the religious scholars of the first

---

34. Ibn 'Abd al-Barr, *Al-Intiqa'*, p. 16.

35. Ibn 'Abd al-Barr, *Al-Intiqa'*, p. 16.

36. Ibn 'Abd al-Barr, *Al-Intiqa'*, p. 15.

37. Ibn al-Athir, *Usd al-ghaba*, volume 5, p. 38.

38. 'Umar ibn al-Khattab institutionalized the recourse to capital punishment for fornication; his contemporaries were not at all in agreement with his position. See Bukhari, *Sahih*, volume 4, pp. 146ff. . . . 'Umar ibn al-Khattab . . . was [also] the instigator of the wearing of the veil and was in complete disagreement with the Prophet about the way to treat women.

centuries toward that misogynistic *hadith* that is presented to us today as sacred, unassailable truth. Even though it was collected as *sahih* (authentic) by al-Bukhari and others, that *hadith* was hotly contested and debated by many. The scholars did not agree on the weight to give that *hadith* on women and politics. Assuredly there were some who used it as an argument for excluding women from decision making. But there were others who found that argument unfounded and unconvincing. Al-Tabari was one of those religious authorities who took a position against it, not finding it a sufficient basis for depriving women of their power of decision making and for justifying their exclusion from politics.[39]

After having tried to set straight the historical record—the line of transmitters and witnesses who gave their account of a troubled historical epoch—I can only advise redoubled vigilance when, taking the sacred as an argument, someone hurls at the believer as basic truth a political axiom so terrible and with such grave historical consequences as the one we have been investigating. Nevertheless, we will see that this "misogynistic" *hadith*, although it is exemplary, is not a unique case.

Throughout my childhood I had a very ambivalent relationship with the Qur'an. It was taught to us in a Qur'anic school in a particularly ferocious manner. But to my childish mind only the highly fanciful Islam of my illiterate grandmother, Lalla Yasmina, opened the door for me to a poetic religion. . . . This dual attitude that I had toward the sacred text was going to remain with me. Depending on how it is used, the sacred text can be a threshold for escape or an insurmountable barrier. It can be that rare music that leads to dreaming or simply a dispiriting routine. It all depends on the person who invokes it. However, for me, the older I grew, the fainter the music became. In secondary school the history of religion course was studded with traditions. Many of them from appropriate pages of al-Bukhari, which the teacher recited to us, made me feel extremely ill at ease: "The Prophet said that the dog, the ass, and woman interrupt prayer if they pass in front of the believer, interposing themselves between him and the *qibla* [the direction of Mecca]."[40] . . .

By lumping [woman] in with two familiar animals, the author of the *hadith* inevitably makes her a being who belongs to the animal kingdom. It is enough for a woman to appear in the field of vision for contact with the *qibla*—that is, the divine—to be disturbed. Like the dog and the ass, she destroys the symbolic relation with the divine by her presence. One has to interrupt one's prayer and begin again.

Arab civilization being a civilization of the written word, the only point of view we have on this question is that of Abu Hurayra [died 678]. According to [Shams al-Din] Ibn Marzuq [1311–1379], when someone invoked in front of 'A'isha the *hadith* that said that the three causes of interruption of prayer were dogs, asses, and women, she answered them: "You compare us now to asses and dogs. In the name of God, I have seen the Prophet saying his prayers while I was there, lying on the bed between him and the *qibla*. And in order not to disturb him, I didn't move."[41] The believers used to come to 'A'isha for verification of what they had heard, confident of her judgment, not only because of her closeness to the Prophet, but because of her own abilities:

> I have seen groups of the most eminent companions of the Prophet ask her questions concerning the *fara'id* [the daily duties of the Muslim, the rituals, etc.], and Ibn 'Ata' said: "'A'isha was, among all the people, the one who had the most knowledge of *fiqh*, the one who was the most educated and, compared to those who surrounded her, the one whose judgment was the best."[42]

Despite her words of caution, the influence of Abu Hurayra has nevertheless infiltrated the most prestigious religious texts, among them the *Sahih* of al-Bukhari, who apparently did not always feel obliged to insert the corrections provided by 'A'isha. The subject of many of these *hadith* is the "polluting" essence of femaleness.

To understand the importance for Islam of that aspect of femaleness, evoking disturbance and sullying, we would do well to look at the personality of Abu Hurayra, who, as it were, gave it legal force. Without wanting to play the role of psychoanalytical detective, I can say that the fate of Abu Hurayra and

39. 'Asqalani, *Fath al-bari*, volume 13, p. 47.
40. Bukhari, *Sahih*, volume 1, p. 99.

41. Bukhari, *Sahih*, volume 1, p. 199.
42. Ibn Hajar al-'Asqalani, *Al-Isaba fi tamyiz al-sahaba* [*A Biographical Dictionary of the Companions of the Prophet*] (Cairo: Maktaba al-Dirasa al-Islamiya Dar al-Nahda, no date), volume 8, p. 18.

his ambivalence toward women are wrapped up in the story of his name. Abu Hurayra, meaning literally "Father of the Little Female Cat," had previously been called "Servant of the Sun" ('Abd al-Shams).[43] The Prophet decided to change that name, which had a very strong sense of idolatry about it. "Servant of the Sun" was originally from Yemen, that part of Arabia where not only the sun, a female star in Arabic, was worshipped, but where women also ruled in public and private life. Yemen was the land of the Queen of Sheba, Bilqis [tenth century B.C.], that queen who fascinated King Solomon [reigned 962–922 B.C.], who ruled over a happy kingdom, and who put her mark on Arab memory, since she appears in the Qur'an:

> [Hud-hud] said: "I have found (a thing) that thou apprehendest not, and I come unto thee from Sheba with sure tidings."

> Lo! I found a woman ruling over them, and she hath been given (abundance) of all things, and hers is a mighty throne.

> I found her and her people worshipping the sun instead of God. . . . (Sura 27, Verses 22–24)

Abu Hurayra came from the Yemeni tribe of the Daws.[44] At the age of 30 the man named "Servant of the Sun" was converted to Islam. The Prophet gave him the name 'Abdallah (Servant of God) and nicknamed him Abu Hurayra (Father of the Little Female Cat) because he used to walk around with a little female cat that he adored.[45] But Abu Hurayra was not happy with this nickname, for he did not like the trace of femininity in it: "Abu Hurayra said: 'Don't call me Abu Hurayra. The Prophet nicknamed me Abu Hirr [Father of the Male Cat], and the male is better than the female.'"[46] He had another reason to feel sensitive about this subject of femininity—he did not have a very masculine job. In a Medina that was in a state of full-blown economic development, where the Medinese, especially the Jews, made an art of agriculture, and the immigrant Meccans continued their commercial activities and managed to combine them with military expeditions, Abu Hurayra preferred, according to his own comments, to be in the company of the Prophet. He served him and sometimes "helped out in the women's apartments."[47] This fact might clear up the mystery about his hatred of women, and also of female cats, the two seeming to be strangely linked in his mind.

He had such a fixation about female cats and women that he recalled that the Prophet had pronounced a *hadith* concerning the two creatures—and in which the female cat comes off much better than the woman. But 'A'isha contradicted him, a Companion recounted:

> We were with 'A'isha, and Abu Hurayra was with us. 'A'isha said to him: "Father of the Little Cat, is it you who said that you heard the Prophet declare that a woman went to hell because she starved a little female cat and didn't give it anything to drink?"

> "I did hear the Prophet say that," responded Father of the Little Cat.

> "A believer is too valuable in the eyes of God," retorted 'A'isha, "for Him to torture that person because of a cat. . . . Father of the Little Cat, the next time you undertake to repeat the words of the Prophet, watch out what you recount."[48]

It is not surprising that Abu Hurayra attacked 'A'isha in return for that. She might be "The Mother of the Believers" and "The Lover of the Lover of God," but she contradicted him too often. One day he lost patience and defended himself against an attack by 'A'isha. When she said to him, "Abu Hurayra, you relate *hadith* that you never heard," he replied sharply, "O Mother, all I did was collect *hadith*, while you were too busy with make-up and your mirror."[49]

One of the constant themes of conflict in Islam from the very beginning is what to do about menstrual periods and the sex act. Are periods the source of sullying? 'A'isha and the other wives of the Prophet never lost any opportunity to insist that the Prophet did not have the phobic attitude of pre-

43. 'Asqalani, *Al-Isaba*, volume 7, p. 427.

44. 'Abd al-Mun'im Salih al-'Ali al-'Uzzi, *Difa' 'an Abi Hurayra* [*In Defense of Abu Hurayra*], second edition (Beirut, Lebanon: Dar al-Qalam; Baghdad: Maktaba al-Nahda, 1981), p. 13.

45. 'Asqalani, *Al-Isaba*, volume 7, p. 426.

46. 'Asqalani, *Al-Isaba*, volume 7, p. 434.

47. 'Asqalani, *Al-Isaba*, volume 7, p. 441.

48. Imam [Muhammad ibn Bahadur al-]Zarkashi [circa 1344–1392], *Al-Ijaba li-irad ma istadrakathu 'A'isha 'ala al-sahaba* [*Collection of 'A'isha's Corrections to the Statements of the Companions*], second edition (Beirut, Lebanon: Al-Maktab al-Islami, 1980), p. 118.

49. 'Asqalani, *Al-Isaba*, volume 7, p. 440.

Islamic Arabia on that subject. Did the Prophet purify himself after making love during the holy month of Ramadan? "I heard Abu Hurayra recount that he whom the dawn finds sullied (*janaban*, referring to sullying by the sex act) may not fast."[50] Upon hearing this new law decreed by Abu Hurayra, the Companions hastened to the wives of the Prophet to reassure themselves about it: "They posed the question to Umm Salama [wife of the Prophet, circa 596–682] and 'A'isha. . . . They responded: 'The Prophet used to spend the night sullied without making any ritual of purification, and in the morning he fasted.'"[51] The Companions, greatly perplexed, returned to Abu Hurayra:

"Ah, so. They said that?" he responded.

"Yes, they said that," repeated the Companions, feeling more and more troubled, because Ramadan is one of the five pillars of Islam. Abu Hurayra then confessed, under pressure, that he had not heard it directly from the Prophet, but from someone else. He reconsidered what he had said, and later it was learned that just before his death he completely retracted his words.[52]

Abu Hurayra was not the only one to report *hadith* about the purification ritual, and this was a real bone of contention between 'A'isha and the Companions. "['Abdallah] ibn 'Umar [died 693] ordered women who were doing the purification ritual to undo their braids [before touching their hair with wet hands]." 'A'isha is supposed to have responded when someone reported to her the teaching that he was propounding: "That's strange. . . . Why, when he was about it, didn't he order them to shave their heads? When I used to wash myself with the Prophet, we purified ourselves with the same bucket of water. I passed my wet hand over my braids three times, and I never undid them!"[53] 'A'isha insisted on these corrections because she was conscious of the implications of what was being said. Pre-Islamic Arabia regarded sexuality, and the menstruating woman in particular, as a source of pollution, as a pole of negative forces. This theory about pollution expressed a vision of femaleness that was conveyed through a whole system of superstitions and beliefs that Muham-

mad wanted to condemn. He saw it as, on the one hand, the essence of the *jahiliya* [pre-Islamic era], and, on the other hand, the essence of the beliefs of the Jewish community of Medina.

The religious scholars who took part in the debate on the subject of pollution, recorded at length in the religious literature, came down on the side of 'A'isha. Their argument was that her version of the *hadith* seemed to agree more with the attitude of the Prophet, who tried by all means to "struggle against superstition in all its forms."[54]

This was not a matter that interested only the *imam*s. The caliphs were also greatly concerned about it: "Mu'awiya ibn Abi Sufyan [reigned 661–680] asked Umm Habiba, the wife of the Prophet [circa 588–680], if the Prophet—may God pray for him—had ever prayed in the garments in which he had made love. She said yes, he had, because he saw nothing bad in it."[55] Imam al-Nasa'i explains to us why he laid such stress on the subject of menstruation in his chapter on the purification ritual. The Prophet, he said, wanted to react against the phobic behavior of the Jewish population of Medina, who declared a woman who was having her period unclean: "He ordered them [the male believers who had asked him questions on this subject] to eat with their wives, drink with them, share their bed, and do everything with them that they wanted except copulate."[56]

The books of *fiqh* devote whole chapters to the purification rituals that every Muslim must carry out five times a day before praying. It is undeniable that Islam has an attitude bordering on anxiety about bodily cleanliness, which induces in many people an almost neurotic strictness. Our religious education begins with attention focused on the body, its secretions, its fluids, its orifices, which the child must learn to constantly observe and control. The sex act imposes a more elaborate ritual for the grown man and woman, and after menstruating the woman must wash her entire body according to a precise ritual. Islam stresses the fact that sex and menstruation are really extraordinary (in the literal meaning of the word) events, but they do not make the woman a negative pole that "annihilates" in some way the pres-

50. Imam Zarkashi, *Al-Ijaba*, p. 112.
51. Imam Zarkashi, *Al-Ijaba*, p. 112.
52. Imam Zarkashi, *Al-Ijaba*, pp. 112, 113.
53. Imam Zarkashi, *Al-Ijaba*, p. 111.

54. Imam Zarkashi, *Al-Ijaba*, p. 115.
55. Imam [Abu 'Abd al-Rahman al-]Nasa'i [830–915], *Sunan* [*Hadith Collection*] (Cairo: Al-Matba'a al-Misriya, no date), volume 1, p. 155.
56. Nasa'i, *Sunan*, volume 1, p. 155.

ence of the divine and upsets its order. But apparently the Prophet's message, 14 centuries later, has still not been absorbed into customs throughout the Muslim world, if I judge by the occasions when I was refused admittance at the doors of mosques in Penang, Malaysia, in Baghdad, Iraq, and in Kairouan, Tunisia.

According to the meticulous al-Nasa'i, Maymuna [circa 593–672], one of the wives of the Prophet (he had nine at the time, that concerns us here, the last years of his life in Medina), said: "It happened that the Prophet recited the Qur'an with his head on the knee of one of us while she was having her period. It also happened that one of us brought his prayer rug to the mosque and laid it down while she was having her period."[57] Already at the time that Imam al-Nasa'i was writing (he was born in year 214 or 215 A.H., 830 A.D.), the scholars suspected that there was a message there that was disturbing the misogyny ingrained in the peoples of the Arab Mediterranean area, before and after the Prophet, and they made great efforts not to betray that very disturbing aspect of the Prophet's message. These religious scholars, who saw in misogyny the danger of betrayal of the Prophet, doubled their precautions and did a thorough investigation of the sex life of the Prophet by listening to the reports of his wives, the only credible sources on this subject. They accumulated details about his life at home as well as in the mosque. Ibn Sa'd devoted a chapter of his book to the layout of the Prophet's house. This chapter, as we shall soon see, is extremely important for the clarification of a key dimension of Islam: the total revolution it represented vis-à-vis the Judeo-Christian tradition and the pre-Islamic period with regard to women. However, very quickly the misogynistic trend reasserted itself among the religious scholars and gained the upper hand. We will see the resurgence in many *hadith* of that superstitious fear of femaleness that the Prophet wanted to eradicate.

One can read among al-Bukhari's "authentic" *hadith* the following one: "Three things bring bad luck: house, woman, and horse."[58] Al-Bukhari did not include other versions of this *hadith*, although the rule was to give one or more contradictory versions in order to show readers conflicting points of view, and thus to permit them to be sufficiently well informed to decide for themselves about practices that were the subject of dispute. However, there is no trace in al-Bukhari of 'A'isha's refutation of this *hadith*:

> They told 'A'isha that Abu Hurayra was asserting that the Messenger of God said: "Three things bring bad luck: house, woman, and horse." 'A'isha responded: "Abu Hurayra learned his lessons very badly. He came into our house when the Prophet was in the middle of a sentence. He only heard the end of it. What the Prophet said was: 'May God refute the Jews; they say three things bring bad luck: house, woman, and horse.'"[59]

Not only did al-Bukhari not include this correction, but he treated the *hadith* as if there was no question about it. He cited it three times, each time with a different transmission chain. This procedure generally strengthens a *hadith* and gives the impression of consensus concerning it. No mention was made of the dispute between 'A'isha and Abu Hurayra on this subject. Worse yet, al-Bukhari followed this misogynistic *hadith* with another along the same lines which reflected the same vision of femaleness as a pole of destruction and ill luck: "The Prophet said: 'I do not leave after me any cause of trouble more fatal to man than women.'"[60] The source of this *hadith* is 'Abdallah ibn 'Umar (the son of 'Umar ibn al-Khattab, the second caliph), who was known for his rare asceticism and for nights interrupted by prayers and purifications.[61] 'Abdallah was a source very highly valued by Bukhari. He was the author of another famous *hadith*, in which he throws women into hell: "'Abdallah ibn 'Umar said: 'The Prophet said: "I took a look at paradise, and I noted that the majority of the people there were poor people. I took a look at hell, and I noted that there women were the majority."'"[62]

What conclusion must one draw from this? That even the authentic *hadith* must be vigilantly examined with a magnifying glass? That is our right, Malik ibn Anas tells us. Al-Bukhari, like all religious scholars, began his work of collecting by asking for God's help and acknowledging that only He is infallible. It is our tradition to question everything and everybody, especially the religious scholars and *imam*s. And it

57. Nasa'i, *Sunan*, volume 1, p. 147.
58. Bukhari, *Sahih*, volume 3, p. 243.

59. Imam Zarkashi, *Al-Ijaba*, p. 113.
60. Bukhari, *Sahih*, volume 3, p. 243.
61. The biography of 'Abdallah ibn 'Umar can be found in 'Asqalani, *Al-Isaba*, volume 4, pp. 182ff.
62. Bukhari, *Sahih*, volume 4, p. 137.

is more than ever necessary for us to disinter our true tradition from the centuries of oblivion that have managed to obscure it. But we must also guard against falling into generalizations and saying that all the imams were and are misogynistic. That is not true today and was not true yesterday. The example of this is Imam Zarkashi, who, luckily for us, recorded in writing all of 'A'isha's objections.

Imam Zarkashi was of Turkish origin, but born in Egypt in the middle of the 14th century A.D. (year 745 A.H.). Like all the scholars of his time, he traveled throughout the Muslim world in search of knowledge. He specialized in religious knowledge and left behind no less than 30 compendiums. Many of these are lost to modern researchers, and we know only their titles. Among those that have come down to us is a book devoted to 'A'isha's contribution to Islam, her contribution as a source of religious knowledge. The book begins as follows:

> 'A'isha is the Mother of the Believers. . . . She is the lover of the Messenger of God. . . . She lived with him for eight years and five months; she was 18 years old at the time of the death of the Prophet. . . . She lived to be 65 years old. We are indebted to her for 1,210 *hadith*s.[63]

And he explains:

> This book is devoted to her particular contribution in this field, especially the points on which she disagreed with others, the points to which she supplied added information, the points on which she was in complete disagreement with the religious scholars of her time . . . . I have entitled this book *Collection of 'A'isha's Corrections to the Statements of the Companions.*[64]

This book remained in manuscript form until 1939. [Jamal al-Din] Al-Afghani [1838–1897] discovered it while doing research for his biography of 'A'isha in the al-Dahiriya Library of Damascus, Syria. Why did Imam Zarkashi, one of the greatest scholars of the Shafi'i school of his time, undertake his work on 'A'isha? A work that, by all accounts, he must have considered extremely important, since he dedicated his book to the Judge of Judges (*qadi al-qudat*)—the equivalent of the Minister of Justice today, the supreme authority in religious matters in a Muslim city. Because, he says, "the Prophet recognized 'A'isha's

importance to such an extent that he said: 'Draw a part of your religion from little *al-humayra* [red woman].'"[65] One of the Prophet's favorite pet names for 'A'isha was *al-humayra*, referring to her very white skin made radiant by a light sunburn, something rather rare in the Hijaz, the northern part of Arabia.[66]

'A'isha disputed many of Abu Hurayra's *hadith* and declared to whoever wanted to hear it: "He is not a good listener, and when he is asked a question, he gives wrong answers."[67] 'A'isha could take the liberty of criticizing him because she had an excellent memory: "I never saw anyone who had so much knowledge about religion, poetry, and medicine as 'A'isha."[68] Abu Hurayra knew how to rile her. "But who has heard about that from Abu al-Qasim [the Prophet's surname]?" she exclaimed when someone recounted to her another of Abu Hurayra's traditions, this time describing what the Prophet did after making love.[69]

It is not wasted effort for us to tarry over the personality of Abu Hurayra, the author of *hadith* that saturate the daily life of every modern Muslim woman. He has been the source of an enormous amount of commentary in the religious literature. But he was and still is the object of controversy, and there is far from being unanimity on him as a reliable source. The most recent book about him, jointly published by a Lebanese and an Iraqi firm, is a tribute written by one of his admirers who devotes not less than 500 pages to defending him. 'Abd al-Mun'im Salih al-'Ali gave his book a rather eloquent title: *In Defense of Abu Hurayra.*[70] It was obviously a success, since a new edition was published in 1983. The author begins by asserting that "the Zionists and their allies and supporters have found another weapon against Islam; it is to introduce doubt about the narrators of traditions . . . and especially about those who were the source of many *hadith*."[71] This gives an idea of the intensity of the controversy surrounding Abu Hurayra. What is certain is that Abu Hurayra, long

---

63. Imam Zarkashi, *Al-Ijaba*, pp. 37, 38.
64. Imam Zarkashi, *Al-Ijaba*, p. 32.

65. Imam Zarkashi, *Al-Ijaba*, p. 31.
66. Zahiya Qaddura, *'A'isha, Umm al-mu'minin* [*'A'isha, Mother of the Faithful*] (Beirut, Lebanon: Dar al-Kitab al-Lubnani, 1976).
67. Imam Zarkashi, *Al-Ijaba*, p. 116.
68. 'Asqalani, *Al-Isaba*, volume 8, p. 17.
69. Imam Zarkashi, *Al-Ijaba*, p. 120.
70. [Al-'Ali] al-'Uzzi, *Difa'*.
71. [Al-'Ali] al-'Uzzi, *Difa'*, p. 7.

before Zionism, was attacked by Companions of his own generation. He had a very dubious reputation from the beginning, and al-Bukhari was aware of it, since he reports that "people said that Abu Hurayra recounts too many *hadith*."[72] 'Abd al-Mun'im, to his credit, cites all the incidents in which he was strongly challenged, including by those other than 'A'isha. He assures us that 'Umar ibn al-Khattab, the second orthodox caliph, did not say that "the worst liar among the narrators of *hadith* is Abu Hurayra."[73] He disputes the claim that 'Umar threatened to exile him, to send him back to his native Yemen, if he continued to recount *hadith*.[74]

'Umar, who enjoyed an unparalleled influence on the Prophet and the Muslim community of yesterday (and still does today) because of his prestige as a man of politics, his boldness in military matters, his strong personality, and his horror of lying, avoided recounting *hadith*. He was terrified at the idea of not being accurate. For that reason, 'Umar was one of those Companions who preferred to rely on their own judgment rather than trust their memory, which they considered dangerously fallible.[75] He was very irritated by the facile manner in which Abu Hurayra reeled off *hadith*: "'Umar al-Khattab," we can read in al-'Asqalani's biography of him, "is supposed to have remarked as follows about Abu Hurayra: 'We have many things to say, but we are afraid to say them, and that man there has no restraint.'"[76]

For the pious Companion the fallibility of memory was an occasion for meditating on the fragility of existence in the face of the flowing river of time, which steals not only youth, but especially memory. 'Umar ibn Hasin [seventh century], another Companion who was conscious of the treacherousness of memory, said:

> If I wanted to, I could recite traditions about the Prophet for two days without stopping. What keeps me from doing it is that I have seen some of the Companions of the Messenger of God who heard exactly what I myself heard, who saw what I saw, and those men recounted *hadith*. Those traditions are not exactly what we heard. And I am afraid of hallucinating, as they hallucinate.[77]

The Arabic word is *yushba*, literally "to hallucinate," that is, to see a reality that does not exist but that has the appearance of reality.

Abu Hurayra, on the contrary, for the three years that he spent in the company of the Prophet, would accomplish the *tour de force* of recalling 5,300 *hadith*.[78] Al-Bukhari listed 800 experts who cited him as their source.[79] Here is how Abu Hurayra explains his excellent memory: "I said to the Prophet: 'I listen attentively, I take in many of your ideas, but I forget many.'"[80] Then the Prophet is supposed to have told him to spread out his cloak while he was speaking to him, and afterwards to pick it up at the end of the session. "And this is the reason that I no longer forgot anything."[81] Telling the story of the cloak was not the best way to be convincing in a religion like Islam, which has a horror of mysteries of all sorts, where Muhammad resisted the pressure of his contemporaries to perform miracles and magical acts, and where the religious scholars became well-versed from very early on in an exaggerated pragmatism.

Abu Hurayra also gave another explanation that was a bit more realistic than the first. The other Companions, he said, put their energy into business matters and spent their time in the bazaars drawing up contracts and increasing their fortunes, while he had nothing else to do but follow the Prophet everywhere.[82] 'Umar ibn al-Khattab, who was well known for his physical vigor and who awoke the city every day to say the dawn prayer, disliked lazy people who loafed around without any definite occupation. He summoned Abu Hurayra on one occasion to offer him a job. To his great surprise, Abu Hurayra declined the offer. 'Umar, who did not consider such things a joking matter, said to him:

> "You refuse to work? Better people than you have begged for work."

> "Who are those people who are better than me?" inquired Abu Hurayra.

> "Joseph, the son of Jacob, for example," said 'Umar to put an end to a conversation that was getting out of hand.

72. Bukhari, *Sahih*, volume 1, p. 34.
73. [Al-'Ali] al-'Uzzi, *Difa'*, p. 122.
74. [Al-'Ali] al-'Uzzi, *Difa'*, p. 122.
75. Muhammad Abu Zahra, *Malik* [Malik ibn Anas, 710–796] (Cairo: Dar al-Fikr al-'Arabi, no date), p. 146.
76. 'Asqalani, *Al-Isaba*, volume 7, p. 440.
77. Abu Zahra, *Malik*, p. 145.
78. 'Asqalani, *Al-Isaba*, volume 7, p. 432.
79. Bukhari, *Sahih*, volume 1, p. 34.
80. Bukhari, *Sahih*, volume 1, p. 34.
81. Bukhari, *Sahih*, volume 1, p. 34.
82. 'Asqalani, *Al-Isaba*, volume 7, p. 517.

"He," said Abu Hurayra flippantly, "was a prophet, the son of a prophet, and I am Abu Hurayra, son of Umayma [his mother]."[83]

With this anecdote we come back to our point of departure, the relationship of "Father of the Little Female Cat" to femaleness and to the very mysterious and dangerous link between the sacred and women. All the monotheistic religions are shot through by the conflict between the divine and the feminine, but none more so than Islam, which has opted for the occultation of the feminine, at least symbolically, by trying to veil it, to hide it, to mask it. Islam as sexual practice unfolds with a very special theatricality since it is acted out in a scene where the *hijab* [veil] occupies a central position. This almost phobic attitude toward women is all the more surprising since we have seen that the Prophet has encouraged his adherents to renounce it as representative of the *jahiliya* and its superstitions. This leads me to ask: Is it possible that Islam's message had only a limited and superficial effect on deeply superstitious seventh-century Arabs who failed to integrate its novel approaches to the world and to women? Is it possible that the *hijab*, the attempt to veil women, that is claimed today to be basic to Muslim identity, is nothing but the expression of the persistence of the pre-Islamic mentality, the *jahiliya* mentality that Islam was supposed to annihilate?

83. ʻAsqalani, *Al-Isaba*, volume 7, p. 517.

14

Qur'an and Woman

Muslims number more than 3 million in the United States and constitute one of the country's fastest-growing religious groups. African-Americans, comprising a third of this Islamic community—most of the rest are immigrants from Islamic countries and their descendants—have traditionally practiced heterodox forms of Islam not recognized as "Islamic" by Muslim scholars in other countries. Since Malcolm X's (1925–1965) famous pilgrimage in 1964, however, many African-American Muslims have adopted more orthodox Islamic practices. At the same time, African-American Muslims have brought their own historical experiences to bear on their Islamic faith.[1] A leading representative of this approach is Amina Wadud-Muhsin (United States, born 1952), a professor at Virginia Commonwealth University in Richmond, Virginia. Wadud-Muhsin combines gendered readings of the Qur'an with the experience of African-American women to argue that Islamic injunctions must be interpreted in relation to specific historical circumstances.

Introduction: How Perceptions of Woman Influence Interpretation of the Qur'an

My objective in undertaking this research was to make a "reading" of the Qur'an that would be meaningful to women living in the modern era. By "read-

ing" I mean the process of reviewing the words and their context in order to derive an understanding of the text. Every "reading" reflects, in part, the intentions of the text, as well as the "prior text"[2] of the one who makes the "reading." Although each "reading" is unique, the understanding of various readers of a single text will converge on many points.

In this "Introduction" I will give the background to this work. In particular, I will look at how the perception of woman influences the interpretations of the Qur'an's position on women. I will give an overview of my own perspective of woman and of the

---

1. Yvonne Yazbeck Haddad and Jane I. Smith, *Muslim Communities in North America* (Albany: State University of New York Press, 1994); Haddad and Smith, "United States of America," in John L. Esposito, editor, *The Oxford Encyclopedia of the Modern Islamic World* (New York: Oxford University Press, 1995), volume 4, pp. 277–284; Aminah Beverly McCloud, *African American Islam* (New York: Routledge, 1995); Kambiz GhaneaBassiri, *Competing Visions of Islam in the United States* (Westport, Conn.: Greenwood Press, 1997), especially pp. 126–131.

2. The perpectives, circumstances, and background of the individual. This concept will be discussed at greater length below.

methods of interpretation I used in analyzing the Qur'an which have led to some new conclusions.

No method of Qur'anic exegesis is fully objective. Each exegete makes some subjective choices. Some details of their interpretations reflect their subjective choices and not necessarily the intent of the text. Yet, often, no distinction is made between text and interpretation. I put interpretations of woman in the Qur'an into three categories: "traditional," reactive, and holistic.

The first category of Qur'anic interpretation I call "traditional." Traditional *tafasir* (exegetical works) give interpretations of the entire Qur'an, whether from the modern or classical periods, with certain objectives in mind. Those objectives could be legal, esoteric, grammatical, rhetorical, or historical. Although these objectives may lead to differences in the *tafasir*, one similarity in these works is their atomistic methodology. They begin with the first verse of the first chapter and proceed to the second verse of the first chapter—one verse at a time—until the end of the Book. Little or no effort is made to recognize themes and to discuss the relationship of the Qur'an to itself, thematically. A brief mention of one verse's relation to another verse may be rendered but these are haphazard with no underlying hermeneutical principle applied. A methodology for linking similar Qur'anic ideas, syntactical structures, principles, or themes together is almost non-existent.[3]

However, what concerns me most about "traditional" *tafasir* is that they were exclusively written by males. This means that men and men's experiences were included and women and women's experiences were either excluded or interpreted through the male vision, perspective, desire, or needs of woman.[4] In the final analysis, the creation of the basic paradigms through which we examine and discuss

the Qur'an and Qur'anic interpretation were generated without the participation and firsthand representation of women. Their voicelessness during critical periods of development in Qur'anic interpretation has not gone unnoticed, but it has been mistakenly equated with voicelessness in the text itself.

The second category of Qur'anic interpretation concerned with the issue of woman consists primarily of modern scholars' reactions to severe handicaps for woman as an individual and as a member of society which have been attributed to the text. In this category are many women and/or persons opposed to the Qur'anic message (or more precisely, to Islam) altogether. They use the poor status of women in Muslim societies as justification for their "reactions." These reactions have also failed to draw a distinction between the interpretation and the text.[5]

The objectives sought and methods used, often come from feminist ideals and rationales. Although they are often concerned with valid issues, the absence of a comprehensive analysis of the Qur'an sometimes causes them to vindicate the position of women on grounds entirely incongruous with the Qur'anic position on woman. This shortcoming must be overcome in order to make use of a most effective tool for the liberation of Muslim women: demonstrating the link between that liberation and this primary source of Islamic ideology and theology.

The interpretations which reconsider the whole method of Qur'anic exegesis with regard to various modern social, moral, economic, and political concerns—including the issue of woman—represent the final category. It is in this category that I place this work. This category is relatively new, and there has been no substantial consideration of the particular issue of woman in the light of the entire Qur'an and its major principles.

I propose to make a "reading" of the Qur'an from within the female experience and without the stereotypes which have been the framework for many of the male interpretations. In the final analysis, this reading will confront some of the conclusions drawn on this subject. Because I am analyzing the text and

3. One notable exception in English is Fazlur Rahman's *Major Themes of the Qur'an* (Chicago and Minneapolis: Bibliotheca Islamica, 1980). In addition, see Mustansir Mir, *Thematic and Structural Coherence in the Qur'an: A Study of Islahi's Concept of Nazm* (University of Michigan Microfilms International, 1987), which gives a comprehensive analysis of the significance of theme to Qur'anic organization and, consequently, its exegesis.

4. See Marjorie Procter-Smith, *In Her Own Rite: Reconstructing Feminist Liturgical Tradition* (Nashville, Tenn.: Abingdon Press, 1990), chapter 1, pp. 13–35, on the significance of inclusion and exclusion of women in religious dialogue.

5. For example, Fatna A[it] Sabbah in her book *Woman in the Muslim Unconscious*, translated by Mary Jo Lakeland from the French (New York: Pergamon Press, 1984), discusses valid points with regard to this issue, but when she discusses the Qur'an, she fails to distinguish between the Qur'an and the Qur'anic interpreters.

not the interpretations of that text, my treatment of this issue differs from many of the existing works on this topic.

Methodology: A Hermeneutical Model

A hermeneutical model is concerned with three aspects of the text, in order to support its conclusions: (1) the context in which the text was written (in the case of the Qur'an, in which it was revealed); (2) the grammatical composition of the text (how it says what it says); and (3) the whole text, its *Weltanschauung* or world-view. Often, differences of opinion can be traced to variations in emphasis between these three aspects.

I argue against some conventional interpretations, especially about certain words used in the Qur'an to discuss and fulfill universal guidance. I render some discussions, heretofore considered as gendered, into neutral terms. Other discussions, heretofore considered as universal, I render specific on the basis of their limitations and on the expression in terms specific to seventh-century Arabia. Some historical information with regard to occasions of revelation and the general period of revelation was considered here.

Thus, I attempt to use the method of Qur'anic interpretation proposed by Fazlur Rahman [Pakistan–United States, 1919–1988]. He suggests that all Qur'anic passages, revealed as they were in a specific time in history and within certain general and particular circumstances, were given expression relative to those circumstances. However, the message is not limited to that time or those circumstances historically. A reader must understand the implications of the Qur'anic expressions during the time in which they were expressed in order to determine their proper meaning. That meaning gives the intention of the rulings or principles in the particular verse.

Believers from another circumstance must make practical applications in accordance with how that original intention is reflected or manifested in the new environments. In modern times this is what is meant by the "spirit" of the Qur'an. To get at that "spirit," however, there must be some comprehensible and organized hermeneutical model.[6]

The initial question behind my research was, why does the Qur'an specify males and females on some occasions (like "Believing males and Believing females"—masculine plural followed by feminine plural forms), while on other occasions it uses a more generic ("Oh you who believe . . ."—masculine plural) form? From my perspective on the Qur'an, every usage of the masculine plural form is intended to include males and females, *equally*, unless it includes specific indication for its exclusive application to males.

The plural in Arabic is used to denote three or more rational beings. Thus the following Arabic sentences:

A. *Al-tullab fi al-ghurfa* (masculine plural noun) means
   (1) three or more students in the room—including at least one male
   (2) three or more *exclusively* male students in the room.
B. *Al-talibat fi al-ghurfa* (feminine plural form) means
   (1) three or more female students in the room.

As there is no form exclusively for males, the only way to determine if the masculine plural form (*al-tullab fi al-ghurfa* [A]) is exclusively for males (2) would be through some specific indication in the text. Thus:

C. *Al-tullab wa al-talibat fi al-ghurfa* indicates that the use of the masculine plural (*al-tullab*) refers exclusively to males since the inclusion of the female plural form distinguishes the female students present.[7]

All the verses which contained any reference to women, separately or together with men, were analyzed with the traditional method of *tafsir al-Qur'an bi al-Qur'an* (interpretation of the Qur'an based on the Qur'an itself). However, I elaborated these particular terms of this method. Each verse was analyzed: (1) in its context; (2) in the context of discussions on similar topics in the Qur'an; (3) in the light of similar language and syntactical structures used

---

of an Intellectual Tradition (Chicago: University of Chicago Press, 1982), Introduction, especially pp. 4–9.

7. This is a direct contradiction of the classical models which propose that the masculine plural form means male (exclusively). Thus, language is used to make male the norm, and by implication, the female must be abnormal.

6. For details of Fazlur Rahman's discussion of the above double movement methodology—"from the present situation to Qur'anic times, then back to the present"—for particular communities, see his *Islam and Modernity: Transformation*

elsewhere in the Qur'an; (4) in the light of overriding Qur'anic principles; and (5) within the context of the Qur'anic *Weltanschauung*, or world-view.

Language and Prior Text

One unique element for reading and understanding any text is the prior text of the individual reader: the language and cultural context in which the text is read. It is inescapable and represents, on the one hand, the rich varieties that naturally occur between readers, and, on the other hand, the uniqueness of each.

Prior text adds considerably to the perspective and conclusions of the interpretation. It exposes the individuality of the exegete. This is neither good nor bad in and of itself. However, when one individual reader with a particular world-view and specific prior text asserts that his or her reading is the only possible or permissible one, it prevents readers in different contexts from coming to terms with their own relationship to the text.

To avoid the potential of relativism, there is continuity and permanence in the Qur'anic text itself as exemplified even through various readings by their points of convergence. However, in order for the Qur'an to achieve its objective to act as a catalyst affecting behavior in society, each social context must understand the fundamental and unchangeable principles of that text, and then implement them in their own unique reflection. It is not the text or its principles that change, but the capacity and particularity of the understanding and reflection of the principles of the text within a community of people.

Thus, each individual reader interacts with the text. However, the assertion that there is only one interpretation of the Qur'an limits the extent of the text. The Qur'an must be flexible enough to accommodate innumerable cultural situations because of its claims to be universally beneficial to those who believe.[8] Therefore, to force it to have a single cultural perspective—even the cultural perspective of the original community of the Prophet—severely limits its application and contradicts the stated universal purpose of the Book itself.

The Prior Text of Gender-Specific Languages

The significance of masculine and feminine forms, whether used distinctively or to make generic indications, was an important part of my analysis. Perspectives on gender, particularly on the understanding of what constitutes feminine or masculine behavior, and the roles of men and women in society, are based on one's cultural context. Gender-specific languages, such as Arabic, create a particular prior text for the speakers of that language. Everything is classified male or female. English, Malay, and other languages do not share this prior text with Arabic. This results in a distinction between the various readings of the Qur'an. This distinction becomes apparent in the interpretation of the text and the conclusions drawn from the function of the text with regard to gender.

With regard to Arabic, the language of the Qur'an, I approach the text from the outside. This frees me to make observations which are not imprisoned in the context of a gender-distinct language.

> There exists a very strong, but one-sided and thus untrustworthy, idea that in order better to understand a foreign culture, one must enter into it, forgetting one's own, and view the world through the eyes of this foreign culture. This idea, as I have said, is one-sided. Of course, a certain entry as a living being into a foreign culture, the possibility of seeing the world through its eyes, is a necessary part of the process of understanding it; but if this were the only aspect of this understanding, *it would merely be duplication and would not entail anything new or enriching.* Creative understanding does not renounce itself, its own place in time, its own culture; and it forgets nothing. In order to understand, it is immensely important for the person who understands to be located outside the object of his or her creative understanding—in time, in space, and in culture.[9] (Emphasis mine.)

A new look at Qur'anic language with regard to gender is especially necessary in the light of the absence of an Arabic neuter. Although each word in Arabic is designated as masculine or feminine, it does not follow that each use of masculine or feminine persons is necessarily restricted to the mentioned gender—from the perspective of universal Qur'anic

---

8. This is the Scripture wherein there is no doubt, a guidance unto those who ward off (evil), who believe in the unseen, establish worship, and spend of that We have bestowed upon them. . . . (Sura 2, Verses 2–3)

9. M. M. Bakhtin, *Speech Genres and Other Late Essays*, translated by Vern W. McGhee, edited by Caryl Emerson and Michael Holquist (Austin: University of Texas Press, 1986), pp. 6–7.

guidance.[10] A divine text must overcome the natural restrictions of the language of human communication. Those who argue that the Qur'an cannot be translated believe that there is some necessary correlation between Arabic and the message itself. I will demonstrate that gender distinction, an inherent flaw, necessary for human communication in the Arabic, is overcome by the text in order to fulfill its intention of universal guidance.

Perspectives on Women

"Most men have at one time or another heard, or perhaps even believed, that women are 'inferior' and 'unequal' to men."[11] I worked against the backdrop of common prejudices and attitudes among Muslims towards women which have not only affected the position of women in Muslim societies but also affected the interpretation of the position of women in the Qur'an. One such belief is that there are *essential* distinctions between men and women reflected in creation, capacity and function in society, accessibility to guidance (particularly to Qur'anic guidance), and in the rewards due to them in the Hereafter.

Although there are distinctions between women and men, I argue that they are not of their essential natures. More importantly, I argue against the *values* that have been attributed to these distinctions. Such attributed values describe women as weak, inferior, inherently evil, intellectually incapable, and spiritually lacking. These evaluations have been used to claim that women are unsuitable for performing certain tasks, or for functioning in some ways in society.

The woman has been restricted to functions related to her biology. The man, on the other hand, is evaluated as superior to and more significant than woman, an inherent leader and caretaker, with extensive capacity to perform tasks that the woman cannot. Consequently, men are *more* human, enjoying completely the choice of movement, employment, and social, political and economic participation on the basis of human individuality, motivation, and opportunity This is actually an institutionalized compensation for the reverse situation.

> Woman alone gives birth to children, nurses them, and is their primary nurturer in their early formative years. Moreover, the social and economic roles that commonly have been defined as the province of the male have never been performed exclusively by men. Subconsciously, men are aware of this fact. . . . *The male has never had an exclusive social or economic role that woman could not participate in too. . . .*
>
> Awareness of woman's monopoly was psychologically repressed and overshadowed by institutionalizing and socially legitimating male values that had the effect of creating self-fulfilling prophecies.[12] (Emphasis mine.)

Distinctions between Men and Women

The Qur'an acknowledges the anatomical distinction between male and female. It also acknowledges that members of each gender function in a manner which reflects the well-defined distinctions held by the culture to which those members belong. These distinctions are an important part of how cultures function. For this reason, it would be unwise if the Qur'an failed to acknowledge and, in fact, sympathize with culturally determined, functional distinctions.

> As they are divided, so genders are also interwoven differently in each culture and time. They can rule separate territories and rarely intertwine, or they can be knotted like the lines in the Book of Kells. Sometimes no basket can be plaited, no fire kindled, without the collaboration of two sets of hands. Each culture brings the genders together in its unique way.[13]

The Qur'an does not attempt to annihilate the differences between men and women or to erase the significance of functional gender distinctions which help every society to run smoothly and fulfill its needs. In fact, compatible mutually supportive functional relationships between men and women can be seen as part of the goal of the Qur'an with regard to

---

10. This recurrent problem in "reading" the Qur'an causes readers to justify limiting to women statements made using feminine forms and figures; see chapter 3 below concerning Bilqis. [Not included in this excerpt.—Editor] Although she is a good leader—that happens to be a woman—she is not taken as a universal example of leadership. Statements using masculine forms or figures are limited to men and extended to women only by *qiyas* (analytical reasoning).

11. Alvin J. Schmidt, *Veiled and Silenced: How Culture Shaped Sexist Theology* (Macon, Ga.: Mercer University Press, 1989), Introduction, p. xiii.

12. Schmidt, *Veiled and Silenced*, pp. 59–60.

13. Ivan Illich, *Gender* (New York: Pantheon Books, 1982), pp. 106–107.

society.[14] However, the Qur'an does not propose or support a singular role or single definition of a set of roles, exclusively, for each gender across every culture.

The Qur'an acknowledges that men and women function as individuals and in society. However, there is no detailed prescription set on how to function, culturally. Such a specification would be an imposition that would reduce the Qur'an from a universal text to a culturally specific text—a claim that many have erroneously made. What the Qur'an proposes is transcendental in time and space.[15]

Gender distinctions and distinct gender functions contribute to the perceptions of morally appropriate behavior in a given society. Since the Qur'an is moral guidance, it must relate to the perceptions of morality—no matter how gender-specified—which are held by individuals in various societies. Yet, the mere fact that the Qur'an was revealed in seventh-century Arabia when the Arabs held certain perceptions and misconceptions about women and were involved in certain specific lewd practices against them resulted in some injunctions specific to that culture.

Some prevailing practices were so bad they had to be prohibited explicitly and immediately: infanticide, sexual abuse of slave girls, denial of inheritance to women, *zihar*,[16] to name a few of the most common. Other practices had to be modified: polygamy, unconstrained divorce, conjugal violence, and concubinage, for example. With regard to some practices, the Qur'an seems to have remained neutral: social patriarchy, marital patriarchy, economic hierarchy, the division of labor between males and females within a particular family.

Some women activists today openly question this neutrality. Why didn't the Qur'an just explicitly prohibit these practices? If the evolution of the text and its *overall* objective is consumed under one—albeit important—aspect of social interaction, say consciousness-raising with regard to women, then the Qur'an is made subservient to that aspect, rather than the other way around. There is an essential acknowledgment of the relationship between men and women as they function in society, but it is not the sole nor primary objective of the text.

In addition, certain practices encouraged by the Qur'an may be restricted to that society which practiced them, but the Qur'an is "not confined to, or exhausted by, (one) society and its history. . . ."[17] Therefore, each new Islamic society must understand the principles intended by the particulars. Those principles are eternal and can be applied in various social contexts.

For example, in Arabia at the time of the revelation, women of wealthy and powerful tribes were veiled and secluded as an indication of protection. The Qur'an acknowledges the virtue of modesty and demonstrates it through the prevailing practices. The principle of modesty is important—not the veiling and seclusion which were manifestations particular to that context. These were culturally and economically determined demonstrations of modesty.[18] Modesty is not a privilege of the economically advantaged only: all believing women deserve the utmost respect and protection of their modesty—however it is observed in various societies.

Modesty is beneficial for maintaining a certain moral fiber in various cultures and should therefore be maintained—but on the basis of faith: not economics, politics or other forms of access and coercion. This is perhaps why Yusuf Ali [1872–1952] translates Sura 24, Verse 31 "what (must ordinarily) appear"[19] (with regard to uncovered parts), to indicate that (ordinarily) there are culturally determined guidelines for modesty.

14. See Sayyid Qutb [1903–1966], *Fi zilal al-Qur'an* [*In the Shade of the Qur'an*] (Cairo: Dar al-Shuruq, 1980), volume 2 (of 6), pp. 642–643, where he discusses the shared beliefs and responsibility between men and women in the Islamic social system of justice.

15. Fazlur Rahman, *Islam and Modernity*, pp. 5–7, discusses the moral values of the Qur'an in "extra-historical transcendental" terms; that is, the moral value extracted from a particular verse goes beyond the time and place of the specific instance at which that verse and its injunction was occasioned.

16. The practice of stating that one's wife was as "the back of my mother," which would make conjugal relations impossible, but would not totally free the woman for remarriage.

17. Wan Mohd. Nor Wan Daud, *The Concept of Knowledge in Islam and Its Implications for Education in a Developing Country* (London: Mansell, 1989), p. 7.

18. See William Robertson Smith, *Kinship and Marriage in Early Arabia*, edited by Stanley A. Cook (London: A. and C. Black, 1907).

19. Translation by A. Yusuf Ali, *The Holy Qur'an: Text, Translation, and Commentary*, U.S. edition (Elmhurst, N.Y.: Tahrike Tarsile Qur'an, 1987).

This method of restricting the particulars to a specific context, extracting the principles intended by the Qur'an through that particular, and then applying those principles to other particulars in various cultural contexts, forms a major variation from previous exegetical methodologies. The movement from principles to particulars can only be done by the members of whatever particular context a principle is to be applied. Therefore, interpretation of the Qur'an can never be final. . . .

Rights and Roles of Women: Some Controversies

Woman Is Not Just Biology

Because woman's primary distinction is on the basis of her childbearing ability, it is seen as her primary function. The use of "primary" has had negative connotations in that it has been held to imply that women can only be mothers. Therefore, women's entire upbringing must be to cultivate devoted wives and ideal mothers in preparation for this function.

There is no term in the Qur'an which indicates that childbearing is "primary" to a woman. No indication is given that mothering is her exclusive role. It demonstrates the fact that a woman (though certainly not all women) is the exclusive human capable of bearing children. This capacity is essential to the continuation of human existence. This function becomes primary only with regard to the continuity of the human race. In other words, since only the woman can bear children, it is of primary importance that she does.

Although it does not restrict the female to functioning as a mother, the Qur'an is emphatic about the reverence, sympathy, and responsibility due to the female procreator. "O humankind . . . have *taqwa*[20] towards God in Whom you claim your rights of one another, and (have *taqwa*) towards the wombs (that bore you)." (Sura 4, Verse 1) This verse is often interpreted as indicating respect for women in general.[21] I specify this verse as indicating respect for the needed procreative capacity of women. I do not diminish

respect from women as a class, but I do specify, from the Qur'anic perspective, the significance of the function of child-bearing, which is exclusively performed by women.[22] The reverence given to the fulfillment of this function helps explain how the Qur'an explicitly delineates a function for males which creates a balance in human relations.[23]

No other function is similarly exclusive to one gender or the other. This brings to mind the popular misconception that since only males have had the responsibility of *risala*,[24] it indicates something special about that class. Both men and women have been included in divine communication as the recipients of *wahy*,[25] but there is no Qur'anic example of a woman with the responsibility of *risala*. However, all those chosen for this responsibility were exceptional.

This is not a biological association with males representing their primary function and expressing a universal norm for all men. In fact, given the difficulty they have faced in getting others to accept the message when these exceptional men have come from poor classes, the likelihood of failure for the message might have been greater if women, who are given so little regard in most societies, were selected to deliver the message. It is strategy for effectiveness, not a statement of divine preference.[26]

Besides the two functions discussed above, every other function has real or potential participation by both males and females. However, there is still a wide range of functional distinctions between individuals considered in the Qur'an. The questions that must be asked then are: What is the value of the functional distinctions between individuals? Do these functional distinctions and the values placed on them delineate specific values for males and females in society? Are these values intra-Qur'anic or extra-Qur'anic?

---

20. [Fear of God.—Editor]

21. It should not be overlooked in my literal interpretation, that "the wombs that bore you" is also used as a metaphor for the blood ties of family relations in general.

22. To further substantiate this point of view, see the discussion of Mary, Mother of Jesus, in chapter 2. [Not included in this excerpt.—Editor]

23. Which I will discuss in detail below.

24. There is a distinction between *wahy*, receiving divine communication, and *risala*, receiving divine communication concerning the destiny of humankind, which includes the obligation to transmit the information of that *wahy* to humankind at large.

25. Maryam [Mary, the mother of Jesus] and Umm Musa [the mother of Moses] among the women.

26. See, for example, Sura 22, Verse 75.

In particular, several verses from the Qur'an have frequently been used to support the claims of the inherent superiority of males over females. These verses contain two terms which have been used to indicate value in the functional distinctions between individuals and groups on earth. I will review these terms, how they have been used in the Qur'an, and in the overall context of Qur'anic justice.

The first term is *daraja* (plural: *darajat*), "step, degree or level." A *daraja* exists not only on earth between people but also between the Hereafter and earth,[27] between levels in Heaven and in Hell. The other term, *faddala*, is often used in conjunction with *darajat*. I have translated *faddala* "to prefer," with a verbal noun (*tafdil*) meaning "preference." Often the preference given is spoken of in terms of *fadl*, which I translate as (God's) "benevolence."

Daraja

An individual or group can earn or be granted a *daraja* over another. The Qur'an specifies, for example, that by striving in the way of God with one's wealth and one's person (Sura 4, Verse 95) or by immigrating for God (Sura 9, Verse 20), one can obtain a *daraja*. However, most often the *daraja* is obtained through an unspecified category of doing "good" deeds (Suras 20, Verse 75; 6, Verse 132; 46, Verse 19).

Distinguishing between individuals or groups on the basis of "deeds" involves problems with regard to the value of women in society and as individuals. Although the Qur'an distinguishes on the basis of deeds, it does not set values for particular deeds. This leaves each social system to determine the value of different kinds of deeds at will. They have always done this and "every society has distinguished men's work from women's work."[28] The problem is that "Men's work is usually regarded as more valuable than women's work, no matter how arbitrary the division of labor."[29]

On the one hand, the Qur'an supports distinctions on the basis of deeds, but on the other hand, it does not determine the actual value of specific deeds. This leads to the interpretation that the Qur'an supports values of deeds as determined by individual societies. Actually, the Qur'an's neutrality allows for the natural variations that exist.

With regard to the *daraja* obtained through deeds, however, the Qur'an has stipulated several points which should affect evaluation in society. First, all deeds performed with *taqwa* are more valuable. Second, "Unto men a fortune from that which they have earned and unto women a fortune from that which they have earned." (Sura 4, Verse 32) The deeds may be different, but recompense is given based on what one does. It does not matter how the deeds are divided between the males and the females in a particular social context.

Another implication of a "fortune from what one earns" is that whenever anyone performs tasks normally attributed to the other gender in addition to his or her own normal tasks, he or she will earn an additional reward. For example, Moses meets two women from Madyan, where ordinarily the males tended the animals. However, because there was no able-bodied male in the family to perform this task according to the norm (the father being an old man), the women were required to be *extraordinarily* useful.

There is no indication that these women were immoral in their performance of this task, because fulfilling the tasks needed for survival takes precedence over socially determined roles. Similarly, in post-slavery America, the Black female was given employment instead of the Black male. In many families, she became the sole supporter. This necessity, in addition to her fulfillment of the ordinary tasks of bearing and rearing children, should have given her more. A flexible perspective on the fulfillment of necessity would have benefited her. Instead, she was subject to a double burden and, often, violence at home from a husband who felt displaced.

Each social context divides the labor between the male and the female in such a way as to allow for the optimal function of that society. The Qur'an does not divide the labor and establish a monolithic order for every social system which completely disregards the natural variations in society. On the contrary, it acknowledges the need for variations when it states that the human race is divided "into nations and tribes that you might know one another." (Sura 49, Verse 13) Then it gives each group, and each member of the

---

27. "See how We prefer one above another, and verily the Hereafter will be greater in *darajat* and greater in preference [*tafdil*]." (Sura 17, Verse 21) [Bracketed terms in Qur'anic quotations are the author's, not the editor's.—Editor]

28. Carol Tarvis and Carole Wade, *The Longest War: Sex Differences in Perspective*, second edition (Orlando, Fl.: Harcourt Brace Jovanovich, 1984), p. 3.

29. Tarvis and Wade, *The Longest War*, p. 20.

group—the males and the females—recompense in accordance to deeds performed.

This is an important social universal in the Qur'an. It allows and encourages each individual social context to determine its functional distinctions between members, but applies a single system of equitable recompense which can be adopted in every social context. This is also one reason why certain social systems have remained stagnant in their consideration of the potential roles of women. The Qur'an does not specifically determine the roles, and the individual nations have not considered all the possibilities.

As for the *daraja* which is "given" by God, it is even more illusive than the *daraja* for unspecified deeds. There is a distinction on the basis of knowledge: "God will exalt those who believe among you, and those who have knowledge, to high ranks [*darajat*]." (Sura 58, Verse 11) "We raised by grades [*darajat*] (of mercy) whom We will, and over all endued with knowledge there is one more knowing." (Sura 12, Verse 76)

There are also social and economic distinctions: "We have apportioned among them their livelihood in the life of the world, and raised some of them above others in ranks [*darajat*] that some of them may take labor from others; and the mercy of God is better than (the wealth) that they amass." (Sura 43, Verse 32)[30] It is also clear, however, that wealth is not a "real" distinguishing characteristic, but a functional distinction apparent to humankind and valued within society.

The *daraja* given by God serves another significant function—to test the inhabitants of the earth: "He it is Who has placed you as viceroys of the earth and has exalted some of you in ranks [*darajat*] above others, that He may try you by (the test of) that which He has given you." (Sura 6, Verse 165)

Finally, it is necessary to discuss the one verse which distinguishes a *daraja* between men and women:

Women who are divorced shall wait, keeping themselves apart, three (monthly) courses. And it is not lawful for them that they conceal that which God has created in their wombs if they believe in God and the Last Day. And their husbands would do better to take them back in that case if they desire a reconciliation. And [(the rights) due to the women are

similar to (the rights) against them, (or responsibilities they owe) with regard to] the *ma'ruf*, and men have a degree [*daraja*] above them (feminine plural). God is Mighty, Wise. (Sura 2, Verse 228)

This verse has been taken to mean that a *daraja* exists between all men and all women, in every context. However, the context of the discussion is clearly with regard to divorce: men have an advantage over women. In the Qur'an the advantage men have is that of being individually able to pronounce divorce against their wives without arbitration or assistance. Divorce is granted to a woman, on the other hand, only after intervention of an authority (for example, a judge).

Considering the details given, *daraja* in this verse must be restricted to the subject at hand.[31] To attribute an unrestricted value to one gender over another contradicts the equity established throughout the Qur'an with regard to the individual: each *nafs* [soul] shall have in accordance to what it earns. Yet, the verse is presumed to state what men have believed and wanted others to believe: that society operates hierarchically with the male on top. Finally, this verse states: "[(the rights) due to the women are similar to (the rights) against them, (or responsibilities they owe) with regard to] the *ma'ruf*". The term *ma'ruf* occurs in other instances with regard to the treatment of women in society. [Muhammad Marmaduke] Pickthall [Britain, 1875–1936] translates it as "kindness," but its implications are much wider than that. It is a passive participle of the verbal root "to know," and as such indicates something "obvious," "well known," or "conventionally accepted."[32] However, with regard to treatment, it also has dimensions of equitable, courteous and beneficial.[33]

In this verse (Sura 2, Verse 228), it precedes the *daraja* statement to indicate its precedence. In other words, the basis for equitable treatment is conventionally agreed upon in society. With regard to this, the rights and the responsibilities of the woman and the man are the same. Again, the expression places

30. This is one of the verses which demonstrates that an Islamic society allows for economic classes.

31. In addition, the preceding verses 221–227 discuss at length other details related to marriage, divorce, and widowhood.

32. Edward William Lane, *An Arab-English Lexicon* (London: Librairie du Liban, 1980), part 5, p. 2017.

33. As defined by Milton J. Cowan, *A Dictionary of Modern Written Arabic*, third edition, edited by Hans Wehr (Ithaca, N.Y.: Spoken Language Services, 1976).

a limitation rather than a universal perspective on this issue because convention is relative to time and place.

Faddala

As with *daraja*, the Qur'an states explicitly that God has preferred [*faddala*] some of creation over others. Like *daraja*, this preference is also discussed in specific terms. First, humankind is preferred over the rest of creation (Sura 17, Verse 70). Then, occasionally, one group of people have been preferred over another.[34] Finally, some of the prophets are preferred over others (Suras 2, Verse 253; 6, Verse 86; 17, Verse 55). It is interesting to note, however, that "preference" is not absolute. Although the Qur'an states that some prophets are preferred over others, it also states that *no distinction* is made between them (Sura 2, Verse 285). This indicates that, in the Qur'anic usage, preference is relative.

Like *daraja*, *faddala* is also given to test the one to whom it is given. Unlike *daraja*, however, *faddala* cannot be earned by performing certain deeds. It can only be given by God, Who has it and grants it to whom He wishes and in the form He wishes. Others do not have it and cannot give it. They can only be recipients of His *fadl*.

With regard to *faddala*, men and women, the following verse is central:

> Men are [*qawwamuna 'ala*] women, [on the basis] of what God has [preferred] (*faddala*) some of them over others, and [on the basis] of what they spend of their property (for the support of women). So good women are [*qanitat*],[35] guarding in secret that which God has guarded. As for those from whom you fear [*nushuz*], admonish them, banish them to beds apart, and scourge them. Then, if they obey you, seek not a way against them. (Sura 4, Verse 34)

Needless to say, this verse covers a great deal more than just preference. This is classically viewed as the single most important verse with regard to the relationship between men and women: "men are *qawwamuna 'ala* women." Before discussing this,

however, I want to point out that this correlation is determined on the basis of two things: (1) what "preference" has been given, and (2) "what they spend of their property (for support of women)," that is, a socioeconomic norm and ideal.

The translation I have inserted, "on the basis of," comes from the *bi*[36] used in this verse. In a sentence, it implies that the characteristics or contents before *bi* are determined "on the basis" of what comes after *bi*. In this verse it means that men are *qawwamuna 'ala* women only if the following two conditions exist. The first condition is "preference," and the other is that they support the women from their means. "If either condition fails, then the man is not '*qawwam*' over that woman."[37]

My first concern then is *faddala*. The verse says the position between men and women is based on "what" God has preferred. With regard to material preference, there is only one Qur'anic reference which specifies that God has determined for men a portion greater than for women: inheritance.[38] The share for a male is twice that for the female (Sura 4, Verse 7) within a single family. The absolute inheritance for all men will not always be more than that for all women. The exact amount left depends on the family's wealth in the first place. In addition, if Sura 4, Verse 34 refers to a preference demonstrated in inheritance, then such a materialistic preference is also not absolute. This connection is often favored because the other condition for *qiwama* is that "they spend of their property (for the support of women)." Thus, there is a reciprocity between privileges and responsibilities. Men have the responsibility of paying out of their wealth for the support of women, and they are consequently granted a double share of inheritance.

However, it cannot be overlooked that "many men interpret the above passage" as an unconditional indication of the preference of men over women. They assert that "men were created by God superior to women (in strength and reason)."

34. For example, the Children of Israel were preferred over "other creatures" (the same term has been translated in chapter 1, the Fatiha, as "the worlds") in Sura 2, Verses 47 and 122; and Sura 7, Verse 40. This preference is usually understood to mean that they were chosen to receive prophets and the revelations.

35. [Obedient.—Editor]

36. This is the *ba al-sababiyya* known in Arabic as the *bi* for a reason or purpose. It establishes a conditional relationship between two parts of a sentence or clause. The first part is conditional upon, and cannot be attributed without, the second part.

37. Azizah al-Hibri, "A Study of Islamic Herstory: Or How Did We Ever Get into This Mess?" *Women and Islam: Women's Studies International Forum*, volume 5, number 2, 1982, p. 218.

38. Which I will discuss in detail below.

However, this interpretation ... is (i) unwarranted and (ii) inconsistent with other Islamic teachings. . . . [T]he interpretation is unwarranted because there is no reference in the passage to male physical or intellectual superiority.[39]

Faddala cannot be unconditional because Sura 4, Verse 34 does not read "they (masculine plural) are preferred over them (feminine plural)." It reads "*ba'd* (some) of them over *ba'd* (others)." The use of *ba'd* relates to what obviously has been observed in the human context. All men do not excel over all women in all manners. Some men excel over some women in some manners. Likewise, some women excel over some men in some manners.[40] So, whatever God has preferred, it is still not absolute.

If "what" God has preferred is restricted to the material (and specifically inheritance), then the extent and nature of the preference is explained by the Qur'an. Even if "what" God has preferred is more than just the preference given in inheritance, it is, nevertheless, still restricted to "some of them" over "some others" by the wording in this context:

> Men are "*qawwamun*" over women in matters where God gave *some* of the men more than *some* of the women, *and* in what the men spend of their money, then clearly men as a class are not "*qawwamun*" over women *as a class*.[41]

However, further understanding of this distinction requires further explanation of *qawwamuna 'ala*. What does it mean, and what are the parameters of its application?

As for the meaning, Pickthall translates this as "in charge of." [Abu'l Qasim Mahmud] Al-Zamakhshari [1075–1144][42] says it means that "men are in charge of the affairs of women." [Abul A'la] Mawdudi [1903–

1979][43] says, "Men are the managers of the affairs of women because God has made the one superior to the other. . . ." Azizah al-Hibri [Lebanon, born 1943] objects to any translation which implies that men are protectors or maintainers because "the basic notion here is one of moral guidance and caring"[44] and also because:

> only under extreme conditions (for example, insanity) does the Muslim woman lose her right to self-determination. . . . Yet men have used this passage to exercise absolute authority over women. They also use it to argue for the male's divinely ordained and inherent superiority.[45]

Some questions beg asking concerning the parameters of application: Are all men *qawwamuna 'ala* all women? Is it restricted to the family, such that the men of a family are *qawwamuna 'ala* the women of that family? Or, is it even more restricted, to the marital tie such that only husbands are *qawwamuna 'ala* wives? All of these possibilities have been given.

Generally, an individual scholar[46] who considers *faddala* an unconditional preference of males over females does not restrict *qiwama* to the family relationship but applies it to society at large. Men, the superior beings, are *qawwamuna 'ala* women, the dependent, inferior beings.

Sayyid Qutb,[47] whose discussion I will consider at length, considers *qiwama* an issue of concern for the family within society. He restricts Sura 4, Verse 34, in some ways, then, to the relationship between the husband and the wife. He believes that providing for the females gives the male the privilege of being *qawwamuna 'ala* the female.

He gives *qiwama* a decided dimension of material maintenance. The rationale behind restricting this verse to the context of husband and wife is partly due to the fact that the remainder of the verse discusses other details of concern to the marital relationship.

---

39. Al-Hibri, "A Study of Islamic Herstory," pp. 217–218.

40. I have translated *ba'd* in its usual meaning of "some" or "a portion of." However, there is also usage of *ba'd* plus masculine plural noun plus *ba'd*, which means "each other" with no particular number or gender implied. In other words, a degree of vagueness surrounds this statement. It could also mean women have a preference over men.

41. Al-Hibri, "A Study of Islamic Herstory," p. 218.

42. *Al-Kashshaf 'an haqa'iq al-tanzil wa 'uyun al-aqawil fi wujuh al-ta'wil* [*The Revealer of the True Meanings of the Revelation and Select Opinions concerning Interpretations of the Text*] (Beirut, Lebanon: Dar al-Ma'arif, no date), volume 1 (of 4), p. 523.

43. *Al-Kashshaf*, volume 2, p. 117.

44. Al-Hibri, "A Study of Islamic Herstory," p. 217.

45. Al-Hibri, "A Study of Islamic Herstory," p. 218.

46. For example, I would include Pickthall because he translates this passage as unrestricted "men are in charge of women." Al-Zamakhshari, in *Al-Kashshaf*, volume 1, p. 523, states the terms he believes of God's preference of men over women. 'Abbas Mahmud Al-'Aqqad [1889–1964], *Al-Mar'a fi al-Qur'an* [*Woman in the Qur'an*] (Cairo: Dar al-Hilal, 1962), p. 7, states the same. Finally, Mawdudi interprets it this way.

47. *Al-Kashshaf*, volume 2, pp. 648–653.

In addition, the following verse uses the dual, indicating that it is concerned with the context between the two: the husband and wife. However, preceding verses discuss terms of relations between male members of society and female members of society.

I apply this verse to society at large but not on the basis of inherent superiority of men over women, or of God's preference of men over women. Rather, I extend the functional relationship which Sayyid Qutb proposes between the husband and the wife towards the collective good concerning the relationship between men and women in society at large. My main consideration is the responsibility and right of women to bear children.

Sayyid Qutb says, "The man and the woman are both from God's creation and God . . . never intends to oppress anyone from His creation."[48] Both the man and the woman are members of the most significant institution of society, the family. The family is initiated by marriage between one man and one woman. Within the family, each member has certain responsibilities. For obvious biological reasons, a primary responsibility for the woman is childbearing.

The child-bearing responsibility is of grave importance: human existence depends upon it. This responsibility requires a great deal of physical strength, stamina, intelligence, and deep personal commitment.[49] Yet, while this responsibility is so obvious and important, what is the responsibility of the male in this family and society at large? For simple balance and justice in creation, and to avoid oppression, his responsibility must be equally significant to the continuation of the human race. The Qur'an establishes his responsibility as *qiwama*: seeing to it that the woman is not burdened with additional responsibilities which jeopardize that primary demanding responsibility that only she can fulfill.

Ideally, *everything* she needs to fulfill her primary responsibility comfortably should be supplied in society, by the male: this means physical protection as well as material sustenance. Otherwise, "it would be a serious oppression against the woman."[50]

This ideal scenario establishes an equitable and mutually dependent relationship. However, it does not allow for many of today's realities. What happens in societies experiencing a population overload, such as China and India? What happens in capitalistic societies like America, where a single income is no longer sufficient to maintain a reasonably comfortable life-style? What happens when a woman is barren? Does she still deserve *qiwama* like other women? What happens to the balance of responsibility when the man cannot provide materially, as was often the case during slavery and post-slavery U.S.?

All of these issues cannot be resolved if we look narrowly at verse Sura 4, Verse 34. Therefore, the Qur'an must eternally be reviewed with regard to human exchange and mutual responsibility between males and females. This verse establishes an ideal obligation for men with regard to women to create a balanced and shared society. This responsibility is neither biological nor inherent, but it is valuable. An attitude inclined towards responsibility must be cultivated. It is easy enough to see the cases in which it has not been acquired.

However, such an attitude should not be restricted to mere material *qiwama*. In broader terms, it should apply to the spiritual, moral, intellectual, and psychological dimensions as well. Such a perspective on *qiwama* will allow men to truly fulfill their *khilafa* (trusteeship) on the earth, as ordained by God upon human creation. Such an attitude will overcome the competitive and hierarchical thinking which destroys rather than nurtures.

Men are encouraged to fulfill their trusteeship of the earth—especially in relationships with women, the child-bearers and traditional caretakers. What women have learned through bearing and caring for children, men can begin to experience, starting with their attitudes to and treatment of women.

---

48. Qutb, *Fi zilal al-Qur'an*, volume 2, p. 650.
49. Qutb, *Fi zilal al-Qur'an*, volume 2, p. 650.

50. Qutb, *Fi zilal al-Qur'an*, volume 2, p. 650.

Islam and the 1995 Beijing World Conference on Women

Muhammad Shahrour (Syria, born 1938) attended primary and secondary school in Damascus. When he was nineteen, he went to Moscow to study engineering. Although not a Marxist, Shahrour was fascinated by Marxist theory and practice, which played a role in shaping his writing on Islamic themes.[1] Shahrour returned to Syria in 1964 but left again in 1968 to study for his master's and doctoral degrees in soil mechanics and foundation engineering at the University College, Dublin, Ireland. He became a faculty member at the University of Damascus on his return to Syria in 1972 and a partner in a successful civil engineering firm. His first book, *Al-Kitab wa-l-Qur'an: qira'a mu'asira* [*The Book and the Qur'an: A Contemporary Reading*], more than 800 pages long and nearly half a month's salary for an educated professional in Syria, became a best-seller throughout the Arab world following its publication in 1990.[2] Using modern linguistics and frequent metaphors and analogies drawn from engineering and the sciences, Shahrour argues that the Qur'an should be read and interpreted, not through the prism of centuries of jurisprudence, but as if "the Prophet just died and informed us of this Book."[3] The essay translated here, originally prepared in response to written questions posed by the editor of a Kuwaiti newspaper, defends the right of Muslim women to participate in the Fourth United Nations Conference on Women, held at Beijing, China, in 1995. More self-contained than Shahrour's books,[4] it shows how he invokes and interprets Qur'anic texts to address contemporary social and religious themes.

1. Interview with Dale F. Eickelman and Sadek J. Sulaiman, Damascus, March 22, 1996.

2. Dale F. Eickelman, "Islamic Liberalism Strikes Back," *Middle East Studies Association Bulletin*, volume 27, number 2, December 1993, pp. 163–168; Peter Clark, "The Shahrur Phenomenon: A Liberal Islamic Voice from Syria," *Islam and Christian-Muslim Relations*, volume 7, number 3, October 1996, pp. 337–341.

3. Muhammad Shahrour, *al-Kitab wa-l-Qur'an: Qira'a mu'asira* (*The Book and the Qur'an: A Contemporary Read-*ing) (Damascus: Al-Ahali li-l-Taba'a wa-l-Nashr wa-l-Tawzi'a, 1990), p. 44.

4. In addition to *Al-Kitab wa-l-Qur'an*, Shahrour is the author of *Dirasat al-Islamiyya mu'asira fi dawla wa-l-mujtama'* (*Contemporary Islamic Studies in State and Society*) (Damascus: Al-Ahali li-l-Taba'a wa-l-Nashr wa-l-Tawzi'a, 1994), which contains an introduction replying to the critics of his first book (pp. 15–46); and *Al-Islam wa-l-iman: Manzuma al-qiyam* (*Islam and Faith: A Treatise on Values*) (Damascus: Al-Ahali li-l-Taba'a wa-l-Nashr wa-l-Tawzi'a, 1996).

I certainly see the need for convening conferences like this one because the issues concern both men and women. Human rights are abused in many countries, and tyranny and political despotism are primary oppressors. From a purely historical perspective, women fall under two forms of oppression. First, like men, they are politically, economically, and socially subjugated; second, they live in a male-oriented society. A quick glance at world statistics shows us that women possess 1/1000th of the world's aggregate wealth and receive 10 percent of the world's total wages despite comprising 50 percent of the world's population. This situation prevails in many countries regardless of people's religion. As Ibn Qayyim al-Jawziyya (1292–1350) wrote, "Wherever justice exists, the rule of God is found."

God is the Lord of all peoples, and all peoples are our brothers in religion and equal to us as God's creations. The cause of justice is served when a conference is convened in Beijing or elsewhere for the purpose of fighting oppression and despotism. Indeed, such a conference promotes justice. The desire for justice is shared by all peoples and open discussion is the principal means of communication among people. Justice and Islam are the basis of this search; violence, oppression, injustice, and despotism are deviations which we are obliged to oppose whether these deviations exist between peoples, individuals, or men and women.

For this reason, separate conferences for women, men, and children would only be opposed by a person of limited vision, a person who is unaware of the information revolution which has occurred in the last half of the 20th century, shortening distances and making the world a small village. Such a person has not realized that the era of concealing information from people with iron curtains has passed, and the time of forbidding people to read, listen and view has vanished forever. The information revolution has given us something important—knowledge. It has helped us move to a new level of awareness, expressing opinions, taking stands, and respecting other opinions.

The Beijing world conference on women embodies the stage of expressing opinion publicly, listening to other opinions, and acknowledging their existence. This positive outcome is not in any way alien to our beliefs as Muslims. We will never forget the slogan—political, intellectual, and social—with which the Prophet Muhammad confronted the polytheists: "Don't block the way between me and my people." People's convictions are not generated by violence and coercion, but by peaceful and open dialogue. Open dialogues do not frighten us as Muslims. Fear is created by a lack of self-confidence and by weak suppositions which cannot be sustained in dialogues with others. We, by the grace of God, possess the self-confidence which enables us to face others without shrinking or questioning motives.

Accepting all participant groups in this conference, no matter how diverse their beliefs, orientations, and perspective, should happen as a matter of principle. This is precisely what I alluded to in my comment on the freedom of opinion and respecting the views of others.

The participation of organizations of sexual deviants and prostitutes in the debates over women's issues—and I refer to debates only—is certainly legitimate. The conference is not able to pass binding resolutions or take measures for resolving the problems of women in any way.

I am speaking of a world conference of women which has 50,000 participants. There will be sexual deviants and prostitutes among them—they might even have organizations—but the conference is not a gathering of prostitutes in either purpose or form. Lust, prostitution and sexual deviancy are as old as history. They will exist in the future. We carry the banner of a true living religion, believing in the coexistence of good and evil, with an unbreakable bond between them. God has tied them together with the phenomenon of death in his wisdom-giving revelation: "Every soul shall have a taste of death, and We test you by evil and by good by way of trial. To Us must ye return." (Qur'an, Sura 21, Verse 35) In other words, as long as there is life and death, good and evil will evolve together. This requires us to abandon the idea that a day will come when all people on earth will become believers, everyone will become atheists, or all women will become virtuous.

Conference recommendations are one thing, and resolutions are something else. There is an important issue here which we must not overlook. There are high ideals, commandments, and general moral laws that tie people together. These high ideals, commandments, and moral laws do not yield to debate in conferences and votes in assemblies, irrespective of religious, political, or national beliefs.

I don't believe that people at the conference wish to subject the issues of false testimony or parental abuse to discussion or vote. These issues do not require deliberation. The role of religious moral principles is evident in such matters, and these religious principles are more basic than political or economic ones.

Respected, remarkable women are taking part in the Beijing conference. I see the need for Muslim women to take part alongside them, so that they will be able to object by reasonable argument to those recommendations which violate moral law and high ideals. It is the right of Muslim women to voice such opposition at these conferences.

When I emphasize high ideals and moral laws as basic to the contemporary Islamic positions, I point implicitly to the need to refrain from making jurisprudential (*fiqh*) rulings the basis for argument. There are two reasons the jurisprudential rulings, especially those related to women, are not an appropriate basis. First, Muslims disagree among themselves about them. Second, jurisprudential ruling bears the historical stamp of the era in which it was created and the society in which it was shaped. These rulings have been forged in the context of political despotism on the one hand, and male authority on the other. A clear case specific to women is *mut'a* marriage [among Shi'i Muslims, a temporary, contractual marriage], which some Muslims accept and others do not.

I believe that it is legitimate to continue developing jurisprudential rulings (*fiqh*) but not the core of Islamic jurisprudence, the divine revelation (*al-shar'*), in matters relating to women's status. I also believe that the development of Islamic jurisprudence should include matters related to men and to society as a whole in accordance with the following premises.

1. Distinguishing between divinely sanctioned (*halal*) and the divinely prohibited (*haram*), the humanly permissible (*masmuh*) and the humanly forbidden (*mamnu'*), and believing that Islam is a religion compatible with human nature. The basic tenet of Islam is that everything not specifically prohibited is permitted.

2. The only authority for divine prohibitions (*tahrim*) is God, although humankind may allow or disallow. Consider God's statement, "Fight those who believe not in God nor the Last Day, nor hold that forbidden which hath been forbidden by God and His Messenger." (Qur'an, Sura 9, Verse 29)

The order to fight in this verse is based on two assumptions. The first [as is clear from the verse's Arabic wording—Translator] is that fighting involves two sides. The second is that the other non-Muslim side is the aggressor. This assumption is derived from God's saying, "If anyone commits aggression against you, then fight him back in exactly the same way." (Qur'an, Sura 2, Verse 194) The command is invoked against those who "do not believe in God and in the Last Day," that is, the atheists who are not concerned with what God and His Prophet have divinely forbidden. A last important observation is in "that which God and His Messenger have forbidden." God's forbidding and the Prophet's forbidding are interconnected. This means that the Prophet forbids that which God forbids. If the Prophet could forbid on his own, the passage would say, "What God forbids and what His Messenger forbids." The Qur'an [Sura 66, Verse 1] confirms this statement: "O Prophet! Why holdest thou to be forbidden that which God has made lawful to thee." No one has the right to forbid that which God has declared divinely lawful. We understand from this that the Prophet allowed and disallowed various things, but did not make lawful the divinely forbidden or forbid the divinely sanctioned. There are good examples in the Prophet's conduct and sayings. If everything that Muhammad did and said was divinely inspired, it would imply that the Prophet had been transformed into a pre-programmed robot, and robots aren't suitable examples for humanity.

Then came the Companions of the Prophet. All that they did and said represents human judgment and does not relate to the divinely sanctioned or forbidden. As such, their actions and words have historical relevance in terms of laying down rules and regulations for their societies without crossing into the realm of the divinely sanctioned and forbidden. Let us illustrate this with a hypothetical example:

If the Prophet had lived in the time of the automobile and had commanded people to keep to the right side of the road when driving, then driving on the right would have become—according to jurisprudential principles—an Islamic law. Australia, for example, where driving is on the left, would have been deemed in violation of Islamic law, and we don't see this interpretation as correct.

3. Islamic revelation began with Noah and ended with Muhammad. One of the goals of Qur'anic stories is to give a clear picture of this development. All messengers and prophets were Muslims. But Islam embodies the capacity to evolve through legislation

and morality. This provides a backbone for Islamic belief and practice. It does not mean that evolution contradicts verses from the wisdom-giving revelation. Rather, the seal of Muhammad's revelation means the achievement of universality with Islam and humankind may adopt such customs not specifically mentioned in the revelation. People are required, however, to remain within the boundaries set forth in revelation. By this process, Islamic jurisprudence develops continuously.

4. The ways in which humankind acquires knowledge in the 20th century influence how it reads and understands divine revelation. For example, now that we know more about procreation, we understand the basic distinctions between genitor and father, genetrix and mother, distinctions that the revelation made,

even though most of the first jurists did not. Recognizing these distinctions gives us new perspectives on jurisprudence, adding to our adjustment of earlier rulings related to such things as inheritance and adoption, while adhering to the text and essence of the revealed verses. What has happened here is that our understanding of these verses has changed in accordance with changes in our objective knowledge.

In this manner, we understand how the course of human history and the development of universal knowledge about humanity and its environment is the only phenomenon that reveals and authenticates the content of the Qur'an. Its authenticity does not depend on knowledge specific to any given era, generation, or individual.

PART IV

Rights of Non-Muslims

Minorities in a Democracy

The partition of the British colonies in South Asia in 1947 left 100 million Muslims in the newly independent nation of India, but Muslim Indians comprise only 12 percent of the population of India. The Muslims of India are therefore keenly interested in protection of the rights of minorities.[1] This theme is prominent in the work of Humayun Kabir (India, 1906–1969), one of the premier political and intellectual leaders of the Muslim community of India. Born and raised in the West Bengal region and educated both in India and at Oxford University, Kabir supported the Indian nationalist movement and opposed Islamic demands for partition. After independence, he served in the Indian parliament for more than a decade, held a series of cabinet posts, and represented India at a variety of United Nations educational programs.[2] At the same time, he wrote and lectured on Islam, developing a modernist and humanist interpretation that emphasized religious tolerance and cross-cultural communication.

Many think that the diversity of India and consequent multiplicity of centers of power is a source of weakness for the country. I have always held the contrary view. I feel that the greater the number of centers of power in a people—provided the centers of power are held in some kind of a balance with one another, and there is harmony among them — the stronger the country. Where you have a completely homogeneous, monolithic society, the chances of survival of that society or community are always less than those of a heterogeneous society in which there are many centers of power, many ways of expression. The reason for this is easy to understand. Since society is changing, circumstances are changing, a monolithic society may not be able to react to a new situation with complete success. But if there is a heterogeneous society, one element or other in that heterogeneous society may respond to the new situation, and help to preserve the community as a whole. Diversity of response and distribution of power are therefore sources of strength, not causes of weakness. The history of India is itself a shining example of this fact.

1. On recent debates within Indian Islam, see Christian W. Troll, "Sharing Islamically in the Pluralistic Nation-State of India: The Views of Some Contemporary Indian Muslim Leaders and Thinkers," in Yvonne Yazbeck Haddad and Wadi Zaidan Haddad, editors, *Christian-Muslim Encounters* (Gainesville: University Press of Florida, 1995), pp. 245–262.

2. *Science, Philosophy and Culture: Essays Presented in Honour of Humayun Kabir's Sixty-Second Birthday* (New York: Asia Publishing House, 1968), pp. xi–xii.

More monolithic societies have disappeared, but the more, shall I say, democratic form of Indian society lives. In spite of the fact that there was no political democracy here, the distribution of power in a number of centers, the existence of different types of communities within what one may call a loose federal social framework, has enabled India to survive. Wherever society shows such diversity, wherever different groups exist side by side, the chances of survival of the entire community are greater.

Now how does this link up with our problem today? Today, there is a common citizenship in India. Power has to be exercised in terms of common programs and common attitudes and common ideals. At the same time there are groups based on the fact of language or religion or political beliefs or economic interests. I would suggest for your consideration that if these groups are rigid and unchangeable, especially at the level of political action, it would create a problem for this country. I have always been against political parties based on religion, political parties based on caste, not because there is anything intrinsically evil in any of them, but because in the modern world, in the kind of society in which we function, this type of attachment of a political program to a group based on birth—which is comparatively rigid and inalienable, which cannot be changed easily—creates difficulties for society as well as the group itself.

One other interesting phenomenon has to be remembered in this context. Wherever group consciousness is strong, it is the minority which suffers most. If group consciousness can be diffused and dispersed, the minorities get many privileges, many advantages, which they would not get, if group consciousness became strong. Majorities are in any case in a position of advantage. I think it should be one of the aims of every minority group to see that the group consciousness of the majority becomes diffused. This can be done only if right issues are selected. If groups are constituted on grounds other than rigid and inalienable factors like religion, caste, tribe, or language, we can change or modify more easily the composition and number of the groups within society.

Even rigid groups may change under the pressure of events, but in their case the changes are far more difficult to effect. Proselytization on a large scale is almost impossible in the modern world. And therefore for any religious group to think that it will convert all the members of some other religious group to its own religion is not practical politics today. Languages can also spread, but here also the experience of history shows that linguistic boundaries are one of the most rigid things in the world. The political boundaries of Europe have changed again and again during the last four or five hundred years, but the linguistic boundaries of Europe have hardly changed. Even political suppression has not been able to stifle the linguistic minorities. If persecution could kill a language, Polish would have been killed many years ago. No language can be killed by persecution without exterminating the people speaking the language. Similarly, we cannot easily change tribal or caste organizations. All such groups suffer from a lack of flexibility. In the modern world, where politics is expanding its scope and where political power is impinging on almost every sphere of life, we have to be specially careful of the way in which interests are organized into groups. If a minority group is based on considerations which cannot be easily changed, it will ultimately be the minority itself which will suffer.

On the other hand, if groups are formed on considerations which are flexible, it will make for greater mobility among groups and therefore ultimately for greater cohesion within the community. Persons from any part of the country or belonging to any birth group can come and join such organizations on the basis of their political belief or economic affiliation. I know that economic classes also have a certain degree of rigidity, but the degree of rigidity in economic stratification is far less than that in a caste or religious or linguistic structure. Similarly, cultural groups show greater flexibility than groups based on the fact of birth. If groups are formed on the basis of cultural ideals, there again the ease in movement from one group to another would be far greater than where there are water-tight compartments based on religion, language or caste.

The greatest danger to national unity arises where a group seeks to combine all these rigid elements. Where a unit based on birth includes all the factors like religion, language, caste, and tribe and links them up with political, economic and cultural affiliations, such a group would seek to repel all other groups and have hardly any cross associations with them. On the other hand, when individuals belong to different groups for different purposes, and there are many cross currents which cut across group loyalties, we have a better balanced and healthier national community. In fact, the more cross associations we have, the better for everyone concerned and the better for the health of a democracy.

I would like to return to the point that the essence of democracy lies in the distribution of power in a number of different centers. Such distribution of power can be on the basis of community groups; it can also be on the basis of interest. I have just suggested that where the distribution is on the basis of community groups, based on the fact of birth, there are dangers to social unity. But having said this, I would also say that groups based on birth cannot be completely overlooked in our national context. We have to face facts as they are, especially in a country like India. Some people resent the existence of linguistic or religious or caste groups and would like to eliminate them. We may disapprove, but the linguistic groups will remain. We may dislike it, but the religious groups will also remain. All that we can do is to see that they do not become too rigid, that all these diversities do not tend to ossify, that they do not tend to combine in a way so that the same group is characterized by all these differences. That would be the greatest danger, but having recognized the danger, we may say that the multiplicity of groups also serves a function in modern democracy in India. . . .

The problem of group relations goes very far back in history. The concept of the secular State is something which is relatively novel. In the days before the dawn of history, the same individual was simultaneously prophet, priest and king. There was no distinction between what we call religious and secular functions. We find this among the Aryans in India and we find it among the Aryans in Europe. This was equally true of the non-Aryan groups who lived in different areas of the world and some of whom developed great and rich civilizations of their own. Anthropology tells us that in almost every social group, the prophet, the priest and the king were rolled into one for a very long time.

It is interesting to note that perhaps the first conscious attempt to differentiate the religious from the secular functions is found in a saying of Jesus Christ. Many of you remember his famous statement: "Render unto Caesar that which belongs to Caesar and render unto God that which belongs to God." I do not remember the exact words, but this is the sense of what Jesus said. Christ thus did attempt to make a distinction between a person's religious loyalties and his obligations in the political field. As far as I recollect, this is perhaps the first recognition of a distinction between religious and political loyalties. It would thus be fair to say that we have the origin of the secular State in this famous statement.

Theoretically, the secular State emerged as late as the time of Jesus, but in practice, the rudiments of the secular State had appeared long before. This was perhaps inevitable. Whenever men professing different faiths were brought under one rule—as in the Persian or the Babylonian Empire, the Assyrian Empire or some of the Empires in India—men following one faith had to make allowances for people professing other faiths. Where men followed different customs, and yet lived within the same territory, it was inevitable that accommodation among them should grow. Without such adjustments the State would break up. Theoretically, the State accepted one particular religion and the king was the defender of that faith. To some extent, this idea persists even today. Practice however differed sharply from theory. Normal men and women want to lead a life of cooperation and friendship with their neighbors and hence some kind of accommodation was established from very early times. That theory still lags behind practice is obvious, when we see that a kingdom like the United Kingdom—very progressive in many ways —still describes its ruler as the Defender of the Faith. A person who does not belong to the Anglican Church cannot be ruler of England. In practice, if not in theory, we find similar restrictions in other parts of the world. Some of you will remember that only seven years ago, when Mr. [John F.] Kennedy [1917-1963] was seeking election to the office of the President of the USA, it was for a long time debated whether he would be elected because of his religious faith. While in practice the idea of a secular State has steadily gained acceptance, in theory it remained for a long time unrecognized and is still unrecognized in large areas of the world.

The practical recognition of the secular State dates back fairly early in India. We have the early division of the people into the Buddhists and the Hindus. Some may object that there were perhaps no Hindus at the time. It has been argued seriously that the idea of the Hindu as such is a comparatively recent development. In any case, there were in ancient India the six orthodox Schools and there were the heterodox Schools like the Buddhists and the Jains.

We find in both the great Mauryan Empire in the north [321–185 B.C.] and the Vijaya Empire in the south [fifth century B.C.–65 A.D.] a great deal of tolerationn of all faiths. It will perhaps amuse some of you to hear of the way in which the principle of toleration operated in South India. In the Vijaya Empire, the kings were mostly Hindus and the queens were generally Buddhists. The kings extended protection and patronage to the Brahmanical priests. The queens extended equal protection and patronage to the Buddhist Sramanas and Bhikshus. As long as this balance was maintained and support given to the Brahmins and the Brahmanical faith as well as to the Buddhists and the Buddhist faith, the Vijaya Empire flourished. When at a later stage, one of the kings started persecuting the Buddhists, the decay of the Empire began. We have parallels in northern India as well, in the pre-Muslim and the Muslim period. The idea of the secular State thus goes back fairly far in Indian history, certainly to the times of Chandragupta Maurya [reigned 321–297 B.C.] and to the times of the great kings of Amaravati and Vijayapuri.

A new situation arose when Muslims first established their rule in India. In the beginning, Muslim political thinking, like the political thinking of almost all nations of the world of the time, recognized no distinction between religion and the State. In fact, every religion then claimed the total allegiance of man. This was true of Christianity, this was true of all the different forms of the Hindu faith, this was true of Islam. In the early days of Islam, the man who was the *khalifa* [caliph] was not only the secular but also the religious head of the State. It was claimed that no one should be selected as the *khalifa* unless he was capable of exercising also the religious leadership of the community. This was of course pure theory. Practice began to differ within a few decades. After the death of the Prophet, even when Abu Bakr *Siddiqi* was elected the *khalifa* [reigned 632–634], there were some protests. There were some followers of 'Ali [son-in-law of the Prophet, circa 596–661] who said that 'Ali should have been the first *khalifa* and not Abu Bakr. 'Ali himself repudiated them and accepted Abu Bakr as the *khalifa* but the voice of dissension had already risen. The same problem arose with greater intensity at the time of the election of 'Umar [ibn al-Khattab, reigned 634–644]. These two elections were however generally welcome but dissensions became much more bitter at the time of the election of 'Uthman [reigned 644–656] and 'Ali himself [reigned 656–661]. Many of you remember the story of Karbala and the martyrdom of Husayn [younger son of 'Ali, 626–680]. Mu'awiya [ibn Abi Sufyan, circa 605–680] had raised the banner of revolt against the election of Hasan [elder son of 'Ali, 624–669] and declared that he should be elected the *khalifa*. There was a compromise by which Mu'awiya was accepted but it was also laid down that after his death, Hasan and Husayn in that order should be elected the *khalifa*. Mu'awiya's son Yazid [circa 642–683] repudiated the agreement and the conflict was resolved by the fighting in Karbala leading to the martyrdom of Hussain. The opposition to Mu'awiya and Yazid was mainly on religious grounds, so that theoretically there was still the demand that the State shall be a religious State and there shall be no distinction between secular and religious duties, obligations and rights.

The situation changed as the Muslim empire spread rapidly through large areas of Asia and many different peoples were brought within its fold. Many practical problems arose and Muslim political thinking had to find a place for non-Muslim subjects in a Muslim State. Their existence was recognized in theory by introducing a novel idea, the idea of *dhimmi*. *Dhimmi* means the protected people, who had to pay a special tax, the *jizya*, because they took no share in guarding the State. Muslims were required to bear arms in defense of the State and were exempted from this tax, but those who were not required to bear arms, or purchased exemption, had to pay the tax. They had thus no obligation to defend the country but enjoyed the security guaranteed by the State and were required to pay a special tax instead. This is the notorious, famous, infamous, whichever way you put it, *jizya*. *Jizya* was thus nothing but a kind of polltax by which a person purchased the right of not being called to arms. Some modern States have the system of draft, by which every adult male has to undergo military training for a specified period. A citizen can however get out of the draft in certain ways. In a sense, the *jizya* was an anticipation of these devices for it provided a mode of payment through which a man could escape the draft, but it had an invidious character as it applied only to non-Muslims.

New considerations came into the picture when the Muslims came to India. Whatever may have been the theory, the men who ruled India found that unless there was accommodation among the different religious communities who lived in the country and a great deal of toleration by the ruler, their rule would not last. History has proved again and again that one cannot rule by might alone. Such rule may last for a while but if the entire people are determined to overthrow a foreign yoke, such foreign rule cannot last very long. Some of these early Muslim rulers in India soon discovered that whatever may be said in theory, in practice they had to accommodate their subjects in many ways. If they sometimes oppressed their Hindu subjects, they oppressed their Muslim subjects with equal gusto. 'Ala'uddin Khalji's [reigned 1296–1316] is a name which readily comes to one's mind in this context. He put a tax on all the nobles and made no distinction between a Hindu noble and a Muslim noble. Nobles could not inter-marry without his permission. Nobles could not keep retainers beyond a certain number. 'Ala'uddin was concerned not with religion nor mainly with the interest of this group or that group. He was interested primarily in maintaining his own power. Whoever challenged his power was immediately curbed and punished. A good deal of the persecution in this period may be explained in terms of this desire to maintain one's own authority. When the ruler felt secure, he tried to give good administration to the people. He recognized that contented subjects were his best protection. Throughout the Pathan period, religious and political toleration grew steadily.

I would like to draw your attention to another interesting feature of the spread of Islam in India. It is noteworthy that the largest concentration of Muslims is not in the capital cities but in the distant regions and in certain special areas. There is a very heavy concentration in East Bengal which is far from Delhi. We find similar heavy concentration in Kerala which hardly ever came under Muslim rule. We find fairly heavy concentration in certain selected areas of Madras. The continuous influx of new groups of Muslims added to the Muslim population of the Punjab but even then the Punjab always had a sizable non-Muslim population. The explanation which has been offered for this fact is that by and large the spread of Islam in India, as in other parts of the world, was due to the teachings of the Sufis and the Saints and not the political power of the rulers. In the case of Indonesia, those of you who are students of Indonesian history will remember that Indonesia was never conquered by Muslims and it was Arab traders who took Islam to Indonesia. Similarly it was Arab traders who brought Islam to

Kerala and Muslim merchants and Sufis who brought it to Sylhet and Chittagong.

We may point to find another interesting pattern in the growth of Islam within India. Wherever the Arabs went, there was a greater cultural assimilation and far greater give and take between the different communities than in areas where Islam was taken by the newly converted Turkish rulers. It was largely these Turks who dominated the political and military fields in North India. Wherever they took Islam, there was a certain amount of persecution, but wherever the Arabs brought Islam, there was on the whole greater accommodation. We thus find that the number of Muslims was greater in the areas under Arab influence, in the areas where Sufis and Saints and Fakirs taught. In these areas the religion generally spread as a revolutionary and liberating force.

We do not always remember today that when Islam first appeared on the stage of world history, it came as a great liberal and democratic movement. It was a revolt of the intellectual as well as a revolt of the underprivileged. It brought a message of equality and fraternity for all sections of the people, and transcended the barriers created by race, color and language. [George] Bernard Shaw [Irish author, 1856–1950] in one of his books has said that the most severe test of race and color equality is the test of marriage. In every other type of contact between different communities, one can cheat. You can once in the year be together in a great religious congregation and fraternize. Once in a year you can dine together, once in a year you can join in a pilgrimage to Kaba or Kashi. The test of marriage is very different. Bernard Shaw points out that this is the test which Islam has passed with credit. Islam did largely break down the barriers of color and the barriers of race. In fact, almost all the human barriers came down once people accepted Islam. This was one reason why large numbers of the underprivileged everywhere accepted and still accept Islam.

Another reason for the rapid spread of Islam was the opening up of opportunity for vast sections of the people. It is again an interesting fact of history that till the advent of Islam, most religions had made education a preserve of the select few. In ancient Egypt and indeed in almost all parts of the world, knowledge was recognized as power and because knowledge was and is power, knowledge was the prerogative of a privileged class. It was Islam which broke that barrier down and made knowledge accessible and indeed obligatory on a universal scale. In practice there was however a great gap between what was laid down and what was actually carried out. It is one of the ironies of history that in India at least, Islam which has declared that it is an obligation for every man and woman to acquire learning, the Muslims are one of the most backward communities so far as education is concerned. This holds for men as well as women, though for women the position is even worse.

For the reasons indicated above, the Muslim population increased rapidly in India. So long as the ruler was either a Muslim or a Hindu, the position was comparatively simple. In Muslim political thought, apart from States where both the ruler and the ruled were Muslims, lawgivers had allowed for two kinds of situation, a situation in which there is a Muslim ruler and a large number of non-Muslim subjects and also the situation in which there is a non-Muslim ruler and Muslim subjects. But Muslim political thought had not provided for the situation which has developed in India today, the situation in which *Muslims are citizens in a secular State*. In this situation, they are neither the sole rulers nor merely the ruled. We can put it in another way and say that they are rulers and ruled simultaneously. As a citizen of India, a Muslim shares in the sovereignty of the people. As a citizen of India, he is subject to the laws of the State like any other citizen professing any religion. In a democratic State, every citizen has a share in sovereignty and therefore we have in India today this unique situation, a situation which has never before faced Muslim people anywhere in the world. They are not merely ruled, but neither are they merely rulers. They are rulers and the ruled at the same time. Further they are not rulers by themselves, they are rulers in association with people of many different religions.

Considered from this point of view, the situation in India today presents a great challenge and also a great opportunity to Muslims and other Indians. We have a recognition of this fact in the Indian Constitution. It is one of the first instances where we have a self-confessed secular State which explicitly recognizes that the State cannot prosper and perhaps cannot even survive without adherence to the secular principle. Here we have to remember another fact. There are some people in India and elsewhere who think that secularism is a concession to the different minority groups. In one sense it certainly is. Over 85 percent of the total population of India belong broadly to what we call the Hindu faith. All the other minorities together number less than 15 percent. If therefore the majority community of India had wished, there was nothing to prevent them from declaring India as a Hindu State or a Brahmanical State. But the framers of the Indian Constitution had great political foresight. They had the wisdom to see that in the peculiar circumstances of India and the scientific developments of the modern world, the concept of a religious State would not work. I will explain this in a moment.

Let us assume that some party comes to power in India which is militantly religious. In the Indian context, such a party can only be a Hindu party. Even if the Muslims become militantly religious, they form only 11 or 12 percent of the population and cannot have a decisive say in the political affairs of the country. Christians with less than two percent will have even less influence. Sikhs, they are less than one percent, will also not make much of an impact. If there can be any militant religious party it can be only a Hindu party. Supposing such a party comes into power and declares that India would not be a secular State, but a State following a particular religion, the Hindu religion, the question would immediately arise: which Hindu religion? Those of you who are familiar with Indian religious thought know that the Hindu faith itself is a great confederation of different beliefs and different religious systems. You have within the Hindu fold people who believe in one God and one God alone, who are as strict monotheists as Muslims or Sikhs or the staunchest Unitarians in the Christian Church. You have also Hindus who believe in three Gods or believe in a thousand Gods. There is in fact a saying that for the 300 million Indian people there are 330 million gods. You have also atheists who are perfectly good Hindus, for there have been Rishis or Saints who professed atheism and are still recognized as Rishis.

If therefore India decided to be a religious State, the question would immediately arise: Will it be Vaishnava? Will it be Saiva? Will it be Lingait? Will it be Jaina? What will be the faith and in which form? The unity of India would probably be shattered again as it has been shattered so often in the past. We have in our past history the record of Kings changing their faith and asking their people to change their faiths. Vaishnava temples were converted into Saiva temples, and vice-versa. In fact you find similar phenomena throughout the world. Not only in India but everywhere in Asia, Europe and Africa. With the change of faith by the King, there was a change of character, a change of beliefs and of religious worship of the people but in the end it led nowhere.

This is not the only difficulty a non-secular religious State would face in India. There would be differences on the basis of caste as well. Caste has no doubt lost ground in recent times. It has lost ground primarily because of industrialization and improvement in means of transport and communication. Certainly ideas have also played a part and we have to remember with gratitude the reformers from Buddha [sixth–fifth centuries B.C.] to [Rabindranath] Tagore [1861–1941] and [Mahatma Mohandas K.] Gandhi [1869–1948]. But a far more important part has been played by the fact of industrialization and improvement in the means of transport and communication. When you are in a country bus in India, probably 50 people are put in a bus which is meant to hold only 30. Questions about caste or untouchability become completely irrelevant in such a situation. The conductor or the driver of the bus will have no sympathy at all if you say: I do not want to sit next to that man. He will in all likelihood ask you to get down and put two more men in your place. Transport and communication, industrialization and urbanization along with the anonymity which towns give are breaking down caste barriers. But if the secular ideal ever breaks down, some of the old ideas would reaffirm themselves, and the result would be that Indian unity will itself be threatened.

A secular State is therefore necessary in India not in the interest of the minorities alone—they also would certainly gain, there is no doubt about it—but it is in the interest of all the people of India including the majority community. That is why in our Constitution we find a guarantee of equal rights and opportunities for every citizen regardless of caste, religion, sex, language or race. The entire list of the differences which distinguish and divide human beings, they are all as far as one can reckon mentioned in the Constitution and it is said: All these distinctions shall be overlooked and as Indian citizens they shall have equal rights and equal opportunities. The highest office is open to any person of any religious profession. Representation in the legislatures, in trade and industry is equally open to all. In fact the Universal Declaration of Human Rights has to a very large extent been incorporated in the Indian Constitution. . . .

While the relations between Hindus and Muslims in India are friendly in normal times, we find time and again outbreaks of violence that result in destruction and death. There must be a reason for this and this can only be some flaw in the attitude of religious toleration which both communities accept as the normal mode of life. For Hindus, this flaw can be traced to caste exclusiveness, which leads to a lack of regard for men of other religious faiths. Indifference and even contempt for men of other religions is perhaps a natural corollary to untouchability within the Hindu social fold. This indifference or contempt may not be conscious or deliberate and there may also be cases where in fact there is no feeling of contempt or hatred, but those who suffer from the effects of untouchability do not make any distinction between conscious and unconscious motives or their absence. For them, the fact of discrimination in everyday life is enough to rouse their resentment and lead to feelings of anger and hatred which break out whenever an opportunity offers.

For historical and political reasons, Muslims feel this sense of discrimination more acutely than members of other Indian communities. It is true that there has been a small Christian community in the country for some two thousand years. It is however small in number and for centuries remained confined to a narrow corner of the land. In addition, Indian Christians never exercised political power and did not therefore pose any challenge to the majority community. Muslims have on the other hand been spread throughout the subcontinent from the day of their first appearance in India. Their number, their distribution and above all their exercise of military and political power made the problem of untouchability between them and the Hindus one full of explosive possibilities.

There is a parallel flaw in the Muslim attitude to other religions. Islam categorically declares that there must be no compulsion in religion and each individual must be left free to follow the faith of his choice. While Muslims thus recognize that there are many religions in the world, there is one basic difference between Hinduism and Islam in their attitude to this diversity. For Hindus, the diverse ways of worship have arisen because of different human needs and all have equal validity. For Muslims, the diversity has arisen because of human failing which has led to the distortion of a single pristine truth. According to Islam, all religions were initially the same, but in course of time became distorted by custom and circumstance. It was to rectify these distortions that prophets appeared in succession in different parts of the world, but no prophet preached a new religion. Thus the Prophet Muhammad was not the originator of Islam, but only the last in a long line of prophets who had all taught an identical faith. Any deviation from this original religion is therefore for Muslims a deviation from Truth.

When these two religious attitudes met in India, there was an attempt at reconciliation from both sides. Hindus have for centuries recognized the validity of different professions and practices in the sphere of religion. Within Hinduism itself, there is the widest variety of faiths and customs. A place has been found in the Hindu pantheon for even those who rebelled against traditional Hinduism. Thus, the Buddha is regarded today as one of the Hindu Avatars. Christ and Muhammad have also found places of honor in the Hindu mind. Similarly, Muslims have condemned compulsion in religion and admitted that different religions must be given due respect. The accommodation achieved in India between Hindus and Muslims is seen in the many instances where Hindus worship at Muslim shrines and Muslims pay homage to Hindu religious teachers and saints.

In spite of such accommodation, the psychological separation between Hindus and Muslims has not however been overcome. Social and political factors have contributed to this, but a major reason is the difference in religious outlook mentioned above. Among orthodox Muslims, there are many who look upon all non-Muslims, particularly Hindus, as *kafir*s or unbelievers. Among Hindus, there are many who look upon Muslims as *mlechha*s or unclean. For Hindus, such an attitude was in the past partially a defense reaction to protect the Hindu community against the political power and religious proselytization of Muslims. After the advent of the British, superiority in education and economic position strengthened such feelings. Among Muslims, political pride and a sense of religious superiority led to the same attitude. This was reinforced by a defense reaction after they lost their economic and political advantages under British rule. The root cause for Hindu-Muslim conflicts in India therefore derives from this attitude of exclusiveness. Because of this Muslims look upon Hindus as *kafir*s and Hindus return the compliment by looking upon Muslims as *mlechha*s.

In order to create the psychological atmosphere where the two communities can develop a sense of national identity while retaining their special group characteristics, it is necessary to bring about a change of attitude among both Hindus and Muslims. In the case of Hindus, what is needed is a change in the snobbery born out of caste exclusiveness. Due to industrialization and urbanization, the process of break-up of caste has already begun. As education spreads, the process is bound to be accelerated, though one has to admit that in recent years caste has had an unexpected lease of life given to it by political forces. The democratic process of elections has in certain cases led to an ossification of caste and this is most marked where elections are in small constituencies. With larger areas and greater mixture of population, the governing power of caste is bound to diminish and ultimately disappear. In fact, we already see the beginning of a new type of social grouping where Hindus and Muslims belonging to the same economic class or educational background tend to draw nearer to one another than to their co-religionists in different social categories. This applies even more to Hindus of different castes.

Among Muslims also, the process of change has begun in the recognition of the philosophic and other truths embedded in Hindu, Buddhist or Christian thought. This recognition has however to be linked up with the Muslim religious belief that prophets have been sent to every country in every age. While Muslim religious thought insists that true religion is one and only one, it also recognizes that this pristine truth has been sent to every people in every age in a form acceptable to them. This has introduced a respect for diversity of faith, but such respect finds easy and wide acceptance only when the people following different faiths claim to be the followers of a recognized prophet. That is why we find throughout the Muslim world a distinction between those who are called the people of the Book and others. According to orthodox Muslim thought, a Christian or a Jew has deviated from the pristine teaching of true religion, but nevertheless he has a position of privilege among non-Muslims and is entitled to special consideration. The clearest evidence of this is found in the law which permits marriage between Muslims and followers of a Book but forbids a Muslim to marry a non-believer.

Once therefore it is accepted that Hindus are *ahl al-kitab* or people of the Book, it would remove one of the major psychological barriers between the two communities. A book is given to a people through a prophet and according to the Qur'an, prophets were sent to every country in every age. It is further stated that no apostle has been sent except to teach in the language of his people so that they might easily understand him. Many such prophets were sent before the Prophet Muhammad, some of whom are mentioned in the Qur'an and others not. The Qur'an does not give their number but according to an authentic tradition [of the Prophet], it was almost two hundred thousand.

The Qur'an also lays down the criteria of a *kitab* or a revealed Book. A revealed Book conveys the message of God and is not the composition of any man. It preaches the unity of God as well as the responsibility of man for his actions. The criterion easily fits in with the Vedas and the Gita. Both, according to Hindu tradition, are *apaurusheya*, i.e., not the handiwork of man but of divine origin. The Qur'an insists on the unity of Godhead and claims that this is the basis of all true religion. The Rig Veda also proclaims, "He is one, though sages call Him by many names." The Atharva Veda declares that renown and glory, force and happiness, splendor, food and nourishment belong to him who only thinks of God as "One without a second. . . . He is the Sole, the simple One, the One alone." One could easily imagine that these passages were taken from the Qur'an.

In the light of the Qur'anic declaration that prophets have been sent to every country in every age to preach in the language of its people, it seems certain that there must have been many prophets in India. Surely when so many prophets were sent to Palestine within a few hundred years, a vast country with so ancient a history as India could not be denied that privilege. In fact we find in the Indian tradition conceptions which fit in with the concepts of revelation and prophethood. The description of the Vedas as *shruti* or heard fits in with the Qur'anic concept of revelation where the prophet hears what is revealed to him. Similarly, the concept of *avatar* in Hinduism appears as an Indian version of the concept of prophet in Islam. A prophet is a man on whom God's message descends. *Avatar* from the root meaning of the word could mean exactly the same thing. It is a matter for interpretation whether the *avatar* is regarded as an incarnation of God or a vehicle through whom God's message is revealed. The role that Christianity has ascribed to Christ is an interesting commentary on this and shows how easily these two interpretations can merge.

The Qur'an states that only some prophets are mentioned but the majority remain unnamed. Among the names that are explicitly mentioned, there is at least one which could refer to an Indian prophet. In Sura 21 [Verse 85; also Sura 38, Verse 48] there is a reference to "Dhu'l Kifl." This can be roughly translated as Prince of Kufl and could very well refer to the Buddha who was Prince of Kapilavastu [sixth–fifth century B.C.]. There is no "p" in Arabic so that "p" sounds are converted either to "f" or "b." Similarly, Dhu'l-Qurnain [Sira 18, Verses 83–98] mentioned in the Qur'an has been differently identified by Sir Syed Ahmad [Khan, 1817–1898] with Chehwang-te, the Chinese emperor-sage [Xuan Di, reigned 74–48 B.C.], with Alexander [Macedonian emperor, 356–323 B.C.] by Abdullah Yusuf Ali [1872–1952], and with Cyrus [Persian emperor, circa 590–529 B.C.] by Maulana [Abu al-Kalam] Azad [1888–1958].

It may be argued that whatever may have been the religion of the Vedas, Hinduism today is not monotheistic and has many idols. Such an argument admits by implication the claim of the Vedas to be a revealed Book. At the most it could therefore be said that the pristine purity of Vedic faith has been distorted. It may be pointed out that a similar development has taken place in Christianity as well. There are pictures and images of Mary and Jesus in most Christian churches. In spite of this, Christians are recognized as *ahl al-kitab*. On the same basis, Hindus should also be regarded as people of the Book.

Images came to the Christian churches at a later date. This is equally true of Hinduism. As far as is known, idol worship was introduced into India in the wake of Alexander's invasion. Even in early Buddhism, there is no image of the Buddha. It is only after the Greeks came to India and brought their statuary that we get the first life-like images of the Buddha. Hinduism borrowed image worship from the later phases of Buddhism. It is interesting to note that the word "*but*" [idol] in Persian as well as in Urdu is a corruption of Budh or Buddha, indicating the close connection between the representation of the Buddha and idol worship. Finally, even in traditional

Hinduism of today, the fact that the idol is discarded and thrown into a river after the religious ceremony proves that the idol is not the object of worship but only a symbol to help the devotee to concentrate.

There are Arabic scholars who hold that the term *kafir* was restricted only to certain idolatrous tribes in Arabia and cannot be applied to those who claim to have a Book. Hindus claim to have a Book and there is no reason to dispute that claim. The description they give of their religion as *Sanatan Dharma* or the perennial faith has a close affinity to the Muslim conception of Islam as the one faith that has persisted through the ages. If in spite of modification and changes, Jews and Christians are recognized as *ahl al-kitab* or people of the Book, is there any reason to deny that title to Hindus?

Universalism in Islam

Since the late 1960s, Malaysia has witnessed tensions and occasionally open conflict between the Muslim community, which comprises a slight majority, and non-Muslim Chinese and South Asians. This communalism has taken both ethnic and religious forms because of the combination of ethnicity (Malay) and religion (Islam) in the identity of Bumiputra (literally, son of the soil).[1] Chandra Muzaffar (Malaysia, born 1947), a political scientist and civic activist, has analyzed Malay communalism in his academic work and combated it in his civic work, in particular, the multicommunal, pro-democracy organization Aliran Kesedaran Negara (National Awareness Movement), which he founded in the late 1970s and led until the early 1990s. In the 1990s, Muzaffar founded an international organization, the Just World Trust, which seeks to promote similar ideals globally, and coauthored a declaration on human rights that was adopted by more than two hundred Asian and Pacific nongovernmental organizations. Muzaffar has been harassed by the Malaysian government for his criticism of its undemocratic practices.[2]

The Universalism of Islam is an open proclamation to everyone—Muslim and non-Muslim alike—that communalism is totally alien to the spirit and philosophy of Islam.

This proclamation is particularly relevant in a society like ours. It is unfortunate that over the decades Islam in Malaysia has come to be seen in com-

1. M. Kamal Hassan, "Malaysia," in John L. Esposito, editor, *The Oxford Encyclopedia of the Modern Islamic World* (New York: Oxford University Press, 1995), volume 3, pp. 35–38; Hussin Mutalib, *Islam and Ethnicity in Malay Politics* (Singapore: Oxford University Press, 1990); Chandra Muzaffar, "Ethnicity, Ethnic Conflict, and Human Rights in Malaysia," in Claude E. Welch Jr. and Virginia A. Leary, editors, *Asian Perspectives on Human Rights* (Boulder, Colo.: Westview, 1990), pp. 107–141; K. J. Ratnam, *Communalism in the Political Process in Malaya* (Kuala Lumpur, Malaysia: University of Malaya Press, 1965); R. K. Vasil, *Ethnic Politics in Malaysia* (New Delhi: Radiant, 1980); Karl von Vorys, *Democracy without Consensus: Communalism and Political Stability in Malaysia* (Princeton, N.J.: Princeton University Press, 1975).

2. Daniel S. Lev, "Human Rights NGOs [Non-Governmental Organizations] in Indonesia and Malaysia," in Welch and Leary, *Asian Perspectives on Human Rights*, pp. 142–161; Amyn B. Sajoo, *Pluralism in "Old Societies and New States": Emerging ASEAN Contexts* (Singapore: Institute of Southeast Asian Studies, 1994), pp. 53–54; and Sajoo, "Pondering the 'Periphery': Pluralist Trends in Southeast Asia," *Muslim Politics Report*, number 8, Summer 1996, p. 5.

munal perspectives. "Communal" in this context does not mean mere association with a particular community. It is perhaps unavoidable that in a situation where all Malays are Muslims, Islam will be perceived as a Malay religion by both Malays and non-Malays. As long as there is sufficient awareness that Islam does not belong exclusively to the Malays and that there are millions upon millions of non-Malays who are also Muslims, no one can say that such a perception is in itself communal.[3]

What makes the prevailing attitude towards Islam communal is the tendency to link the religion with what I shall call Malayism and Bumiputraism when it is apparent that both the premises of these two almost identical "isms" and their implications have nothing to do with Islam. By Malayism I mean that whole philosophy that argues that, as the indigenous community, the Malays have certain political, economic and cultural rights that distinguish them from the non-indigenous communities [primarily Chinese and South Asians]. Bumiputraism rests upon the same premise except that it also encompasses indigenous non-Malay, non-Muslim communities whose interests may, at certain points, conflict with those of the Malays.[4] A clear instance would be the political pre-eminence of the Malays, which is not just pre-eminence in relation to the non-indigenous communities but also pre-eminence in relation to the non-Malay, non-Muslim indigenous communities.[5]

Since both Malayism and Bumiputraism are founded upon the notion of an indigenous people, let us consider this factor from the point of view of Islam. The Islamic party of Malaysia (PAS [*Partai Islam Se-Malaysia*, or Pan-Malaysian Islamic Party]) has all along demanded the "restoration of Malay sovereignty" primarily because of the indigenous status of the community.[6] What is important to us is that its demand has invariably been presented in the name of Islam. Even a cursory analysis of PAS's philosophy will reveal that its insistence upon Malay political pre-eminence, Malay economic pre-eminence and Malay cultural pre-eminence have been articulated as a way of protecting the integrity of Islam.[7]

Now Islam does not recognize an indigenous/non-indigenous dichotomy as the basis of any social system. If terms like indigenous (Bumiputra) and non-indigenous (non-Bumiputra) are used merely as descriptions of categories within the population which have emerged as a result of the evolution of the Malaysian nation, it would not be altogether antithetical to Islamic principles. For then the categories concerned would be of historical rather than social relevance. But since the PAS argument is that public life should be conducted on the basis of an indigenous/non-indigenous dichotomy one would be right in describing it as an un-Islamic stance. There are three important reasons for saying so. Firstly, it is seldom realized that by distinguishing the indigenous community from the non-indigenous communities one is, in fact, dividing the Muslims since there are Muslims who are non-Bumiputras just as there are Bumiputras who are non-Muslims. Islamic teachings are opposed to any covert or overt attempt to divide Muslims. This is borne out by the importance attached to the very well-known principle in Islam that "the Believers are but a single Brotherhood, so make peace and reconciliation between your two contending brothers" (Qur'an, Sura *Al-Hujurat* [Sura 49], Verse 10).[8] Lest this idea of Muslim unity be misunderstood it must be stressed that Islam does not advocate an obscurantist sort of unity without considering the ethical foundations of that unity. As proof, it is stated in the Qur'an that "God will not

3. There is this awareness, though non-Malays who become Muslims are sometimes referred to as people who have "*masuk Melayu*" (become Malays). "*Masuk Melayu*," however, need not be interpreted literally; it could simply mean those who have adopted the religion of the Malays.

4. These communities would be the Kadazans, Ibans, and others of East Malaysia in the main and some of the Orang Asli of West Malaysia.

5. In both Sabah and Sarawak, for instance, the Chief Ministership and certain other important political offices are held by indigenous Muslims, though non-Muslim indigenous communities are numerically stronger in both states. For a fuller discussion of politics in these states, see K. J. Ratnam and R. S. Milne, *New States in a New Nation* (London: Frank Cass, 1974).

6. See "Amanat Yang di-Pertua Agong PAS Ulang Tahun 1958" [The 1958 Anniversary Speech of the President of the PAS], in *Cenderamata Pembukaan Bangunan PAS Kelantan & Kongres PAS ke 13* [*Souvenir Program in Conjunction with the Opening of the PAS's Building in Kelantan and the Thirteenth PAS Congress*].

7. For a detailed analysis see my "Protection of the Malay Community: A study of UMNO's Position and Opposition Attitudes," Masters Thesis, Universiti Sains Malaysia, 1974.

8. See A. Yusuf Ali [1872–1952], *The Holy Qur'an: Text, Translation and Commentary* (Lahore, Pakistan: Sh. Muhammad Ashraf, 1972).

leave the Believers in the state in which ye are now until He separates what is evil from what is good." (Sura *Al-'Imran* [Sura 3], Verse 179) Dividing non-indigenous Muslims from indigenous Muslims in matters relating to politics, economics, education and culture is certainly not a case of separating evil from good! Secondly, even if all Bumiputras were Muslims and all non-Bumiputras non-Muslims, it would still be wrong to differentiate between the two groups in employment, education, and other similar areas where the paramount consideration should be the welfare of the human being. The Qur'an itself prohibits such discrimination (Sura *Al-Baqara* [Sura 2], Verse 272). The constitution of Medina formulated by Prophet Muhammad (may peace be upon him) provided equal rights and responsibilities to Muslims and non-Muslims alike.[9] Illustrious caliphs in early Islam like Abu Bakr [reigned 632–634], 'Umar [reigned 634–644], and 'Ali [reigned 656–661] took great pains to ensure that their non-Muslim citizens were well looked after. According to the 8th century Hanafi jurist Abu Yusuf, the second caliph 'Umar even fixed special pensions for the non-Muslims living in Damascus.[10] Thirdly, by placing the whole Bumiputra/non-Bumiputra dichotomy at the center of things one has, in a sense, elevated ethnicity and ancestry to a level which is repugnant to genuine Islamic values. One of the *hadith*s (sayings of Prophet Muhammad) reminds mankind that "there is no pride whatsoever in ancestry; there is no merit in an Arab as against a non-Arab nor in a non-Arab as against an Arab."[11] What is at the kernel of Islam is not ethnicity or ancestry but the unity of God. And the one most significant implication of that unity is the unity of the whole of mankind. The Qur'an for instance, observes,

O mankind! We created you from a single pair of a male and a female, and made you into nations and tribes, that ye may know each other, not that ye may despise each other. Verily, the most honored of you in the sight of God is he who is the most righteous of you. (Sura *Hujurat* [Sura 49], Verse 13)

This concept of unity is in fact linked to the idea of equality within the human community as suggested in Sura *Al-'Imran* [Sura 3], Verse 195.[12] In other words, the very endeavor to sustain and strengthen ethnic dichotomies like the indigenous/non-indigenous distinction amounts to a denunciation of the central principle of Islam itself—the principle of the unity of God or *towhid*.

Obviously then, PAS cannot justify Bumiputraism by using or misusing Islam. Of course it is not just PAS that advocates Bumiputraism. It is, as we know, the whole basis of public policy formulation. However, in all fairness to the UMNO-led [United Malays National Organization] government which is responsible for this, it must be recognized that it does not justify Bumiputraism in the name of Islam.[13]

That Bumiputraism cannot be defended from an Islamic point of view is something that very few Muslims in Malaysia are aware of. Even where there is some awareness, there doesn't seem to be a willingness to articulate such a view in public. This is true of almost all Muslim groups in the country, including those who argue that PAS is un-Islamic and that they represent pure, pristine Islam. That is why I have never believed for one moment that the tremendous interest in Islam manifested in recent years by educated youths and others who are part of the urban environment reflects the emergence of a genuine Islamic consciousness.[14] To establish this point, I shall undertake a brief analysis of the so-called "rising tide of Islam" of the 1970s. I hope to show

9. For a discussion on the Constitution of Medina, see Zainal Abidin Ahmad, *Piagam Nabi Muhammad s.a.w.* [*Charter of the Prophet Muhammad, Peace Be upon Him*] (Jakarta, Indonesia: Bulan Bintang, 1973).

10. See Sayyid Abul A'la Mawdudi, *The Islamic Law and Constitution* (Lahore, Pakistan: Islamic Publications Ltd.), p. 312.

11. Mawdudi, *The Islamic Law and Constitution*, p. 159.

12. In commenting upon that sura, Yusuf Ali notes, "In Islam, the equal status of the sexes is not only recognized but insisted on. If sex distinction, which is a distinction in nature, does not count in spiritual matters, still less of course would count artificial distinctions such as rank, wealth, position, race, color, birth, etc." A. Yusuf Ali, *The Holy Qur'an*, p. 175.

13. For the UMNO leadership as a whole, Bumiputraism is apparently justified on its own basis. Some analysis of this is available in my "The New Economic Policy and the Quest for National Unity," *Fifth Malaysian Economic Convention* (Malaysian Economic Association, 1978).

14. Two points, however, must be made. Firstly, there are without any doubt a number of Muslim youths who understand genuine Islamic principles. See, for instance, the view of Anwar Ibrahim [born 1947] (President, *Angkatan Belia Islam Malaysia* [Muslim Youth Movement of Malaysia], or ABIM), in *Bintang Timur* [*Eastern Star*], 1st March 1979. Secondly, the world-wide interest in Islam among young Muslims has also had some bearing upon the Malaysian situation, but I do not consider it a crucial factor.

that Islam in Malaysia is still clothed in communal garb; that Muslims in Malaysia have yet to understand what the universal spirit of Islam means in reality.

It is no mere coincidence that this "Islamic tide" has risen in the 1970s. For the 1970s has seen the emergence of the Malay community as a significant component of the urban environment, especially the Kuala Lumpur environment.[15] It is estimated that by 1980, 32 percent of the urban population would be Malay.[16] In a society where ethnic consciousness is pervasive, Malays who have just become part of a largely non-Malay milieu are bound to develop an awareness of their ethnic background which may not have been there when they were amongst their own ethnic kind in the rural areas. One can argue that even in societies where ethnic consciousness is not as pervasive, a first-generation community in a somewhat alien setting is expected to manifest a similar psychological response. A sense of insecurity, a feeling of suspicion, of distrust, are some of the accompanying elements of this increased ethnic awareness. Islam provides a useful channel for the expression of this awareness since it touches the life of an ordinary Malay in a thousand different ways. No other cultural symbol of the Malay community can be as effective. The Malay language expresses only one dimension of Malay identity and besides, since 1970, it has become increasingly the language of social communication of non-Malays as well.[17] It cannot therefore be used as an avenue for expressing "Malayness." But Islam on the other hand, as it is understood here, can be used as the rationale for dressing in a certain way, staying away from certain groups, avoiding certain places and, most of all, adhering to certain beliefs and ideas. More specifically, this explains why some Muslim women in colleges and universities, firms and factories—more than their counterparts in the padi-fields and rubber small-holdings—are so concerned about dressing in the "proper Islamic way," about avoiding male company, about staying away from cinemas and so on. It also explains, I suppose,

why there is so much concern among certain Muslim circles in the cities about whether "*tanggung halal*" [that which is permissible] signs displayed in some non-Muslim eating shops are genuine or not.[18]

What all this shows is that as a reaction to the non-Malay, non-Muslim dominated urban environment, certain segments of the urban Malay community are seeking to carve out a distinctive identity, establish a separate ethnic presence. As I have tried to explain, this search is not the outcome of a sudden realization of what it is to be a Muslim in terms of dress or social intercourse; rather it stems from a feeling of deep insecurity that compels the individual concerned to protect his "Malayness." This is why he chooses only those elements from Islam which will help him maintain his separateness, his distinctiveness. After all, an Islamic identity is much more than dress forms or modes of social intercourse. Is not a Muslim also defined on the basis of his commitment to truth and justice, his readiness to fight oppression and corruption, his willingness to help the poor, the weak, his capacity for charity, for kindness? There are numerous verses in the Qur'an that support such an idea of a Muslim identity. One such verse says,

> And show him the two highways? But he hath made no haste on the path that is steep, and what will explain to thee the path that is steep? It is freeing the bondman; or the giving of food in a day of privation, to the orphan with claims of relationship, or to the indigent down in the dust. Then will he be of those who believe and enjoin patience (constancy and self-restraint), and enjoin deeds of kindness and compassion. Such are the Companions of the Right Hand. (Sura *Al-Balad* [Sura 90], Verses 10–18)

Another verse says,

> Seest thou one who denies the Judgment (to come)? Then such as the (man) who repulses the orphan (with harshness). And encourages not the feeding of the indigent. So woe to the worshippers who are neglectful of their prayers. Those who (want but) to be seen (of man) but refuse (to supply) (even) neighborly needs. (Sura *Al-Ma'un* [Sura 107], Verses 1–7)

---

15. This is due to both the rural-urban drift which has been on since Merdeka [Independence, 1957], and the New Economic Policy (NEP) [since the early 1970s] which among other things emphasizes Malay participation in commerce and industry.

16. See *The Star*, 20 March 1979.

17. This is partly due to the implementation of Malay as the main medium of education since 1970.

18. The crucial word here is "*halal*" (legitimate). "*Halal*" signs therefore refer to foods that Muslims are allowed to eat. There has been a great deal of discussion about this in *Utusan Malaysia* [*Malaysian Messenger*] and *Utusan Melayu* [*Malay Messenger*, daily newspapers in Kuala Lumpur] in the last two years or so.

Of course, defining the identity of a Muslim in terms of his kindness to the poor will not serve the purpose of maintaining a separate identity since kindness like compassion is a sentiment, a value, which any human being, Muslim or non-Muslim, Malay or non-Malay, is capable of. If, on the other hand, one emphasizes dress or food or various rituals which are specific and exclusive to the religion, one would be highlighting forms and practices which others cannot share. Thus, one would be able to sustain a Muslim/non-Muslim dichotomy which at the emotional-psychological level equals a Malay/non-Malay, a Bumiputra/non-Bumiputra dichotomy.

So far, I have shown that the interest in Islam in the 1970s is closely aligned to the crystallization of ethnic consciousness in a new urban environment. Insecurity has been suggested as one of the propelling forces behind this consciousness. There is, however, another psychological force which is also at work at the same time—a force which superficially at least appears to contradict the feeling of insecurity we have just analyzed. The political climate of the 1970s with its emphasis upon Malay interests and aspirations in the economy, in politics, and in the cultural life of the nation has bestowed various Malay groups with a sense of confidence about the legitimacy of their demands.[19] Confidence of this sort derived from an overall political situation where the Malay position is undoubtedly strong and powerful can, of course, co-exist quite happily with insecurity generated by a specific urban environment where the Malay position is neither strong nor powerful as yet. It is because there is this confidence that Malay groups are more vocal than ever before in demanding an Islamic administration based upon the Qur'an and the *sunna* (the way of the Prophet), Islamic laws, an Islamic economic system, an Islamic education system, indeed, a total Islamic society.[20] There are a number of things about these demands which must be noted. Firstly, as I have mentioned, the stronger Malay political position—an ethnic phenomenon—

is at the root of these demands. Secondly, like the obsession with dress and rituals, the interest in Islamic laws cannot possibly evoke any empathy from the non-Muslims since Islamic laws are also, on the whole, very specific to the religion. It would have been different if the concern was with fighting exploitation or ensuring self-reliance—goals which are highly cherished in Islam—since they have an appeal that transcends religious boundaries. The emphasis given to Islamic laws and Islamic administration only helps to underline the differences that exist between Muslims and non-Muslims and, by implication, Malays and non-Malays. In that sense, it reveals the true character of the whole agitation for an Islamic state. Thirdly, if it were a genuine Islamic movement inspired by a genuine Islamic consciousness there would have been an increasing endeavor to study and analyze the structure and content of an Islamic society in Malaysia. This is particularly important in our context because the non-Muslim segment is a little more than half of the total population. How this large number of non-Muslims would fit into an Islamic society, what their rights and roles would be, what responsibilities they would share with the Muslims, how they would relate to an Islamic legislature or judicial system—all these and a number of other issues should have been debated and discussed in depth and detail. The fact is there has been no such effort. This lack of interest in the position and status of the non-Muslims among the so-called "Champions of Islam" of the 1970s is no different from the total lack of concern for the non-Muslims and non-Malays exhibited by PAS in the 1950s and 1960s. It is because there isn't this concern, that no Muslim group in the country has taken up cudgels on behalf of the non-Muslim poor. Yet, the humanitarian ideals which lie at the heart of Islam, the noble examples of the Prophet Muhammad (may peace be upon him) and the great caliphs which I had alluded to earlier, would demand such a response.

Once again, this negative attitude of various Muslim groups exposes the real nature of their political struggle. It is just another way of preserving Malayism. To understand this better, one has to compare the situation here with the attitudes that prevailed among Islamic groups in Indonesia from the 1930s right up to the 1960s. In spite of a smaller non-Muslim population, leaders of the Masyumi [party] in particular, like Muhammad Natsir [1908–1993], spent so much time and effort elucidating the

19. The genesis of this whole atmosphere is discussed in my "Some Political Perspectives on the New Economic Policy," *Fourth Malaysian Economic Convention* (Malaysian Economic Association, 1977).

20. The development of these demands finds some mention in my "Dominant Concepts and Dissenting Ideas on Malay Society and Malay Rule from the Malacca Period to the Merdeka Period," Doctoral Thesis, University of Singapore, 1977.

rights and responsibilities of non-Muslims in the Islamic state they envisaged for Indonesia.[21] One of their more important intellectual commitments was the quest for common principles that could unite Muslims and non-Muslims—a commitment which conforms with Qur'anic ideals.[22] In this connection, no Muslim group in Malaysia has ever bothered to embark upon such a mission, though, at the level of social philosophy, there are many outstanding similarities between Islam and aspects of Chinese culture and Hindu thought.[23] The reason is, of course, obvious. It is because Islam is seen from a communal angle—not a universal perspective. Finally, one would have thought that those who seek to establish an Islamic state would first examine critically the ideas, beliefs and attitudes of the Muslim community itself, in order to discover if these are elements which need to be jettisoned in the endeavor to create a genuine Islamic spirit. Apart from the occasional blast at some insignificant ritual like Mandi Safar or puja ceremonies,[24] Muslim groups have maintained an embarrassing silence in relation to more fundamental ideas and attitudes within Malay society. These are ideas and attitudes which need to be rectified in the interest of Islam. One such important idea which I have already analyzed is the whole notion of Bumiputraism. If the post-1970 Muslim movement was genuinely Islamic it would have at least attempted to show Muslims how a concept based upon ethnicity and ancestry—or upon residence and territory if you like—does not synchronize with Islamic values. The willingness to live with Bumiputraism, and worse still, defend it at times, shows that the real spirit of Islam has not crystallized. After all, Islam is a religion which has

even questioned nationalism—let alone the perpetuation of communal dichotomies within a nation. Muhammad Iqbal [1877–1938], one of the greatest Muslims of this century, argued that territorial or racial nationalism was foreign to the spirit of Islam. As one writer on Iqbal put it,

> He [Iqbal] was convinced now that it would be a tragically retrograde step if the Muslim World began to try to remedy its frustrations by replacing the global Islamic sentiment by aggressive nationalism of the Western type. He conceived of Islam as a universal religion which envisaged all humanity as a unity. But the Islam of his time had become narrow, rigid and static. He conceived of life as evolutionary and dynamic. He came to the conclusion that a fossilized religious dogmatism could not generate an outlook that would lead to the self-realization of individuals and communities.[25]

It is this universal character of Islam, its conception of humanity as a unity, that we have attempted to present in this book. For this purpose we have chosen four illustrious names from Islamic history [Jalal al-Din Rumi (1207–1273), Shah Wali Allah Dihlawi (1702–1762), Abul Kalam Azad (1888–1958), and Ameer Ali (1849–1928)]. . . . ALIRAN hopes that through the writings of these great thinkers the Malaysian public will achieve a deeper understanding of Islam. Because the views they have espoused are hardly known in our country, we can expect a number of our readers to express some misgivings.

But whatever their misgivings, it is our fervent prayer that they will go on looking for the truth in a sincere and rational manner. For in this quest for truth lies the future of Islam.

---

21. See various parts in Muhammad Natsir, *Capita Selecta* [*Selected Works*], volumes I and II (Jakarta, Indonesia: Pustaka Pendis, 1957).

22. The Qur'anic call for common principles is contained in Sura *Al-'Imran* [Sura 3], Verses 64–66.

23. For some discussion of common values, see my "Values in the Education System," *New Directions* (Singapore), March 1976.

24. "Mandi Safar" is a sort of purification bath confined mainly to Muslim groups in Malacca. It is pre-Islamic in origin and has some roots in Hindu custom. One of the better known puja ceremonies was the puja conducted for fishermen going out to sea. It was once popular in Kelantan. The former PAS government banned it.

25. See Khalifah Abdul Hakim's "Renaissance in Indo-Pakistan: Iqbal," in M. M. Sharif, editor, *A History of Muslim Philosophy*, volume 2 (Wiesbaden, Germany: Otto Harrassowitz, 1966), p. 1619.

Religious Liberty

Mohamed Talbi (Tunisia, born 1921) received his doctorate in history from the Sorbonne in 1968. Now a professor emeritus at the University of Tunis, Talbi began teaching there in the late 1950s and served as dean of Arts and Sciences in the late 1960s. In his retirement, Talbi has turned from his professional focus on medieval Islamic history to an enthusiastic participation in interreligious dialogue. His contributions to a variety of European and North American conferences and journals argue that Islam allows freedom of religion and that the traditional death penalty for apostasy involves a misreading of the Qur'an.

From Old Relations to a New Context

Religious liberty, as a common human concern and international preoccupation, is relatively new. In the old ages the problem was irrelevant. During antiquity all people felt it natural to worship the deities of their city. It was the job of these deities to protect the house and to look after the family and the welfare of the state. The deities of Carthage were by nature the enemies of the deities of Rome. In that context refusal to worship the deities of the city was disloyalty to the state.

The situation was almost the same inside the biblical tradition. In the Bible Yahweh acts as the Jews' God. He constantly warns His people not to worship any other deity and to obey His law. This people, with one God, is also a physical entity—the twelve tribes descended from Abraham by Isaac and Jacob with a land, Palestine. The Jewish community is an ideal prototype of unity: it obeys the law of blood, place, and religion. Judaism is the perfect prototype of an ethnically homogeneous community rooted in religion and shaped into a land and a state. To speak of religious liberty in such a case is absurd. There is no choice other than sticking to the state-community, or leaving it. Jews who convert to another religion cease *ipso facto* to belong to their state-community. So their conversion is felt as betrayal, and as such it warrants the penalty of death. If we dwelt on the case of the Jewish community as a prototype, it is because that case is not without similarity to the classical Islamic *umma* [community] as it has been shaped by traditional theology.

For historical reasons the situation changed with the appearance of Christian preaching. From the beginning this preaching was not linked with the state, and Jesus' people, the Jewish community, rejected the call. Jesus ordered his disciples "to render unto Caesar the things which are Caesar's, and unto God the things which are God's." (Gospel of Matthew,

Chapter 22, Verse 21) This revolutionary attempt to dissociate state from religion, and to ensure freedom of individual conscience, failed. The time was not yet ripe. Consequently the Roman state considered the first Christians to be disloyal subjects, because of their refusal to pay honor to the deities of their city and of their social group. Accordingly, they were treated as rebels. The right to self-determination and to religious liberty was denied them. They could not act freely in accordance with conscience.

To condense much history: church and state soon found that they needed each other. Intolerance of the dominant social or religious group soon asserted itself everywhere with internal and external wars, and many forms of discrimination and persecution. Of course the Islamic world, though relatively tolerant, was not an exception. As everywhere else, human rights have been violated or ignored. But that does not mean, as we shall see, that Islam as such authorizes violation of these fundamental rights.

Now, to avoid looking on the dark side of things, we have to add that our common past was not entirely ugly and somber. We can also cite eras of tolerance, respect, comprehension, and dialogue. Nevertheless, not until the 19th century do we see the right to free-thinking claimed. Political liberalism and the philosophical studies were then in vogue, and in fact what was claimed was not the right to think freely, but the right not to believe. So religious liberty became a synonym of secularism, agnosticism, and atheism. Consequently, a stubborn fight has been waged against religious liberty because of misidentification. To deal with the subject honestly and dispassionately, we must free ourselves from this false conception.

It must be admitted that religious liberty is today rooted in our social life. Since the Declaration of the Human Rights in 1945, this concept has emerged as an essential part of international law.

On the other hand, we live in a pluralistic world destined to be increasingly so. I wrote elsewhere that each human has the right to be different and already our planet is too small for our ambitions and dreams. In this new world, which is in rapid gestation, there is no more room for exclusiveness. We have to accept each other as we are. Diversity is the law of our time. Today, by virtue of expanding and sophisticated mass media, *every human is truly the neighbor of every human*.

In our Islamic countries we have been, since the beginning, in the habit of living side-by-side with communities of different faiths. It has not always been easy—as past and recent events could document. But only recently have we begun to be confronted with secularism. It is now our turn to experience from within the growth of agnosticism and atheism. We have to be conscious of this overwhelming change in our societies and, accordingly, exercise our theological thinking in this new and unprecedented context.

But first, and before going any further, what is religious liberty? Is it only the right to be an unbeliever? One may indeed say that religious liberty is but one aspect of the question—and from my point of view the negative one. In fact, religious liberty is basically the right to decide for one's self, without any kind of pressure, fear, or anxiety; the right to believe or not to believe; the right to assume with full consciousness one's destiny; the right, of course, to rid oneself of superstitions inherited from the Dark Ages; but also the right to espouse the faith of one's choice, to worship and to bear witness freely. Is this definition in harmony with the Qur'an's basic teachings?

Qur'an: The Basic Principles

Religious liberty is founded, from a Qur'anic perspective, first and foremost, on the divinely ordered nature of the human. The human is not a being among many others. Among the whole range of creatures only humans have duties and obligations. They are an exceptional being. They cannot be reduced to their body, because humans, before everything else, are a spirit, a spirit given the power to conceive the Absolute and to ascend to God. If humans have this exceptional power and this privileged position inside the Creation, it is because God "breathed into them something of His spirit." (Qur'an, Sura 32, Verse 9) Of course humans, like all living animals, are matter. They have a body created "from sounding clay, from mud molded into shape" (Sura 15, Verse 28). But they received the Spirit. They have two sides: a lower side—their clay—and a higher side—the Spirit of God. This higher side, comments A. Yusuf Ali [1872–1952], "if rightly used, would give man superiority over other creatures."

Humankind's privileged position inside the order of Creation is illustrated in the Qur'an in the scene where we see the angels receiving the order to prostrate themselves before Adam (Sura 15, Verse 29; Sura 38, Verse 72), the heavenly prototype of humankind. In a way, and provided we keep humans in their place as creature, we may say as Muslims—in harmony with Abraham's other spiritual descendants, Jews and Christians—that God created humans in His image. A *hadith*, saying of the Prophet, although questioned, authorizes this statement. So we can say that on the level of the Spirit, all persons, whatsoever may be their physical or intellectual abilities and aptitudes, are really equal. They have the same "breath" of God in them, and by virtue of this "breath" they have the ability to ascend to Him and to respond freely to His call. Consequently they have the same dignity and sacredness, and because of this dignity and sacredness they are equally and fully entitled to enjoy the right to self-determination on earth and for the hereafter. So from a Qur'anic perspective we may say that human rights are rooted in what every human is by nature, and this is by virtue of God's plan and creation. Thus the cornerstone of all human rights is religious liberty.

From a Muslim perspective humans are not the mere fruit of "hazard and necessity." Their creation obeys a plan and a purpose. Through the "breath" they have received the faculty to be at one with God; and their response, to have meaning, must be free. The teachings of the Qur'an are clear: Humans are privileged beings with "spiritual favors" (Sura 17, Verse 70); they had not been "created in jest" (Sura 23, Verse 115); they have a mission and they are God's "Viceregent on Earth" (Sura 2, Verse 30). They proceed from God with a mission to fulfill, their destiny is ultimately to return to Him. "Whoso do right, do it for their own soul; and whoso do wrong, do so to its detriment. Then to your Lord will you all be brought back." (Sura 45, Verse 15)

It is necessary that all persons may choose their way freely and without coercion. All persons must conscientiously fulfill their own destiny. The Qur'an states clearly that compulsion is incompatible with religion.

> There should be no compulsion in religion. Truth stands out clear from Error. Whosoever rejects Evil and believes in God hath grasped the most trustworthy hand-hold, that never breaks. God is All-Hearing, All-Knowing. (Sura 2, Verse 256)

To my best knowledge, among all the other revealed texts, only the Qur'an stresses religious liberty so unambiguously. The reason is that faith, to be true and reliable, must be a voluntary act. In this connect it is worthwhile to underline that the quoted verse was used to reprove some Jews and Christians, newly converted to Islam in Medina, who were willing to convert their children also to their new faith. So it is clearly stressed that faith is an individual concern and commitment, and that even parents must refrain from interfering with it. Faith, as stressed in the basic text of Islam in clear and indisputable words, is a voluntary act born out of conviction and freedom.

In fact, even God refrains from subduing against His will. This too is clearly expressed in the Qur'an. Faith is a free gift, God's gift. Humans can accept or refuse it. They have the faculty to open their heart and their reason to God's gift. Guidance (*hudan*) has been sent to them. They are warmly invited to listen to God's call. God warns them in clear and non-ambiguous terms. As it is underlined in the quoted verse stressing human freedom: "Truth stands out clear from Error." It is up to human to make their choice. The human condition—and that is the price of human dignity and sacredness—is not without something tragic in it. Humans can be misled. They are able to make the wrong choice and to stray from the right path.

In a word, they have the capacity to resist God's call, and this capacity is the criterion of their true freedom. Even the Messenger whose mission is properly to convey God's call and message is helpless in such a situation. He is clearly and firmly warned to respect human freedom and God's mystery. "If it had been thy Lord's will, all who are on the earth would have believed, all of them. Wilt thou then compel mankind, against their will, to believe!" (Sura 10, Verse 99) A. Yusuf Ali, in his translation of the Qur'an, comments on that verse in this way:

> Men of faith must not be impatient or angry if they have to contend against Unfaith, and most important of all, they must guard against the temptation of forcing Faith, that is, imposing it on others by physical compulsion, or any other forms of compulsion such as social pressure, or inducements held out by wealth or position, or other adventitious advantages. Forced faith is no faith.

The Apostle's mission—and all the more ours—is strictly restricted to advise, warn, convey a message, and admonish without compelling. He is ordered: "Admonish, for thou art but an admonisher. Thou hast no authority to compel them" (Sura 88, Verses 21–22). In other words, God has set humans truly and tragically free. What He wants is, in full consciousness and freedom, willing and obedient response to His call—and that is the very meaning of the Arabic word "*Islam*."

I do not mean that we should adopt an attitude of abandon and indifference. In fact, we have to avoid extremes. We have, of course, to refrain from interfering in the inner life of another, as I have stressed. It is time to add that we must avoid also being indifferent or careless about one another. We must convey God's message. This obligation of faith also needs stressing.

We are tempted today to shut ourselves up and to live comfortably wrapped in our own thoughts, indifferent to our neighbors. But this is not God's purpose. God Himself sets the example. He is nearer to humankind "than humans' own jugular vein" (Sura 50, Verse 16) and He knows better than we do our inmost desires, and what these desires "whisper" (*tuwaswisu*) to us (Sura 50, Verse 16). So He stands by us, and He speaks unceasingly to each of us, warning and promising with a divine pedagogy that fits all persons of different social and intellectual classes, using images, symbols, and words that He only may use with total sovereignty.

And God urges us to follow His example, and to turn our steps towards all our brothers in humanity, beyond all kinds of frontiers, the confessional ones included.

> O mankind! We created you from a male and a female; and We have made you into nations and tribes that you may know each other. Verily, the most honorable among you, in the sight of God, are those who are the most righteous of you. And God is All-Knowing, All-Aware. (Sura 49, Verse 13)

A. Yusuf Ali comments:

> This is addressed to all mankind, and not only to the Muslim brotherhood, though it is understood that in a perfect world the two would be synonymous. As it is, mankind is descended from one pair of parents. Their tribes, races, and nations are convenient labels by which we may know certain differing characteristics. Before God they are all one, and he gets most honor who is most righteous.

In other words humans are not created for solitariness and impervious individuality. They are created

for community, relationship, and dialogue. Their fulfillment is in their reconciliation both to God and to people. We have to find the way, in each case, to realize this double reconciliation, without betraying God and without damaging the inner life of the other. To do so, we have to listen to God's advice:

> Do not argue with the People of the Book unless it is in the most courteous manner, except for those of them who do wrong. And say: "We believe in the Revelation which has come down to us and in that which came down to you. Our God and your God is one, and to Him we submit." (Sura 29, Verse 46)

The Arabic word used in this verse, and rendered in the translation by the verb "to submit," is "*Muslimun*"—"Muslims." To be a true Muslim is to live in courteous dialogue with peoples of other faiths and ideologies, and ultimately to submit to God. We must show concern to our neighbors. We have duties to them, and we are not islands of loneliness. The attitude of respectful courtesy recommended by the Qur'an must be expanded to embrace all mankind, believers and unbelievers, except for those who "do wrong"—the unjust and violent, who resort deliberately to fist or argument. In such a case it is better to avoid so-called dialogue.

In short, from my Muslim perspective, our duty is to bear witness courteously and respectfully for the inner liberty of our neighbors and for their sacredness. We must also be ready to give them an honest hearing. We have to remember, as Muslims, that a *hadith* of our Prophet states: "The believer is unceasingly in search of wisdom, wherever he finds it he grasps it." Another saying adds: "Look for science everywhere, even as far as in China." And, finally, it is up to God to judge, for we, as limited human beings, know only in part. Let us quote:

> To each among you, have We prescribed a Law and an Open Way. And if God had enforced His Will, He would have made of you all one people. But His plan is to test you in what He hath given you. So strive as in a race in all virtues. The goal of you all is to God. Then will He inform you of that wherein you differed. (Sura 5, Verse 51)

> Say: "O God! Creator of the heavens and the earth! Knower of all that is hidden and open! It is thou that wilt judge between Thy Servants in those matters about which they have differed." (Sura 39, Verse 46)

Beyond the Limits Imposed
by Traditional Theology

Though all Muslims are bound by the Qur'an's basic teachings, Muslim traditional theology, for historical reasons, in my opinion, does not always reflect the spirit of the Qur'an. I'll cite briefly two important cases: the case of the *dhimmis*—the confessional minorities in the medieval Islamic empire—and the case of apostates.

Let us start with the *dhimmis*. If the doors of many countries have been opened by force or *jihad* [religious struggle], to pave the way for Islam, Islam itself has never been imposed by compulsion. From this point of view the teachings of the Qur'an have been observed. They protected the *dhimmis* against the most unbearable forms of religious intolerance. In particular, with two or three exceptions, the *dhimmis* have never been prevented from following the religion of their choice, from worshipping, or organizing their communities in accordance with their own law. Their situation has even been improved by Islamic conquest. They enjoyed long periods of tolerance and real prosperity, often holding high positions in the administration, in the court, and in economic activities.

But it is a fact that they suffered, from time to time, here and there, from discrimination. Things worsened after the reign of al-Mutawakkil (847–861). Discrimination, especially in dress, was openly humiliating. The oppression culminated in Egypt during the reign of al-Hakim (966–1021), who may not have been sane.

In the medieval context of wars, hostilities, and treacheries, discrimination or open oppression has always been prompted, or strongly backed, by the theologians. We have to remember that it was not then a virtue—according to the medieval mentality wherever—to consider all human beings as equal. How, then, to consider equal truth and error, true believers and heretics!

So in appraising the past we must always take circumstances into account. Above all, we must strive to avoid the same situations and errors. In any case, the Qur'an's basic teachings lay down a clear line of conduct. They teach us to respect the dignity and freedom of one another. In a world where giant holocausts have been perpetrated, where human rights are still manipulated or blandly ignored, our modern Muslim theologians must denounce all forms of discriminations as crimes strictly and explicitly condemned by the Qur'an.

On the other hand, we must consider the case of the apostate. In this field, too, traditional theology did not stick to the spirit of the Qur'an; rather, it abridged the liberty to choose one's religion.

According to this theology, though conversion to Islam must be, and is in fact, without coercion, it is practically impossible, once inside Islam, to get out of it. Conversion from Islam to another religion is considered treason, and the apostate is subject to the death penalty. For their interpretation, the traditional theologians rely on the precedent of the first caliph of Islam, Abu Bakr ([reigned] 632–634), who energetically fought the tribes that rejected his authority after the Prophet's death, and refused to pay him the alms taxes. He likened their rebellion to apostasy. Also, they cite the authority of this *hadith*: "Anyone who changes religion must be put to death."

During the history of Islam, I am not aware of any historical or current application of the law condemning the apostate to death. However, during the 1970s, in Egypt, the Islamists narrowly failed to enforce this law against Copts who converted to Islam, generally to marry Muslim women, and then, if the marriage failed, returned to their Coptic religion. Recently some Tunisian atheists have expressed their concern about this law.

So the case of the apostate in Islam, though mostly theoretical, needs to be cleared up. First, the *hadith* upon which the theologians assert the death penalty is always more or less mixed, in the books of *hadith*, with rebellion and highway robbery. The cases of "apostates" killed during the Prophet's life or shortly after his death are without exception those persons who, as a consequence of their "apostasy," turned their weapons against the Muslims, whose community was at that time small and vulnerable. The penalty of death appears in these circumstances as an act of self-defense. It is undoubtedly for that reason that the Hanafi School of *fiqh* [Islamic jurisprudence] does not condemn to death the woman apostate, "because women, contrary to men, are not fit for war."

On the other hand, the *hadith* authorizing the penalty of death is not technically *mutawatir* [epistemologically in the clear], and consequently it is not, according to the traditional system of *hadith*, binding. And above all, from a modern point of view, this *hadith* can and must be questioned. In my opinion, we have many good reasons to consider it a forgery.

It may been forged under the influence of Leviticus, Chapter 24, Verse 16, and Deuteronomy, Chapter 13, Verses 2–19, where the Israelites were ordered to stone the apostate to death.

In any case, the *hadith* in question is at variance with the teachings of the Qur'an, where there is no mention of the death penalty required against the apostate. During the life of the Prophet apostasy presented itself at various times, and several verses [of the Qur'an] deal with it. In all, without exception, punishment of the apostate who persists in rejection of Islam is left to God's judgment and to the afterlife. The cases mentioned in the Qur'an and by the commentators concern, on the one hand, individuals and tribes who become turncoats, and, on the other hand, persons attracted by the "Peoples of the Book," Jews and Christians, to their faith (Sura 2, Verse 109; Sura 3, Verses 99–100). Taking into account the special situation, the Qur'an argues, warns, or recommends the attitude to take, without ever threatening death.

1. The Qur'an Argues

From a Muslim perspective, the Qur'an recognizes all previous revelations, authenticates and perfects them.

> Say: "We believe in God, and in what has been revealed to us, and what was revealed to Abraham, Ishmael, Jacob, and the Tribes, and in that which was given to Moses, Jesus, and the Prophets, from their Lord. We make no distinction between anyone of them, and to God we submit (*Muslimun*)." (Sura 3, Verse 84)

It does not follow that one is permitted, at the convenience of the moment, to change religion as one changes a coat. Such behavior denotes lack of true faith. It is for this reason that the following verse insists on the universal meaning of Islam, a call directed to all of mankind: "If anyone desires a religion other than Islam, never will it be accepted of him; and in the Hereafter he will be among the losers." (Sura 3, Verse 85)

Accordingly, apostates are warned: those who choose apostasy, after being sincerely convinced that Islam is the Truth, are unjust, and as such they are bereaved of God's guidance, with all the consequences that follow for their salvation. "How shall God guide those who reject faith after they accepted it, and bore witness that the Apostle was true, and that clear signs had come to them? But God guides not a people unjust." (Sura 3, Verse 86; see too the following Verses 87–91)

On the other hand, the Qur'an denounces "Peoples of the Book" who exert pressure on Muslims to induce them to retract. There is no doubt that polemics between the emerging Islam and the old religions were sharp. In this atmosphere the Qur'an urges people who espouse Islam to stick firmly to their new faith until their death; to close their ranks, to refuse to listen to those who strive to render them apostates, and to keep out of their trap. They are also reminded of their former state of disunion, when they were "on the brink of the Pit of Fire"; and they are exhorted to ensure their final salvation:

> Say, "O People of the Book: Why obstruct ye those who believe, from the Path of God, seeking to make it crooked, while ye were yourselves witness thereof? But God is not unmindful of all that ye do."
>
> O ye who believe! If you obey a faction of those who have been given the Book, they will turn your back into disbelievers after you have believed.
>
> And how would you disbelieve, while to you are rehearsed the signs of God, and His Messenger is among you? And he who holds fast to God is indeed guided to the Right Path.
>
> O ye who believe! Fear God as He should be feared, and die not except in the state of Islam.
>
> And hold fast, all together, by the Rope of God, and be not divided, and remember God's favor on you: for ye were enemies, and He joined your Hearts in love, so that by His Grace, ye became brethren; and ye were on the brink of the Pit of Fire, and He saved you from it. Thus doth God make His Signs clear to you, that ye may be guided.
>
> Let there arise out of you a Community inviting to all that is good, enjoining what is right, and forbidding what is wrong. They are the ones to attain felicity. (Sura 3, Verses 99–104)

Thus, unceasingly and by all means, the Qur'an strives to raise new Muslims' spirit, in order to prevent them from falling into apostasy. The argumentation is only moral. The Qur'an goes on: It is "from selfish envy" that "quite a number of the People of the Book wish they could turn you back to infidelity" (Sura 2, Verse 109; see too Sura 3, Verse 149); you have not to fear them. "God is you Protector, and He is the best of helpers, soon shall He cast terror into the hearts of the unbelievers" (Sura 3, Verses 150–151); "your real friends are God, His Messenger, and the believers . . . therefore take not for friends those who take your religion for a mockery or sport." (Sura 5, Verses 58–60) And, finally, those who in spite of all this counsel allow themselves to be tempted by apostasy, are forewarned: If they desert the Cause, the Cause will not fail. Others will bring it to a head.

> O ye who believe! If any from among you turn back from their faith, soon will God produce a people whom He will love as they will love Him, lowly with the Believers, mighty against the Rejecters, striving in the way of God, and never afraid of the reproaches of a fault finder. That is the grace of God, which He will bestow on whom He pleaseth. And God is Bountiful, All-Knowing. (Sura 5, Verse 57; see too Sura 47, Verse 38)

Finally, the apostates are given this notice: they "will not injure God in the least, but He will make their deeds of no effect." (Sura 47, Verse 32)

2. The Qur'an Warns

The young Muslim community is thus given many reasons to stick to the new religion. Members are also warned that their salvation depends on their not departing from their faith. They are urged to follow the true spirit of Islam, which is defined in two ways: First, they will love God and God will love them; second, they will be humble among their brethren, but they will not fear wrong-doers and they will not consort with them. If by fear, weakness, or time-serving, they fall into apostasy, the loss will be theirs and punishment will be hard in the Hereafter. "And if any of you turn back from their faith, and die in unbelief, their works will bear no fruit in this life. And in the Hereafter they will be companions of the Fire, and will abide therein." (Sura 2, Verse 217) The apostates lay themselves open to "the curse of God, of His angels, and of all mankind" (Sura 3, Verse 87), except for "those who repent thereafter, and amend, for God is Oft-Forgiving, Most Merciful." (Sura 3, Verses 89–91). They will "taste the penalty for rejecting faith" (Sura 3, Verse 106; see too Verse 140). Such people are entirely in the hands of Evil (Sura 47, Verse 25). They secretly plot with enemies (Sura 47,

Verses 26–27), and "they obstruct the way to God." (Sura 47, Verses 32, 34) As a result "God will not forgive them." (Sura 47, Verse 34)

3. The Qur'an Advises

How to deal with obstinate and ill-disposed apostates? How to treat those who try to draw them into their camp, or to manipulate them? Let us underline once more that there is no mention in the Qur'an of any kind of penalty, including death. To use the Arab technical word, we say that there is no specific *hadd* [limitation] in this matter.

On the contrary, Muslims are advised to "forgive and overlook till God accomplishes His purpose, for God hath power over all things." (Sura 2, Verse 109) In other words, no punishment on earth. The case does not answer to the Law. The debate is between God and the apostate's conscience, and it is not our role to interfere in it.

Muslims are authorized to take up arms in only one case, self-defense, when they are attacked and their faith seriously jeopardized. In such a case "fighting" (*al-qital*) is "prescribed" (*kutiba*), even if they "dislike it" (*kurhun lakum*) (Sura 2, Verse 194). To summarize—Muslims are urged not to yield, when their conscience is at stake, and to take up arms against "those who will not cease fighting you until they turn you back from your faith, if they can." (Sura 2, Verse 217)

Conclusion

It is thus evident that religious liberty, with all its ramifications, is not new inside Islam. The Qur'an deals at length with it. In the core of this problem we meet the ticklish subject of apostasy. We have seen that the Qur'an argues, warns, advises, but never resorts to the sword. The reason is that argument is meaningless in matters of faith. In our pluralistic world our theologians must take that into account.

We can never underline enough that religious liberty is not an act of charity or a tolerant concession to mislead persons. It is a fundamental right for everyone. To claim it for myself, implies *ipso facto* that I am disposed to claim it for my neighbor too.

Religious liberty is not the equivalent of atheism. My right, and my duty also, is to bear witness, by fair means, of my own faith, and to convey God's call.

Ultimately it is up to each person to respond or not to respond to this call.

From a Muslim perspective, and on the basis of the Qur'an's teachings, religious liberty is fundamentally and ultimately an act of respect for God's Sovereignty and for the mystery of His plan for humankind, who have been given the terrible privilege of building on their own responsibility, their destiny on earth and for the hereafter. Finally, to respect human freedom is to respect God's plan.

To be a True Muslim is to submit to this plan. It is, in the literal sense of the word, to put one's self, voluntarily and freely, with confidence and love, in the hands of God.

19

Ali Bulaç

The Medina Document

Ali Bulaç (Turkey, born 1951) is a leading figure among the growing group of Muslim intellectuals in Turkey. His first book, published in the late 1970s, achieved the status of "a kind of manifesto of the Muslim intellectuals."[1] Bulaç argues that Islam represents a viable alternative to Western political systems that solves many of the social and political ills associated with the West, but only if Muslim intellectuals undertake a systematic analysis of Islam's applicability to modern problems. His more recent work has attempted to supply some of this analysis[2] and begun to focus on the issue of pluralism, particularly ethnic and religious pluralism. Bulaç's basis for analysis is the Medina Document, a contract signed by the Prophet Muhammad, Jews, and polytheists granting Muslims the right to rule in the Arabian city and at the same time protecting the rights of other groups.

With the *hijra* [the exodus of the Muslims from Mecca to Medina in 622] and subsequent developments, there were three main social groups in Medina: Muslims, Jews and the Polytheist Arabs.

The Muslim group consisted of refugees from Mecca and the Ansar [literally "helpers," these were Medinans who accepted Islam]. The Ansar were composed of the Aws [tribe] and the Khazraj [tribe]. This kind of social structure was alien to the ancient traditions of the whole Arabian peninsula. In traditional tribal life social organization depended on blood and kinship ties, while in Medina, for the first time, people from totally divergent geographical, ethnic and cultural backgrounds gathered and identified themselves as a distinct social group. Later the Roman Suhayl, the Persian Salman and the Kurdish Gavan would be added to this group. Indeed, the second article of the Medina Document [translated and discussed in this chapter] would designate this social group as "an *umma* [community] distinct from other people" on a religious and legal basis.

Yet, of course, Medina did not consist only of Muslims. There were its ancient inhabitants: Jews and the Arabs who did not accept Islam. *Hazrat* [his excellency] Muhammad (peace be upon him) faced the important problem of reconciling and unifying these social groups, of discovering the formula for co-existence.[3] But how was he going to do it?

---

1. Michael E. Meeker, "The New Muslim Intellectuals in the Republic of Turkey," in Richard Tapper, editor, *Islam in Modern Turkey* (London: I. B. Tauris, 1991), pp. 197–198.

2. For instance, Ali Bulaç, *İslam ve Demokrasi* (*Islam and Democracy*) (Istanbul: Beyan Yayınları, 1993).

3. A. Himmet Berki and Osman Keskioğlu, *Hatemü'l Enbiya Hz. Muhammed ve Hayatı* [*The Seal of the Prophets, Hazrat Muhammad, and His Life*], 7th edition (Ankara, Turkey, 1978), p. 204; S. M. Ahmed Nedvi and S. S. Ansari, *Asr-ı Saadet* [*The Era of Prosperity, Namely the Reign of the*

It now appears that Hazrat Muhammad started out by tracing the social, religious and demographic composition of Medina. For this purpose, he had a population census taken, an undertaking quite strange for its time. Can we say that, in addition to the [pioneering] Medina Document, we encounter the first census here, where the inhabitants of the town were recorded one by one (man, woman, child, the old) in a notebook? Whatever the answer, there is no doubt that the act was "new and strange" for Arabs. According to a report from Huzayfa [ibn al-Yaman, companion of the Prophet]: "God's Messenger said to us: 'Bring me the names of (each of) the people who chose Islam as their religion and those who became Muslims.' And we wrote down and brought 1500 names to him."[4]

From the census they found that 10,000 people lived in Medina, of which 1,500 were Muslims, 4,000 were Jews and 4,500 were Polytheist Arabs. The Prophet took another step and determined the physical city boundaries of Medina by marking its four corners. In this way he specified the land included in a "city-state," which was to be designated as the "protected area (*harem*) remaining within the Medina (Yathrib) valley" in article 39 of the Medina Document.

Naturally Muslims were pleased with this undertaking, and the Jews also seemed pleased with this social and political organization. Only the *Mushrik*s (Polytheists) of Medina were disturbed. They perceived a potential threat,[5] which is not difficult to understand. Since the Prophet and his followers had had to migrate [from Mecca to Medina] due to unbearable pressures exerted by the Polytheists of Mecca, it is unthinkable that he would be on good terms with other unbelievers. Moreover, right after the *hijra*, news had started to arrive from Mecca that the Quraish [tribe of Mecca] would continue chasing them and was planning an attack on Medina soon.

In the event of such a struggle, what would the position of the Polytheists of Medina be? Would not the Quraish blame them, asking why they accepted Muhammad? Might not a conflict arise between them and the Muslims even before such an attack? There was a de facto possibility. How was co-existence possible in such a conjuncture?

Hazrat Muhammad was preoccupied with the settlement of the migrant Meccans and their adaptation to the new environment, while on the other hand he was trying to gain the confidence of the Jews and the Polytheist Arabs. He declared that his aim was not to establish an absolute rule over Medina, but to assure the security of his religious community as well as the necessary conditions for the propagation of the new religion. In fact, even in the [earlier Qur'anic] revelations of Mecca, a political principle had been adopted stating, "To you your religion, to me my religion." (Sura 109, Verse 6) However, the Quraish, refusing this multireligious pluralist project, had blocked the spread of the religious message and tortured those who wanted to become Muslims.

Because of these factors, one would not expect the Prophet to change the strategy he had been following. Under these conditions, his life in Medina would implement the Meccan revelations on the social, legal, and institutional levels. It would transform the vision of Mecca into practice in Medina; and this was what happened. In other words, he demonstrated, to every one and every community, possible ways of co-existing through the realization of a pluralist social project based on religious and legal autonomy. Of course, the religious message would be propagated; but no one would be coerced to convert through force and pressure; those who converted would meet no opposition, as they had in Mecca.

When they first arrived in Medina, the Ansar of Medina and the chiefs of the families (*naqib*) from Mecca gathered in a big meeting. . . . The first 23 articles of the Medina Document, decided upon in this meeting, established the social and legal relationships of the new Muslim group in written decrees.

After the completion of the work, *Hazrat* Muhammad, peace be upon him, consulted the representatives of the non-Muslim social groups, just as he had consulted the Muslim leaders. All of them agreed upon the basic principles constituting the foundations of a new "city-state" in a gathering in the house of Anas [ibn Malik, Companion of the Prophet, 710–796]. The "constitution" of this new state was recorded in writing and this is the Document that we hold in our hands now.

Prophet], translated [into Turkish] by A. Genceli (Istanbul, 1985), volume 1, p. 64.

4. [Muhammad ibn Isma'il] Bukhari [810–870, *hadith* compiler], 56/181, number 1; M. Tayyib Okiç, "İslamiyette İlk Nüfus Sayımı" [The First Census in Islam], *Ankara Üniversitesi İlahiyat Fakultesi Dergisi* [*Ankara University Theology Faculty Review*], volume 7, 1958–1959, pp. 11ff.

5. S. M. Ahmed Nedvi and S. S. Ansari, volume 1, p. 64.

Now let us take a closer look at the decrees of the Document in order to render the subject more comprehensible:

The Medina Document[6]

In the name of God, the compassionate, the merciful.

1. This book (document) has been prepared by Muhammad the Prophet of God, on behalf of the believers of Quraysh [the emigrants from Mecca] and Yathrib [Medina], the Muslims and those who have joined them, and those fighting along with them.
2. Surely, they form an *umma* (group) apart from the rest of humankind.
3. The migrants of Quraysh shall defray the cost of bloodshed among themselves as has been the custom and shall join in ransoming their war prisoners according to the proper and approved principles of justice among the believers.
4. The Banu 'Awf shall continue to pay the costs of their bloodshed as they have been accustomed, and each group shall participate in ransoming their war prisoners according to the proper and approved principles of justice among the believers.
5. The Banu'l-Harith shall continue to pay the costs of their bloodshed as they have been accustomed, and each group shall participate in ransoming their war prisoners according to the proper and approved principles of justice among the believers.
6. The Banu Sa'ida shall continue to pay the costs of their bloodshed as they have been accustomed and each group shall participate in ransoming their war prisoners according to the proper and approved principles of justice among the believers.
7. The Banu Jusham shall continue to pay the costs of their bloodshed as they have been accustomed to and each group shall participate in ransoming their war prisoners according to the proper and approved principles of justice among the believers.

8. The Banu'n-Najjar shall continue to pay the costs of their bloodshed as they have been accustomed to and each group shall participate in ransoming their war prisoners according to the proper and approved principles of justice among the believers.
9. The Banu 'Amr ibn 'Awf shall continue to pay the costs of their bloodshed as they have been accustomed to and each group shall participate in ransoming their war prisoners according to the proper and approved principles of justice among the believers.
10. The Banu'n-Nabit shall continue to pay the costs of their bloodshed as they have been accustomed to and each group shall participate in ransoming their war prisoners according to the proper and approved principles of justice among the believers.
11. The Banu'l-Aws shall continue to pay the costs of their bloodshed as they have been accustomed to and each group shall participate in ransoming their war prisoners according to the proper and approved principles of justice among the believers.
12. The Muslims shall not leave anyone among them under financial burden (in this situation), and shall pay the debts thereof, arising from ransoms for war prisoners and costs of bloodshed, according to the proper and approved principles.
12B. No Muslim shall oppose the *mawla* (person with whom a contractual brotherhood has been established) of another Muslim. (According to another reading: No Muslim may enter into an agreement with the *mawla* of another Muslim, so as to harm the latter.)
13. All God-fearing Muslims shall be against the person who intends to commit an aggressive and unjust act among them, or who aims to infringe one's right or to cause turmoil among believers. And even if this person is the offspring of one of them, they shall all raise their hands against him.
14. No Muslim shall kill another Muslim for the sake of an unbeliever and shall assist an unbeliever at the expense of a Muslim.
15. God's possession (protection and assurance) is one; (a protection acknowledged by the least important of the Muslims) applies to them all. This is because a Muslim is the *mawla* (brother) of another, apart from rest of the people.
16. Among Jews, those who submit to us shall receive our assistance and protection; they shall not be oppressed, nor shall we give assistance to their enemies.

6. We owe our recognition of the Document in the Islamic world to Professor Muhammad Hamidullah. . . . See his *İslam Peygamberi* [*The Prophet of Islam*], translated [into Turkish] by Professor Salih Tuğ, fifth edition (Istanbul, 1990), volume 1, pp. 200ff. [The following is translated from Bulaç's Turkish rendition.—Editor]

17. Peace is one among Muslims. No Muslim, in a war fought in the path of God, may agree to a peace accord by excluding other believers. This peace shall only be made among them (Muslims) according to the principles of generalizability and justice.

18. All those (military) groups joining us in war shall be relieved in turn.

19. Muslims shall take revenge for each other of the blood shed for (the sake of) God.

20. Surely, God-fearing Muslims follow the best and the straightest path.

20B. No polytheist may protect the life and property of one of the Quraish and can intervene with a believer in this matter (may not prevent an attack on the Quraish).

21. If it is proven with certainty that one person has killed a Muslim and the guardian (defender) of the victim does not grant a pardon, rules of retaliation shall operate; in this case all Muslims shall be against him. It is only *halal* (right) for them to act in compliance (with this rule).

22. It is not *halal* (right) for any Muslim believing in God and the Day of Judgment, accepting the contents of this sheet (document), to assist a murderer and to provide protection for him; whoever helps him and provides protection shall receive the curse and wrath of God on the Day of Judgment, when financial compensation or sacrifice shall no longer be accepted.

23. Any issue over which you are divided shall be taken to God and Muhammad.

24. Jews along with Muslims shall bear (their own) war expenses during war.

25. The Jews of Banu 'Awf, together with Muslims[7] constitute an *umma* (group). The religion of the Jews is for themselves, the religion of Muslims for themselves. This includes both their *mawla* and themselves personally.

25B. But whoever performs an unjust action or commits a crime shall harm solely himself and members of his family.

26. The Jews of Banu'n-Najjar shall have the same (rights) as the Jews of Banu 'Awf.

27. The Jews of Banu'l-Harith shall have the same (rights) as the Jews of Banu 'Awf.

28. The Jews of Banu Sa'ida shall have the same (rights) as the Jews of Banu 'Awf.

29. The Jews of Banu Jusham shall have the same (rights) as the Jews of Banu 'Awf.

30. The Jews of Banu'l-Aws shall have the same (rights) as the Jews of Banu 'Awf.

31. The Jews of Banu Tha'laba shall have the same (rights) as the Jews of Banu 'Awf. But whoever performs an unjust action or commits a crime shall harm solely himself and members of his family.

32. The Jafna (family) is a branch of the Tha'laba [tribe] and because of this they shall be considered as the Tha'laba.

33. Banu'sh-Shutaiba shall have the same (rights) as the Jews of Banu 'Awf. (The rules) shall be obeyed absolutely; no one shall break them.

34. The *mawla* of the Tha'laba shall be considered as Tha'laba themselves.

35. Those who have taken refuge with the Jews (*bitana*) shall be considered as Jews themselves.

36. Among them (Jews) none may go (on a military campaign with the Muslims) without the permission of Muhammad.

36B. It shall not be forbidden to take revenge of a wound. Surely if a person happens to kill another, both he and his family shall be responsible as a consequence, otherwise there shall be injustice (meaning any person not obeying this rule shall have been unjust). God is with those who best obey this Document.

37. (In case of war) Jews bear their expenses and the Muslims theirs. Surely they shall cooperate among themselves, in opposing those who wage war against the people designated on this sheet (document). There shall be benevolence and good behavior between them. (The rules) shall be obeyed absolutely; no one shall break them.

37B. No one may commit a crime against his ally; surely the oppressed shall receive help.

38. Jews along with Muslims shall bear the expenses of wars fought together.

39. On behalf of a person designated by this sheet (document), the Yathrib valley (*jawf*) constitutes a *harem* (protected) territory.

40. Any person under protection (*jar*) is like the protector himself; he shall not be oppressed nor shall he commit any crime.

41. Excepting those with permission to give protection, no one may be given the right to protection.

42. All cases of murder and fighting that occur among the people designated in this sheet (Document) shall be taken to God and His Messenger Muhammad. God is with those who best obey this Document.

7. In ['Abd al-Malik] Ibn Hisham [died 833] this is written as *ma'a* (with), and in Abu 'Ubayd [al-Qasim ibn Sallam, 770–838] as *min* (of). [These two authors, the most important sources for the text of the Medina Document, disagree on wording in a number of places.—Editor]

43. Neither the Quraish nor those assisting them shall receive protection.

44. There shall be cooperation among them (Muslims and Jews) against those who invade the Yathrib.

45. If they (the Jews) are invited (by the Muslims) to adhere to a peace agreement or to take part in a peace agreement, they shall either directly sign it or participate in it. If they (the Jews) suggest the same things (to the Muslims), they shall have the same rights from the Muslims; excepting cases of war over religious issues.

45B. Each group is responsible for the area belonging to it (with regards to its defense and other needs).

46. The Jews of al-Aws, meaning their *mawla* and themselves, shall have the same rights agreed upon on this sheet (document), with strict and complete obedience from the people designated on this sheet (document). (The rules) shall be obeyed absolutely; no one shall break them. God is with those who best and truly observe the rules described on this sheet (document).

47. This book (document) shall not protect the perpetrator of an unjust act or a crime from punishment. Whoever goes to war shall have security and whoever remains in Medina shall also have security; except those who commit an unjust act or a crime. God and His Messenger Muhammad shall protect those who observe (this sheet) with complete loyalty and care.

Constitutive Principles Implicit in the Articles

According to [Muhammad] Hamidullah [born 1908], "This constitution carries the title and privilege of being not only the first Islamic state constitution but also the first constitution on earth announced by a state."[8] The Italian historian [Leone] Caetani [1869–1935] calls it a "document" without using the term "constitution" and adds, "The document is a book of the Prophet Muhammad so that it is not anyone else but Muhammad himself who wrote (or who had it written). Others, meaning Muslims, Jews and Polytheists, have adopted it."[9] It should not be deduced from these words of Caetani that the Prophet dictated

to others a text prepared by himself, or that he made them sign it by default. Information from [Malik ibn] Anas [Companion of the Prophet, 710–796] and other sources indicates that the Document took shape as a result of negotiations and as a product of social consensus.

And this is the true interpretation, because it is unimaginable that a person who snuck out of Mecca in the middle of the night to migrate to Medina would be able to impose the text of an agreement that serves his own purposes and interests on people stronger both militarily and numerically. It should be remembered that his [the Prophet's] supporters made up only 15 percent of the total city population. No, this does not make sense.

One of the main factors contributing to the acceptance of this social contract was the chaotic and insecure condition of Medina, which was worn out by 120 years of wars and conflicts. It is as if Medina awaited its savior. It could not, by itself and through the existing social forces, find a political and social formulation for peace and stability. Because of war Medina stagnated economically, and it appeared to be generating even more new conflicts. At just such a critical period a stranger showed all groups how to coexist in partnership, inviting everyone to exist on legal foundations, according to the principle of "you are what you are."

The fact that terms like "wounding," "killing," "costs of bloodshed," "ransom for freedom" are uttered frequently in the text reflects the normal condition of a society shaken and worn out by long years of internal strife. The urgent problem of the day was to end the conflicts and to find a formulation for the co-existence of all sides according to the principles of justice and righteousness. In this respect, the Document is epochal. Its historical nature and the small number of the people signing it are insignificant with respect to its constitutive principles.

The second important point is the fact that such a project enabled everyone to be accepted by each other as a natural reality without resorting to domination, the legalization of respect for each other's ways of living and thinking, and protection under the law.

Another point to be noted is this: The Medina Document proposes a social project not based on

8. Hamidullah, volume 1, p. 189.

9. L. Caetani, *Annali [dell'Islam]* [*The History of Islam*] (Milan, Italy, 1903), translated [into Turkish] by Hüseyin Cahit [Yalçın, 1874–1957] as *İslam Tarihi* [*The History of Islam*] (Istanbul, 1924), volume 3, p. 112.

"domination" but on "participation" by all social groups. According to the project offered by the Document, Muslims will live as free people in the direction indicated by God and *Hazrat* Muhammad, in safety, and will propagate their religion. The same rights apply to the Jews and others.

Here we underline the first constitutive principle that can be drawn from the Document:

A righteous and just, law-respecting ideal project aiming for true peace and stability among people cannot but be based on a contract among different groups (religious, legal, philosophical, political, etc.). During the preparation of the contract, the members or the representatives of the social groups should be present, the articles of the contract (basic principles) should be decided in a free environment, involving discussions and negotiations of the different parties involved. . . .

Since the groups in the social scene are heterogeneous, each article should reflect a common interest and should be settled democratically. Every common interest constitutes an article of the covenant, and every article concerning points of disagreement is left to the groups themselves. Commonalities belong to the sphere of the covenant; differences belong to the autonomous sphere. This is a rich diversity within unity, or a real pluralism.

The second constitutive principle is the selection of the concept of participation as the starting point, rather than domination, because a totalitarian or unitarian political structure cannot allow for diversities. The Medina Document cites Muslims and Jews tribe by tribe (one by one). It deals with the Polytheists in a different article (Article 20B). Immigrants, the Ansar, Banu 'Awf, Banu'l-Harith, Banu Sa'ida, Banu Jusham, Banu'n-Najjar, Banu 'Amr ibn 'Awf, Banu'n-Nabit, Banu'l-Aws (Articles 1–11); and again, among the Jews, the tribes Banu 'Awf, Banu'n-Najjar, Banu'l-Harith, Banu Sa'ida, Banu Jusham, Banu'l-Aws, Banu Tha'laba, Jafna, Banu'sh-Shutaiba (Articles 25–33) and their *mawla* —all are cited one by one.

Mawla [brothers] are a tribe, family or group connected to or in contract with another tribe without having a blood or kinship relationship to it. In other words, each social group that becomes a party to the contract by affixing its name and signature represents the other groups connected to it while acknowledging equivalent rights and responsibilities for them.

However Article 20B adopts special decrees for the Polytheists, supported by Article 43. This is in order to prevent the Polytheists of Medina from establishing any political or military relationships with the Polytheists of Mecca. Actually, the Polytheists of Medina did not intend to ally with the Meccans; in fact, they feared its consequences. Yet, they too, like the others, wanted to have all the rights and freedoms permitted within the City, as described in Article 39. The Document guarantees the right to demand these rights as well. Consequently, we know that after the battles of Badr and Uhud fought against the Meccans, the Polytheist parties to the contract continued to live in Medina without serious conflicts occurring between them and the Muslims.

The mentioning of the tribes one by one is in order to acknowledge the identities of the religious and ethnic collectivities existing in the society. The tribal leaders probably demanded this in particular.

The conclusion to be drawn here is this: each religious and ethnic group enjoys complete cultural and legal autonomy. In other words, in such areas as religion, law-making, judiciary, education, trade, culture, art, and the organization of daily life, each group will remain as it is and will express itself through the cultural and legal criteria it defines. The guarantee of this religious and legal autonomy is Article 25, which declares: "The religion of the Jews is for themselves, the religion of Muslims for themselves. This includes both their *mawla* and themselves personally."

The decree demanding that possible conflicts should be taken to *Hazrat* Muhammad, in Article 42, was proposed by the Jews and the Polytheists, as we know both from the Qur'an and the *hadith* [traditions of the Prophet] as well as from other sources. For reasons mentioned above, the chaotic conditions in Medina had disrupted the trust between tribes. With this specific article, the groups agree to carry the case to a "higher judiciary authority" whenever they cannot solve the conflicts among themselves. This higher judiciary authority is *Hazrat* Muhammad, being trustworthy, impartial and an outsider to Medina. The Qur'an granted to the Prophet the authority to handle their cases, if he was willing to do so (Sura 5, Verse 42). As a result, the Prophet left them free to choose every time they consulted him, asking them, "How do you want me to decide, according to the Qur'an or the Torah?" In this arrangement, the Prophet did not act as a "judge" but as a "referee." It should be added that the practice of resolving the cases of non-Muslims or leaving them with their own courts and laws has formed part of the *dhimmi* [minority groups] law since then, lasting until the final days of the Ottomans [reigned 1281–1924].

Another constitutive principle emerges here: in a pluralist society, several legal systems, not necessarily one single system, may coexist. Of course if conflicts arise among groups due to contradictions between laws—which are expected to arise—in these cases either the Court of *Mazalim* [Injustice] extends its authority to decide the case, as was the case historically; or higher courts formed by the legal representatives of all legal communities may be established. In my opinion, the best solution is to leave the injured party free to choose among legal systems; this is possible from the perspective of Islamic law.

The 23rd article of the Document makes the Prophet the absolute ruler of the Muslim social group. This is natural, since the Muslims have agreed to follow him from the beginning by giving allegiance to him. This is an attitude consistent with the basic Islamic assumption of not separating religious practice, belief and law from each other. The constitutive principle behind these decrees underlines the fact that Islam is a religion binding only on the Muslims.

Those who claim that the Islamic model is totalitarian are not sufficiently aware of this fact. If the people have the right to freely choose their religion, their laws and ways of living must of necessity be consistent with their beliefs and ideas. In this sense, Islamic religion and law binds Muslims; it does not include or bind others, nor does it expect others to behave according to this law. In fact *Hazrat* 'Umar [second caliph, reigned 634–644] was not pleased to see a non-Muslim female slave covering her head, saying that covering the head is a decree relevant for those who accept Islam in its entirety.

On the other hand, the Document transcends all religious and social groups with its objective rulings. In other words, Muslims, Jews and Polytheists cannot break its general guidelines. In this sense, the Document, erected as a result of mutual agreement, stands above the Qur'an, the Torah and the established customs.

Articles 4 and 11 endorse the autonomy of the social groups. According to these, the tribes shall compensate for bloodshed, as was customary, and shall ransom war prisoners. They will settle their financial liabilities among themselves, where these will be determined through mutual agreements (Articles 3, 12, and 37). However, the guilty will not be protected by tribal ties of blood and kinship, as they were in the old system; when someone commits a crime, the individuals of the tribe will not be held responsible. Thus the crime and the punishment will become individualized (Articles 22 and 31B). This was a revolution by itself. In this new structure, where the guilty and the criminal are not protected—no matter which group they belong to—the consolidation of justice and safety is raised to the status of a common and collective responsibility; the parties—individuals within a bloc—being held responsible to each other (Articles 12, 13, 21). Following this, Article 12B concedes the possibility of individuals making contracts with *mawla* of other individuals, separately. As I understand it, this and other decrees take the right of granting visas away from the state and accord it directly to individuals and groups.

Other articles of the Document can be briefly summarized as follows: The concept of country and defended frontiers were introduced by Article 39, an innovation in those historical circumstances. The tribal structure based upon blood and kinship ties was thus transcended, as people gathered around a higher political association ordered in groups (or legal collectivities), and any kind of conflict and violation of law among families and tribes of Medina was prohibited. The term *haram* used in the Document means defended frontier, and refers to the territorial integrity of a political union. The term corresponding to this political union in the Document is *umma* (Articles 2, 25). In this sense *umma* is the political union consisting of Muslims, Jews and Polytheists. This union is a social project which does not discriminate on the basis of race, language, religion, sect and ethnic origins (Articles 1, 2, 16 and 25), since it is founded upon religious, cultural and legal autonomy.

In relationships among individuals and groups, universally transcendent ideals agreed by all and basic ethical principles rule (Article 47). Still, in order for these to operate, a written legal text regulating the entirety of social relationships is needed. Because of this, the Document presents itself as "book" (Articles 1, 47) or "sheet" (Articles 22, 39, 42, 46, etc.), two terms which connote a sense of obligation in the traditional culture of the day. The

Qur'an, too, defines itself as "the book" and states that various books and sheets were revealed to past prophets.[10]

While the Document demands full obedience to the rule of law, binding everyone (Articles 37, 37B), the act of war has been removed from the realm of single individuals and tribes and has been passed to the central government (Articles 17, 18). War will be announced by a decision of the central government reached through consent. One of the most important reasons for war can be to form a front of solidarity against external attacks. In such a war of defense, the parties to the agreement undertake mutual financial and military responsibilities, fighting all together (Articles 15, 18, 19, 24). However, common responsibility does not exist in wars fought in the name of religion (Article 45). Accordingly, if Muslims happen to be warring with others—outside Medina—for religion, the Jews and the Polytheists of Medina do not have to join them. The battles of Badr and Uhud took place outside of Medina, because of this article.

Justice in social life, the organization of legal procedures and the judiciary will be taken care of by delegating these powers to the central authority and not to the judgments and initiatives of individuals (Article 13).

While the Document transfers power to the central authority (the state?) in judiciary, defense, and the proclamation of war—legislation, culture, science, arts, economy, education, health and other services are left to civil society. Through other reports from the Prophet, we know that the government is restricted to such areas as taxing, judiciary, and defense; whereas other areas remain with civil society.

Other conclusions can be drawn from the general decrees of the Document, yet this is not the proper place. The importance of the Document for us lies in the fact that it was written as a result of negotiations and deliberations among three different religious and social groups in year 622, and put into practice.

Personally, I believe that some constitutive principles can be reached by generalization and abstraction from the decrees of the Document, and that these principles can, in the last analysis, support a possible pluralist project. Islamic law, when considered apart from the Qur'an, the *hadith*, and the specific local-

historical experience of Muslims, carries decrees that support and extend such a project. In our region [the Middle East], where the Arab-Israeli war of many years, the recent Azeri-Armenian war, the feuding religious communities in Lebanon, the ethnic predicament in the Balkans, the Kurdish problem, et cetera, exist, we need pluralist projects allowing the coexistence of all religious, ethnic and political groups based on partnership, choice, and participation.

The Possible Project of Living Together

What is the best form of government? . . . One of the miraculous works of the Prophet, the Medina Document, is a historical and concrete example [of how to answer this question]. The document concerned is not an artificial utopia or a theoretical political exercise. It has entered written history as a legal document employed systematically and concretely from 622 to 632.

The principles of this legal document establish the framework of political unity, and the meanings they bestow upon the concepts of politics and power are still important today.

Briefly defined, *the Medina Document is the legal manuscript for political unity*. The general framework of this document presents itself as a social project [for Islamic intellectuals today].

First of all, the document defines the parties entered into the contract (the Muslims, the Jews, and non-believers) as distinct "*umma*s" (Medina Document, Articles 2 and 25). Here, *umma*, as a technical term, corresponds to a political unit. If the term had meant the political unit of the Muslims in the traditional sense, the Jews and the non-believers in Article 25 would have been accepted as Muslims; and this is inconceivable. . . .

When we look at the issue of power from the perspective of the Muslims—who are, like others, naturally sociable,[11] who have to live together and enter into political organization—the question under what conditions they become powerful becomes important. The answer to this question lies in the totality of meaning bestowed by Islam as a religion on life in general. And no doubt, for any Muslim the meaning of life is living according to God's satisfaction

---

10. See Sura 6, Verse 154; Sura 17, Verse 2; Sura 53, Verse 36; Sura 87, Verse 19; et cetera.

11. [Earlier sections of the article discussed humans' natural sociability.—Editor]

and worshipping him. For a Muslim, there is no nobler and more legitimate meaning of life. Muslims learn how to live in accordance with God's pleasure from the holy *shari'a*, promulgated and concretely shown to them by the Prophet. *Shari'a* is the manuscript of Divine Law, and the sum total of the principles and laws of living in accordance with the divine will.

For a Muslim, the desire to live according to the divine legal order of Islam never diminishes. On the contrary, as he enters more and more into the universe of knowledge of the religion to which he belongs, this desire increases. Besides this, the second big task of a Muslim is to promulgate to others the truths of the religion, which he accepts as the source of all Truth. A Muslim can never avoid or neglect this duty. . . . If a Muslim can fulfill this dual mission within the social organization he finds himself in, he is powerful.

The final objective of the difficult struggle that filled the lives of all prophets and the final Prophet Muhammad, peace be upon him, was to make possible the free milieu, the conducive social environment where this mission can realize itself. What Muslims understand of *freedom* is nothing but the eradication of the obstacles that prevent them from living their religion completely and promulgating it to others. . . .

The fact that the Prophet migrated to the free environment of Medina and suggested to other religious-ethnic groups that they sign a contract based on these two demands is the first step showing that political power can be configured outside the central ideology. If a central ideology is not to be imposed on groups belonging to different religions and beliefs, if they are given the freedom to choose their religion and ideology, and if there is no interference with the lifestyles that correspond to their choice, then the concrete guarantee of this lies not in a singular, but in a pluralistic legal system.

In this respect, Islam gives preeminence to the principle that law cannot be separated from religion. According to this principle, if there is no official religion or ideology represented by the governing apparatus and imposed from the top down, then it would be contradictory for the same apparatus to impose an official and single legal system. As a natural extension, if there is no coercion in the choice of religion (Qur'an, Sura 2, Verse 256), then there should be no pressure and compulsion on the laws embraced by

different religions, philosophical beliefs, or ideologies. A person who chooses this or that religion, chooses, at the same time, the legal system which is a manifestation of that particular religion. Leaving people free to choose their religion, yet creating obstacles in their choice of a legal system—and that is precisely what the modern [secular] state is doing—means interference with the essence of religion. Any interference with religion divides the personality of the believer and makes him culturally schizophrenic. Witness the widespread schizophrenia we see in every realm of life today. . . .

As long as they do not enter into war with Muslims (Qur'an, Sura 60, Verses 8–9), those who belong to different religions and beliefs can lead their lives according to their own religious and legal systems.[12] Just like those non-believers who entered into a contract with the Prophet in Medina, those who do not want to be Muslims—they can be Jewish, Christian, secular, atheist and so on—choose their own religion, world view, ideology or some other thought system, and declare what kind of a legal system they foresee in accordance with their religion or secular system.

Within the framework of the Medina Document, those who choose a religion and a legal system and declare their choices compose a legal group, and these groups are accepted as parties to the establishment of political unity.

In this model we propose, political power is internalized by the contractors in terms of choice of religion and declaration of a legal system. Politics in this model is understood as a technique or art of governance that makes the organization of the parties possible. . . .

In this respect, realms of activities such as legislation, culture, education, science, economy, health and the like, are left to the legal groups and the governing apparatus is limited to the executive. Since the executive branch undertakes *common and indivisible*

---

12. This conceptual frame should be considered as distinct from the Islamic treatment of *dhimmi* law, because the *dhimmi* status explains the legal order appropriate for non-Muslims who did not want to live amongst the Muslims and warred with them and were defeated. Our concern here is the conditions of non-Muslims, like those in Medina, who wanted to live amongst the Muslims and participated as equal parties to the political organization, in the form of legal groups, free people according to the general principles of the legal contract which they signed [with the Muslims].

services at the material, routine, and technical level, financial resources (taxes) and a certain amount of legislation will be necessary. Each of the parties, proportional to their financial means and population potential, will participate in the expenses. The legislative assemblies within the executive domain (village, town, province, region, nation) will consist of members elected by the legal groups.

Since the founding principles which establish the model of political unity are based on the free selection by the groups of their religion and legal systems, there will be no need for ghettos or religious and ethnic purification. As historical experience demonstrates to us [discussed in an earlier section], where there are no reasons for the organization of ghettos and for mass purifications, people show a great desire to live together.

The productive debate[13] that began when the Medina Document came onto the current agenda leads to a reconsideration of certain basic assumptions and concepts that appear to have enjoyed universal consensus. The Document has a potential richness which makes it conducive to bringing new dimensions to the concepts of politics, power, and state. In addition, one should add that the Document, which was implemented by the Prophet, peace be upon him, is not independent of the Qur'an and something outside of it. Rather, as part of the Prophet's *sunna* [practices], it is a manifestation of the Qur'an and a practical model of the Qur'an's life-giving and redeeming principles.

If the totality of the relationships between profound contemporary problems and the founding principles of the legal document signed by distinct social groups 1400 years ago are read correctly, then we can conceive of the state as something beyond an apparatus controlling every aspect of life.

This blueprint of an alternative social project—which requires maturation through widespread and continual discussions—contributes to the solution of the problem by reducing the state to executive activity and limiting the executive to the provision of common and indivisible services. However, what opens the door to real pluralism is the fact that individuals and groups can define their own identities and choose their own religion and legal systems. Experience shows that unless the realms of economy, culture, science, education, art, health, communication and so on are taken away from the control of the centralized state and transferred to groups with different religions and identities, real pluralism cannot be envisioned. The precondition for such a revolutionary design is to bring the singular quality of law to an end and to leave this realm, among others, to the discretion of legal groups.

What material form government should take, based on the principles discussed above, is an issue that ought to be determined by the legal groups that are the founders of political unity. In this respect, the fact that this political organization is based on *participation from the bottom up, rather than on singular sovereignty*, distinguishes it from other forms of government.

Finally, one further reason why we emphasize the Medina Document is the necessity to *transcend* modernity itself. The Medina Document is the source of a blueprint that may be an alternative to a modern state that is becoming more totalitarian, overtly and covertly, through raw or sophisticated methods and means. Whoever deals with the "state" or "modernity" realizes immediately that one has to deal with both.

---

13. [A long footnote listing recent publications on this issue has been deleted.—Editor]

The Downhill Path *and* Defense, Not Surrender

Rusmir Mahmutćehajić (Yugoslavia-Bosnia, born 1948), a professor of electrical engineering, served in several cabinet posts in the first years of Bosnia-Herzegovina's independence from Yugoslavia, 1991–1993. During this period, Bosnia's Serb and Croat minorities—supported by the neighboring countries of Serbia (the dominant remaining segment of Yugoslavia) and Croatia—embarked on secessionist campaigns that involved the "ethnic cleansing" of Bosnian Muslims, who comprise almost 40 percent of the nation's population, in areas under Serb and Croat control. The mass eviction, pillage, rape, and murder of Muslims drove the Bosnian government to adopt an increasingly strident Islamic identity. Mahmutćehajić and other Bosnian Muslims objected to this response as inconsistent with Bosnia's destiny of "unity within diversity."[1] As he explains in the second excerpt here, Mahmutćehajić protested by resigning from the cabinet in 1993 and has turned to the historical study of Islam in Bosnia, particularly its Sufi traditions. While Mahmutćehajić defends multicultural pluralism, he appears to identify "democracy" with its most virulent, xenophobic expressions, as exemplified for Mahmutćehajić by contemporary Serbia and Croatia.

The Downward Path

I.

Speaking in 1924 about the book *D'Orient et et Occident* [*On East and West*] by René Guénon [French author, 1886–1951], Léon Daudet [French author, 1867–1942] indicates, *inter alia*, the possibility of summarizing Guénon's statement as follows:

Since the time of Encyclopaedists [eighteenth century], and even earlier—since the Reformation [sixteenth century]—the West has been brought into a state of intellectual anarchy, which is true inhumanity.

Civilization, on which the West prides itself so greatly, relies on a sum of material and industrial achievements which multiply the chances of war and invasion; these are built on a very fragile moral and

1. Khalid Durán, "Bosnia: Background to a Tragedy," *Church and Society*, volume 84, number 3, January–February 1994, pp. 72–82; Smail Balić, "Bosnia: The Challenge of a Tolerant Islam," translated by John Bowden, in Hans Küng and Jürgen Moltman, editors, *Islam: A Challenge for Christianity* (London: SCM Press; Maryknoll, N.Y.: Orbis Books, 1994), pp. 3–10; Rusmir Mahmud-Ćehajić, "Understanding the Suffering: A Sufi Perspective on the Plight of Bosnia's Muslims," *Islamic World Report*, volume 1, 1996, pp. 51–63.

intellectual base, and on no metaphysical base whatsoever. The West is in greater danger from within, through feeble-mindedness, than from the outside, where it has to be admitted that its situation is not totally safe either. . . .

Since Bosnia is "the West's soft underbelly," it inevitably suffers from the effects of this "intellectual anarchy," this "multiplication of chances for war and invasion," this "danger from within," et cetera, in that it relies on solutions and solvers from outside that are alien to the true nature of Bosnia's expression of unity in diversity.

In spite of Bosnia's vast and indisputable inner power, Bosnian politics still has not found its path. Yet this path, which leads in the opposite direction to today's long downhill slope, must exist. But how can it be found without the courage to face up to and fight one's own weaknesses, which hold one back first from understanding and then from acting?

2.

Today, when the greater part of Bosnia is under military occupation and outside the control of the Bosnian authorities, we must return to the contradictory plans from which the conflicts and the anti-Bosnian onslaught arose. Bosnia's awareness of herself as a country has emerged from the long course of history, turning gradually to a memory and a prophecy of a state. When the Croat and Serb peoples tied their ethnic identities to plans for statehood, Bosnia became an arena for efforts to extend the Croat and Serb states. The response to these claims was an increased awareness of Bosnia's statehood, which because of Bosnia's personality, could not possibly be the same as the states being planned around it. Serbia launched a fullscale onslaught on Bosnia, intending to absorb Bosnia into its own state, and destroying everything that stood in its way. According to the Croat national plan, part of Bosnia was needed to round out the boundaries of the hypothesized Croatian nation-state. Thus Bosnia, as a single entity, found itself under attack by twin schemes for Greater States, which had taken to heart the world's cynical deviation from transcendent principles. Bosnia's unity in diversity is founded in religious tradition, and is thus seen as outdated. It is closer to the transcendent origins of justice, therefore it is seen as a potential threat to the Supreme God of Western civilization: global stability based on modern-day secularism.

3.

The shape of nationalist rule in Serbia and Croatia, the source of their anti-Bosnian claims, is only a reflection of the present shape of power in the modern world. Bosnia cannot oppose them if she remains a mere reflection of the governmental systems of her enemies. Bosnian statehood, which is at present fighting for its survival, is also grappling with the question of the foundations of its governmental system and the direction of its development. This indicates a need to re-examine the entire structure of power, in order to assess whether changes for the better or for the worse have taken place.

In the modern world, many would claim that only two forms of rule can be discerned—democracy and dictatorship. In order to determine how the Bosnian power structure reflects the opinion of the majority—starting from the principle that any people gets the government it deserves—we should first point to two essential features of the power hierarchy to which both democracy and dictatorship belong.

4.

Plato [Greek philosopher, circa 427–347 B.C.], in his *Politea*—which can be translated as "State" or "System of State"—poses the question: What is the ideal form of rule? Although many of his conclusions can be disputed in detail, they generally correspond to solutions which have arisen throughout history. For the purposes of this overview, it is important to determine the full distance between the ideal concept and the lowest reality to which it can degenerate. According to Plato, this goes from *aristocracy* (the rule of the best)—which for him is the ideal form of rule—through *timocracy*, *oligarchy*, and *democracy* to *tyranny*. To express Plato's idea in modern political jargon, the terms used nowadays would be theocracy for aristocracy, and dictatorship or demagogy for tyranny; the remaining two forms of rule can be disregarded for the purposes of clarity. These forms of rule were in most cases oligarchic, expressed as various forms of rule by a monarch and his nobility or an elite. Such forms of rule could in principle be called autocracies, since they recognize transcendent principles, regardless of how far they may be violated in practice. They are, in any case, less principled than theocracy, which is a higher-order system of rule. Principled autocracy is constantly in danger of becoming a *de facto* unprincipled dictatorship. The next step in the process of degeneration from principled autocracy is democracy, in which, according to Plato, the dominant concepts are those of freedom and equality. Democracy, by its very nature, is a forerunner of dictatorship or demagogy. (Whether modern advocates of democracy like it or not, history since the Plato's time has at least not proved him wrong.) Since the course of degeneration is not straight down a slippery slope, but oscillates around an underlying trend, apparent deviations from what Plato describes are possible, so that chaos may be interrupted by principled autocracy, which is always less evil than the dangers of demagogy.

5.

As for Bosnia and its neighbors, a somewhat primitive principled autocracy in communist Yugoslavia was followed by formal democracy—a transition phase before the establishing of unprincipled autocracies in Belgrade and Zagreb, whose course was one of obvious degeneration into dictatorship and demagogy. Their aim was to have the same degeneration, preferably at an even faster rate, take place in Bosnia, because this would enable them to draw a long-desired borderline between "Serbdom" and "Croatdom" in the shape of two nation-states, whose appearance would mean the disappearance of Bosnia. Preserving Bosnian rule within a democratic framework was therefore the best way of opposing the aggressive and hostile claims of her neighbors. Guiding the Bosnian people through a "narrow gate" [Qur'an, Sura 7, Verse 40; Bible, Gospel of Matthew, Chapter 7, Verses 13–14] with a "steep uphill path" to follow [Qur'an, Sura 90, Verses 11–12] should lead to a common weal manifested through transcendent principles—a fact that the best amongst us realize. This is how to safeguard the sources of power to oppose the destruction of Bosnia. It demands, however, discipline plus a thorough and hard-headed examination and restriction of low-level freedoms as conditions for the struggle against total destruction, which is exacerbated by the power of self-degeneration. As a condition for staying true to their original goals, Bosnia's forces need to be able to recognize the various forms of rule, both at grassroots and national level. The schemes of destruction launched against Bosnia tend nowadays to be labeled "fascist." Thus a complex phenomenon manifested

in a certain system of rule is simply given the external label of "utterly evil," without recognizing or analyzing the essential features of what we call "fascist" or "nazi." Such a recognition and analysis requires an insight into the position of each ruling system on a scale which determines its position vis-à-vis others, its direction of change, and its relative relationship to the modalities of political reality or its absolute relationship towards systems based on principles.

6.

The three most representative forms of fascist ideology—in Italy in the 1920s, in Germany at the beginning of the 1930s, and in Spain by their end—appeared in conditions of social upheaval and turmoil. Although they reflect distortions of individual consciousness and society which are to be found throughout the history of mankind, their links with the geopolitical concepts and the extraordinary technological and organizational possibilities of the modern world indicate the need for further study.

Bosnia is today in a state of social upheaval, and the turmoil that is now in its third year shows no sign of coming to an end. The tide of fascism in Serbia and amongst Serbs throughout the South Slav region has prompted the growth and build-up of fascism in neighboring countries, primarily in Croatia and among the Croats. Bosnia therefore found herself caught between, and finally in, the two fascist maelstroms. Both have tried, whether consciously or subconsciously, to generate fascisms among the peoples they see as an obstacle to their imperialist goals. For fascism amongst Bosnian Muslims could never gain enough power to threaten Serb and Croat fascism. However, its existence is of great importance, since it justifies the crimes perpetrated by Serb and Croat fascists against Bosnian Muslims. The military and economic power at the disposal of the Serb and Croat fascists and their expectations of world support all favor the Greater Serb and Greater Croat grand plans. Bosnian Muslims, therefore, find themselves pushed from both sides, directly and indirectly, into nationalist exclusivity and a fascism of their own. Such a possibility reared its ugly head with the first signs of Greater Serb and Greater Croat designs for the destruction of Bosnia. Bosnian Muslims were offered, as a reward for giving up a united Bosnia and Herzegovina, a hypothetical "Muslim state," an "Islamic *jamahiriya*" [republic], the "tutelage of certain distant countries," and so on. At the same time, both in public and in secret, the very people who made these offers also made allegations against Bosnian Muslims to the members of the ruling elite, allegations about what they themselves had forced then Muslims into, by which means they hoped to justify their military attacks against Bosnia and Herzegovina. But the politics of the Bosnian Muslims successfully managed to outmaneuver the tactics of their enemies.

Since the ambitions of the Greater Serb and Greater Croat nationalists to break up Bosnia and Herzegovina as an integral state will never go away, the danger of a potential Bosnian Muslim (or simply "Muslim") fascism will not disappear either. It is therefore of great political importance to be ever-vigilant in unmasking all forms of fascist consciousness amongst Bosnian Muslims and its manifestations in the political life of our country.

7.

The first characteristic of fascism is the adulation of the collective, usually personified as the state, at the expense of the individual. This leads one to despise and persecute all forms of liberalism, rationalism, democracy, promoting instead the sovereignty of an individual identified with one political party, one race and one state. Political decisions and discussions in such conditions take on a mystic tone, while destruction, persecution and murder become a framework which supports the Messianic role of the individual and those loyal to him. There is no collective decision-making and consequently public performances aim at promoting the illusion that this is precisely what the people wants and that it firmly supports the individual's every act. The able are suppressed and withdraw, while the incapable and the power-hungry enter the political stage. Empty apologies for the leader take the place of discussion and advice, creating the illusion that the majority is on his side. This environment of chaos and social dramatics enable the ruler to turn the desperate expectations of the majority into a cheap source of assumed support. What is gained is simply support in the struggle against the "enemy of the people and the country," who tends to be anyone disloyal to the leader. In such an atmosphere, a utopian vision of a new world order replaces the active management of state and society. Those in his entourage counter any justifiable criticism of the political actions of the "leader," assuming they accept the evidence, with the words: "Everything considered, he simply has no alternative."

Today there are many who, betraying their unconscious support of a nascent Bosnian Muslim fascism, speak of a "political reality" in which a united Bosnia and Herzegovina is an impossibility. As an alternative they offer—to be frank, without the necessary courage and determination—a "Muslim state." Thus they indirectly conceal the obviously less-than-perfect abilities of our leaders to defend the state they have been entrusted with. For with their appeal to *Realpolitik* they aim to spread the falsehood that the present situation is our inescapable destiny, and that salvaging what we can from it is our best option. . . .

Defense, Not Surrender: An Interview

The book *Living Bosnia* was published after my decision to withdraw from all areas of the governmental activities. I believe that all I do can only be explained by my allegiance to Bosnia and my implacable hostility to its destroyers. These thugs and criminals fabricated a cunning scheme to raze Bosnia to the ground. Part of this plan was to inveigle forces within Bosnia into believing that Bosnia is not an organic unity, but a mechanistic assembly of several components; and once certain organic elements of Bosnia's unity have accepted that they are just parts in some mechanism, it will not be difficult to set them against each other in such a way that they are forced to split up into separate but dead components. Bosnian Muslims are the focus of this plan. According to this evil scheme, they must be prompted to withdraw to their own "ethno-religious space," thus providing their own evidence for the impossibility of Bosnia. In this they must be made to believe that in accepting the lie about the impossibility of Bosnia, they are not accepting the impossibility of their own existence. Yet it is obvious that in so doing they are working directly against themselves and their own existence. The pressures from outside and the plots from within are aimed at inciting the break-up or dissolution of Bosnia—which the warriors of the anti-Bosnian onslaught see as their ideal. This dangerous trick is intended to incite Bosnian Muslims into forgetting about her Serbs or Croats, and anything that does not transparently belong to their religion, people or poli-

tics. Their hopes are to be focused on imaginary res-
cuers from outside, intervention from heaven, the
mercy and charity of the world's mighty, and so on.
Their determination to organize for the purposes of
their own defense should be constantly weakened,
and what is closest to them should be made the most
distant; they should be fed false hopes and prevented
from looking ahead and being concerned about their
future. Wherever our enemies have put their plan into
action, they have done an effective job of destroying Bosnia and her Muslims. Our answer to their plan
should be to reverse the sequence: first our own duty,
then that of the world; first think of the traitors and
the criminals in our midst, and only then of the enemy
without; first organize ourselves, and only then dis-
organize our enemies; first use up our own resources
and only then beg for alms, and so on. This is how,
from the very outset, I saw the enemy's strategy of
destroying Bosnia and our response to it. As early
as 1990 I pointed this out in my political writings,
trying to explain this evil deception. However, it is
obvious that there are some today whose lack of insight into the course of history and inability to
see ahead have led them to side with our enemy's
trickery, thus allying themselves with the campaign
against Bosnia and the Bosnians. The scope of
enemy operations does not end at the front line where
they do battle with our soldiers. Enemy action is not
only spent on destroying everything in our territories that their jackboots have marched over. The
enemy is not satisfied with raining lethal missiles at
a distance down on our cities. His intention is to
affect and undermine, by means of well-planned and
shrewdly-organized actions, our politics and opinions as a whole, in order to assist him in achieving
his final goal—the destruction of Bosnia and her
Muslims. You must be familiar, I expect, with how
often my views have been falsified and misinter-
preted. The sheer amount of lies about myself and
my words has confused even my friends. In the attitude of our enemies to what I have said or written, I
have seen a confirmation of their fears lest their plans
be revealed. This made me happy, not worried. But
I am unhappy and worried at all the distorted views
and inability to see deception which are expressed
amongst us. In order to point out these deceptions
even more directly, some of my friends suggested
publishing a selection of my texts and interviews that
came into existence before I decided to withdraw

from national politics. And so that's why
Oslobođenje's Ljubljana office published my book
Living Bosnia: Political Essays & Interviews.[2] . . .

Bosnia nowadays is still seen by neighboring
states only as a space for them to expand into. But
then they come up against strong resistance from
Bosnia's unity in diversity. The external anti-Bosnian
forces need to destroy this unity, in order to use the
rubble of Bosnia as material for the building of new
states unlike any that have ever existed in this region.
These plans are neither feeble-minded or simplistic.
They are skillfully thought through. They are often
backed by powerful high priests of evil, chosen by
nationalist politics as the "most prestigious and leading intellectuals of our race." After four years of war
and the two or three years preceding it, it is quite
possible to reconstruct the key elements of the secret
plans for the destruction of Bosnia. They almost certainly have the following features: firstly, their starting point is the fact that three separate elements
exist in Bosnia: Muslim, Croat and Serb; the future
of the latter two should be joined to Croatia and
Serbia, while the Muslim element should be depicted
as something dangerous, whose nature makes it un-
fit to be part of European civilization. These plans
mean that Bosnian Muslims have to be depicted as
carriers of noxious ambitions and ideologies, thus
setting them against the whole of Western sensibilities and politics. But portraying them in this light is
not enough to guarantee their destruction. Pseudo-
Islamic fanaticism, displays of rhetoric, exclusivity
under the veil of religion, and so on, should also be
fomented amongst them. This will be perceived as a
peril threatening both Bosnia's Croats and Bosnia's
Serbs with humiliation and destruction. This will
inevitably result in the "legitimate right of the Bosnian Croats and Bosnian Serbs to ask for assistance
and support from Croatia and Serbia, who have both
the right and the moral obligation to lend such assistance." The enemy plan as described above aims
to reduce the totality of Bosnia and Herzegovina's
culture, history and statehood to that of her Muslims;
and the more convincingly her Muslims can be portrayed as "Islamic radicals"—a label for pseudo-
Islam, instigated and cherished by Islam's enemies—

2. [The author wrote a column for the independent
newspaper *Oslobođenje* in Sarajevo, Bosnia-Herzegovina.
—Editor]

the easier her enemy's final goal will be to attain. This is the strategy by which the enemies of Bosnia aim to destroy all the bridges between Bosnia's individual elements and rip out the threads that bind them into a unity. When the bridges and the threads within Bosnia's unity grow few and far between and the break-up of Bosnia is clear for all to see, then the question of global stability will be raised in world politics. All in all, Serbia and Croatia seem to play a much more significant role in the protection of global stability than the survival of Bosnian Muslims and the Bosnia-Herzegovinian state. The Bosnian Muslims as a political concept, are, according to the plotters of Bosnia's destruction, a potential threat to global stability; their allegiance to Islam (or rather pseudo-Islam) should, their enemies claim, justify their eventual destruction for the sake of world stability. . . .

So why did I decide to withdraw from the Government? When I did not manage to convince the people I was working with on strengthening and defending the Bosnian political process about what I saw as essential, it was only logical for me to withdraw from that process. I felt it was my moral obligation to express my disagreement and refuse to participate further in such a political set-up. Power is perhaps the worst vice of all. All who aspire to it speak about goodness, justice and beauty, and so on as goals, with power only an indispensable means to these ends. When they get this power, many of them completely forget the goals which justified their ambitions. Power itself becomes their supreme good. They worship it as if it were a god. All those who do not praise and support them are their opponents and enemies. Their obsession with power clouds their reason. When I no longer had a contribution to make through my belief in a free Bosnia as unity in diversity, I refused to participate in the structure of power just for the sake of power. And I thank God for having being able to resist power as a vice and having stayed faithful to my beliefs.

PART V

Freedom of Thought

21

Humanity and Islam

'Ali Shari'ati (Iran, 1933–1977) may be one of the most popular figures in Iran today. During the Iranian Revolution of 1979, his photograph and his writings appeared throughout the country, and the subsequent cold shoulder he received from the clerical leaders of the Islamic Republic of Iran may have served to improve his reputation. Shari'ati was born and raised in northeastern Iran, the son of a religious scholar but educated in secular schools, including the Sorbonne, where he received his doctorate. Upon his return to Iran, Shari'ati launched a career as a lecturer—first at the University of Mashhad, then at the Hosseiniyeh Ershad in Tehran, a religious educational institution, where he built a large following, especially among university students, for his critique of oppressive political and religious establishments. After being tolerated by the Pahlavi regime for several years, he was imprisoned in 1973, and the Hosseiniyeh was shut down. Soon after his release from prison, he died in London. The following lecture from around 1969 defends the concept of free will in Islam.[1]

Ladies and Gentlemen: Today I want to talk about humankind.[2] At present, humankind is more enigmatic and more unknown than any other period. And ever since the end of the 19th century, scientists, writers, and thinkers have each evaluated humankind in various ways. Yes, humankind's position today is shakier than any other period in history.

My basic thesis is that today's humankind is generally incarcerated within several prisons, and naturally it becomes a true human being only if it can liberate itself from these deterministic conditions. What are these determinisms and how can humankind free itself from their grip? Before I can answer these inquiries, I must define humankind.

1. Among the numerous treatments of Shari'ati's life and work, the following are notable for going beyond hagiography: H. E. Chehabi, *Iranian Politics and Religious Modernism* (Ithaca, N.Y.: Cornell University Press); Hamid Dabashi, *Theology of Discontent: The Ideological Foundations of the Islamic Revolution in Iran* (New York: New York University Press, 1993), pp. 102–146; Shahrough Akhavi, "Shari'ati, 'Ali," in John L. Esposito, editor, *The Oxford Encyclopedia of the Modern Islamic World* (New York: Oxford University Press, 1995), volume 4, pp. 46–50; Abdulaziz Sachedina, "Ali Shariati: Ideologue of the Iranian Revolution," in John L. Esposito, editor, *Voices of Resurgent Islam* (New York: Oxford University Press, 1983), pp. 191–214.

2. [Because the word *insan* has no gender, it is translated here as "humankind" rather than as "man."—Editor]

A friend of mine who was doing some research on the Qur'an, once stated that there are two words for humankind in the Qur'an: *bashar* and *insan*. For instance, sometimes the Qur'an states, "I am a *bashar* like you" (Sura 18, Verse 110) and at other times it states, "*Insan* was created impatient." (Sura 17, Verse 11) Thus, by using *bashar*, the Qur'an is talking about the two-footed creature that emerged at the end of the evolutionary chain of which there are two billion on earth now. On the other hand, *insan* is that unusual and enigmatic being that has a special definition that does not apply to any other phenomena in nature. So, there are two kinds of humans; one who is the subject-matter of poets, philosophers, and religion, and another that is the subject-matter of biology. Further, the first kind, *bashar*, is that particular being that contains physiological, biological, and psychological characteristics which are shared by all humans, regardless of whether they are black, white, yellow, Western, religious or non-religious; it is based upon physical laws that medicine, physiology, psychology, and so forth have discovered. Meanwhile, humankind in its second connotation consists of the truth of being *insan*, possessing exceptional characteristics which cause each member of the human race to attain certain degrees of *insaniyat* [humanness, humanity]. Accordingly, we are all *bashar* but not necessarily *insan*. Thus, from among all humans, everyone is as much *bashar* as the rest, but there are some who have attained *insaniyat*, and there are others who are in the process of becoming an *insan*; either little or to an exalting degree.

Bashar is a "being" while *insan* is a "becoming." *Insan* differs from *bashar* and all other natural phenomena such as animals, trees, et cetera, because it is a "becoming." Take, for instance, the termites. If we inspect their buildings in Africa, we notice that ever since a million years ago they have been building the same thing over and over again. Thus, a termite is (exists), no matter how many more years it is going to live on earth; it will always have an immutable definition. The same is true of other creatures, including *bashar*. A science fiction writer has written about this type of human in the account of a scientist from earth who went to Mars:

> While walking on the streets of Mars, the scientist found out that there was a conference in one of the universities about a Martian scientist who had traveled to earth. He attended the conference. The Martian scientist went behind the lectern and said:

"The theory about life on earth was confirmed. The latest findings show that there is life, one of which is called *bashar*. Of course, I cannot exactly define what *bashar* looks like since you don't have the slightest inkling of it in your heads. In short, it looks like a *kheek* [sheepskin bag] that contains two holes and four little [feet] and hands. They crawl hither and thither on earth with such an amazingly wild struggle unseen anywhere in the firmament. *Bashar*s have a lust for killing one another. Sometimes large groups of them (who are unrelated to the other parts of the earth) get armed with modern weaponry, leave their houses and jobs and attack one another. At first, I thought all was done for obtaining food, but later I noticed they just killed one another and left. *Bashar* has a history of self-mortification and suicide. And all its energy goes towards killing one another without reason. They don't need each other's flesh and blood since their staples come from other sources. After massacring one another they leave with pride and invent epics. For collecting food they use their little hands. They do not eat all their aromatic and delicious fruits, they take them home and set them on fire and boil them and consequently they become sick and plead doctors to pull them out of their stomachs. This is why doctors are very rich and respectable on earth. While *bashar* has dominated the earth, they have lunacies unseen in any other animal!"

Although it is embarrassing, this is an accurate description of what we mean by *bashar*. When we study human history—I mean the history of human stupidities—it is longer and consistently more interesting than the history of his understandings. This *bashar* is a monkey that has not evolved since time immemorial. Its weapons, clothing, and food all have changed but its characteristics are very much the same. There is no difference between Genghis Khan [Mongol monarch, 1162–1227] ruling over the wild tribes, the great emperors ruling over the great civilized societies, and those individuals who are at the present reigning over the great civilized civilizations. Of course, the only difference is that Genghis was honestly saying that he had come to kill, while today's civilized leaders assert that they want to make peace. And so, it is the mode of talking and explanation which has evolved; otherwise, lying, disparity, murder, and looting have intensified. This is *bashar*.

But humankind in its essence, as an exalted truth, consists of ideal and sublime qualities that we must strive to attain. Namely, they are the types of characteristics that do not exist in *bashar* . . . and the aim of humanity is to become *insan*. Mind you that becoming *insan* is not a stationary event, rather, it is a perpetual process of becoming and an everlasting evolution towards infinity.

The Qur'anic verse "To God we belong, and to Him we return" (Sura 2, Verse 156)[3] is a philosophy of anthropology. Unlike Sufism, which claims that man reaches God and imagines Him to be stationary, the word "*ilaihi*" [in this verse] means "towards Him" rather than "in Him." For instance, [Abu'l-Mughith] Hallaj [Persian mystic executed for heresy, 857–922] claimed that he reached God, and he implied that God was a fixed point. God is infinite, everlasting, and absolute. Thus humankind's journey towards Him is perpetual and eternal; there is no pause. This is the connotation of becoming an *insan*.

Insan has three characteristics: (a) self-consciousness, (b) the ability to make choices; and, (c) the ability to create. All of humankind's other characteristics derive from these three. We are, therefore, *insan* relative to the degree of our self-consciousness and our creativities. Accordingly, when the characteristics of an ideal *insan* is clarified, we must try to identify the factors that hinder humankind in its becoming, and by removing them we can pursue our inherent and instinctive movement in the process of becoming an *insan*.

[René] Descartes [French philosopher, 1596–1650] once said, "I think, therefore I am." He doubted everything but his own existence. And he built his whole philosophical work upon this doubt. A second statement was made by [André] Gide [French intellectual, 1869–1951], "I feel, therefore I am," and a third by [Albert] Camus [French intellectual, 1913–1960], "I revolt, therefore I am." All these assertions are correct, but the most exalting becoming, peculiar to humankind, is referred to by Camus.

So long as Adam was in Heaven and had not sinned he was not an *insan*, he was an angel. In Heaven, he was just a consumer. Once he ate the fruit of wisdom, vision, and rebellion, he was kicked out. He descended to earth to struggle in order to shoulder his own life, just like parents who kick their child out; this is an indication that children have to accept responsibility for their own life. This is on a par with

[Jean-Paul] Sartre's [French philosopher, 1905–1980] "*délaissement*," which means "left on its own." In other words, humans, unlike animals—which are guided by their instincts and do not choose their own lives—have to bear responsibility for their own life. This is *insan*, who has attained consciousness by revolting against Heaven, and even God. This is a new creation in the universe, capable of attaining salvation by obeying God and praying to Him through choice. And so, the praying of an unaware individual who can't revolt, just like an animal, is useless. What is expected, then, is the obedience of someone who has sinned. And *insan* is the only creature in nature who can choose (and disobedience is indicative of the ability to choose). This is what Camus meant by revolt; either against a social order or against one's own nature; while Descartes' "I think, therefore I am" and Gide's "I feel, therefore I am" confirm the "is-ness" of humankind rather than its "becoming." To summarize what I have said so far:

1. *Insan* is a conscious creature, that is, the only creature in all of nature who has attained self-consciousness, which I define as "perceiving one's quality and nature, perceiving the quality and the nature of the universe, and perceiving one's relationship with the universe." We are *insan* to the extent that we are conscious of these three principles.

2. Humankind is a chooser, that is, the only being who is not only capable of revolting against nature and the order which is ruling over it, but can revolt against its own natural, physical, and psychological needs. Humans can choose things which have neither been imposed on them by nature, nor is their body fit to choose them. This is the most sublime aspect of *insaniyat*. Accomplishing such tasks is peculiar to God alone. Animals are mere machines whose instincts push them to all directions. For instance, exactly once a year the sexual urges in a sheep emerge; this is a compulsion and the animal has no choice. Once the appetite is gone the animal forgets its love. This is a deterministic characteristic in a sheep.

It is only humans who can revolt, contrary to the demands of their nature. Despite their selfishness, they can commit suicide, and despite their natural instincts which call on them to protect their life and body, they sacrifice themselves for others. Or, despite all the natural characteristics which call them to a comfortable life, they can revolt, sin, or resort to

---

3. Nowadays this verse is said when a death occurs! When progressive and logical ideas fall into the hands of a corrupt and fanatic society, they, too, cause corruption. This applies to this Qur'anic verse.

asceticism and piousness. These are indications that humankind is the only being who can choose.

3. Humans are creatures who create; from the smallest to the largest thing is the manifestation of God's power in their nature. Unlike some who define the human as an animal who makes tools, it is only humans who can make things that go beyond tools.

Humans' creativity emerges when their needs evolve to the point that what their wants are does not exist in nature. This is indicative of the fact that humankind was created. So long as humans are contented with what nature offers them, they are a natural animal pursuing what nature provides them. If, however, they reach a point when nature alone cannot satisfy them, their needs and feelings evolve beyond the totality of nature's powers, creativities, and possibilities. This is the point at which, as [Martin] Heidegger [German philosopher, 1889–1976] stated, "humankind feels lonesome" because it feels that it does not belong here, and realizes that its genius is different than its materialistic nature and that humans are different from other animals. They feel that they are attracted towards ideals which do not exist in nature. Thus they want to fly, but nature did not give them wings; they begin to build a ship, plane, satellite, or space-ship.

Technology is the totality of humankind's creativity by which it tries to harness the forces of nature which are not within its easy reach. For instance, although oil is in the ground, humans cannot extract it with the possibilities that nature has provided for them. Thus, the petroleum industry offers new possibilities which nature withheld from them.

Humankind's second creation is of a different kind; it is the artistic creation which is one of the Divine's manifestations of humankind's soul, and the definition of humankind as a "tool-making animal" falls apart here. Art, just like technology, is the manifestation of humankind's creative aptitude in nature. Technology is the creation of humankind so that it can reach the things that already exist in nature, while art is the creativity of humankind so that it can have the things that it needs, but that do not exist in nature; it is an extra-natural activity. So, constructiveness and ingenuity are two of humankind's characteristics which are the third dimension of the human soul.

In short, humans are a three-dimensional being with three aptitudes; they are conscious of themselves and the world, they can choose, and they can create.

All these attributes belong to the Lord and humankind is in the likeness of Him. Since I do not want to create a partner for God, by "likeness" I mean humans are creatures who are capable, unlike nature, of utilizing and nourishing God's sublime attributes in themselves and of continuing to evolve. The famous saying of the Prophet Muhammad—"Adapt your character to that of God"—tells us that we must assimilate the Lord's attributes. That is, *insan*—not *bashar*—becomes God's vicegerent on earth; the latter is the vicegerent of monkeys as well as the extension of their evolution. It is only *insan* who can revolt, choose, gain consciousness, and create in a relative way (God creates in the absolute sense).

At the present, these "choosers" are incarcerated within several determinisms—prisons—that prevent them from gaining self-consciousness, making choices, and creating. Unfortunately the grandest tragedy facing humans today is that, to the extent that various ideologies do away with their needs and bestow relative self-consciousness upon them and give power and evolution to their societies, to the same extent they leave the "self" out and send humans to oblivion. How can such ideologies forget humankind? Some of these ideologies are as follows:

Materialism. Materialism recognizes humankind to be composed of material essence. With this definition it imprisons humans within the evolutionary frame limited to being matter. If this is the case, it is impossible for them to evolve beyond the capacity of the matter's dimensions itself.

Naturalism. This is another victimizer of humankind which burgeoned from the 18th century to the beginning of the 19th century. Naturalism believes that originality belongs to a living being, though without consciousness, which is called nature, and humankind is one of its products. Thus, I am free, I can choose, and I can feel because of nature's will. As we can see, humans' freedom is once again limited to the possibilities which nature has bestowed upon their disposition and aptitude. . . .

Existentialism. Although the existentialism of Sartre, Heidegger, and [Søren] Kierkegaard [Danish philosopher, 1813–1855] is non-theistic, it believes that humankind's makeup is different and contrary to all other creatures in nature; this is especially true of Sartre's. But it is surprising since Sartre does not believe in God and metaphysics, yet he separates humankind from all other creatures in nature. He believes that animals' total essence appeared first but humankind's essence emerged later. Why does he say this? "Because," he states, "when we remove God, we have to fit humankind into material nature," and consequently we sacrifice it. Therefore, in order not to sacrifice humankind, Sartre resorts to this line of reasoning: "In animals essence precedes existence, while in humans existence precedes essence." For instance, if I ask a carpenter, "What are you making?" he would respond, "A chair." "What is a chair?" I ask. He continues, "A chair has four legs, a seat," and so on. Such descriptions are the essence of the chair, although it is not in existence yet.

However, according to Sartre, humankind is unlike a chair. Its existence emerged first. But what is it now? Nothing! We do not know yet! Humankind's "how-ness and who-ness" will emerge later; they depend upon human will. Thus, according to existentialism humans shape their own essence any way they wish. This is why Sartre believes that if we strip humans of their volition and choice they will no longer remain *insan*. Sartre is scared, and justly so, since, if we take materialism and naturalism as foundations, as we do today, we incarcerate humankind in petrified molds.

Pantheism. Despite the fact that Pantheism is a theistic idealism, it, too, sacrifices humankind. Pantheism (providential determinism) exists among some Muslim sects, Indians, Sufis, and Catholics. For instance, Catholics believe that God determined humans' fate before they came to this world. Here again, humankind is sacrificed by predestination. As Hafiz [Persian poet, circa 1325–1390] said:

Since the destiny was determined without our
      presence,
Don't carp if it is a bit disagreeable.

That is, when we were being created, no one asked our opinion; God made us the way He pleased. And later He let us loose on earth. Another poet parodied Hafiz, "Don't find fault if all of it displeases thee!" This is determinism; what can we do? Even objecting is considered wrong! It is like Camus's objection. They asked him:

QUESTION: Who are you protesting against?

CAMUS: God.

QUESTION: Do you believe in God?

CAMUS: No!

QUESTION: . . . Then who are you protesting against? You do not seem to believe in any

responsible force in the universe, yet you are protesting.

CAMUS: Yes, I am protesting. I am protesting against no one, yet I am protesting![4]

This is like throwing punches in the air. When God's will does not take human choice and will into account, then humankind is not responsible. And when humans have no responsibility, they are not *insan*.

Historicism. This school believes that humankind is the product of history. The Iranian, Islamic, and Shi'ite histories have molded my personality. "If I were living during the French revolution, instead of my actual position in history, I would have had a different language, sentiment, and characteristics." So, human characteristics fall in the hands of a will that is called Historicism. How do I make a choice then? Any way history wishes for me. Accordingly, if I am a Muslim and I speak Persian, it is due to the will of history; that is, by the same token that nature chooses the color of our skin, history chooses the color of our soul.

Sociologism. This school believes that social environment and social order are the shapers of humankind. If I am generous it is due to my feudalistic order, and if I am brave it is due to the tribal environment under which I was reared. Further, it is believed that the social order, composed of social relations, productive order, ownership order, the tools of production, and the bureaucracy of the ruler—which all make up my society—are all factors that shape my personality any way they want.

There is no "individual" or a "chooser" in sociologism; so, there is no *insan*, since the latter is capable of saying, "I," or, "I chose this for such and thus reasons. . . ."

Biologism. This school tries to elevate humankind a little from its petrified and materialistic frame. This is an indication that 20th-century scientists can no longer understand and explain humankind through their dry and narrow materialistic definitions of the 17th, 18th, and the 19th centuries. Biologism consists of the originality of the totality of the physiological characteristics that, in a complex and developed amalgam, make up the human.

Although biologism looks at humankind as more exalted than a common natural or material phenomenon, it still negates humans as conscious and free beings. When I am a victim of my own unconscious

4. [Shari'ati is paraphrasing.—Translator]

and biological forces, then I am no longer an "I." For instance, biology believes fat people are kind, or thin people are intelligent. Thus it appears that intelligence is related to body weight and kindness is related to biological makeup and so on.[5]

I am not negating naturalism, sociologism, or historicism; I accept them all, but I believe that humans are capable of choice. This being—humankind—throughout its evolutionary process is a natural, historical, and material phenomenon; it is shaped by its environment. When people live, for instance, in a tribe, it is not because they chose this mode of living (no one has). The fact that these individuals live in a tent, migrating from place to place, is due to a particular social and productive order which made them tent-dwellers. Or, the natural order forces some people to hunt, fish, and live in jungles. When villagers become city-dwellers their traditions, morality, and morale also change, and such changes are not due to their choice, rather they are due to the prevailing productive system which required a change of characteristics in them. In short, humankind is what nature, history, and society make of it, and if we change the environment humankind will also change. . . .

What I am saying is that humans, throughout their evolutionary processes—their transformation from *bashar* to *insan*—liberates themselves from such determinism. For instance, the originality of geography was so popular in the 19th century that one of its harbingers, Ibn Khaldun [Tunisian historian, 1332–1406], proposed that the form of societies changed relative to their geographic conditions. Of course, he was right then, but it is not so today. Today, to the extent that humans evolve, to that extent they can free themselves from such determinism.

Well, how can humans . . . free themselves from naturalism? This is easier to understand because in this century we are just beginning to free ourselves from naturalism.[6] Today, industry and the new civilization are freeing humans from naturalism more than any other time in the past. People who live in the African Sahara are capable—despite the natural

conditions imposed upon them—of creating modern living conditions on par with North Americans' for themselves. Or take the earth's gravity, which is another determinism. Gravity was so natural to us that we thought it was part of our bodies. But today we are no longer a slave to gravity. In addition, we are no longer bound to the style of climatic (regional) agriculture. In the past, humans had to live where there was river, jungle, water, and so forth, otherwise they would die. Today, however they can live in a desert and build themselves a great civilization. How do humans free themselves from determinism? By becoming familiar with nature's determinism and the laws which rule over nature and their effects upon themselves. The way to study these is science. Familiarity with nature or science has made it possible for humans to create technology which has one aim; to save humans from nature's determinism. Those who attack technology as an agent which has metamorphosed and sacrificed humankind have a point. But the same technology can also save humankind. In the past, in order to have food and clothing, humans had to work 10–12 hours a day. This was a natural determinism. However, technology stepped up the rate of production and consequently working hours were reduced. Today, if we are witnessing individuals who are working longer hours than the pre-technological period, it is because the bourgeoisie keeps creating more consumption and consequently production must be stepped up.

How can we save ourselves from the prison of history? If humans can (with the aid of science) discover the laws and the variables that reign over history, and if we can find out how such variables affect our thinking processes, our wills, our sentiments and our morals, we can certainly save ourselves from historical determinism. At the present there are societies in Asia, Africa, and Latin America that have covered several historical cycles in one leap without having had to go through each separate stage. Historically, societies must pass through certain stages. But to the extent that such societies find historical self-consciousness and their free-thinkers become familiar with their particular historical epoch and its makeup, to that extent these societies can skip several cycles. We are now witnessing societies which were tent-dwellers or slaves, but suddenly, by revolting against history, they leaped to the bourgeois stage. This is the process of getting rid of society by knowing the determinism of history, movement of

5. This is not a new subject. From time immemorial these ideas have been popular among common people. [The best-known morphologist is W. H. Sheldon, *The Varieties of Temperament* (New York: Harper and Row, 1942).—Translator]

6. The belief that water, weather, mountainous climate, and so forth shape our character.

history, and the discovery of the deterministic laws of history.

With regards to sociological determinism we know that in the past individuals grew relative to their societal demands. However, today, to the extent that sociology grows and discovers social and class relations and understands political philosophy and governance and becomes socially aware, to that extent, as [Karl] Jaspers [German philosopher, 1883–1969] states, "Men who are shaped by their societies become the builders of societies." In the past, a tent-dwelling and a feudal community or a backward village did not have the slightest doubt about its religions, traditions, or governments. These were held to be as sacred, immutable, and self-evident as the sun. It never entered the minds of these people that it was possible to live differently, or that they could revolt against their own beliefs. But today's humans can consciously choose as well as reject their religion.

Religion is one of those factors that society either offers or imposes upon its members. But today it is different. The productive, economic, and ownership orders as well as traditions, social and class relations, rights and family privileges, and social groups, relative to today's self-conscious humans, are all unlike the past, when they were held to be immutable, everlasting, sacred, and Heavenly facts. Rather, they are phenomena which humans can think about, change, reform, choose, and negate. All these revolutions, changes, and reforms bear witness to the fact that today's humans have freed themselves from the prison of society. Humans accomplished this task by studying sociology and comparative studies of different social orders. Science can help them to completely free themselves.

One's Self

The last prison, one's self, is the worst of all, since it is the one that has rendered humankind the most helpless prisoner. It is surprising that now, more than any other time in history, although humans have been able to save themselves from the aforementioned prisons, they are more helpless than ever in the face of this last prison. And it is the existence of this prison which has rendered the others vain and futile. Why have today's humans, who have freed themselves from the prison of nature, history and society, reached this absurdity? Today's humans,

though they are more knowledgeable and capable than any other time in history, know less than ever what to do. Why can't humans leave their cell? It is too hard. In the past, the aforementioned prisons placed four walls around my existence and I was aware of my own incarceration. For instance, when humans were primitive, they were aware of the existence of a river or a jungle next to them; they had to become a fisherman or a hunter. They felt the presence of such determinism in the past, but with respect to this last one there is no wall around human existence. It is a prison that I carry within myself. This is why becoming self-conscious and familiar with this prison is the hardest task of all. Here, the prison and the prisoner are the same; that is, the disease and the patient have merged together. This is why getting rid of the malaise is so arduous!

Another problem is that humans can break out of the prison of history, nature, or an existing social order with the help of science. But, unfortunately, they cannot extricate themselves from the prison of the self by seeking help from science, since the latter is the possession of the prisoner. This is why the "self" does not feel that it has buried a free "I" in it. Rather, the self feels that, as an absolute being, it must free itself from the prison of nature, society, and history; it can free itself but it reaches futility. At this point I would like to present general principles: (a) at first, all humans have needs; (b) they fulfill their needs and embrace comfort; (c) comfort terminates in futility; (d) futility ends up in rebellion; and (e) rebellion ends up in asceticism and subjectivity. These principles have been true ever since Adam. Today's hippie-ism, existentialism, our past aristocracy which ended up in Sufism, the Indochinese aristocracy which terminated in Sufism and *nirvana* (negating the material life), and the new bourgeoisie which has ended up in negating the material life, confirm the veracity of my generalizations.

Humans value their material ideals so long as they have not accomplished them. Once they have them, they reach futility. Thus human ideals must be so lofty that they cannot reach a dead end; if they do they will end in futility. And it is obvious that prisoners of their own determinism—even if they conquer nature—will still be "armed but helpless." Jean Izoulet [French author, 1854–1929] states that, "A writer wrote about a prince who wallowed in gold and riches, yet suffered from an incurable inner sickness. The France of today is like this prince." But I believe that it is today's humankind that is like that prince; it is more helpless than ever.

In the middle of the large Rotterdam square in Holland there is an interesting statue whose parts are all displaced. For instance, its neck has slipped a bit to one side, its arms have popped out of their joints, and so on. The whole thing is distorted in such a way that viewers think it is about to collapse. But the statue is made of stone. The sculptor wanted to personify post–World War II humankind, the humans of our age who have become as strong as rock, but more than ever in danger of being annihilated. Why? Because freedom from the earlier prisons have left him with a great deal of unprecedented power, so much that they are able to bombard Mars and guide an intricate machine into outer space, yet so weak that if you add an extra $12.00 to their salary they will work for you against their boss!

Once I heard that slavery is still popular in some parts of Africa; people capture the primitive tribes and sell them somewhere else. But I have seen slavery with my own eyes in the West. At Cambridge and the Sorbonne the best human brains are being auctioned off. The entrepreneurs from America, Europe, Russia, and elsewhere all come to buy the talented students. They all offer attractive prices, a car, a chauffeur, and whatnot. Finally, students choose the best offer. Why? Because they are slaves. The company wants these students to save society from the prison of nature or history while they themselves are helpless beings and slaves of their own selves. The difficulty is that, since this last prison is part of humankind's own dimensions, it cannot rebel against itself.

As you see, it is not possible to get out of this last prison with the aid of science. How is it possible then? With love. What is love? I don't mean Sufi and theosophic love and whatnot, which are different kinds of prisons. By love I mean an Almighty force (beyond my rational and discretionary faculties) in the very depth of my being that can blow me apart and help me to rebel against my self. Since the prison is inside me, my insides must be set aflame. How? Why fire? Why can't I liberate myself from this prison by utilizing my rational faculties? [Vilfredo] Pareto [Italian philosopher and social scientist, 1848–1923] believes that problems can be divided into three categories: (1) logical acts like living, receiving a salary, putting clothes on, thinking, studying, and whatnot; (2) illogical acts carried out by crazies and screwballs; and (3) alogical acts that belong to neither of the two former categories. Logic consists of discovering causalities so that I can employ them in my needs. But sometimes humans destroy all their worldly belongings and ambitions for something more exalting. For instance, they may set themselves on fire (without anything in return) so that their society can be saved.[7] This is not a logical act. The roots of such act go to morality. Love consists of a power which invites me to go against my profits and well-being and sacrifice myself for others and the ideals that I hold so dear.

If I don't lie to you, it is because I don't want you to lie to me in the bazaar. Or, I don't write bad checks because I want to establish good credit. These are called discretionary virtues, business based upon rationality and logic. On the other hand, when I tell a truth that I know will cost my life or belongings, my "*insaniyat*" will emerge and my "I" will stand tall. Which *insan*? The one (that was buried in the dungeon of my own self a while ago) and is now walking towards becoming an *insan* under the sun of faith and love.

[Friedrich] Nietzsche [1844–1900] was a great philosopher and genius. . . . But in his youth he was an arrogant man who said, "Force is genuine, truth belongs to the powerful," and so on. However, in his old age he changed to a kind humanist, so much so that he did a strange thing. The same man who believed that helping others was a sign of weakness and weak men should be forgotten,[8] one day, while he was passing through the streets he saw an overturned cart. The loaded cart had fallen on the horse and the cart driver was trying to get the horse up on its feet by flogging the animal ruthlessly. The horse would jump periodically under the heavy lashes but would again collapse under the burden with a broken leg. Nietzsche was angered and asked the cart driver not to beat the horse. He advised the man that he should empty the cart first, but the man did not pay attention and continued beating the animal. Finally, Nietzsche grabbed the collar of the driver, who turned around and kicked Nietzsche so hard that he went home and died. This story may strike us as contradictory. In the

---

7. [During the war in Vietnam, some Buddhist monks immolated themselves in public as a political statement.— Translator]

8. Like Eskimos who abandon their elders in ice and snow to die because they can no longer produce.

"I" of every human there are two dimensions: one that becomes excited at the beauty and grandeur of Nietzsche's soul that sacrificed himself in order to help an animal, and the other that mocks such a stupid incident in which a genius died in order to keep a horse alive. This act is neither logical nor illogical; it is alogical, beyond logical analysis. This is ethics and love. When we love someone in order to be loved, or when we are kind to someone so that we can receive a favor, we are businesspeople. Love consists of giving up everything for the sake of a goal and asking nothing in return. This requires one to make a great choice. What is that choice? To choose to die—or some other objective—so another can live and some ideals can be realized.

After a logical stage, the fourth stage is to sacrifice oneself. At this point humans enter the stage of "*ithar*" [self-sacrificing generosity], a word that does not exist in any other language. Here, humans choose someone else over themselves, in other words, they sacrifice themselves for others. It is obvious that from among the two deaths—another person's and their own—they have chosen their own death. This may be the end of one's life, profit, fame, happiness, comfort, bread, and whatnot.

Thus all humans can free themselves from the last prison—which is frightening and contains invisible walls—through the power of *ithar*. It is a love which, beyond rationality and logic, invites us to negate and rebel against ourselves in order to work towards a goal or for the sake of others. It is in this stage that a free human is born, and this is the most exalting level of becoming an *insan*.

Humans as liberators, creators, and conscious choosers can free themselves from the prison of nature and history with the aid of science. They can free themselves from their social order with the aid of sociology. But in order to free themselves from the prison of their selves, as [Sarvepalli] Radhakrishnan [Indian philosopher, 1888–1975] states, "They need religion and love."

We humans have been invited to this world with a duty and a responsibility to devise a plot. What plot? A scheme in which humankind, God, and love are involved to initiate a new creation and a new *insan*. This is what I mean by human responsibility.

Extremism

Yusuf Al-Qaradawi (Egypt-Qatar, born 1926), dean of the law school at the University of Qatar, wrote the following essay in 1981 as an attempt to undermine rising Islamic extremism, especially in his home country of Egypt. In particular, Al-Qaradawi's work is an extended critique of a small radical organization, the Society of Excoriation and Exodus, which kidnapped and killed an Egyptian religious official in 1977. Al-Qaradawi argues that, while extremist religious practices are allowed in Islam, they may not be forced on others.

Logicians argue that one cannot pass a judgment on something unless one has a clear conception of it, because the unknown and the undefined cannot be judged. Therefore, we first have to determine what "religious extremism" means before we can condemn or applaud it. We can do so by considering its reality and its most distinguishing characteristics. Literally, extremism means being situated at the farthest possible point from the center. Figuratively, it indicates a similar remoteness in religion and thought, as well as behavior. One of the main consequences of extremism is exposure to danger and insecurity.[1] Islam, therefore, recommends moderation and balance in everything: in belief, worship, conduct, and legislation. This is the straightforward path that God, the most exalted, calls *al-sirat al-mustaqim*

[the straight path], one distinct from all the others which are followed by those who earn God's anger and those who go astray. Moderation, or balance, is not only a general characteristic of Islam, it is a fundamental landmark. The Qur'an says: "Thus have we made of you an *umma* [community] justly balanced, that you might be witnesses over the nations, and the Messenger a witness over yourselves." (Sura 2, Verse 143) As such, the Muslim *umma* is a nation of justice and moderation; it witnesses every deviation from the "straightforward path" in this life and in the hereafter. Islamic texts call upon Muslims to exercise moderation and to reject and oppose all kinds of extremism: *ghuluw* [excessiveness], *tanattu'* [transgressing, meticulous religiosity], and *tashdid* [strictness, austerity]. A close examination of such texts shows that Islam emphatically warns against, and discourages, *ghuluw*. Let us consider the following *hadith*s [traditions of the Prophet]:

1. "Beware of excessiveness in religion. [People] before you have perished as a result of [such] ex-

---

1. This notion was expressed in a couplet [quoted in the original text] by an Arabian poet who believed that his tribe was safe and a haven before becoming vulnerable when nibbled by calamities and forced into an extreme position.

cessiveness."[2] The people referred to above are the people of other religions, especially *ahl al-kitab* [the people of the book]—Jews and Christians, mainly the Christians. The Qur'an addresses these people:

> Say: "O People of the Book! Exceed not in your religion the bounds [of what is proper], trespassing beyond the truth, nor follow the vain desires of people who went wrong in times gone by who misled many, and strayed [themselves] from the even Way." (Sura 5, Verse 77)

Muslims have therefore been warned not to follow in their steps: he who learns from the mistakes of others indeed lives a happier life. Furthermore, the reason behind the above *hadith* is to alert us to the fact that excessiveness may crop up as an insignificant action that we unwittingly allow to continue and develop into a menace. After reaching Muzdalifa [a town in Arabia] during his last *hajj* [pilgrimage], the Prophet, peace be upon him, asked ['Abdallah] Ibn 'Abbas [619–686] to gather some stones for him. Ibn 'Abbas selected small stones. Upon seeing the stones, the Prophet, peace be upon him, approved of their size and said: "Yes, with such [stones do stone Satan]. Beware of excessiveness in religion."[3] This clearly indicates that Muslims should not be so zealous as to believe that using larger stones is better, thus gradually allowing excessiveness to creep into their lives. Al-Imam Ibn Taymiyya [1263–1328] argues that this warning against excessiveness applies to all forms of belief, worship, and transactions, and notes that since the Christians are more excessive in faith and in practice than any other sect, God, the most exalted, admonishes them in the Qur'an, "Do not exceed the limits of your religion " (Sura 4, Verse 171)

2. "Ruined were those who indulged in *tanattu'*." And he [the Prophet] repeated this thrice.[4] Imam al-

Nawawi [1233–1277] said that the people referred to here, "those indulging in *tanattu'*," i.e., those who go beyond the limit in their utterance as well as in their action. Evidently the above two *hadith*s emphatically assert that the consequence of excessiveness and zealotry will be the complete loss of this life and of the hereafter.

3. The Prophet, peace be upon him, used to say: "Do not overburden yourselves, lest you perish. People [before you] overburdened themselves and perished. Their remains are found in hermitages and monasteries."[5] Indeed, the Prophet Muhammad, peace be upon him, always condemned any tendency toward religious excessiveness. He cautioned those of his companions who were excessive in worship, or who were too ascetic, especially when this went beyond the moderate Islamic position. Islam seeks to create a balance between the needs of the body and those of the soul, between the right of man to live life to its full, and the right of the Creator to be worshipped by man, which is man's reason for being. . . .

The Qur'an disapproves of and rejects the tendency to prohibit worldly goods and ornaments which God has provided for his servants. In a verse revealed in Mecca, God, the most exalted, says:

> O Children of Adam! Wear your beautiful apparel at every time and place of prayer. Eat and drink, but waste not by excess, for God loves not those who waste.

> Say: "Who has forbidden the beautiful gifts of God which He has produced for His servants, and the things clean and pure which He has provided for sustenance?" (Sura 7, Verses 31–32)

In another *sura*, revealed in Medina, God, the most exalted, addresses the believers similarly:

> O you who believe! Make not unlawful the good things which God has made lawful for you. But commit no excess, for God does not like those given to excess. Eat of the things which God has provided you, lawful and good, but fear God, in Whom you believe. (Sura 5, Verses 86–88)

2. Reported by Ahmad [ibn Hanbal, 780–855], [Abu 'Abd al-Rahman] al-Nasa'i [830–915], and [Abu 'Abdallah] Ibn Maja [824–887] in their *Sunan* [*Hadith* collections].

3. Reported by al-Imam Ahmad [ibn Hanbal], in his *Musnad* [*Hadith* collection], al-Nasa'i and ['Imad al-Din] Ibn Kathir [circa 1300–1373] in their *Sunan* [*Hadith* collections], and [Muhammad ibn 'Abdallah] al-Hakim [al-Naysaburi, 933–1014] in his *Mustadrak* [*'ala sahihayn*] [supplement to the authentic *Hadith* collections], on the authority of ['Abdallah] Ibn 'Abbas.

4. Reported by Muslim [ibn al-Hajjaj, *hadith* compiler, circa 821–875]. [Jalal-al-Din] Al-Suyuti [died 1505] attrib-

uted this *hadith* to both Ahmad [ibn Hanbal] and Abu Dau'd [al-Sijistani, 817–889].

5. Reported by Abu Ya'la [Ibn al-Fara', died 1066] in his *Musnad* [*Hadith* collection], on the authority of Malik ibn Anas [companion of the Prophet, 710–796]. Cited by Ibn Kathir in his interpretation of Sura 57, Verse 27, namely: "But the monasticism which they themselves invented, We did not prescribe for them."

These verses explain to the believers the true Islamic way of enjoying worldly goods and of resisting the excessiveness found in other religions. It is reported that the situational context for the revelation of these two verses was when a group of the Prophet's companions decided to castrate themselves and to roam the land like monks.

Ibn 'Abbas, may God be pleased with him, also reported: "A man came upon the Prophet, peace be upon him, and said, 'O Messenger of God, whenever I eat of this meat I [always] have a desire to make love, therefore, I have decided to abstain from eating meat.'" Consequently the verses were revealed.[6] . . .

1. Defects of Religious Extremism

All these warnings against extremism and excessiveness are necessary because of the serious defects inherent in such tendencies. The first defect is that excessiveness is too disagreeable for ordinary human nature to endure or tolerate. Even if a few human beings could put up with excessiveness for a short time, the majority would not be able to do so. God's legislation addresses the whole of humanity, not a special group who may have a unique capacity for endurance. This is why the Prophet, peace be upon him, was once angry with his eminent companion Mu'adh [ibn Jabal, died 627], because the latter led the people one day in prayer and so prolonged it that one of the people went to the Prophet and complained. The Prophet, peace be upon him, said to Mu'adh: "O Mu'adh! Are you putting the people on trial?" and repeated it thrice.[7]

On another occasion he addressed an *imam* [prayer leader] with unusual anger: "Some of you make people dislike prayer. So whoever among you leads people in prayer should keep it short, short because amongst them are the weak, the old, and the one who has business to attend to."[8] . . .

The second defect is that excessiveness is short-lived. Since man's capacity for endurance and perseverance is naturally limited, and since man can easily become bored, he cannot endure any excessive practice for long. Even if he puts up with it for a while, he will soon be overcome by fatigue, physically and spiritually, and will eventually give up even the little he can naturally do, or he may even take a different course altogether substituting excessiveness with complete negligence and laxity. I have often met people who were known for their strictness and extremism; then I lost contact with them for a while. When I inquired about them after a period of time, I found out that they had either deviated and taken the opposite extreme, or had, at least, lagged behind like the "hasty one" referred to in the following *hadith*: "He [the hasty one] neither covers the desired distance nor spares the back [of his camel]."[9] . . .

How superb is the Prophet's advice to all Muslims not to overburden themselves in worship and to be moderate so that they will not be overcome by fatigue and finally fail to continue. He said: "Religion is very easy, and whoever overburdens himself will not be able to continue in that way. Be right [without excessiveness or negligence], near [perfection], and have good tidings [in being rewarded for your deeds]."[10]

The third defect is that excessive practice jeopardizes other rights and obligations. A sage once said in this respect: "Every extravagance is somehow bound to be associated with a lost right."

When the Prophet, peace be upon him, learned that 'Abdallah ibn 'Umar [died 693] was so absorbed in worship that he even neglected his duty toward his wife, he said to him: "O 'Abdallah! Have I not been correctly informed that you fast during the day and offer worship throughout the night?" 'Abdallah replied, "Yes, O Messenger of God!" The Prophet, peace be upon him, then said: "Don't do that. Instead, fast and then break your fast; worship during the night but also sleep. Your body has a right on you, your wife has a right on you, and your guest has a right on you."[11] . . .

6. *Mukhtasar* [*The Handbook*] of Ibn Kathir, volume 1, p. 541.

7. Reported by [Muhammad ibn Isma'il] Al-Bukhari [810–870, *hadith* compiler].

8. Reported by Al-Bukhari.

9. Reported by [Abu Bakr Muhammad] al-Bazzaz [died 965], on the authority of Jabir [ibn 'Abdallah, Companion of the Prophet, died 697], with a weak *isnad* [authentic oral history].

10. Reported by al-Bukhari and al-Nasa'i on the authority of Abu Hurayra [Companion of the Prophet, died 678]. Explained by ['Abd al-Ra'uf ibn Taj al-'Arifin] al-Munawi [died 1621].

11. Reported by al-Bukhari.

2. The Concept of Religious Extremism

I would like at this point to draw attention to two important observations. First: The degree of a person's piety as well as that of the society in which he lives affect his judgment of others as far as extremism, moderation, and laxity are concerned. A religious society usually produces a person sensitively aversive to any deviation or negligence, however slight it may be. Judging by the criteria of his own practice and background, such a person would be surprised to find that there are Muslims who do not worship at night or fast. This is historically obvious. When examining the deeds and practices of people, the nearer one gets to the time of the Prophet, peace be upon him, his companions and the first generation of Muslims, the less worthy seem the deeds and practices of the pious among the later generations. Hence the gist of the saying: "The merits of those nearest to God are but the demerits of the righteous." . . .

Second: It is unfair to accuse a person of "religious extremism" simply because he has adopted a "hard-line" juristic opinion of certain religious scholars. If a person is convinced that his opinion is right and that he is bound by it according to religious law, he is free to do so even if others think that the juristic evidence is weak. He is only responsible for what he thinks and believes even if, in so doing, he overburdens himself, especially since he is not content with only limiting himself to the categorical obligations required of him but seeks God's pleasure through supererogatory performances. People naturally differ on these matters. . . .

3. Manifestations of Extremism

The *first* indications of extremism include bigotry and intolerance, which make a person obstinately devoted to his own opinions and prejudices, as well as rigidity, which deprives him of clarity of vision regarding the interests of other human beings, the purposes of religious law, or the circumstances of the age. Such a person does not allow any opportunity for dialogue with others so that he may compare his opinion with theirs, and chooses to follow what appears to him most sound. We equally condemn this person's attempt to suppress and discard the opinions of others, just as we condemn the similar attitude of his accusers and opponents. Indeed, we emphatically condemn his attitude if he claims that he alone is right and everybody else is wrong, accusing those who have different ideas and opinions of ignorance and self-interest, and those with different behavior of disobedience and sin, as if he were an infallible prophet and his words were divinely revealed. This attitude contradicts the consensus of the Islamic community, that what every person says can be totally or partly accepted or rejected, except, of course, the *hadith*s of the Prophet Muhammad, peace be upon him.

Strangely, though some of these people take liberty in exercising *ijtihad* [Islamic interpretation] in the most complicated matters and issues and pass notional and whimsical judgments, yet they would deprive the contemporary expert religious scholars—singly or collectively—of the right to exercise *ijtihad* regarding statements which contradict theirs. Some of them never hesitate to give ridiculous opinions on, and interpretations of, the Qur'an and *sunna* [practices of the Prophet]; opinions which are contradictory to those handed down to us by our forefathers, or subsequently arrived at by contemporary scholars. This indifference is due to their presumption to be on an equal footing with Abu Bakr [first caliph, reigned 632–634], 'Umar [second caliph, reigned 634–644], 'Ali [fourth caliph, reigned 656–661], and Ibn 'Abbas, may God be pleased with them. This presumption might be less grave if these people admitted that their contemporaries who hold different views or approaches are also capable of *ijtihad* like themselves; but they would not.

Bigotry is the clearest evidence of extremism. An extremist seems to address people in this way: "I have the right to speak, your duty is to listen. I have the right to lead, your duty is to follow. My opinion is right, it cannot be wrong. Your opinion is wrong, it can never be right." Thus, a bigot can never come to terms with others. Agreement is possible and can be reached when people hold moderate positions, but a bigot neither knows nor believes in moderation. He stands in relation to people as the East stand in relation to the West—the nearer you get to one, the further you move away from the other.

The issue becomes even more critical when such a person develops the tendency to coerce others, not necessarily physically but by accusing them of innovations, laxity, unbelief, and deviation. Such intellectual terrorism is as terrifying as physical terrorism.

The *second* characteristic of extremism manifests itself in a perpetual commitment to excessiveness, and in attempts to force others to do likewise, despite the existence of good reasons for facilitation and the fact that God, the most exalted, has not ordained it. A person motivated by piety and caution may, if he so wishes, choose a hard-line opinion in some matters and on certain occasions. But this should not become so habitual that he rejects facilitation when he needs it. Such an attitude is not in keeping with the teachings of the Qur'an or *sunna*, as is clear from the following verse: "God intends every facility for you; He does not want to put you to difficulties." (Sura 2, Verse 185)

The Prophet, peace be upon him, also said . . . "Facilitate [matters] and do not make [matters] difficult." The Prophet also said: "God loves that His dispensations [to make matters easier] be accepted, as He dislikes [to see people] committing disobedience."[12] It is also reported that "Whenever the Prophet, peace be upon him, was given a choice between two options, he always chose the easiest, unless it was a sin."[13] . . .

A bedouin once asked the Prophet, peace be upon him, about the obligatory prescriptions required of him. The Prophet, peace be upon him, mentioned only three: prayer, *zakat* taxation, and fasting during Ramadan. When the bedouin asked if there was anything else he must do, the Prophet, peace be upon him, replied in the negative, adding that the bedouin could volunteer to do more if he so wished. As he was leaving, the bedouin swore never to increase or decrease what the Prophet, peace be upon him, had asked him to do. When the Prophet, peace be upon him, heard this he said, "If he is saying the truth, he will succeed" or "he will be granted paradise."[14]

If a Muslim in this age observes the religious obligations, maintains loyalty to God, the most exalted, and His Messenger, peace be upon him, and eschews the most heinous of sins, he should be accommodated in the fold of Islam and regarded as one of its advocates. Even if he commits some minor sins, the merits gained by his observance of the five daily prayers, the Friday [Sabbath] prayers, fasting [during the month of Ramadan], and so on will expiate his small faults.

The Qur'an says: "Good deeds remove those that are evil" (Sura 11, Verse 114), and in another verse: "If you eschew the most heinous of the things which are forbidden, We shall expel out of you all the evil in you and admit you to a state of great honor." (Sura 4, Verse 31) In view of the above evidence from the Qur'an and *sunna*, how could we expel a Muslim from the fold of Islam merely because of his commitment to certain controversial matters that we are not sure are permissible or forbidden, or because of his failure to perform practices that we are not certain are obligatory or recommended. This is why I object to the tendency of some pious people to adopt and cling to hard-line opinions, not only in their own personal practice but also in influencing others to do the same. I also object to the charges leveled by such people against any Muslim scholar who disagrees with their line of thought by opting for facilitation in the light of the Qur'an and *sunna* in order to relieve people of distress and undue restrictions in their religious practice.

The *third* characteristic of extremism is the overburdening of others without regard for time and place—applying Islamic principles to people in non-Muslim countries or to people who have only recently converted to Islam, as well as to Muslims who are newly devout. With all these, emphasis should not be put on minor or controversial issues, but on fundamentals. Efforts should be made to correct their concepts and understanding of Islam before anything else. Once the correct beliefs are firmly established, then one can begin to explain the five pillars of Islam and gradually to emphasize those aspects which make a Muslim's belief and practice compatible, and his entire life an embodiment of what is pleasing to God, the most exalted. This fact was recognized by the Prophet Muhammad himself, peace be upon him, when he sent Mu'adh, may God be pleased with him, to Yemen. He told him:

> You are going to [meet] people of a [divine] scripture, and when you reach them call them to witness that there is no god but God and that Muhammad is His Messenger. And if they obey you in that, then tell them that God has enjoined on them five prayers to be performed every day and night. And if they obey you in that, then tell them that God has enjoined upon

12. Reported by al-Imam Ahmad [ibn Hanbal] and [Abu'l-Fadl Muhammad Katib ibn] al-Bayhaqi [995–1077] on the authority of ['Abdallah] Ibn 'Umar, and by [Abu Ja'far Muhammad] al-Tabari [died 922] on the authority of Ibn 'Abbas.

13. Reported by al-Bukhari and [Abu 'Isa Muhammad] al-Tirmidhi [*hadith* compiler, died 892].

14. Reported by al-Bukhari.

them taxation, to be taken from the rich amongst them and given to the poor amongst them.[15]

Notice the gradation in the Prophet's advice to Mu'adh, may God be pleased with him.

I was shocked and dismayed during a tour of North America to find that devout young Muslims have initiated a great controversy because Muslims sit on chairs during the Saturday and Sunday lectures in mosques instead of sitting on mats on the ground, and do not face Mecca as Muslims do, and also because those who attend wear shirts and trousers rather than loose outer coverings, and sit at dining tables to eat rather than on the ground. I was angered by this kind of thinking and behavior in the heart of North America. I therefore addressed these people:

> It would be more worthwhile in this materialistic society to make your paramount concern the call to monotheism and the worship of God, the most exalted, to remind people of the hereafter, of the noble Islamic values, and to warn them of the heinous acts in which the materially developed countries have been totally immersed. The norms of behavior and improvements in religious practice are governed by time as well as place, and should be introduced only after the more necessary and fundamental tenets have been firmly established.

In another Islamic center, people were creating a considerable fuss over the showing of a historical or educational film in a mosque, claiming that "mosques have been turned into movie theaters," but forgetting that the purpose of the mosque is to serve the worldly as well as spiritual interest of Muslims. During the time of Prophet Muhammad, peace be upon him, the mosque was the center of religion and of the state, as well as of social activities. We are all aware of the Prophet's granting permission to a group of people from Abyssinia to sport with their spears in the middle of his mosque, and that he allowed 'A'isha [wife of the Prophet, circa 614–678], may God be pleased with her, to watch them.[16]

The *fourth* characteristic of extremism manifests itself in harshness in the treatment of people, roughness in the manner of approach, and crudeness in calling people to Islam, all of which are contrary to the teachings of the Qur'an and *sunna*. God, the most

exalted, commands us to call to Islam and to His teachings with wisdom, not with foolishness; with amicability, not with harsh words: "Invite [all] to the Way of your Lord with wisdom and beautiful preaching, and argue with them in ways that are best and most gracious." (Sura 16, Verse 125) [The Qur'an] also describes the Prophet, peace be upon him, thus: "Now has come unto you a Messenger from among yourselves. It grieves him that you should perish, ardently anxious is he over you. To the believers he is kind and merciful." (Sura 9, Verse 128) The Qur'an also addressed the Prophet, peace be upon him, defining his relationship with his companions: "It is part of the mercy of God that you [Muhammad] deal justly with them. If you were severe and hard-hearted they would have broken away from you." (Sura 3, Verse 159)

. . . [The call to Islam] cannot succeed without wisdom and amicability, and without taking into consideration human nature—man's obstinacy, resistance to change, and argumentativeness. These characteristics necessitate the exercise of kindness and gentleness when attempting to reach man's heart and mind so that his hardness can be softened, his rigidity abated and his pride checked. This approach was described for us in the Qur'an as having been followed by earlier prophets and sincere believers who called people to the worship of God, the most exalted. Examples can be found in Abraham's call to his father and people, in Shu'aib's call to his people [the ancient people of Midyan], in Moses' call to the Pharaoh . . . in [Muhammad's] call (Sura 36, Verse 20), as well as in the calls of others who directed people to the truth and righteousness. . . .

No wonder then that people experienced in the call reject and disapprove of the young people's manner in arguing with those who hold different opinions! Rather than calling people to the Way of God, the most exalted, with wisdom, they are quite often harsh, rough, and crude. No distinction is made between the old and the young; no special consideration is given to those whose age or status deserves special respect, that is, parents, teachers, the learned, or those who have precedence in the call and the struggle. Nor do the young people differentiate between those sectors in the community—such as the laity, the illiterate, and the misled—who are ceaselessly battling to earn a living, and those who actively resist Islam out of malice or treason, not ignorance.

15. Authenticated by all authorities.
16. Reported by al-Bukhari and others.

Such lack of insight is still dominant in Muslim society, despite the fact that the early scholars of *hadith* literature distinguished very clearly between common innovators who do not call others to their innovation, and those who deliberately publicize and defend their innovations. The reports of the former were accepted, while those of the latter were rejected.

Suspicion and distrust are also manifestations of extremism. An extremist readily accuses people and quickly passes judgment contrary to the generally accepted norm: "innocent until proven guilty." He considers a person guilty the moment he suspects him of something. He jumps to conclusions rather than looking for explanations. The slightest mistake is blown out of all proportion; a mistake becomes a sin, and a sin a mortal sin. Such a reaction is a stark violation of the spirit and teachings of Islam which encourage Muslims to think well of other Muslims, to try to find an excuse for their misbehavior, and to help them improve their words and deeds.

The religious sincerity and integrity of those who disagree with such an extremist are always called into question. An extremist would depict people as being guilty of transgression, innovation, or disrespect for the Prophet's *sunna* even if their views are solidly based upon authentic Islamic texts.

One could cite many examples: If you argue that carrying a stick or eating while sitting on the ground has nothing to do with the *sunna*, you would be accused of disrespect for the Prophet himself, peace be upon him. Not even learned Muslim scholars are spared such accusations. If a scholar renders a decision that facilitates matters for Muslims, he is considered lax on religious issues; if a Muslim preacher tries to call people to Islam in a manner suitable to the spirit and the taste of the age, he is accused of succumbing to and patronizing Western civilization.

Moreover, these accusations are not only hurled at the living but also at the dead, who are unable to defend themselves. No one holding a different opinion can escape unjust indiscriminate accusations, such as being a Freemason, a predeterminist Jahmi, or a rationalist Mu'tazilite.[17] Even the four great jurists of Islam who established the main Islamic juristic schools and who have earned the respect of the majority of Muslims throughout the centuries have not escaped the venomous slander of the extremists.

Indeed, the whole history of the Muslim community after the fourth century A.H., with its glorious legacy and unprecedented civilization, has been a target of unjustified criticism. It is considered by the extremists as being the source of contemporary evils, the roots of our malaise. To some extremists, it was a period of conflict and discord, of struggle for personal power; for others, a period of ignorance and even mortal sin.

This destructive tendency is not new. Extremists existed even during the time of the Prophet, peace be upon him. Once, an extremist among the *Ansar* [literally helpers, meaning the Muslims of Medina] accused the Prophet, peace be upon him, of favoritism in his division and distribution of the spoils of war.

The gravest shortcoming of the contemporary extremists is suspicion. If they understood and comprehended the Qur'an and *sunna*, they would discover that both seek to foster in the mind of each and every Muslim the confidence and trust of other fellow Muslims.

A Muslim is not even allowed to publicize the minor mistakes and faults of others or become blind to their merits, though some people are interested in criticizing others and in praising themselves. "Therefore, justify not yourselves: He knows best who it is that guards against evil." (Sura 53, Verse 32) Indeed, Islam strongly warns against two characteristics: despairing of God's mercy and suspecting fellow human beings. God, the most exalted, says: "O you who believe! Avoid suspicion as much [as possible]: for suspicion in some cases is a sin." (Sura 49, Verse 12) The Prophet, peace be upon him, also says in this respect: "Avoid suspicion, for suspicion is the false element in talk."[18] . . .

Extremism reaches its utmost limit when a single group deprives all people of the right to safety and protection, and instead sanctions their killing and the confiscation of their lives and property. This, of course, occurs when an extremist holds all people—except those in his group—to be unbelievers. This kind of extremism severs any bond between such a person and the rest of the Islamic community. This is the trap into which the Khawarij fell during the dawn of Islam, although they were known for their strict observance of religious duties such as prayer, fasting, and recitation of the Qur'an. However, their

---

17. [The latter two are theological positions historically dismissed as heretical.—Editor]

18. Authenticated by all authorities.

thinking rather than their conscience was distorted and corrupt. Hence they were so infatuated with their belief and behavior that they unintentionally deviated from the right path.

The Prophet, peace be upon him, described the devotion of such people by saying: "Any of you would hold insignificant his own prayer compared with their [the Khawarij's] prayer, and his nightly devotions compared with their nightly devotions, his recitation [of the Qur'an] compared with their recitation."[19] Nevertheless, he said of them: "They would recite the Qur'an but it would not go beyond their throat, and they pass through religion without a mark."[20] This means that they slip out of religion as an arrow slips out of its bow. The Prophet, peace be upon him, also said of them that they regard it as their duty to "destroy adherents of Islam and save the idol-worshippers."[21]

This is why when a Muslim fell into their hands and was asked about his identity, he replied that he was a polytheist curious to find out about God's message and book. On hearing this the Khawarij told the man that they would protect him and grant him safe passage. In support of their decision, they recited the following verse from the Qur'an:

If one amongst the pagans asks you for asylum, grant it to him, so that he may hear the Word of God; and then escort him to where he may be secure. That is because they are men without knowledge. (Sura 9, Verse 6)

The irony is that if the man had admitted that he was a Muslim they would have killed him. Unfortunately, some Muslims have not yet learned this lesson. The *Jama'at al-Takfir wa al-Hijra* [Society of Excoriation and Exodus, a militant Islamic group in Egypt] seems to be following in the footsteps of the Khawarij. They readily brand as an unbeliever anybody who commits a sin and does not immediately repent. Even more worthy of condemnation, in their view, are the rulers who do not implement the *shari'a*, as well as people who submit to such rulers. Still more sinful in their view are the religious scholars who do not openly condemn such people as unbelievers, as well as those who reject the group's beliefs and submit to the laws elaborated by the four

great jurists of Islam on the basis of consensus: logical deduction, public welfare, or fairness. Moreover, anyone who first pledges support for their cause and joins their group, then decides to leave it—for one reason or another—is considered an apostate and must be put to death. Indeed, they hold all history after the fourth century A.H. as periods of ignorance and unbelief, worshipping the idol of tradition rather than God, the most exalted.[22]

In this way, the group became so excessive in accusing people of unbelief that they spared neither the dead nor the living. The group has thus run into deep trouble, because accusing a Muslim of unbelief is a very serious matter, with very serious consequences—his killing and the confiscation of his property become lawful. As an apostate, he must be separated from his wife and children; there can be no bond between him and other Muslims; he must be deprived of his inheritance and cannot bequeath to others; he must be denied Islamic burial and the prayer for the deceased; and he must not be buried in a Muslim graveyard.

The Prophet, peace be upon him, said: "When a Muslim calls another Muslim an unbeliever, then surely one of them is such."[23] This means that unless the accusation is validated and substantiated, it will fall back on the accuser, who will face great danger in this world and in the hereafter.

Usama ibn Zayd [Companion of the Prophet, died circa 673] said: "If a man says, 'I witness that there is no god but God,' he has embraced Islam, and his life and property should be granted safety. If he said so in fear or to protect himself from the sword, he will account for that before God. We should [judge] the apparent.'"[24] The Prophet, peace be upon him, rebuked Usama when he discovered that the latter had killed a man who had uttered the *shahada* [acceptance of Islam] following a battle in which the man's tribe was defeated. When Usama argued that he thought—at the time—that the man did so to save himself, out of fear, the Prophet, peace be upon him, said: "Did you look into his heart after he had confessed that there is no god but God?" Usama relates: "He [the Prophet] continued repeating this to me till I wished I had not embraced Islam before that day."

---

19. Reported by Muslim [ibn al-Hajjaj].
20. Reported by Muslim [ibn al-Hajjaj].
21. Reported by Muslim [ibn al-Hajjaj].

22. See 'Abd al-Rahman Abu al-Khayr, *Dhikrayati ma'a Jama'at al-Muslimin (al-Takfir wa al-Hijra)* [*My Memoires of the Society of Muslims (Society of Excoriation and Exodus)*].
23. Reported by al-Bukhari.
24. Reported by al-Bukhari.

Religious law teaches that those who embrace Islam with certainty of mind can only be expelled from its fold by proven and substantiated evidence. Even major sins such as murder, fornication, and drinking alcohol do not justify the accusation of unbeliever, provided that the person concerned does not show disrespect for, reject, or refuse to recognize religious law.

This is why the Qur'an established brotherly love between the person who commits a premeditated murder and the next of kin of the victim, as this verse shows: "And for him who is forgiven somewhat by his [injured] brother, prosecution according to usage and payment unto him in kindness." (Sura 2, Verse 178)[25]

The Prophet, peace be upon him, also addressed a person who cursed an alcoholic who had already been punished several times for alcoholism: "Do not curse him; he loves God and His Messenger."[26]

Further, religious law has prescribed different punishments for crimes such as murder, fornication, and drunkenness. Had all of these been unbelief, then they would have been punished in accordance with the law of apostasy.

All the obscure and vague evidence on which the extremists base their accusations are refuted by fundamental and categorical texts in both the Qur'an and *sunna*. This issue was settled by the Islamic community centuries ago—it is futile to try to revive and renew it.

---

25. Translation by Muhammad Asad [born Leopold Weiss, Austria-Pakistan, born 1900].

26. Reported by al-Bukhari.

Rethinking Islam Today

Mohamed Arkoun (Algeria-France, born 1928) received his doctorate at the Sorbonne in Paris and joined the faculty there as Professor of Islamic Thought in 1963. In a series of works since the early 1970s, Arkoun has attempted to reshape Islamic interpretation through the use of contemporary social-scientific, particularly linguistic, methods. "One of the most articulate . . . liberal Muslims,"[1] Arkoun has embarked on "an intellectual crusade,"[2] engaging Islamic radicals in debate and arguing for pluralism within Islam, acceptance of multiple interpretations of the sacred texts, and a more self-conscious attitude toward one's own interpretation.[3] The following chapter serves as an introduction to and summary of Arkoun's work; its style is somewhat more accessible than his French work.

Shall I seek other than God for Judge, when He is who hath revealed unto you the Book, fully explained? Those unto whom we gave the Book know that it is revealed from thy Lord in truth. So be not (O Muhammad) of the waverers. Perfected is the word of thy Lord in truth and justice. There is naught that can change His word. He is the Hearer, the Knower. (Qur'an, Sura 6, Verses 114–115)

Islam holds historical significance for all of us, but at the same time, our understanding of this phenomenon is sadly inadequate. There is a need to encourage and initiate audacious, free, productive thinking on Islam today. The so called Islamic revivalism has monopolized the discourse on Islam; the social scientists, moreover, do not pay attention to what I call the "silent Islam"—the Islam of true believers who attach more importance to the religious relationship with the absolute of God than to the vehement demonstrations of political movements. I refer to the

1. Wm. Montgomery Watt, "A Contemporary Muslim Thinker," *The Scottish Journal of Religious Studies*, volume 6, number 1, Spring 1985, pp. 5–10.

2. Fedwa Malti-Douglas, "Arkoun, Mohammed," in John L. Esposito, editor, *The Oxford Encyclopedia of the Modern Islamic World* (New York: Oxford University Press, 1995), volume 1, pp. 139–140.

3. Robert D. Lee, *Overcoming Tradition and Modernity* (Boulder, Colo.: Westview Press, 1997), pp. 143–174. Among Arkoun's works are *Lectures du Coran (Readings from the Qur'an)* (Paris: G. P. Maisonneuve et Larose, 1982); *Pour une critique de raison Islamique (For a Critique of Islamic Reason)* (Paris: G. P. Maisonneuve et Larose, 1984); *L'Islam: Morale et politique (Islam: Morals and Politics)* (Paris: UNESCO and Desclée de Brouwer, 1986); and *Ouvertures sur l'Islam* translated by Robert D. Lee, as *Rethinking Islam* (Boulder, Colo.: Westview Press, 1994).

Islam of thinkers and intellectuals who are having great difficulties inserting their critical approach into a social and cultural space that is, at present, totally dominated by militant ideologies.

My own ambition as a Muslim intellectual is not the result of my academic training; rather, it is rooted in my existential experience. I entered high school in Oran and then the university in Algiers. It was the colonial time in Algeria, and like all Algerians, I was continually shocked by the sharp, hard confrontation between the conquering French culture and language and my own Algerian culture. (I speak Berber and Arabic.) When I heard lectures on Islam at the University of Algiers I was, like others, deeply disappointed by the intellectual poverty of the presentation, especially when burning issues were raised in Algerian society between 1950 and 1954. The national movement for liberation was countering the colonial claim to represent modern civilization by emphasizing the Arab-Muslim personality of Algeria. As a result of this brutal confrontation I resolved (1) to understand the Arab-Muslim personality claimed by the nationalist movement, and (2) to determine the extent to which the modern civilization, represented by the colonial power, should be considered a universal civilization.

These are the roots of my psychological concerns. As a scholar and a teacher at the Sorbonne since 1961, I have never stopped this *ijtihad* [Islamic interpretation], my intellectual effort to find adequate answers to my two initial questions. At the same time, this explains my method and my epistemology. For me, as a historian of Islamic thought, there is one cultural space stretching from the Indian to the Atlantic Oceans. This space is, of course, extremely rich in its languages and ethno-cultural variety. It also has been influenced by two axial traditions of thinking: the ancient Middle Eastern culture, which has a special place for Greek thought, and the monotheism taught by the prophets. I learned to discover Islam in this wide, rich, intricate space, which is why I am not comfortable with the English title imposed on me for this lecture. I could not find a relevant translation of the French *Penser l'Islam* or the Arabic *Kayfa na'qilu al-Islam*. *Penser l'Islam* suggests the free use of reason aimed at elaborating a new and coherent vision which integrates the new situations faced by societies and the living elements of Muslim tradition. Here I emphasize freedom. *Rethinking* Islam could suggest that I am repeating the well-known position

of the *islahi*—the reformist thinking represented since the 19th century by the *salafi* school [revivalists, literally followers of the pious ancestors]. I want to avoid any parallel between the modern perspective of radical critical thought applied to any subject and the *islahi* thinking which, in the Islamic tradition, is a mythical attitude more or less mixed with the historical approach to the problems related to religious vision.

I favor the historical approach, with its modern enlarged curiosities, because it includes the study of mythical knowledge as being not limited to the primitive archaic mentality, according to the definitions imposed by the positivist historicist school since the 19th century. On the contrary, the main intellectual endeavor represented by *thinking* Islam or any religion today is to evaluate, with a new epistemological perspective, the characteristics and intricacy of systems of knowledge—both the historical and the mythical. I would even say that both are still interacting and interrelated in our modern thought after at least three hundred years of rationalism and historicism. There is no need to insist on the idea that *thinking* Islam today is a task much more urgent and significant than all the scholastic discussions of Orientalism; the ultimate goal of the project is to develop—through the example set by Islam as a religion and a social-historical space—a new epistemological strategy for the comparative study of cultures. All the polemics recently directed against Orientalism show clearly that so-called modern scholarship remains far from any epistemological project that would free Islam from the essentialist, substantialist postulates of classical metaphysics. Islam, in these discussions, is assumed to be a specific, essential, unchangeable system of thought, beliefs, and non-beliefs, one which is superior or inferior (according to Muslims or non-Muslims) to the Western (or Christian) system. It is time to stop this irrelevant confrontation between two dogmatic attitudes—the theological claims of believers and the ideological postulates of positivist rationalism. The study of religions, in particular, is handicapped by the rigid definitions and methods inherited from theology and classical metaphysics. The history of religion has collected facts and descriptions of various religions, but religion as a universal dimension of human existence is not approached from the relevant epistemological perspective. This weakness in modern thought is even more clearly illustrated by the poor, conformist, and sometimes polemical literature on the religions of the Book, as we shall see.

For all these reasons, it is necessary to clear away the obstacles found in Islamic as well as Orientalist literature on Islam and to devote more attention in our universities to teaching and studying history as an anthropology of the past and not only as a narrative account of facts. I insist on a historical, sociological, anthropological approach not to deny the importance of the theological and philosophical, but to enrich them by the inclusion of the concrete historical and social conditions in which Islam always has been practiced. My method is one of deconstruction. For centuries religions have dominated the construction of different, intricate *Weltanschauungen* [worldviews] through which all realities were perceived, judged, classified, accepted, and rejected without the possibility of looking back at the mental-historical process which led to each *Weltanschauung* [worldview]. The strategy of deconstruction is possible only with modern critical epistemology. Reason needs to be free from the ontology, transcendentalism, and substantialism in which it has made itself a prisoner, especially in the various theologies elaborated through Greek logic and metaphysics.

Thus presented, the enterprise of *thinking* Islam today can only be achieved—if ever—by dynamic teams of thinkers, writers, artists, scholars, politicians, and economic producers. I am aware that long and deeply-rooted traditions of thinking cannot be changed or even revised through a few essays or suggestions made by individuals. But I believe that thoughts have their own force and life. Some, at least, could survive and break through the wall of uncontrolled beliefs and dominating ideologies.

Where can we start under these conditions? Where is the authorized voice or the accepted theory which could give expression to an Islam integrated into our modern, scientific mentality and at the same time into the religious experience of Muslims? In other words, is it possible to articulate a modern vision of Islam which could have the same impact on the community as the *Risala* [*Treatise*] of [Abu 'Abdallah Muhammad] Shafi'i [767–820] or *Ihya' 'ulum al-din* [*Revival of the Religious Sciences*] of [Abu Hamid Muhammad] Ghazzali [1058–1111]? I refer to these two major books because they illustrate the same intellectual initiative as the one I propose, namely, to integrate, as Shafi'i and Ghazzali did, new disciplines, new knowledge, and new historical in-

sights into Islam as a spiritual and historical vision of human existence.

Actually, I started this project with an article written in 1969 in which I asked "How to read the Qur'an?" One necessarily has to start with the Qur'an because, historically, everything started with what I called the "Experience of Medina," including the communication of the Qur'an received as revelation and the historical process through which a social group, named believers (*mu'minun*), emerged and dominated other groups—named unbelievers, infidels, hypocrites, polytheists (*kafirun, munafiqun, mushrikun*). For the first time in the history of Qur'anic exegesis, I raised the crucial issue of reading texts according to the new epistemology introduced by modern linguistics and semiotics. When I applied this epistemology to the reading of the Fatiha, I received the usual response that there is nothing new in this essay; everything already has been well explained through classical exegesis. Other essays collected in my book, *Lectures du Coran* [*Readings of the Qur'an*] (Paris, France: Maisonneuve-Larose, 1982), did not evoke more interest either among Orientalists or Muslims who read French. I mention this fact because it illustrates clearly the concept of epistemological space.

It is true that I use grammatical and lexicographic material collected by classical exegeses. However, the epistemological perspective of linguistic analysis is totally different from the theological postulates accepted without discussion in the Islamic, Christian, and Jewish traditions of thought. This will appear in the following analyses.

I shall not insist any longer here on the decisive importance of linguistics and semeiotics in rethinking the cognitive status of religious discourse. Rather, I would like to stress various views already developed in several essays which I collected in my *Critique de la raison Islamique* [*Critique of Islamic Reason*] (Paris, France: Maisonneuve-Larose, 1984). I shall tackle the following points:

1. Tools for new thinking.
2. Modes of thinking.
3. From the unthinkable to the thinkable.
4. Societies of the Book.
5. Strategy for deconstruction.
6. Revelation and history.

Many other problems must be raised and solved because Islam has regulated every aspect of individual and collective life; but my wish here is to indicate a general direction of thinking and the main conditions necessary to practice an *ijtihad* recognized equally by Muslims and modern scholars.

1. Tools for New Thinking

Periodization of the history of thought and literature has been dictated by political events. We speak currently of the Umayyad, 'Abbasid, and Ottoman periods [661–750, 750–1258, and 1281–1924, respectively]. However, there are more enlightening criteria that we can use to distinguish periods of change in the history of thought. We must consider the discontinuities affecting the conceptual framework used in a given cultural space. The concepts of reason and science (*'ilm*) used in the Qur'an, for example, are not the same as those developed later by the *falasifa* [philosophers], according to the Platonic and the Aristotelian schools. However, the concepts elaborated in Qur'anic discourse are still used more or less accurately today because the *episteme* introduced by the Qur'an has not been intellectually reconsidered.

Episteme is a better criterion for the study of thought because it concerns the structure of the discourse—the implicit postulates which command the syntactic construction of the discourse. To control the epistemological validity of any discourse, it is necessary to discover and analyze the implicit postulates. This work has never been done for any discourse in Islamic thought (I refer to my essay "Logocentrisme et verité religieuse selon Abu al-Hasan al-'Amiri" [Logocentrism and Religious Truth according to Abu al-Hasan al-'Amiri], in *Essais sur la pensée Islamique* [*Essays on Islamic Thought*], Paris, France: Maisonneuve-Larose, third edition, 1984). This is why I must insist here on the new *episteme* implicit in the web of concepts used in human and social sciences since the late sixties.

It is not possible, for example, to use in Arabic the expression "problem of God," associating God and *mushkil* (problem); God cannot be considered as problematic. He is well-known, well-presented in the Qur'an; man has only to meditate, internalize, and worship what God revealed of Himself in His own words. The classical discussion of the attributes has not been accepted by all schools; and finally the attributes are recited as the most beautiful names of God

(*asma' Allah al-husna*) but are neglected as subjects of intellectual inquiry.

This means that all the cultures and systems of thought related to pagan, polytheistic, *jahili* (pre-Islamic), or modern secularized societies are maintained in the domain of the *unthinkable* and, consequently, remain *unthought* in the domain of "orthodox" Islamic thought or the *thinkable*. In European societies since the 16th century, the historical role that the study of classical antiquity played in initiating the modern ideas of free thinking and free examination of reality is significant; based on this link we can understand the intellectual gap between Muslim orthodoxy and Western secularized thought (see Marc Augé, *Génie du paganisme* [*The Genius of Paganism*], Paris, France: Gallimard, 1982).

Tradition, orthodoxy, myth, authority, and historicity do not yet have relevant conceptualizations in Arabic. Myth is translated as *ustura* [plural: *asatir*], which is totally misleading because the Qur'an uses the word for the false tales and images related in "the fables of the ancient people," and these *asatir* are opposed to the truthful stories (*qasas haqq* or *ahsan al-qasas*) told by God in the Qur'an. The concept of myth as it is used in contemporary anthropology is related more to *qasas* than to *ustura*, but even anthropology has not yet clarified the difference between myth and mythology, mystification and mythologization, as well as the semantic relationship between myth and symbol and the role of the metaphor in mythical and symbolic discourse.

We still approach these concepts and use them with a rationalist positivist system of definitions, as the Qur'an did with *asatir al-awwalin* (pre-Islamic mythology of the ancient people). However, the Qur'an created a symbolic alternative to the competing mythical and symbolic constructions of the ancient cultures in the Middle East. Our positivist rationalism criticizes symbols and myths and proposes, as an alternative, scientific conceptualism. We have neither a theory of symbol nor a clear conception of the metaphor to read, with a totalizing perspective, the religious texts. Religious tradition is one of the major problems we should *rethink* today. First, religions are mythical, symbolic, ritualistic ways of being, thinking, and knowing. They were conceived in and addressed to societies still dominated by *oral* and not written cultures. Scriptural religions based on a revealed Book contributed to a decisive change with far-reaching effects on the nature and functions of religion itself. Christianity and Islam (more than Judaism, until the creation of the Israeli state) became official ideologies used by a centralizing state which created written historiography and archives.

There is no possibility today of *rethinking* any religious tradition without making a careful distinction between the mythical dimension linked to oral cultures and the official ideological functions of the religion. We shall come back to this point because it is a permanent way of thinking that religion revealed and that social, cultural, and political activity maintained.

Tradition and *orthodoxy* are also unthought, unelaborated concepts in Islamic traditional thought. Tradition is reduced to a collection of "authentic" texts recognized in each community: Shi'i, Sunni, and Khariji. If we add to the Qur'an and *hadith* [traditions of the Prophet], the methodology used to derive the *shari'a* [Islamic law] and the *corpus juris* [body of law] in the various schools, we have other subdivisions of the three axes of Islamic tradition. I tried to introduce the concept of an *exhaustive tradition* worked up by a critical, modern confrontation of all the collections used by the communities, regardless of the "orthodox" limits traced by the classical authorities ([Muhammad ibn Isma'il] Bukhari [810–870] and Muslim [ibn al-Hajjaj, circa 821–875] for the Sunnis; [Abu Ja'far Muhammad] Kulayni [died 940], [Abu Ja'far Muhammad] Ibn Babawayh [923–991], [Muhammad al-Hasan] al-Tusi [995–1067] for the Imamis; ['Abdallah] Ibn 'Ibad [seventh century] and others for the Kharijis). This concept is used by the Islamic revolution in Iran, but more as an ideological tool to accomplish the political unity of the *umma* [community of Muslims]. The historical confrontation of the corpuses, and the theoretical elaboration of a new, coherent science of *Usul al-fiqh* [principles of Islamic jurisprudence] and *Usul al-din* [principles of religion], are still unexplored and necessary tasks.

Beyond the concept of an *exhaustive tradition* based on a new definition of the *usul* [principles], there is the concept of tradition as it is used in anthropology today—the sum of customs, laws, institutions, beliefs, rituals, and cultural values which constitute the identity of each ethno-linguistic group. This level of tradition has been partially integrated by the *shari'a* under the name of *'urf* [custom] or *'amal* [judicial practice] (like *al-'amal al-fasi* in Fas), but it is covered and legitimized by the *Usuli* methodology of the jurists. This aspect of tradition can be expressed in Arabic by *taqalid* [plural of *taqlid*, the imitation of leading religious scholars], but the concept of exhaustive tradition can be expressed by the word *sunna* only if it is re-elaborated in the perspective I mentioned.

Likewise, *orthodoxy* refers to two values. For the believers, it is the authentic expression of the religion as it has been taught by the pious ancestors (*al-salaf al-salih*); the "orthodox" literature describes opposing groups as "sects" (*firaq*). For the historian, orthodoxy refers to the ideological use of religion by the competing groups in the same political space, like the Sunnis who supported the caliphate—legitimized afterwards by the jurists—and who called themselves "the followers of the tradition and the united community" (*ahl al-sunna wa-al-jama'a*). All the other groups were given polemical, disqualifying names like *rawafid* [Shi'is, literally rejectors], *khawarij* [Kharijites, literally withdrawers], and *batiniyya* [Isma'ilis, literally seekers of hidden meanings]. The Imamis called themselves "the followers of infallibility and justice" (*ahl al-'isma wa-al-'adala*), referring to an orthodoxy opposed to that of the Sunnis.

There has been no effort (*ijtihad*) to separate orthodoxy as a militant ideological endeavor, a tool of legitimation for the state and the "values" enforced by this state, from religion as a way proposed to man to discover the Absolute. This is another task for our modern project of *rethinking* Islam, and other religions.

2. Modes of Thinking

I would like to clarify and differentiate between the two modes of thinking that Muslim thinkers adopted at the inception of intellectual modernity in their societies (not only in thought), that is, since the beginning of the *Nahda* [Renaissance] in the 19th century. I do not need to emphasize the well-known trend of *salafi* reformist thought initiated by Jamal al-Din al-Afghani [1838–1897] and Muhammad 'Abduh [1849–1905]. It is what I call the *islahi* way of thinking which has characterized Islamic thought since the death of the Prophet. The principle common to all Muslim thinkers, the *'ulama' mujtahidun* [religious scholars qualified to conduct *ijtihad*], as well as to historians who adopted the theological framework imposed by the division of time into two parts—before/after the *hijra* [the exodus of Muslims from

Mecca to Medina in 622] (like before/after Christ)—
is that all the transcendent divine Truth has been
delivered to mankind by the Revelation and concretely realized by the Prophet through historical
initiatives in Medina. There is, then, a definite model
of perfect historical action for mankind, not only for
Muslims. All groups at any time and in any social
and cultural environment are bound to *go back* to this
model in order to achieve the spirit and the perfection shown by the Prophet, his companions, and the
first generation of Muslims called the pious ancestors (*al-salaf al-salih*).

This vision has been faithfully adopted and assumed by the program of the International Institute
of Islamic Thought (founded in 1981 in Washington, D.C., "for the reform and progress of Islamic
thought"). The publication of the Institute's International Conference in the Islamicization of Knowledge
notes that the "human mind by itself with its limitations cannot comprehend the totality of the matter."
This means that there is an "Islamic framework"
constantly valid, transcendent, authentic, and universal in which all human activities and initiatives ought
to be controlled and correctly integrated. Since the
Islamic framework is part of the "Islamic legacy," one
must always *look back* to the time when the Truth
was formulated and implemented either in the model
set in Medina by the Prophet and the Revelation or
by recognized *'ulama' mujtahidun* who correctly
derived the *shari'a* using the rules of valid *ijtihad*.

This is at the same time a methodology, an epistemology, and a theory of history. It is certainly an
operative intellectual framework used and perpetuated by generations of Muslims since the debate on
authority and power started inside the community
according to patterns of thinking and representing the
world specific to the *islahi* movement. I do not want
to engage in a discussion of the intellectual and scientific relevance of this mental attitude which is now
generalized on a worldwide scale by so-called
Islamic revivalism.

To rethink Islam one must comprehend the socio-
cultural genesis of *islahi* thinking and its impact on
the historical destiny of the societies where this thinking has been or is actually dominant. To assess the
epistemological validity of *islahi* thinking, one has
to start from the radical and initial problems concerning the generative process, the structure and the ideological use of knowledge. By this, I mean any kind
and level of knowledge produced by man living,

acting, and thinking in a given social-historical situation. Radical thinking refers to the biological,
historical, linguistic, semiotic condition shared by
people as natural beings. From this perspective, the
Revelation of Islam is only one attempt, among many
others, to emancipate human beings from the natural limitations of their biological, historical, and linguistic condition. That is why, today, "Islamicizing
knowledge" must be preceded by a radical epistemological critique of knowledge at the deepest level of
its construction as an operative system used by a
group in a given social-historical space. We need
to differentiate ideological discourses produced by
groups for assessing their own identity, power, and
protection, from ideational discourses, which are
controlled along the socio-historical process of their
elaboration in terms of the new critical epistemology.

Given the sociological diffusion today of *islahi*
thinking, I must insist on the characteristics of this
critical epistemology applied not only for thinking Islam, but also, beyond the rich example of
Islamic tradition, for a rationality based on a comparative theory of all cultural traditions and historical experiences.

Any attempt to think an object of knowledge
relies on epistemic postulates, as I have said. The difference between the new emerging rationality and all
inherited rationalities—including Islamic reason—
is that the implicit postulates are made explicit and
used not as undemonstrated certitudes revealed by
God or formed by a transcendental intellect, but as
modest, heuristic trends for research. In this spirit,
here are six fundamental heuristic lines of thinking
to recapitulate Islamic knowledge and to confront
it with contemporary knowledge in the process of
elaboration.

1. Human beings emerge as such in societies
through various changing uses. Each use in the society is converted into a sign of this use, which means
that realities are expressed through languages as systems of signs. Signs are the radical issue for a critical,
controlled knowledge. This issue occurs prior to any
attempt to interpret Revelation. Holy scripture itself
is communicated through natural languages used as
systems of signs, and we know that each sign is a lo-
cus of convergent operations (perception, expression,
interpretation, translation, communication) engaging
all of the relations between language and thought.

Remark 1.1: This line of research is directly opposed to a set of postulates developed and shared by

Islamic thought on the privilege of the Arabic language elected by God to "teach Adam all the names." The ultimate teaching is the Qur'an as revealed in the Arabic language. These postulates command the whole construction of *Usul al-din* and *Usul al-fiqh* as a correct methodology with which to derive from the holy texts the divine laws. The core of Islamic thought is thus represented as a linguistic and semantic issue. (This is true for all religious traditions based on written texts.)

Remark 1.2: This same line is equally opposed to the philological, historicist, positivist postulates imposed by Western thinking since the 16th century. That is why we have made a clear distinction between the modernity (or rationality) of the Classical Age and the heuristic trends of the present rationality (Prefigurative Age). (I refer to my book, *L'Islam hier-demain* [*Islam Yesterday–Tomorrow*], second edition, Paris, France: Buchet-Chastel, 1982.)

2. All semiotic productions of a human being in the process of his social and cultural emergence are subject to historical change which I call historicity. As a semiotic articulation of meaning for social and cultural uses, the Qur'an is subject to historicity. This means that there is no access to the absolute outside the phenomenal world of our terrestrial, historical existence. The various expressions given to the ontology, the first being the truth and the transcendence by theological and metaphysical reason, have neglected historicity as a dimension of the truth. Changing tools, concepts, definitions, and postulates are used to shape the truth.

Remark 2.1: This line is opposed to all medieval thinking based on stable essences and substances. The concept of Revelation should be reworked in the light of semiotic systems subjected to historicity. The Mu'tazili theory of God's created speech deserves special consideration along this new line.

Remark 2.2: The Aristotelian definition of formal logic and abstract categories also needs to be revised in the context of the semiotic theory of meaning and the historicity of reason.

3. There are many levels and forms of reason interacting with levels and forms of imagination as is shown in the tension between *logos* [words subject to debate] and *mythos* [unquestioned words], or symbol and concept, metaphor and reality, or proper meaning, *zahir* [literal external meaning] and *batin* [inner meaning] in Islam.

Recent anthropology has opened up the field of collective social *imaginaire*[4] not considered by traditional historiography and classical theology. Imagination and social *imaginaire* are reconsidered as dynamic faculties of knowledge and action. All the mobilizing ideologies, expressed in a religious or a secular framework, are produced, received, and used by social *imaginaire*, which also is related to imagination. The concept of social *imaginaire* needs more elaboration through many societies and historical examples. In Muslim societies, its role today is as decisive as in the Middle Ages because rationalist culture has less impact and presence there than in Western societies, which, nevertheless, also have their own *imaginaire* competing with various levels and forms of rationality.

4. Discourse as an ideological articulation of realities as they are perceived and used by different competing groups occurs *prior* to the faith. Faith is shaped, expressed, and actualized in and through discourse. Conversely, faith, after it has taken shape and roots through religious, political, or scientific discourse, imposes its own direction and postulates to subsequent discourses and behaviors (individual and collective).

Remark 4.1: The concept or notion of faith given by God and the classical theories of free will, grace, and predestination need to be re-elaborated within the concrete context of discourses through which any system of beliefs is expressed and assimilated. Faith is the crystallization of images, representations, and ideas commonly shared by each group engaged in the same historical experience. It is more than the personal relation to religious beliefs; but it claims a spiritual or a metaphysical dimension to give a transcendental significance to the political, social, ethical and aesthetic values to which refers each individual inside each unified social group, or community.

5. The traditional system of legitimization, represented by *Usul al-din* and *Usul al-fiqh*, no longer has epistemological relevance. The new system is not yet established in a unanimously approved form inside the *umma*. But is it possible today, given the principles of critical epistemology, to propose a system of knowledge or science *particular* to Islamic

---

4. I prefer to use the French word for this important concept because it has no exact correspondent in English. See C. Castoriadis, *L'Institution imaginaire de la société* [*The Imaginary Institution of Society*] (Paris: Seuil, 1977).

thought? What are the theoretical conditions of a modern theology not only for political institutions, but also for universal knowledge, in the three revealed religions? We are in a crisis of legitimacy; that is why we can speak only of heuristic ways of thinking.

Remark 5.1: This line is opposed to the dogmatic assurance of theology based on the *unquestionable* legitimacy of the *shari'a* derived from Revelation or the classical ontology of the first Being, the neo-Platonic One, the Origin from which the Intellect derives and to which it desires to return. That is why the problem of the state and civil society is crucial today. Why should an individual obey the state? How is the legitimacy of power monopolized by a group over all other established groups?

6. The search for ultimate meaning depends on the radical question concerning the relevance and existence of an ultimate meaning. We have no right to reject the possibility of its existence. What is questionable is how to base all our thoughts on the postulate of its existence. Again, we encounter the true responsibility of the critical reason: To reach a better understanding of the relationship between meaning and reality, we must, first, improve our intellectual equipment—vocabulary, methods, strategies, procedures, definitions, and horizons of inquiry.

To illustrate all these theoretical perspectives, let us give an example from classical Islamic thought. Ghazzali (died 505 A.H./1111 A.D.) and [Abu'l-Walid Muhammad] Ibn Rushd (died 595 A.H./1198 A.D.) developed an interesting attempt to *think* Islam in their historical context. We do not need an exhaustive analysis of their discussion. The most relevant to our project is to be found in *Faysal al-tafriqa bayn al-Islam wa-al-zandaqa [The Decisive Criterion for Distinguishing between Islam and Unbelief]* by Ghazzali and *Fasl al-Maqal [On the Harmony of Religion and Philosophy]* written as an answer by Ibn Rushd. Ghazzali declared the *falasifa* infidels on three bases: They deny the resurrection of the body; they deny the knowledge of particulars (*juzi'yyat*) by God; and they claim that God is anterior ontologically, not chronologically, to the world. These three theses are matters of belief, not demonstrative knowledge. The *falasifa* have been wrong in trying to transfer to demonstrative knowledge matters which, in fact, depend on belief. Ibn Rushd used the methodology of *Usul al-fiqh* to solve a philosophical question; even the formulation of the problem, at the beginning of the *Fasl*, is typically juridical.

This does not mean that Ghazzali chose the right way to tackle the question. Actually, the most significant teaching for us is to identify, through the discussion, the epistemic limits and the epistemological obstacles of Islamic thought as it has been used by its two illustrious representatives. The new task here is not to describe the arguments (see G. H. Hourani, editor and translator of *Fasl*), but to *think* the consequences of the epistemic and epistemological discontinuities between classical Islamic thought (all included in medieval thought) and modern thought (Classical Age, from the 15th to the 20th century, up to the 1950s; Prefigurative Age of a new thought, since the 1950s). Before we move ahead in the search for an unfettered way of *thinking* Islam today, it is worth noting some theories on the medieval system of intelligibility as it is shown in Ghazzali and Ibn Rushd's discussion.

1. Both thinkers accept the cognitive priority of revealed truth in the Qur'an. Reason has to be submitted totally to this clearly formulated truth (Ghazzali) or to be elaborated as a coherent articulation of the truth established through demonstrative knowledge (in the conceptual and logical framework of Aristotelian methodology and philosophy) and the revealed truth. This last contention is served by intermingling or interweaving juridical and philosophical methodologies.

2. Both mix at different degrees but with a common psychology commanded by beliefs between religious convictions and legal norms on one side (*ahkam*, explicated by the science of *Usul al-din* and *Usul al-fiqh*) and philosophical methodology and representations on the other side. Left to themselves, the milk-sisters (*shar'* [religious law] and *hikma* [wisdom]) are "companions by nature and friends by essence and instinct" (*Fasl*, p. 26).

3. Both ignore the decisive dimension of historicity to which even the revealed message is subjected. Historicity is the unthinkable and the unthought in medieval thought. It will be the conquest—not yet everywhere complete—of intellectual modernity.[5]

4. Historiography (*tarikh*) has been practiced in Islamic thought as a collection of information, events, biographies (*tarajim, siyar*), genealogies (*nasab*), knowledge of countries (*buldan*), and

---

5. See my *Tarikhiyyat al-fikr al-'arabi al-Islami [Historicity of Arab Islamic Thought]* (Beirut, Lebanon: Dar al-Inma' al-'Arabi, 1985).

various other subjects. This collection of facts is related to a chronology representing time as *stable*, without a dynamic movement of change and progress. No link is established between time as a historical dynamic process (historicity) and the elements of knowledge collected by his toriography. Ibn Khaldun [Tunisian historian, 1332–1406] can be cited as the exception who introduced the concept of society as an object of knowledge and thought,[6] but even he could not think of religion, society, history, or philosophy as related levels and ways to achieve an improved intelligibility. On the contrary, he contributed to eliminating philosophy and to isolating the Ash'ari vision of Islam from history as a global evolution of societies influenced by various theological expressions of Islam.

5. In the case of Islamic thought, the triumph of two major official orthodoxies with the Sunnis (since the fifth century A.H.) and the Shi'a (first with the Fatimids and second with the Safavids in Iran) imposed a mode of thinking narrower than those illustrated in the classical period (first to fifth century A.H.). Contemporary Islamic thought is under the influence of categories, themes, beliefs, and procedures of reasoning developed during the scholastic age (seventh to eight century A.H.) more than it is open to the pluralism which characterized classical thought.

6. The historical evolution and intellectual structure of Islamic thought create the necessity of starting with a critique of Islamic reason (theological, legal, historiographical) as well as of philosophical reason as it has been understood and used through Aristotelian, Platonic, and Plotinist traditions (or legacies).

We shall not do this here.[7] We have to think more clearly about new conditions and ways to *think* Islam today.

Intellectual modernity started with Renaissance and Reform movements in 16th-century Europe. The study of pagan antiquity and the demand for freedom to read the Bible without the mediation of priests (or "managers of the sacred," as they are sometimes called) changed the conditions of intellectual activities. Later, scientific discoveries, political revolutions, secularized knowledge, and historically criticized knowledge (historicism practiced as philosophies of history) changed more radically the whole intellectual structure of thought for the generations involved in the Industrial Revolution with its continuous consequences.

This evolution was achieved in Europe without any participation of Islamic thought or Muslim societies dominated, on the contrary, by a rigid, narrow conservatism. This is why Muslims do not feel concerned by the secularized culture and thought produced since the 16th century. It is legitimate, in this historical process leading to intellectual modernity, to differentiate between the ideological aspects limited to the conjunctural situations of Western societies and the anthropological structures of knowledge discovered through scientific research. Islamic thought has to reject or criticize the former and to apply the latter in its own contexts.

We cannot, for example, accept the concept of secularization or *laïcité* as it has been historically elaborated and used in Western societies. There is a political and social dimension of this concept represented by the struggle for power and the tools of legitimization between the church and the bourgeoisie. The intellectual implications of the issue concern the possibility—political and cultural—of separating education, learning, and research from any control by the state as well as by the church. This possibility remains problematical everywhere.

Similarly, we cannot interpret religion merely as positivist historicism and secularism did in the 19th century. Religion is addressed not only to miserable, uncultivated, primitive people who have not yet received the light of rational knowledge; human and social sciences, since 1950–60, have changed the ways of thinking and knowing by introducing a pluralist changing concept of rationality, according to which religion is interpreted in a wider perspective of knowledge and existence.

The project of *thinking* Islam is basically a response to two major needs: (1) the particular need of Muslim societies to think, for the first time, about their own problems which had been made unthinkable by the triumph of orthodox scholastic thought; and (2) the need of contemporary thought in gen-

6. Miskawayh [932–1030] did this before in his philosophical and historiographical works. See my *Humanisme arabe au IVe/Xe siècle* [*Arab Humanism in the Fourth Century* A.H./Tenth Century A.D.], second edition (Paris: Vrin, 1982).

7. See my essays in *Critique de la raison Islamique* [*Critique of Islamic Reason*] (Paris: [G. P. Maisonneuve et Larose], 1984); and *L'Islam: Morale et politique* [*Islam: Morals and Politics*] (Paris: UNESCO-Desclée de Brouwer, 1986).

eral to open new fields and discover new horizons of knowledge, through a systematic cross cultural approach to the fundamental problems of human existence. These problems are raised and answered in their own ways by the traditional religions.

3. From the Unthinkable to the Thinkable

Islam is presented and lived as a definite system of beliefs and non-beliefs which cannot be submitted to any critical inquiry. Thus, it divides the space of thinking into two parts: the unthinkable and the thinkable. Both concepts are historical and not, at first, philosophical. The respective domain of each of them changes through history and varies from one social group to another. Before the systemization by Shafi'i of the concept of *sunna* and the *Usuli* use of it, many aspects of Islamic thought were still thinkable. They became unthinkable after the triumph of Shafi'i's theory and also the elaboration of authentic "collections," as mentioned earlier. Similarly, the problems related to the historical process of collecting the Qur'an in an official *mushaf* [complete text of the Qur'an] became more and more unthinkable under the official pressure of the caliphate because the Qur'an has been used since the beginning of the Islamic state to legitimize political power and to unify the *umma*. The last official decision closing any discussion of the readings of the received orthodox *mushaf* was made by the *qadi* [judge] [Ahmad ibn Musa] Ibn Mujahid after the trial of [Abu'l-Hasan Muhammad] Ibn Shanabudh (fourth century A.H./ tenth century A.D.).

We can add a third significant example to show how a thinkable is transformed into an unthinkable by the ideological decision of the leading politico-religious group. The Mu'tazila endeavored by their *ijtihad* to make thinkable the decisive question of God's created speech, but in the fifth century A.H. the caliph al-Qadir [bi-'llah, 947–1031] made this question unthinkable by imposing, in his famous *'Aqida* [Creed], the dogma of the uncreated Qur'an as the "orthodox" belief (see G. Makdisi, *Ibn 'Aqil et la resurgence de l'Islam traditionaliste au XIe siècle* [*Ibn 'Aqil and the Resurgence of Traditionalist Islam in the Eleventh Century*], Damascus, Syria, 1963).

As we have said, the unthinkable or the not yet thought (*l'impensé*) in Islamic thought has been enlarged since intellectual modernity was elaborated in the West. All the theories developed by sociology and anthropology on religion are still unknown, or rejected as irrelevant, by contemporary Islamic thought without any intellectual argument or scientific consideration.

It is true that traditional religions play decisive roles in our secularized, modernized societies. We even see secular religions emerging in industrialized societies, like fascism in Germany and Italy, Stalinism and Maoism in the communist world, and many new sects in liberal democracies. If we look at the revealed religions through the parameters set by recent secular religions, we are obliged to introduce new criteria to define religion as a universal phenomenon. To the traditional view of religion as totally revealed, created, and given by God, we cannot simply substitute the sociological theory of religion generated by a sociohistorical process according to the cultural values and representations available in each group, community, or society. We must rethink the whole question of the nature and the functions of religion through the traditional theory of divine origin and the modern secular explanation of religion as a social historical production.

This means, in the case of Islam, rewriting the whole history of Islam as a revealed religion and as an active factor, among others, in the historical evolution of societies where it has been or still is received as a religion. Orientalist scholars have already started this study, inquiring even into the social and cultural conditions of the *jahiliya* period in which Islam emerged; but I do not know any Orientalist who has raised the epistemological problems implicit in this historicist approach. No single intellectual effort is devoted to considering the consequences of historicist presentations of the origins and functions of a religion *given* and *received* as being *revealed*.[8]

We need to create an intellectual and cultural framework in which all historical, sociological, anthropological, and psychological presentations of

---

8. *Given* and *received* are technical terms in linguistic and literary analyses. Islam is given as revealed in the grammatical structure of Qur'anic discourse, and it is received as such by the psychological consciousness generated by this discourse and the ritual performances prescribed by it. For more thorough elaboration of this approach, I refer to my essay, *The Concept of Revelation: From Ahl al-Kitab to the Societies of the Book* ([Claremont, Calif.:] The Claremont Graduate School, 1987).

revealed religions could be integrated into a system of thought and evolving knowledge. We cannot abandon the problem of revelation as irrelevant to human and social studies and let it be monopolized by theological speculation. One has to ask, then, why sociology and anthropology have been interested in the question of the sacred and in ritual, but not in revelation. Why, conversely, has theology considered revelation, but not so much the sacred and the secular, until it has been influenced by anthropology and social sciences?

To move a step further in these complex interrelated difficulties and theories, let us try to work out the concept of the "Societies of the Book" (*Sociétés du Livre*).

4. The Societies of the Book

I introduce this concept as a historical category to deepen the analysis of the revealed religions. I emphasize first the significant fact that the three revealed religions have not yet been studied comparatively as we have suggested above. Instead, there is an ancient polemical literature. A descriptive literature, especially on Islam and Christianity, is being developed in line with the Islamic-Christian dialogue. but the theological postulates received in each tradition are still dominating the analyses of the revealed religions.

Scholarship has not yet contributed to changing the intellectual approach in this field of research and reflection. Departments of history of religion or of comparative religions devote a larger place to Judaism and Christianity than to Islam. There are many departments in very famous universities, like Princeton or the Sorbonne, where no chair exists for teaching Islam, and I know that these departments do not even utilize the existing departments of Near Eastern studies or languages because they have different scientific concerns. The books written by Orientalists on Islam are limited and irrelevant. They do not show any comparative curiosity or epistemological critique beyond the traditional theological definitions of the different schools.[9]

This is why the problem of revelation is one of the key topics, but it has been neglected by modern scholarship despite its fundamental role in the historical genesis of societies where Judaic, Christian, and Islamic expressions are found.

I call Societies of the Book those that have been shaped since the Middle Ages by the Book as a religious and a cultural phenomenon. The Book has two meanings in this perspective. The Heavenly Book preserved by God and containing the entire word of God is called *Umm al-Kitab* [Mother of the Book] in the Qur'an. Geo Widengren [born 1907] has demonstrated the very ancient origin of this conception in Near East religious history (see his *Muhammad, The Apostle of God and the Heavenly Book*, Uppsala, 1955). The importance of this belief for our purpose is that it refers to the verticality which has constituted the religious *imaginaire* in the Near East. Truth is located in Heaven with God, who reveals it in time and through the medium He chooses: the prophets, Himself incarnated in the "Son" who lived among people, the Book transmitted by the messenger Muhammad. There are different *modalities* for the delivery of parts (not the whole) of the Heavenly Book, but the Word of God as God Himself is the same from the point of view of the anthropological structures of religious *imaginaire*.

The modalities for the delivery of parts of the Heavenly Book have been interpreted by each community, raised and guided by a prophet, as the absolute expression of God Himself. The cultural, linguistic, and social aspects of these modalities were unthinkable in the mythical framework of knowledge particular to people who received the "revelations." When theologians came to systematize in conceptual, demonstrative ways the relations between the Word of God (*Umm al-Kitab*) and its manifested forms in Hebrew, Aramaic, and Arabic, they used either literalist exegesis of the scripture itself or rational categories and procedures influenced by Greek philosophy. Grammar and logic have been used as two different ways to reach and to deliver the meaning of the manifested revelation in relation to the grammatical and logical "reading," but they did not

9. The comparative approach, attempted by L. Gardet and G. Anawati in their *Introduction à la théologie musulmane*

[*Introduction to Islamic Theology*] [Paris: I. Vrin, 1948], is commanded by the postulates of Thomist theology. W. C. Smith has tried to open the field, including the case of Islam. See the recent book by Hans Küng, J. Van Ess, H. Von Stietencron, and H. Bechert, *Le Christianisme et les religions du monde, Islam, Hindouisme, Bouddhisme* [*Christianity and the Religions of the World. Islam, Hinduism, Buddhism*], translated from German by Joseph Feisthauer (Paris: Seuil, 1986).

lead to a radical critique of the postulates used in the different exegeses developed in the Middle Ages. This issue needs to be rethought today in light of the new knowledge of language, mind, logic, and history, which means that all the ancient exegesis has to be reworked, too. We are obliged today to consider differently the second meaning of the concept of Book in our expression "Societies of the Book." The Mu'tazila touched on this point in their theory of God's created speech. The *Mushaf*, as well as the Bible, are the manifested, *incarnated* word of God in human languages, transmitted orally by human voices, or fixed in written material. One has to answer here to a Christian objection on the specificity of Christian revelation made through Jesus as the incarnated God, not through human mediators. As I said, this is a difference in modality, not in the relation between the Heavenly Book and its terrestrial manifestations through religious *imaginaire*. Theological theorization transformed into substantial transcendental truths revealed by God what, in fact, had been historical, social, and cultural events and manifestations. The delivery of the Word of God by Jesus in a given society and period of history, using the Aramaic language, is a historical event just like the delivery of the Qur'an by Muhammad. That Jesus is presented as the "Son of God" and the Qur'an a speech worded by God Himself are theological definitions used in systems of beliefs and non-beliefs particular to Christian and Islamic dogma. These definitions do not change the linguistic and historical fact that the messages of Jesus, Muhammad, (and, of course, the prophets of Israel) are transmitted in human languages and collected in an "orthodox" closed corpus (Bible, Gospels, and Qur'an) in concrete historical conditions. Then, the Heavenly Book is accessible to the believers *only* through the *written* version of the books or scriptures adopted by the three communities. This second aspect of the Book is then submitted to all the constraints of arbitrary historicity. The books or scriptures are read and interpreted by the historical communities in concrete, changing, social, political, and cultural situations.

The societies where the Book—or Holy Scriptures —is used as the revelation of the divine will developed a global vision of the world, history, meaning, and human destiny by the use of hermeneutic procedures. All juridical, ethical, political, and intellectual norms had to be derived from the textual forms of the revelation. The Torah, Canon Law, and the *shari'a*

have been elaborated on the basis of the same vision of revealed Truth and "rational" procedures from which norms have been derived. There is a common conception of human destiny commanded by the eschatological perspective (the search for salvation by obedience to God's will) and guided in this world by the norms of the law.

The new dimension which I aim to explain by the concept of the Societies of the Book is the process of *historicization* of a divine category: Revelation. The believers in the three religions claim, even in the context of our secularized culture, that divine law derived from Revelation is not subject to historicity. It cannot be changed by any human legislation and it is a totally *rationalized* law. Scientific knowledge cannot demonstrate that this belief is based on a wrong assumption, but it can explain how it is possible psychologically to maintain the affirmation of a revealed law in the form presented in the Torah, Canon Law, and the *shari'a*, against the evidence of its historicity.

Traditional theological thought has not used the concept of social *imaginaire* and the related notions of myth, symbol, sign, or metaphor in the new meanings already mentioned. It refers constantly to *reason* as the faculty of true knowledge, differentiated from knowledge based on the representations of the imagination. The methodology elaborated and used by jurists-theologians shares with the Aristotelian tradition the same postulate of rationality as founding the true knowledge and excluding the constructions of the imagination. In fact, an analysis of the discourse produced by both trends of thinking—the theological and the philosophical—reveals a simultaneous use of reason and imagination. Beliefs and convictions are often used as "arguments" to "demonstrate" propositions of knowledge. In this stage of thinking, metaphor is understood and used as a rhetorical device to add an aesthetic emotion to the *real* content of the words; it was not perceived in its creative force as a semantic innovation or in its power to shift the discourse to a global metaphorical organization requiring the full participation of a coherent imagination. The philosophers, however, recognized the power that imagination as a faculty of privileged knowledge bestowed on the Prophet especially. [Abu 'Ali al-Husayn] Ibn Sina [980–1037] and [Abu Bakr Muhammad] Ibn Tufayl [died 1185] used this faculty in each of their accounts of *Hayy ibn Yaqzan* [character in a philosophical allegory], but this did not create a trend comparable to the logocentrism of the jurists, the theologians, and the *falasifa* who favored Aristotelianism.

This lack of attention to the imagination did not prevent the general activity of social *imaginaire*—the collective representations of the realities according to the system of beliefs and non-beliefs introduced by revelation in the Societies of the Book. The social *imaginaire* is partially elaborated and controlled by the *'ulama'* with their *'Aqa'id* [Creeds] (like the one written by Ibn Batta [917–997], French translation by H. Laoust, *La profession de foi d'Ibn Batta* [*The Profession of Faith of Ibn Batta*], Damascus, Syria [Institut français de Damas], 1958); but it is structured as well by beliefs and representations taken from the cultures preceding Islam. In all Islamic societies, there are two levels of traditions—the deepest archaic level going back to the *jahiliya* of each society and the more recent level represented by Islamic beliefs, norms, and practices as they have been developed since the foundation of the Muslim state. The revealed Book assumed a great importance because it provided a strategy of integration for all norms, beliefs, and practices proper to each social group. This means that the social *imaginaire* is generated by the interacting layers of traditions, so that it is not correct from an anthropological point of view to describe the Societies of the Book as if they were produced exclusively by the Book used as their constitution. The revealed Book had an influence on all cultural activities and political institutions to some extent. It generated a civilization of written culture opposed to, or differentiated from, the oral civilization.

The key to the Societies of the Book is thus the intensive dialectic developed everywhere between two strongly competitive forces: On the one hand, there is the state using the phenomenon of the Book in its two dimensions—the transcendent, divine, ontological message and the written literature and culture derived from it. This comprises the official culture produced and used under the ideological supervision of the state, that is, the orthodox religion defined and enforced by doctors of law (jurists-theologians). On the other hand, there are the non-integrated, resisting groups using oral, non-official culture and keeping alive non-orthodox beliefs (called heresies and condemned by the official *'ulama'*). The struggle between the reformed church and the Catholic church in the 16th century is a typical example of this competition. In Islam, we have many examples in history from the first century to the contemporary revivalist movements. The segmentary groups perpetuating oral cultures and traditions and adhering to archaic beliefs under the name of Islam, have resisted to their integration into the Muslim state. This is why the *'ulama'*—ancient and contemporary—regularly condemned the "superstitions" and "heresies" of these groups, as long as they resisted the norms of the Societies of the Book.

This model is more than a contemplative *Weltanschauung*; it is and remains an active paradigm of historical action with which the Societies of the Book generated their structure and destiny. Religions are superior to any scientific theory because they give imaginative solutions to permanent issues in human life, and they mobilize the social *imaginaire* with beliefs, mythical explanations, and rites. (For more explanations, see my *Lectures du Coran.*)

5. Strategies for Deconstruction

Thus far, we have presented elements and forces acting in the Societies of the Book. This is not sufficient for thinking in new ways about the opposition between Societies of the Book and secularized societies. Thinking about this opposition is thinking from a new perspective about human destiny with two major historical results. The Societies of the Book, as well as the secularized societies, have shown the intellectual limits and the empirical failures of their respective paradigms for historical action.

Thinking about our new historical situation is a positive enterprise. We are not aiming for a negative critique of the previous attempts at the emancipation of human existence as much as we wish to propose relevant answers to pending and pressing questions. This is why we prefer to speak about a strategy for deconstruction. We need to deconstruct the social *imaginaire* structured over centuries by the phenomenon of the Book as well as the secularizing forces of the material civilization[10] since the 17th century.

We speak of one social *imaginaire* because secularization has not totally eliminated from any society all the elements, principles, and postulates organizing the social *imaginaire* in the Societies of the Book.

10. I use this expression according to its historical elaboration by F[ernand] Braudel [1902–1985].

This is, I know, a controversial point among historians. Karl Lowith (*Meaning in History*, 1968) has shown that so-called modern ideas are just the secularized reshaping and re-expressing of medieval Christian ideas. More recently, Regis Debray (*Critique de la raison politique* [*Critique of Political Reason*], Paris: Gallimard, 1981) underlined the Christian origins of the present socialist utopia.

Hans Blumenberg tried to refute these positions in his dissertation on *The Legitimacy of the Modern Age* (Cambridge, Mass.: MIT Press, 1983). He showed how modernity is an alternative to Christian medieval conceptions. According to him, the modern idea of progress is the product of an imminent process of development rather than a messianic one. Long-term scientific progress guided by pluralist method and experimentation, continuity of *problems* rather than *solutions*, and history as a positive whole process cut from the transcendent God, are characteristics of the modern age. Should one, then, accept the definition of secularization as a long-term process through which religious ties, attitudes toward transcendence, the expectation of an afterlife, ritual performances, firmly established forms of speech, a typical structure of the individual *imaginaire*, specific articulation and use of reason and imagination, become a private concern separated from public life? One could add the triumph of *pragmatism*, which gives priority to action over contemplation, verification over truth, method over system, logic over rhetoric, future over past, and becoming over being.

Along this line of thinking, secularization is usually presented as one of the following: a decaying of the former capacity for receiving divine inspiration and guidance; a cultural and political program of emancipation from theological thinking and ecclesiastical dominance; the domination of nature to increase the powers of man; or the substitution of a public system of education for the private one. This is known in France as *laïcité*, which often has been expressed as a militant attitude against the religious vision of the world, as we saw during 1982–1983 when the socialist government wanted to "unify" the national educational system (see Guy Gautier, *La laïcité en miroir* [*Secularism in the Mirror*], Paris: Grasset, 1985).

Whatever the relevance of these observations to the long-term process of change undertaken first in Western societies and extended more and more to the rest of the world, two remarks are in order. First, references to traditional religions—especially the three revealed religions—are frequent and even dominating everywhere. Second, secular "religions," like fascism, Stalinism, and Maoism, are produced by contemporary societies and govern the social *imaginaire* with their so-called values, norms, aims, beliefs, and representations. Secularism appears, then, as a change of methods, styles, procedures, and forms of expression in human existence; but it does not affect the ultimate force structuring and generating the human condition through the existential and historical process.

How can we obtain a clear vision of this force and describe it? Religions have mobilized it, shaped it, and formulated it by using various cultural systems, myths, rites, beliefs, and institutions. Modern ideologies do the same by using secularized languages and collective organizations. What is the common unifying reality of all these religious and ideological constructions? To answer this question we must avoid the usual opposition between the "true" religious teaching and the "false" secularist conceptions. We will be better able to discover the reality if we deconstruct methodically all the manifested cultural constructions in the various societies. Returning to the Societies of the Book, we can show a deep, common mechanism described by Marcel Gauchet (*Le désenchantement du monde* [*The Disenchantment of the World*], Paris: Gallimard, 1985) as "the debt of meaning."

All known societies are built on an *order*, a hierarchy of values and powers maintained and enforced by a political power. On what conditions is a political power accepted and obeyed by the members of the society? How is it legitimized? There is no possible legitimation of any exercised power without an authority spontaneously internalized by each individual as an ultimate reference to the absolute truth. In traditional societies, authority is the privilege of a charismatic leader able to mediate the meaning located in an extra- or super-worldliness, meaning possessed by a god (or gods), and this leader delivers it in various ways to human beings. Thus, this process creates a recognition of *debt* in each individual consciousness and, consequently, an adherence to all the commandments of the leader.

The example of Islam gives a clear illustration of this general mechanism, one which is at the same time psychological, social, political, and cultural. A very small group of believers followed Muhammad, a charismatic leader related to the known paradigm of prophets and messengers of God in the history of salvation common to the "People of the Book." Muhammad, supported and inspired by God, had the ability to create a new relationship to the divine through two simultaneous and interacting initiatives as all charismatic leaders do with different levels of success and innovation. He announced the absolute truth in an unusual Arabic form of expression, and he engaged the group in successive, concrete experiences of social, political, and institutional change. The Revelation translated into a sublime, symbolic, and transcendental language the daily public life of the group whose identity and *imaginaire* were separated from the hostile, non-converted groups (called infidels, hypocrites, enemies of God, errants, and bedouins). We can follow in the Qur'an the growth of a new collective social-cultural *imaginaire* nourished by new systems of connotation whose semantic substance was not primarily an abstract vision of an idealistic dreaming mind but the historic crystallization of events shared at the time by all the members of the group.

The "debt of meaning" incurred in such conditions is the most constraining for the individuals who are the actors of their own destiny. The relation to the source of authority is not separated from obedience to the political power exercised in the name of this authority. But already, in this first stage of setting up and internalizing the debt of meaning, we must pay special attention to a structural process not yet deconstructed by historians and anthropologists.

When we write the history of these twenty years (612–632) during which Muhammad created a new community, we mention the principal events in a narrative style. We neglect to point out the use made of these events by later generations of believers. In other words, how does the "debt of meaning" historically operate on the collective *imaginaire* to produce the concrete destiny of each group in each society? There is, in fact, a double line to follow in writing the history of societies commanded by an initial "debt of meaning" incurred in the Inaugural Age. The first is to index, describe, and articulate all the significant events and facts that occurred in each period; the second is to analyze the mental representations of these events, facts, and actions shaping the collective *imaginaire* which becomes the moving force of history. This study of psychological discussions of history is more explanatory than the positivist narration of "objective" history. It shows the powerful capacity of imagination to create symbolic figures and paradigms of meaning from very ordinary events and persons, at the first stage, then the transformation of these symbols into collective representations structuring the social *imaginaire*.

Thus, the idealized figures of Muhammad, 'Ali [son-in-law of the Prophet, circa 596–661], Husayn [son of 'Ali, 626–680], and other *imam*s have been constructed to enlighten and legitimize the historical development of the community. The biographies (*sira*) of Muhammad and 'Ali, as they have been fixed in the Sunni and Shi'i traditions, are the typical production of the same social *imaginaire* influenced by a highly elaborated mythical vision provided by the Qur'an. The whole Qur'anic discourse is already a perfect sublimation of the concrete history produced by the small group of "believers" in Mecca and Medina.

The point I want to make here is that historians of Islam, so far, have not considered the question of the *imaginaire* as an important historical field. I have mentioned this concept several times because it is unavoidable when we want to relate political, social, and cultural events to their psychological origins and impacts. The narrative history suggests that all the events are understandable according to a "rational" system of knowledge. No one historian raises the question: How does one rationalize, for example, the history of Salvation as it is proposed by the Holy Scriptures—Bible, Gospels, and Qur'an–and as it is received, integrated, and used by the individual and the collective *imaginaire*? There is no possibility to interpret the whole literature derived from those Scriptures without taking into account the representations of Salvation perpetuated in the behaviors and the thinking activity of all believers, so that all history produced in the Societies of the Book is legitimized and assimilated by the *imaginaire* of Salvation, not by any "rational" construction. The theological and juridical systems elaborated by so-called "reason" are also related to the *imaginaire* of Salvation.

The writing and the understanding of the so-called "Islamic" history would change totally if we accept to open the field of research on social *imaginaire*, and the anthropological structures of this *imaginaire* as we can describe it, for example, through *Ihya 'ulum al-din* of Ghazzali, the literature of Qur'an exegesis, the present discourse of Islamist movements (I refer to my essay, "L'Islam dans l'histoire" [Islam in History], in *Maghreb-Mashreq*, number 102, 1985).

6. Revelation and History

The strategy of deconstruction leads to the ultimate decisive confrontation in the Societies of the Book. When we discover the function of social *imaginaire* as producing the history of the group, we cannot maintain the theory of revelation as it has been elaborated previously, that is, as images produced by the complex phenomenon of prophetic intervention.

The Qur'an insists on the necessity of man to listen. to be aware, to reflect, to penetrate, to understand, and to meditate. All these verbs refer to intellectual activities leading to a kind of rationalization based on existential paradigms revealed with the history of salvation. Medieval thought derived from this an essentialist, substantialist, and unchangeable concept of rationality guaranteed by a divine intellect. Modern knowledge, on the contrary, is based on the concept of social-historical space continuously constructed and deconstructed by the activities of the social actors. Each group fights to impose its hegemony over the others not only through political power (control of the state) but also through a cultural system presented as the universal one. Seen from this perspective, the Qur'an is the expression of the historical process which led the small group of believers to power. This process is social, political, cultural, and psychological. Through it, the Qur'an, presented as the revelation and received as such by the individual and the collective memory, is continuously reproduced, rewritten, reread, and re-expressed in a changing social-historical space.

History is the actual incarnation of the revelation as it is interpreted by the *'ulama'* and preserved in the collective memory. Revelation maintains the possibility of giving a "transcendent" legitimization to the social order and the historical process accepted by the group. But this possibility can be maintained only as long as the cognitive system, based on social *imaginaire*, is not replaced by a new, more plausible rationality linked to a different organization of the social-historical space. This is one reason for the known opposition between *falasifa* and *mutakallimun*, or *fuqaha'* [religious jurisprudents].

The struggle between the inherited thinkable and the not yet thought has become more intense in Muslim societies since the violent introduction of intellectual modernity; but, as we have seen, the same struggle between the paradigms of knowledge and action started in Western societies in the 16th century. The result has been the inversion of the priorities fixed by the revelation. Economic life and thought had been submitted to ethical-religious principles until the triumph of the capitalist system of production and exchange, which replaced the symbolic exchanges practiced in traditional societies with the rule of profit.

Within this new value system, ethical thinking has less relevance than the technical regulations of the market and the efficient control of productive forces. Democracy limits the source of authority to the acquiescence expressed in different circumstances of various professional or political groups. There is no longer any reference to the transcendental origin of authority. The question of revelation is thus eliminated; it is neither solved intellectually nor maintained as a plausible truth according to the pragmatic reason prevailing in so-called modern thought. All relations are based on the respective power of nations, groups, and individuals; ethical principles, founded on metaphysical or religious visions, lose their appeal. I do not mean that we have to go back to the "revealed" truth according to *islahi* thinking. I am stressing a major difficulty of our time: the rupture between ethics and materialism. At the same time, social *imaginaire* is not more controlled or used in a better way by "scientific" knowledge. Rather, it is mobilized more than ever by ideologues who take advantage of the modern mass media to disseminate slogans taken from religious (in Muslim societies) or secular ideologies, or from a mixture of both (in the so-called socialist regimes).

If we sum up the foregoing analysis and observations, we can stress the following propositions:

1. The social-historical space in which religions emerged, exercised their functions, and shaped cultures and collective sensibilities is being replaced by the secular positivist space of scientific knowledge, technological activities, material civilization, individual pragmatic ethics and law.
2. Scientific knowledge is divided into separate, technical, highly specialized disciplines. Religions, on the contrary, have provided global, unified, and unifying systems of beliefs and

non-beliefs, knowledge and practice, as well as pragmatic solutions to the fundamental problems of human destiny: life, death, love, justice, hope, truth, eternity, transcendence, and the absolute. The nostalgia for a unified vision explains the re-emergence of religion.

3. Positivist scientific knowledge has discredited or eliminated religious functions in society without providing an adequate alternative to religion as a symbol of human existence and a source of unifying ethical values for the group. This happened in Western societies under the name of secularism (or *laïcisme* in French), liberalism, and socialism.

4. Present thought has not yet recognized the positive aspect of secularism as a cultural and intellectual way to overcome fanatic divisions imposed by the dogmatic, superstitious use of religion. At the same time, the specific role of religion as a source for symbols in human existence also goes unrecognized.

5. Islam is not better prepared than Christianity to face the challenge of secularism, intellectual modernity, and technological civilization. The so-called religious revivalism is a powerful secular movement disguised by religious discourse, rites, and collective behaviors; but it is a secularization without the intellectual support needed to maintain the metaphysical mode of thinking and to search for an ethical coherence in human behavior. Theological and ethical thinking has reappeared in contemporary Islamic thought in the form of the ideology of liberation (political and economic). There is little intellectual concern with genuine religious issues like the consciousness of culpability, the eschatological perspective, or revelation as a springboard for mythical or symbolic thinking.

6. The concept that the Societies of the Book could help to build a new humanism which would integrate religions as cultures and not as dogmas for confessional groups (or *tawa'if*, as in Lebanon or Ireland) is not taken seriously either in theology or in the social scientific study of religions. But there is hope that semiotics and linguistics can create the possibility of reading religious texts in the new way we have mentioned.

7. The study of Islam today suffers particularly from the ideological obstacles created, since the 19th century, by the decay of the Muslim intellectual tradition, as it had developed from the first to the fifth century A.H., and by the economic pressure of the West, the general trend of positivist rationalism and material civilization, the powerful impact of demography since the late 1950s and the necessity of building a modern state and unifying the nation.

8. World system economists insist on the opposition between the center and the periphery. Likewise, in intellectual evolution, we should pay attention to the increasing domination of Western patterns of thought which have not been duly criticized, controlled, or mastered in Western societies themselves. Islam, which has a rich cultural tradition, is facing major issues in a generalized climate of semantic disorder; our thinking should be directed to the dangers resulting from this threat.

9. We should not forget that man agrees to obey, to be devoted, and to obligate his life when he feels a "debt of meaning" to a natural or a supernatural being. This may be the ultimate legitimacy of the state understood as the power accepted and obeyed by a group, community, or nation. The crisis of meaning started when each individual claimed himself as the source of all or true meaning; in this case, there is no longer any transcendent authority. Relations of power are substituted for relations of symbolic exchanges of meaning. To whom do we owe a "debt of meaning"?

It is our responsibility to answer this question after man has changed himself by his own initiatives, discoveries, performances, and errors. It seems that the answer will be conjectural and more and more bound to empirical research instead of to divine guidance taught by traditional religions. I learned through the Algerian war of liberation how all revolutionary movements need to be backed by a struggle for meaning, and I discovered how meaning is manipulated by forces devoted to the conquest of power. The conflict between meaning and power has been, is, and will be the permanent condition through which man tries to emerge as a thinking being.

In the full light of this experience, the question arises again: Should we Islamicize knowledge according to the revealed discourse, or should we consider Islam in the context of a universal quest for meaning? Many paths are open again. Let us explore them with confidence, hope, and lucidity.

Shari'a and Basic
Human Rights Concerns

'Abdullahi Ahmed An-Na'im (Sudan–United States, born 1946) is a legal scholar and human-rights activist. He was until recently head of Africa Watch, a human-rights organization in Washington, D.C. He received law degrees from the University of Khartoum in the Sudan and Cambridge University in England and a doctorate in law from the University of Edinburgh in Scotland. He has taught at law schools in the Sudan, Canada, and the United States. An-Na'im's legal training may define his work less than his identity as a prominent follower of Mahmoud Mohamed Taha (see chapter 28), an innovative—some would say heterodox—Islamic reformer, whose work An-Na'im has translated into English. He has focused his own contributions on the compatibility of Taha's interpretation of Islam and Western notions of human rights.[1]

Some of the issues discussed [in earlier chapters of An-Na'im's book] in relation to constitutionalism and criminal justice can be seen as issues of human rights in the domestic context of the modern nation-state. In that context, however, they are commonly known as fundamental constitutional rights. As used in this chapter, the term *human rights* refers to those rights recognized by and promoted through international law and institutions. Thus, although fundamental constitutional rights and international human rights are both concerned with the same type of claim or entitlement, the former deals with these claims and/or entitlements in the context of a domestic legal system while the latter deals with them in the context of the international legal system.

In accordance with the fundamental purpose of this book—to enable Muslims to exercise their right to self-determination without violating the rights of others to the same—this chapter will attempt to identify areas of conflict between *shari'a* [Islamic law] and universal standards of human rights and seek a reconciliation and positive relationship between the two systems. The hypothesis of this chapter, like that of the preceding chapters, is that if they implement historical *shari'a*, Muslims cannot exercise their right to self-determination without violating the rights of others. It is possible, however, to achieve a balance within the framework of Islam as a whole by developing appropriate principles of modern Islamic public law.

Stating the objectives of the chapter in this way raises the initial question of the relevance of so-called universal human rights to *shari'a*, or for that matter

1. Ann Elizabeth Mayer, *Islam and Human Rights* (Boulder, Colo.: Westview Press, 1991), pp. 54, 113.

to Islam itself. Why should universal human rights be a criterion for judging *shari'a* and an objective of modern Islamic public law?

Universality of Human Rights

Article 1.3 of the Charter of the United Nations . . . imposes on all members of the United Nations the obligation to cooperate in promoting and encouraging respect for human rights and fundamental freedoms for all without distinction as to race, sex (gender), language, or religion. But the charter did not define the terms *human rights* and *fundamental freedoms*. That task was undertaken by the United Nations in a series of declarations, conventions, and covenants drafted and adopted since 1948.[2] The U.N. human rights documents and regional documents of Europe, the Americas, and Africa[3] all have the same premise—that there shall be universal standards of human rights which must be observed by all countries of the world, or countries of the region in the case of regional documents.

There is some debate as to the genuine universality of some of these standards,[4] and there are some serious problems of enforcement. This does not mean, however, that there are no universal and binding standards or that enforcement efforts should be abandoned. The position adopted here is that there are certain universal standards of human rights which are binding under international law and that every effort should be made to enforce them in practice. Thus the principle of respect for and protection of human rights has been described as *jus cogens*, that is, such a fundamental principle of international law that states may not repudiate by their agreement.[5] This would, of course, be true of respect for and protection of human rights in principle. It is easier to give examples of human rights of this stature, such as the prohibition of genocide and slavery, than to define the concept in a categorical fashion. Nevertheless, such a definition, or at least a criterion by which human rights may be identified, will be attempted below.

The main difficulty with working to establish universal standards across cultural, and particularly religious, boundaries is that each tradition has its own internal frame of reference because each tradition derives the validity of its precepts and norms from its own sources. If a cultural, especially religious, tradition relates to other traditions at all, it is likely to do so in a negative and perhaps even hostile way. To claim the loyalty and conformity of its members, a cultural or religious tradition would normally assert its own superiority over other traditions.[6]

Nevertheless, there is a common normative principle shared by all the major cultural traditions which, if construed in an enlightened manner, is capable of sustaining universal standards of human rights. That is the principle that one should treat other people as he or she wishes to be treated by them. This golden rule, referred to earlier as the principle of reciprocity, is shared by all the major religious traditions of the world. Moreover, the moral and logical force of this simple proposition can easily be appreciated by all human beings of whatever cultural tradition or philosophical persuasion.

It is not easy to place oneself in the exact position of another person, especially if that other person is of a different gender or religious belief.[7] The

2. See generally, *United Nations Action in the Field of Human Rights*, United Nations Document ST/HR/2/Rev. 1, United Nations sales number E.79.XIV.6 (1980); and B. G. Ramcharan, editor, *Human Rights Thirty Years after the Universal Declaration of Human Rights* (The Hague, Netherlands: Martinus Nijhoff, 1979).

3. These are the European Convention for the Protection of Human Rights and Fundamental Freedoms of 1950, the American Convention on Human Rights of 1969, and the African Charter on Human and Peoples' Rights of 1981.

4. See, for example, Jack Donnelly, "Human Rights and Human Dignity: An Analytic Critique of Non-Western Conceptions of Human Rights," *American Political Science Review*, volume 76, June 1982, p. 303; and Rhoda Howard and Jack Donnelly, "Human Dignity, Human Rights and Political Regimes," *American Political Science Review*, volume 80, September 1986, p. 801.

For a survey of the main problems and theories in justification and support of universal standards of human rights, see Jerome J. Shestack, "The Jurisprudence of Human Rights," in Theodore Meron, *Human Rights in International Law: Legal and Policy Issues* (Oxford: Clarendon, 1985), p. 69.

5. Warwick McKean, *Equality and Discrimination under International Law* (Oxford: Clarendon, 1983), pp. 280–281.

6. Official spokesmen of the Islamic Republic of Iran have voiced their belief that they are bound by Islamic law and not international human rights standards. See a collection of these statements in Edward Mortimer, "Islam and Human Rights," *Index on Censorship*, volume 12, number 5, 1983, pp. 5–6.

7. The same would be true of other differences such as race or ethnicity, language, and so on. But because *shari'a* does not sanction discrimination on any other grounds except gender and religion, this chapter will focus on these two grounds of discrimination.

purpose of the principle of reciprocity, as applied to the present argument, is that one should try to achieve the closest possible approximation to placing oneself in the position of the other person. Assuming that one is in the exact position of the other person in all material respects, including gender and religious belief or other convictions, what basic human rights would one demand?

It should be emphasized that reciprocity is mutual so that when one identifies with another person, one would ascribe equivalent reciprocity to the belief system of the other person. Thus, when person X accepts the status or belief of person Y for the purposes of conceding Y's right to the same treatment which X would demand for himself, X would assume that Y accepts the same principle of reciprocity toward X by conceding to X the same rights he would demand for himself. In other words, X should not be entitled to deny Y's rights on the grounds that Y is unlikely to afford X the same rights because Y's belief system does not impose that obligation upon Y. If Y's belief system in fact fails to accord X the same rights, the answer would be for X to insist on reciprocity from Y rather than abdicate his obligation to afford Y the same rights he would claim for himself.

The problem with using the principle of reciprocity in this context is the tendency of cultural, and particularly religious, traditions to restrict the application of the principle to other members of its cultural or religious tradition, if not to a certain group within the given tradition.[8] The historical conception of the principle of reciprocity under *shari'a* did not apply to women and non-Muslims to the same extent that it applied to Muslim men.[9] In other words,

by granting women and non-Muslims a lower status and sanctioning discriminatory treatment against them, *shari'a* denies women and non-Muslims the same degree of honor and human dignity it guarantees to Muslim men.

This general problem will have to be addressed within each cultural tradition. In the case of Islam, for example, one must be able to establish a technique for reinterpreting the basic sources, the Qur'an and *sunna* [practice of the Prophet], in a way that would enable us to remove the basis of discrimination against women and non-Muslims. The technique I find most promising has already been explained in [an earlier section] and applied to questions of constitutionalism, criminal justice, and international relations. In the remainder of this chapter, I hope to explain the inadequacy of *shari'a* as a basis for human rights in the Muslim context and propose an alternative Islamic foundation for universal human rights.

Without going into the details of arguments that may be too closely identified with a particular cultural tradition,[10] one can make the following basic transcultural justification for universal standards of human rights. The criteria I would adopt for identifying universal human rights is that they are rights to which human beings are entitled by virtue of being human. In other words, universal standards of human rights are, by definition, appreciated by a wide variety of cultural traditions because they pertain to the inherent dignity and well-being of every human being, regardless of race, gender, language, or religion.[11] It follows that the practical test

---

8. In the context of the modern nation-state, this tendency is reflected in general intolerance of minorities, whether religious or otherwise. Thus it has been said that "the ideals of national unity manifested by a central concentration of power; by a common language, culture and religion; and by economic and geographical limits, all so fundamental to the self-identification of the new states, tended also to express themselves in intolerant and repressive attitudes toward those who were perceived or perceived themselves as 'others'" (Patrick Thornberry, "Is There a Phoenix in the Ashes? International Law and Minority Rights," *Texas International Law Journal*, volume 15, Summer 1980, p. 421).

9. Although this is the unavoidable conclusion of the briefest survey of the relevant principles and rules of *shari'a*, it is rarely admitted by contemporary Muslim writers on the subject.

One of the rare exceptions in modern Muslim writings is Sultanhussein Tabandeh, *A Muslim Commentary on the Uni-*

versal Declaration of Human Rights (London: F. T. Goulding and Company, 1970), pp. 17–20 and *passim*, where the author states clearly and defends the exclusion of women and non-Muslims from the full range of human rights under *shari'a*.

10. For example, the theories surveyed by Shestack, "Jurisprudence of Human Rights," pp. 85 and forward, appear to be primarily based on the Western tradition. In fact, the available literature on the philosophical notions of "rights" and "universal human rights," reviewed in Shestack, pp. 70–85, is not very useful for our purposes because it is primarily based on Western cultural tradition.

11. Oscar Schachter, in his editorial comment, "Human Dignity as a Normative Concept," *American Journal of International Law*, volume 77, 1983, p. 853, has suggested that it may be philosophically significant to derive human rights from the inherent dignity of human beings. But as Schachter himself has shown, the term *human dignity* has its own definitional problems.

by which these rights should be identified is whether the right in question is claimed by the particular cultural tradition for its own members. Applying the principle of reciprocity among all human beings rather than just among the members of a particular group, I would argue that universal human rights are those which a cultural tradition would claim for its own members and must therefore concede to members of other traditions if it is to expect reciprocal treatment from those others.

In content and substance, I submit that universal human rights are based on the two primary forces that motivate all human behavior, the will to live and the will to be free.[12] Through the will to live, human beings have always striven to secure their food, shelter, health, and all other means for the preservation of life. Moreover, people have always striven to improve the quality of their lives through the development and manipulation of available physical resources and through political struggle to achieve the fair and equitable distribution of wealth and power among the members of the particular community. At one level, the will to be free overlaps with the will to live, in that it is the will to be free from physical constraints and to be secure in food, shelter, health, and other necessities of a good life. At another level, the will to be free exceeds the will to live in that it is the driving force behind the pursuit of spiritual, moral, and artistic well-being and excellence.

The right to seek the satisfaction of the legitimate claims of these two forces is granted by every cultural tradition to its own members and must therefore, in accordance with the principle of reciprocity, be granted to the members of other traditions. This is, in my view, the basis of the universality of certain minimum human rights. By applying this simple criterion, we can identify those rights, claims, and entitlements that ought to be protected as human rights even if they are not identified as such by any formal document.

Relevant Standards of Human Rights

Our primary concern here is to establish cross-cultural foundations for the universality of human

rights. Consequently, other major and important issues, such as the relationship between strategic goals and tactical means, the question of hierarchy and trade-offs between different sets of rights, and the legitimacy of permitting derogations from certain obligations in times of emergency are not discussed in this book.

Being consistent with its own historical context, *shari'a* restricted the application of the principle of reciprocity in relation to women and non-Muslims. As frequently suggested throughout this book, the inadequacy of the public law of *shari'a* can only be understood and supplemented through a consideration of the impact of the historical context within which *shari'a* was constructed by the founding jurists of the eighth and ninth centuries A.D. out of the original sources of Islam. In that historical context, it was natural for the Muslim jurists to restrict the "other person" in the reciprocity rule to other Muslim men. This is a common feature of all historical cultural traditions and is also reflected in attitudes and policies of modern nation-states. It is for this aspect of the historical interpretation of the principle of reciprocity that I have said earlier that this principle can sustain universal human rights "if it is construed in an enlightened manner." An enlightened construction would extend the "other person" to all human beings, regardless of gender, religion, race, or language.

If such an enlightened construction is to be effective in changing Muslim attitudes and policies, two conditions must be satisfied. First, the proposed broad construction of the other person has to be valid and credible from the Islamic point of view. This can be done only through Islamic arguments that repudiate the historical restrictive construction and support the alternative broader construction. Second, other cultural and religious traditions must undertake a similar process of enlightened construction. It seems to me that the historical restriction of the other person to male members of one's own culture was unavoidable when other cultural traditions practiced similar exclusion of women and nonmembers of the particular culture. It would therefore seem to follow that we need to overcome historical hostility and resentment through concurrent action, each working within his or her own cultural tradition toward the same goal.

In the following outline of the relevant universal human rights, it is useful to quote international custom and treaties that recognize these rights because

---

12. Here I am adopting the analysis of *Ustadh* [Teacher] Mahmoud Mohamed Taha, *Second Message of Islam* (Syracuse, N.Y.: Syracuse University Press, 1987), pp. 80 and forward.

they establish norms that are binding on Muslim states under international law. In quoting these documents, however, it is not suggested that the given rights are accepted as universal simply because they are recognized as such by the documents. Rather, the rights are recognized by the documents because they are universal human rights, that is, rights to which every human being is entitled by virtue of being human.

Slavery is one of the most serious impediments on both the will to live and the will to be free. Although it has been practiced by every major human civilization throughout history, slavery, in the sense of institutionalized and legal ownership of human beings as chattel, has finally come to be universally condemned and outlawed by both domestic and international law.[13] More effort is needed to eradicate all shades and forms of economic exploitation and degradation reminiscent of slavery. In the present context, however, we are concerned with slavery as a legal institution.

The abolition of slavery may well be the first example of the acceptance of an international human right as a limitation on domestic jurisdiction.[14] In other words, the antislavery movement established a precedent for recognizing the principle that the violation of a universal human right by one country is the legitimate concern of other countries.[15] As a result of this movement, a series of international agreements was concluded, culminating in one of the most widely ratified conventions condemning and prohibiting slavery under international law.[16] More-over, several major international treaties have since reiterated the prohibition of slavery and required signatory states to outlaw and eliminate its practice in their domestic jurisdictions.[17]

Another early example of international cooperation in the field of human rights is the movement to eliminate the persecution of and discrimination against religious minorities.[18] Besides the moral abhorrence of such practices, persecution and discrimination on grounds of religion were perceived to be among the major causes of international conflict and war.[19] Consequently, a number of international treaties declared such persecution and discrimination a violation of human rights.[20]

A third area of emerging universal human rights, as defined above, is the prohibition of discrimination on grounds of gender. Although this right did not receive international attention as early as the other two rights, it has now come to be recognized as a

13. Myles S. McDougal, Harold D. Lasswell, and Lung-chu Chen, *Human Rights and World Public Order* (New Haven, Conn.: Yale University Press, 1980), pp. 473–508; and V. Nanda and C. Bassiouni, "Slavery and the Slave Trade: Steps towards Eradication," *Santa Clara Law Review*, volume 12, 1972, p. 424.

Article 8 of the Supplementary Convention on the Abolition of Slavery, the Slave Trade, and Institutions and Practices Similar to Slavery of 1956 requires states party to the convention to communicate to the secretary general of the United Nations copies of any laws, regulations, and administrative measures enacted or put into effect to implement the provisions of this convention. This documentation is to be used by the Economic and Social Council of the United Nations as a basis for further recommendations on this subject.

14. McKean, *Equality and Discrimination under International Law*, pp. 116–21.

15. Louis Henkin, et al., *International Law: Cases and Materials*, second edition (St. Paul, Minn.: West Publishing, 1987), p. 982.

16. The main current slavery convention was signed on September 25, 1926, and entered into force on March 9, 1927 (60 L.N.T.S. 253). More recent international treaties on the subject include the Supplementary Convention on the Abolition of Slavery, the Slave Trade and Institutions and Practices Similar to Slavery, which was signed on September 7, 1956, and entered into force on April 30, 1957 (18 T.I.A.S. No. 6418, 266 U.N.T.S. 3).

17. See, for example, Article 5 of the African Charter on Human and Peoples' Rights and Article 8 of the International Covenant on Civil and Political Rights. This last article is exempt by Article 4 of the convention from derogation, that is, no state party to the convention may ever derogate from its obligation to prohibit slavery and the slave trade and servitude under any circumstances. Moreover, Articles 6 and 7 of the International Covenant on Economic, Social and Cultural Rights, providing for the right to work, render slavery obsolete.

18. Arcot Krishnaswami, *Study of Discrimination in the Matter of Religious Rights and Practices* (New York: United Nations, 1960), pp. 11–12; and Francisco Capotorti, *Study of the Rights of Persons Belonging to Ethnic, Religious and Linguistic Minorities* (New York: United Nations, 1979), pp. 1–3.

19. This was true among states professing different sects within the same religion as well as among those adhering to different religions. Thus various European peace treaties since the 17th century have provided for the protection of Protestants within Catholic territory and vice versa. See Thornberry, "Is There a Phoenix in the Ashes?" p. 426 and accompanying notes.

20. See, for example, Articles 1.3 and 55(c) of the United Nations Charter, Article 2 of the African Charter, and Article 2 of the Civil and Political Rights Covenant.

For a comprehensive survey and analysis of current treaty-based guarantees against such discrimination since the end of World War II, see Capotorti, *Study of the Rights*, pp. 26–41.

universal human right under a variety of international conventions.[21]

The principle of nondiscrimination does not preclude all differential treatment on grounds such as race, gender, or religion. In this respect, I would agree with the proposition that one has to judge the nature of differential treatment in light of its purpose. "If the purpose or effect is to nullify or impair the enjoyment of human rights on an equal footing, the practice is discriminatory."[22] In this way, one would accept action that has the purpose or effect of enhancing rather than impairing the enjoyment of human rights on an equal footing.[23] It is not necessary to go into these issues in detail in this context. What is being affirmed here is that discrimination on grounds such as gender and religion violates human rights. . . .

Shari'a and Human Rights

In [an earlier chapter] it was argued that the historical context within which shari'a was constructed and applied by the early Muslims explained and justified its sanction of Muslim antagonism toward non-Muslims and its countenance of the use of force against them. By the same token, shari'a's position on what is known in modern terminology as human rights was also justified by the historical context. During the formative stages of shari'a (and for the next millennium at least) there was no conception of universal human rights anywhere in the world. Slavery was an established and lawful institution in many parts of the world throughout this period. Until the 19th century

A.D., moreover, it was normal throughout the world to determine a person's status and rights by his religion. Similarly, up to the 20th century A.D., women were not normally recognized as persons capable of exercising legal rights and capacities comparable to those enjoyed by men. Full citizenship and its benefits were to be restricted to the men of certain ethnic or racial groups within a particular polity in the same way that status and its benefits were restricted by shari'a to Muslim men. The most that shari'a could do, and did in fact do, in that historical context was to modify and lighten the harsh consequences of slavery and discrimination on grounds of religion or gender.[24]

Once again, to argue that shari'a's restrictive view of human rights was justified by the historical context and that it was an improvement on the preexisting situation is not to say that this view is still justified. On the contrary, my position is that since shari'a's view of human rights was justified by the historical context, it ceases to be so justified in the present drastically different context. By the same token that shari'a as a practical legal system could not have disregarded the conception of human rights prevailing at the time it purported to apply in the seventh century, modern Islamic law cannot disregard the present conception of human rights if it is to be applied today. In an early short piece, Khadduri said: "Human rights in Islam, as prescribed by the divine law [shari'a], are the privilege only of persons of full legal capacity. A person with full legal capacity is a living human being of mature age, free, and of Moslem faith. It follows, accordingly, that non-Moslems and slaves who lived in the Islamic state were only partially protected by law or had no legal capacity at all."[25] While accepting this statement as a substantially accurate presentation of the position

---

21. The principle of nondiscrimination provided for in the articles cited in the previous note apply equally to discrimination on grounds of gender. Moreover, several specialized conventions specifically apply to the rights of women, such as the Convention on the Political Rights of Women of 1953 (193 U.N.T.S. 135). The most comprehensive of this class of international treaties is the Convention on the Elimination of All Forms of Discrimination against Women of 1979.

22. Vernon Van Dyke, Human Rights, Ethnicity and Discrimination (Westport, Conn.: Greenwood Press, 1985), p. 194.

23. This differential treatment, known as affirmative action or positive discrimination, has its own problems in practice. See, for example, Marc Galanter, Competing Equalities (Berkeley: University of California Press, 1984), for an explanation of these problems as they have arisen through the recent application of this principle in the Indian context.

24. As was explained in chapter 4, the status of dhimmi [protected peoples] under shari'a guaranteed non-Muslims security of person and property and a degree of communal autonomy.

Shari'a also recognized for women an independent legal personality, including the full capacity to hold and dispose of property in their own right and certain minimum rights in family law and inheritance. See generally, Jane I. Smith, "Islam," in Arvind Sharama, editor, Women in World Religions (Albany: State University of New York Press, 1987), p. 235.

25. Majid Khadduri, "Human Rights in Islam," Annals of the American Academy of Political and Social Science, number 243, 1946, p. 79.

under *shari'a*,[26] I would add the following qualification with respect to the status of Muslim women: although it is true that they have full legal capacity under *shari'a* in relation to civil and commercial law matters, in the sense that they have the requisite legal personality to hold and dispose of property and otherwise acquire or lose civil liabilities in their own independent right, Muslim women do not enjoy human rights on an equal footing with Muslim men under *shari'a*. Moreover, in accepting Khadduri's statement of the position under *shari'a*, I would also reiterate my often-stated position that this aspect of *shari'a* is not the final word of Islam on the subject. As I shall argue at the end of this chapter, an alternative formulation of Islamic public law which would eliminate these limitations on human rights is both desirable and possible.

When we consider writings by contemporary Muslim scholars, we find that most of the published expositions of human rights in Islam are not helpful because they overlook the problems of slavery and discrimination against women and non-Muslims.[27]

One of the better discussions of human rights in Islam, which shows sensitivity to gender discrimination, is that by Riffat Hassan entitled "On Human Rights and the Qur'anic Perspectives."[28] The problem with this article is that it is selective in its choice of the Qur'anic perspectives. In overlooking some relevant verses of the Qur'an, the author fails to confront those Qur'anic perspectives which are not consistent with her vision of the Qur'anic perspectives on human rights. As will be suggested at the end of this chapter, the only effective approach to achieve *sufficient* reform of *shari'a* in relation to universal human rights is to cite sources in the Qur'an and *sunna* which are inconsistent with universal human rights and explain them in historical context, while citing those sources which are supportive of human rights as the basis of the legally applicable principles and rules of Islamic law today.

In contrast to the generally evasive approach of the majority of Muslim writers on human rights issues, a few other Muslim writers have adopted a more honest and candid approach. A good example of this approach is Sultanhussein Tabandeh's *Muslim Commentary on the Universal Declaration of Human Rights*. This short book has the merit of clearly indicating the inconsistencies between *shari'a* and the 1948 Universal Declaration of Human Rights in relation to the status of women and non-Muslims.[29] Tabandeh notes these inconsistencies to argue that Muslims are not bound by the Universal Declaration of Human Rights in these respects, whereas I am suggesting that it is *shari'a* which should be revised, from an Islamic point of view, to provide for these universal human rights. I welcome the clear statement of the inconsistencies between *shari'a* and universal human rights as part of my argument for Islamic law reform. It should be recalled, however, that the proposed reform must maintain its Islamic legitimacy if it is to be effective in changing Muslim attitudes and policies on these issues.

For our purposes here, we need not go into an exhaustive statement of all human rights because there are no fundamental problems with *shari'a* except for slavery and discrimination on grounds of gender and religion. It is more to the point to focus on those human rights standards which are violated by *shari'a*, the prohibition of slavery and discrimination on grounds of gender and religion.

Slavery

It is obvious that *shari'a* did not introduce slavery, which was the norm throughout the world at the time. *Shari'a* recognized slavery as an institution but sought to restrict the sources of acquisition of slaves, to improve their condition, and to encour-

26. In a recent substantially revised version of this paper Khadduri omitted the above-quoted statement. Though emphasizing the need for reform and compliance with current international standards of human rights, Khadduri's revised version does not dispute the accuracy of the statement from his 1946 paper. See Majid Khadduri, *The Islamic Conception of Justice* (Baltimore: Johns Hopkins University Press, 1984), p. 233.

27. See, for example, Ali Abdel Wahid Wafi, "Human Rights in Islam," *Islamic Quarterly*, Volume 11, 1967, p. 64; Khalid M. Ishaque, "Human Rights in Islamic Law," *International Commission of Jurists Review*, volume 12, 1974, p. 51; and Isma'il al-Faruqi, "Islam and Human Rights," *Islamic Quarterly*, volume 27, 1983, p. 12.

28. Riffat Hassan, "On Human Rights and the Qur'anic Perspectives," *Journal of Ecumenical Studies*, volume 19, 1982, p. 51.

29. Tabandeh, *Muslim Commentary on the Universal Declaration of Human Rights*, pp. 18–20 and 35–45. Reference to these and other points made in this book was made [in an earlier chapter].

age their emancipation through a variety of religious and civil methods.[30] Nevertheless, slavery is lawful under *shari'a* to the present day.[31] It is unlikely today that institutionalized slavery will be formally sanctioned in any Muslim country.[32] If the right conditions under which slaves may be acquired should arise today and someone was made a slave under those conditions, *shari'a* would protect the "rights" of both the master and the slave in the same way it did 13 centuries ago. In this respect, one would appreciate the candid and honest statement of the situation under *shari'a* by Tabandeh, who noted the absence of any possibility of finding confirmation of the legality of the enslavement of any person today, and then proceeded to say:

> Nonetheless, should the legal condition for the enslavement of anyone be proven (because he had been taken prisoner fighting against Islam with a view to its extirpation and persisted in invincible ignorance in his sacrilegious and infidel convictions, or because there did exist legal proof that all his ancestors without exception had been slaves descended from a person taken prisoner conducting a warfare of such invincible ignorance) Islam would be bound to recognize such slavery as legal, even though recommending the freeing of the person and if possible his conversion, in this modern age.[33]

In accepting this as an accurate statement of *shari'a*, I am not accepting this aspect of *shari'a* as the final and conclusive law of Islam. In this light, it would be lawful, from *shari'a*'s point of view, if slavery is reestablished in a modern Islamic state. As I have argued in [a previous chapter], however, there is the possibility of replacing these dated and archaic aspects of *shari'a* with modern and humane principles of Islamic law. Such an enlightened construction would

prohibit slavery as a matter of *Islamic* law. Thus it is *shari'a* and not Islam that "would be bound to recognize such slavery" under Tabandeh's statement.

To make an Islamic argument for the prohibition of slavery, we first need to know the circumstances under which slavery is permitted by *shari'a* and its rules regarding the treatment and emancipation of slaves.

There is no verse in the Qur'an which directly sanctions the enslavement of any person, but many verses do so by implication when, for example, the Qur'an speaks of a Muslim's right to cohabit with his slave concubine, which clearly presupposes the existence of such slave women. The same can be said of *sunna* on the subject.[34] The only way a person who is born free may be brought into slavery under *shari'a* is through military defeat in a war sanctioned by *shari'a*.[35] According to the founding jurists, subjecting the vanquished unbelievers to slavery is one of the options open to Muslims under *shari'a*. Thus the Shafi'i school allowed the *imam* [leader] four options in dealing with prisoners of war: immediate execution, enslavement, or release with or without ransom. The Maliki school restricted the options to execution, enslavement, or release with ransom, and the Hanafi school reduced them further to either execution or enslavement.[36]

Once a person is brought into slavery through military conquest or is born to slave parents, he or she remains a slave until emancipated. While a slave, he or she may be employed in whatever manner deemed fit by his or her master but must be treated with kindness and compassion as required by *shari'a*.[37] That does not preclude the sale of slaves in principle, but it may place some limitations on the conditions

---

30. Fazlur Rahman, *Islam* (Chicago: University of Chicago Press, 1979), p. 38; and Majid Khadduri, *War and Peace in the Law of Islam* (Baltimore: Johns Hopkins University Press, 1955), p. 130.

For a comprehensive treatment of slavery in *shari'a* and in history see R. Brunschwig, "'Abd," in *Encyclopedia of Islam*, new edition, volume 1, pp. 24–40. See also Reuben Levy, *The Social Structure of Islam* (Cambridge: Cambridge University Press, 1957), pp. 73–85.

31. Modernist arguments that slavery should have been abolished by *shari'a* will be considered below.

32. I am not concerned here with secret slavery and semislavery, which exist in many parts of the world.

33. Tabandeh, *Muslim Commentary on the Universal Declaration of Human Rights*, p. 27.

34. For reports of *sunna* and other early traditions showing the free practice of slavery during the Prophet's time see Majid Khadduri, *The Islamic Law of Nations* (Baltimore: Johns Hopkins University Press, 1966), pp. 80 and forward.

35. This, of course, does not cover the purchase of slaves, which is treated by *shari'a* jurists as part of the law of sale. See Brunschwig, "'Abd."

36. Majid Khadduri and Herbert Liebesny, *Law in the Middle East* (Washington, D.C.: Middle East Institute, 1955), pp. 355–356. For a documented account of these options and differences of opinion among the jurists in matters of detail see Khadduri, *War and Peace in the Law of Islam*, pp. 126–130.

37. For example, Sura 4, Verse 36 of the Qur'an instructs Muslims to "do good" and to treat their parents, relatives, orphans, slaves, and others well.

under which the sale is concluded, such as a requirement not to separate a mother and child when they are sold as slaves.[38]

Shari'a encouraged the emancipation of slaves through a variety of methods. The emancipation of slaves is designated by Sura 9, Verse 60, and Sura 2, Verse 177, of the Qur'an as one of the prescribed items of expenditure of the official treasury or private charity. Moreover, the emancipation of a slave is prescribed by some verses of the Qur'an, such as Sura 4, Verse 92, and Sura 58, Verse 3, as religious penance and atonement for some sins, and recommended by others, such as Sura 2, Verse 177, and Sura 89, Verses 11–13, as a most meritorious act. Sura 24, Verse 33, of the Qur'an encourages a Muslim to grant the wish of a slave who wants to contract with the master for emancipation in exchange for the payment of a certain sum of money or performance of certain services.

Given the entrenched position of slavery throughout the world at the time, Islam had no choice but to recognize the institution of slavery in that historical context and do its best to improve the conditions under which slaves were to endure their unfortunate status. It can also be argued that Islam was aiming at the elimination of slavery by restricting its incidence and encouraging its termination. But since there was no internal mechanism by which slavery was to be rendered unlawful by *shari'a*, it continued to be lawful under that system of law up to the present day.

Riffat Hassan quoted with approval the argument made by G. A. Parwez [India-Pakistan, born 1903] to the effect that since the Qur'an restricted the source of slavery to prisoners of war, and then prescribed in Sura 47, Verse 4, that prisoners of war were to be set free either for ransom or as a favor, it follows that "the door for future slavery was thus closed by the Qur'an forever. Whatever happened in subsequent history was the responsibility of the Muslims and not of the Qur'an."[39] Similarly, it is sometimes argued by modern Muslims that this verse of the Qur'an prohibits the enslavement of captives after a war with Muslims. The relevant part of this verse may be translated as follows: "When you meet the unbelievers [in battle], smite at their necks [kill them]. Once you

have thoroughly subdued them, then [hold] and bind [them]. Thereafter [practice] either generosity [by freeing them without compensation] or [for] ransom, until war is terminated."

These arguments are, in my view, examples of selective citation of *shari'a* sources leading to serious distortion and confusion. When we consider that both the Qur'an and *sunna* did recognize and regulate slavery in a number of ways, that the Prophet himself and leading Companions had slaves, and that all the founding jurists of *shari'a* took the existence of slavery for granted and elaborated rules for its regulation, we cannot dismiss the matter as the alleged failure of generations of Muslims to implement the intention of the Qur'an to abolish slavery. Despite the apparent limitation by this verse of the options open to Muslims over their captives, it is a historical fact that Muslim armies, during and after the Prophet's time, have continued to exercise the option to enslave their captives. Moreover, it should be emphasized that the founding jurists of *shari'a* did not perceive this verse as excluding the option of enslavement of captives.[40] This verse may now be used in an argument for prohibiting enslavement as a matter of Islamic law, but this possible construction of the verse should not be confused with the position under *shari'a* as it has been established by early Muslim practice and authoritatively stated by the founding jurists.

I believe that the early Muslims were correct in interpreting the Qur'an and *sunna* as recognizing the institution of slavery *in the historical context* of early Islam. In the current historical context and with a new principle of interpretation such as the one proposed in the present study, the basic premise of the argument by modern Muslims against slavery may now be used to abolish slavery under Islamic law in an authoritative manner. Although those arguments cannot be accepted to alter the legal and historical fact that *shari'a* recognized slavery, and continues to do so to the present day, they provide a very significant indication of the eagerness of modern Muslims to abolish slavery in Islamic law.

38. Khadduri, *War and Peace in the Law of Islam*, pp. 131–32.

39. Hassan, "On Human Rights and the Qur'anic Perspectives," p. 59.

40. In his explanation of this verse, ['Imad al-Din] Ibn Kathir [circa 1300–1373] does not mention any implication of prohibition of the enslavement option. Rather, he quotes [Abu 'Abdallah Muhammad] Shafi'i's [767–820] statement of the four options open to the ruler over captives of war: execution, enslavement, or release with or without ransom.

Modern Muslims should welcome the evolutionary approach proposed by *Ustadh* [Teacher] Mahmoud Mohamed Taha. As applied to slavery, for example, that principle would conclude that though *shari'a* implemented the transitional legislative intent to permit slavery, subject to certain limitations and safeguards, modern Islamic law should now implement the fundamental Islamic legislative intent to prohibit slavery forever.

When slavery was eventually abolished in modern Muslim states, in some cases as late as the 1960s and after, that result was achieved through secular law and not *shari'a*.[41] Given the formal abolition of slavery in all Muslim countries, some may argue that it is no longer an issue. I disagree and believe that slavery is a fundamental human rights issue for Muslims until it is abolished in Islamic law.

In my view, it is utterly abhorrent and morally indefensible for *shari'a* to continue to sanction slavery today, regardless of the prospects of its practice. Moreover, the fact that slavery is permissible under *shari'a* does have serious practical consequences not only in perpetuating negative social attitudes toward former slaves and segments of the population that used to be a source of slaves but also in legitimizing forms of secret practices akin to slavery. In the Sudan, for example, images of slavery under *shari'a* and Islamic literature continue to support negative stereotypes of Sudanese from the southern and western parts of the country, which were sources of slaves until the late 19th century. Moreover, recent news reports indicate that Muslim tribesmen of southwestern Sudan feel justified in capturing non-Muslims from southern Sudan and keeping them in secret slavery.

Discrimination on Grounds of Gender and Religion

A similar analysis applies to discrimination against women and non-Muslims under *shari'a*. Both types of discrimination were the norm at the time.[42] While accepting such discrimination in principle, *shari'a* restricted its incidence and reduced its scope.[43] Nevertheless, when viewed in modern perspective, principles of *shari'a* sanctioning serious and unacceptable discrimination on grounds of gender and religion are, in my view, untenable today.

According to *shari'a*, non-Muslims may live within a Muslim state either under the status of *dhimmi* [protected religious groups] for non-Muslim subjects or the status of *aman* (pledge of security or safe-conduct) for non-Muslim aliens.[44] Various examples of discrimination under the public law of *shari'a* on grounds of religion were given in the chapters on constitutionalism and criminal justice. As explained earlier, personal and private law matters for non-Muslims within an Islamic state were left to their own personal law and communal arrangements for administration. Should the matter involve a Muslim, *shari'a* would apply.

Discriminatory *shari'a* rules of personal and private law include the following:

- A Muslim man may marry a Christian or Jewish woman, but a Christian or Jewish man may not marry a Muslim woman.[45] Both Muslim men and women are precluded from marrying an unbe-

43. On the relative improvements in the status of women introduced by *shari'a* see Sayed Ameer Ali, *The Spirit of Islam* (London: Christophers, 1922), pp. 222–257; Fazlur Rahman, "Status of Women in the Qur'an," in Guity Nashat, editor, *Women and Revolution in Iran* (Boulder, Colo.: Westview, 1983), p 37; and Noel Coulson, *A History of Islamic Law* (Edinburgh, Scotland: Edinburgh University Press, 1964), pp. 14–15.

44. On the acquisition of the status of *aman* and its consequences see Muhammad Hamidullah, *Muslim Conduct of State*, fifth edition (Lahore, Pakistan: Sh. M. Ashraf, 1966) pp. 201–202; Khadduri and Liebesny, *Law in the Middle East*, pp. 361–62; and Ibrahim Shihata, "Islamic Law and the World Community," *Harvard International Club Journal*, volume 4, 1962, pp. 108–109.

45. Although this is the position of all major schools of Islamic jurisprudence, it is not based on direct Qur'anic prohibition of such marriages. Rather, it is based on the derivative argument that since Sura 4, Verse 34 of the Qur'an entitles the husband to exercise authority over his wife while stating, as in Sura 4, Verse 141, that a non-Muslim may never exercise authority over a Muslim, it follows that a man from the People of the Book, such as a Christian or Jew, may never marry a Muslim woman.

This reasoning will be repudiated at the end of this chapter through the application of the evolutionary principle of construction of Islamic sources.

41. Slavery was abolished in Bahrain in 1937, Kuwait in 1947, and Qatar in 1952. See C. W. W. Greenidge, "Slavery in the Middle East," *Middle Eastern Affairs*, December 1956, p. 439.

42. Levy, *Social Structure of Islam*, pp. 91–134 and passim, for comparisons between various aspects of the status of women before and during the early Islamic period.

liever, that is, one who does not believe in one of the heavenly revealed scriptures.[46]

- Difference in religion is a total bar to inheritance. Thus a Muslim may neither inherit from nor leave inheritance to a non-Muslim.[47]

Examples of discrimination on grounds of gender in family and private law include the following:[48]

- A Muslim man may be married to up to four wives at the same time but a Muslim woman can only be married to one man at a time.[49]
- A Muslim man may divorce his wife, or any of his wives, by unilateral repudiation, *talaq*, without having to give any reasons or justify his action to any person or authority. In contrast, a Muslim woman can obtain divorce only by consent of the husband or by judicial decree for limited specific grounds such as the husband's inability or unwillingness to provide for his wife.[50]
- In inheritance, a Muslim woman receives less than the share of a Muslim man when both have equal degree of relationship to the deceased person.[51]

We are not concerned here with the historical justification of these instances of discrimination on grounds of religion or gender. Reasonable people may differ in their view of the historical sufficiency of any justifications that may be offered for any particular instance of discrimination. For example, it may be argued that economic and social conditions of seventh-century Arabia did not justify some or all of the discriminatory rules cited above. It is my submission, however, that regardless of differences over the historical sufficiency of justifica-

tions, these instances of discrimination against women and non-Muslims under *shari'a* are no longer justified.

It should be emphasized here that such unacceptable discrimination exists despite the modern reforms of personal law in several Muslim countries. As explained in [a previous chapter], these efforts cannot achieve the desired degree of reform because of the internal limitations of reform within the framework of historical *shari'a*. Moreover, the limited benefits achieved through these modern reforms are constantly challenged and threatened by more fundamental principles of *shari'a* which remain intact in the jurisprudence and legal practice of the countries that introduced those reforms.

In light of the preceding discussion, the following conclusions seem justified. First, in continuing to recognize slavery as a lawful institution, even if only in theory, *shari'a* is in complete violation of a most fundamental and universal human right. It is very significant that slavery was abolished in the Muslim world through secular law and not *shari'a* and that *shari'a* does not object to the reinstitution of slavery under its own conditions regarding the source of slaves and conditions for their treatment. Although the vast majority of contemporary Muslims abhor slavery, it remains part of their religious law.

Second, discrimination on grounds of religion and gender under *shari'a* also violates established universal human rights. Discrimination on grounds of religion has been found to be one of the major causes of international conflict and war because other countries that sympathize with the persecuted non-Muslim minority are likely to be prompted into acting in support of the victims of religious discrimination, thereby creating a situation of international conflict and possibly war. More important, it is my submission that discrimination on grounds of either gender or religion is morally repugnant and politically untenable today.

These are, in my view, the most serious points of conflict and tension between *shari'a* and universal human rights as defined in the present study. Before proceeding to an application of the method of reconciliation adopted in this book, it may be helpful to highlight the relevance of this conflict and tension. Is it of purely historical interest or is it relevant to the current policy and practice of Muslim states?

---

46. This was the construction given by the founding jurists to Sura 2, Verse 21; Sura 5, Verse 5; and Sura 9, Verse 10, of the Qur'an.

47. Joseph Schacht, *An Introduction to Islamic Law* (Oxford: Clarendon, 1964), p. 170.

48. On the contrast between *shari'a* view of the status and rights of women and that envisaged by Article 16 of the Universal Declaration of Human Rights see Tabandeh, *Muslim Commentary on the Universal Declaration of Human Rights*, pp. 35–67.

49. Sura 4, Verse 2, of the Qur'an. See Coulson, *History of Islamic Law*, pp. 18–19.

50. This is the construction given by the founding jurists to Sura 2, Verses 226–232 of the Qur'an. Look under *talaq* in H. A. R. Gibb and J. H. Kramers, editors, *Shorter Encyclopedia of Islam* (Leiden, The Netherlands: E. J. Brill, 1953), pp. 564–567.

51. Sura 4, Verses 11 and 176, of the Qur'an.

Current Muslim Ambivalence on Human Rights

The basic inconsistency between a historical, religiously determined conception of individual and collective rights under *shari'a* and a contemporary universalistic conception of human rights is clearly reflected in the ambivalence of modern Muslim states on the issue. The policies of these countries are influenced, whether consciously or unconsciously, by inherently contradictory forces. On one hand, there is the pull of historical religious traditions which sanction discrimination on grounds of religion and gender. On the other hand, there is the push of modernist domestic and international forces in favor of human rights and against discrimination on grounds of religion or gender. This ambivalence is reflected, in my view, in the subscription by some Muslim countries to international human rights documents which they are unable to uphold within their national jurisdictions because of the role of *shari'a* in the domestic legal systems of those countries.

It is difficult to provide detailed and conclusive documentation of human rights violations in many countries, especially in the Muslim world, because of the lack of verifiable records.[52] Moreover, it is much more difficult to link those violations, to the extent that they are documented, to the influence of *shari'a*.[53] Nevertheless, the ambivalence of Muslim countries in the field of human rights can be illustrated by comparing the content of the international human rights documents to which a particular Muslim country has subscribed and the *shari'a* rules being enforced in that country as a matter of domestic law. A clear example can be found by contrasting Egypt's international obligation to eliminate discrimination on grounds of gender with rules

of *shari'a* personal law that apply to Muslims in Egypt.[54]

Article 1 of the 1979 International Convention on the Elimination of All Forms of Discrimination against Women, to which Egypt is a party, defines discrimination against women as "any distinction, exclusion or restriction made on the basis of sex which has the effect or purpose of impairing or nullifying the recognition, enjoyment or exercise by women, irrespective of their marital status, on a basis of equality of men and women, of human rights and fundamental freedoms in the political, economic, social, cultural, civil or any other field." Articles 3 to 16 of the convention implement this definition through very specific and precise provisions for the elimination of discrimination against women in the fields of political and public life, education, employment, health care, and others.

In ratifying this convention, Egypt entered reservations on Articles 9, 16, and 29. Although the reservations on Articles 9 and 29, dealing with nationality of children and submission to arbitration under the convention, may be based on national policy not necessarily related to *shari'a*, the one on Article 16 is expressly related to *shari'a*. Whereas the article requires complete equality between men and women in all matters relating to marriage and family relations during the marriage and upon its dissolution, Egypt's reservation states that its obligations "must be without prejudice to the Islamic *shari'a* provisions." In this way, it can be said that Egypt is aware of the conflict between the international obligation established by that article and its own *shari'a* personal law for Muslims. As long as this is the only aspect of Egyptian law based on *shari'a* which is inconsistent with Egypt's obligation under this convention and other international human rights instruments, it can be said that Egypt is honest in its position and serious in its intention to honor its international human rights obligations. That is not enough. Egypt and all other Muslim countries should bring every aspect of their law, including personal law for Muslims, into complete conformity with human rights standards.

52. Reports by nongovernmental organizations, such as Amnesty International and the Arab Human Rights Organization, and other monitoring documentation, such as Human Rights Internet Reporter, may be the best available sources of documentation for human rights violations. But because most Muslim countries are governed by authoritarian regimes, information about human rights violations is difficult to obtain.

53. For an effort to do so see James Dudley, "Human Rights Practices in the Arab States: The Modern Impact of *Shari'a* Values," *Georgia Journal of International and Comparative Law*, volume 12, 1982, p. 55.

54. *Shari'a* is the family law for Muslims in Egypt. See Maitre A. El-Kharboutly and Aziza Hussein, "Law and the Status of Women in the Arab Republic of Egypt," *Columbia Human Rights Law Review*, volume 8, 1976, p. 35.

Given the various ways in which *shari'a* discriminates against women and non-Muslims and the powerful influence of *shari'a* on private as well as official Muslim behavior throughout the world, however, it is reasonable to conclude that more serious consequences of Muslim ambivalence on human rights are unavoidable. Moreover, this ambivalence is likely to increase in scope and degree if the current trend toward greater Islamization of public life in Muslim countries should continue.

The relevance of *shari'a* to contemporary Muslim practice raises the basic issue of how to reconcile *shari'a* with universal standards of human rights. As in the case of similar issues raised in our discussion of questions of constitutionalism, criminal justice, and international law, reconciliation can be achieved only through the drastic reform of *shari'a*. It now remains to be seen how the reform technique explained earlier operates in achieving the desired reconciliation between Islamic law and universal human rights from within the Islamic tradition.

Universal Human Rights in Islam

Once again, and in culmination of the basic argument of this book, we come to the same conclusion. Unless the basis of modern Islamic law is shifted away from those texts of the Qur'an and *sunna* of the Medina stage,[55] which constituted the foundations of the construction of *shari'a*, there is no way of avoiding drastic and serious violation of universal standards of human rights. There is no way to abolish slavery as a legal institution and no way to eliminate all forms and shades of discrimination against women and non-Muslims as long as we remain bound by the framework of *shari'a*. As stated in [a previous chapter] and explained in relation to constitutionalism, criminal justice, and international law, the traditional techniques of reform within the framework of *shari'a* are inadequate for achieving the *necessary* degree of reform. To achieve that degree of reform, we must be able to set aside clear and definite texts of the Qur'an and *sunna* of the Medina stage as having served their transitional purpose and implement those texts of the Meccan stage which were previously inappropriate

55. [The distinction between the Mecca and Medina stages is derived from the work of Mahmoud Mohamed Taha, who is also included in this volume.—Editor]

for practical application but are now the only way to proceed.

A similar approach is proposed for achieving the reconciliation of Islamic law with the full range of universal human rights identified through the criteria indicated earlier in this chapter. The key to the success of this part of the effort is to convince Muslims that the other person with whom they must identify and accept as their equal in human dignity and rights includes all other human beings, regardless of gender and religion. This would require an explanation of why the verses of antagonism which instructed Muslims to be *awliya*, friends and supporters, of each other and disassociate themselves from all non-Muslims, should not apply today. It would also require showing that Sura 4, Verse 34, of the Qur'an, which establishes general male guardianship over women, and other verses which establish specific instances of discrimination against women, should not be implemented today.

In accordance with the logic of the evolutionary principle proposed by *Ustadh* Mahmoud Mohamed Taha, the texts of the Qur'an emphasizing exclusive Muslim solidarity were revealed during the Medina stage to provide the emerging Muslim community with psychological support in the face of the violent adversity of non-Muslims. In contrast to these verses, the fundamental and eternal message of Islam, as revealed in the Qur'an of the Mecca period, preached the solidarity of all humanity. In view of the vital need for peaceful coexistence in today's global human society, Muslims should emphasize the eternal message of universal solidarity of the Qur'an of the Mecca period rather than the exclusive Muslim solidarity of the transitional Medina message. Otherwise, Muslims would only provoke counter exclusive solidarity by non-Muslims, thereby repudiating the prospects for peaceful coexistence and cooperation in promoting and protecting universal human rights.

The application of *Ustadh* Mahmoud's evolutionary principle to male *qawwama*, guardianship, over women has already been explained. Male guardianship over women has been rationalized by Sura 4, Verse 34, as following from the economic and security dependence of women on men. Because such dependence is no longer necessarily true, argued *Ustadh* Mahmoud, male guardianship over women should be terminated. Both men and women should now be equally free and equally responsible before the law, which guarantees economic opportunity and security for all members of the community.

The application of this evolutionary principle of interpretation to specific instances of discrimination against women and non-Muslims can be illustrated by the rule of *shari'a* prohibiting marriage between a Muslim woman and a non-Muslim man. This rule is based on the combined operation of the guardianship of the man, in this case the husband, over his wife, and that of a Muslim over a non-Muslim. Since a non-Muslim husband may not be the guardian of his Muslim wife, *shari'a* prohibits such a marriage. If either form of guardianship, of a husband over his wife or of a Muslim over a non-Muslim, is repudiated, there would be no justification for prohibiting marriage between a Muslim woman and a non-Muslim man. The evolutionary principle of *Ustadh* Mahmoud would repudiate both types of guardianship.

The evolutionary principle will also repudiate another possible rationale of the prohibition of marriage between a Muslim woman and a non-Muslim man, namely, the assumption that a wife is more susceptible to influence by her husband than vice versa. In other words, it appears to be assumed that if such a marriage is permitted, it is more likely that the non-Muslim husband will draw his Muslim wife away from Islam than that she will draw him to Islam. This rationale is, of course, part of the wider sociological phenomenon, namely, the lack of confidence in a woman's integrity and good judgment. Educational and other efforts are needed to repudiate this sociological phenomenon in all its manifestations. Besides its immediate practical impact, legal reform can also be an effective tool of education and leadership. This task can be begun by removing, through the application of the evolutionary principle of *Ustadh* Mahmoud, all aspects of the law which discriminate against women, thereby encouraging and sustaining a positive view of women.

Conclusion

Salman Rushdie [born 1947], an Indian-born Muslim novelist who became a British citizen, published in Britain a novel entitled *Satanic Verses* in September 1988. In various parts of the novel, and especially in a dream sequence therein, irreverent references are made to the Prophet of Islam, his wives, and leading Companions. Although made in metaphorical fictitious form, the associations and negative connotations are obvious.

Within a few months, thousands of Muslims were demonstrating in various parts of the Muslim world, burning copies of the book, and demanding that it be banned not only in their own countries but throughout the world. Some of the demonstrators called for the death of Rushdie. In mid-February 1989, Imam [Ruhollah] Khomeini of Iran [1902–1989] issued a declaration in which he called on Muslims to kill Rushdie and any person associated with the publication and sale of the book. When Rushdie issued a statement a few days later expressing his regrets for any affront and anguish his book may have caused Muslims, Khomeini responded by saying that Rushdie's apology would not be accepted and that he should be killed even if he repented and recanted his insults to Islam and the Muslims. These events were widely reported in the media all over the world.

In the following remarks, I am assuming, for the sake of argument, that Rushdie's book is extremely offensive to Muslims. I am also assuming that freedom of expression is not absolute. It is conceivable that a published work, whether claiming to be a work of fiction or scholarship, can cause such harm to some identifiable private or public interest as to justify the banning or restriction of its circulation. Although I believe that it should be extremely difficult to make a convincing case for banning a work, I am assuming that it is not impossible to do so. Moreover, I am also assuming that Rushdie's book warrants examination with a view to its possible banning by the appropriate authorities.

Assuming all this, I find it extremely disturbing that thousands of Muslims in many parts of the world are demanding not only the banning of the book but also the murder of the author. What is even more disturbing is that a head of a Muslim country, Imam Khomeini of Iran, has called on Muslims to seek out and murder a citizen of another country, and a non-Muslim country at that, without the benefit of trial and a chance to defend himself. Khomeini does not speak for all the Shi'i Muslims of the world, let alone the Sunni Muslims, who are by far the vast majority of Muslims today. Nevertheless, since the vast majority of Muslims have failed to condemn Khomeini's action, they are to be taken as acquiescing to it.

Even though *shari'a* rules of procedure are extremely underdeveloped, many Muslims would argue that sufficient authority can be found to support the conclusion that Khomeini's action is totally wrong and invalid in *shari'a* for at least three reasons. First, assuming that Khomeini is the undisputed ruler of an Islamic state (*dar al-Islam*), his jurisdiction under *shari'a* does not extend to a non-Islamic state (*dar al-harb*). In modern terms, *shari'a* does not give the ruler of an Islamic state the power to punish the citizen of a non-Islamic state. Second, even if Khomeini were to have jurisdiction over Rushdie on the absurd ground that the ruler of an Islamic state has universal jurisdiction over Muslims anywhere in the world, *shari'a* requires that a person be charged with an offense and allowed a chance to defend himself before he may be punished. Third, repentance and recantation of heretic views is always a complete defense against a charge of apostasy (*ridda*), which is presumably the offense Rushdie is supposed to have committed.

All of these objections to Khomeini's action are procedural and formal in nature. That thousands of Muslims in many parts of the Muslim world have demanded the death of Rushdie can only mean that they continue to perceive this to be the appropriate penalty for apostasy. In other words, Muslims are saying that if Rushdie is subject to the jurisdiction of an Islamic state, was duly charged and tried, and refused to recant his views, he should be put to death. This is the prevailing view of *shari'a*, which is not disputed by the vast majority of Muslims, who are demanding the application of *shari'a* today as the public law of Muslim countries. Even those Muslims who argue that the death penalty is not required by *shari'a* for peaceable nonviolent apostasy would still have to concede the variety of other negative legal consequences to the apostate noted earlier, including the possibility of a discretionary punishment (*ta'zir*) short of death.

Although I know this to be the position under *shari'a*, I am unable *as a Muslim* to accept the law of apostasy as part of the law of Islam today. If the prevailing view of apostasy remains valid today, a Muslim could be put to death for expressing views in a given Muslim country which are deemed by the dominant view in that country to be tantamount to apostasy. For example, from some Sunni perspectives, the views of many Shi'i Muslims amount to apostasy; and from some Shi'i perspectives, the views of many Sunni Muslims amount to apostasy. If the *shari'a* law of apostasy is to be applied today,

it would be conceivable for some Shi'i Muslims to be sentenced to death in a Sunni country and vice versa.

Furthermore, it is conceivable for a Muslim within the Sunni tradition, for example, to be put to death for apostasy by the authorities even though many contemporary Muslims regard that person to be an exemplary Muslim. Numerous examples can be cited from Muslim history of leading Sufi (Muslim mystic) men who were killed for apostasy despite their large following among Muslims at the time. Other examples can be cited of currently respected scholars, such as Ibn Taymiyya [1263–1328], who could have been put to death under the pretext of the *shari'a* law of apostasy if their opponents were in control of the machinery of the state at the time. Many modern Muslim intellectuals, such as 'Ali 'Abd al-Raziq [1888–1966], have been denounced and threatened with death for expressing profound scholarly views. *Ustadh* Mahmoud Mohamed Taha was executed for apostasy in the Sudan in January 1985 for his views on Islamic reform.

These instances would suggest to me that toleration of unorthodoxy and dissent is vital for the spiritual and intellectual benefit of Islam itself. The *shari'a* law of apostasy can easily be abused and has been abused in the past to suppress political opposition and inhibit spiritual and intellectual growth. This aspect of *shari'a* is fundamentally inconsistent with the numerous provisions of the Qur'an and *sunna* which enjoin freedom of religion and expression.

Another aspect of the historical experience of Muslims brought into focus by the Rushdie affair is the tradition of direct violent action and self-help, which goes back to the earliest times of Islam. Examples can be cited of the Prophet instructing Muslims to kill someone on sight or to correct an injustice by direct action. Unless these instances are identified and explained in their specific historical contexts or other special circumstances, they will continue to be used to undermine the rule of law and motivate terrorist action.

The Rushdie affair has attracted much attention because of its international, especially Western, dimension. Although I am fully aware of the realities of international power politics, I still believe that this affair is useful in publicizing the drastic incompatibility between *shari'a* and modern standards of international relations and human rights. Some of those who rushed to defend Rushdie no doubt had their ulterior motives; some may have acted out of spite for Islam and Muslims. As a Muslim, however, I have to concede that it was Muslim actions that gave occasion for such reactions. More important, I am concerned with the views of men and women of goodwill and sensitivity and wish to emphasize the value of this affair in illustrating the need for Islamic reform.

Although many contemporary Muslims would privately object to *shari'a*'s suppression of freedom of belief and expression, very few are willing to express their objections publicly for fear of being branded as apostates themselves—guilt by association. Other Muslims would find it difficult to admit their objections, even to themselves, for fear of losing their faith in the process. As long as the public law of *shari'a* continues to be regarded as the only valid view of the law of Islam, most Muslims would find it extremely difficult to object to any of its principles and rules or to resist their practical implementation, however repugnant and inappropriate they may find them to be.

The public law of *shari'a* has not been applied for many generations in most parts of the Muslim world. Moreover, the nature and style of classical treatises on *shari'a* make them generally inaccessible even to the highly educated contemporary Muslim. As a result of these and other factors, the vast majority of Muslims today are unaware of the full implications of the modern application of the public law of *shari'a* If contemporary Muslims can clearly envisage the ways in which the application of *shari'a* would affect their daily lives, and if they were given a free choice in opposing the application of *shari'a* without the threat of prosecution for apostasy or the fear of losing their faith in Islam, I believe that most of them would strongly oppose the application of *shari'a* today.

The fundamental objective of this book is to start a process of drastic reform of Islamic law that would enable Muslims to seek to achieve their right to self-determination in terms of an Islamic identity (whether Sunni, Shi'i, or variations thereof), including the application of Islamic law, without violating the rights of others to self-determination. To this end, the book explains the negative consequences of the modern application of *shari'a* to demonstrate that it is *not* the appropriate vehicle for Islamic self-determination in the present context. An Islamic alternative to *shari'a* is provided as the appropriate framework for Muslims to exercise their right to

self-determination while fully respecting the rights of others, whether within their own countries or in other lands.

Reference has already been made to the difficulties facing Muslims who would otherwise criticize *shari'a* and oppose its application today. To help these Muslims overcome their inhibitions, I have shown that *shari'a* was in fact *constructed* by Muslim jurists over the first three centuries of Islam. Although derived from the fundamental divine sources of Islam, the Qur'an and *sunna*, *shari'a* is not divine because it is the product of *human interpretation* of those sources. Moreover, this process of construction through human interpretation took place within a specific historical context which is drastically different from our own. It should therefore be possible for contemporary Muslims to undertake a similar process of interpretation and application of the Qur'an and *sunna* in the present historical context to develop an alternative public law of Islam which is appropriate for implementation today.

In addition to explaining and documenting the validity of this premise, I have suggested that the reform methodology developed by the late Sudanese Muslim reformer *Ustadh* Mahmoud Mohamed Taha appears to be the most appropriate means for constructing the modern public law of Islam out of the Qur'an and *sunna* as interpreted in the present historical context. Whether this particular methodology is accepted or rejected by contemporary Muslims, the need for drastic reform of the public law of *shari'a* is beyond dispute.

Optimism is a necessity of life, especially for a Muslim today. As a Muslim optimist, I believe in the power of ideas, when expounded in the right way at the right time, to inspire significant social and political change. I also believe in the progressive force of life and the ability of people to struggle for and achieve a quality of life compatible with their human dignity and well-being. It would be irresponsible wishful thinking on my part, however, to overlook the power of reactionary forces or to underestimate the difficulties facing the struggle for human dignity and well-being.

I am painfully aware that the vast majority of the Muslim peoples throughout the world live at a superficial level of both Islam and modern civilization. Although they claim adherence to Islam and exhibit apparent commitment to its ritualistic formalities, most contemporary Muslims fail to appreciate and live up to its moral and spiritual essence. Moreover, although they have grown accustomed to enjoying the benefits of modern technology and claim adherence to modern institutions, the majority of Muslim peoples have little appreciation of the values and ways of thinking that underlie and sustain that technology and those institutions. Many distinguished modern Muslim scholars have lamented this state of affairs in the Muslim world, but as long as it persists, the voices of fanaticism will find receptive ears and the forces of regression will have eager followers.

It may therefore appear presumptuous to expect a book that is written in English and is likely to be banned in some Muslim countries to have any significant impact in the Muslim world. Despite the oppressive nature of most political regimes and the conservative orientation of many societies in the Muslim world, however, I believe that the ideas expressed here will reach the hearts and minds of many Muslims. For one thing, most of these ideas already exist, perhaps in somewhat rudimentary and reticent form, in the hearts and minds of many Muslims, especially the younger generations, who are the more active agents of social change. It is my hope and expectation that this book will act as a catalyst for change in the Muslim world by presenting these ideas in a systematic and comprehensive fashion and providing them with an Islamic rationale, Moreover, the cultural interdependence of the modern world is making it increasingly difficult to exclude ideas and diminish their impact.

Contemporary Muslims are not the only audience for this book. Although issues of Islamic law reform and social and political change in the Muslim world are primarily the business of the peoples of Muslim countries, these matters are the legitimate concern of all humankind because of their impact on the human rights and fundamental freedoms of human beings. Conversely, the peoples of Muslim countries should be concerned with similar matters in non-Muslim lands. Humanity can no longer disclaim responsibility for the fate of human beings in any part of the world. This is the glorious achievement of the modern international human rights movement. All the peoples of the world are hereby invited to assist Muslims in their predicament and to accept the assistance of Muslims to non-Muslims in their predicaments. It should be emphasized, however, that these efforts of mutual assistance must be undertaken with due sensitivity and goodwill if they are to be most effective.

It is my conviction as a Muslim that the public law of *shari'a* does not represent the law of Islam which contemporary Muslims are supposed to implement in fulfillment of their religious obligation. I also strongly believe that the application of the public law of *shari'a* today will be counterproductive and detrimental to Muslims and to Islam itself. I hope that this book, with the help and guidance of God, will contribute in bringing all Muslims to a clear realization of these facts and in enabling them to develop and implement the appropriate public law of Islam for today.

My trust in God leads me to believe that current efforts to implement the public law of *shari'a* will fail because they are harmful to the best interests of Islam and the Muslims. These efforts will fail because the public law of *shari'a* is fundamentally inconsistent with the realities of modern life. This is my firm conviction as a Muslim. My only concern is to avoid the human suffering which is likely to be caused by this doomed endeavor. May this book, by the grace of God, contribute to minimizing that suffering.

Alhaji Adeleke Dirisu Ajijola

The Problem of *'Ulama'*

Islamic reformers in Nigeria are divided in numerous factions, some of them liberal and most of them not. The more moderate reformers tend to be members of the political elite, which has ruled Nigeria for much of the independence period through military dictatorship; their religious liberalism does not always carry over into their political beliefs.[1] By contrast, Alhaji Adeleke Dirisu Ajijola (Nigeria, born 1932), an attorney and prolific author on Islamic themes, espouses reform in both the political and religious arenas. In this text, Ajijola forcefully defends the right of all Muslims to interpret religious doctrine, contesting the monopoly of the *'ulama'* (religious scholars).

The *'ulama'* in Islam simply form a category of citizens specialized in Islamic humanistic culture and little knowledge of Muslim law. Those who are advanced in Islamic legal studies are given the name of *fuqaha'* or jurists. Normally disputes or cases pertaining to religious matter may be referred to them.

It must, however, be noted that *'ulama'* are not what clerics are in Christian communities or in any other religions, for in Islam, there is neither clergy nor an intermediary between man and God.

But today in Nigeria, the *'ulama'* have taken over as the leaders of Muslim communities—a job they are not equipped to handle properly. It must be conceded that the survival of Islamic learning in the present-day Nigeria is due to their uncompromising efforts. Credit must also be given to them for religious education.

Nevertheless, at the present time they are giving wrong education to our young men and women, for any young person who devotes himself only to religious education as presently thought without incorporating professional education as it is imparted today, is ill equipped for the struggle of life and the race for progress in fast-changing Nigeria.

Many of the *'ulama'* who have become Muslim leaders have themselves lost the true spirit of Islam. They do not have the ability to interpret the principles and law of Islam in the light of changing conditions. They have little juristic insight or practical wisdom. They lack the power of action and are utterly incapable of reducing the external and flexible principles of Islam from the book of God, and the teaching of the Prophet to the changing conditions of life.

On the contrary, they are obsessed with the past and addicted to uncritical acceptance and blind imi-

1. Peter Clarke, "Islamic Reform in Contemporary Nigeria," *Third World Quarterly*, volume 10, number 3, April 1988, p. 521.

tation of ancient dead Muslim jurists' views, especially those of the Maliki school of [Islamic] law on all issues. Some of the so-called learned and highly [educated] government officials among the so-called *qadi*s [Islamic judges] equate the Qur'an with the work of ancient jurists—with the consequence that whenever any problem arose, they did not turn to the divine book, the Holy Qur'an which is above the limitation of time and space, but instead devoted their attention to books produced by the ancient jurists who are men like themselves.

With great respect to the ancient jurists who have made great contributions to Islam, these men with all their great qualities were not apostles of God. Their wisdom and foresight could never transcend the limitations of their time and condition and varying circumstances of life of their age.

The teaching of these jurists, however wise and pious, are not at all capable of guiding the Muslim on the eve of the 21st century of the Christian era, at a time when the conditions as well as the practical fields of human activities have undergone a revolutionary change, which only God Almighty could know and which could not possibly have been foreseen centuries earlier by any person not endowed with prophetic insight and powers.

The *'ulama'* were not equipped with the required instruments to proffer alternative lines of development. They were merely interested in condemning the evils of Western civilization without appreciating the good in it. This has led to inertia and inaction. They forget that the trend of events in the modern world cannot be countered with outdated logic, outworn argument; the *'ulama'* cannot gain anything by closing their eyes to the reality of modern Nigeria.

It is a pity that our *'ulama'* did not try seriously to comprehend the prevailing trends and the mental make-up of modern men and women in Nigeria. They are incapable of proffering solutions to the various complicated intellectual economic, political and practical problems that the new conditions of life have created for the Muslim of the present age. They merely go to Mecca without noticing the legal, economic and social evolution that is taking place in Saudi Arabia.

Even in the manner in which they are trying to explain, the teaching and law of Islam appear to be calculated to repel rather than attract the modern educated mind. Indeed some of their explanations are so crude that they are a disservice to Islam.

Many of these *'ulama'* still live in the past. *'Ulama'* were the standard bearers of Islamic learning and culture of the past, but because of deficiencies in their education they are incapable of leading and guiding modern Muslims in any spheres of life.

Their concern is to force Nigerian Muslims to apply the so-called Maliki school of law in all legal matters. To them this is the panacea solution to the problem facing the Muslims.

There are other groups of Muslims who have Western education and whose motto is to succeed in world affairs. These groups join other similar groups of non-Muslim religion [primarily Christianity] in controlling the intellectual, literary, economic and political affairs of Nigeria.

But unlike their non-Muslim counterparts who take active part in their religion, they are ignorant of the principles and essential features of Islam. They are alien to the spirit of Islamic culture and are unaware of the character of communal organization of Islam and its social law, except for its spark of faith in the recesses of their mind.

The Muslim in this group does not at all differ from a non-Muslim. When there is any conflict between Muslims and non-Muslims, they immediately condemn their fellow Muslims, branding them as intolerant. Yet, it is this group of Muslims that have Western education and possess intellectual, technical and practical power, and it is they alone, with non-Muslims of the other group, that possess the capacity and the strength to govern the affairs of Nigeria. The *'ulama'* and the Western-educated Muslims are diametrically opposed and often at loggerheads with each other. This is a dangerous situation which must be resolved in the interests of Islam. This situation is blamed on *'ulama'* and Muslim leaders whose duty right at the onset of colonization of Nigeria was to bestir themselves and try to comprehend the principles and essential future of the new civilization of the West, and make the best use of their sons and daughters who acquired this education.

This should have avoided the present struggle between the stagnant and backward cultural position of Muslim leaders, the *'ulama'*, and the civilization of the West, which the Western-educated Muslims have acquired, throbbing with life and zeal with light of knowledge and the vigor of activities.

This problem can be solved only through the interpretation of the principle of Islamic theology and law in the light of changing conditions. The Muslims must go back to the Qur'an to find remedy to their problems. . . . But it is tragic that Nigerian *'ulama'* seem to shun any such endeavors calling them to revert to the principal source of Islamic civilization to find solutions to Muslims' problems.

To progress, the educated Muslim has to study the intellectual and scientific foundation on which the edifice of Western civilization has been raised.

With the help of *ijtihad* [Islamic interpretation], they should [seek] to persuade the Muslims to accept and press into service the useful practical knowledge and scientific discoveries that enable Western nations to achieve such remarkable material progress. They should fit these new instruments of progress in keeping with the principles of Islam, into the educational system and social life of Muslims.

Islam resolves the supposed conflicts between science and religion; it does not ask Muslims to ignore the law of nature and reject what is established through positive scientific observation and calculations. On the contrary, it exacts its followers to study the law of nature and derive benefits from them.

Rational speculation is the foundation of Islam. The Qur'an, which urges men to consider the universe for themselves, laid the foundation of scientific research. The Qur'an stresses scientific investigation by urging people to find out the secrets of creation for themselves. "Do they not consider how camels have been created, nor how the sky has been lifted, nor how the mountains have been created, not even how the earth has been flattened?" [Sura 88, Verses 17–20].

The Qur'an reconciles science and religion, [while] the stand accepted today as materialism appears to have reached its climax and has found itself in urgent need of spiritual values.

In order to awaken man's faith in one God, it does not use miracles but ordinary faculty of human reason. Later on, in order to awaken belief in the prophets and in the divine revelations, Islam presents that great miracle known as the Qur'an (which in itself is both an understandable science and the intelligible word of God).

It does not expect that man should accept Islam with passive faith, without the active application of his intelligence. Rather, it invites him to understand it, to meditate on it to the limit which human intelligence and reason permit, and it challenges him to find a way to deny its superiority, or find a work which could be its equal (Sura 2, Verse 24).

The importance which is assigned to reason and difference of opinion in Islam is such that for the majority of Muslims, when there is an irreconcilable conflict between an alleged tradition and reason, the latter must prevail and the tradition must be rejected as spurious. Difference of opinion has been described by the Qur'an as a continuous aspect of human life and even as a purpose of creation. "And if thy Lord had willed, he verily would have made mankind one nation, yet they cease not to differ, save those on whom thy Lord hath mercy, and for that He did create them" (Sura 11, Verses 118–119). Now, a religion which has its basis in rational speculation, and which gives such a broad scope to reason, a religion that orders the use of all the faculties bestowed upon man by God, and consequently the one which is greatest of all, namely, his intelligence, how could such a religion be an obstacle in the way of science and philosophy?

When the courts and schools of Islam were lighthouses, when knowledge reached Europe which was at that time in the midst of the darkness of the Middle Ages; when the thoughts of Muslim philosophers reached such heights that they led the way for Western scholars; when Harun ar-Rashid [caliph, circa 763–809] required a school for the study of various sciences to be attached to each mosque; and when libraries rich in hundreds and thousands of books were opened to scholars all over the Islamic world, were the Muslims not the first to apply experimental methods, long before Francis Bacon [English scientist, 1561–1626] proclaimed their necessity?

The development of chemistry, of astronomy, the propagation of Greek science, the promotion of the study of medicine and the discovery of various physical laws—are not these to the credit of the Muslims?

It is an admitted fact that Muslims made notable contributions in the fields of mathematics, chemistry and physical sciences, the greatest being the use of objective experiments to test the veracity of facts. The achievements of Jabir Ibn Hayyan (Geber) [Syrian scientist, 721–776] were outstanding and constituted, until the eighteenth century, the foundation of modern chemistry. The name of the anthropologist and free thinker Abu 'Uthman 'Amr Ibn Bahr Al-Jahiz (died 869) is ranked amongst the most distinguished pioneers of this discipline. He was a radical theologian, whose books are still read for the elegance of his Arabic prose.

If this is so, then it is wrong to say as many Christians in Nigeria assume, that it is in the nature of Islamic religion to create obstacles in the way of the progress of science. Let us say instead that at times statesmanship was compelled, in order to preserve peace in certain territories, to repress currents of thoughts which the rulers believed could become dangerous to the public order, that political and sometimes personal struggles, rather than religious causes, have in the past determined the attitudes of theologians, lawmakers, traditionalists and philosophers.

It must, however, be recognized that even today in certain Muslim environments, there are strong objections to rational science and to modern industry. Such traditional Muslims remain strongly bound to their old traditions, based on their school of law.

Some Muslims are even filled with exaggerated fanaticisms. There are still jurists who are so attached to the literal expressions of juristic work which they regard as fundamental that they refuse to express an opinion when a new case appears for which no clue is to be found in these juristic work; or they try to keep the case in abeyance until they succeed in agreeing on a well-accepted opinion of one of their preferred authors—but it is not fair to accuse the spirit of Islam of rigidity and immobility, simply because of certain local situations and customs that are to be found in particular historical conditions today, or because of the over-rigid mentality of certain Muslim groups who accepted the juristic work as divine law.

But, unfortunately, many Muslim leaders in Nigeria have not adopted scientific methods, but follow blindly the views of the ancient jurists, particularly those of the Maliki school of law. They argue only that they want to establish an Islamic way of life; they forget that this way of life must relate to the reality of life in Nigeria, otherwise this ideal will remain a mere slogan and deception.

The Islamic way of life to me means scientific advancement and progress coupled with Islamic principles which should make Muslims remain spiritually and morally human beings and not machines.

The Nigerian Muslims like their non-Muslims brothers are engaged in a titanic struggle against poverty, hunger and disease. They know that their lot can be improved only by superior knowledge which science and technology bring with them.

At the beginning of Islam, there was cross-fertilization of knowledge existing in the Orient and Occident. It is an interesting fact of history that at that time the stimulation for scientific development flowed from Muslims to non-Muslims and today it must flow from non-Muslims to Muslims.

I do not think that it is derogatory to learn science and technology from a non-Muslim, but in learning new things from others, the Muslim should retain those good things that are wonderful and beautiful in Islamic teaching, doctrines that are capable of removing friction amongst individuals and nations.

The Muslim should have an open mind and an open heart in adopting good things from other people. Muslim scientists must develop critical minds and use initiative, independence and persistence when dealing with European scientific discovery.

European scientists were able to lay the foundation of technological and industrial power because they devoted themselves to further inquiry and research. Muslim scientists similarly have to acquire knowledge with continuous and painstaking efforts at extending the frontiers of knowledge.

Today is the age of science and the civilization of science. Anyone desirous of living an honorable life cannot escape the use of modern science. The quicker the *'ulama'* and Muslims enter the age of science the better.

The basic problems of Nigeria today in the field of science and technology are associated with a search for greater productivity and a higher standard of living for its populace. This is why Muslims must lay emphasis on scientific education with a bias towards Islamic studies.

Why Islamic Law Should Be Applied

Modern man is threatened by a world created by himself; he is faced with the conversion of mind to naturalism, dogmatic secularism and opposition to belief in the Transcendent.

The true remedy, therefore, for the ills that affect mankind and threaten to overwhelm it today and tomorrow is for man to turn to God with single-minded purpose and make his peace with Him, having sincerely determined that in all matters, whatever, His guiding rule shall be. . . .

That is why the Muslims all over the world want the application of Islamic civil law. Islamic civil law sets forth and places at man's disposal a most effective and potent means of achieving the purpose of life. It is the best of all God's numberless bounties bestowed upon man; it is indispensable for the beneficent growth of man in the epoch now unfolding before him. . . .

But, the real question is not whether Islamic civil law should be applied or not, which all Muslims accept, but whether Nigeria should continue to apply classical juristic work without any modification or whether Islamic civil law in Nigeria should be applied within the primary source of Islamic law, i.e. the Qur'an and tradition of the Prophet. . . .

The problem of Muslims in Nigeria is that many of the so-called Arabists believe that juristic work is so comprehensive that it provides solutions to all human problems for all times.

But, with all the comprehensiveness of the juristic works, this system is after all an individual interpretation and as such cannot claim any finality. Did the founders of our schools of laws ever claim finality for their reasoning and interpretation? "Never."

The teaching of the Qur'an that life is a process of progressive creation necessitates that each generation, guided but unhampered by the work of its predecessors, should be permitted to solve its own problems.

Unfortunately many Muslims and non-Muslims regard the systems [prescribed] by various juristic school as the *shari'a* [Islamic law], although the juristic works constitute a long development of interpretation of the term *ijtihad* or reasoning. But this reasoning, to be accepted, must always rest on the texts of the Qur'an and the accepted *sunna* [practices of the Prophet]. But this juristic reasoning is always apt to vary from jurist to jurist and from time to time. The variety of opinion within juristic reasoning implics on the one hand a wealth of juridical [sources] and the remarkable techniques of interpreting the *shari'a* to solve the problems of their days. This, however, must be subordinated to the binding texts of the *shari'a*. A particular juristic notion may be rigid or may be wrong, nor should any juristic school or group of schools be identified with the Holy Qur'an and Prophet of Islam.

The principles in the Qur'an have great potentialities of expansion and development by interpretation from age to age to meet the changing conditions of man. It seeks to guide its followers in secular as well as spiritual affairs. It gave the world a sound conception of state, society and law unrivaled by any other religion or civilization.

Today it is recognized that Islamic civil law is a living force and, progressing in many Muslim countries within its accepted limits imposed by the divine command, is capable of meeting the challenge of the modern age.

Islamic civil law takes the whole of human conduct for its field. The verse conspectus of the jurists' work was not contained in Qur'an or the *sunna*. The jurists used their reason to interpret the law to solve the problem of their days. The problem facing the Muslim today could hardly have been conceived by the classical writers. Why then should the Muslims of today consider the jurists' views as divine law, and as such regard it as basically immutable?

The Qur'an and the *sunna* have always been regarded by the early doctors of Muslim laws as providing them a ground work of legal principles which far from leaving no scope for thought and legislative activities, had enabled them to evolve a practical legal system. The most significant is that there is no comparative system of civil law even in the so-called developed countries that can rival the excellency of Islamic civil law. . . .

The Muslims of the present age must find solutions to their problems from the Holy Qur'an and the *sunna*. This they can only do by exerting their energy and reasoning in conducting research into the Holy Qur'an and interpreting it in the light of modern scientific knowledge. But the Muslims will never develop as long as they blindly follow and accept as final the view of juristic works which were meant to solve the problems of 700 to 1300, which in my view is not relevant to the problems of the Muslims on the eve of 21st century of the Christian era.

It is tragic for the Muslims of Nigeria that Muslim leaders, particularly the Arabists occupying high official positions, have themselves lost the true spirit of Islam. They do not have the ability to interpret the principles and laws of Islam in the light of the changing conditions. . . . On the contrary, they are obsessed with the past and addicted to uncritical acceptance and blind imitation of antique Muslim juristic works as a final authority on Islam. . . .

I am not advocating for the total rejection of juristic opinion, but I am opposed to following them blindly as if they are the final authority on Islam. The present generation of Muslims may gain from their work on how they have interpreted the *shari'a* to meet and solve the problems of their days. But present-day Muslims must never regard juristic reasoning as final. They must use their own intelligence to interpret the *shari'a* to meet the problems of today.

The Evolution and Devolution
of Religious Knowledge

Abdul-Karim Soroush (Iran, born 1945), a pharmacologist and philosopher educated in Iran and England, was until recently a dean at the Research Institute for Human Sciences in Tehran and "one of the most prominent speakers in Iran in the 1990s," lecturing at mosques, universities, and over the radio.[1] Soroush used this prominent position to argue forcefully for a rethinking of Islam's relationship to the non-Muslim West. In particular, his studies in the philosophy of science have led him to suggest that Islamic nations can and must allow scientific advance, including relatively free conditions for researchers, and that religion can be studied "rationally" like other phenomena.[2] In this essay, Soroush argues that religion is divine but religious interpretation is human, fallible, and even sociologically determined. Such positions have put Soroush at odds with other Islamic scholars in Iran. In the mid-1990s, Soroush received death threats for his theological positions, was physically attacked on two occasions, has been banned from public lectures, and may lose his job.[3]

The science of nature is a human endeavor to understand nature, and the science of religion is a human endeavor to understand religion. All understanding assumes suppositions and entails "categorization," that is, subsuming the particular under universal categories and concepts. Understanding religion is no exception. It is preceded by certain assumptions and principles which are necessary conditions for its intelligibility and interpretation.

1. Farhang Rajaee, "Islam and Modernity: The Reconstruction of an Alternative Shi'ite Islamic Worldview in Iran," in Martin E. Marty and R. Scott Appleby, editors, *Fundamentalisms and Society* (Chicago: University of Chicago Press, 1993), p. 111.

2. Mehrzad Boroujerdi, "The Encounter of Post-Revolutionary Thought in Iran with Hegel, Heidegger, and Popper," in Şerif Mardin, editor, *Cultural Transitions in the Middle East* (Leiden, The Netherlands: E. J. Brill, 1994), pp. 236–259; Yann Richard, "Clercs et Intellectuels de la République Islamique d'Iran" (Clerics and Intellectuals of the Islamic Republic of Iran), in Gilles Kepel and Yann Richard, editors, *Intellectuels et militants de l'Islam contemporain* (*Intellectuals and Militants of Contemporary Islam*) (Paris: Seuil, 1990), pp. 48–58; Valla Vakili, *Debating Religion and Politics in Iran: The Religions Thought of Abdolkarim Soroush* (New York: Council on Foreign Relations, occasional paper no. 2, 1996).

3. *Index on Censorship*, volume 25, number 4, July–August 1996, pp. 165–178.

This seemingly Kantian position is more than familiar today, but a century ago not only was it a blasphemous view concerning religion, but a dubious one even in the case of natural sciences. The positivism of [John Stuart] Mill [English philosopher, 1806–1873] and [Francis] Bacon [English philosopher, 1561–1626] based itself on the idea that "brute facts" were available and only needed an open eye to be captured by observation. But later developments in the philosophy of science demonstrated clearly, to their utter disappointment, that these "brute facts" existed nowhere except in the barren lands of wild hallucinations of speculators. Even in simple inductive research, where the regular association of successive events is under scrutiny, one cannot be sure of the complete list of the relevant factors nor of the right aspects of the events subject to generalization. In all these cases one has to be equipped with a preassumed picture of the scene of research in order to know where to begin and where to end, what to include and explain and what to exclude as irrelevant or unimportant. These schemes are not sacrosanct; they can be criticized, modified, refined or perhaps redefined, but two things are absolutely certain about them: number one, their absolute inevitability in the field of research and for the purpose of understanding; number two, their transcendence and independence relative to the world of experiment.

Now, more important than all that is their impact on the whole context of the final product of the research. Preassumptions are not like chemical catalysts whose function is only to facilitate an otherwise slow chemical reaction, but rather like a matchmaker whose mediation determines who marries whom and shapes the whole structure of the ensuing family, within the conceivable and available possibilities of the age. The main and radical difference between positivist and post-positivist philosophy is the recognition of the fact, on the part of philosophers, that observation does not stand alone; it is theory-laden. In other words it is, of necessity, preceded by theories on the one hand and colored by the same theories on the other. Interestingly enough, scientific instruments which seem to provide us with careful observation and measurements, such as microscopes and nuclear magnetic resonance devices, are nothing but complex theoretical assumptions arranged and objectified in such a way as to allow us to put certain questions to nature and obtain answers therefrom.

The theory-ladenness of observations has been shown to be a fact of the history of science, as well as an implicit requirement of the method of science, that is, the logic of the understanding of nature. This important and pivotal insight, permeating the whole body of science, has been able to link areas as far apart from each other as logic, history, and the sociology of science, re-molding them into a unified whole, namely the contemporary post-positivistic philosophy of science.

In the same sense and exactly for the same reasons, one can say that the text does not stand alone, it does not carry its own meaning on its shoulders, it needs to be situated in a context, it is theory-laden, its interpretation is in flux, and presuppositions are as actively at work here as elsewhere in the field of understanding. Religious texts are no exception. Therefore their interpretation is subject to expansion and contraction according to the assumptions preceding them and/or the questions enquiring them. These assumptions can be of very different nature, ranging from philosophical, historical, and theological to the more specific assumptions such as linguistic and sociological ones. (These are part of the worldview of the age, which need not and do not usually enter the mind through formal education, but are utilized inadvertently and fluently.)

Now, since presuppositions are age-bound, can change and do change in fact, religious knowledge, or the science of religion which is the product of comprehending it, will be in continuous flux, and since it is only through those presuppositions that one can hear the voice of revelation—hence the religion itself is silent— and since the interpretation of the text is social by nature and depends on the community of experts, like all learned activities it will be an independent dynamic entity, abstracting from individual interpreters; containing right and wrong, certain and dubious ideas—the wrong ones being as important as the right ones from the evolutionary point of view. It is a branch of knowledge, no less, no more.

The outcome of the preceding concise arguments can be briefly listed as follows:

1. Religion, or revelation for that matter, is silent.
2. The science of religion is relative, that is, relative to presuppositions.
3. The science of religion is age-bound, because presuppositions are.

4. Revealed religion itself may be true and free from contradictions, but the science of religion is not necessarily so.
5. Religion may be perfect or comprehensive, but not so for the science of religion.
6. Religion is divine, but its interpretation is thoroughly human and this-worldly.

That is the story of religion. All this implies that religion is always surrounded by a host of contemporaneous data and deliberations, in constant give and take with them, the interpretation of which remains constant so long as these external elements are constant; once they change, the change will be reflected in the understanding of religion as well. Therefore it is not because of conspiracy or aberration of mind or illegitimate manipulation or extravagant interpretations that the science of religion changes. Rather, it is the natural product of the evolution of human understanding in non-religious fields and contexts that forces religion to be comprehended differently. And as mentioned above, external factors are responsible not only for the change, but also for the constancy of religious interpretation throughout the ages.

The worldview of classical humanity—its view of nature, man, God, history, language, society, happiness, certainty, reason, knowledge and the like—was reflected in its understanding of religion in the same manner and to the same extent as the worldview of modern humanity has exerted its influence on the science of religion. Each interpretation, of course, seems as natural and as true as the other to the party concerned.

This rough statement of the position of the "evolution and devolution of religious knowledge" may seem a pretty straightforward a priori piece of epistemology, not unfamiliar to hermeneuticists and philosophers of science. But it has two serious shortcomings. First, it may not look convincing or revealing enough to more historically minded scholars, who may ask for more historical data and a posteriori justification in support of the suggested doctrine. Second, it may seem a flatly false and even blasphemous idea about religion, whose revelatory nature, according to true believers, guarantees its constancy, relevance, and truth throughout history. Relativity and change are characteristics of man-made systems whose application to divine revelation would be utterly misplaced. In addition to that, it seems as if the

doctrine puts religion at the mercy of extra-religious principles whose truth and accuracy are not certain, compromising the whole message of religion, whose main mission is to offer fallible humanity an infallible source of certainty and information.

Both questions are too complex to be treated here in depth and in full. But certain remarks are in order.

First, as to the demand of historians. The conflict between science and religion in Europe from the 16th century onwards is a very telling case. At first glance science made mincemeat of religion, disproved it in an unsurpassed manner, and demonstrated its reactionary nature forever. (This is clearly a positivistic orientation that makes the meaning transparent for the unarmed observer.) But for more serious thinkers, religious and otherwise, and from an epistemological standpoint, it was a matchless opportunity to uncover the essence of those epoch-making champions. It showed at least that the clergy, trying in earnest to comprehend revelation, had generously and undeliberately utilized their medieval and premedieval worldviews to acquire the "true" interpretation of the Book, and of course they could not have done otherwise. All they should have realized, and it was later realized thoroughly indeed, thanks to the blessed conflict, was that a new constellation of suppositions was also conceivable in which religion might seem more consistent with the wisdom of the age. Reinterpretations began, and they were as we now know, nothing but revisions made in light of extra-religious shifts. It was seldom the case that words were found to be mistranslated from Greek or Syriac. Rather, debates on the language of religion revealed the depth of the indebtedness of textual interpretation to the implicit principles and presuppositions of the believers. It should be obvious by now that it is not enough for an interpreter to give simply a consistent interpretation of a whole text; interpretation must also be consistent with the received wisdom of the age.

Horrifying as this might sound, one has to notice that this has been the actual practice of all serious religious thinkers of all ages. In Iran, for instance, [Molla] Sadroddin Shirazi [1571–1640] and his followers are proud that they have successfully reconciled shari'a [Islamic law], 'irfan [mysticism], and philosophy—in short, revelation and reason. This can only occur through a reinterpretation of shari'a according to the principles of philosophy, that is, to subsume it under philosophical categories. Some might think that Sadroddin's rational justification of the dogmas of religion is the proper essence of his efforts to reconcile reason and revelation. But to put matters this way is to put the cart before the horse. In order to justify a statement rationally, one has to rationalize it first, that is, define its concept and categories in such a way as to render them liable to rational justification. Take the case of bodily resurrection (*ma'ad*). Sadroddin says quite explicitly that it does not become a true philosopher to be content with a simple belief in *ma'ad*; rather he must secure a rational understanding thereof. He must accept, for instance, an Aristotelian definition of the body as consisting of form and matter, and he must also accept Sadroddin's principle that the form, rather than the matter, is the primary constituent element of the body, in order to justify bodily resurrection in a rational metaphysical way (bodies being resurrected in form rather than in matter). In other words, philosophical understanding of the text precedes the philosophical justification of it.

Therefore, the desired reconciliation between religion and philosophy cannot be purchased except at the expense of one being colored by the other; that is, only a conceptually philosophical religion (or, more meticulously put, a philosophized comprehension of a religious text) can be reconciled with philosophy, and a conceptual mystification of the religion would always precede the mystical justification of it, and so forth.

Mystical and philosophical Islam are but two conceivable kinds of Islam, better articulated and refined than others at the present, but in practice there are virtually innumerable types of Islam, all sharing the common feature of being in balance with the believers' extra-religious system of thought. Now, disputing the validity of those mystical and philosophical interpretations of the text is missing the point completely. These are parts and moments of the history of religion; all science is a mixture of right and wrong ideas. Despite the fact that every scientist tries hard to secure hard facts and true ideas, science itself, transcending the beliefs and opinions of this or that particular scientist, cannot but consist of errors, misunderstandings, dubious hypotheses, arguments and counterarguments, side by side with firmly established facts and conclusions. To see only the good side of the story is to distort history. There, defeats are as important as victories, and both are of the same value as far as the evolutionary life of science is con-

cerned. The science of religion, to repeat the same point again, is no exception.

As another example take the case of *tafsir bi-ra'y*, that is, the interpretation of the Qur'an according to one's wishes and views (*ra'y* comes from *ru'ya*, meaning "to see," so that "view" is the exact rendering of the word). Muslims have been severely warned against this kind of interpretation, and a tradition of the Prophet has it that he who interprets the Qur'an in conformity with his views, his dwelling place (in the hereafter) will be filled with fire.

Controversies over the exact meaning and applicability of *tafsir bi-ra'y* are never-ending. Everybody claims to have avoided it while at the same time accusing others of committing the sin of subjecting the Qur'an to his own views, and rightly so, and no one really shows the way out. It has proved to be a hard nut to crack. In our own time 'Allama Mohammad Husayn Tabataba'i [1903–1981], the author of *Tafsir al-Mizan* [*The Scale, an Analysis of the Qur'an*, 20 volumes, 1954–1972], suffered from the same charge despite his own warning in the introduction to his commentary against mixing up *tatbiq* (conforming) and *tafsir* (commenting).

The gracious advice of some of the uninitiated, that the objective commentator accomplishes the impossible task of wiping from mind every idea and opinion, except perhaps grammar and vocabulary, should be taken with a grain of salt. It is impossible because the history of religion demonstrates clearly that no one has ever been able to comply with this advice. Even more disastrously, to do so would be undesirable as well, because it would render the whole task of interpretation unrealizable. One has, at the least, to take a position as to whether God speaks in figurative language or not. Surely this position cannot be derived from the texts of religion themselves, or we will be trapped in a vicious circle. Therefore the position and its negation are both views (*ra'y*) to be adopted prior to the act of interpretation. So how are we to understand the threatening warning about objective and opinion-free interpretation of the Qur'an? Isn't it the case that all interpretations are theory-laden? If so, then isn't it better to take the warning as meaning simply not to base our interpretation on unsubstantiated theories? Yes. That is all. Therefore, everything hinges upon the extratextual positions again.

Tabataba'i, in his commentary, names theologians, philosophers, Sufis, and modernists as four groups who did not take care to extract the exact meaning of the text, but rather tried to impose their own views upon it, and committed *ta'wil* [claiming an internal meaning in contrast to the outward meaning], which is the paradigmatic case of *tafsir bi-ra'y*, in order to make verses of the Qur'an conform to their positions. In the case of modernists he specifically mentions the *ta'wil* they made about *'arsh* (throne), *kursi* (chair), *lowh* (tablet), *qalam* (pen), interpreting these terms so as to imply material things (Tabataba'i, p. 7). He goes on to say that all these methods have one serious shortcoming in common, namely, imposing extratextual scientific and/or philosophical meanings on verses, thereby converting some of the literal meanings of the words into metaphors and some of the direct meanings into *ta'wil*.

His own method, according to Tabataba'i, is to collate one part of the text to another in order to construct the meaning through this hermeneutical circle. But he gives us at least one explicit hint as to the implicit foundations of his method, namely, that the language of the Qur'an is not to be taken too materialistically, because neither the materiality nor the actual structure of things are included in the meanings of words, only their functions are intended. Take the word "scale" (*mizan*), for instance, whose meaning does not include "having pans." Digital scales are scales too. Perhaps future generations will witness totally different kinds of scales that we cannot dream of today. But one thing is certain: so long as something functions as a scale, it can be called a scale, no matter what it is made from or how it works. This paves the way, according to Tabataba'i, for us to grasp the true meaning of words like *mizan* (scale), *lowh* (tablet), and *arsh* (throne) in the Qur'an, and for us to avoid repeating the mistakes of those superficial theologians and traditionalists who took the words to imply familiar material things. The idea, of course, comes from Abu Hamid al-Ghazzali [philosopher, 1058–1111] (and later [Jalal al-Din] Rumi [poet, 1207–1273] and Fayz Kashani [Mulla Muhsin, circa 1598–1680]). Al-Ghazzali is adamant in his *Mishkat al-Anwar* [*The Niche of Lights*] that the word "light" (*nur*), for instance, literally implies the immaterial light, and that its application to familiar physical light is entirely metaphorical.

Again, disputing the validity of these conclusions is totally irrelevant. What matters from the vantage point of epistemology is to notice the lofty suppositions that are at work here, and the testimony of one of the great members of the dynasty of commentators, namely, Tabataba'i, about the history of *tafsir* [textual analysis] (indeed, the whole history of religion) as being tampered with by the uneducated views and improper wishes of mystics, philosophers, theologians, traditionalists and modernists alike. Modifying tone and terms, we can state the same fact as follows: the science of religion has been under continuous construction and reconstruction by various commentators and interpreters during its long history, and religion is nothing but the history of the science of religion, of course.

We come to the conclusion then that the whole history of the sincere efforts of commentators to liberate Qur'anic commentary from the infiltration of external ideas have ended in one sharp and important result, namely, the practical unavoidability of such infiltration, together with its epistemological inevitability. In other words, it is in practice unavoidable because it is epistemologically inevitable.

Another example may serve the purpose better. The commentator Tabataba'i, who is at the same time also a metaphysician of the first rank, tries laboriously to show that the principle of causality is endorsed by the Qur'an, whereas Jalal al-Din Rumi, the great Iranian mystic poet of the 7th century A.H., points exactly in the opposite direction, that is, that indeterminism is the lesson to be drawn from the Qur'an:

> The prophets came in order to cut the cord of causes:
> They flung their miracles at Saturn.

> The whole of the Qur'an consists in the cutting off of causes. Its theme is the glory of the poor and the destruction of Abu Lahab [early enemy of Islam].

> In like manner, from the beginning of the Qur'an to the end, is the abandonment of causes and means. (*Mathnavi* [Couplets], volume 3, verses 2517, 2520, 2525)

Also of some interest is the criticism that Tabataba'i levels against [Mulla Mohammad Baqer] Majlesi, the great traditionalist (*muhaddith*) of the 11th century A.H. [1627–1698 A.D.] and the compiler of *Bihar al-anwar* [*Seas of Light*] in 110 volumes. Majlesi's persuasion was anti-philosophical—hence his rejection of words like *ruh* [spirit] and *nafs* [soul] as referring to immaterial entities. Tabataba'i takes issue with him not on the literal meanings of words but on one of the main suppositions he imputes to Majlesi, namely, the idea that the language of religion is addressed only to laymen. According to Tabataba'i, this is not the case, that some of the sayings of the Prophet (peace be upon him) and his progeny are addressed to experts as well, so that one must look at them with a trained eye. Tabataba'i thinks that Majlesi's mistrust of philosophy and philosophers has led him to infer incorrect and superficial meanings from some of the deepest and most exalted texts of Islam.

The case of *mutashabihat* is even more telling. According to Sura *Al-'Imran* (Sura 3, Verse 7), the verses of the Qur'an are divided into two major classes, *muhkamat* and *mutashabihat*, roughly referring to verses having certain and uncertain implications, respectively. Few verses in the Qur'an are as controversial as this one. Commentators' major controversies revolve around two central points: first, the exact meaning of these terms; second, the secret and the expediency of those "ambiguous" verses revealed to the Prophet. Some have argued that only the disconnected characters in the beginning of each *sura* are *mutashabih*, and all else is *muhkam*. Some have held that all verses covering resurrection and the attributes of God are *mutashabih*; still others have maintained that only verses concerning practical rituals and observances are *muhkam*; others consider only abrogated verses to be *mutashabih*; and one can find various other views as well.

As to the second point, namely, the question why the Qur'an contains such unclear verses, one comes across many curious hypotheses. These are but a few of them:

1. *Mutashabihat* are there in order for the believers to be distinguished from unbelievers. Faith cannot be but blind. True believers approve of all verses of the Qur'an, despite the fact that some of them offer no clear interpretation, but nonbelievers rely on their own reason and reject verses with unjustifiable or unclear meanings.
2. *Mutashabihat* are instrumental in mobilizing and cultivating reason, which is so dear to the Creator; hence their importance and their need to be incorporated in the Qur'an.
3. *Mutashabihat* attract the ill-hearted to the Qur'an in order to find materials for their devilish purposes; but this very act may sometimes lead them to the right path and may enlighten their hearts through the study of the Qur'an as a whole, both *mutashabihat* and *muhkamat*.
4. Religion and revelation are intended for all people, learned and otherwise; therefore, some very exalted ideas have to be conveyed in a very simple language, in the process mutilating facts and

statements. *Mutashabihat* are verses in which language is under severe strain, due to the loftiness of the guest and the tininess of the nest (to borrow an analogy from Rumi).

As can be seen, none of these views really deals with the requirements of textual interpretation; therefore all of them miss the important point that the presence of *mutashabihat* in the Qur'an is something inherent in the text, emerging in the context of interpretation, and has nothing to do with testing unbelievers and so on. The issue of *mutashabihat* is not confined to the Qur'an alone. All texts, especially revealed ones, should be expected to contain *muhkamat* as well as *mutashabihat*, whose existence is the clear cause and effect of the expansion and contraction of the science of religion. Once one looks carefully at the process of understanding texts, which is always to subject to presuppositions, the true meaning of and reason for their presence in the Qur'an becomes evident. Interestingly enough, the Qur'an itself does not give any clue as to how *mutashabihat* can be determined and distinguished from other verses, and the whole history of Islam clearly shows that virtually every verse of the Qur'an has been suspected at one time or another of being *mutashabih*, which is clear evidence in favor of the suggestion that all this stems from the nature of interpretation and interpreters' presuppositions.

As an instance of a non-linguistic presupposition, I may point to the problems one expects religion to solve—in brief, the question of expectations. Now this has got a very long and well-known theological ancestry reaching back to the vexed question of why people are in need of prophets. This is clearly an extra-religious question, the answer to which can have a profound impact on the way one interprets the text. Theologians who think that people cannot lead a happy life, individually and socially, without receiving guidance from prophets, naturally expect religions to advise people not only how to purify their souls and worship their creator, but also how to marry, wash, clean, eat, transact business, hire employees, lend money, punish criminals, and—above all—rule the country. These expectations of course induce one to search the text carefully and meticulously, lest one miss the minutest point alluding faintly to these anticipated matters, taking every hint seriously and building an entire edifice out of it. This is of course the dominant view in the Muslim world today.

But to those theologians who think otherwise, the content of the text is to be divided into two parts, essentials and accidentals, accidentals being functions of the cultural, social, and historical environment of the delivery of the main message, and more generally those points and allusions which are considered to be beyond the proper field of expectations. There are many *hadith*s (sayings of the Prophet) concerning treatment of diseases, say, but nobody really considers them essential to Islam because that is not what makes people needy of prophets. People themselves can find the facts about diseases and drugs through trial and error. If that is so, then what about philosophy, economics, politics, and the like? Are these also beyond the proper field of the mission of prophets? These are very crucial and hotly debated questions among Muslim intellectuals today, but the main issue sometimes remains untouched or unattended, namely the extra-textuality of the question of expectations. These problems are not to be decided on the strength of text and tradition or historical facts. On the contrary, tradition and the text should be explained in light of the expectations.

Treating these questions requires a good deal of philosophy, politics, sociology, and history, and that is what gives the science of religion the flavor of the age. That also explains why the true *ijtihad* (rational adjudication) in disciplines such as *fiqh* [Islamic jurisprudence] cannot materialize unless a true *ijtihad* in first principles has taken place beforehand. This, in turn, shows why *fiqh* has been so stagnant in religious seminaries in recent centuries. Since *fiqh* is a "consumer" science, its stagnation is due to the lack of dynamism on the part of the "producer" disciplines like economics, political philosophy, and *'Ilm al-Imran* (the sociology of Ibn Khaldun [1332–1406]). These constitute the relevant reasons for the stagnation. The story of the causes is different, of course.

The status and significance of religious revivalism and intellectualism can now be better understood. Broadly speaking, revivalism can transpire in two different manners, positive and negative. Negative revivalism consists in purging and purifying current religious understanding of alien elements and doing justice to the more neglected dimensions thereof— the great champion of the field being al-Ghazzali, no doubt. Positive revivalism, by contrast, is more attentive to and more deeply concerned with the extra-religious factors and foundations required for and relevant to the time-bound comprehension of the text.

The most prominent representative of this orientation is Muhammad Iqbal [India, 1877–1938], whose main complaint was directed to the dominance of Greek thought over Islamic culture. Both al-Ghazzali and Iqbal serve the same purpose, of course, namely, to keep the mission of religion alive. The difference is due to the first-order and second-order epistemological outlooks of the two forms of reform.

This brings me to the end of my treatment of the first question. But before leaving this part of the discussion, I would like to emphasize the point that religious reform in our time cannot succeed unless one is vigilant to the continuous new developments taking place in the different areas of thought. Mottos like "back to the roots" or "try the neglected sources" or "find a brave inspired thinker" can be very misleading. No reform can take place without re-shuffling the traditional suppositions, and no re-shuffling will be forthcoming unless one is well acquainted with both revelation and ideas developed outside the sphere of revelation. The truths uncovered inside and outside the sphere of revelation sooner or later approach an equilibrium. To combat the stagnation one has to mobilize the external sources. Muslims' decadent understanding of the sacred texts was a consequence of the decadent civilizational, cultural, and social climate, rather than vice versa.

Now as to the second charge, namely, betraying the sacredness of the text, sacrificing its eternal message at the doorstep of the vagaries of the age, and undermining the certitude of faith, I'd better start with a short dialogue which took place recently between a friend and myself. "What is your position on the Islamization of knowledge?" he asked me quite seriously, and then added in a jocular way, "Perhaps you opt for a scientization of Islam rather than Islamization of knowledge?" "Neither of the two," I replied. "I opt for the humanization of religion." That was my reply, and in fact it is the basic foundation on which the whole edifice of "The Evolution and Devolution of Religious Knowledge" is erected. Revealed religion, of course, is divine, but not so for the science of religion, which is a thoroughly human production and construction. It is human in the sense that it is imprinted by virtually all characteristics of human beings, both noble and mean.

Rationality, prejudice, egoism, truth-seeking, obliviousness, greed, fallibility, partiality, complacency, easygoingness, acquisitiveness, and the like all have their due share in the science of religion and all influence it in one way or another. True, the revelation is divine, but what about the interpretation of the revelation?

The interpretation no doubt may be conjectural, fallible, changeable, partial, fallacious, one-sided, misguided, prejudiced, culture-bound, and incomplete, but this is what the Source of Revelation has ordained it to be. We are fallible human beings and that is our lot from Truth. The case of religion is no better than the case of nature. There also we are captives of our humanity. No human science is sacred, the science of religion being no exception. But of course, the revelation itself is different. Therefore the dichotomy of the revelation/interpretation should be kept intact. We are all immersed in an ocean of interpretations, and whenever one tries to offer the "true" interpretation of the text, he makes himself even more engaged. To capture the true intention of the Revelator is an ideal toward which all of us approach collectively, but in the end we may discover that the true intention of the Revelator was nothing but the collective endeavor of mankind itself. Here the action and its telos coincide. This is not to desacralize the sacred or to secularize religion; it is the simple and at the same time subtle instance of the naturalization of the supernatural, or if you like, the manifestation of the supernatural as and in the natural.

The secular view is blind to the supernatural, but here we look at human interpretation as revelation descended anew, from the heaven of the text to the earth of interpretation through the angel of the reason of the age, after being revealed to the Prophet once in the past. In other words we look at revelation in the mirror of interpretation, much as a devout scientist looks at creation in the mirror of nature. Of progress we are not certain, but evolution is certainly guaranteed.

Now there is a sharp difference between faith and knowledge. Faith is always personal and private, and firmer or less firm, but knowledge cannot be but collective, public, and fallible. A higher-order look at the historical process of the evolution of knowledge shows us that despite the firm belief of individual believers in their own interpretation of revelation, the caravan of knowledge, informed by all kinds of complexities and contrarieties, is breaking its way ahead, feeding on the controversies, competitions, and cooperations of its members, irrespective of their individual desires and faiths. Our lot is nothing but to hope. That is what Jalal al-Din Rumi has exhorted us:

> The merchant of timid disposition and frail spirit
> Neither gains nor loses in his quest.
> Nay, he suffers loss, for he is deprived and despicable.
> Only he that is an eater of flames will find the light.
> Inasmuch as affairs turn upon hope,
> The affairs of religion are most worthy.
> Here it is most permitted to knock at the door.
> Naught but hope is possible. (*Mathnavi*, volume 3, verses 3084–3092)

Once that is understood, the way for religious democracy and the transcendental unity of religions, which are predicated on religious pluralism, will have been paved—these being but two fruits of that auspicious tree.

> Seest thou not how God sets forth a parable: a goodly word like a goodly tree, whose root is firmly fixed and whose branches reach to the heavens. It brings forth its fruits at all times by the leave of its Lord. (Qur'an, Sura 14, Verses 24–25)

PART VI

Progress

The Principle of Movement in the Structure of Islam

Muhammad Iqbal (India, 1877–1938)—poet, philosopher, lawyer—is widely considered the spiritual father of Pakistan. His presidential address to the Muslim League in 1930 helped to launch the movement toward the partition of British South Asia into two nations, the predominantly Muslim Pakistan and the predominantly Hindu India.[1] As important as his political legacy is Iqbal's position as "a driving force for Islamic modernism in South Asia."[2] Iqbal leveled sharp criticism against the rigidity of traditional religious exegesis and called for a renewed emphasis on "movement" in the interpretation of Islam.

As a cultural movement Islam rejects the old static view of the universe, and reaches a dynamic view. As an emotional system of unification it recognizes the worth of the individual as such, and rejects blood-relationship as a basis of human unity. Blood-relationship is earth-rootedness. The search for a purely psychological foundation of human unity becomes possible only with the perception that all human life is spiritual in its origin. Such a perception is creative of fresh loyalties without any ceremonial to keep them alive, and makes it possible for man to emancipate himself from the earth. Christianity which had

originally appeared as a monastic order was tried by Constantine [Roman emperor, reigned 306–337] as a system of unification. Its failure to work as such a system drove the Emperor Julian [reigned 361–363] to return to the old gods of Rome on which he attempted to put philosophical interpretations. A modern historian of civilization has thus depicted the state of the civilized world about the time when Islam appeared on the stage of History:

> It seemed then that the great civilization that it had taken four thousand years to construct was on the verge of disintegration, and that mankind was likely to return to that condition of barbarism where every tribe and sect was against the next, and law and order were unknown. The old tribal sanctions had lost their power. Hence the old imperial methods would no longer operate. The new sanctions created by Christianity were working division and destruction instead of unity and order. It was a time fraught with tragedy. Civilization, like a gigantic tree whose foliage had overarched the world and whose branches

1. This speech and several essays on Iqbal's political thought appear in C. M. Naim, editor, *Iqbal, Jinnah, and Pakistan* (Syracuse, N.Y.: Maxwell School of Citizenship and Public Affairs, Syracuse University, 1979).

2. Mumtaz Ahmad, "Pakistan," and Hafeez Malik, "Iqbal, Muhammad," in John L. Esposito, editor, *The Oxford Encyclopedia of the Modern Islamic World* (New York: Oxford University Press, 1995), volume 3, p. 296, and volume 2, pp. 221–224.

had borne the golden fruits of art and science and literature, stood tottering, its trunk no longer alive with the flowing sap of devotion and reverence, but rotted to the core, riven by the storms of war, and held together only by the cords of ancient customs and laws, that might snap at any moment. Was there any emotional culture that could be brought in to gather mankind once more into unity and to save civilization? This culture must be something of a new type, for the old sanctions and ceremonials were dead, and to build up others of the same kind would be the work of centuries.

The writer then proceeds to tell us that the world stood in need of a new culture to take the place of the culture of the throne, and the systems of unification which were based on blood-relationship. It is amazing, he adds, that such a culture should have arisen from Arabia just at the time when it was most needed. There is, however, nothing amazing in the phenomenon. The world-life intuitively sees its own needs, and at critical moments defines its own direction. This is what, in the language of religion, we call prophetic revelation. It is only natural that Islam should have flashed across the consciousness of a simple people untouched by any of the ancient cultures, and occupying a geographical position where three continents meet together. The new culture finds the foundation of world unity in the principle of *towhid* [one-ness]. Islam, as a polity, is only a practical means of making this principle a living factor in the intellectual and emotional life of mankind. It demands loyalty to God, not to thrones. And since God is the ultimate spiritual basis of all life, loyalty to God virtually amounts to man's loyalty to his own ideal nature. The ultimate spiritual basis of all life, as conceived by Islam, is eternal and reveals itself in variety and change. A society based on such a conception of Reality must reconcile, in its life, the categories of permanence and change. It must possess eternal principles to regulate its collective life; for the eternal gives us a foothold in the world of perpetual change. But eternal principles when they are understood to exclude all possibilities of change which, according to the Qur'an, is one of the greatest "signs" of God, tend to immobilize what is essentially mobile in its nature. The failure of Europe in political and social science illustrates the former principle; the immobility of Islam during the last 500 years illustrates the latter. What then is the principle of move-

ment in the structure of Islam? This is known as *ijtihad* [Islamic interpretation].

The word literally means "to exert." In the terminology of Islamic law it means to exert with a view to form an independent judgment on a legal question. The idea, I believe, has its origin in a well-known verse of the Qur'an—"And to those who exert We show Our path." [Sura 29, Verse 69] We find it more definitely adumbrated in a tradition of the Holy Prophet. When Mu'adh [ibn Jabal, died 627] was appointed ruler of Yemen, the Prophet is reported to have asked him as to how he would decide matters coming up before him. "I will judge matters according to the Book of God," said Mu'adh. "But if the Book of God contains nothing to guide you?" "Then I will act on the precedents of the Prophet of God." "But if the precedents fail?" "Then I will exert to form my own judgment." The student of the history of Islam, however, is well aware that with the political expansion of Islam systematic legal thought became an absolute necessity, and our early doctors of law, both of Arabian and non-Arabian descent, worked ceaselessly until all the accumulated wealth of legal thought found a final expression in our recognized schools of law. These schools of law recognize three degrees of *ijtihad*: (1) complete authority in legislation which is practically confined to the founders of the schools, (2) relative authority which is to be exercised within the limits of a particular school, and (3) special authority which relates to the determining of the law applicable to a particular case left undetermined by the founders. In this paper I am concerned with the first degree of *ijtihad* only, i.e. complete authority in legislation. The theoretical possibility of this degree of *ijtihad* is admitted by the Sunnis, but in practice it has always been denied ever since the establishment of the schools, inasmuch as the idea of complete *ijtihad* is hedged round by conditions which are wellnigh impossible of realization in a single individual. Such an attitude seems exceedingly strange in a system of law based mainly on the groundwork provided by the Qur'an which embodies an essentially dynamic outlook on life. It is, therefore, necessary, before we proceed farther, to discover the causes of this intellectual attitude which has reduced the Law of Islam practically to a state of immobility. Some European writers think that the stationary character of the Law of Islam is due to the influence of the Turks. This is an entirely superficial view, for the legal schools of Islam had been finally established long before the Turkish influence began to work in the history of Islam. The real causes are, in my opinion, as follows:

1. We are all familiar with the Rationalist movement which appeared in the church of Islam during the early days of the 'Abbasids [caliphs, reigned 750–1258], and the bitter controversies which it raised. Take for instance the one important point of controversy between the two camps—the conservative dogma of the eternity of the Qur'an. When Rationalists denied it because they thought that this was only another form of the Christian dogma of the eternity of the word; on the other hand, the conservative thinkers whom the later 'Abbasids, fearing the political implications of Rationalism, gave their full support, thought that by denying the eternity of the Qur'an the Rationalists were undermining the very foundations of Muslim society. [Ibrahim ibn Sayyar] Nazzam [circa 775–845], for instance, practically rejected the traditions [*hadiths*], and openly declared Abu Hurayra [a Companion of the Prophet, died 678] to be an untrustworthy reporter. Thus, partly owing to a misunderstanding of the ultimate motives of Rationalism, and partly owing to the unrestrained thought of particular Rationalists, conservative thinkers regarded this movement as a force of disintegration, and considered it a danger to the stability of Islam as a social polity. Their main purpose, therefore, was to preserve the social integrity of Islam, and to realize that the only course open to them was to utilize the binding force of *shari'a* [Islamic law], and to make the structure of their legal system as rigorous as possible.

2. The rise and growth of ascetic Sufism, which gradually developed under influences of a non-Islamic character, a purely speculative side, is to a large extent responsible for this attitude. On its purely religious side Sufism fostered a kind of revolt against the verbal quibbles of our early doctors. The case of [Abu 'Abdallah] Sufyan Sauri [715–778] is an instance in point. He was one of the acutest legal minds of his time, and was nearly the founder of a school of law; but being also intensely spiritual, the dry-as-dust subtleties of contemporary legists drove him to ascetic Sufism. On its speculative side which developed later, Sufism is a form of freethought and in alliance with Rationalism. The emphasis that it laid on the distinction of *zahir* and *batin* (Appearance and

Reality) created an attitude of indifference to all that applies to Appearance and not to Reality.

This spirit of total other-worldliness in later Sufism obscured men's vision of a very important aspect of Islam as a social polity, and offering the prospect of unrestrained thought on its speculative side it attracted and finally absorbed the best minds in Islam. The Muslim state was thus left generally in the hands of intellectual mediocrities, and the unthinking masses of Islam, having no personalities of a higher calibre to guide them, found their security only in blindly following the schools.

3. On the top of all this came the destruction of Baghdad—the center of Muslim intellectual life—in the middle of the 13th century. This was indeed a great blow, and all the contemporary historians of the invasion of Tartars describe the havoc of Baghdad with a half-suppressed pessimism about the future of Islam. For fear of further disintegration, which is only natural in such a period of political decay, the conservative thinkers of Islam focused all their efforts on the one point of preserving a uniform social life for the people by a jealous exclusion of all innovations in the law of *shari'a* as expounded by the early doctors of Islam. Their leading idea was social order, and there is no doubt that they were partly right, because organization does to a certain extent counteract the forces of decay. But they did not see, and our modern *'ulama'* [religious scholars] do not see, that the ultimate fate of a people does not depend so much on organization as on the worth and power of individual men. In an overorganized society the individual is altogether crushed out of existence. He gains the whole wealth of social thought around him and loses his own soul. Thus a false reverence for past history and its artificial resurrection constitute no remedy for a people's decay. "The verdict of history," as a modern writer has happily put it, "is that worn out ideas have never risen to power among a people who have worn them out." The only effective power, therefore, that counteracts the forces of decay in a people is the rearing of self-concentrated individuals. Such individuals alone reveal the depth of life. They disclose new standards in the light of which we begin to see that our environment is not wholly inviolable and requires revision. The tendency to overorganization by a false reverence of the past as manifested in the legists of Islam in the 13th century and later, was contrary to the inner impulse of Islam, and con-

sequently invoked the powerful reaction of Ibn Taymiyya, one of the most indefatigable writers and preachers of Islam, who was born in 1263, five years after the destruction of Baghdad.

Ibn Taymiyya was brought up in Hanbalite tradition. Claiming freedom of *ijtihad* for himself he rose in revolt against the finality of the schools, and went back to first principles in order to make a fresh start. Like [Abu Muhammad 'Ali] Ibn Hazm [994–1064] —the founder of Zahiri school of law—he rejected the Hanafite principle of reasoning by analogy and *ijma'* [consensus] as understood by older legists for he thought agreement was the basis of all superstition. And there is no doubt that, considering the moral and intellectual decrepitude of his times, he was right in doing so. In the 16th century [Jalal-al-Din] Suyuti [died 1505] claimed the same privilege of *ijtihad* to which he added the idea of a renovator at the beginning of each century. But the spirit of Ibn Taymiyya's teaching found a fuller expression in a movement of immense potentialities which arose in the 18th century from the sands of Nejd [Arabia], described by [Duncan Black] Macdonald [Orientalist, 1863–1943] as the "cleanest spot in the decadent world of Islam." It is really the first throb of life in modern Islam. To the inspiration of this movement are traceable, directly or indirectly, nearly all the great modern movements of Muslim Asia and Africa, e.g., the Sennusi movement, the Pan-Islamic movement, and the Babi movement, which is only a Persian reflex of Arabian Protestantism. The great puritan reformer, Muhammad Ibn 'Abd al-Wahhab, who was born in 1700, studied in Medina, traveled in Persia, and finally succeeded in spreading the fire of his restless soul throughout the whole world of Islam. He was similar in spirit to [Abu Hamid] Ghazzali's [1058–1111] disciple, Muhammad Ibn Tumart [1077–1130]—the Berber puritan reformer of Islam who appeared amidst the decay of Muslim Spain, and gave her a fresh inspiration. We are, however, not concerned with the political career of this movement, which was terminated by the armies of Muhammad 'Ali Pasha [ruler of Egypt, circa 1768– 1849]. The essential thing to note is the spirit of freedom manifested in it: though inwardly this movement, too, is conservative in its own fashion. While it rises in revolt against the finality of the schools, and vigorously asserts the right of private judgment, its vision of the past is wholly uncritical, and in matters of law it mainly falls back on the traditions of the Prophet.

Passing on to Turkey, we find that the idea of *ijtihad*, reinforced and broadened by modern philosophical ideas, has long been working in the religious and political thought of the Turkish nation. This is clear from Halim Sabit's [Şibay, Ottoman Empire and Turkey, 1883–1946] new theory of Islamic Law, grounded on modern sociological concepts. If the renaissance of Islam is a fact, and I believe it is a fact, we too one day, like the Turks, will have to re-evaluate our intellectual inheritance. And if we cannot make any original contribution to the general thought of Islam, we may, by healthy conservative criticism, serve at least as a check on the rapid movement of liberalism in the world of Islam.[3]

I now proceed to give you some idea of religio-political thought in Turkey which will indicate to you how the power of *ijtihad* is manifested in recent thought and activity in that country. There were, a short time ago, two main lines of thought in Turkey represented by the Nationalist Party and the Party of religious reform. The point of supreme interest with the Nationalist Party is above all the State and not Religion. With these thinkers religion as such has no independent function. The state is the essential factor in national life which determines the character and function of all other factors. They, therefore, reject old ideas about the function of State and Religion, and accentuate the separation of Church and State. Now the structure of Islam as a religio-political system, no doubt, does permit such a view, though personally I think it is a mistake to suppose that the idea of state is more dominant and rules all other ideas embodied in the system of Islam. In Islam the spiritual and the temporal are not two distinct domains, and the nature of an act, however secular in its import, is determined by the attitude of mind with which the agent does it. It is the invisible mental background of the act which ultimately determines its character. An act is temporal or profane if it is done in a spirit of detachment from the infinite complexity of life behind it; it is spiritual if it is inspired by that complexity. In Islam it is the same reality which appears as Church looked at from one point of view and State from another. It is not true to say that Church and State are two sides or facets of the same thing. Islam is a single unanalyzable reality which is one or the other as your point of view varies. The point is extremely far-reaching and a full elucidation

---

3. [Iqbal equates "liberalism" with secularism.—Editor]

of it will involve us in a highly philosophical discussion. Suffice it to say that this ancient mistake arose out of the bifurcation of the unity of man into two distinct and separate realities which somehow have a point of contact, but which are in essence opposed to each other. The truth, however, is that matter is spirit in space-time reference. The unity called man is body when you look at it as acting in regard to what we call the external world; it is mind or soul when you look at it as acting in regard to the ultimate aim and ideal of such acting. The essence of *towhid* as a working idea is equality, solidarity, and freedom. The state, from the Islamic standpoint, is an endeavor to transform these ideal principles into space-time forces, an aspiration to realize them in a definite human organization. It is in this sense alone that the state in Islam is a theocracy, not in the sense that it is headed by a representative of God on earth who can always screen his despotic will behind his supposed infallibility. The critics of Islam have lost sight of this important consideration. The ultimate Reality, according to the Qur'an, is spiritual, and its life consists in its temporal activity. The spirit finds its opportunities in the natural, the material, the secular. All that is secular is therefore sacred in the roots of its being. The greatest service that modern thought has rendered to Islam, and as a matter of fact to all religion, consists in its criticism of what we call material or natural—a criticism which discloses that the merely material has no substance until we discover it rooted in the spiritual. There is no such thing as a profane world. All this immensity of matter constitutes a scope for the self-realization of spirit. All is holy ground. As the Prophet so beautifully puts it: "The whole of this earth is a mosque." The state according to Islam is only an effort to realize the spiritual in a human organization. But in this sense all state, not based on mere domination and aiming at the realization of ideal principles, is theocratic.

The truth is that the Turkish nationalists assimilated the idea of the separation of Church and State from the history of European political ideas. Primitive Christianity was founded, not as a political or civil unit, but as a monastic order in a profane world, having nothing to do with civil affairs, and obeying the Roman authority practically in all matters. The result of this was that when the State became Christian, State and Church confronted each other as distinct powers with interminable boundary disputes between them. Such a thing could never happen in Islam; for Islam was from the very beginning a civil society, having received from the Qur'an a set of simple legal principles which, like the twelve tables of the Romans, carried, as experience subsequently proved, great potentialities of expansion and development by interpretation. The Nationalist theory of state, therefore, is misleading inasmuch as it suggests a dualism which does not exist in Islam.

The Religious Reform Party, on the other hand, led by Said Halim Pasha [1863–1921; Ottoman Grand Vizier, or prime minister, 1913–1916], insisted on the fundamental fact that Islam is a harmony of idealism and positivism; and, as a unity of the eternal verities of freedom, equality, and solidarity, has no fatherland. "As there is no English Mathematics, German Astronomy or French Chemistry," says the Grand Vizier, "so there is no Turkish, Arabian, Persian or Indian Islam. Just as the universal character of scientific truths engenders varieties of scientific national cultures which in their totality represent human knowledge, much in the same way the universal character of Islamic verities creates varieties of national, moral and social ideals." Modern culture based as it is on national egoism is, according to this keen-sighted writer, only another form of barbarism. It is the result of an over-developed industrialism through which men satisfy their primitive instincts and inclinations. He, however, deplores that during the course of history the moral and social ideals of Islam have been gradually de-Islamized through the influence of local character, and pre-Islamic superstitions of Muslim nations.

These ideals today are more Iranian, Turkish, or Arabian than Islamic. The pure brow of the principle of *towhid* has received more or less an impress of heathenism, and the universal and impersonal character of the ethical ideals of Islam has been lost through a process of localization. The only alternative open to us, then, is to tear off from Islam the hard crust which has immobilized an essentially dynamic outlook on life, and to rediscover the original verities of freedom, equality, and solidarity with a view to rebuild our moral, social, and political ideals out of their original simplicity and universality. Such are the views of the Grand Vizier of Turkey. You will see that following a line of thought more in tune with the spirit of Islam, he reaches practically the same conclusion as the Nationalist Party, that is to say, the freedom of *ijtihad* with a view to rebuild the law of *shari'a* in the light of modern thought and experience.

Let us now see how the Grand National Assembly [Turkey's parliament] has exercised this power of *ijtihad* in regard to the institution of *khilafat* [caliphate]. According to Sunni Law the appointment of an *imam* [leader] or *khalifa* [caliph] is absolutely indispensable. The first question that arises in this connection is this—Should the Caliphate be vested in a single person? Turkey's *ijtihad* is that according to the spirit of Islam the Caliphate or Imamate can be vested in a body of persons, or an elected Assembly. The religious doctors of Islam in Egypt and India, so far as I know, have not yet expressed themselves on this point. Personally, I believe the Turkish view is perfectly sound. It is hardly necessary to argue this point. The republican form of government is not only thoroughly consistent with the spirit of Islam, but has also become a necessity in view of the new forces that are set free in the world of Islam.

In order to understand the Turkish view let us seek the guidance of Ibn Khaldun [1332–1406]—first philosophical historian of Islam. Ibn Khaldun, in his famous *Prolegomena*, mentions three distinct views of the idea of Universal Caliphate in Islam: (1) That Universal Imamate is a Divine institution, and is consequently indispensable; (2) that it is merely a matter of expediency; (3) that there is no need of such an institution. The last view was taken by the Khawarji.[4] It seems that modern Turkey has shifted from the first to the second view, i.e., to the view of the Mu'tazila[5] who regarded Universal Imamate as a matter of expediency only. The Turks argue that in our political thinking we must be guided by our past political experience which points unmistakably to the fact that the idea of Universal Imamate has failed in practice. It was a workable idea when the Empire of Islam was intact. Since the break-up of this Empire independent political units have arisen. The idea has ceased to be operative and cannot work as a living factor in the organization of modern Islam. Far from serving any useful purpose it has really stood in the way of a reunion of Independent Muslim States. Persia has stood aloof from the Turks in view of her doctrinal differences regarding the *khilafat*; Morocco

has always looked askance at them, and Arabia has cherished private ambition. And all these ruptures in Islam for the sake of a mere symbol of a power which departed long ago. Why should we not, he can further argue, learn from experience in our political thinking? Did not *Qazi* Abu Bakr Baqilani [Iraq, died 1013] drop the condition of *qarshiyat* [membership in the Quraysh tribe of the Prophet] in the *khalifa* in view of the facts of experience, i.e., the political fall of the Quraysh and their consequent inability to rule the world of Islam? Centuries ago Ibn Khaldun, who personally believed in the condition of *qarshiyat* in the *khalifa*, argued much in the same way. Since the power of the Quraysh, he says, has gone, there is no alternative but to accept the most powerful man as Imam in the country where he happens to be powerful. Thus Ibn Khaldun, realizing the hard logic of facts, suggests a view which may be regarded as the first dim vision of an International Islam fairly in sight today. Such is the attitude of the modern Turk, inspired as he is by the realities of experiences, and not by the scholastic reasoning of jurists who lived and thought under different conditions of life.

To my mind these arguments, if rightly appreciated, indicate the birth of an International ideal which, though forming the very essence of Islam, has been hitherto overshadowed or rather displaced by Arabian Imperialism of the centuries of Islam. This new ideal is clearly reflected in the work of the great nationalist poet Zia [Gökalp] [Turkey, 1875–1924], whose songs, inspired by the philosophy of Auguste Comte [French social theorist, 1798–1857], have done a great deal in shaping the present thought of Turkey. I reproduce the substance of one of his poems from Professor [August] Fischer's [1922] German translation:

> In order to create a really effective political unity of Islam, all Moslem countries must first become independent: and then in their totality they should range themselves under one Caliph. Is such a thing possible at the present moment? If not today, one must wait. In the meantime the caliph must reduce his own house to order and lay the foundation of a workable modern state.
>
> In the international world the weak find no sympathy; power alone deserves respect.

These lines clearly indicate the trend of modern Islam. For the present every Moslem nation must sink into her own deeper self, temporarily focus her vision on herself alone, until all are strong and powerful to

---

4. [The Khawarji, or Kharijites, were an early Islamic sect often called "puritanical" for their focus on the extirpation of sin.—Editor]

5. [The Mu'tazilites were an early Islamic sect that helped to found Islamic philosophy on ancient Greek philosophical methods.—Editor]

form a living family of republics. A true and living unity, according the nationalist thinkers, is not so easy as to be achieved by a merely symbolical over-lordship. It is truly manifested in a multiplicity of free independent units whose racial rivalries are adjusted and harmonized by the unifying bond of a common spiritual aspiration. It seems to me that God is slowly bringing home to us the truth that Islam is neither Nationalism nor Imperialism but a League of Nations which recognizes artificial boundaries and racial distinctions for facility of reference only, and not for restricting the social horizon of its members.

From the same poet the following passage from a poem called "Religion and Science" will throw some further light on the general religious outlook which is being gradually shaped in the world of Islam today:

Who were the first spiritual leaders of mankind? Without doubt the Prophets and Holy men. In every period religion has led philosophy; From it alone morality and art receive light. But then religion grows weak, and loses her original ardor! Holy men disappear, and spiritual leadership becomes, in name, the heritage of the Doctors of Law! The leading star of the Doctors of Law is tradition; They drag religion with force on this track; but philosophy says: "My leading star is reason: you go right, I go left."

Both religion and philosophy claim the soul of man and draw it on either side!

When this struggle is going on pregnant experience delivers up positive science, and this young leader of thought says, "Tradition is history and Reason is the method of history! Both interpret and desire to reach the same indefinable something!"

But what is this something?

Is it a spiritualized heart?

If so, then take my last word—Religion is positive science, the purpose of which is to spiritualize the heart of man!

It is clear from these lines how beautifully the poet has adopted the Comtian idea of the three stages of man's intellectual development, i.e., theological, metaphysical, and scientific—to the religious outlook of Islam. And the view of religion embodied in these lines determines the poet's attitude towards the position of Arabic in the educational system of Turkey. He says:

The land where the call to prayer resounds in Turkish; where those who pray understand the meaning of their religion; the land where the Qur'an is learnt in Turkish; where every man, big or small, knows full well the command of God; O! Son of Turkey! that land is thy fatherland!

If the aim of religion is the spiritualization of the heart, then it must penetrate the soul of man, and it can best penetrate the inner man, according to the poet, only if its spiritualizing ideas are clothed in his mother tongue. Most people in India will condemn this displacement of Arabic by Turkish. For reasons which will appear later the poet's *ijtihad* is open to grave objections, but it must be admitted that the reform suggested by him is not without a parallel in the past history of Islam. We find that when Muhammad Ibn Tumart—the Mehdi of Muslim Spain—who was a Berber by nationality, came to power, and established the pontifical rule of the Mawahidin, he ordered for the sake of the illiterate Berbers, that the Qur'an should be translated and read in the Berber language; that the call to prayer should be given in Berber; and that all the functionaries of the Church must know the Berber language. In another passage the poet gives his ideal of womanhood. In his zeal for the equality of man and woman he wishes to see radical changes in the family law of Islam as it is understood and practiced today:

There is the woman, my mother, my sister, or my daughter; it is she who calls up the most sacred emotions from the depths of my life! There is my beloved, my sun, my moon and my star; it is she who makes me understand the poetry of life! How could the Holy Law of God regard these beautiful creatures as despicable beings? Surely there is an error in the interpretation of the Qur'an by the learned?

The foundation of the nation and the state is the family!

As long as the full worth of the woman is not realized, national life remains incomplete.

The upbringing of the family must correspond with justice;

Therefore equality is necessary in three things—in divorce, in separation, and in inheritance.

As long as the woman is counted half the man as regards inheritance and one fourth of man in matrimony, neither the family nor the country will be elevated. For other rights we have opened national courts of justice;

The family, on the other hand, we have left in the hands of schools.

I do not know why we have left the woman in the lurch?

Does she not work for the land? Or, will she turn her needle into a sharp bayonet to tear off her rights from our hands through a revolution?

The truth is that among the Muslim nations of today, Turkey alone has shaken off its dogmatic slumber, and attained self-consciousness. She alone has claimed her right of intellectual freedom; she alone has passed from the ideal to the real—a transition which entails keen intellectual and moral struggle. To her the growing complexities of a mobile and broadening life are sure to bring new situations suggesting new points of view, and necessitating fresh interpretations of principles which are only of an academic interest to a people who have never experienced the joy of spiritual expansion. It is, I think, the English thinker Hobbes who makes this acute observation that to have a succession of identical thoughts and feelings is to have no thoughts and feelings at all. Such is the lot of most Muslim countries today. They are mechanically repeating old values, whereas the Turk is on the way to creating new values. He has passed through great experiences which have revealed his deeper self to him. In him life has begun to move, change, and amplify, giving birth to new desires, bringing new difficulties and suggesting new interpretations. The question which confronts him today, and which is likely to confront other Muslim countries in the near future is whether the Law of Islam is capable of evolution—a question which will require great intellectual effort, and is sure to be answered in the affirmative; provided the world of Islam approaches it in the spirit of 'Umar [Companion of the Prophet and second caliph, 592–644]— the first critical and independent mind in Islam who, at the last moments of the Prophet, had the moral courage to utter these remarkable words: "The Book of God is sufficient for us."

We heartily welcome the liberal movement in modern Islam; but it must also be admitted that the appearance of liberal ideas in Islam constitutes also the most critical moment in the history of Islam. Liberalism has a tendency to act as a force of disintegration, and the race-idea which appears to be working in modern Islam with greater force than ever may ultimately wipe off the broad human outlook which Muslim people have imbibed from their religion. Further, our religious and political reformers in their zeal for liberalism may overstep the proper limits of reform in the absence of a check on their youthful fervor. We are today passing through a period similar to that of the Protestant revolution in Europe, and the lesson which the rise and outcome of [Martin] Luther's [16th-century Protestant Reformation] movement teaches should not be lost on us. A careful reading of history shows that the Reformation was essentially a political movement, and the net result of it in Europe was a gradual displacement of the universal ethics of Christianity by systems of national ethics. The result of this tendency we have seen with our own eyes in the Great European War [World War I] which, far from bringing any workable synthesis of the two opposing systems of ethics, has made the European situation still more intolerable. It is the duty of the leaders of the world of Islam today to understand the real meaning of what has happened in Europe, and then to move forward with self-control and a clear insight into the ultimate aims of Islam as a social polity.

I have given you some idea of the history and working of *ijtihad* in modern Islam. I now proceed to see whether the history and structure of the Law of Islam indicate the possibility of any fresh interpretation of its principles. In other words, the question that I want to raise is—Is the Law of Islam capable of evolution? [Max] Horten [born 1874], Professor of Semitic Philology at the University of Bonn, raises the same question in connection with the Philosophy and Theology of Islam. Reviewing the work of Muslim thinkers in the sphere of purely religious thought he points out that the history of Islam may aptly be described as a gradual interaction, harmony, and mutual deepening of two distinct forces, i.e., the element of Aryan culture and knowledge on the one hand, and a Semitic religion on the other. The Muslim has always adjusted his religious outlook to the elements of culture which he assimilated from the peoples that surrounded him. From 800 to 1100, says Horten, not less than one hundred systems of theology appeared in Islam, a fact which bears ample testimony to the elasticity of Islamic thought as well as to the ceaseless activity of our early thinkers. Thus, in view of the revelations of a deeper study of Muslim literature and thought, this living European Orientalist has been driven to the following conclusion: "The spirit of Islam is so broad that it is practically boundless. With the exception of atheistic ideas alone it has assimilated all the attainable ideas of surrounding peoples, and given them its own peculiar direction of development."

The assimilative spirit of Islam is even more manifest in the sphere of law. Says Professor [C. Snouck] Hurgronje [1857–1936], the Dutch critic of Islam:

When we read the history of the development of Islamic Law we find that, on the one hand, the doctors of every age, on the slightest stimulus, condemn one another to the point of mutual accusations of heresy; and, on the other hand, the very same people, with greater and greater unity of purpose, try to reconcile the similar quarrels of their predecessors.

These views of modern European critics of Islam make it perfectly clear that, with the return of new life, the inner catholicity of the spirit of Islam is bound to work itself out in spite of the rigorous conservatism of our doctors. And I have no doubt that a deeper study of the enormous legal literature of Islam is sure to rid the modern critic of the superficial opinion that the Law of Islam is stationary and incapable of development. Unfortunately, the conservative Muslim public of this country is not yet quite ready for a critical discussion of *fiqh* [Islamic jurisprudence], which, if undertaken, is likely to displease most people, and raise sectarian controversies; yet I venture to offer a few remarks on the point before us.

1. In the first place, we should bear in mind that from the earliest times, practically up to the rise of the 'Abbasids, there was no written law of Islam apart from the Qur'an.

2. Secondly, it is worthy of note that from about the middle of the first century up to the beginning of the fourth not less than nineteen schools of law and legal opinion appeared in Islam. This fact alone is sufficient to show how incessantly our early doctors of law worked in order to meet the necessities of a growing civilization. With the expansion of conquest and the consequent widening of the outlook of Islam these early legists had to take a wider view of things, and to study local conditions of life and habits of new peoples that came within the fold of Islam. A careful study of the various schools of legal opinion, in the light of contemporary social and political history, reveals that they gradually passed from the deductive to the inductive attitude in their efforts at interpretation.

3. Thirdly, when we study the four accepted sources of Islamic Law and the controversies which they invoked, the supposed rigidity of our recognized schools evaporates, and the possibility of a further

evolution becomes perfectly clear. Let us briefly discuss these sources.

(a) The Qur'an. The primary source of the Law of Islam is the Qur'an. The Qur'an, however, is not a legal code. Its main purpose, as I have said before, is to awaken in man the higher consciousness of his relation with God and the universe. No doubt the Qur'an does lay down a few general principles and rules of a legal nature, especially relating to the family—the ultimate basis of social life. But why are these rules made part of a revelation the ultimate aim of which is man's higher life? The answer to this question is furnished by the history of Christianity which appeared as a powerful reaction against the spirit of legality manifested in Judaism. By setting up an ideal of other-worldliness it no doubt did succeed in spiritualizing life, but its individualism could see no spiritual value in the complexity of human social relations. "Primitive Christianity," says [Friedrich] Naumann [1860–1919] in his *Briefe über Religion*, "attached no value to the preservation of the state, law, organization, production. It simply does not reflect on the conditions of human society." And Naumann concludes: "Hence we either dare to aim at being without a state, and thus throwing ourselves deliberately into the arms of anarchy, or we decide to possess, alongside of our religious creed, a political creed as well." Thus the Qur'an considers it necessary to unite religion and State, ethics and politics in a single revelation much in the same way as Plato [Greece, 427–347 b.c.], does in his *Republic*.

The important point to note in this connection, however, is the dynamic outlook of the Qur'an. I have fully discussed its origin and history. It is obvious that with such an outlook the Holy Book of Islam cannot be inimical to the idea of evolution. Only we should not forget that life is not change, pure and simple. It has within it elements of conservation also. While enjoying his creative activity, and always focusing his energies on the discovery of new vistas of life, man has a feeling of uneasiness in the presence of his own unfoldment. In his forward movement he cannot help looking back to his past, and faces his own inward expansion with a certain amount of fear. The spirit of man in its forward movement is restrained by forces which seem to be working in the opposite direction. This is only another way of saying that life moves with the weight of its own past on its back, and that in any view of social change the value and function of the forces of conservatism cannot be lost sight of. It is with this organic insight into the essential teaching of the Qur'an that modern Rationalism ought to approach our existing institutions. No people can afford to reject their past entirely; for it is their past that has made their personal identity. And in a society like Islam the problem of a revision of old institutions becomes still more delicate, and the responsibility of the reformer assumes a far more serious aspect. Islam is non-territorial in its character, and its aim is to furnish a model for the final combination of humanity by drawing its adherents from a variety of mutually repellent races, and then transforming this atomic aggregate into a people possessing a self-consciousness of their own. This was not an easy task to accomplish. Yet Islam, by means of its well-conceived institutions, has succeeded to a very great extent in creating something like a collective will and conscience in this heterogeneous mass. In the evolution of such a society even the immutability of socially harmless rules relating to eating and drinking, purity or impurity, has a life-value of its own, inasmuch as it tends to give such society a specific inwardness, and further secures that external and internal uniformity which counteracts the forces of heterogeneity always latent in a society of a composite character. The critic of these institutions must therefore try to secure, before he undertakes to handle them, a clear insight into the ultimate significance of the social experiment embodied in Islam. He must look at their structure, not from the standpoint of social advantage or disadvantage to this or that country, but from the point of view of the larger purpose which is being gradually worked out in the life of mankind as a whole.

Turning now to the groundwork of legal principles in the Qur'an, it is perfectly clear that far from leaving no scope for human thought and legislative activity the intensive breadth of these principles virtually acts as an awakener of human thought. Our early doctors of law taking their clue mainly from this groundwork evolved a number of legal systems; and the student of Islamic history knows very well that nearly half the triumphs of Islam as a social and political power were due to the legal acuteness of these doctors. "Next to the Romans," says [Alfred] Von Kremer [Orientalist, 1828–1889], "there is no other nation besides the Arabs which could call its own a system of law so carefully worked out." But with all their comprehensiveness, these systems are after all individual interpretations, and as such cannot claim any finality. I know the *'ulama'* of Islam claim finality for the popular schools of Islamic Law, though they never found it possible to deny the theoretical possibility of a complete *ijtihad*. I have tried to explain the causes which, in my opinion, determined this attitude of the *'ulama'*; but since things have changed and the world of Islam is today confronted and affected by new forces set free by the extraordinary development of human thought in all its directions, I see no reason why this attitude should be maintained any longer. Did the founders of our schools ever claim finality for their reasonings and interpretations? Never. The claim of the present generation of Muslim liberals to re-interpret the foundational legal principles, in the light of their own experience and the altered conditions of modern life is, in my opinion, perfectly justified. The teaching of the Qur'an that life is a process of progressive creation necessitates that each generation, guided but unhampered by the work of its predecessors, should be permitted to solve its own problems.

You will, I think, remind me here of the Turkish poet Zia, whom I quoted a moment ago, and ask whether the equality of man and woman demanded by him, equality, that is to say, in point of divorce, separation, and inheritance, is possible according to Islamic Law. I do not know whether the awakening of women in Turkey has created demands which cannot be met without a fresh interpretation of foundational principles. In the Punjab [region in northern India], as everybody knows, there have been cases in which Muslim women wishing to get rid of undesirable husbands have been driven to apostasy. Nothing could be more distant from the aims of a missionary religion. The Law of Islam, says the great Spanish jurist Imam [Abu Ishaq al-]Shatibi [died 1388] in his *Al-Muwafiqat [fi usul al-shari'a]* [*The Correspondences on the Methodology of Islamic Law*], aims at protecting five things—*din* [religion], *nafs* [soul], *'aql* [intellect], *mal* [property], and *nasl* [progeny]. Applying this test I venture to ask: "Does the working of the rule relating to apostasy, as laid down in the *hidaya* [guidance], tend to protect the interests of the Faith in this country?" In view of the intense conservatism of the Muslims of India, Indian judges cannot but stick to what are called standard worlds. The result is that while the peoples are moving the law remains stationary.

With regard to the Turkish poet's demand, I am afraid he does not seem to know much about the family law of Islam. Nor does he seem to understand the economic significance of the Qur'anic rule of inheritance. Marriage, according to Islamic Law, is a civil contract. The wife at the time of marriage is at liberty to get the husband's power of divorce delegated to her on stated conditions, and thus secure equality of divorce with her husband. The reform suggested by the poet relating to the rule of inheritance is based on a misunderstanding. From the inequality of their legal shares it must not be supposed that the rule assumes the superiority of males over females. Such an assumption would be contrary to the spirit of Islam. The Qur'an says: "And for women are rights over men similar to those for men over women" [Sura 2, Verse 228].

The share of the daughter is determined not by any inferiority inherent in her, but in view of her economic opportunities, and the place she occupies in the social structure of which she is part and parcel. Further, according to the poet's own theory of society, the rule of inheritance must be regarded not as an isolated factor in the distribution of wealth, but as one factor among others working together for the same end. While the daughter, according to Islamic Law, is held to be full owner of the property given to her both by the father and the husband at the time of her marriage; while, further, she absolutely owns her dower-money which may be prompt or deferred according to her own choice, and in lieu of which she can hold possession of the whole of her husband's property till payment, the responsibility of maintaining her throughout her life is wholly thrown on the husband. If you judge the working of the rule of inheritance from this point of view, you will find that there is no material difference between the economic position of sons and daughters, and it is really by this apparent inequality of their legal shares that the law secures the equality demanded by the Turkish poet. The truth is that the principles underlying the Qur'anic law of inheritance—this supremely original branch of Islamic Law as Von Kremer describes it—have not yet received from Muslim lawyers the attention they deserve. Modern society with its bitter class-struggles ought to set us thinking; and if we study our laws in reference to the impending revolution in modern economic life, we are likely to discover, in the foundational principles, hitherto unrevealed aspects which we can work out with a renewed faith in the wisdom of these principles.

(b) The *hadith* [traditions of the Prophet]. The second great source of Islamic Law is the traditions of the Holy Prophet. These have been the subject of great discussion both in ancient and modern times. Among their modern critics Professor [Ignácz] Goldziher [Orientalist, 1850–1921] has subjected them to a searching examination in the light of modern canons of historical criticism, and arrives at the conclusion that they are, on the whole, untrustworthy. N. P. Aghnides [born 1883], after examining the Muslim methods of determining the genuineness of a tradition, and pointing out the theoretical possibilities of error, arrives at the following conclusion:

> It must be said in conclusion that the preceding considerations represented only theoretical possibilities and that the question how far these possibilities have become actualities is largely a matter of how far the actual circumstances offered inducements for making use of the possibilities. Doubtless the latter, relatively speaking, were few, and affected only a small proportion of the entire *sunna* [practice of the Prophet, a chief source of Islamic law]. It may therefore be said that for the most part the collections of *sunna* considered by the Muslims as canonical are genuine records of the rise and early growth of Islam. (*Mohammedan Theories of Finance*)

For our present purposes, however, we must distinguish traditions of a purely legal import from those which are of a non-legal character. With regard to the former, there arises a very important question as to how far they embody the pre-Islamic usages of Arabia which were in some cases left intact, and in others modified by the Prophet. It is difficult to make this discovery, for our early writers do not always refer to pre-Islamic usages. Nor is it possible to discover that the usages, left intact by express or tacit approval of the Prophet, were intended to be universal in their application. Shah Wali-Ullah [India, 1703–1762] has a very illuminating discussion on the point. I reproduce here the substance of his view. The prophetic method of teaching, according to Shah Wali-Ullah, is that, generally speaking, the law revealed by a prophet takes especial notice of the habits, ways, and peculiarities of the people to whom he is specifically sent. The prophet who aims at all-embracing principles, however, can neither reveal different principles for different peoples, nor leaves them to work out their own rules of conduct. His method is to train one particular people, and to use them as a nucleus for the building up of a universal *shari'a*. In doing so he accentuates the principles underlying the social life of all mankind, and applies them to concrete cases in the light of the specific habits of the people immediately before him. The *shari'a* values (*ahkam*) resulting from this application (e.g., rules relating to penalties for crimes) are in a sense specific to that people; and since their observance is not an end in itself they cannot be strictly enforced in the case of future generations. It was perhaps in view of this that Abu Hanifa [circa 699–767], who had a keen insight into the universal character of Islam, made practically no use of these traditions. The fact that he introduced the principle of *istihsan*, i.e., juristic preference, which necessitates a careful study of actual conditions in legal thinking, throws further light on the motives which determined his attitude towards this source of Islamic Law. It is said that Abu Hanifa made no use of traditions because there were no regular collections in his day. In the first place, it is not true to say that there were no collections in his day, as the collections of Abdul Malik [Ibn Jurayj, 699–767] and [Muhammad ibn Muslim] Zuhri [670–circa 737] were made not less than thirty years before the death of Abu Hanifa. But even if we suppose that these collections never reached him, or that they did not contain traditions of a legal import, Abu Hanifa, like Malik and Ahmad ibn Hanbal [780–855] after him, could have easily made his own collection if he had deemed such a thing necessary. On the whole, then, the attitude of Abu Hanifa towards the traditions of a purely legal import is to my mind perfectly sound; and if modern Liberalism considers it safer not to make any indiscriminate use of them as a source of law, it will be only following one of the greatest exponents of Islamic Law in Sunni Islam. It is, however, impossible to deny the fact that the traditionists, by insisting on the value of the concrete case as against the tendency to abstract thinking in law, have done the greatest service to the Law of Islam. And a further intelligent study of the literature of traditions, if used as indicative of the spirit in which the Prophet himself interpreted his Revelation, may still be of great help in understanding the life-value of the legal principles enunciated in the Qur'an. A complete grasp of their life-value alone can equip us in our endeavor to re-interpret the foundational principles.

(c) The *ijma'* [consensus]. The third source of Islamic Law is *ijma'* which is, in my opinion, per-

haps the most important legal notion in Islam. It is, however, strange that this important notion, while invoking great academic discussions in early Islam, remained practically a mere idea, and rarely assumed the form of a permanent institution in any Islamic country. Possibly its transformation into a permanent legislative institution was contrary to the political interests of the kind of absolute monarchy that grew up in Islam immediately after the fourth caliph. It was, I think, favorable to the interest of the Umayyad and the 'Abbasid caliphs [reigned 661–750 and 750–1258, respectively] to leave the power of *ijtihad* to individual *mujtahid*s [religious scholars] rather than encourage the formation of a permanent assembly which might become too powerful for them. It is, however, extremely satisfactory to note that the pressure of new world forces and the political experience of European nations are impressing on the mind of modern Islam the value and possibilities of the idea of *ijma'*. The growth of republican spirit and the gradual formation of legislative assemblies in Muslim lands constitute a great step in advance. The transfer of the power of *ijtihad* from individual representatives of schools to a Muslim legislative assembly which, in view of the growth of opposing sects, is the only possible form *ijma'* can take in modern times, will secure contributions to legal discussion from laymen who happen to possess a keen insight into affairs. In this way alone we can stir into activity the dormant spirit of life in our legal system, and give it an evolutionary outlook. In India, however, difficulties are likely to arise; for it is doubtful whether a non-Muslim legislative assembly can exercise the power of *ijtihad*.

But there are one or two questions which must be raised and answered in regard to the *ijma'*. Can the *ijma'* repeal the Qur'an? It is unnecessary to raise this question before a Muslim audience; but I consider it necessary to do so in view of a very misleading statement by a European critic in a book called *Mohammedan Theories of Finance*—published by Columbia University. The author of this book says, without citing any authority, that according to some Hanafi and Mu'tazila writers the *ijma'* can repeal the Qur'an. There is not the slightest justification for such a statement in the legal literature of Islam. Not even a tradition of the Prophet can have any such effect. It seems to me that the author is misled by the word *naskh* in the writings of our early doctors to whom, as Imam Shatibi points out in *Al-Muwafiqat*, volume 3, page 65, this word, when used in discussions relating to the *ijma'* of the companions [of the Prophet], meant only the power to extend or limit the application of a Qur'anic rule of law, and not the power to repeal or supersede it by another rule of law. And even in the exercise of this power the legal theory, as ['Ali ibn Abi 'Ali] Amidi—a Shafi'i doctor of law who died about the middle of the seventh century [A.H., or 1233 A.D.], and whose work is recently published in Egypt—tells us, is that the companions must have been in possession of a *shari'a* value (*hukm*) entitling them to such a limitation or extension.

But supposing the companions have unanimously decided a certain point, the further question is whether later generations are bound by their decision. [Muhammad ibn 'Ali] Shaukani [circa 1760–1839] has fully discussed this point, and cited the views held by writers belonging to different schools. I think it is necessary in this connection to discriminate between a decision relating to a question of fact and the one relating to a question of law. In the former case, as for instance, when the question arose whether the two small *sura*s [chapters] known as "*Mu'awwazatan*" formed part of the Qur'an or not, and the companions unanimously decided that they did, we are bound by their decision, obviously because the companions alone were in a position to know the fact. In the latter case the question is one of interpretation only, and I venture to think, on the authority of [Abu'l-Hasan] Karkhi [died 952], that later generations are not bound by the decision of the companions. Says Karkhi: "The *sunna* of the companions is binding in matters which cannot be cleared up by *qiyas* [analogical reasoning], but it is not so in matters which can be established by *qiyas*."

One more question may be asked as to the legislative activity of a modern Muslim assembly which must consist, at least for the present, mostly of men possessing no knowledge of the subtleties of Islamic Law. Such an assembly may make grave mistakes in their interpretation of law. How can we exclude or at least reduce the possibilities of erroneous interpretation? The Persian constitution of 1906 provided a separate ecclesiastical committee of '*ulama*'—"conversant with the affairs of the world"—having power to supervise the legislative activity of the *majlis* [parliament]. This, in my opinion, dangerous arrange-

ment is probably necessary in view of the Persian [Shi'i] constitutional theory.[6] According to that theory, I believe, the king is a mere custodian of the realm which really belongs to the Absent Imam. The '*ulama*', as representatives of the Imam, consider themselves entitled to supervise the whole life of the community; though I fail to understand how, in the absence of an apostolic succession, they establish their claim to represent the Imam. But whatever may be the Persian constitutional theory, the arrangement is not free from danger, and may be tried, if at all, only as a temporary measure in Sunni countries. The '*ulama*' should form a vital part of a Muslim legislative assembly helping and guiding free discussion on questions relating to law. The only effective remedy for the possibilities of erroneous interpretations is to reform the present system of legal education in Islamic countries, to extend its sphere, and to combine it with an intelligent study of modern jurisprudence.

(d) The *qiyas*. The fourth basis of *fiqh* is *qiyas*, i.e., the use of analogical reasoning in legislation. In view of different social and agricultural conditions prevailing in the countries conquered by Islam, the school of Abu Hanifa seem to have found, on the whole, little or no guidance from the precedents recorded in the literature of traditions. The only alternative open to them was to resort to speculative reason in their interpretations. The application of Aristotelian logic, however, though suggested by the discovery of new conditions in Iraq, was likely to prove exceedingly harmful in the preliminary stages of legal development. The intricate behavior of life cannot be subjected to hard and fast rules logically deducible from certain general notions. Yet looked at through the spectacles of Aristotle's logic it appears to be a mechanism pure and simple with no internal principle of movement. Thus the school of Abu Hanifa tended to ignore the creative freedom and arbitrariness of life, and hoped to build a logically perfect legal system on the lines of pure reason. The legists of Hijaz [Arabia], however, true to the prac-

6. [Persia, now called Iran, is the primary home of the minority Shi'i sect of Islam, as distinct from the majority Sunni sect. Shi'is, unlike Sunnis, believe that the Prophet's twelfth successor, referred to as the Absent or Hidden Imam, has been in occultation since the ninth century and will return as the messiah.—Editor]

tical genius of their race, raised strong protests against the scholastic subtleties of the legists of Iraq, and their tendency to imagine unreal cases which they rightly thought would turn the Law of Islam into a kind of lifeless mechanism. These bitter controversies among the early doctors of Islam led to a critical definition of the limitations, conditions, and correctives of *qiyas* which, though originally appeared as a mere disguise for the *mujtahid*'s personal opinion, eventually became a source of life and movement in the Law of Islam. The spirit of the acute criticism of Malik and [Abu 'Abdallah Muhammad] Shafi'i [767–820] on Abu Hanifa's principle of *qiyas*, as a source of law, constitutes really an effective Semitic restraint on the Aryan tendency to seize the abstract in preference to the concrete, to enjoy the idea rather than the event. This was really a controversy between the advocates of deductive and inductive methods in legal research. The legists of Iraq originally emphasized the eternal aspect of the "notion," while those of Hijaz laid stress on its temporal aspect. The latter, however, did not see the full significance of their own position, and their instinctive partiality to the legal tradition of Hijaz narrowed their vision to the "precedents" that had actually happened in the days of the Prophet and his companions. No doubt they recognized the value of the concrete, but at the same time they eternalized it, rarely resorting to *qiyas* based on the study of the concrete as such. Their criticism of Abu Hanifa and his school, however, emancipated the concrete as it were, and brought out the necessity of observing the actual movement and variety of life in the interpretation of juristic principles. Thus the school of Abu Hanifa which fully assimilated the results of this controversy is absolutely free in its essential principle and possesses much greater power of creative adaptation than any other school of Islamic Law. But contrary to the spirit of his own school the modern Hanafi legist has eternalized the interpretations of the founder or his immediate followers much in the same way as the early critics of Abu Hanifa eternalized the decisions given on concrete cases. Properly understood and applied, the essential principle of this school, i.e., *qiyas*, as Shafi'i rightly says, is only another name for *ijtihad* which, within the limits of the revealed texts, is absolutely free; and its importance as a principle can be seen from the fact that, according to most of the doctors, as Qazi Shaukani tells us, it was permitted even in the lifetime of the Holy Prophet. The closing of the door of *ijtihad* is pure fiction suggested partly by the crystallization of legal thought in Islam, and partly by that intellectual laziness which, especially in the period of spiritual decay, turns great thinkers into idols. If some of the later doctors have upheld this fiction, modern Islam is not bound by this voluntary surrender of intellectual independence. Sarkashi writing in the 10th century of the *Hijra*[7] rightly observes:

> If the upholders of this fiction mean that the previous writers had more facilities, while the later writers had more difficulties in their way, it is nonsense; for it does not require much understanding to see that *ijtihad* for later doctors is easier than for the earlier doctors. Indeed the commentaries on the Qur'an and *sunna* have been compiled and multiplied to such an extent that the *mujtahid* of today has more material for interpretation than he needs.

This brief discussion, I hope, will make it clear to you that neither in the foundational principles nor in the structure of our systems, as we find them today, is there anything to justify the present attitude. Equipped with penetrative thought and fresh experience the world of Islam should courageously proceed to the work of reconstruction before them. This work of reconstruction, however, has a far more serious aspect than mere adjustment to modern conditions of life. The Great European War bringing in its wake the awakening of Turkey—the element of stability in the world of Islam, as a French writer has recently described her—and the new economic experiment tried in the neighborhood of Muslim Asia, must open our eyes to the inner meaning and destiny of Islam. Humanity needs three things today—a spiritual interpretation of the universe, spiritual emancipation of the individual, and basic principles of a universal import directing the evolution of human society on a spiritual basis. Modern Europe has, no doubt, built idealistic systems on these lines, but experience shows that truth revealed through pure reason is incapable of bringing that fire of living conviction which personal revelation alone can bring. This is the reason why pure thought has so little influenced men, while religion has always elevated individuals, and transformed whole societies. The idealism of Europe never became a living factor in her life, and the result is a perverted ego seeking itself through mutually intolerant democracies whose

7. [Possibly Muhammad ibn Bahadur Zarkashi, eighth century A.H./fourteenth century A.D.—Editor]

sole function is to exploit the poor in the interest of the rich. Believe me, Europe today is the greatest hindrance in the way of man's ethical advancement. The Muslim, on the other hand, is in possession of these ultimate ideas on the basis of a revelation, which, speaking from the inmost depths of life, internalizes its own apparent externality. With him the spiritual basis of life is a matter of conviction for which even the least enlightened man among us can easily lay down his life; and in view of the basic idea of Islam that there can be no further revelation binding on man, we ought to be spiritually one of the most emancipated peoples on earth. Early Muslims emerging out of the spiritual slavery of pre-Islamic Asia were not in a position to realize the true significance of this basic idea. Let the Muslim of today appreciate his position, reconstruct his social life in the light of ultimate principles, and evolve, out of the hitherto partially revealed purpose of Islam, that spiritual democracy which is the ultimate aim of Islam.

The Second Message of Islam

Mahmoud Mohamed Taha (Sudan, circa 1910–1985) received his university degree in Khartoum, Sudan, and worked for many years as a civil engineer, specializing in irrigation. At the same time, he was active in the Sudanese independence movement. In 1945, he helped to found the Republican Party and then spent several years in jail as a result of his activism. After independence, his followers founded the Republican Brothers, which Taha led until his execution in 1985. The founding document of this organization, first drafted in the early 1950s and published in 1967—excerpted here—presents Taha's unorthodox view that the earlier Qur'anic revelations (revealed in Mecca before the Prophet gained political power) should be granted greater importance than the later revelations, which refer more narrowly to the conditions of the Prophet's rule in Medina. This view brought Taha into conflict with the Sudanese government's implementation of more orthodox Islamic laws in the 1980s. His protest against these policies led to his arrest and execution.[1]

Introduction to the Third Edition

This is the introduction to the third edition of *The Second Message of Islam*. The first edition was published in January 1967 A.D., in the revered month of

---

1. Abdullahi Ahmed An-Na'im, "Translator's Introduction," in Mahmoud Mohamed Taha, *The Second Message of Islam* (Syracuse, N.Y.: Syracuse University Press, 1987); Khalid Duran, "An Alternative to Islamism: The Evolutionary Thought of Mahmud Taha," *Cross Currents*, volume 42, number 4, Winter 1992–1993, pp. 453–467; Paul J. Magnarella, "Republican Brothers," in John L. Esposito, editor, *The Oxford Encyclopedia of the Modern Islamic World* (New York: Oxford University Press, 1995), volume 3, pp. 429–430.

Ramadan 1386 A.H. The second edition was published in April 1968 A.D., in the month of Muharram 1388 A.H. At the time of the second edition we were, however, preoccupied with other business and could not give that edition an introduction of its own.

This book, *The Second Message of Islam*, is new in every respect. . . . Besides being new, it is also totally "strange," that is, unexpected, since it proclaims the return of a renewed Islam. Such "strangeness," however, is to be expected, especially by informed Muslims. The Prophet is reported to have said: "Islam started as a stranger, and it shall return as a stranger in the same way it started. Blessed are the strangers! They asked: Who are the strangers, O Messenger of God? He replied: Those who revive my *sunna* [practice of the Prophet] after it had been abandoned."

Thus, the return of a revived Islam is by nature strange, that is to say, mysterious and unexpected. Those who criticize this book for its "strangeness," therefore, reveal both a lack of understanding and of patience. We need not concern ourselves here with those who oppose this book's message out of misunderstanding and deliberate distortion out of bad faith. But we must emphasize that the apparent "strangeness" of this message is inherent in the nature of Islamic revival. Understanding this book requires patience, diligence, and close scrutiny. If the reader is able to persist, his mind shall be open to a new understanding of the Qur'an and Islam, and he shall be rewarded for his perseverance, God willing.

Sunna *and* Shari'a

In the above quoted *hadith* [tradition of the Prophet], the Prophet referred to the strangers and said they were those who revive his *sunna* after it had been abandoned. Those who call for such a revival become strangers amongst their own people, because such a call involves a divergence from what people are accustomed to. They are strangers by virtue of their adherence to the truth amongst people for whom the truth is a stranger. If people have experienced falsehood for so long, then because of their long unfamiliarity with the truth, they come to accept falsehood as the truth.

It is mistakenly believed by some that the *sunna* consists of all the acts and words of the Prophet, as well as his approval of the action of others. This is not true, because his teachings to others and approval of their conduct relate to *shari'a* [Islamic law]. Only the Prophet's personal deeds, and his utterances that reflect the state of his heart in its knowledge of God, constitute *sunna*. The Prophet's statements which were designed to teach the people their religion are *shari'a*. The difference between *shari'a* and *sunna* is the difference between the Message and the Prophethood. In other words, it reflects the difference between the standard of the generality of Muslims of all levels, and the standard of the Prophet, which is a tremendous difference indeed.

Sunna relates to the personal practice of the Prophet, while in *shari'a* the Prophet descends from the level of his own personal practice to the level of his people in order to teach them according to their capabilities, thereby requiring them to act within their capacities. *Sunna* is his prophethood, while *shari'a* is his message. With respect to his message, the Prophet said: "We the prophets have been instructed to address people in accordance with the level of their understanding."

Al-Islam *and* Al-'Iman

There is a common failure to appreciate the fine distinction between *islam* [submission to God] and *'iman* [faith]. *'Iman* is widely and mistakenly believed to be superior to *islam*. This mistaken belief is due to an inability to appreciate the circumstances of the time. The time when such belief sufficed is over, as we have now reached a point when the understanding of religion has developed and evolved from the level of *'iman* to the level of *islam*. The distinction can be explained as follows:

Islam is an intellectual process by which the diligent worshiper proceeds on a ladder of seven steps, the first being *islam*, secondly *'iman*, thirdly *ihsan* [beneficence], fourthly *'ilm al-yaqin*, fifthly *'ilm 'ayn al-yaqin*, sixthly *'ilm haqq al-yaqin*, and seventhly *islam* once more.[2] But *islam* at the higher stage differs in degree from *islam* at the initial stage. At the initial stage, *islam* is merely external or apparent submission, while in the final state it is both external and internal (genuine) submission. *Islam* at the initial stage concerns speech and action, while in the final stage it is intelligent surrender and submission and acceptance of God both in private and in public. At the initial stage *islam* is inferior to *'iman*, while at the final stage it is superior to *'iman*. Many theologians whom we know today are unable to make this distinction.

Religious scholars have been confused by the *hadith* involving Gabriel, reported by 'Umar ibn al-Khattab [Companion of the Prophet, 592–644], who said:

As we were seated with the Messenger of God, peace be upon him, there came a man wearing [clean][3]

2. [These somewhat technical terms refer to the various degrees of piety and perfection of conduct and lifestyle, in accordance with religious and moral norms and ethics.—Translator]

3. [The bracketed words in this quotation and throughout this chapter, with several exceptions, have been inserted by the translator.—Editor]

white clothes, with very dark hair. None of us knew him, yet he did not show the signs of travel. He sat near the Messenger of God, peace be upon him, and placed his knees next to his [the Prophet's] knees, and placed his hands on his [the Prophet's] thighs and said: O, Muhammad, tell me about *islam*. . . . He [the Prophet] said: *islam* is to declare that there is no god but God, and that Muhammad is the Messenger of God; to say the prayers; pay *zakat* taxes; fast the month of Ramadan, and do pilgrimage to the House [of God], if you can afford it. He said: You are right. We wondered how he could ask him and then confirm he was right. Then he [the man] said: Tell me about *'iman*. He [the Prophet] replied: *'iman* is to believe in God, His angels, His Books, Messengers, fate whether good or bad, and the hereafter. He [the man] said: you are right. Then he asked: tell me about *ihsan*. He [the Prophet] replied: *ihsan* is to worship God as if you see Him, and although you do not see Him, be certain that He can see you. He [the man] said: you are right. Then he said: Tell me when is the final hour? He [the Prophet] replied: the one being asked does not know of it more than the one who asks. He [the man] said: Tell me of its signs? He [the Prophet] replied: When the woman gives birth to her mistress, and when you see the bare-footed and naked shepherds practice extravagance. He said: You are right. Then he left. We stayed a while, then the Messenger, peace be upon him, said: O 'Umar, do you know the one who was asking the questions? I replied, God and His Messenger know better. He said: This is Gabriel, who came to teach you your religion.

Many religious scholars interpreted this to mean that Islam proceeds in three stages: *islam*, *'iman*, and *ihsan*. Since it is said in the Qur'an, concerning the Bedouins, "The Bedouins said *amanna* (we believe); tell them you have not believed, but say *aslamna* (we submit) and *'iman* (true belief) did not enter your hearts yet" (Sura 49, Verse 14), it seems obvious to these scholars that *'iman* is higher in degree than *islam*. Those scholars failed to appreciate that the issue needs close consideration.

The Truth of the Matter

The truth of the matter is that *islam*, as conveyed in the Qur'an, comes in two stages: the stage of dogma (*'aqida*) and the stage of the truth (*haqiqa*) or knowledge. Each of these two stages has three levels.

The levels of dogma are *islam*, *'iman*, and *ihsan*, while the levels of knowledge are *'ilm al-yaqin*, *'ilm 'ayn al-yaqin*, and *'ilm haqq al-yaqin*. Finally, there is a seventh stage in the ladder of evolution, which is *islam*, which completes the cycle. The end of religious evolution resembles the beginning, yet they are not identical. The beginning is *islam* and the end is *islam*, but there is a vast difference between *islam* at the beginning of religious evolution and *islam* at the end. The stage of *'aqida* is the stage of the nation of *Mu'minin* [Believers], which is the nation of the First Message of Islam.

The stage of knowledge is the stage of the nation of *Muslimin* [Muslims, literally Those Who Submit], which is the nation of the Second Message of Islam. This nation has not come yet, although its vanguard have appeared individually throughout human history, in the form of prophets, with the final prophet being the Prophet Muhammad ibn Abdullahi, may he receive the highest blessing and utmost peace. It was Muhammad who prophesied the coming of the nation of *Muslimin* and brought its message, as contained in general terms in the Qur'an, and detailed it in the *sunna*. When the nation of *Muslimin* comes, it shall begin at the same point as the nation of *Mu'minin*, namely at a stage of dogma or *'aqida*. But it shall not stop at the third step of the ladder, where Gabriel stopped in his questions. It shall continue to evolve to the end of the ladder, thereby combining both dogma as well as knowledge. In other words, the coming nation is a nation of both *Muslimin* as well as *Mu'minin* at one and the same time, while the first nation was one of *Mu'minin* (believers) and not *Muslimin* (submitters) in the final sense of *islam* [as total and intelligent surrender to God].

It must be noted that Gabriel stopped in his questions at the end of the level of dogma, *'aqida*, because he had come to explain religion to the nation of *Mu'minin*, and not to the nation of *Muslimin*, which had not yet come.

Muhammad is the Messenger of the First Message, and he is also the Messenger of the Second Message. While he explained the First Message in detail, he only outlined the Second Message. Its elaboration now requires a fresh understanding of the Qur'an. That is the purpose of this book.

Those who approach this book with an open mind will be guided along the right path. We ask God for rectification and success in our endeavor; He is the best Lord. . . .

The First Message of Islam

Nation of Mu'minin

We have said that the Qur'an was divided between *'iman* and *islam*, as well as being revealed in two parts as Meccan and Medinese. The Meccan Qur'an was revealed first. In other words, people were invited to adopt Islam [in the ultimate sense] first, and when they failed to do so, and it was practically demonstrated that they were below its standard, they were addressed in accordance with their abilities. This offer of the higher standard is the conclusive argument against people referred to in the verse: "And We will surely try you until We make manifest those among you who strive [for the cause of God] and those who are steadfast. And We will make known the truth about you." (Sura 47, Verse 31) This experiment and consequent practical experience is for the benefit of mankind because God's knowledge does not occur afresh (*hadith*).[4] The phrase "those who strive" means major *jihad*, namely, striving to control the self.[5] "And those who are steadfast" refers to endurance of the state of distance from God. "And We will make known the truth about you" means to extract thoughts that are repressed in your subconscious—your *sir al-sir*.

The verses which demonstrate descent from ultimate Islam to the level of *'iman* are numerous—for example, the verse, "O believers (*mu'minin*), fear God as He ought to be feared, and become true submitters (*muslimin*) before you die." (Sura 3, Verse 102) When the believers (*mu'minin*) said "which of us can fear God as He ought to be feared?" the Qur'an descended in another verse to the level of "Fear God as much as you can, listen and obey and pay alms,

as that is good for yourselves, and those who are rid of their own selfishness are the truly successful ones." (Sura 64, Verse 16)

When the verse, "Those who believe without obscuring their belief with unfairness have security, and they are truly guided" (Sura 6, Verse 82) was revealed, people found it too difficult to comply with, and they said: "O Messenger of God, which one of us is not unfair to himself?" He replied: "It is not what you mean. Did you not hear what God's true slave (Luqman) said: O son, do not disbelieve in God, such disbelief is great unfairness. The verse means disbelief." The believers were relieved because they knew that they had not disbelieved since the time they came to believe. In fact the Prophet explained the verse to them at the level of *mu'minin*, knowing that its explanation at the level of the *muslimin* was above their ability, because "unfairness" then means subtle polytheism in the sense mentioned in the verse of the *sir al-sir*. "All shall submit to the living and all-sustaining God. And he indeed has failed who holds iniquity." (Sura 20, Verse 111)

It is reported about the verse, "Those who believe without obscuring their belief with unfairness have security, and they are truly guided," that the Prophet said: "I was told that I am one of them." The Prophet is not merely one of the believers (*mu'minin*), as he is the first of the true submitters to God (*muslimin*); "Say: 'My prayer and my worship and my life and my death are [all] for God the Lord of all creation. He has no partner. And so am I commanded, and I am the first of those who submit (*muslimin*).'" (Sura 6, Verse 163)

We have said that the nation of the First Message are *muslimin*. While the Qur'an described *muslimin* at the time of Moses as the Jews, and at the time of Jesus as Christians, it describes them at the time of the First Muhammadan Message as *mu'minin* or "those who believed." Listen to the Qur'an: "Surely, those who believe and the Jews and the Christians and the Sabians who so believe in God and the Last Day, and do good deeds shall have their reward with their Lord, and no fear [shall come] upon them, nor shall they grieve." (Sura 2, Verse 62) Again, it says, "Surely, those who have believed, and the Jews, and the Sabians, and the Christians who so believe in God and the Last Day and do good deeds—on them [shall come] no fear, nor shall they grieve." (Sura 5, Verse 69) Another instructive verse reads:

4. [God in His comprehensive and all-preceding knowledge already knew that Islam would be rejected when first offered in Mecca, but He conducted the experiment for our sake, so that we should know with certainty. God's knowledge is ancient and external beyond time, *qadim* and not *hadith*.—Translator]

5. [Reference here is to the *hadith* where the Prophet describes self-control as the primary and major *jihad* or self-exertion.—Translator]

O believers (*mu'minin*), believe in God, His Messenger, and the Book that He revealed to His Messenger, and the Book revealed previously. He who disbelieves in God, His angels, books, messengers, and the Final Day, has grossly strayed from the path. (Sura 4, Verse 136)

So He calls them *mu'minin* (believers) and yet invites them to further belief, more *'iman*.

The verses: "O believers (*mu'minin*), fear God as He ought to be feared, and become true submitters (*muslimin*) before you die," and "Fear God as much as you can, and listen and obey and pay alms, as that is good for yourselves, and those who are rid of their own selfishness are the truly successful ones" clearly have two different meanings—one setting an original precept and the other a subsidiary one. It is also clear that the real objective is the achievement of the original precept. When it was shown that it was impracticable to do so, it was postponed and the intermediate objective of implementing the subsidiary precept was sought. When the conditions necessary for achieving the original objective, that is to say, when both individual as well as collective human capacities are sufficiently mature, the original precept shall be restored. This is the reason why the original precepts of religion were postponed, and the subsidiary precepts were implemented [as transitional measures] as shall be explained below.

Jihad *Is Not an Original Precept in Islam*

Islam's original view is that a person is free until it is shown, in practice, that he or she is unable to properly discharge the duty of such freedom. Freedom is a natural right corresponding to a duty, namely, its proper exercise. Once a free person is unable to fulfill the duty of his or her freedom, such freedom shall be withdrawn under a law which is consistent with the constitution, that is, a law which reconciles the need of the individual for absolute individual freedom, and the need of the community for total social justice. As already stated, this is the law of *mu'awada* (reciprocity).

This was Islam's original and fundamental principle. The propagation of Islam began with the verses of persuasion in Mecca where the verse "Propagate the path of your Lord in wisdom and peaceable advice, and argue with them in a kind manner. Your Lord is more knowledgeable of those who stray from His path, and He is more knowledgeable of the

guided ones" (Sura 16, Verse 125) and many other similar verses were revealed. This approach was continued for 13 years, during which time much of the miraculous Qur'an was revealed, and many men, women, and children were transformed under the guidance of the new discipline. The early Muslims curtailed their own aggression against the unbelievers, endured hurt, sacrificed their comforts sincerely and self-denyingly in the cause of spreading their religion, without weakening or submitting. Their lives were the supreme expression of their religion and consisted of sincere worship, kindness, and peaceful coexistence with all other people.

God says: "I have created *jinn* [spirits] and people for no reason except that they may worship Me." (Sura 51, Verse 56) And He favored people with the mind, body, and comforts that enable them to worship Him and appreciate His Grace. He also says: "God enjoins *'adl* [justice], *ihsan*, the doing of good to others, and benevolence to the next of kin; and forbids indecency, lewdness, manifest evil, and transgression. He admonishes you that you may take heed." (Sura 16, Verse 90) Again, God says:

> and that you slay not your children for fear of poverty—it is We who provide for you and for them—and that you approach not foul deeds, whether open or secret; and that you slay not the self, which God has forbidden save in accordance (with the demands of) justice. That is what He has enjoined upon you, that you may understand. (Sura 6, Verse 151)

All this the Qur'an produced in the new religion, and the Prophet and his Companions delivered by their words and example, all to the best interest and advantage of their people.

Nevertheless, their people persisted in worshiping the stone they carved, severing relations with the next of kin, destroying life, and burying girls alive,[6] thereby abusing their freedom, and rendering it liable to be withdrawn. Since at that time there was no law except the sword, the sword was used to that effect [abridging freedom]. Thus, implementation shifted from the verse, "Then remind them, as you are only a reminder. You have no dominion

---

6. [In pre-Islamic days, the Arabs used to bury their daughters alive to avoid any shame they might cause to them, if taken by their enemies, and to avoid having to defend and feed them generally.—Translator]

over them" (Sura 8, Verses 21–22), to the verse, "except he who shuns and disbelieves, on whom God shall inflict the greatest suffering." (Sura 88, Verses 23–24) It is as if God said, "We have granted you, Muhammad, dominion over anyone who shuns and disbelieves, so that God shall subject him to minor suffering at your hands through fighting, then God shall also subject him to the greatest suffering in hell." "It is to Us that they shall return. Then We shall hold them to account." (Sura 88, Verses 25–26) Thus the two first verses were abrogated or repealed by the two second verses. In this way, all the verses of persuasion, though they constitute the primary or original principle, were abrogated or repealed by the verses of compulsion (*jihad*). This exception was necessitated by the circumstances of the time and the inadequacy of the human capability to discharge properly the duty of freedom at that time. Hence the Prophet said:

I have been instructed to fight people until they declare that "There is no god but God," and that Muhammad is the Messenger of God (et cetera). Once they do, they will have secured their lives and property, unless they violate the law. And I leave their sincerity to be judged by God.

Some Muslim scholars believe that Islamic wars were purely defensive wars, a mistaken belief prompted by their keenness to refute claims by the Orientalists that Islam spread by means of the sword. In fact, the sword was used to curtail the abuse of freedom.

Islam used persuasion for 13 years in propagating its clearly valid message for the individual and the community. When the addressees failed to discharge properly the duties of their freedom, they lost this freedom, and the Prophet was appointed as their guardian until they came of age. However, once they embraced the new religion and observed the sanctity of life and property, and the social claims of their kith and kin, as they had been instructed, the sword was suspended, and abuses of freedom were penalized according to new laws. Hence the development of Islamic *shari'a* law, and the establishment of a new type of government.

In justifying the use of the sword, we may describe it as a surgeon's lancet and not a butcher's knife. When used with sufficient wisdom, mercy, and knowledge, it uplifted the individual and purified society. God said to this effect:

We have sent Our Messengers with the clear signs, and revealed with them the Book and the scales, so that people should maintain the fair balance, and decreed iron with much hardship and benefits to people, so that God may discover who supports Him and His Messengers sincerely. God is All-Powerful and Self-Sufficient. (Sura 57, Verse 25)

"We have sent Our Messengers with the clear signs" indicates the conclusive proof of the validity of their messages; "and revealed with them the Book" refers to the principle that "There is no god but God." "The scales" means the *shari'a* to adjudicate between slave [man] and the Lord on the one hand, and between one slave and another on the other hand, "so that people should maintain the fair balance," that is to say, be fair in their dealings.

The part "and decreed iron with much hardship and benefits to People" signifies that God has enacted fighting with the sword in order to curtail the freedom of those who abuse it, so that the sword brings them to their senses, thereby allowing them to earn their freedom and benefit from their life. That is, of course, besides other benefits which may be derived from iron, which we need not enumerate here. The part "so that God may discover who supports Him and His Messengers sincerely" is to discover out of practical experience for man's own benefit, because fighting is hateful and difficult. In other words, the object was to see who would endure the hardship of war for the sake of God and in support of the oppressed, by maintaining the fair balance between each individual and himself, and between himself and others. "God is All-Powerful and Self-Sufficient" implies that He is so Powerful that He needs no support from anyone else, and nothing can be gained from Him except through His own Grace.

What can be gained from Him in this context is victory. So the verse refers in a subtle way to another verse: "O believers, if you support [the cause of] God, He will help you and will make your steps firm." (Sura 47, Verse 7) So if you support the cause of God by supporting His Prophet in order to maintain the balance, God shall help you and give you victory over your own lower selves. In other words, if you stand by the cause of God in minor *jihad* (fighting), He shall support You and give you victory in the major *jihad* (self-control) where one is helpless without God's help, and no one can give you victory except Him. To "make your steps firm" means tranquillity and peace of mind, and includes, of course, physical courage in battle.

In treating ailments of the heart it is wise to begin with gentle means, and to resort to strict measures only when absolutely necessary, deferring drastic treatment to the very end. Suffering death by the sword in this life is really an aspect of suffering hell in the next life, since both are punishments for disbelief. Whoever adds to his own disbelief by inciting others to disbelief or to shun the path of God must be suppressed before he takes up arms in the cause of disbelief. God says:

> Those who spend their money in order to shun the path of God shall spend it, achieve only sorrow, and still be defeated. The infidels shall be gathered in hell, so that God may distinguish the bad from the good and set the bad apart and cast them all in hell. These indeed are the losers. Tell the infidels that if they repent, they shall be forgiven for what they have done, but if they persist, then they shall be dealt with as were similar people before them. Fight them to prevent chaos, and so that all religion is rendered unto God; if they give up, then God has insight in what they do. (Sura 8, Verses 36–39)

When we consider God's expression, "the infidels shall be gathered in hell, so that God may distinguish the bad from the good," we can readily appreciate that the cause of suffering is disbelief. "God has no need for your suffering if you are thankful and believing, God is All-Thankful and All-Knowledgeable." (Sura 4, Verse 147) The part of the above text, "Fight them to prevent chaos," means so that there will be no disbelief, its propagation, or the shunning of the path of faith. "[S]o that all religion is rendered unto God" reflects the original purpose of fighting: "Your Lord commanded [that you] worship none but Him." (Sura 17, Verse 23) This is the design which He shall accomplish regardless of the wishes of the infidels.

In another verse God says: "Fight them to prevent chaos, and in order to render religion unto God; if they desist, then there can be no hostility except against the wrongdoers." (Sura 2, Verse 193) The wrongdoers are of two levels. On one level there are those who worship other than God, and persist in doing so, while on the other level there are those who appear to submit to God in obedience, but transgress upon the rights of other people and do them injustice. The verse decrees that freedom be withdrawn from those who abuse it, such withdrawal being proportionate to the degree of abuse: for the disbelievers the law of war, and hard-ship of iron, while to the transgressors, the law of peace and adjudication of rights. This is the meaning of the expression "then there can be no hostility except against the wrongdoers."

Postponement from the original principles to the subsidiary principles signifies descent from the level of *islam* to the level of *'iman*. This is referred to in the verse "And We have revealed to you the Reminder [the Qur'an] so that you may explain to mankind that which has been sent down to them, and that they may reflect." (Sura 16, Verse 44) The phrase "we have revealed to you the Reminder" means the whole of the Qur'an including the original principle—*islam*—as well as the subsidiary (*'iman*). "So that you may explain to mankind that which has been sent down to them" means to detail through legislation, and to explain, in various other ways, to the believers (*mu'minin*) what has been brought down to their level. "[T]hat they may reflect," means that perhaps such reflection, while implementing the subsidiary principle, may lead them to the original principle they were unable to implement at the beginning. Here is a subtle reference to the ascent up the various levels of Islam, starting with initial Islam, and ascending by means of clear thinking, guided speech, and sincere action: "Unto Him ascends the pure words, being elevated by good deeds." (Sura 35, Verse 10)

Thus we reach an extremely important conclusion: many aspects of the present Islamic *shari'a* are not the original principles or objectives of Islam. They merely reflect a descent in accordance with the circumstances of the time and the limitations of human ability.

Slavery Is Not an Original Precept in Islam

Islam's original principle is freedom. But the Islamic religion was revealed to a society in which slavery was an integral part of the socioeconomic order. It was also a society that was shown in practice to be incapable of properly exercising its freedom, and therefore its individual members needed guidance; hence the consequent enactment of *jihad*. In Islamic *jihad*, the Muslims first had to offer to the unbelievers the new religion. If they refused to accept it, they had the second option of paying *jizya* [tax] and living under Muslim government, while practicing their own religion and enjoying personal security. If they also refused the option of *jizya*, the Muslims would fight them and if victorious take some of them as slaves, thereby adding to the number of those already in slavery.

The rationale of such servitude is to be found in the principle of reciprocity (*mu'awada*). If an individual is invited to become the slave of God but refuses, such refusal is symptomatic of ignorance that calls for a period of training. The individual prepares to submit voluntarily to the servitude of God by becoming the slave of another person, thereby learning obedience and humility, which are becoming of a slave. Reciprocity (*mu'awada*) here rules that if a free person refuses to become the slave of God, he may be subjugated and made the slave of a slave of God, in fair and just retribution: "And whoso does an atom's weight of evil will also see it" (Sura 99, Verse 8). . . . .

The Second Message of Islam

The Second Message is Islam. The Prophet himself imparted this Second Message without elaboration or detail, except for such overlaps between the First Message and the Second Message as *'ibadat* and *hudud* [worship practices and the specified penalties]. God says: "Today I have perfected your religion for you, completed My grace upon you, and sanctioned Islam as your religion " (Sura 5, Verse 3) That day was the day of *'arafa* [ninth day of the month Dhu'l-Hijja] on *hajat al-wada'* (the farewell pilgrimage) of the eighth year A.H., which was a Friday. This verse is the last verse of the Qur'an to be revealed, and is the ultimate word of the Divine Message.

God has accepted Islam for mankind so that we may accept it, because anything that is not initiated by Him cannot be undertaken by us. God says: "Then He forgave them in order that they may repent." (Sura 9, Verse 118)[7]

Many people considered the phrase, "Today I have perfected your religion for you," as implying that Islam itself has been fully achieved by mankind on earth on that day. The verse "And We have revealed to you the Reminder [the Qur'an] so that you may explain to mankind that which has been sent down to them" (Sura 16, Verse 44) was also taken to mean that the Qur'an has already been finally and

7. [That is to say, people's repentance is initiated by God before it can be undertaken by them.—Translator]

conclusively explained. Nothing, however, is further from the truth than this view. "Explanation" of the Qur'an has been only in terms of [expedient] legislation, the *shari'a*, and interpretation to the extent appropriate for the time of such explanation and in accordance with the capacity of the audience and the abilities of the people.

The Qur'an can never be finally and conclusively explained. Islam, too, can never be concluded. Progress in it is eternal: "Surely, the [true] religion with God is Islam." (Sura 3, Verse 19) "With God" [is eternal] beyond time and space. Progress into Islam by means of the Qur'an is progress towards God in infinitude (*itlaq*). As such it has not been, and can never be, fully and conclusively explained. It is its revelation into *mashaf* [Arabic text] as a Book that has been concluded, but its explanation has not.

This is how one should understand the difference between "revealed" and "explain" in the verse "And we have revealed to you the Reminder [the Qur'an] so that you may explain to mankind that which has been sent down to them, and they may reflect." According to the prevailing understanding of Muslim scholars, the two notions are synonymous, while in fact they are not. The level of understanding in the phrase "that which has been sent down to them" does not refer to the whole of the Qur'an but only to the part subject to explanation, namely, the First Message, and sections where the First and the Second Messages overlap.

The Qur'an was revealed with dual meanings. God says in this connection:

God has revealed the best speech in a Book of similar and dual meanings, from which the skin of those who fear their Lord creeps! Then their skin and hearts soften to *dhikr* [remembrance through worship of God]. That is the guidance of God with which He guides whomsoever He wishes, and he whom God misguided has no other guide. (Sura 30, Verse 23)

The word "similar" implies that there is some similarity between the Qur'an at its base and at its peak, its front and back. Its *zahir* and *batin*, "dual meanings," refer to its two levels of meaning: a distant meaning with the Lord, and a nearer meaning that has come down to the slave [of God].

The whole of the Qur'an is of dual meanings: every verse and word and even every letter has a dual meaning. The reason for this is that the Qur'an is the Lord's speech to His slave. The similarity in the

Qur'an is due to the similarity between the Lord and the slave, expressed by the Prophet in the *hadith*, "God has created Adam [man] after His Own image." God expresses the same meaning in the verse: "O people, fear your Lord, Who has created you from a single Self." (Sura 4, Verse 1) That "single Self" means His Own Blessed and Exalted Self.

The word Islam, for example, has a near meaning exposed by the Qur'an in the verse, "The Bedouins said *amanna* [we believe]; tell them you have not believed, but say *aslamna* [we submit] and *'iman* [true belief] did not enter your hearts yet." (Sura 49, Verse 14) This is what we termed initial Islam which, we said, is not taken by God as significant. Islam has a further meaning which lies with God in infinity. To this further meaning comes the reference in the verse: "Oh believers [*mu'minin*], fear God as He ought to be feared and become true submitters [*muslimin*] before you die." (Sura 3, Verse 102)

It goes without saying that no one fears God as He ought to be feared except God Himself. This is, therefore, a methodology of ascent to God through many levels of servitude, humility, and submission. Servitude is infinite, just like Lordship. Absolute servitude to God requires absolute knowledge of God, and this only God can achieve. "Say no one knows what is in heaven and earth, the Unknown, except God." (Sura 27, Verse 65) The Unknown here means God Himself, so it is as if He said, "No one knows God except God Himself." In our book *Rasalat al-salah* [*The Message of Righteousness*], which may be consulted in this context, we have shown how servitude [to God] is freedom.

Islam is a method of ascent to servitude, and the Qur'an is the Book which leads the way. This quality of the Qur'an is the reason it was revealed, as indicated in the verse, "And, indeed, We rendered the Qur'an for the sake of *dhikr*, remembrance through worship, is there anyone who would take heed?" (Sura 54, Verse 17) The Qur'an reminds us of servitude which we have accepted and then forgotten:

And [remember] when thy Lord brought forth from Adam's children—out of their loins—their offspring and made them bear witness against their own selves saying, "Am I not your Lord?" They said: "Yes, we admit this." [This He did] lest you should say on the Day of Resurrection, "we were surely unaware of this." Or [lest] you should say, [it was] only our fathers [who] associated co-partners [with God] in the past and we were merely a generation after them.

Will Thou then destroy us for what those, who lied, did? And thus do We make clear the Signs, [that they may be admonished] and that they may return [to God]. (Sura 7, Verses 172–174)

So that they may return to God in servitude and submission, through Islam.

As the Qur'an is the methodology of ascent to God, "We said: Go forth hence, all of you. And if there comes to you guidance from Me, then whoso shall follow My guidance, on them [shall come] no fear, nor shall they grieve." (Sura 2, Verse 38) Since the Qur'an is that guidance, then it has its beginning with God, and its end with us. If we proceed properly through its levels, we shall recover the paradise we lost through the sin of Adam, and ascend into infinity (*itlaq*). God said of the Qur'an: "*Alif lam min*.[8] That is certainly the Book which contains guidance for the God fearing." (Sura 2, Verses 1–2) Of those who fear God who are guided by the Qur'an, He said: "Those who fear God are in paradise, and a river, on a seat of truth, with the Most Able King." (Sura 54, Verse 54) These are levels or grades, beginning with paradise, then the river, then the seat of truth, and finally with the Most Able King in infinity. Such levels vary from physical paradise—which is the paradise lost through sin, to the Absolute in His *itlaq*. The Qur'an guides to all this, hence it is inexhaustible: "Say, if every sea became ink for the words of my Lord, surely, the sea would be exhausted before the words of my Lord were exhausted, even if a similar amount is brought as additional supply." (Sura 18, Verse 109) For this reason it is false to assert that the Qur'an may be finally and conclusively explained. The Qur'an is God's *dhat* [Self or Soul] which has descended, out of pure grace, to levels comprehensible by the slaves, thereby becoming the Qur'an in its various levels of descent: *dhikr*, *Qur'an*, and *furqan*.[9] *Furqan* was the most effective form of Arabic expression to indicate the two levels of *Qur'an* and *dhikr*. The Qur'an was rendered into the form of Arabic expression so that we might understand from God. God says in this respect: "We have rendered it into Arabic so that you may understand." (Sura 43, Verse 3) This verse and other similar verses

8. [Three letters of the Arabic alphabet. 28 of 114 *suras* of the Qur'an begin with letters.—Editor]

9. [These terms refer to the Qur'an at different levels of knowledge and understanding of the truth in its *batin*, beyond the superficial *zahir* meaning of the text.—Translator]

have misled many Muslim scholars into believing that the Qur'an itself is Arabic, in the sense that its meanings may be exhaustively understood through the Arabic language. It is not so, as we have explained when discussing Qur'anic chapters starting with letters of the alphabet, above.

Being so supreme, Islam has never been achieved by any nation up to the present day. The nation of *muslimin* has not yet come. It is expected to come, however, in the future of humanity. Its day of emergence shall be the day of the ultimate pilgrimage, the day when the Divine statement "Today I have perfected your religion for you, completed My grace upon you, and sanctioned Islam as your religion" (Sura 5, Verse 3) is realized in practice.

Muhammad, in his time, was the pioneer of the *muslimin* to come. It was as if he came to his nation, the nation of the *mu'minin* from the future. He was not one of them, as he was the only Muslim amongst them. "Say: My prayer and my worship and my life and my death are [all] for God the Lord of all creation. He has no partner. And so am I commanded, and I am the first of those who submit [*muslimin*]." (Sura 6, Verse 163) Abu Bakr [died 634], the second best man, was the most superior of all the believers (*mu'minin*), yet there was a huge gap between him and the Prophet. It was to future *muslimin* that the Prophet referred, when he said:

"How I long for my brothers who have not come yet." And Abu Bakr said: "Are we not your brothers, O Messenger of God?" He replied: "No, you are my Companions!" Then he said again: "How I long for my brothers who have not come yet!" Then Abu Bakr said: "Are we not your brothers, O Messenger for God?" He said: "No, you are my Companions!" Then He said for the third time: "How I long for my brothers who have not come yet!" They asked: "Who are your brothers, O Messenger of God?" He said: "A people who come at the end of time, of whom the active one shall have seventy times as much reward as you have." They asked: "Seventy times as much as we have or they have?" He replied: "As you have." They asked: "Why?" He replied: "Because you find assistance in doing good, and they find no assistance."

The Muslims (Muslimin)

The Muslims, as a nation, have not yet come, but the Prophet prophesied their coming, towards the end of time, when circumstances are suitable, and God's promise is fulfilled: "And he who seeks a religion other than Islam, it shall not be accepted of him and in the Hereafter he shall be among the losers." (Sura 3, Verse 85) On that day all people shall embrace religion and find no alternative, because religion provides the only answers.

We believe that the earth is preparing for the emergence of the Islamic *shari'a* of the true submitters (*muslimin*), which shall establish the new civilization. In view of the bankruptcy of contemporary social philosophies, there is no alternative. As stated at the outset of this book, the whole of humanity today is in an ideological wilderness, with Western civilization lost and bankrupt,[10] and with issues of democracy, socialism, and individual freedom persistently demanding answers. Yet there is no answer except through the cross-fertilization of Western civilization, or to be more precise, Western material progress, with a new spirit, namely, the spirit of Islam. Islam appears to be the only ideology capable of resolving the existing conflict between the individual and the community and between the individual and the universe, as we have already demonstrated.

We should not confuse the name Muslims with the traditional name given to the present nation. We have already stated that the present nation derives its name from the initial Islam. Actually, present Muslim society is the nation of the *mu'minin* [believers]. No nation up to now has deserved the name *muslimin*. Any mention of Islam with respect to previous nations refers merely to initial Islam, except for the pioneers of humanity who achieved ultimate Islam, or rather a degree of the ultimate Islam, as the ultimate Islam can never be exhaustively achieved. Such pioneers are, therefore, the pioneers of the nation of *muslimin* which has not come yet. God says in this connection:

And [remember the time] when Abraham and Ishmael raised the foundations of the House [praying]: "Our Lord, accept [this] from us for Thou art the All-Hearing, the All-Knowing. Our Lord, make both of us submissive to Thee and make of our offspring a people submissive to Thee. And show us our ways of worship and turn to us with mercy; for Thou art Oft-Returning [with compassion, and art] Merciful. And, Our Lord, raise up among them

10. [As indicated earlier in his book, the author includes both the Marxist and liberal traditions when he refers to Western civilization.—Translator]

a Messenger from among themselves, who may recite to them Thy Signs and teach them the Book and Wisdom and may purify them; surely, Thou art the Mighty, the Wise." And who will turn away from the religion of Abraham but he who makes a fool of himself. Him did We choose in this world, and in the next he will surely be among the righteous. When his Lord said to him, "Submit," he said, "I [hereby] submit to the Lord of the worlds." The same did Abraham enjoin upon his sons—and Jacob [also— saying,] "O my sons, truly God has chosen this religion for you; so let not death overtake you except when you are in a state of complete submission." Were you present when death came to Jacob, when he said to his sons, "What will you worship after me?" They answered, "We will worship thy God, the God of thy fathers, Abraham and Ishmael and Isaac, the One God; and to Him we submit ourselves." (Sura 2, Verses 127–133)

The phrase "Our Lord, make both of us submissive to Thee" refers to ultimate Islam, and they [Abraham and Ishmael] were in fact *muslimin* [in this sense of ultimate Islam]. But the phrase "and make of our offspring a people submissive to Thee" indicates, in the short run, a Muslim nation in the sense of initial Islam, which shall evolve and develop into the ultimate Islam. Their prayers have been answered. Abraham advised his sons that there is no god except God, and so did Jacob: "O my sons, truly God has chosen this religion for you; so let not death overtake you except when you are in a state of complete submission"—that is to say, remain holding fast to the creed and maintain that "there is no god but God" until your death. Their answer, "we will worship thy God, the God of thy fathers Abraham and Ishmael and Isaac, the One God; and to Him we submit ourselves," refers to the initial Islam.

God also said: "As I inspired the disciples [of Jesus] to believe in Me, and in My Messengers, they said: We do believe, and You shall bear witness that we have submitted (*muslimin*)." (Sura 5, Verse 111) Their Islam here is synonymous with *'iman* [faith], as required in the revelation. God in the revelation required them to believe. When they did believe and declared this, they thought that their *'iman* was Islam, so they said: "You shall bear witness that we have submitted (*muslimin*)." A knowledgeable person can hear the Lord replying: "Do not say we have surrendered, but say we believe." They had not surrendered

in the sense of the ultimate Islam. They merely surrendered in the sense of the initial Islam.

The disciples were Muslims in the sense of initial Islam, since even the first stage of ultimate Islam requires moving out of the law for the community as a whole, and entering upon *shari'a fardiya*, the law for the individual. Individuality is achieved only after perfect compliance with the law for the community, until one is able to properly exercise his absolute individual freedom. The ultimate Islam is the level of individualities.

Individuality cannot be achieved by anyone who is divided within himself. When the conscious mind is no longer in conflict with the subconscious, unity of being is attained, and this is characterized by wholesomeness of the heart, clarity of thought, and beauty of body, thereby realizing a full and comprehensive intellectual and emotional life. "The next life is the ultimate life if they only know." (Sura 29, Verse 64) Ultimate life, free from defects, disease, and death, indeed the opposite of death.

To restore unity to one's being is for an individual to think as he wishes, speak what he thinks, and act according to his speech. This is the objective of Islam: "O believers, why do you say what you do not do? It is most hateful to God that you say what you do not do." (Sura 61, Verses 2–3)

The Good Society

This superior state can only be reached through a two-fold method: first, the good society, and secondly, the scientific educational method to be adopted by the individual in order to liberate himself from inherited fear.

The good society is one that is based on three equalities: economic equality, today known as socialism, or the sharing of wealth; political equality or democracy, or sharing in political decisions which affect daily life; and social equality which, to some extent, results from socialism and democracy, and is characterized by a lack of social classes and discrimination based on color, faith, race, or sex. In the good society, people are judged according to their intellectual and moral character, as reflected in their public and private lives and demonstrated in the spirit of public service at all times and through every means. Social equality aims at removing social classes and differences between urban and rural life by providing equal opportunities for cultural refinement. The criterion of social equality is that marriage [the most fundamental and intimate relation] is possible between any man and any woman. This is the accurate test of social equality.

A good society also enjoys tolerant public opinion, permitting different life-styles and manners, as long as these are beneficial to society.

Public opinion has its own judgments over and above those of the law and may be more effective than legislation itself in deterring deviants and offenders. Public opinion may, of course, condemn any type of conduct it disapproves, but it must always do so only by nonviolent means, since violence usually results in one of two evil responses: counterviolence or hypocrisy. Sometimes public opinion can be enacted as legislation if this is consistent with the constitution as described above [that is, legislation that reconciles the individual need for absolute individual freedom and society's need for complete social justice]. . . .

Political Equality: Democracy

Again, we will not discuss democracy in detail here, as it will be discussed in our book *Islam Is Democratic and Socialist*. Just as socialism is the product of the struggle between the "haves" and the "have nots" in the material sphere, democracy is the product of the struggle between those same extremes in the political sphere. Its purpose is the sharing of power. Democracy parallels socialism; they are as two wings of society. In the same way that a bird does not fly with one wing, so does society need the two wings of democracy and socialism.

Socialism, which requires greater social awareness, is preceded by democracy which, in the beginning, may be exercised by only a few enlightened individuals. Scientific socialism also needs, as a base, the riches of developed capitalism as well as the advances of modern technology. Primitive, native socialism, however, has its origins in ancient history.

Democracy was born in Athens, the most culturally advanced of the Greek city-states. Each of those cities had its own independent government. As the city-states were small, it was easy for the entire population to participate in government through public assemblies. Greek democracy was, therefore, direct democracy, with no need for an elected house of representatives or executives of modern democratic governments. In Greece officials were elected annually, and elections were often conducted by poll. The Athenians believed that participation in public affairs was the right and duty of every citizen. (However, they did not regard women and slaves as citizens). Pericles [circa 495–429 B.C.], their greatest orator, speaking on behalf of Athenian democracy in the funeral oration following the war against Sparta in the year 430 B.C., described Athenian democracy as follows:

[Our government] favors the many instead of the few; this is why it is called a democracy. If we took to the laws, they afford equal justice to all in their private differences; if to social standing, advancement in public life falls to reputation for capacity, class considerations not being allowed to interfere with merit; nor again does poverty bar the way; if a man is able to serve the state, he is not hindered by the obscurity of his condition. The freedom which we enjoy in our government extends also to our ordinary life. There, far from exercising a jealous surveillance over each other, we do not feel called upon to be angry with our neighbor for doing what he likes, or even to indulge in those injurious looks which cannot fail to be offensive, although they inflict no positive penalty. But all this ease in our private relations does not make us lawless as citizens. Against this fear is our chief safeguard, teaching us to obey the magistrates and the laws, particularly such as regard the protection of the injured, whether they are actually on the statute book, or belong to that code which, although unwritten, yet cannot be broken without acknowledged disgrace.

Further, we provide plenty of means for the mind to refresh itself from business. We celebrate games and sacrifices all the year round, and the elegance of our private establishments forms a daily source of pleasure and helps to banish the spleen; while the magnitude of our city draws the produce of the world into our harbor, so that to the Athenian the fruits of other countries are as familiar a luxury as those of his own.

. . . We cultivate refinement without extravagance and knowledge without effeminacy; wealth we employ more for use than for show, and place the real disgrace of poverty not in owning to the fact but in declining the struggle against it. Our public men have, besides politics, their private affairs to attend to, and our ordinary citizens, though occupied with the pursuits of industry, are still fair judges of public matters, for, unlike any other nation we regard him who takes no part in these duties not as unambitious but as useless. We Athenians are able to judge at all events if we cannot originate, and instead of looking on discussion as a stumbling-block in the way of action, we think it an indispensable preliminary to any wise action at all.[11]

Athenian democracy, as described by Pericles, continued to grow and develop in various parts of the world after the city's demise. This type of democracy manifested certain principles and a distinctive approach to life—recognizing the dignity of man and attempting to manage human affairs in accordance with justice, truth, and popular acceptance. Modern democracy has established certain principles, the most important of which may be summarized as follows:

1. Recognition of basic equality between all individuals.
2. The value of the individual as above that of the state.
3. Government as the servant of the people.
4. The rule of law.
5. Appeal to reason, experiment, and experience.
6. The rule of the majority, with utmost respect for rights of the minority.
7. Democratic method and procedures used to achieve objectives.

Democratic methods and procedures are not an end in themselves, but rather means to an end that lies behind them. The object of democracy is not simply to establish legislative, executive, and judicial organs, since all these are but means to realize the dignity of man. Democracy is not merely a way of government; it is also a way of life. The individual human being is the end, and everything else is a means to that end. The respect and high regard which people have for the democratic approach to government are due to the fact that it is the best approach to achieving the dignity of the individual.

There remain, however, some inadequacies in the present democratic approach, although these are much less pronounced than the deficiencies of Marxism. We leave its detailed examination for our coming book, *Islam Is Democratic and Socialist*.

The dignity of man is derived from the fact that he is the most capable of all living things in learning

11. These extracts, corresponding roughly to the part quoted by the author in Arabic, are quoted here as translated by Joseph Govorse, in *The Complete Writings of Thucydides: The Peloponnesian War* (New York: Modern Library, 1934), pp. 104–105.

and developing. The value of democracy is that it is the type of government most capable of providing opportunities for man to realize his dignity and honor. In a dictatorship, however, the government denies individuals the right to experiment and assume responsibility, thereby retarding their intellectual, emotional, and moral growth. In contrast to dictatorship, democracy is based on the right to make mistakes. This does not mean that individuals are encouraged to make mistakes for the sake of making mistakes, but rather it is recognition of the fact that freedom requires a choice between various modes of action. Democracy implies learning how to choose, choosing well, and correcting previous mistakes. In fact, all self-discipline and the true exercise of freedom are a series of individual actions in choice and implementation. In other words, freedom of thought, freedom of speech, and freedom of action all require that one accepts responsibility for mistakes in speech and action in accordance with law that is consistent with the constitution.

Democracy is therefore the right to make mistakes, as we learn from the *hadith* of the Prophet: "If you do not make mistakes, and then ask for forgiveness, God shall replace you by people who make mistakes, ask for forgiveness, and are forgiven."

Human dignity is so dear to God that individual freedom is not subject to any guardianship, not even that of the Prophet, irrespective of his impeccable morality. God says: "Then remind them, as you are only a reminder. You have no dominion over them." (Sura 88, Verses 21–22) Reference here is made to the polytheists who refused to worship God and tended the idols, worshipping them and sacrificing to them. Even the Messenger Muhammad, who was not seeking power for himself and whom God described in the Qur'an: "You are of great moral character" (Sura 68, Verse 4) [was not allowed to have dominion even over such a backward people]. This indicated that no man is perfect enough to be entrusted with the freedom of others, and that the price of freedom is continuous individual vigilance in safeguarding such freedom. In fact, individual freedom is a fundamental right with a corresponding duty, namely, the proper exercise of such freedom.

Since the society of *mu'minin* was incapable of exercising individual freedom in choice and action, the Prophet was appointed as a guardian to prepare them for the responsibility of absolute individual freedom. While exercising such guardianship, he insisted on giving them the right to make mistakes, whenever possible, without subjecting them to undue hardship or difficulty. In that way he was preparing them for democracy, for which they had to be sufficiently mature and intelligent. Such was the order of God when He said:

> And it is by the Great Mercy of God that you are kind towards them, and if you had been rough and hard-hearted, they would surely have dispersed from around you. So pardon them and ask forgiveness for them, and consult them; and when you are resolved, then put your trust in God. Surely, God loves those who put their trust [in Him]. (Sura 3, Verse 159)

This is the verse of *shura* [consultation], and consultation, whenever mentioned, whether in this verse or in the following verse—"those who answered the call of their Lord, and perform the prayer, and their affairs are [decided] by *shura* [mutual consultation] and pay alms from what We have provided for them" (Sura 42, Verse 38)—does not refer to democracy. *Shura*, however, was a necessary stage in preparation for democracy, in due course.

Shura is not an original Islamic precept, but rather a subsidiary one. It is not democracy, but rather the rule of the mature individual who is preparing the nation to become democratic. The original precept of democracy is based on the verse, "Then remind them, as you are only a reminder.

You have no dominion over them." (Sura 88, Verses 21–22)

By the same token, *zakat* [Islamic taxation] is not a socialist practice; it is rather capitalist and is based on the verse, "Take alms out of their wealth, so that you may cleanse them and purify them thereby. And pray for them; your prayer indeed is [a source of] tranquillity for them. And God is All-Hearing, All-Knowing." (Sura 9, Verse 103) Thus, *zakat* is not an original precept of Islam, but rather a subsidiary one. Its purpose is to prepare people psychologically and materially for socialism in due course. The original precept which the verse of *zakat* abrogated is that which reads, "When they ask you what to give away, say all that you do not need" (Sura 2, Verse 219), as explained above.

The Second Message calls for a return from the subsidiary verses to the original verses, which were temporarily abrogated because of circumstances and material and human limitations. We must now elevate legislation by evolving and basing it on the original Qur'anic verses. In this way we shall welcome the age of socialism and democracy and open the way to absolute individual freedom through worship and humane dealing with other people. This is the *shari'a* law of the nation of the Muslims (*muslimin*) that is yet to come, as the earth is now preparing to receive it. It is the duty of the people of the Qur'an [present-day Muslims] to pave the way for *muslimin*. And that is the purpose of this book. . . .

The Necessity of Renewing Islamic Thought *and* Reinvigorating Religious Understanding

A native of Java, educated through college level at Islamic schools, Nurcholish Madjid (Indonesia, born 1939) rose to national prominence in the late 1960s as leader of the Islamic Students Association. In a speech of January 2, 1970, the first of two translated here, Madjid called for deep-seated changes in Islam to keep pace with changes in the world, even using the controversial term *secularism*.[1] He had not intended for this speech to be circulated or published—indeed, he later called the talk's bluntness "a tactical blunder"—but he did not disavow the ideas expressed in the speech.[2] The second talk translated here, delivered in 1972, was an attempt to develop these ideas further, and his 1984 doctoral dissertation under Fazlur Rahman at the University of Chicago (see chapter 31)—on the thirteenth-to-fourteenth–century Islamic reformer Ibn Taymiyya—sought to "reexplain" his views with greater historical and philosophical sophistication.[3] Still an active and controversial figure in Indonesian Islamic debates, Madjid now heads a private Islamic research institute.[4]

The Necessity of Renewing
Islamic Thought and the Problem of
the Integration of the Umma

1. Introduction

The incentive to discuss the problem as reflected in the title stems from the established fact that Indonesian Muslims are again experiencing inertia in

thought and development of Islamic teachings, and the loss of "psychological striking force!" in their

the Indonesian Social Context (Clayton, Australia: Centre of Southeast Asian Studies, Monash University, Annual Indonesian Lectures, number 15, 1991).

2. Nurcholish Madjid, "The Issue of Modernization among Muslims in Indonesia," pp. 143–155 in Gloria Davis, editor, *What Is Modern Indonesian Culture?* (Athens, Ohio: Center for International Studies, Ohio University, 1979).

3. Howard M. Federspiel, *Muslim Intellectuals and National Development in Indonesia* (New York: Nova Science Publishers, 1992), p. 42.

4. Douglas E. Ramage, *Politics in Indonesia: Democracy, Islam, and the Ideology of Tolerance* (London: Routledge, 1995), p. 218; Amyn B. Sajoo, "Pondering the 'Periphery': Pluralist Trends in Southeast Asia," *Muslim Politics Report*, number 8, Summer 1996, p. 5.

1. For differing interpretations of Madjid's views, see Muhammad Kamal Hassan in *Muslim Intellectual Responses to "New Order" Modernization in Indonesia* (Kuala Lumpur, Malaysia: Dewan Bahasa dan Pustaka, Kementerian Pelajaran, Malaysia, 1980), pp. 89–99; and Greg Barton, "The International Context of the Emergence of Islamic Neo-Modernism in Indonesia," pp. 69–82 in M. C. Ricklets, editor, *Islam in*

struggle. The *umma* [Islamic community] is immediately confronted with a dilemma: should it choose to blaze the trail of regeneration within itself at the expense of long-coveted integration, or should it cling to the preservation of efforts toward integration even though it has to bear the consequences of inertia in thought and the loss of invulnerable moral forces? The incompatibility between the need for renovation and the need for integration is seen in the fact that when a section of the community takes the initiative in renewal, another section will react unfavorably towards it. History has repeatedly shown the truth of this phenomenon.

2. Islam Yes, Islamic Party No?

One of the encouraging facts about Islam in Indonesia at present is its rapid expansion, particularly in terms of its (formal) adherents. Areas which previously had not known the religion are now accepting it; in fact (in some areas) they are making it the principal religion of the inhabitants alongside the other religions which already existed there. A greater interest in Islam is being shown by people in the higher social classes; even if they do not practice it themselves they at least show such an interest in their official attitudes. But we have a question that still needs to be answered, that is, to what extent is that development a result of genuine attraction to the ideas of Islam as presented by its leaders, verbally or in written form?

Or can this Islamic quantitative growth be regarded as nothing more than a phenomenon of social adaptation because of recent political developments in the country, namely, the defeat of the communists which gave the impression of Muslim victory? (Such social adaptation occurred in the period of *Orde lama* [Old Order, 1945–1965] as well, because at that time President Sukarno was always demonstrating, with great enthusiasm, his interest in Islam and, similarly, toward Marxism—whatever people might have speculated about the motives behind this.)

The answer to the above questions might be found by putting down the next question: to what extent were they attracted to Islamic parties and organizations? Except for a few, it is clear that they were not attracted to Islamic parties or organizations. Their attitude might be formulated thus, more or less: "Islam yes, Islamic party no!" So if Islamic parties

constitute a receptacle of ideas which are going to be fought for on the basis of Islam, then it is obvious that those ideas are now unattractive. In other words, those ideas and Islamic thinking are now becoming fossilized and obsolete, devoid of dynamism. Moreover these Islamic parties have failed to build a positive and sympathetic image; in fact they have an image that is just the opposite. (The reputation of a section of the *umma* with respect to corruption, for example, is, as time passes, mounting.)

3. Quantity versus Quality

It is usually regarded as a truism that quality is more important than quantity. But what the *umma* is now doing in Indonesia is precisely the opposite: giving more importance to quantity than quality. It cannot be denied that unity gives a greater guarantee of achieving the aims, of a struggle than disunity. But can that unity exist in a dynamic form and become a dynamic force if it is not based on dynamic ideas? ("There cannot be revolutionary actions without revolutionary theories," said [Vladimir Ilich] Lenin [Russian socialist, 1870–1924].) Dynamism is, at any rate, more decisive than a static state, even though the latter means a greater number of people. The paralysis of the *umma* these days is due, among other things, to the fact that it is closing tight its eyes to the defects on its body. This necessitates the existence of a movement aimed at the renovation of ideas so that the defects may be removed.

4. Liberalization of Outlook towards the Present "Teachings of Islam"

If we have reached the decision to undertake renovation within the *umma*, then where do we start? In connection with this problem we might quote the statement of André Beaufre [French military strategist, 1902–1975]: "Our traditional lines of thought must go overboard, for it is now far more important to be able to look ahead than to have large scale of force whose effectiveness is problematical." The reminder that a small group can triumph over a larger group shows the importance of dynamics in comparison with quantity. No doubt what is still better is a combination of both. But if this is not possible, then the choice has to be between the two of them, and that choice has to be "dynamics." We would like to deduce from the above quotation the meaning that renewal has to start with two closely related actions, that is, freeing oneself from traditional values and seeking values which are oriented toward the future. The orientation to the past and excessive nostalgia have to be replaced by a forward-looking attitude. To that end we need a process which, for the sake of simplicity, we shall call the liberalization process. That process will be applied to the "teachings and views of Islam" which exist today. It involves other processes:

a. Secularization. By "secularization" is not meant the application of secularism, because "secularism" is the name for an ideology, a new closed worldview which functions very much like a new religion. What is meant here is all forms of "liberating development." This liberating process is particularly needed because the *umma*, as a result of its own historical growth, is no longer capable of distinguishing— among the values which they consider Islamic— those that are transcendental from those that are temporal. In fact the hierarchy of values is often the reverse; the transcendental becomes temporal and vice versa, or everything becomes transcendental and valued as *ukhrawi* [pertaining to the hereafter] without exception. Even though they (the Muslims) perhaps do not express it in words, or may even deny it, still that attitude is reflected in their day-to-day activity. The consequences of this, as we already know, are most injurious: Islam assumes the same value as tradition, and to be Islamic is the same in degree as being traditionalist. Since the defense of Islam has come to be the same as the defense of tradition, an impression is created whereby Islamic strength is seen as the reactionary strength of tradition. The glasses through which Muslims see the scale of values have made them unable to respond properly to the development of thought in the world today.

So, by "secularization" one does not mean the application of secularism and the transformation of Muslims into secularists. What is intended is the "temporalizing" of values which are in fact worldly, and the freeing of the *umma* from the tendency to spiritualize them. In this manner the mental readiness to always test and retest the truth of a value in the face of material, moral or historical facts [may] become a characteristic of Muslims.

Further, it is intended by "secularization" that the temporal role of man as God's "vicegerent" (caliph)

on earth be fully consummated. Acting as vicegerent of God provides man with enough space for his freedom to choose and decide for himself, in the context of improving his life on this earth, whatever steps and measures [he deems fit], and at the same time it acknowledges man's responsibility for those actions before God.

But what has happened now is that the *umma* has lost its creativity in this temporal life to the extent that it leaves the impression that it has decided not to act rather than [risk making a] mistake. In other words it has lost the spirit of *ijtihad* [Islamic interpretation].

In fact, as a logical consequence of *towhid* [belief in the unity of God], Muslims should automatically possess an attitude that is realistic and in accordance with what is towards the world and its problems. The fact that absolute transcendence pertains solely to God should actually give rise to an attitude of "desacralization" towards that which is other than God, namely, the world, its problems and values which are related to it. For to sacralize anything other than God is, in reality, *shirk* [polytheism], the opposite of *towhid*. So now secularization acquires its concrete meaning, that is, desacralization of everything other than that which truly possesses divine attributes, in other words, the world.

The object of the process of desacralization is everything pertaining to the world, both moral and material. Values are included among moral worldly objects, while matter constitutes the material objects. Now, if one hears the statement that "Islam is Bolshevism plus God" (Muhammad Iqbal [1877–1938]), one of its meanings is that the outlook of Islam regarding the world and its problems is the same as that of the communists (realistic, in accordance with what is, and without giving a value to the object more than that which it actually possesses). The only difference is that Islam postulates the existence of a transcendental being—God. The Islamic *Weltanschauung* [worldview] regarding the relationship between the universe and God is like that of the body, with the head above and the legs below (terms used by [Karl] Marx [German socialist, 1818–1883]). This means that [for Muslims] faith in God forms the basis of [their] outlook towards the universe, and not the reverse as in dialectical materialism.

b. Intellectual Freedom. One liberal Islamic institution of higher learning, Balai Pendidikan "Darussalam" at Gontor, Ponorogo (East Java), has as its motto, "Freedom of Thought"—following "Lofty Character," "Healthy Body," and "Broad Knowledge." Among the freedoms of the individual, the freedom to think and to express opinions are the most valuable. We must have a firm conviction that all ideas and forms of thought, however strange they may sound, should be accorded means of expression. It is by no means rare that such ideas and thoughts, initially regarded as generally wrong, are [later] found to be right. This has been the experience of every reform movement, whether individual or organizational, everywhere in the world. Furthermore, in the confrontation of ideas and thoughts, even error can be of considerable benefit, because it will induce truth to express itself and grow as a strong force.

Perhaps it was not entirely small talk when our Prophet said that differences of opinion among his *umma* were a mercy [from God]. Freedom of thought was very well explained by Oliver Wendell Holmes [U.S. judge, 1809–1894] when he said: "The ultimate good desired is better reached by free trade in ideas— that the best test of truth is the power of thought to get itself accepted [in the] competition of the market, and that truth is the only ground upon which their wishes can safely be carried out."

Because of the absence of fresh ideas we have lost what we described above as "psychological striking force." This is due to the fact that there is not a single free-thinking body which focuses its attention on the immediate needs of continuously developing social conditions, whether in the economic, political or social arenas. Be that as it may, we still have to admit that our Islamically based ideas can best solve those problems if they are adjusted, refreshed, renewed and organized (coordinated) in such a way that they are in step with the realities of the present age. For example, the [Islamic] teaching concerning *shura* or *mushawara* [consultation] has been generally accepted by the *umma* as almost if not exactly identical with the concept of democracy that originated in the West. But on the other hand, the principal teachings of Islam on social justice and the care and protection of the weak, the poor, and the oppressed, as contained in many passages of the Qur'an, has yet to find expression in ideas formulated for practical application in dynamic and progressive terms. This is so because the *umma*, it appears, still views with horror the word "socialism," which like "democracy" originated in the West, and has a meaning which is quite similar to the corresponding Islamic concepts.

If this is not due to the absence of freedom of thought, then what psychological impediment is there within the *umma*? It has also made the *umma* incapable of taking initiatives in the development of this worldly society. Initiatives are always taken by others first, and as a result strategic positions that have to do with concepts and ideas fall into their hands. Islam is then excluded from those [strategic positions]. It is indeed important to realize that just as in military operations, wherein one vies for a vantage position on the battlefield and by capturing it prevents the enemy from occupying it, so also in the psychological game of politics one may capture positions of intellectual influence and hold on to them only to prevent them from falling into the hands of the enemy or other people. It is in this aspect that we see the main weakness of the *umma*. All of this is, once again, the consequence of the absence of freedom of thought, confusion in the hierarchy of values as to what constitutes the transcendental and what the temporal, the mode of thinking which is too encrusted with taboos, presumptions, and so on.

c. The "Idea of Progress" and Open Attitudes. In point of fact, if a Muslim is truly consistent with the teachings [of Islam], then the value of the "idea of Progress," like all other values of truth, need not be stated, because it is, in fact, already part of these teachings.

The idea of progress springs from the concept that man is intrinsically good, pure, and yearns for truth and progress (man was created by God with *fitra* [natural disposition to the good] and endowed with the *hanif* quality [that is, inclined to truth]).

Because of this, one of the manifestations of the existence of the idea of progress is the belief in the future of man throughout his history. So there is no need to be afraid of the changes which always occur in the temporal value system of man. A reactionary attitude and a closed mentality in fact stem from a pessimistic view of history.

Therefore, consistent with the idea of progress is an open mental attitude, in the form of a readiness to accept and to take (temporal) values from whatever source as long as they contain truth. In accordance with the intellectual freedom mentioned above we have to be ready to observe the development of ideas concerning man across the widest possible spectrum, and then choose among them those which, according to objective criteria, contain truth. It is very difficult to comprehend why, in spite of the fact that their Holy Book clearly lays down that they "should give their ears to ideas and follow the best of them" (Sura 39, Verse 18), the *umma* today is more closed in its mental attitude. It is also stated that an open attitude is an indication that the person possessing it has received guidance from God, while the "closed" mentality described as " . . . bosom close and narrow as if he were engaged in sheer ascent" (Sura 6, Verse 126)[5] is one of the signs of being in error. If Islam is indeed neither a culture nor a civilization but a foundation for both, then where will Islamic culture and civilization find the materials to build themselves up if not from the entire surface of the earth, in the form of the universal human heritage. History provides unquestionable testimony to this fact. The Muslims came out of the Arabian peninsula having only a strong faith derived from the Qur'an and the *sunna* [practice of the Prophet]. Then from the newly conquered regions they discovered the legacies of humanity both from the West (Greek and Roman) and from the East (Persian). They later developed those legacies on the basis of principles which they brought from the desert of the Arabian peninsula and made them as their own. Was it not this creation of theirs that eventually gave birth to what we now know as the culture and civilization of Islam, of which we are so proud?

5. A "Liberal" Group of Renovators Is Needed

Reform movements have been emerging on the stage of history, both in Indonesia and in the world at large. We have now, in Indonesia, organizations with the renovatory aspirations such as the *Muhammadiya* [The Muhammadiya Association, founded 1912], *Al-Irshad* [Society for Reform and Guidance, founded 1920s], and *Persis* [Islamic Union, founded 1926]. But history also records—and we must frankly admit—that they have now ceased to be renovators. Why?

The reason is that, in the long run, they have become rigid, probably as a result of not being able to capture the spirit of dynamism and progressiveness from the idea of renovation itself. On the other hand, organizations which history records as counterreformist such as *Nahdlatul Ulama* [Renaissance of

5. [Note the author's liberal interpretation of the verse.— Translator]

the Religious Scholars, founded 1926], *Al-Washliya* [Unshakeable Association, founded 1930], *Persatuan Ulama Indonesia* [Union of Indonesian Religious Scholars, founded 1917], and others, have now acted on their own, and have accepted values that previously were the monopoly of the renovators, although this attitude of theirs is due to the pressure of unavoidable historical laws. Moreover, they did not adopt those values with the requisite degree of seriousness or accept them formally as a principal viewpoint. The consequence of this is that a general state of stagnancy has now struck the *umma*: Islamic organizations that, at the time of their inception, were antitraditional and opposed to sectarianism have become traditionalist and schismatic, while other organizations, which originally rejected new values but have now accepted them, at no time intended to adopt the new values as principal attitudes in life. Hence a new and liberal group of Islamic renovators is required. As for the meaning of the word *liberal*, we have already given it above. But the term has further implications, as a logical consequence, namely, nontraditionalism and nonsectarianism.

What is further demanded here is that there has to be the capability and the courage constantly to review the group's (sect's) own values. Those values need not be brought forth again if only the Islamic community is consistent with its own teachings. For nontraditionalism is nothing more than the converse of the attitude: "We found our fathers subscribing to a particular set of values, and we receive guidance from their legacies" (Sura 43, Verse 22), while nonsectarianism is the converse of the attitude: "each group prides itself with what it has." (Sura 30, Verse 32) Both attitudes are condemned in the Holy Book. To return to what we referred to earlier, the values of Islam are in fact dynamic, not static. Apart from the articles of faith (the most important of which is belief in God) and the fundamentals of worship coupled with some of the most fundamental social values which are deemed not likely to undergo change, Islam does not provide definitive formulations so far as temporal actions are concerned. Except for the fundamental value of *taqwa* [fear of God], which grows out of faith in God and worship of Him, there are no fixed values. [Most] values are cultural values which have, of necessity, to develop continuously in accordance with the laws of change and development (everything other than God undergoes destruction or change) (Sura 28, Verse 88).

Therefore the values of Islam are those that conform to humanity's true nature or to universal truths and are supported by *taqwa* towards God. Those values are Islamic if they basically do not contradict *'iman* [faith] or *taqwa*, and are good according to humanity and its development.

Today, the struggle to improve the welfare of mankind is not the monopoly of the *umma*. The whole of mankind, by relying on reason and the mind, has become involved in the attempts to discover the best ways of improving collective human life. In this modern age such expressions of human thought are encountered in those terms now heard so often, such as democracy, socialism, citizenship, communism and so forth.

However erroneous these ideas may later be proved by history, they nevertheless represent the summit of human intelligence concerning our own social life, as a result of the realistic and intellectually stimulating observation of social and historical phenomena. Now we have to learn to employ the best of these ideas according to Islamic yardsticks and endeavor to develop them further with the same realism and the same diligence in thinking. This is the essence of the meaning of the *ijtihad* or renewal which we desire. Therefore *ijtihad* or renewal ought to be a continuous process of original thinking based on the evaluation of social and historical phenomena which, from time to time, need to be reviewed in order to determine whether they are really erroneous. *Ijtihad* is a process such that misunderstanding or its problems will result in a bitter fruit—failure. Nevertheless it is still much lighter than the burden of social and historical stagnation brought about by absence of renewal. Hence it is not possible for *ijtihad* and a meaningful renovation to take place if we do not have research organizations with strong foundations; if we do not have a first-rate method of analyzing all kinds of situations; and if we do not have accurate knowledge of the developments of human discoveries in the social or natural spheres. It appears that we are still far away from that comforting situation.

To sum up, the renewal effort is the task of those who come from that section of society that has the greatest capability to understand and to think. In other words it is the task of the educated. So the responsibility of educated people is indeed heavy—before mankind in history and before God in the hereafter. It is hoped that the major knowledge- and education-oriented organizations within the Islamic community . . . can act as pioneers in promoting and carrying out this stupendous task through a kind of relationship which is more solid and better coordinated, without forgetting other liberal elements among existing Islamic associations.

With God alone are success and guidance.

Reinvigorating Religious Understanding in the Indonesian Muslim Community

Preface

The opportunity given to me by the Dewan Kesenian Jakarta [Jakarta Arts Council] to take part in the present literary program is indeed a great honor. For this honor I should like to thank the D.K.J., especially the Daily Activities Council.

This opportunity must be put to use in the best possible way. I shall use it to restate my thesis. I have earlier presented that thesis under the heading, "The Necessity of Renewing Islamic Thought and the Problem of the Integration of the Umma" [see previous section] on January 13, 1970. Now I shall present it again under a slightly different title, as may be seen above.

It is felt necessary to restate that thesis so that the misconceptions which then developed may be minimized. The thesis is being presented here with a simplification in the use of terms in addition to improvement—wherever possible—in the arrangement of words.

Hopefully that aim is still in keeping with the theme decided by the D.K.J. for this program, namely, "The Younger Generation and Religious Thinking in Islam," as is printed in the Calendar of Events, October 1972.

Introduction

The reinvigoration of religious understanding is presently felt to be extremely important by those who are aware of it, particularly within the Indonesian Muslim community. The conceptions which are available at present are somewhat crippled. In the face of the criticisms of the younger generation, those crippled ideas have become unattractive and "withered."

Every conception or idea will determine the shape of the social character of its adherents. That social character will then color their actions and life behavior, and will consequently direct the course of their life's destiny. So if a change in their lot is desired, then there has to be first and foremost a transformation in the conceptions and ideas which rule over their community.

In the case of Islam, the sources of its teachings are in our hands. Those sources, particularly the Qur'an, have been preserved, in terms of sounds and pronunciation, from the beginning. But (Muslim) man's understanding of the principal teachings contained in them is always growing. This happens because of developments in human civilization which regularly provide new inputs to the world of ideas.

But not all this growing understanding is creative and correct. Sometimes it is extremely vulgar or coarse, to the extent that it renders religious concepts superficial. Examples of this are the ideas of modern apologetics. The apology came about as a means of defending Islam against the invasion of modern Western culture. In that situation Muslims confronted the invasion from a position of weakness. This apology, originating from a weaker position, sometimes revealed an inferiority complex. This is the reason why all apologetic ideas, in their essence, do not contain original creativeness.

Not every apologetic idea, however, was a failure. Some of them have, in fact, been so influential that they have given satisfaction to the Muslim community, calmed its restlessness and restored its spirit to endure and fight against the influence of foreign culture. But precisely because they were basically no more than apology, their potentialities were limited.

It is ironical that these apologetic tendencies are found at their strongest among modern Muslims, or—to be more exact—pseudomodern Muslims. These are precisely the people who know of and have enjoyed the blessings of Western civilization—both moral and material—but they do not possess within themselves the inner certitude of being Muslim. This is either due to their background or, more important, to their inability to make the adjustment between modern civilization and the religion they desire to believe in so firmly.

The Principle of 'Iman

To begin with, Islam is obviously a religion. As a religion its kernel is conviction. There is no need to dwell here on the necessity of having a conviction,

whatever its form and content may be. It is a fact that life is impossible without conviction at all.

Right conviction, in Islam, is called "'iman." Literally this means belief. In this matter belief in God stands first and above everything else. This is not a mere belief in God's existence. What is more important is the believing attitude, or having faith in God.

'Iman is more of a product of an inner spiritual response than rational deduction. It is the state of the soul which is full of appreciation of God. This appreciation develops through a complete assimilation of God's qualities as contained in His "beautiful Names" (Arabic al-asma' al-husna).

The attitude which is appreciative of God constitutes the core of human religious experience. This attitude is also known as "taqwa." It is the spirit of God-consciousness in a faithful man. It represents one of the highest forms of spiritual life. . . .

And now we note a point which is pertinent to this discussion; that is, that 'iman, taqwa, and the religious experience of the appreciation of divinity, as explained above, are spiritual in nature. This means that these values are connected to something that is entirely intrinsic in a person, namely, sincerity. Hence they have to grow out of free and independent choice. For this reason, these religious values are highly individual in nature. They may vary [in quality], especially if there is external pressure. They are man's most personal and most deep-rooted possessions. They are perfectly preserved in the innermost chambers of the heart or moral conscience. Such religiosity is so perfectly hidden and preserved in the breast that only God knows of it and only He can evaluate it. The person concerned can only feel it, but is not able to explain or reveal it to others properly because of the limitations of the mind and language.

The Principle of 'Amal Salih

We mentioned earlier that when someone has the consciousness of God, it will become a strong and stable guiding principle and foundation of life. The reason for this is that when taqwa takes possession of the inner self and its attitudes, it will determine, out of the state of spiritual purity, the form and value of motivation for all acts in life or culture. This cannot but come from the desire to achieve a higher level of divine appreciation, toward the ultimate completion of the sense of purity—the "consent" or *rida* of God Himself.

Indeed the motivation, desire, and inclination to attain the good, the pure, and the true are qualities intrinsic to man because of his humanity. In accordance with his *fitra* or "original nature" which is pure, man is intrinsically inclined to that which is holy (*hanif*). He is further inclined, naturally, to yearn for the ultimate and absolute purity, namely, God, who is absolutely Pure, True, Good, and Absolute in all His qualities.

But it is precisely because God is the Ultimate Absolute, that He is beyond the ken of human comprehension. Man can only reach toward Him by following a way that channels his innate yearning and longing. Although man cannot hope, in this life, to reach God, he can, however, obtain God's consent or *rida*, which would be felt by him spiritually in the form of divine appreciation. Indeed the highest stage of a spiritual life is that inner attitude which is wholly appreciative of God, coupled with the feeling of being contented with and resignation in God. This experience is a sign that God too is pleased and has given His assent. It should be borne in mind, however, that the forms of religious experience are highly individual in nature, and carry with them the implications we described earlier.

Since God, the goal of life and object of appreciation, is the Ultimate Absolute, and as such His essence is beyond comprehension, then what can be done—and should be done—is continuously to approach Him by following a way that leads to Him. This means that man should always strive to develop and expand his religious appreciation through "exploration" which will yield new experiences. This process cannot stop even for one moment, for each stop means finalization and absolutization, and this would mean, indirectly, laying claim to having attained and comprehended God, the Absolute. This would imply that God was being brought into the area of human comprehension, in which He becomes relative, loses His Absoluteness and assumes the relativity of nature and man himself with all its limitations. So it is in this process that knows no surcease that we Muslims are taught to make supplication to God every moment, particularly in our moments of formal communication (especially the canonical prayers) with God so that He may always guide them on the straight and right path.

Let us return to the question of man and humanity. It is already explained that man possesses an intrinsic inclination to that which is holy in accordance with his pure original self. Now this spiritual tendency expresses itself outwardly in the form of character. Man is basically a moral creature and when *taqwa* or appreciation of God is in accord with one's humanity or *fitra* then it also means strengthening this humanity or *fitra* and sharpening its innate inclination to the holy. Hence religion and religiosity function as the perfecter of man's noble character which intrinsically resides in him.

What then is the tangible form of that sublime character? None other than actions (or *'amal*) and deeds that are harmonious and consonant or *salih* [appropriate] in their comprehensive relationship with the living environment, especially in interpersonal relationships. . . .

But how does man understand and know the God-created laws that control the domain of life, whose vastness is unlimited? Since the universe is limitless, the laws which govern it must also be limitless. Such indeed is the case: God's laws repose in His knowledge, which embraces the whole universe. [So vast is God's knowledge that] "if every piece of wood on this earth were to become a pen in order to write down God's knowledge, and all the seas became ink, added to by seas seven times over, it would still not be possible to finish writing down the knowledge of God." Such is the picture given in the Qur'an (Sura 30, Verse 27).

It is inconceivable that God would teach man all His knowledge. Neither man nor any other creature has the capacity to understand it all at once. But man still needs to know and understand to some degree the scheme of God in order to assist himself somewhat in creating a life that is coherent, harmonious, and happy. Out of His mercy, God gave man an instrument by which he could come to some understanding of these laws. That instrument is the specifically human faculty called "mind," "reason," or "intellect." With that instrument the opportunity to undertake the task of developing this world opens up for man. This intellectual faculty truly constitutes man's superiority over other creatures, including angels, to such an extent that he is honored as God's vicegerent on earth.

So, with that faculty man is given the opportunity to understand the domain of his life, both the natural and the social aspects. If his understanding is correct and he follows it conscientiously, then he will be able, to some extent, to shape the good earthly life. That ability is, no doubt, limited. The knowledge that he can acquire is likewise meager. But even that limited amount of knowledge is highly beneficial to man, because it is useful in his life. It is only by marshalling his rational capacity that man can, to some degree, develop his earthly existence in a better way. . . .

Let us return to the aspect of material life mentioned above. Unlike the aspect of spiritual life which is inward and personal, the aspect of rational life is not personal in nature, at least not all of it. For it can be tackled together with others. In fact, in many respects it certainly depends on others. All the more so when it is realized that the rational faculty is limited in such a way that its findings in the form of knowledge are relative in nature, that is, they may be wrong. So a cooperative effort among men is necessary to counter-balance these weaknesses or reduce them. That cooperation expresses itself in openness of attitude toward criticisms, evaluations or improvements, in keeping with the development of overall human knowledge. So there are two principles, *'iman* and *'amal salih*, and a subprinciple, that of joint effort in search of truth and progress.

Owing to its relativity as a rational product of limited capacity, knowledge is always developing from moment to moment. One who closes himself to the development of his knowledge is really denying the relativity and limitations of his reason. This means that he is making his knowledge and reason absolute. In truth he becomes an absolutist man. And since only God is absolute, he is thereby competing with God. It has already been explained that this is an extraordinarily grave evil against man's true nature. The sin of *shirk* is unpardonable. We realize that absolutism is damaging to the human race, since it closes all doors to progress and development, whereas all things change. Only the Absolute, God, does not undergo change. Certainly there is no greater evil than to block the historical development of the human race, for that means destroying it totally.

So the dimension of material earthly life pertains to knowledge (*'ilm*) while that of spiritual transcendental life pertains to faith (*'iman*). For that reason their respective approaches have to be differentiated. As we have argued at great length, obviously these two aspects of life cannot be separated. The acts of every individual are, first of all, inseparable from the inner self, the spirit. The forms of their relationship do have influence and consequence; in fact they determine the nature of his life in the hereafter. Nevertheless, their respective approaches must be differentiated on account of the differences in dimension.

The dimensional differences between these two types of life correspond with the dimensional difference between *'iman* and *'ilm*. The former grows and develops on the basis of revelation (belief), while the latter owes its growth to rationality. Because of this difference in dimension, the approach to either could be made in abeyance of the other. For example, in the approach to worldly existence, or knowledge, there is nothing to hinder two persons of different faiths working together. Or a man may achieve a low or high level of achievement without the influence of the spiritual aspect. . . . But, of course, man has to strive for the highest possible status in both aspects of life. Hence although the Qur'an, for example, contains many references to the transitoriness and deceptions of worldly life, it enjoins, nevertheless, that man should work for "the good in this world and the good in the hereafter." (Sura 2, Verse 201) Since the two dimensions and approaches are different, the two kinds of happiness cannot be achieved simultaneously by means of one method. Whoever aims for the dimensions of earthly life will attain [the good of that life] and whoever aims for the dimensions of transcendental life will attain [the good thereof]. Pursuing either one does not automatically result in getting the other as well. One is reminded that anyone who strives only for the worldly life will not receive any returns in the hereafter. Similarly, those who strive only for happiness in the hereafter are reminded not to forget their portion in this world (Sura 28, Verse 77). . . . It is putting faith and knowledge together that enables man to perform *'amal salih*, thereby attaining the highest degree of his humanity. . . .

Apologia concerning the Islamic State

This is an additional discussion, by way of an observation on one of the forms of religious concept within the *umma*. It is necessary to discuss this because of the urgent need to undertake some clarification concerning it.

The idea of the "Islamic state" has been in the habit of emerging with great force within the Muslim community at certain periods in the past. We are grateful that it does not exist now—at least, so it seems outwardly, although remnants of it still linger.

Viewed from the perspective of the history and development of thought, the emergence of the idea of the Islamic state represents, in reality, a kind of apologetic tendency, as indicated in the heading. That apology arose from at least two bases:

The first was an apology in relation to modern Western ideologies such as democracy, socialism, communism and others. These ideologies are often totalitarian in character, in the sense that they are comprehensive in scope and cover every sphere of life in detail, particularly the political, social, economic, and cultural spheres, and others besides. The apology in relation to modern ideologies gave rise to an ideological-political understanding of Islam which then led to the ideal of an "Islamic state" just as there existed democratic states, socialist states, communist states, and so forth. This totalitarian ideological-political apperception led to the emergence of apologetic thinking which declared that Islam was not merely a religion, such as Buddhism, Hinduism, Christianity, and others, whose domains of efficacy are the spiritual, wherein is arranged the relationship between God and man. Islam, it was claimed, is "*din*" [religion]. With the word "*din*" it was hoped and intended that a totalitarian meaning would be conveyed, which would include all aspects of life—political, economic, social, cultural, and so on. The apology, it seems, was deemed necessary because in modern life, dominated by Western patterns, the most important aspects of life are the political, economic, social, and the rest, other than spiritual. It is understandable that this dangerous cultural invasion destroyed the self-esteem of the *umma*, which was backward in precisely those above-mentioned aspects, and brought about a sense of inferiority. Thus the apology was a compensation for an inferiority complex. The reason for this was that the *umma* (through its apologists) tried, with apologia that produced the totalitarian ideological-political appreciation, to prove that Islam was actually superior to or at least on par with Western civilization, whose modern ideologies embraced the economic, political, social, and other domains—precisely those in which the Muslims failed.

As an apology, these ideas had only a brief span of life. After having temporarily satisfied the Muslims and restored their self-respect, the ideas were finally proved to be false. Like a boomerang they struck back at the *umma*. Its condition now is probably more pathetic than at the beginning. Such is the fate of ideas resulting from apology, whether they have been put down in writing or not.

The apology that Islam is "*din*," that it is not merely political appreciation—is untenable from several points of view. First of all, from the linguistic point of view, there is obvious inconsistency. The word "*din*" in the Qur'an is used also to designate other religions, including the polytheism of the Meccan Quraish tribe. So the word simply means religion; Islam is therefore a religion.

Secondly, there is the question of point of departure. Although it is not realized or, more exactly, not admitted, it can be clearly seen that the motive force behind the apology is an inferiority complex. This is the feeling that unless Islam, in addition to dealing as a religion with the spiritual domain, also embraces other spheres of life, it does not stand on a par with Western ideologies. This means indirectly admitting the superiority of the political, economic, social, and other aspects of material life over the spiritual or religious. This mode of thinking clearly represents a Muslim's total defeat before the onslaught of the Western materialistic way of thinking. Actually, if a Muslim truly realizes the position of the religious or spiritual aspect of life and is really cognizant and convinced of the superiority of Islam, he will not experience this sense of inferiority. On the contrary, he will have a sense of self-respect in facing anyone. Fortified by a firm conviction in himself and in his religion, he would then become creative in other fields, and with his mind freed from any sense of inferiority, he would readily learn from others who are superior in these fields. Another point is that it can be proved that in the sources of Islamic teaching—particularly the Qur'an—the domain of efficiency in which Islam is most emphatic and most lucid is the spiritual, the domain of religious matters.

Legalism represents the second factor which led some sections of the Muslim community to the apologetic concept of an "Islamic state." This legalism produced an understanding of Islam which was wholly legalistic, in the form of an Islamic perspective which portrayed Islam as a structure and compendium of law. This legalism is an extension of "*fiqh*-ism." *Fiqh* is the codification of [Islamic] law resulting from the labors of Muslim savants in the second and third centuries of the Muslim era [eighth and ninth centuries A.D.]. The codification was undertaken to fulfill the needs of a legal system which regulated the government and the state which, at that time, embraced a very large region and a huge populace. This "*fiqh*-ism" is so dominant in the Muslim community that even reformist movements for the most part still concentrate their objectives in that domain. This legal composition is sometimes also called *shari'a* [Islamic law]. The "Islamic state" is likewise an apology by which the Muslim *umma* hopes to be able to manifest laws and regulations, Islamic *shari'a*, that are superior to other laws. But it is already clear that, despite the renovations of the reformists, *fiqh* has lost its relevance to the present mode of living. Its complete renovation, however, such that it might become suitable for modern life, would require a comprehensive knowledge of modern life in all its aspects, so that this does not become an interest and a [matter of the] competency of the Muslim *umma* alone, but also of others. Its result, then, does not have to be in the form of Islamic law per se, but a law which embraces everybody for the regulation of a life shared by all.

From a more fundamental point of view, the concept of "Islamic state" is a distortion of the [properly] proportioned relationship between state and religion. The state is one of the aspects of worldly life whose dimension is rational and collective, while religion is an aspect of another kind of life whose dimension is spiritual and personal.

Of course, it is not possible, as explained earlier, to separate state and religion. Through the individual citizen an inseparable connection exists between motivation (or inner attitude derived from being part of a state) and action (or outward stance derived from being part of a state).

Islam and Humanism

Mamadiou Dia (Senegal, born 1911) was a schoolteacher, a headmaster, and a journalist before turning to politics in the mid-1940s. He served as a senator of the French Republic, representing Senegal; then after independence, he was prime minister of Senegal for four years. Dia's long collaboration with President Léopold Sédar Senghor, a non-Muslim, symbolized the relative absence of religious strife in Senegal, where the population is more than four-fifths Muslim. Nonetheless, Dia broke with Senghor in 1962 and was jailed for a dozen years. During his incarceration, Dia turned from politics to religion, integrating his fervent socialism into a theory of "Islamic humanism."[1] In a series of books on Islam published after his release from prison, Dia argues that interpretation of Islam must respond positively to the modern world, as Christianity has. Dia refers frequently to recent French theology for inspiration and methodological guidance—the effect being an opacity somewhat different from the Qur'anic exegesis of other works in this book.

Theological Bases of Islamic Humanism

All projects of Islamic renovation, in order to survive, must be based on solidly established theoretical foundations that call for a reflection on [the original] sources. The Islamic humanism that is being sought cannot forget this lesson, which results from the history of modernist reformism itself. In order to face the problems of the day, Islam needs first to affirm itself as ethical and religious value as much as spiritual personality. To resolve its own problems and confront the modern ideologies, it requires an adequate ideological apparatus built on an authentic Islamic philosophy. Islamic authenticity requires a return to the sources, that is, to the Qur'an and to the [sunna], not to take shelter there, to drown current cares there, but to draw from thence elements for the renovation and revitalization of Islamic philosophy. It is thus to a confrontation with the sources which we must submit any reformism, in order to know if there exist or not, in Islam, the ideological bases of a humanism integrating reason, the person, history; and if so, to try to determine in what measure the ideology of Islam lends itself to an enlargement to the dimensions of a universal humanism. . . .

1. Kenneth Cragg, "Mamadou Dia of Senegal," in *The Pen and the Faith: Eight Modern Muslim Writers and the Qur'an* (London: George Allen & Unwin, 1985), pp. 33–52; René Luc Moreau, *Africains Musulmans (African Muslims)* (Paris: Présence Africaine; Abidjan: Inades, 1982), pp. 275–279.

Islam and History

Historicity and Qur'anic Exegesis

A correct exegesis of the Qur'an, as we have already indicated, leads to a consideration of Islam as both esoteric and exoteric, *haqiqa* [truth] and *shari'a* [Islamic law], meta-history and history. Man, in accepting the burden of the *amana* [faith] on the day of the Covenant, has affirmed his Promethean character before God. It matters little that this event cannot be dated, since it is situated in pre-existence: the Muslim retains the symbol of it; he knows that he is the inheritor of this celestial being that had the crazy audacity to designate him for conquest. This spiritual filiation leaves him no doubt about his Promethean vocation and exempts him from asking God to descend to earth in order to make history. If he tried to forget this vocation, the *shahada* [acceptance of Islam][2] and the *shari'a* remind him of it at all times. First, the *shahada*—which, as we already know, is not pure contemplation, pure spiritualization, but Promethean effort to be faithful to the pact concluded with God. The history which was in virtuality in the celestial sojourn of man, begins, not with Islam, nor with Christianity or Judaism, but well before, with Adam descended to earth, less to expiate a sin than to accomplish the promise made to God: the promise to witness out of benevolence and out of his creative power through imitation of the creation, on a human scale. The continuity of destiny born of meta-history obliges the Muslim to adopt a conquering and creative attitude towards the world. In inviting him to meditate on the beauties of creation, on universal harmony, in exciting his curiosity, the Qur'an engages him—one cannot deny this— in the path of discovery and creativity which leads to salvation. But if the *shahada* appears thus *as the source of the Islamic philosophy of history*, as the ontological foundation of the Promethean vocation of Islam, if it is historic conscience, it is through the *shari'a* that it becomes praxis, concrete history, lived experience, acted faith. Through the *shari'a* the Muslim descends from the peaks of spirituality, installs himself in temporality, takes possession of the world, not to transform it into an eternal dwelling, but to set it up as a way station necessary for the pursuit of his transhistorical voyage. With the *shari'a* are born the written event, dated, the countability of time passing from qualitative to quantitative, the organization of a living community, the edification of a *culture of totality* responding to the needs of the *totality* which is *man*. It is the Muslim response, on the temporal plane, to the appeal of the *shahada* which invites us to remain faithful to the totality, to reject any dualist worldview, and to realize the earthly vocation of man in a trans-historical perspective.

The Islamic Response to History

It is thus a positive response to history that the sources prescribe, and in fact the Islamic response is marked by positivity. It appears in the dynamism of Islam which, scarcely 15 years after the death of the prophet, extends its influence over three continents, contributing thereafter to the origin of the modern international economy; in the glory of the experimental sciences of the 'Abbasids [reigned 750–1258], which introduced "the foreign themes of Greek aesthetic statistics" with the utilization "of singular numbers, irrationals, trigonometry and algebra" (Louis Massignon). It is written in the vitality and liberalism of the political institutions that inspired democratic constitutions while remaining faithful to theocracy, giving birth sometimes to secular regimes such as the Socialist Republic of Lahsa [presumably al-Ahsa', capital of the Qarmati state in eastern Arabia, tenth to eleventh centuries], whose revolutionary zeal bordered on heresy; [and the] the caliphate of Baghdad [762–1258], during the same epoch, whose caliphs remained content to be no more than "president of Islam," renouncing theocratic privileges, including the Friday sermon.[3] It bursts through "this gushing of creative power" (Wilfred Cantwell Smith) of medieval Islam, which not only built new empires, doubling by its conquest the geographic sphere of influence of classical Islam, but favored the blossoming of the cultures of the converted peoples: Persians, Turks, Indonesians. It is that Islam becomes very quickly—alas!—the faith and the raison d'être of a

---

2. [The *shahada*, which translates literally as witnessing, is repeated at all prayers.—Editor]

3. Aly Mazahéri, *La vie quotidienne des musulmans au Moyen Age* [*The Everyday Life of Muslims in the Middle Ages*, 1951].

ruling class, overflowing with dynamism and entre-preneurial spirit. From a religion of adversity, of sal-vation in defeat, it transformed into a "religion of triumph in success, of salvation in victory, accom-plishment, and power," a religion of effectiveness, of the creation of the project whereby history con-firms faith. During this conquering period . . . the "*shahid*, that is, the martyr who fights and dies in the path of God," gives his life, "not against history but with it, for the historic and earthly success of Islam, for the triumph of its cause, for the expansion of its domination in the world."[4] It is significant that a pious theologian as classical as ['Ali ibn Muhammad] al-Mawardi [Iraq, circa 974–1058] comes to con-struct an *abad* [eternity; here, utopia] of the world based on the fecundity of the soil as the source of ease and riches; on hope as a grace "placed in the heart of man," so that civilization extends itself over the world, and to prefigure, even before [Henri de] Saint-Simon [French social theorist, 1760–1825], the com-mon exploitation of the natural resources unequally distributed throughout the earth, on the basis of mu-tual aid. But for our purpose, the positive character of the response of Islam manifests itself above all in the idea of progress that Islamic thinkers and philoso-phers have brought to light. These are, above all, secular thinkers and philosophers. It is the physi-cian [Abu Bakr Muhammad] Razi [Persia, 864–925], whose philosophy is founded on the notions of "demiurge," of "materia prima," of "space and time," who distinguishes between absolute time and limited time, who proclaims the mission of the phi-losophers "to awaken souls." It is the mathematician [Abu Rayhan] Biruni [Persia, 973 circa 1050] who professes a philosophy of history based, in imitation of the yogas of India, on the cycles corresponding to the periods of universal cataclysms. It is [Abu Yusuf Ya'qub] Al-Kindi [Arabia, circa 801–866] who, ral-lying to the idea of a creation *ex nihilo*, established the distinction between the divine world and the world of nature, the world of becoming and that of change, between the revealed truth and the philo-sophical truth. It is Averroes (Ibn Rushd) [Spain-Morocco, died 1198] who by his Aristotelian ratio-nalism—that in reality never abandoned the dialectic of esoteric *ta'wil* [interpretation]—will give rise after

the live curiosity of Middle Age Christianity, to the enthusiasm of Ernest Renan [French Orientalist, 1823–1892], who will make a free thinker out of him, when he was never anything but an *Islamic free thinker*. But, at least as much as secular thought, it is reli-gious thought itself that is affected by the philosophi-cal idea of progress. It is that which attests to the audacious enterprise of the Isma'ili gnosis, which, after Al-Kindi, allows itself to calculate the cycle of the revelation, throws itself into the science of balance, "quantitative science," who proposes to measure "the intelligence, the soul of the world, na-ture, forms, stars," without forgetting "the animal, the vegetable, the mineral" and above all the letters (Henry Corbin, p. 186), which presents itself as an anticipation of "the energy of the soul," manifest-ing even the ambition to "build robots, artificial hu-mans" (Louis Massignon).

One may also say that it is this Islam which, with pan-divine Averroism, is at the root of the "scien-tism" that has contaminated the West through the mediation of medieval Christianity. The fact that Islamic orthodoxy does not repudiate Averroism, nor Averroes, nor even the Isma'ili quantitatism, is the proof that in Islam, philosophical progress is not necessarily a heresy. On the contrary, through the richness of its philosophical culture, the result of a synthesis of diverse elements, autochthonous and foreign, Islam shows that it is open to cross-fertilization, that it can make itself "woman" and be-come the matrix of a historic, progressive, original culture, which is something else than the product of syncretism. . . .

Islam Confronts Contemporary Humanism

Elements for an Islamic Humanism of the Twentieth Century

Islam has not, truly, remained indifferent in the face of the problem of its adaptation to the modern world. Reformism represents a praiseworthy effort, both of secular elites and progressive *'ulama'* [religious scholars], to elaborate a constructive and dynamic version of Islam. Unfortunately, the responses of reformism are false responses to the problems which it confronts. The effort of the *'ulama'* is shackled by the vision of the past from which they do not suc-ceed in detaching themselves; reform is conceived

4, W[ilfred Cantwell] Smith, *Islam In Modern* [History, 1957].

in relation to the past and not as a function of the present. It is the institutions of the past that are asked to respond to the needs of the present; it is the past which they wish to revive in the present, or, in other words, the present is viewed as past, as attested to by the attitude of modernist exegesis which exhausts itself demonstrating the Qur'anic origin of the most modern discoveries. The reformism of the *'ulama'*, far from situating itself in our world, cannot respond to its challenges.

The modernists of Western inspiration, in sacrificing the unitary character of Islam to a dualist point of view which is totally foreign to it, propose less a reform than a dissolution and, in the greatest of their hypotheses, a Christianization of Islam. They do not believe, nor renew; they destroy in servile imitation. This "reformism" poses more problems than it resolves. In its more moderate form, it puts fidelity to institutions before fidelity to faith. Its modernism is nothing more than a facade of modernism which pastes modern ideas on a foundation of archaism. The paradox of Islamic modernism is that it totally ignores modern problems, which are confused with ancient themes dressed up as modernity. Thus, traditional theology remains at the center of modernist thought, with the old debate on free will which has lost none of its formal character since the Mu'tazilites,[5] the old debate on power, on *imamat* [leadership], which is modernized by the name secularity. No doubt reformism has sensed the necessity of reopening *ijtihad* [Islamic interpretation] as preliminary to the development of all free thought and all philosophical progress. But the fact even of posing this demand that it must satisfy bears witness to a fidelity to established hierarchy and institutions, taking precedence over fidelity to God and to authentic Islam, which excludes all authority. What reformism lacks is the spirit of reform: the debate over *ijtihad* in a world where free discussion poses no theoretical problem is the clear proof of the subordination of modernism to the traditional. Modernist Islam is more attuned to the Ancients than to the Moderns, more attached to written and fixed witness than to the living word of God, more concerned about material identity than about creative originality. Its responses concern our world less than the world of the

5. [The Mu'talizites were an early Islamic sect that helped to found Islamic philosophy on ancient Greek philosophical methods.—Editor]

past: they are worth less for our history than for the history of previous Islamic generations.

For a New Signification of Islam Founded on a Creative Vision of God

Islam the creator is founded not on a God cut off from the world and from men, imposing His Law from outside, instituting His Justice externally, but on the contrary, on a living God, present in heaven and on earth. Islam is a gift of God, a guide-book, a light on behalf of man. It is God going towards His creature, responding to its anguish; it is word, message of benevolence directed towards all of humanity. Fidelity to Islam is thus, first of all, fidelity to the word of God, fidelity to the Messages which must be attested to by the institutions, the rules of life conforming to His directive. That is to say, by its temporal and spiritual manifestation on earth, Islam cannot be anything but *the creation of the Muslims*, both response to God, response to their own problems and to the problems of the world. It is, for the Muslims, the place where history is made, according to the designs of God, under His protective gaze and his benevolent *guidance*: "the straight path." Institutional Islam—manifestation of the faith to the Message—is thus a human product, a product of successive generations of Muslims, carrying necessarily the imprint of the epochs, obeying the dynamics of evolution, in order to be a worthwhile response for the different ages of humanity. Faithfulness to God cannot be, therefore, a loyalism with regard to the institutions of the brilliant Islamic Middle Ages, which accomplished its mission with the means of its time, but the will to create for the Islam of the 20th century efficacious institutions in conformity with *the spirit of the Message*, that is, institutions introducing the Justice of God in a dehumanized universe, institutions endowed with the power to *make heard the message of fraternity* in a world where a mechanical and irresponsible human order tends to be substituted for a rational, fraternal human order. To witness God in such a world is to restore His living reality, to rediscover the *sense of divine engagement*, the sentiment of the *divine presence among us*, to respond to divine grace with an *active piety* which is the only thing we can offer of ourselves. We must restore the idea of a personal God, without anthropomorphism, in affirming as against modernism that in a desacralized world where God is banished, man cannot recognize man, but his shadow, and as against Mu'tazilite rationalism and its survivors that transcendentalism well understood cannot suppress that which makes God a living reality for man in this world. The new humanism calls for a theology which, renewing the authentic spirit of Islam, which is a philosophy before being a juridical construct, defines God not as a *given*, but as a *giver*, "an absolute demand on the heart of the subject," implying at all moments a liaison with God, reclaiming a continuous effort to invent a solution to the problem, to discover the truth.[6] Only an Islamic theology that gives God the image of a modern Divinity, a theology which is founded on a God "nearby, progressive, universal" (Pierre Teilhard de Chardin [French philosopher-anthropologist, 1881–1955]), which humanizes faith, which aids us in discovering a supernatural accorded to our century, which makes Islam and human coincide, can become the source of a real renewal, capable of avoiding "the schism" which threatens us. The shock which the rise of the great modern myths of socialization, progress, alienation have provoked among the Muslim masses and in the consciences of the elites, tends to constitute, in the wise remark of Teilhard de Chardin, "a veritable religion not of joyous adoration but of disinterested conquest, undoubtedly generating high spiritual forces," substituting in people's consciences "the sense of the world" for God, makes urgent the elaboration of a new signification of religion which incorporates in its perspectives the sense of progress, the sense of humanity, the sense of the earth. Contemporary Islam clearly has more need of theological purpose, of philosophical creation, than of juridical erudition.

The elaboration even of *this new theology* calls for *a renewed conceptual apparatus*. Neither utilitarian and superficial rationalism, the Mu'tazilite inspiration that the most liberal juridical schools have not managed to break free of, nor the modernist doctrines, so poor in the scheme of thought, can serve as a foundation for such an enterprise. It is a matter of forging a new conceptual apparatus. First, with properly Islamic elements, in making an appeal to the Islamic gnosis, particularly to Shi'i gnosis.[7] This

school has given us the *notion of Plénôme*, "the mysterious synthesis of the Uncreated and the Created," which Sunni prudence has put at the bottom of the barrel, a fertile development capable of constituting the base *of a theology of the dynamic relations of God to the Universe*, worthy of our times; the Ismaili notion of *hadd* [limitation], which expresses a *metaphysical hierarchy*, interpreted in the same sense as transcendence, allows one to understand, without heresy, how God can reveal Himself as a *Person*, with which becomes possible a *relation of knowing and love*.

But to be adaptable to the needs of a modern theology, the conceptual apparatus must borrow from outside. Only a vigorous Muslim thought, endowed with sophisticated conceptual tools, can respond to the questions that the modern conscience poses. Contemporary Islam cannot content itself with the science of *hadith* [traditions of the Prophet] and *fiqh* [Islamic jurisprudence]: it must add to the traditional knowledge the knowledge of the great modern philosophies: religious philosophies and secular philosophies. It must integrate modern knowledge into its ancestral knowledge. To this end, it must reserve a place of honor for *the study of contemporary Christianity*, instruct itself better in its dogmas, including that of Incarnation, study systematically its thinkers: first, its theologians whose thought is no less an enrichment of all humanity for being of the Church; next, its lay writers who are nourished at its maternal breast and whose works, so profoundly convergent, resound in our universe of violence like a veritable Gospel of new times. Modern Islamic humanism cannot ignore the philosophy of the new Church, for lack of a more complete knowledge of Christian philosophy: it cannot ignore Saint-Simonian thought, Teilhardian thought, Samaritan thought, that of Emmanuel Mounier [French social philosopher, 1905–1950], that of François Perroux [French economist, born 1903], the thoughts of visionaries who, in the Christian world, respond to the anguish and to the interrogations of a world that wishes to be total in order to survive. In particular, Islamic theology must lean on the recent aspects of Christian theology, on the sacralization and dynamization of dogmas such as the cult of the heart of Jesus, which, responding to the prayer of Teilhard de Chardin, seems to evolve from Christ the King, "external power that could not be but juridical and static," to Christ the Universal, "Saving Mover, Master and End of evolution," bind-

6. To take up the admirable formulas of J. Lacroix in a different context.

7. I speak as a Sunni—a Sunni convinced that doctrinal pluralism cannot exclude fraternal exchange in the heart of the *umma* [Islamic community].

ing to the reality of his human nature "the personality of elements which it reunites, though without the danger of pantheism, without pagan naturalism leading to the materialist conquest of the Earth." It is the living example of a theology which poses itself "as savior of the most current hopes of the Earth," which associates "the spirit of detachment and the spirit of conquest; the spirit of tradition and the spirit of adventurous research; the spirit of the Earth and the spirit of God." In this line of thought, the works of the last Council appear to carry elements of meditation richer for Islam than the declaration on the Jews.

Islamic theology must also be open to secular thought, to contemporary human sciences: philosophy, history, sociology, economics, even when they are of materialist and atheist inspiration. First, because to refute atheism and materialism, one must know them. Next, because atheist materialism—as we have just shown—is far from eliminating all spirituality and all cosmicity; on the contrary, it demands a positive humanism, a new religion, all the more formidable in that it responds concretely to the aspirations of man today. Its critique of traditional religions has more than a negative aspect: it has a purifying and methodological role that is not foreign to the progress of the observed doctrines, where one is sensitive to its influence. As Jean Lacroix notes, "The negative dialectic is an essential element of the knowledge of God." But what makes atheism a force to contend with at this time is that it is no longer a critique, but constructive. It is no longer materialist, but spiritualist. It has become a place for the formation of universalizing human values which no modern religion can allow itself to ignore. Islamic humanism cannot ignore either the contribution of Marxism or the contribution of contemporary existentialisms, the new concepts with which they have enriched dialectical analysis and thought, the forces of humanization that they have worked up and which are far from contradicting their theoretical foundations. Without a doubt, it is often a matter of formulas that translate metaphysical intentions which the materialist language hardly seizes on for their communicative value, the propulsive force necessary for any modern theology. In insisting on the *complex totality of being*, on *participation* as a condition of existence, in refusing the Aristotelian dualism for a dialectic of unity that "reestablishes in its continuity the living tissue that an imprudent analysis has disjoined (Gabriel Marcel [French philosopher, 1889–1973]),

the contemporary existential formulas open the path to a fertile meditation on ontological mystery and give a new foundation to a theory of metaphysical knowledge, which integrates Cartesian thought in order to surpass it, in reconstituting the destroyed totality, the link with existence, in correcting the discussion through love" (Jeanne Delhomme). Let us take care that it is not a matter of a syncretism, but of a *re-creation* demanding immense work, both critical and constructive, in order to reconcile all this with our specific experience. It is in speaking the language of the 20th century, in using the conceptual tools of modern man, in making theology an original synthesis of spiritual and intellectual elements equal to the needs of our time, emerging in a *philosophy* both of *truth* and of *reality* that is reconciled with objectivity and allows [us]—no longer to look at the world from outside as a spectacle, but to participate in the drama that is being played. By assuming both cosmic and new earthly responsibilities, Islam will have a real significance for the men of our world.

For an Islamic Praxis Founded on the Renewal of Historic Reality

To live in the world is to think and act together, it is to think in order to act, it is to act in thinking.[8] To be of this world, Islam must—at the same time that it elaborates a new theory of knowledge—construct a praxis based on the total renewal of historic reality.

History has proved [Islam's] capacity for adaptation to sociological and human realities, but here too, one should not be content with a reference to the past. In a world transformed by science and technology, such as never before, it must respond to new challenges with bold and constructive innovations such as never before. Let us repeat once more: the golden age of Islamic civilization that was the Middle Ages, knew how to confront its problems of the scientific and technological revolution. It knew how to generate economic and social institutions and structures adapted to its level, as demonstrated by its model of socialization founded on a structure of work which was not embarrassed to appeal to servile labor. Ancient Islam, of the age of economic and financial take-off, was able to pass from a primitive economy of plunder to a modern economy by resolving the

8. We are paraphrasing a formula of Eric Weil's.

problem of capital formation, contrary to Islamic law, through the official practice of shifting the sin of usury onto its Jewish and Christian compatriots. Contemporary Islam finds itself confronted with an economic and social structure that excludes the recourse to slavery, even for utilization towards collective ends, the recourse to the pernicious process of the shifting of sin onto the Other: the modern economy is an entirely different economy, with a new employment structure and a new capital structure that put [even] the best prepared secular organizations to a harsh test. To witness God in the 20th century is to make *history with the tools* and *the organizational structures* of our times. God is neither anachronistic nor archaic: He is eternal Life, the Life whose complexion is that of the times. To bear witness to His presence is to render possible the reading of His Signs in a universe of machines that strips away all signs. *To bear witness with the means of the epoch*, that is, to adopt modern science and technology, not as new divinities but as means of realization of an efficacious human praxis, as means of liberation and disalienation as much as instruments of conquest. It is to make the world of believers not a universe of pariahs, of the powerless and the resigned, but an efficacious world, dynamic, enterprising, responsive to the challenges of hunger, poverty, illness, and ignorance, which the promises of a better in the beyond cannot satisfy for so many of the human masses who suffer in the world, where the faith of the faithful, instead of confining [them] to hopelessness, gives the right to share in the hopes which science and technology bring. To make Islam significant in a world . . . whose rationality informs all men, which "judges others and judges itself according to quantifiable results in its struggle with external nature, according to their wealth in the means of production" (Eric Weil)—this forms a vital and concrete element of the new humanism by rendering it capable of making dams rise up from the ground, atomic energy plants, modern working cities, no longer of course with the rod of Moses or the sword of 'Ali [son-in-law of the Prophet and fourth caliph, circa 596–661], but with this modern grace of God that is contemporary technology. It is no longer a matter of being assisted, but of being initiated, of being introduced to the sanctuary of the secrets of modernity, of becoming a demiurge both without idolatry and without perverse vanity, in drinking at the source of the new knowledges, in entering in direct relation with Prometheus, jeering

the divinities but giving grace to God. It involves, in a word, inaugurating the era of true cooperation in rising to the level of scientific and technological creator, for "the inherited cultural objects that were not made by us, are not, strictly speaking, ever made by us: they only become ours in the form that we invent [them] and by the new meanings that we give them."[9] A progressive Islam that moves deliberately and resolutely towards science, in the shadow of which it has grown, nourishing itself from its sap, armed with a renovated conceptual tool lofty enough to serve as an "animating revelation" for research. By incorporating science and technology, Islam gives itself the means to contribute to the restoration of the reign of the Spirit on earth, the means of maintaining theology at the side of anthropology, of making their meanings coincide, and of rescuing the Islamic world from the temptation of a new metaphysics. By incorporating modern science—which is essentially "open," disinterested, relativist, endowed with a power of acceleration that communicates to spirits, to technologies and to industries—Islam binds itself to universal dialogue, ties itself to contacts and communications between men and their groups, enables itself to assure the extension and deepening of the "existence together" that is characteristic of our historic epoch, to favor "the opening of closed doctrines, closed institutions, and closed groups,"[10] to help to liberate itself from the excesses of subjectivism and of traditional dogmatisms. The accomplishment of the new responsibilities of Islam demands reconciliation with a science once again modest and comprehensive. . . .

For a New Islamic Culture

Any Islamic renovation worthy of the name must make Islamic culture more than a "culture-ornament," but an operative culture which allies production and belief in being; more than a culture-affirmation, better than a culture-heritage, but a "culture-opening on the whole of the real of the becoming"; a culture which turns towards reconciliation, which becomes a place where each has the possibility of "meeting the man" in the other; a culture which would be in accord with a world in evolution where man knows how to live

9. F. Perroux, "Aliénation et création collective" [Alienation and Collective Creation], ISEA, June 1964, p. 40.
10. F. Perroux, op. cit.

for something other than what he makes, for other beings who he is[11]; a culture, finally, which would have the will to center the new society on man and his double vocation, historic and transhistoric, which returns, in sum, to a theory of man as the inevitable philosophical immediacy.

To pose the problem of a culture of creation and of metaphysical fidelity, that is to say, the whole problem of humanism, in the face of classical humanism, is to pose the problem of means, the problem of new men, the emergence of new structures and mentalities, the reestablishment of equilibrium between the new culture and the new nature, between the historic conscience and the semantic conscience, the junction between "a certain modernity" and "a certain tradition": it is the instrument, the technology of the awaited revolution. It presupposes a new pedagogy, a new spirit, appealing to innovation, generating curiosity and disagreement, developing the taste for research, drawing its themes from history and elaborating them; a pedagogy freed from criticism considered as an end in itself, freed from this sort of "hierotropism" that polarizes thought, invests it wholly in religious sciences, which disparages the natural world to exalt only the supernatural world; a pedagogy that puts an end to the dichotomy of Islamic culture in order to create a unified culture thanks to cultural values, unified, notably in the domain of language, of literature, and of art, where the two worlds coexist, ignoring one another. The new education—essentially unifying, formative, permanent, creative—will have as its home the school: the school open to all; the University: the University open to all; but also the workshop, the factory, the fields, the cooperatives; penetrating in all milieux, everywhere introducing progress, that is to say, the spirit of invention and the spirit of truth, thus rendering the entire society educational, pedagogical. It will be the education of the teacher as much as the student, education of the teacher himself, who must make for himself a new mentality in order to be in a position to renovate his teaching, to invent a new dialect of teacher to student, transforming this teaching in a "possibility of future teachings and diverse communications,"[12] to accept, by means of inevitable ruptures, the innovations that permit survival while modifying the system. If it [education] remains committed to tolerance, it will not proclaim itself neutral for long, it will be openly normative in order to be faithful to the wager implied by the culture that it has a mission to dispense: it will teach, along with the sense of the historic, the sense of the technological, the living tradition, confronting it with life in order to make it bear fruit, the language of signs and symbols. When necessary, it will defend the social semantic, both against the excesses of contemporary formalist exegesis and against "the historicizing or idealist references of the traditional modes of thought" (Jacques Berque [1910–1995]). It will make Islamic culture a fertile and original synthesis in realizing the reconciliation of man's being and nature's being, that violated and disfigured nature which must become "the garden of causes and effects" but also grace, communion, "the proximity of the cosmic." The new education, in order to be the instrument of a culture-opening on the world, will teach, finally, worldliness, universality, but not without attending to the creation of a distinct personality, to the affirmation of the specificity that makes sense of the response of Islamic society to history. Insofar as it is revealed as capable of accommodating all of human existence, of founding a personality that is flexible and available in a "mobile world," the new education will accomplish its creative and universalizing mission.

To win the combat of the new humanism, that is, the real combat of history, contemporary Islam definitely has nothing to lose at the level of fundamentals: at the level of the infrastructure which in this dialectic is nothing but metaphysics. But if words have meaning, if *to restore* is something other than adding block to block, *superimposing* superstructures, but *making anew* that which is at the same time *authentic*, then, it will have to resolve to replace the ancient edifice by a *new, reconstructed elaboration on the fundamentals*. It is more than a reform, it is a revolution in the structures of the Islamic world that the triumph of humanism, and the pursuit by Islam of its earthly responsibilities, demand. After the revolution against the Other, which was nothing but a revolt, a negation, the revolution against the Self, the real revolution: that of the positivity of the second birth, which has a constructive mission. To design itself less for desacralization than for demanding that the sacred integrate the human and the new; to renounce the transformation of Islam into a fundamentalist (*intégrée*) religion in favor of *re-making an*

---

11. Georges Guéron, Perspective no. 5.
12. The expression is J. Lacroix's.

integrating religion, companion of man and world; to propose to Islam, mobilizing the creative power of the Qur'an, a new finality on the scale of our universe, instead of absolving it of its temporal mission, which is inseparable from its spiritual mission. To make of the world of Islam (*dar al-Islam*) an immense people and a vast chorus, a Temple where each servant of the Cult is also a creator, a Promethean hero; to make a world of objectification and adoration at the same time, a land of having and being where each act of production is an act of surpassing which returns to a dialect of verticality, significance, and creativity—such is the profound sense of the new challenge that Islam must face in order to respond to the hopes of 400 million men and women. Through the boiling that is agitating the Islamic world, through the proliferation of experiences and attempts, even aborted ones, something is giving a sign that, though it be still a stammer, is unmistakable in its meaning: a "yes," poorly articulated, but absolute and definitive.

Islam and Modernity

Fazlur Rahman (Pakistan–United States, 1919–1988) was born and raised in the British colonies that would later become Pakistan. He embarked on an academic career that took him to graduate degrees at Punjab University and Oxford and teaching positions in Islamic philosophy in England and Canada. He returned to Pakistan in 1961 to lead the Central Institute of Islamic Research in Karachi, a state-sponsored organization that Rahman mobilized to battle religious traditionalists and radicals. Rahman's modernist views were controversial: "his detractors referred to him as 'the destroyer of *hadiths* [traditions of the Prophet]' because of his insistence on judging the weight of *hadith* reports in light of the overall spirit of the Qur'an."[1] Rahman returned to academia in 1968 as a professor at the University of Chicago, where he continued to argue for a modern reinterpretation of Islam.[2] "A measure of this leading thinker's impact," a colleague wrote after Rahman's death in 1988, "is that wherever I have traveled in the world . . . I have never met a Muslim scholar or other specialist on Islam who has not heard of Fazlur Rahman or who is neutral about his contributions."[3]

Muhammad Shibli Nu'mani [Islamic reformer, India, died 1914] wrote in his *Safarnama* [*Travelogue*] (his own account of his visit to the Middle East, May–October 1892), after talking about the potential benefits of the Dar al-'Ulum [university] at Cairo, "But

those people who have been once as much as touched by traditional education, remain forever irreconcilably estranged from modern learning."[4] In the same work he quotes Muhammad 'Abduh [Egyptian modernist, 1849–1905] as saying to him, after bemoaning the plight of al-Azhar [University in Cairo], about the Egyptian products of Western education, "These are even more misguided."[5] This dilemma that characterized education in the days of Shibli and 'Abduh in the "forward" lands of Islam—lands that had a

1. Tamara Sonn, "Rahman, Fazlur," in John L. Esposito, editor, *The Oxford Encyclopedia of the Modern Islamic World* (New York: Oxford University Press, 1995), volume 3, p. 408.

2. Tamara Sonn, "Fazlur Rahman's Islamic Methodology," *The Muslim World*, volume 81, numbers 3–4, July–October 1991, pp. 212–230.

3. Frederick Mathewson Denny, "Fazlur Rahman: Muslim Intellectual," *The Muslim World*, volume 79, number 2, April 1989, pp. 91–101.

4. Muhammad Shibli Nu'mani, *Safarnama* (Lahore, Pakistan: Ghulam 'Ali and Sons, 1961), pp. 285–286.

5. Shibli Nu'mani, p. 349.

highly developed traditional education as well as a recently adopted modern Western-style education—is, as the preceding pages have demonstrated, still as real today. The reason is that, despite a widespread and sometimes deep consciousness of the dichotomy of education, all efforts at a genuine integration have so far been largely unfruitful.

Let us first analyze more closely the basic features of the attempts at reforming education insofar as Islam is concerned. There are basically two aspects of this reformist orientation. One approach is to accept modern secular education as it has developed generally speaking in the West and to attempt to "Islamize" it—that is, to inform it with certain key concepts of Islam. This approach has had two distinct goals, although they are not always distinguished from one another: first, to mold the *character* of students with Islamic values for individual and collective life, and, second, to enable the adepts of modern education to imbue their respective fields of learning at higher levels, using an Islamic perspective to transform, where necessary, both the content and the orientation of these fields. The two goals are closely connected in the sense that molding character with Islamic values is naturally undertaken basically at the primary level of education when students are young and impressionable. However, if nothing is done to imbue fields of higher learning with an Islamic orientation, or if attempts to do so are unsuccessful, when young boys and girls reach the higher stages of education their outlook is bound to be secularized, or they are very likely to shed whatever Islamic orientation they have had—which has been happening on a large scale.

"Imbuing higher fields of learning with Islamic values" is a phrase whose meaning must be made more precise. All human knowledge may be divided into what are called "natural" or exact sciences, whose generalizations are called "laws of nature," and the fields of learning that have been called "humanities" and "social sciences." Although the *content* of physical or exact sciences cannot by definition be interfered with—else they will be falsified—their orientation can be given a value character. Sometimes certain mistaken ideological attitudes try to interfere with the content of these sciences as well, as, for example, when Stalin ordered Russian biologists to emphasize the influence of environment at the expense of heredity. Under such influences or pressures, science must become a mockery, but it is possible and highly desirable for a scientist to know the consequences his investigations have for mankind. It is also equally and, indeed, urgently important for scientific knowledge to be a unity and to give an overall picture of the universe in order to answer the all-important questions, "Does it mean anything? Does it point to a higher will and purpose?" Or is it, to use Whitehead's famous words, "a mere hurrying of material endlessly, meaninglessly"? The first is a practical question, the second a "theoretical" one but with obvious practical implications.

Social sciences and humanities are obviously relevant to values, and values are relevant to them. This is of course not to say that they are subjective, although subjectivism often does enter into them, sometimes palpably. But to be value-oriented is certainly not by itself to be subjective, provided values do not remain mere assumptions but are "objectified." Although metaphysical speculation is the area of human intellectual endeavor that is perhaps the remotest from factual objectivity, yet it need not be, as [F. H.] Bradley [English philosopher, 1846–1924] put it, "the finding of bad reasons for what we already believe on instinct." If metaphysics enjoys the least freedom from assumed premises, man enjoys the least freedom from metaphysics in that metaphysical beliefs are the most ultimate and pervasively relevant to human attitudes; it is consciously or unconsciously the source of all values and of the meaning we attach to life itself. It is therefore all-important that this very ground of formation of our attitudes be as much informed as possible. Positivism may be negative enough to dismiss it as "meaningless"; yet positivism had rendered great service to a genuine metaphysics by exploding the empty thought shell in which the greatest human minds used to incarcerate themselves. Metaphysics, in my understanding, is the unity of knowledge and the meaning and orientation this unity gives to life. If this unity is the unity of knowledge, how can it be all that subjective? It is a faith grounded in knowledge.

There has not been much by way of an Islamic metaphysics, at least in modern times. In the medieval centuries there were Muslim metaphysicians, some of them brilliant, original, and influential; but the primary basis of their entire *Weltanschauung* [worldview] was Hellenic thought, not the Qur'an. Some of their doctrines were repugnant to the orthodoxy, which took such fright that down the centuries all metaphysical thought became anathema to it.

Among the orthodox there has not been a lack of men of deep insight, but there has been no systematic and coherent body of metaphysical thought fully informed by the Qur'anic *Weltanschauung*, which is itself remarkably coherent. In modern times, Muhammad Iqbal's *Reconstruction of Religious Thought in Islam*[6] is the only systematic attempt. But, despite the fact that Iqbal had certain basic and rare insights into the nature of Islam as an attitude to life, this work cannot be said to be based on Qur'anic teaching: the structural elements of its thought are too contemporary to be an adequate basis for an ongoing Islamic metaphysical endeavor (although I certainly disagree with H. A. R. Gibb's assessment according to which Ash'arite theology, for example, is more faithful to the Qur'anic matrix of ideas than Iqbal's thought). What is true is that Iqbal's thought, like all modern liberal thought, is essentially a *personal* effort, while [Abu'l-Hasan] Ash'ari's [873–935] theology, as a credal system, consisted of certain formal principles that he claimed to have drawn from the Qur'an and on the basis of which he elaborated a full-fledged theological system. But, besides the question whether a modern outlook can have room for hard-and-fast and cut-and-dried formal creeds, this does not mean that Ash'arite theology represented Islam more faithfully than did Iqbal; on the contrary, that theology represents, in my view, an almost total distortion of Islam and was, in fact, a one-sided and extreme reaction to the Mu'tazilite rationalist theology.

However, to resume what I was saying about the Muslims' aim of Islamizing the several fields of learning, this aim cannot be really fulfilled unless Muslims effectively perform the intellectual task of elaborating an Islamic metaphysics on the basis of the Qur'an. An overall worldview of Islam has to be first, if provisionally, attempted if various specific fields of intellectual endeavor are to cohere as informed by Islam. In medieval Islam, even if Ash'arite theology was Islamically wayward, it certainly tried—sometimes with remarkable efficiency—to permeate the intellectual disciplines of Islam, like law, Sufism, and even the outlook on history. In modern times, however, although many Muslims are conscious of the desirability and even necessity of investing factual knowledge with Islamic values, the result is so far perhaps less than negligible—although there is

no dearth of booklets and pamphlets on "Islam and this" and "Islam and that," which occasionally do contain valuable insights and often a good deal of ingenuity but are essentially marred by an apologetic attitude. More recently, a number of conferences and seminars have been held in Saudi Arabia and Pakistan (the former's latter-day spiritual client) on such topics as "Islam and Education," "Islam and Economics," or "Islam and Psychology." I have not seen any publications so far, if any have resulted from this feverish activity. One cannot, of course, expect any spectacular results as yet, but the effort is worth continuing.

I said earlier that the effort to inculcate an Islamic character in young students is not likely to succeed if the higher fields of learning remain completely secular, that is, unpurposeful with regard to their effect on the future of mankind. Indeed, even in the West, attempts at molding young students' character have failed because when these boys and girls grow up they find all life around them practically secular, and they become disillusioned with their childhood orientation, which comes to seem a kind of "pious fraud." In fact, they often grow up with a vengeance and, barring other factors to the contrary, become more secular-minded than their parents. The same is very much true of Muslim children, although in Muslim society the social temper still plays a major role in curbing open deviations and utter secularization. But if moral values are to be observed or at least not flouted under social pressure, this hardly goes altogether to the credit of the efficacy of the Islamic spirit. We shall have to come back later to this all-important issue; in the meantime, we must discuss the problem of what is meant by reforming Islamic education itself since, unless some solution to this is forthcoming, it is futile even to raise the question of the Islamization of knowledge: it is the upholders of Islamic learning who have to bear the primary responsibility of Islamizing secular knowledge by their creative intellectual efforts.

In essence, then, the whole problem of "modernizing" Islamic education, that is, rendering it capable of creative Islamic intellectual productivity in all fields of intellectual endeavor together with the serious commitment to Islam that the *madrasa* system has generally been able to impart, is the problem of expanding the Muslim's intellectual vision by raising his intellectual standards. For expansion of vision is a function of rising to heights; the lower down you

6. [A chapter of Iqbal's work is included in this volume.—Editor]

come the less space you can see, and the more you think yourself master of that little space under your narrow vision. And here appears the stark contrast between the actual Muslim attitudes and the demands of the Qur'an. The Qur'an sets a very high value on knowledge, and the Prophet himself is ordered to pray to God: "O Lord! increase my knowledge." (Sura 20, Verse 114) Indeed, the Qur'an itself is firmly of the view that the more knowledge one has, the more capable of faith and commitment one will be. There is absolutely no other view of the relationship of faith and knowledge that one can legitimately derive from the Qur'an. It is true that the Qur'an is highly critical, for example, of Meccan tradesmen who "know well the externalities of the lower (that is, material) life but are heedless of its ends." (Sura 30, Verse 7) But this is precisely the point I am making here—that a knowledge that does not expand the horizons of one's vision and action is truncated and injurious knowledge. But how can one have knowledge of the "ends" of life—that is, of higher values—without knowing actual reality? If the Muslim modernist has done nothing else, he has adduced such formidable evidence from the Qur'an for the absolute necessity to faith of a knowledge of the universe, of man, and of history, that all Muslims today at least pay lip service to it.

But, by contrast, the Muslim attitude to knowledge in the later medieval centuries is so negative that if one puts it beside the Qur'an one cannot help being appalled. According to this attitude, higher knowledge and faith are mutually dysfunctional and increase at each other's expense. Knowledge thus appears to be purely secular, as is basically the case with all "modern" positive knowledge—indeed, even modern "religious" knowledge is secular, or else it is considered positively injurious to faith. Sometimes an arbitrary distinction is drawn between "religious" and "nonreligious" sciences; the former have, of course, to be acquired at the expense of the latter. Sometimes a distinction is drawn between the "more urgent" knowledge—that of law and/or theological propositions—and "the less urgent or less important" positive sciences. And often enough, indeed, a distinction is drawn between "good" knowledge and "bad" knowledge, for example, of philosophy or music, while a third category is posited of more or less "useless" knowledge such as mathematics. There are several causes of these pernicious distinctions. One of these I have already pointed out, namely, the

fear of philosophy and of intellectualism in general. Another important reason certainly was, as I indicated in chapter 2 [not included in this excerpt], that a knowledge of orthodox disciplines, particularly of law, was an almost sure passport to employment, whereas mathematics or astronomy brought little by way of a livelihood, let alone of fame, and medicine was accepted as a necessary though inferior endeavor. [Abu Hamid Muhammad] Al-Ghazzali [1058–1111], in his criticism of a slogan of medical men—"First [attend to] your body and then [to] your religion [or soul]"—typifies the medieval orthodox attitude to medicine when he says that by such catchy slogans these people want to deceive the simple-minded public as to the real order of priorities.

Whatever the reason, the stark contrast between the Qur'an and the medieval Muslim pursuits of knowledge is obvious. During approximately the past one hundred years . . . Muslims have displayed an increasing awareness of reforming traditional education and integrating the old knowledge with the modern. But this development has been marred by certain important, indeed, fundamental weaknesses that it is essential to elucidate before we can look at the future with greater clarity and a more constructive outlook. The first important block to any reform is the phenomenon I have called neorevivalism or neofundamentalism. Before the advent of classical modernism, there had existed a revivalism or fundamentalism since the 18th century. The "Wahhabi" movement [in Arabia] and other kindred or parallel reform phenomena wanted to reconstruct Islamic spirituality and morality on the basis of a return to the pristine "purity" of Islam. The current postmodernist fundamentalism, in an important way, is novel because its basic élan is anti-Western (and, by implication of course, anti-Westernism). Hence its condemnation of classical modernism as a purely Westernizing force. Classical modernists were, of course, not all of a piece, and it is true that some of these modernists went to extremes in their espousal of Western thought, morality, society, and so on. Such phenomena are neither unexpected nor unnatural when rapid change occurs, particularly when it derives from a living source like the West. But just as the classical modernist had picked upon certain specific issues to be considered and modernist positions to be adopted thereupon—democracy, science, status of women, and such—so now the neofundamentalist, after—as I said before—borrowing certain things from classical modernism, largely rejected its content and, in turn, picked upon certain specific issues as "Islamic" par excellence and accused the classical modernist of having succumbed to the West and having sold Islam cheaply there. The pet issues with the neofundamentalist are the ban on bank interest, the ban on family planning, the status of women (contra the modernist), collection of *zakat* taxes, and so forth—things that will most distinguish Muslims from the West. Thus, while the modernist was engaged by the West through attraction, the neorevivalist is equally haunted by the West through repulsion. The most important and urgent thing to do from this point of view is to "disengage" mentally from the West and to cultivate an independent but understanding attitude toward it, as toward any other civilization, though more particularly to the West because it is the source of much of the social change occurring throughout the world. So long as Muslims remain mentally locked with the West in one way or the other, they will not be able to act independently and autonomously.

The neorevivalist has undoubtedly served as a corrective not only for several types of excesses in classical modernism but, above all, for secularist trends that would otherwise have spread much faster in Muslim societies. That is to say, neorevivalism has reoriented the modern-educated lay Muslim emotionally toward Islam. But the greatest weakness of neorevivalism, and the greatest disservice it has done to Islam, is an almost total lack of positive effective Islamic thinking and scholarship within its ranks, its intellectual bankruptcy, and its substitution of cliché mongering for serious intellectual endeavor. It has often contended, with a real point, that the learning of the conservative traditional *'ulama'*, instead of turning Muslims toward the Qur'an, has turned them away from it. But its own way of turning to the Qur'an has been no more than, as I said above, picking upon certain selected issues whereby it could crown itself by "distinguishing" Muslims from the rest of the world, particularly from the West. The traditionalist *'ulama'*, if their education has suffered from a disorientation toward the purposes of the Qur'an, have nevertheless built up an imposing edifice of learning that invests their personalities with a certain depth; the neorevivalist is, by contrast, a shallow and superficial person—really rooted neither in the Qur'an nor in traditional intellectual culture, of which he knows practically nothing. Because he

has no serious intellectual depth or breadth, his consolation and pride both are to chant ceaselessly the song that Islam is "very simple" and "straightforward," without knowing what these words mean. In a sense, of course, the Qur'an is simple and uncomplicated, as is all genuine religion—in contradistinction to theology—but in another and more meaningful sense a book like the Qur'an, which gradually appeared over almost twenty-three years, is highly complicated—as complicated as life itself. The essence of the matter is that the neorevivalist has produced no Islamic educational system worthy of the name, and this is primarily because, having become rightly dissatisfied with much of the traditional learning of the *'ulama'*, he himself has been unable to devise any methodology, any structural strategy, for understanding Islam or for interpreting the Qur'an.

Second, the reform efforts that have taken place so far have been in two directions. In one direction, this reform has occurred almost entirely within the framework of traditional education itself. Generated largely by the premodernist reform phenomena whose impetus still continues to some extent, this reform has tended to "simplify" the traditional syllabus, which it finds heavily loaded with "extraneous" materials such as medieval theology, certain branches of philosophy (such as logic), and a plethora of works on Islamic law. This simplification consists in dropping most or all works in these medieval disciplines and accentuating *hadith* [traditions of the Prophet], occasionally Arabic language and literature, and, in certain cases, principles of Qur'anic interpretation (but not the Qur'an—that is, its text—as such), in consistency with the religious ideology of these premodernist reformist movements that aimed to "purify" Islam from later accretions. This is confirmed by the developments concerning the subcontinent that I sketched out toward the end of chapter 1 [not included in this excerpt].

In the second direction, a variety of developments have occurred that can be summed up by saying that they all represent an effort to combine and integrate the modern branches of learning with the old ones. In such cases, the years of curriculum have been extended and brought in line with the curricular span of modern schools and colleges, or, as I noted for Indonesia, supplemented by afternoon classes held after the modern lay education of the present-day schools—thus lengthening the day rather than increasing the number of curricular years. At the college level, however, even in the Indonesian experiment, the effort is directed at combining modern subjects with the old.

The most important of these experiments are undoubtedly those of al-Azhar of Egypt and the new system of Islamic education introduced in Turkey since the late 1940s. Al-Azhar has behind it a long tradition of medieval Islamic learning, and therefore, understandably, its conservatism in the field of religious studies is still very strong. Consequently, the modern subjects like philosophy, sociology, and psychology do not seem to have a deep impact, since they essentially trail behind the medieval learning. In Turkey, on the other hand, where traditional education had been completely destroyed, it is being reintroduced afresh, while the modern disciplines are almost at the same level as in the lay schools—indeed, all over in the developing countries. Turkey is fortunate in having to make a fresh start because it has the opportunity to interpret the medieval intellectual heritage and give it a new shape—which, as we shall see presently, is a basic desideratum in all current attempts to integrate the modern and the traditional and which has been satisfied only to a limited degree at al-Azhar in the fields of theology and law.

At present, the "integration" I spoke of above is basically absent because of the largely mechanical character of instruction and because of juxtaposition of the old with the new. It is true that all these reforms are confronted with a vicious circle in that, on the one hand, unless adequate teachers are available with minds already integrated and creative, instruction will remain sterile even given goodwill and talent on the part of students, while, on the other, such teachers cannot be produced on a sufficient scale unless, substantively speaking, an integrated curriculum is made available. This vicious circle can be broken only at the first point—if there come into being some first-class minds who can interpret the old in terms of the new as regards substance and turn the new into the service of the old as regards ideals. This, then, must be followed by the writing of new textbooks on theology, ethics, and so forth. Such minds cannot be produced at will, but something can certainly be done in this respect—namely, to recruit from the best talent available and to provide the necessary incentives for a committed intellectual career in this field. Today, most of the students who are attracted to this field are those who have failed to gain

entrance to more lucrative careers. This shows how little awareness there is that creating minds is both more difficult and, in the last analysis, more urgent than constructing bridges. There is little doubt that most Eastern societies have been laboring under the false and totally self-deceptive impression that they suffer from an over-plenitude of spirituality and spiritual insights while the West, barren in this respect, has outstripped them in material technology and that now they need only get the latter. That the West has outstripped the East in science and technology is correct; what seems to be a fiction is that the East is replete with spirituality, for, if this were so, why should the East—or the Muslim societies—suffer from the mental and spiritual dichotomy of which I have mainly been speaking here?

Second, an important problem that has plagued Muslim societies since the dawn of democracy in them is the peculiar relationship of religion and politics and the pitiable subjugation of the former to the latter. Indeed, it was this pernicious phenomenon that forced Kemal Atatürk [founder of modern Turkey, 1881–1938] to opt for secularism. Secularism is not the answer—quite the opposite. But the politics being waged most of the time in these countries is hardly less pernicious in its effects than secularism itself. For, instead of setting themselves to genuinely interpret Islamic goals to be realized through political and government channels—which would subjugate politics to interpreted Islamic values (whether these values or goals turn out to be conservative or liberal, fundamentalist or modern for different parties)— what happens most of the time is a ruthless exploitation of Islam for party politics and group interests that subjects Islam not only to politics but to day-to-day politics; Islam thus becomes sheer demagoguery. Unfortunately, the so-called Islamic parties in several countries are the most blatantly guilty of such systematic political manipulation of religion. The slogan "in Islam religion and politics are inseparable" is employed to dupe the common man into accepting that, instead of politics or the state serving the long-range objectives of Islam, Islam should come to serve the immediate and myopic objectives of party politics. Reform and reconstruction of that powerful instrument for the shaping of minds—education—is inconceivable in these circumstances. The secularist, who is in any case already alienated from Islam, becomes all the more confirmed in his cynicism about men of religion, the dislocation between their aims and their claims, even though secularism itself may be a child of incurable cynicism about man's real nature.

And yet the most important single channel of both these latter reforms—the correct envisioning of priorities and the saving of religion from the vagaries of day-to-day politics—is education itself. I must therefore turn to a consideration of the possible solution to the problems I have raised in the field of the reform of Islamic education itself: how it can become meaningful in the modern intellectual and spiritual setting, not so much to save religion from modernity—which is, after all, only a partisan interest—but to save modern man from himself through religion.

Some Considerations toward a Solution

Toward an Understanding of Islam

The first essential step to relieve the vicious circle just mentioned is, for the Muslim, to distinguish clearly between normative Islam and historical Islam. Unless effective and sustained efforts are made in this direction, there is no way visible for the creation of the kind of Islamic mind I have been speaking of just now. No amount of mechanical juxtaposition of old and new subjects and disciplines can produce this kind of mind. If the spark for the modernization of old Islamic learning and for the Islamization of the new is to arise, then the original thrust of Islam—of the Qur'an and Muhammad—must be clearly resurrected so that the conformities and deformities of historical Islam may be clearly judged by it. In the first chapter I indicated by what process this normative Islam had understandably, perhaps inevitably, but often by no means justifiably passed into its historical forms. In that chapter I also indicated how this resurrection may be accomplished—namely, by studying the Qur'an's social pronouncements and legal enactments in the light of its general moral teaching and particularly under the impact of its stated objectives (or principles, if one prefers this expression) on the one hand and against the background of their historical-social milieu on the other. Since this method has been made fairly clear in that chapter and particularly in the Introduction, there is no need to repeat it here, but certain other questions concerning it must be answered.

Is this method not yet another form of fundamentalism that will once again, in a new and more "scientific" way, create another idol to arrest Muslims' forward progress? After all, all fundamentalists, like the Wahhabis and subsequently their neofundamentalist successors such as the *Ikhwan* [Muslim Brotherhood], have just said this, namely, that Muslims must go back to the original and pristine Islam; yet they have been arrested at a certain point. Again, the Muslim modernist has also explicitly held that Muslims must go back to the original and pristine Islam; yet they have come up with certain doctrines that both the fundamentalist and the conservative have failed to recognize as Islamic—indeed, as anything but Western, that is, un-Islamic! What is, then the guarantee, or at least the likelihood, that the pursuit of the new solution will not be arrested at a certain point, or that the results reached will not be so bewilderingly chaotic and contradictory?

The answer is that neither the fundamentalist nor the modernist had a clear enough method. That fundamentalist movements in Islam have been arrested is not due to their claims, for they claimed *ijtihad*, that is, new thinking in Islam. How can anyone arrest new thought, particularly when it is claimed that the essence of the Islamic thought process rests on *ijtihad*? Actually it is even something of a misnomer to call such phenomena in Islam "fundamentalist" except insofar as they emphasize the basis of Islam as being the two original sources: the Qur'an and the *sunna* [practice] of the Prophet Muhammad. Otherwise they emphasize *ijtihad*, original thought, which is something forbidden by Western fundamentalists who, while emphasizing the Bible as the "fundament," reject original or new thought. It is also something of an irony to pit the so-called Muslim fundamentalists against the Muslim modernists, since, so far as their acclaimed procedure goes, the Muslim modernists say exactly the same thing as the so-called Muslim fundamentalists say: that Muslims must go back to the original and definitive sources of Islam and perform *ijtihad* on that basis.

To resume my answer to this important question: the so-called fundamentalists and modernists have come up with radically different answers to some basic issues according to their respective environments, but neither has had a clear enough method of interpreting the Qur'an and the *sunna*. As I pointed out in the previous section, the neorevivalist has no method worthy of the name except to react, on certain important social issues, to the classical modernist. I also pointed out earlier that the classical modernist had no method except to treat ad hoc issues that seemed to him to require solution for Muslim society but that were historically of Western inspiration and that he attempted to solve, often with remarkable plausibility, in the light of Qur'anic teaching. As for the premodernist revivalist, he had certainly worked within the traditional perimeters of Islam and had found that Muslim individual and collective life had become permeated with degrading superstitions that, according to the Qur'anic monotheism, were a form of *shirk* [polytheism] and must therefore be eradicated. This was undoubtedly sound, but for the rest the premodernist revivalist neither had nor bothered to seek a methodology of Qur'anic interpretation that would be sound in scholarship, rationally reliable, and faithful to the Qur'an itself.

Although the method I have advocated here is new in form, nevertheless its elements are all traditional. It is the biographers of the Prophet, the *hadith* collectors, the historians, and the Qur'an commentators who have preserved for us the general social-historical background of the Qur'an and the Prophet's activity and in particular the background (*sha'n al-nuzul*) of the particular passages of the Qur'an—despite the divergence of accounts about the latter in some cases. This would surely not have been done but for their strong belief that this background is necessary for our understanding of the Qur'an. It is strange, however, that no systematic attempt has ever been made to understand the Qur'an in the order in which it was revealed, that is, by setting the specific cases of the *shu'un al-nuzul*, or "occasions of revelation," in some order in the general background that is no other than the activity of the Prophet (the *sunna* in the proper sense) and its social environment. If this method is pursued, most arbitrary and fanciful interpretations will at once be ruled out, since a definite enough anchoring point will be available. It is only because the Qur'an was not treated as a coherent whole by many Muslim thinkers that the metaphysical part, which should form the necessary backdrop to a coherent elaboration of the moral, social, and legal message of the Qur'an, in particular received the wildest interpretations at the hands of the so-called esoteric school, be they Sufis, Batinis, philosophers, or even some *mutakallimun* (theologians), while the majority of the orthodox became dusty-dry

literalists far removed from any genuine insight into the depths of the Qur'an. The Qur'an, despite its distinction within its own body of "firm" and "ambiguous" verses (Sura 3, Verse 7)—which has been made so much of by several speculative minds, but which seems to refer to verses of specific and general import—categorically states in numerous places that it is coherent and that it is free from inconsistencies— a claim that is well attested by any closer study of it, which is not vitiated by extravagant preconceived notions (for example, Sura 11, Verse 11; Sura 22, Verse 52; Sura 4, Verse 82; and all such verses where the Qur'an speaks of itself as *tafsil*, that is, a "firm exposition"). Indeed, Sura 3, Verse 7 itself strongly suggests—and it has very often been so interpreted— that the "ambiguous" verses are to be taken in the light of, although in turn as being matricial to, the "firm" ones.

Yet none of this means that any significant interpretation of the Qur'an can be absolutely monolithic. Nothing could be further from the truth. For one thing, we know from numerous reports that the Prophet's Companions themselves sometimes understood certain Qur'anic verses differently, and this was within his knowledge. Further, the Qur'an, as I have often reiterated, is a document that grew within a background, from the flesh and blood of actual history; it is therefore both as "straightforward" and as organically coherent as life itself. Any attempt to take it with a literalist, partialist superficiality and lifeless rigidity will, to use A. J. Arberry's phrase, "crush its gossamer wings to powder." For example, on the question of murder, the Qur'an essentially confirms the pre-Islamic Arab forms of settlement either by blood money or by "life for life," adding that forgiveness is better. From this, all our lawyers deduced the principle that murder is a private crime against the bereaved family, which has therefore to decide whether the murderer will be forgiven, whether he should pay for the murder in money, or whether he should be killed in revenge. However, the Qur'an also enunciates a more general principle stating that "whosoever kills a person unrightfully or without a mischief (that is, a war) on the earth, it is as though he has killed all humanity; while he who saves one person, it is as though he has saved all humanity" (Sura 5, Verse 32), which obviously makes murder a crime against society rather than a private crime against a family. But our lawyers never brought this verse to bear on the issue of murder

To insist on absolute uniformity of interpretation is therefore neither possible nor desirable. What is important is first of all to use the kind of method I am advocating to eliminate vagrant interpretations. For the rest, every interpreter must explicitly state his general assumptions with regard to Qur'anic interpretation in general and specific assumptions and premises with regard to specific issues or passages. Once his assumptions are made explicit, then discussion among differing interpreters is possible and subjectivity is further reduced. But the kinds of differences about the conception of God—whether he is the ground of the being that manifests itself through every existent and is therefore to be contemplated, or whether he is the ultimate and transcendent principle that has simply to be established and "proved" like a mathematical formula, or whether he is the creator-commander who has to be worshipped and obeyed, and so forth—should surely be capable of being sorted out for public and collective life at least, leaving scope for private idiosyncrasies, which in any case cannot cease.

Such interpretive attempts can be made by individual scholars, but they can obviously be made by teamwork as well. What is certain is that there have to be several attempts so that, through discussion and debate, the community at large can accept some interpretations and discard others. It is obviously not necessary that a certain interpretation once accepted must continue to be accepted; there is always both room and necessity for new interpretations, for this is, in truth, an ongoing process. But such bona fide attempts by competent scholars are, as I said before, the only way to break the vicious circle of "where to start" the process of reform in Islamic education. For the first logical step now is the creation of new intellectual materials, since the mechanical part of the process of reform in terms of combining old and new subjects in new reformed schools or setting up afternoon Islamic schools to supplement the morning "regular schools" is by now well underway in virtually all Muslim lands.

Nor is this first step impossible to achieve. The greatest difficulty that will be experienced is not the new step itself but extricating one's feet from the stagnant waters of the old Qur'anic exegesis, which may contain many pearls but which, on the whole, impedes rather than promotes a real understanding of the Qur'an. Qur'an commentaries are, of course, not all of the same value, some being purely subjective distortions, others of real importance in providing both insight and historical information; but the approach being advocated herein is new—although, as I said before, its elements are all in the tradition itself. The new step simply consists in studying the Qur'an in its total and specific background (and doing this study systematically in a historical order), not just studying it verse by verse or passage by passage with an isolated "occasion of revelation" (*sha'n al-nuzul*).

Reconstruction of the Islamic Sciences

The Historical Period

The proposition that the *shari'a* [Islamic] law and institutions have to be derived methodically and systematically from the Qur'an and the example of the Prophet (i.e., his total performance) in the manner described above does not mean that Islamic sciences, as they have originated and developed historically, have to be ignored or discarded. Indeed, they cannot be ignored or discarded for certain basic reasons. First of all, it is historic Islam that gives continuity to the intellectual and spiritual being of the community. No community can annul its past and hope to create a future being for itself—as that community. A basic fallacy of an Atatürkish kind of "reform" consists precisely in an effort to shed the historical being of the community and to seek a future without it. It is important, however, to understand precisely the meaning of what I am saying, which is not that we should necessarily go slow with reform through gradual steps by a process of partial and ad hoc adjustments. My argument has been, in fact, against an ad hoc policy, because, whatever its practical wisdom (which is dubious), it necessarily distorts vision by making it myopic. And it is, in any case, a policy Muslims can ill afford at the present juncture, since the gap between what is and what ought to be is much too great. It must also constantly be borne in mind that the Muslim community has developed over the centuries (say, since the tenth/eleventh) a temper whereby it can swallow small changes without perceptibly moving forward. The factor that has produced this tremendous digestive power can be called conservatism or the spirit of *ijma'* (consensus), depending upon the point of view one chooses to adopt, but the fact remains that it is extremely difficult to move the community as a whole. If one studies the vast and rich juristic and speculative literature of Islam (even leaving out the protean Sufism), one finds startling, indeed, revolutionary ideas in the writings of men who were high "orthodox" authorities, but none of these have left any trace on the being of the community. Changes in the community have always occurred when the cumulative process has reached a stage of outburst that literally re-forms orthodoxy. For this reason also, I am against a partialist, patchy, slow adjustment approach.

The meaning of my proposition that historic formulations of Islam—juristic, theological, spiritual—can be neither ignored nor discarded consists of two parts. The first, as I just hinted above, is that if we took the Qur'an at this point of history, as though it had been revealed just now—for that is what discarding historical Islam would mean (from this perspective, the *sunna* or the performance of the Prophet himself serves, in part, as historical Islam for an understanding of the Qur'an)—we would not be able even to understand it. Religiously speaking, no doubt, the Qur'an has to be taken as though it were revealed to the conscience of every believer—and Sufis have sometimes taken this to an extreme—but it can be so revealed to the conscience of a believer only after it has been properly understood, which requires putting its legal and social enunciations in their historical setting. Besides, within historical Islam differences in religious attitude can be discerned, for, as I pointed out early in chapter 1, the Companions of the Prophet—his immediate audience—understood the Qur'an and the Prophet's own performance more pragmatically than did the later generations, who increasingly became prisoners of their own principles, on the basis of which they elaborated the Qur'anic teaching. Such early history is also involved in our understanding of Islam, not in terms of accepting all of its content but as a general pragmatic guide.

The second part of the meaning of this proposition is that we must make a thorough study, a *historically* systematic study, of the development of Islamic disciplines. This has to be primarily a critical study that will show us on the screen, as it were, the career of Islam at the hands of Muslims. But in religious terms it will be finally judged by the criterion of the Qur'an itself—the Qur'an as we will have understood it by the procedure described above. The need for a critical study of our intellectual Islamic past is ever more urgent because, owing to a peculiar psychological complex we have developed vis-à-vis the West, we have come to defend that past as though it were our God. Our sensitivities to the various parts or aspects of this past, of course, differ, although almost all of it has become generally sacred to us. The greatest sensitivity surrounds the *hadith*, although it is generally accepted that, except the Qur'an, all else is liable to the corrupting hand of history. Indeed, a critique of *hadith* should not only remove a big mental block but should promote fresh thinking about Islam. Further, if a certain *hadith* is shown to be historically unsound, it need not be discarded, for it may contain a good principle, and a good principle, no matter where it comes from, should be adopted. This is not the place to go into details, which I have elaborated in chapter 2 of my *Islamic Methodology in History* (Karachi, 1965). . . .

Systematic Reconstruction

Theology. A historical critique of theological developments in Islam is the first step toward a reconstruction of Islamic theology. This critique, as I said before, should reveal the extent of the dislocation between the worldview of the Qur'an and various schools of theological speculation in Islam and point the way toward a new theology. Leaving aside the various extravagant speculative theological doctrines of the Batinis (Muslim esotericists) and many Sufis, the opposing schools of "rational" (Mu'tazilite) and "traditionalist" (the Ash'arite) theology teach a student an effective lesson on this highly sensitive issue. While admitting that all theological formulations necessarily carry on their brows the dust of time, one still must demand that such formulations be faithful at least to the basic structure of ideas of the religion they claim to represent. But who would claim that the Mu'tazilite doctrines of the negation of attributes of God, of the necessity of excluding God's power from the sphere of human actions and limiting it to the realm of nature, of denial of God's forgiveness of sins, are faithful to the teaching of the Qur'an? And, even more so, who can claim that the Ash'arite reaction in terms of the doctrines of the omnipotence of God at the expense of all human power and will, of the purposelessness of divine commands and prohibitions, of making works essentially irrelevant to faith, of the denial of cause and effect, and, consequently, the elevation of atomism to the position of a cardinal principle of the Islamic creed was representative of the Qur'anic teaching on God, man, or nature? A system of theology may be logically coherent yet totally false to the religion it claims to formulate, for what can one say of a theological system that reigned supreme in the greater part of the Islamic world for the best part of a millennium and whose votaries—some of them august names in the history of Islamic thought like al-Ghazzali and [Fakhr al-Din] al-Razi [1149–1209]—vied with one another in producing ever fresh arguments to prove that man can be said "to act" only metaphysically, not really, since the only real "actor" is God?

It is to the credit of premodernist revivalism and modernism that they tried to undermine this thousand-year-old sacred folly and to invite Muslims back to the refreshing fountain of the Qur'an. But whereas premodernist fundamentalism was good at demolishing the choking prison and letting in fresh air, it refused to build any new edifice. Rather, it believed that all edifices are really prisons, or inevitably become so, and that religion is better off without a theology, which in its eyes amounted to a crime against religion. As for modernism, it has, for the most part, dealt with matters social and political issue by issue, not as a social or political philosophy. Democracy is Islamic, but concepts like human rights and social justice (which are certainly declared to be Islamic) are not much discussed; egalitarianism is emphasized, but its nature and limits, if any, do not come up as problems; Islam has given women rights, but why and what kinds of rights and by what rationale are not clear. Most modernists are very reticent about a theology, a philosophy, a worldview. In Muhammad 'Abduh's work theology is minimal, although he did much to resurrect Mu'tazila-type rationalism; Sayyid Ahmad Khan [Indian modernist, 1817–1898] called desperately for a new *kalam* (theology) consonant with the requirements of the age and felt sure that, unless theology was reformulated afresh, Islam would be in real and grave danger—like all other religions. At his instance, Muhammad Shibli wrote two books in Urdu—a history of theology in Islam called *'Ilm al-Kalam* and a systematic theology called *Kalam*—wherein he attempted to restate arguments for God's existence, prophethood, revelation, and such, relying heavily, like Sayyid Ahmad Khan himself, upon medieval Muslim philosophers like [Abu 'Ali al-Husayn] Ibn Sina [1908–1037].

It was the philosopher-poet Muhammad Iqbal who essayed a new approach to Islamic theology in his *Reconstruction of Religious Thought in Islam.* Iqbal was a keen student of modern Western philosophy as well as of Islamic mysticism (essentially in Persian), but he was not a scholar of the Islamic theological tradition or of the Qur'an (which, however, he read a great deal for inspiration). Iqbal appears to me to have very rightly perceived that the basic impulse of the Qur'an was dynamic and action oriented—seeking to direct history on a spiritual value pattern and attempting to create a world order. As I said earlier, I do not accept the judgment of the late H. A. R. Gibb that one cannot consider Iqbal's work even as a point of departure for building a new Islamic theology; it seems to me that Gibb was probably thinking in terms of a new system of Islamic *credal formulae.* It is, however, correct to say that Iqbal's attempt is very much dated, since he took seriously his contemporary scientists who tried to prove a dynamic free will in man on the basis of the new subatomic scientific data, which they interpreted as meaning that the physical world was "free" of the chain of cause and effect! It is true too that Iqbal did not carry out any systematic inquiry into the teaching of the Qur'an but picked and chose from its verses—as he did with other traditional material— to prove certain theses at least some of which were the result of his general insight into the Qur'an but which, above all, seemed to him to suit most the contemporary needs of a stagnant Muslim society. He then expressed these theses in terms of such contemporary evolutionary theories as those of [Henri] Bergson [1859–1941] and [Alfred North] Whitehead [1861–1947]. My disagreement with Iqbal is therefore not over his concept of God—as the ultimate source of creative energy that can be appropriated by individuals and societies in certain ways—but with his formulation of this concept and the method by which he attempts to deduce it from the Qur'an.

This account further demonstrates the necessity of the procedure I have advocated for a systematic interpretation of the Qur'an. For the theological or metaphysical statements of the Qur'an, the specific revelational background is not necessary, as it is for its social-legal pronouncements, nor do the commentators usually give it, but certainly without a systematic study the Qur'anic worldview cannot emerge. It cannot be denied that any such interpretation will necessarily be influenced by contemporary modes of thought; this is also required in the sense that only in this way can the message of the Qur'an become relevant to the contemporary situation. But it is quite another thing to couch the Qur'anic message in terms of a particular theory, no matter how attractive, sensational, or popular it may seem—in fact, the more topical a theory is, the less suitable it is as a vehicle of expression of an eternal message. It is also possible that this is what Gibb meant by his critique of Iqbal, but then it is possible to separate Iqbal's basic insights into the nature of Islam from the doctrines in terms of which he has formulated them.

Law and ethics. Muslim scholars have never attempted an ethics of the Qur'an, systematically or otherwise. Yet no one who has done any careful study of the Qur'an can fail to be impressed by its ethical fervor. Its ethics, indeed, is its essence, and it is also the necessary link between theology and law. It is true that the Qur'an tends to concretize the ethical, to clothe the general in a particular paradigm, and to translate the ethical into legal or quasi-legal commands. But it is precisely a sign of its moral fervor that it is not content only with generalizable ethical propositions but is keen on translating them into actual paradigms. However, as I have repeatedly pointed out, the Qur'an always explicates the objectives or principles that are the essence of its laws.

The Muslims' failure to make a clear distinction between Qur'anic ethics and law has resulted in a confusion between the two. Neither ethics nor law ever became a discipline in itself. Islamic law, in fact, is not law in a modern sense; it is a treasure of legal materials thrown up during long centuries of endless discussions, upon which modern Islamic legal systems can certainly be built, but only a part of which could ever be enforced in court. No doubt the mixing together of law and morality gave a certain character to Islamic law that is uniquely precious— namely, it kept the moral motivation, without which any law must become a plaything of legal tricksters and manipulators, alive within the law. However, to keep law permeated with a living moral sense it is not necessary to ignore the distinction between the two, only to keep law *organically* related to morality, that is, to keep law Islamic and prevent its secularization.

The Qur'an calls itself "guidance for mankind" (*hudan li'l-nas*) and by the same term designates

earlier revealed documents. Its central moral concept for man is *taqwa*, which is usually translated as "piety" or "God-fearingness" but which in the various Qur'anic contexts may be defined as "a mental state of responsibility from which an agent's actions proceed but which recognizes that the criterion of judgment upon them lies outside him." The whole business of the Qur'an appears to be centered on the attempt to induce such a state in man. The idea of a secular law, insofar as it makes this state indifferent to its obedience, which is consequently conceived in mechanical terms, is the very abnegation of *taqwa*. The increasingly chaotic state of affairs in Western societies and the gradual erosion of an inner sense of responsibility represent a complex situation, but this situation is undoubtedly linked with a process through which law ceased to maintain any organic relation to morality.

Nor is Islamic theology, for that matter, a case of pure intellectualism, unaffective and ineffective, a pure artificial construct that tries to vie with philosophy, which at least claims to start from assumptions of natural reason rather than from given dogmatic beliefs that it claims "to prove." Islamic theology is certainly an intellectual endeavor, but it is so in the sense that it gives a coherent and faithful account of what is there in the Qur'an so that a believing person or a person prone to believe can give consent both from the mind and from the heart and make this world view his or her mental and spiritual home. Insofar as it provides that intellectual home for the mind, it can be taught; insofar as it provides a spiritual haven for the heart, it can be preached. A theology that can perform neither of these two functions is the stark bone of religion. Al-Ghazzali had long ago condemned the official "science of theology" because it was neither spiritually satisfying nor intellectually satisfactory—he called it the game of intellectual children! Yet this seems to be the fate of most historical theologies.

Just as preaching is an expression of theology for the heart, even so must it give rise to morality or an ethical value system to guide man and to instill in him the sense of moral responsibility that the Qur'an calls *taqwa*. A God that speaks neither to the intellect of man nor to his heart, nor yet can generate a system of values for man, is considerably worse than nothing and is better off dead. The moral values are the crucial pivot of the entire overall system, and from them flows the law. The law is therefore the last part in this chain and governs all the "religious," social, political, and economic institutions of the society. Because law is to be formulated on the basis of the moral values, it will necessarily be organically related to the latter. But because it governs the day-to-day life of the society, with necessary social change it has to be reinterpreted. Should the process of reinterpretation stop, obviously the society must either stagnate or else rebel and take the road of secularism. In either case the whole structure of theology, morality, and law will eventually collapse.

The question of who should interpret law has been acute in Islamic societies because of the historical accident that the so-called law (*fiqh*) has been the result of the work of private lawyers, while in the later medieval centuries governments—particularly the Ottoman government—had to promulgate laws on issues not covered by the *shari‘a* law. Although the state-made law was basically sanctioned by certain general principles in the *shari‘a* law itself, nevertheless a dichotomy of the sources of law was unavoidable, and this process paved the way for the secularization of law in several Muslim countries—most systematically in Turkey. With the introduction of parliamentary institutions, law-making has become the business of lay parliamentarians, but there are large-scale protests from the *‘ulama’* and their supporters that law-making must be vested in the *‘ulama’* institutions. For centuries, however, law-making in the *‘ulama’* institutions has been stagnant, and it is no longer feasible to reverse the new arrangements. The only way to produce genuine Islamic law is to enlighten public conscience, particularly that of the educated classes, with Islamic values. This, in fact, underlines the necessity of working out Islamic ethics systematically from the Qur’an and making such works accessible to the general reader. There is no shortcut to this process for the production of Islamic law. There is no doubt that a wider study of earlier works of Islamic jurisprudence and law will help. If first-rate works on the history of Islamic law and jurisprudence are written—as I have argued must be done—these should be made required reading in the schools of law as part of the normal curriculum. In this way, key Islamic legal and moral concepts would gradually come to inform the legal profession. In many Muslim countries the lawyers themselves are keen to learn more about Islamic law. Perhaps an international committee of Muslim jurists could be organized with first-rate traditionalist scholars of law and jurisprudence of various medieval schools to undertake major works in the field. At present, al-Azhar happens to be the most hopeful center for such a development.

Philosophy. In medieval Islam, a series of brilliant and original men had built, on the basis of Greek philosophical thought, a comprehensive and systematic view of the universe and of man, which they were able to synthesize with certain key concepts and doctrines of Islam to the satisfaction of themselves and many of the sophisticated Muslim intelligentsia. As I said earlier, this body of thought, called philosophy (*falsafa*), gave violent affront to the orthodoxy on several issues, and since then philosophy has been a discipline non grata in the Muslim educational system throughout a large part of the Muslim world. As I pointed out earlier, this was only one type of philosophy, with which nevertheless the fate of all philosophy was bound up in the eyes of the orthodox, and this circumstance caused a great deal of harm both to the orthodoxy (which suffered from a lack of ideas and their challenge) and to philosophy. Philosophy did continue to be cultivated at a high level in Iran, but this was done away from the orthodox fold—and even the Shi‘i orthodox fold—and therefore the two hardly ever met. Philosophy is, however, a perennial intellectual need and has to be allowed to flourish both for its own sake and for the sake of other disciplines, since it inculcates a much-needed analytical-critical spirit and generates new ideas that become important intellectual tools for other sciences, not least for religion and theology. Therefore a people that deprives itself of philosophy necessarily exposes itself to starvation in terms of fresh ideas—in fact, it commits intellectual suicide.

The generation of ideas by philosophy is basically a function of its critical-analytical activity. This activity has to be free. Most probably, philosophy as such cannot create any beliefs about reality and its nature, since its function is to analyze data of experience—sense experience, aesthetic experience, or religious experience. Philosophy, therefore, is not a rival of theology but should be helpful to it, for the object of the latter is to build a worldview on the basis of the Qur’an with the help of the intellectual tools provided, in part, by philosophy. Certain philosophical views may create tensions with certain theological doctrines; in this case either that particular philosophical view may be Islamically questionable or it may be that a particular theological doctrine is questionable. In any case, possible or actual tensions are not an excuse for banning philosophy in the name of a self-righteous theology, or vice versa: I have said already, and my argument has assumed all along in this work, that difference of opinion, provided it is meaningful, has to be assigned a high positive value, for it is only through confrontation of different and opposing views that truth *gradually* emerges. In fact, there is no privileged point in the process of human thought where *the Truth* can be said to have dawned.

Because medieval Muslim philosophy was a particular type of philosophical system, one must ask whether it is correct or wise to ban all philosophy (*falsafa*) as such. There can be any number of philosophies depending on point of view, the assumptions a particular philosopher makes, and the problems he starts out to solve, namely, those that seem to him to be most important, whether in the field of metaphysics, or ethics, or epistemology, or logic, or whatever. To say that all philosophy must of necessity contradict theology or its suppositions is to play not only a naive game but a dangerous one. I can say without fear of contradiction that, for the Qur'an, knowledge—that is, the creation of ideas—is an activity of the highest possible value. Otherwise why did it ask the Prophet to continue to pray for "increase in knowledge"? Why did it untiringly emphasize delving into the universe, into history, and into man's own inner life? Is the banning or discouragement of pure thought compatible with this kind of demand? What does Islam have to fear from human thought and why? These are questions that must be answered by those "friends of religion" who want to keep their religion in a hothouse, secluded from the open air.

The social sciences. Social sciences, as systematized bodies of knowledge, that is, as disciplines, are a modern phenomenon. They are undoubtedly a very important development, since, the object of their study being man in society, they can they tell us so much about how collectivities actually behave in various fields of human belief and action. At the beginning of this chapter I said something about Muslims' desire to Islamize these sciences or bodies of knowledge. There is no doubt that here again the vicious circle I have repeatedly spoken of can be broken only at the level of an intellectual activity where works are produced not only to inform how societies actually behave but to show how they can

be imbued with Islamic values conducive to the establishment of an ethical social order in the world.

As a system of values, Islam naturally cannot favor a laissez-faire society. On the other hand, Islam knows well that coercion does not pay or even work. As for indoctrination in the sense of brainwashing, I have already pointed out that this technique of creating future generations of the faithful in fact ultimately backfires. If in the past social pressures helped indoctrination in the sense that people rarely rebelled openly, this situation is increasingly changing, since social pressures are weakening and, owing to a number of apparently irreversible factors, are bound to continue to weaken. In fact, an intense and irrational faith in a subjective humanism among several present-day "liberated" circles has led many to "leave our children alone when they are young so that they can choose their own way of life when they are adults" and the like. Such statements, often made in good faith (although at least as often they are merely a cheap cover for disowning parental responsibility), in fact betray a lack of concern for the future of humanity. For, if humans could grow by themselves, highly sophisticated religious and educational systems would not have developed in the first place. And what we are seeing develop in societies whose liberals think they are the first secular liberals in human history is that, instead of growing into humans, many of the new generation are in fact growing into animals. To remedy the crudity and even cruelty of a self-righteous traditional system is one thing. To throw out the baby with the bath water is quite another.

Indoctrination, however, necessarily occurs only where dogmas come in: the greater the dogma content, the greater the need for indoctrination; the greater the ethical content, the less the need for indoctrination. It is a pity of pities that the ethical content of societies is being washed out because of a general rebellion against dogmas. Dogmas, again, are not all of the same level, for there are relatively "rational" dogmas, that is, such as are tied to the ethical content of a system. In any case, universal ethical values are the crux of the being of a society: the debate about the relativity of moral values in societies is born of a liberalism that in the process of liberalization has become so perverted as to destroy those very moral values it set out to liberate from the constraints of dogma. From my point of view, which is confessedly and necessarily normative, therefore, the best of social sciences is history—if done well and objectively. This is because history, being long range, contains lessons in a way that a study of the contemporary aborigines of Australia, for example, does not. Macrohistory, if done really well, is the best service a social scientist can do for mankind. This is the reason the Qur'an invites us again and again "to travel on the earth and see the end of nations." Microhistory—for example, a study of the postal service in the United States in the 1850s—is of use only insofar as it contributes to our knowledge of the behavior of man and its consequences; otherwise it is pure curiosity or a means to securing an academic post in a modern institution of learning.

Modern societies have acquired far more complexity than ancient and medieval societies. Particularly in the fields of economics, politics, communication, and education, modern societies have evolved thought, institutions, and structures incomparably more complex and sophisticated than those of any society within human experience. Yet we must not be deluded into thinking that because of their sophistication and complexity modern societies are any less subject to the basic laws of right and wrong. Part of modern sophistication, in fact, means that these societies have become more aware, or at least have the means to become more aware, of the possible sources of such social dislocations as might threaten to derange it. All such dislocations are finally rooted in the sense of right and wrong that is the conscience of the social mind. But it is always touch and go whether the conscience of a given social mind does in fact manage to reflect right and wrong with adequate objectivity. Since modern societies are, then, subject to the laws of rights and wrong just as were earlier, and in many ways simpler, societies, the lessons of history are as relevant to them as they were to the earlier ones. But, despite the increasingly sophisticated warning systems of today, the ethical impulse in certain important respects seems to have become, if anything, weaker. It is true that earlier societies were much more dogmatic in certain respects and therefore exposed themselves to dangers, while modern sophistication means less dogmatism, overtly at least. But this competence of modern societies to adjust to necessary change is often like a doctor who treats symptoms rather than the disease. No matter how much a doctor gains competence in treating symptoms while ignoring or being ignorant of the under-

lying disease, the life of his patient cannot be much prolonged. It is to be feared that modern civilization, while sophisticating means and methods to almost no end, has developed cardinal deficiencies in basic insights into human nature.

It is therefore essential that social scientists who study contemporary societies be exposed to the sobering lessons of history, for the history of mankind, whether earlier societies were aware of this or not, is indivisible in the sense that the basic human forces—and it is the human forces that are basic to history—are the same all over the globe. This is certainly the view of the Qur'an, which is singularly free of genetics and genes. If Muslim social scientists are to be involved in social engineering, this is all the more necessary. There is a considerable body of what may be called social thought in the Qur'an, which talks incessantly about the rise and fall of societies and civilizations, of the moral decrepitude of nations, of the succession of civilizations or "the inheritance of the earth," of the function of leadership, of prosperity and peace and their opposites, and especially of "those who sow corruption on the earth but think they are reformers." This body of thought should be organized next to the pure moral thought of the Qur'an and the lessons from history upon which the Qur'an is so insistent. Unless the material of the Qur'an is well systematized, it can be dangerously misleading to apply individual and isolated verses to situations, as most Muslim preachers and even many intellectuals tend to do.

The views of the Qur'an will also remain at the level of pure abstraction unless a thorough *factual* survey is made of the relevant social data. It is of the greatest importance to determine exactly where society is at present before deciding where it can go. To talk about reforming society without scientifically determining where the society is, is certainly like a doctor treating a patient without taking his case history or examining him. In fact, there is a sense in which even a meaningful formulation of Qur'anic thought will be dependent upon such a factual study and a proper method for interpreting facts; the converse, as I underlined in the Introduction, is also true. In other words, as with other fields discussed above, the study of the social sciences is a process, not something that is established once and for all. In fact, it is more so than any other field, for its subject matter—social behavior—is constantly in the process of creation.

Islam and the Challenge
of the Modern World

Shabbir Akhtar (Pakistan-England, born 1960) attended college in England and received his doctorate in the philosophy of religion in Canada. He worked for a time as a local community relations officer in England, but his calling appears to be broader in scope. Since the late 1980s, Akhtar has published a series of books that aim to speak for the Islamic community of England. At the same time, Akhtar has also taken on the role of religious reformer within this community. One of his primary themes is the need to confront and learn from modernity—a challenge that contemporary Islamic theology has shied away from, he argues.[1] In A Faith for All Seasons, excerpted here, Akhtar is so successful at representing secular perspectives that "a number of Muslims felt he had lost his faith, and he was heavily criticised in the Muslim press."[2]

"There are two ways of getting home," wrote G. K. Chesterton [English author, 1874–1936], "and one of them is to stay there."[3] No doubt that is the safer option; for some it is the only option. But there is another itinerary too. In this book I have urged Muslims to leave, if temporarily, the House of Islam, to venture through the alien world of rejection and rival patterns of religious conviction: to venture beyond dogma and unargued assumption, in the larger attempt to become acquainted not only with the a priori theologies of scripture but also with the sometimes recalcitrant realities of a world and human nature under their usual tuition.

The journey thus far has not been easy; and the rest is harder still. For we must now make our way back to the household of faith, back on the road to Mecca. And yet we have, of course, traversed the forbidden ground; we have seen the vast disarray of conflicting beliefs and ideologies vying with one another for our allegiance. An untested faith that prefers the security of unargued assumption, a faith whose votaries never lift their heads above the dogmatic parapet—that is no longer for us. "Thou shalt think!" is the first commandment of a characteristically modern piety. For in seeking to come to terms with modernity, we must develop a new rationalism, one that must reverently and conscientiously refuse to cherish the unempirical or otherwise questionable

1. Philip Lewis, *Islamic Britain: Religion, Politics and Identity among British Muslims* (London: I. B. Tauris, 1994).

2. David Herbert, "Shabbir Akhtar on Muslims, Christians and British Society," *Islam and Christian-Muslim Relations*, volume 4, number 1, June 1993, p. 104.

3. *The Everlasting Man* (London: Burns and Oates, 1974), originally published in 1925, p. 9.

assumptions still so innocently enjoyed by a traditional piety. Can we, then, find a way back to the House of Islam and take our place in it as authentic members and genuine adherents?

I

Perceptive Western listeners to Arab radio services relaying the Qur'an in the month of Ramadan can sense the competing noise and impact of more powerful neighboring stations as these intermittently drown out the reciter's voice. A somewhat fanciful observation; but it may well serve to symbolize Islam seeking an audience in the contemporary world of profane leisure, irreligious confidences, opposed values, and most characteristically, louder voices.

The voice of God in the daily life of Muslims is often only faintly and intermittently heard. But it is, at least within the range of transmission, still heard. It is rare that the noisy turbulence of the vicinity drowns out the entire recited sequence; the partial segment reaches the alert ear. But it has to be an attentive intelligence, given to what the Qur'an calls reflection (*tadabbur*).

Equally, one might say, it has to be a message worthy of our attention, couched in a relevant idiom, voiced in an appropriately attractive way. The Qur'an, like proper Christian preaching, has an exceptionally intelligent earnestness at its core. The art of beautiful recitation of the Qur'an is a mature and extensively cultivated one in Islam, especially Arab Islam, giving Qur'an reciters the same kind of kudos in Muslim society as opera singers have in Western culture. The concern with achieving a dramatic impact upon contemporary audiences is utterly central to any attempt to repossess the legacy of Muhammad for the needs of the age of reason. Yet the message seems increasingly irrelevant. Even its intelligent earnestness these days is often mistaken, particularly by outsiders, as being at one remove from, if not identical with, unworthy passion: in a word, fanaticism.

Yet the need for the preacher and the reciter has rarely been greater. For religions are not saved or even best served by intellectual efforts alone. If the thinker has a word in this affair, the preacher has the decisive one. It is the preacher who is forever exhorting, warning, advising in the accents of scripture—thereby creating disciples who are, by God's grace, inwardly repentant and outwardly concerned to effect social righteousness.

The scripture of Islam aims to persuade and educate us and thereby motivate right conduct. In its striking Arabic eloquence, it registers powerfully even on the rejecting and uncomprehending mind. But the full force of its compassionate coercion, if we may so term it, is felt only by the thoughtful listener.

The Qur'an frequently calls upon its audiences to give heed to its sequences. And much is done to facilitate its reception in the wayward human constituency. Thus, for example, the Qur'an weaves backwards and forwards into the fabric of the present a concern with the past—a past that is dead as history yet alive as a source of guidance. The text is sprinkled with heart-searching meditations that serve to give the reader pause—and the text, too, as it were—in midstream for deliberation. The result is the concise argumentativeness of prosaic literature but the charmingly incongruous effect of poetry in the dramatic impact of the sentences. In fine, the author has found the right tone of "voice" for preaching to the unconverted.

The voice from the radio conveys the word of God, received as proclamation and directive, delivered as sermon and imperative. It is piety and devotion in the highest sense, a reminder of mission and vocation. Through it breathe the allied ethical accents of demands unfulfilled, the intimations of nemesis, and the urgency of repentance, both individual and collective. The interval between birth and death—life itself—is to be properly punctuated by reflection on its elemental seriousness. Reminder is needed here constantly. Profane distraction must be subdued; the voice of mission must speak even when the listeners refuse to listen or when pressures, external or internal, conspire to silence, absorb or deflect it.

II

"Don't bother about being modern. Unfortunately it is the one thing that, whatever you do, you cannot avoid." Can't you? This remark of the late Salvador Dali [Spanish artist, 1904–1989], in his rather pretentious autobiography, *The Diary of a Genius*,[4] is

4. *Diary of a Genius* (London: Pan Books, Picador edition, 1976), p. 52.

oddly thoughtful, even discerning, especially if we may borrow it for our purposes here as a comment on modern religious conviction. For even "traditional" believers are far more secularized today than they themselves might imagine. Modernity, the circumstance of being "modern," is, in a central sense, inescapable. It is the necessary context for every tolerably well-informed life-journey undertaken in the contemporary world.

Yet there is a choice. One need not be too eager to catch up on the facts; one can cultivate a kind of deliberate and bloody-minded will to obscurantism. Indeed even that is unnecessary once innate security of mind strikes alliance with laziness. The results, in the case of Islam, are well known. At least since the end of the 19th century, the entire House of Islam has been surviving on an intellectual overdraft.

A signal hindrance to the development of Islamic thought in the West in the coming years is what may be called "the problem of temperament." An ideology, especially one aiming at the common good, must avoid reactionary and polemical impulses as the chief sources of its motivation. Unless Muslim reflection is actuated by motives nobler than an undifferentiated dislike of the West and all things Western, it has no chance of a hearing. (Remember that "the West" is no longer some amorphous realm, some abstract foe, out there in some distant land: Muslims are *in* the West.) We are all in search of an audience these days; and it is not easy to get anyone to listen, let alone to listen for long. A modern preacher either captures or loses an urbanized audience within the first *three* minutes of his sermon.

To cultivate "rejectionist" and isolationist attitudes is to invite accusations of apology. Moreover, such attitudes severely sap the energy of the faithful intellect. In any case, a shrill voice is an unworthy accompaniment of truth.

Many Muslims believe that contempt for our current situation of secularity and religious pluralism is an adequate substitute for an intellectual reckoning with it. Throughout this work, I have excoriated such a conceit. Here it is sufficient to pass summary judgment and pass on. That Muslim believers have always placed a sturdy trust in the ultimate truth of the Islamic scripture is all well and good. But such security of conviction must itself reckon, if it is intellectually aware and morally honest, with the facts of post-Enlightenment culture. Modern faith

should properly allow room for a pertinent variety of anxiety: an anxiety free from contempt for hostile challenge, an anxiety devoid of hatred of alien belief. For there are secular and religious groups whose members sometimes reject Islamic presuppositions for reasons that cannot be dismissed as shallow or trivial.

The reason for this "new" style in Islamic religiosity is itself specifically Islamic in complexion. The didactic element in Islam is least properly presented in a shrill and unreflective tone precisely because it is then deracinated from the Islamic scripture's own deeply meditative context with all its constant calls for reverent reflection (*tadabbur*). The current Muslim tendency to discuss narrowly dogmatic issues in an unrelievedly authoritarian mood is the best way of imprisoning latently massive scriptural powers. A cramped and degradingly minor Muslim intellectual ambition today effectively gives the lie to the Islamic claim that the Qur'an is a "miracle of reason and speech" vouchsafed to "the best community ever brought forth among mankind." There is work to be done; and, notwithstanding Dali, there is merit in being modern, for it is possible to continue to live in the past—a past that is both a fetter and a release.

III

Is contemporary man then indeed the measure of all things? Should he be? I have argued that the starting point of our modern attempt to achieve an eternal perspective—a modern theology must be an attempt to take the full measure of man. We begin with men and women under an empty sky. Such an emphasis is categorically foreign to a traditional Islamic piety that both begins and ends with God. But there is, as I argued in part 2, some Qur'anic warrant for taking the human condition seriously, if only as an index to God and the transcendent. Within the Qur'an of course any attempt to give man his due necessarily involves giving God his due, so to speak.

This new style of religiosity may strike one as entailing an unduly large concession to modern thought. But there is no real cause for alarm in the Muslim theological camp. Wherever we may begin, we religious thinkers can safely be trusted (as Marxists well know) to arrive finally at God. Naturally, one supposes; for that is our job. And, more seriously, because a correct theology must contain in its premises (and hence in its conclusion) a true statement about man and hence about God. There is a really good conceptual mix here: if theological conclusions about deity are false, the implied theological statements about humanity must also have been untrue. If theological statements about the nature of God are true, a valid anthropology must already have been implicit in the premises.

To understand the nature of God is not equivalent to providing a sound anthropology. But any full understanding of the nature of God will involve some understanding of the created order placed under a divine sovereignty. The theist will argue that any full understanding of man would imply some fundamental if implicit reference to God. For the consciousness of the divine alone constitutes the authentically human.

The starting point is of great importance. But, as in the formation of some systems of mathematics, we should begin where we need to begin. Thus, for example, if we are engaged in the development of Muslim theology and expounding it for the needs of the traditional pious mind confident of faith's claims, there is no harm in beginning—and even ending—with God. For many deeply religious people, man is, at every level, tributary to the divine Creator. However, in other areas, the starting point may well have to be different. For example, in Christian-Muslim dialogue, it is preferable, though not necessary, to begin at the level of the human condition and then explore as to which of the two faiths gives the most "satisfying" characterization of the human and hence of God. God can enter the picture indirectly or, if you like, as an inference from the premises implied or stated. When it comes to the non-theistic faiths and atheistic humanism, God cannot be the starting point of responsible exchange with the rejector. There, man is necessarily, in the first instance at least, the measure of all faiths. We must begin with man; the theist hopes, naturally, that we need not end there. But that must be the hope of a valid epistemology, not the presumption of a dogmatic temper.

Wherever we may begin, we must end with God. Modern Protestant thought, of a reductionist and revisionist vintage, has sometimes lost God in the intricate procedures of theology. Fortunately the supernatural emphasis remains integral to Islam; the human and natural remain tributary and derivative.

A due recognition of the importance of man is likely to be misunderstood in many ways. For example, to say, with Christian thinkers like the Reverend Kenneth Cragg, "Let God be God," is to endow man with an excessive significance and thereby misunderstand Islam or, for that matter, any theism.[5] For God is God—independent of our recognition or acceptance. Even if God's truth can, at worst, fail to be accepted in a sinful human constituency, it remains truth none the less. On every score, this is the Qur'an's message. "Let man be man" is the true creed of Islam. For *man* is debased, denatured, disfigured, devalued by *kufr* (disbelief) and idolatry; *man* attains authentically human stature via Islam. It is man, not God, who must submit his will. God is not a Muslim; he does not need anything and certainly not anything from us in order to be truly divine. He is, in a manner of speaking, necessarily Himself.

To come to terms with modernity is one thing; changing a revealed Islam to suit human whim shaped by passing fashion is quite another. It is a rarely noted tribute to the authentic conviction of the religious intelligentsia of Islam that they suppressed the very conditions in which a neo-Islamic belief could take root. Islam is Islam and remains so. An Islam molded under the concentrated pressures of secularity and interreligious encounter must nevertheless be recognizably a faith bearing a family resemblance to traditional Islam. My attempt at a reverent skepticism in these pages is in the service of rediscovering the old Islam, not of inventing a new heresy. The only dogmatism which is charming and profound, in religions as in individuals, is the one at once aware both of itself as well as of alternative patterns of belief. To learn to face fully the skeptical gaze of modernity is not a license for any wholesale disowning of authentically Muslim dogmas in the tradition. It is only because we today still wish to retain Islam as a complete vision that we need to identify, record and religiously contend with various new theological puzzles. Once we simply sacrifice the problematic parts of revealed scripture—as some Protestant Christians do—we either alter altogether the grounds of our puzzlement or else feel no need to be puzzled at all.

---

5. Kenneth Cragg, *The Pen and the Faith* (London: Allen and Unwin, 1985), chapter 7.

IV

A true Muslim is never a man of many dogmas. For, at the end of the chapter, there is only one dogma, concerning which he has no option: *Allah-u-akbar* [God is great]. This confession of the greatness of God is central to the Muslim imagination. It punctuates the prayer and, when sincerely confessed, transforms the heart and mind. Indeed, even the most obscure and flickering recognition of its worth adds dignity to a life being lived in a complex industrial-commercial society that sets great store by worthless ephemera.

The confession of the overwhelming greatness of God is by no means distinctive to Islam. Every theism is grounded in such a recognition. But it is the manner in which such a conviction continues to leaven the whole of an authentic Muslim life which seems to set Islam apart today as a pre-eminently practical faith.

There is no necessary triumphalism about such a claim. For one can state the strength of Islamic conviction as a fact rather than as a boast. In any case, the Qur'an is concerned with both sides of the idolatrous coin: if the profane is to be repudiated as profane, the sacred is to be worshipped as sacred. If we should categorically refuse to worship forces unworthy of it, we must equally categorically embrace worship of forces worthy of it. "There is no God but God" is a twofold declaration, vigilantly denying the efficacy of purely profane realities while categorically enjoining a trust in the power of the unique Deity. To utter, therefore, with meaning and conscious intent, the creed of Islam is to discover the full nature and bounds of one's duty as a created being.

Modern living is a tall order: a personal quest for fulfillment limited by all the tortured choices of an age of uncertainty, an attempt to recognize and fulfill obligations to oneself, the family, the nation and the global society of mankind. For the Muslim believer these attempts are themselves secondary to a larger attempt to please his Creator, who is to be actively recognized as being greater (*akbar*) than this purely human network of expectations, duties and hopes. A tall order indeed! In such a context, the Muslim sees his Islam as a unified enterprise of private faith and public practice, which cultivates the fullest appreciation of whatever is good and wholesome while actively inviting the most permanent quarrel with the forces of what the Qur'an calls *zulm*

(wrongdoing), whether personal or communal. For what is the worth of a piety that retires from the real world of varied voices, whether innocent and caring, or, more frequently, irate and tired?

What, then, is it to be religious today? To be religious is to see oneself continuously as an exile in the midst of natural existence. This is not to say— it would be plainly untrue—that one is not of this world or in this world nor, most importantly, that one is under a religious obligation to entertain hopes of a false Utopia here or elsewhere. Nor is true religion a warrant for uprooting oneself from the soil of existence by refusing to give personal passions their due: faith has its own resources for easing the burden of private emotion, such as the natural desire for legitimate power and (licit) sexual gratification. It is certainly not for Islam to undermine the normal aspirations of human beings by demanding some deliberate and sustained detachment from the sensuous, the natural, the immediate and the temporal. No, the truly religious ideal involves an intense effort to pass through ordinary human experience and sanctify every episode, whether immediately or retrospectively, by celebrating the good while turning the realization of wrongdoing into an occasion for repentance. In doing that, one is merely practicing the conviction that "God is greater."

V

Such a religious view of the universe would merely indulge our speculative ingenuity— unless it had practical consequences. And these are legion. Choice here settles on three motifs that are dominant in any contemporary discussion of the Islamic religion as a relevant charter for human society. All three are authentically Qur'anic, proclaiming as each does the greatness of God; all are increasingly significant as this century draws to a close: man as custodian of Nature and technology, man as a socio-sexual creature, and man as a tenant with a fixed lease on physical life in this world. We may, for convenience, call these the problems of technology, sexuality and mortality, respectively. The first two are explored briefly here, the third in section VI.

Some of the Qur'an's comments on the religious significance of Nature and an auxiliary technology are profound in a way we today more readily appreciate than did Muhammad's own contemporaries.

Within the scripture of Islam there is, in the Reverend Kenneth Cragg's apt phrase, "a theology of ecology."[6] Unless technology is itself placed under a constraining sovereignty—unless *Allah-u-akbar* is also the scientists' slogan—all our scientific achievements may well radically come to grief. A merciful creator has placed the natural world in our trust. Do we know the duties of stewardship? Can we discharge these properly if we recognize no responsibility to forces greater than the human? The Qur'an's implied verdict is unequivocal. A science and technology freed of all reference and responsibility to the transcendent will cause irreversible damage even while, paradoxically, aiming to confer immeasurable benefit. For a generation that lives under the increasingly darkening shadow of global nuclear holocaust, such a verdict is neither extreme nor rooted in some outdated dogma.

Man too is part of a universal order of mercy and provision. The inaugural revelation already, if we may move on to our second theme, makes a reference to the basic mystery of procreation. "Recite in the name of thy Lord who created man from a blood-clot (*'alaq*)" (Sura 96, Verses 1–2; interpreted). Throughout the Qur'an, there are many reverent allusions to human sexuality and its consequences as among the signs of God for a people given to sustained reflection (*tadabbur*). The male-female division and the benefits of mutual love and compassion flowing from it are divine portents.

Within the Muslim scripture, the sacred and the sexual are often discussed in association. It is as though sexuality is next to godliness in the Islamic lexicon! There is no doubt that the sexual act hides within it deeply religious significances, notwithstanding its essentially legal as opposed to sacramental status in Islam. At the very least, it is an invitation to reflection. For the Qur'anic confidence seems to be that a destiny brought close to the texture of its own origin and dependence (its biological root and the promise of the human fruit) could hardly fail to register the power and caring wisdom of its creator. Humility is certainly not out of place in an area of deep mutual vulnerability. Given the large and varied liabilities and significances of the sexual office—the delicacy of an intimacy that conceals temptations to exploitation, the inevitability of far-reaching consequences of our choices here—the Qur'anic stress is surely salutary.

This is particularly true today. For within the area of the sexual demand upon the human frame, the Qur'anic warning against reducing "the best form" (*akhsani-taqwim*, Sura 95, Verse 4; interpreted) to "the lowest of the low" (*asfala-safilin*, Sura 95, Verse 5; interpreted) acquires impressively contemporary meanings. When we survey the opposed modern view of sexuality as an arena for the celebration of our emancipation—a form of recreation—we can well understand why the fear of God is an appropriate concomitant of the will to sexuality. The prostitution of sex, serving and served by profane interests, notably commercial pornography, is an almost inevitable consequence of the rupture of the traditional liaison between the sexual and the sacred. Given the peculiarly powerful proclivity of the sexual demand to degenerate into what is, stripped of the garment (*libas*)[7] of piety and compassion, merely base and humiliating, the fear of God, in recognition of his greatness, is the best possible background to the activities of the sexual instinct.

It is in this context that one should broach the vexed subject of Islam's legal charter for a truly erotic society. The traditional Muslim custom of segregating men and women in order to protect women against aggressive kinds of male desire has led to charges of sexual apartheid. But one must not judge too hastily here. The aim of Islam's admittedly paternalistic provisions for women is to secure valid norms of modesty, male and female, so that sexual appetite can be indulged with wholesome enjoyment. Within recognized and appropriately liberal limits, men and women can develop a sexual potential, enjoying it without fear of private sin or public reproach. Beyond that there is a clear and legally enforced recognition of the dangers of injury to the dignity of involved parties. Given the power of sex as an instinctual energy, the need for control and harness is virtually axiomatic. Any kind of irresponsible adventurism here spells disaster. Certainly, the recent Western experiment, with all its auxiliary techniques for sexual gratification, has produced an increasingly sordid sensuality retro-

---

6. "The Great Perhaps," in *Resurgence*, number 137, 1990, pp. 47–48.

7. The term is Qur'anic. A man and woman are said to be like garments for each other [Sura 2, Verse 187].

spectively embittered by its own paradoxical loss of natural eroticism.

It is, ironically, the Islamic wish for an authentically erotic, a properly sensual, culture that has led to its endorsement of severely scrupulous, almost puritanical, attitudes towards the abuse of the sexual instinct. Traditional Islam's notorious "extreme" (*hudud*) ordinances for sexual offenses cannot be properly understood without a compelling sense of the scripture's own high estimate of the sexual office.

The veil is no doubt an apt symbol for the sexual culture the Qur'an sanctions and encourages men and women to cultivate. For it well captures the idea of a reverent invitation that, variously, in the hands of female adventurism or male-sponsored desires, may deteriorate into what is irreverently suggestive, even base. The invitation is also a liability, just as in the case of Nature whose religious significance may well be lost in the more superficial invitation to seek control and technological dominion. The veil could enslave, cramp or distort even valid sexual ambition; or it could successfully serve as an index to the truly erotic culture.

VI

In that largely unaccountable desire for immortality which is a unique feature of our species, religious believers may claim a distinctively rational ground. Theism offers, through its faith in the immortality of the soul, important hopes and distinctive ambitions. Though many conceptual difficulties beset this religious belief in survival beyond the grave, it is not clear that it is incoherent. At any rate, acceptance of this conviction has given an overriding purpose to countless human beings throughout history. Certainly, by standing robust witness to an afterlife, Islam has produced an impressive record of zestful bravery and purposeful courage in the context of holy struggle against militant forms of evil.

The Qur'an is alert, on multiple levels, to the fact of transience. All things, including human generations, pass away. Only "thy Lord, full of majesty" is exempt from the indifferent ravages of time. As for the rest of us, God has decreed time as an index to the fragility of all, especially the sinful, society.

In these meditative contexts, where the Qur'anic mood is in dangerous proximity to the forbidden impulse of tragedy, there is a peculiarly moving beauty in the language which translation drastically reduces. It is a language, at any rate, that indelibly impressed those in the contemplative traditions of Islamic theism. For the Arabs, the Qur'an is the first document to impose a specifically religious significance on the facts of human impermanence and mortality. No adequate philosophy of man and his place in the titanic immensity called the universe could conceivably omit references to this centrally relevant truth of our condition. The pre-Islamic Arabs were naturally impressed by the transience of all things mortal; most entertained tragic notions. In the event Islam was destined to frustrate the will to tragedy while radically satisfying the residual desire for a conclusive triumph over the limitations of physical extinction.

That there was in Muhammad's Arabia a national longing for some successful transcendence of the natural and human order is amply evidenced in pagan poetry. The Qur'an offers in conscious opposition to such pagan poetry, a new approach to physical extinction. For Islam, like every responsible metaphysic of man, accepts and psychically reckons with the fact of death. It completely changed its significance for the Arabs. The Qur'an distances itself from the martial ethos of pre-Islamic Arabia with its strong traditions of *muru'a* (virility) displayed in courage and recklessness. But, in a manner typical of its religious genius, it effectively transformed the protest against death by recruiting the old recklessness for a new cause, thereby dignifying the recklessness while ensuring the cause.

If Islamic history overflows with episodes of courageous sacrifice of life for the cause of faith, it is at least partly because a due recognition of the greatness of God, according to the Qur'an, necessitates such dramatic gestures. Though there are many, including unspectacular, ways of pleasing God, martyrdom is, according to all learned authorities, unquestionably the best. Tradition has confidently maintained that martyrs for the cause of Islam are the only exceptions to the rule of strict reckoning on the awful day of judgment. (Muhammad, incidentally, will be judged like anyone else since he died a natural death.)

The Qur'an takes martyrdom seriously. It denies that martyrs are dead; rather, believers are instructed to say, martyrs are living in the presence of God, satisfied and rejoicing in their new state. This is no reductionist sentimentalism that merely allows the dead to live in the memories of the living—with good and evil leaving some permanent heritage while its agents have long left the scene. The Qur'an has a strikingly robust doctrine about an afterlife, with contrasted fates awaiting the good and the bad. Those who endorse the greatness of God may validly entertain high hopes of entering Paradise. As for the rest, for whom their own whims were greater (*akbar*) than God, the sacred volume has a clear message. Their destination is Hell, which is, [Jean-Paul] Sartre [1905–1980] notwithstanding, by no means just other people.

VII

"Every path," declared the late Ayatollah [Ruhollah] Khomeini [Iranian leader, 1902–1989], "can lead to Hell." Some paths much quicker than others, one might immediately add. (The comment is as true, if not more so, than the maxim that inspires it.) Khomeini himself goes on to list science, mysticism, theology, ethics and, surprisingly, even monotheism as all capable of leading to perdition. It is an apt observation for our purposes here, intimating as it does the dangers of abusing powerful and profound faiths. The potential threat of "political religion," for want of a better phrase, is all too obvious, especially when it strikes alliance with human arrogance and lust for domination.

There can be no easy complacency these days, arguing as we do for the necessity of religion to generations that barely care. There are many today who have no wish to be "saved," to be "successful" in the eyes of God. Islam offers spiritual success to those who prefer failure. It is no small paradox; but there we have it. It is a religious puzzle we must accept on faith and move on. But it is always right and unequivocally just to seek, no matter how painful, a full and permanent controversy with those who reject Islam without adequate basis, who disbelieve in its inspiration while cynically exploiting it for purely political or personal ends.

Such an engagement with the rejectors, however, does not allow us to impose upon them any militancy of our own persuasion. That way lies Hell and alienation. For the interests of Islam are not properly served by encouraging the hypocritical element, already extremely large among the educated and secularized classes in the House of Islam. In such a

rendezvous, painful as it is to the committed Muslim, God has the last word. For them their works, and to us ours.

VIII

"What should it profit a house in the night that a lamp is set forth on its roof—when all is dark within?" Sheikh Abu Hamid al-Ghazzali's [1058–1111] rhetorical question, attributed to Jesus of Nazareth,[8] brings us to the last turn on the road to Mecca. I have already remarked in the Preface that Muslims have clearly failed to interpret and appropriate Islam properly for the needs of the modern age. There are many reasons for this failure; the chief ones are the shallowness of intellectual responses to the challenges of modernity and an increasing shallowness in the life of faith.

Al-Ghazzali's question well catches the problem. A little religion is a very dangerous thing. Within the House of Islam, there is today a great need for self-criticism and introspection, both severely jeopardized by the emphasis on a purely external, somewhat legalistic, religious observance. Muslims are religiously obliged to turn inward, to take the full measure of their own failings, and try to effect social and personal criticism in the larger attempt to seek the mercy of God. Islam may well be the best religion with the worst followers.

The pen may be mightier than the sword; but prayer is certainly so. Muslims need to develop, deepen the life of faith. A deeper spirituality, with prayer at its core, will constitute an important part of the characteristically religious reckoning with secularity. Religions are not saved by mental efforts alone. We must live as faithful people; we must strengthen our style of dealing with modernity by living within the parameters of faith, by actively striving for a genuine religiosity that seeks and finds resources for honest, including intellectually honest, living in a difficult age. There are many theological puzzles on our hands; the silence of God is increasingly oppressive, heavier each day on the heart of every reflective believer. And yet here too prayer has

---

8. *The Revival of the Religious Sciences*, book 111, section 198, Cairo edition. Compare the passage in Matthew, chapter 23, verse 27.

its place: "Our Lord, burden us not with what we have not the strength to bear." (Sura 2, Verse 286)

Faith needs to move mountains: the mountains of doubt, hesitation, unclarity, weakness of will. The opening chapter of the Qur'an well captures the flavor of this religious imperative, one that underlines one entirely indispensable mood of the authentically religious temper. "Thee alone we worship, Thee alone we ask for help," says the *sura* [Sura 1, Verse 4]. Could there be a better way of imposing an embargo on every false ideal, an operative veto on any attempt to seek support from purely human sources? This indeed is the voice of the truly iconoclastic conscience. But to attain here the right kind of trust in God—an effortless trust—requires effort, sustained labor. "Guide us in the straight path," the *sura* continues [Sura 1, Verse 5]. The mood for submission (*islam*) is well captured in the imperative "*Ihdena*" (Guide us!)—gracefully requesting the grace of God, yet enjoining human effort in the making of the plea.

There may be certainties and consolations when we get to the heavenly city—but there are few left on the road to it. It will be a difficult journey; and we have miles to go before we sleep. But I hope Muslims can improve on these admittedly rudimentary beginnings.

It is a revealing feature of the Muslim mind that, though the Muslim calendar has put an end to it [in 1979], the 14th century [A.H.] still lingers on. There is a curious kind of finality about this century in the voice of the simple believer as well as in that of the sophisticated religionist. There is a very keen sense of an impending crisis in this world, heightened by prophetic warnings of imminence of judgment.

The Muslim 14th century has, however, ended; and the 15th has already reached a tenth of its span. Islam is now fully in a modern world of competing ideologies and penetrating skepticisms, mostly of Anglo-American provenance, that look with justified suspicion on any exclusivist dogmatic claim. Trust in God is no longer enough; we must tie the camel first. Muslim destinies today need to be shaped partly by conscious choice and struggle. We must earn the right to a future.

Glossary

ahl al-kitab, People of the Book (Christians, Jews, Muslims)

akbar, greater

Allah-u-akbar, God is great

Ansar, literally "helpers," meaning the Muslims of Medina accompanying the Prophet

'aqida (plural: *'aqa'id*), creed

asatir, myths

asma' Allah al-husna, the beautiful names of God

bashar, human

batin, inner meaning

dar al-harb, land of war, non-Islamic lands

dar al-Islam, land of Islam, Islamic lands

daraja, degree, rank

dhikr, remembrance of God

dhimmi, protected religious minorities

faddala, to prefer

fulasifa, philosophers

falsafa, philosophy

faqih (plural: *fuqaha'*), religious scholar

fardu (plural: *fara'id*), Islamic duty

fiqh, Islamic jurisprudence

fitna, civil war

fitra, natural disposition to the good

hadd, limitation

hadith, tradition of the Prophet

hajj, pilgrimage

halal, divinely sanctioned

hanif, inclined to truth

haqiqa, truth

haram, prohibited, protected

hazrat, excellency

hijab, veil

hijra, migration of the Muslims from Mecca to Medina in year 622

hudan, guidance

hudud, Islamic penalties

hukm (plural: *ahkam*), judgment, rule, government

ihsan, beneficence

ijma', consensus

ijtihad, Islamic interpretation

'ilm, science, knowledge

imam, leader

'iman, faith

insan, human being

insaniyat, humanity

islam, submission to God

ithar, self-sacrificing generosity

itlaq, infinity

jadid, new, modern

jahiliya, the pre-Islamic era

jihad, religious struggle

jizya, tax on *dhimmi*

kafir (plural: *kafirun*), unbeliever

khilafa, trusteeship, caliphate

kitab, book

kufr, disbelief

mal, property

ma'ruf, common decency

maslaha, public interest

mawla, blood brother

mu'amalat, Islamic civil law, code of behavior

mu'awada, reciprocity

mujtahid, religious scholar

mu'min (plural: *mu'minin*), believer
mushrik, polytheist
muslimin, Muslims; literally, those who submit
mutashabih, uncertain
nafs, soul
qadi (or *qazi*), Islamic judge
qawwam, in charge of
qiwama, responsibility
qiyas, analogical reasoning
risala, divine inspiration
shahada, witnessing, acceptance of Islam
sha'n al-nuzul (plural: *shu'un*), occasion of revelation
shar', divine revelation, Islamic law
shari'a, Islamic law
shirk, polytheism
shura, consultation
sunna, practice of the Prophet
sura, chapter of the Qur'an

tadabbur, reverent reflection
tafasir, exegetical works
tafsir, interpretation, analysis
tanattu', trangressing, meticulous religiosity
taqlid (plural: *taqalid*)
taqwa, fear of God, piety
tasamuh, tolerance
ta'wil, intepretation
ta'zir, civil penalties
towhid, unity
'ulama', religious scholars
umm, mother
umma, community
ustadh, teacher
usul, principles
zahir, external meaning
zakat, Islamic tax

Index of Qur'anic Citations

Index of Personal Names